Also By The Terminal Press:

The J.G. Ballard Book
Deep Ends: The J.G. Ballard Anthology 2014
Deep Ends: The J.G. Ballard Anthology 2015
Deep Ends: The J.G. Ballard Anthology 2016
Deep Ends: A Ballardian Anthology 2018
Dominika Oramus - Grave New World: The Decline of the West in the Fiction of JG Ballard
Lawrence Russell - Radio Brazil
Lawrence Russell - Outlaw Academic
Rick McGrath - Straight Man: Rock Star Interviews, Reviews & Photos From The 1970s Underground Press
Rick McGrath - The Disenchanted Forest

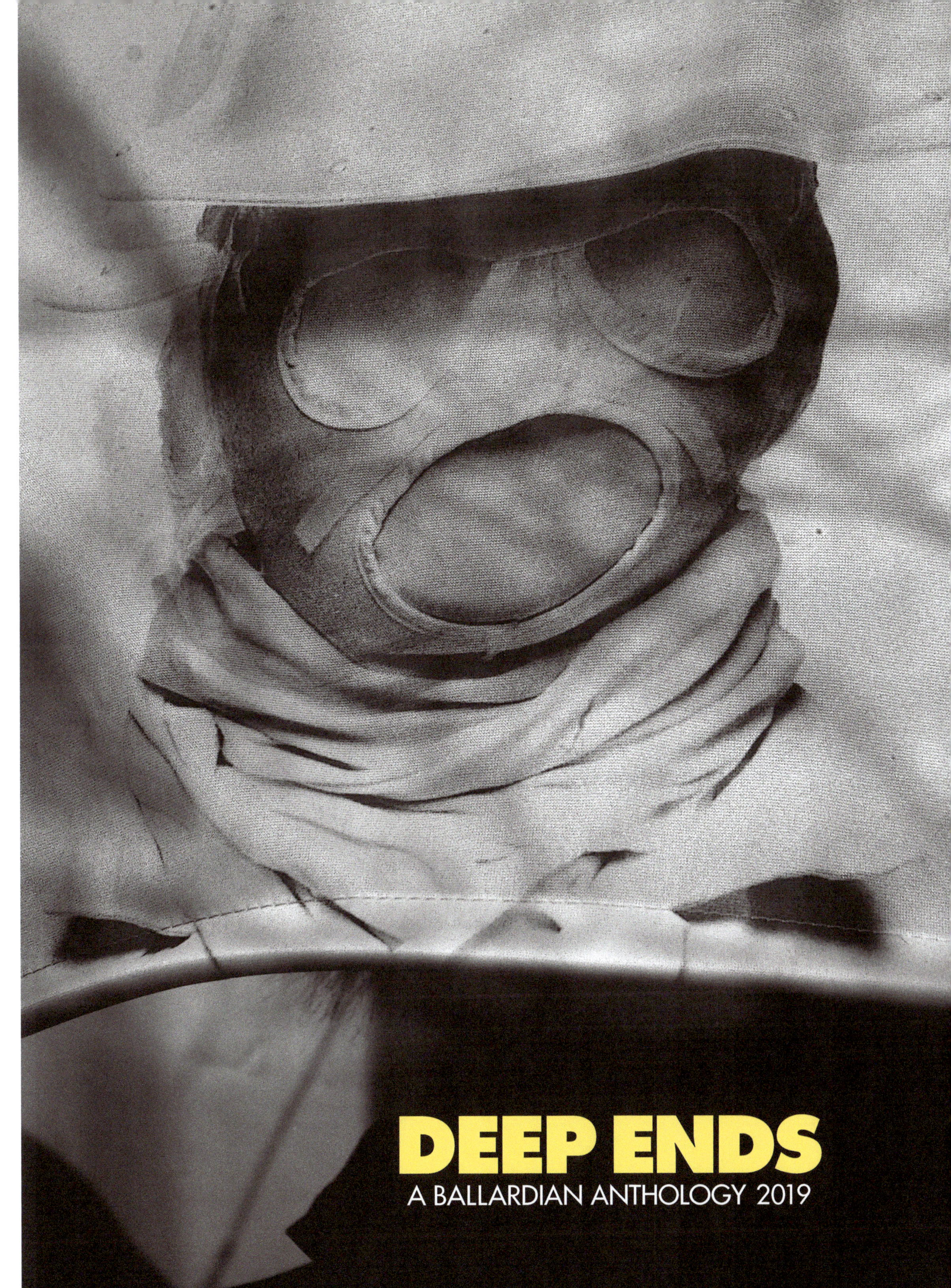
DEEP ENDS
A BALLARDIAN ANTHOLOGY 2019

First Edition

Published By
The Terminal Press
Powell River, BC, Canada
September 2019

Editor & Designer: Rick McGrath

Editorial Board: Thomas Knowles and David Paddy

ISBN: 978-1-7753679-1-8

Visit us: www.facebook.com/theterminalpress
Email: theterminalpress@shaw.ca

Contents:

Front Cover Painting *Love and Napalm*: **Luca Del Baldo** | Back Cover: **Rick McGrath**

Contributors:

David Pringle. David probably needs less introduction than any Ballardian alive, and has been featured in every *Deep Ends*, most importantly for his ongoing chronology of JGB which started in *Deep Ends 2015* and continues in this edition. David was the editor of *Foundation*, an academic journal, from 1980 through 1986, during which time he became one of the prime movers of the collective which founded *Interzone* in 1982. By 1988 he was the sole publisher and editor of *Interzone*, a position he retained until 2004. For two-and-a-half years, in 1991–1993, he also edited and published a magazine entitled *Million: The Magazine About Popular Fiction. Interzone* was nominated several times for the Hugo award for best semiprozine, winning the award in 1995. In 2005, the Worldcon committee gave David a Special Award for his work on *Interzone*. He wrote the first short monograph on Ballard, *Earth is the Alien Planet: J.G. Ballard's Four-Dimensional Nightmare* (Borgo Press, 1979) and compiled *J.G. Ballard: A Primary and Secondary Bibliography* (G.K. Hall, 1984). He has aso written *Science Fiction: The 100 Best Novels* (1985) and *Modern Fantasy: The 100 Best Novels* (1988). David published a newsletter, first titled *News From The Sun* then *JGB News*, from 1981 until 1996.

Mike Holliday. Mike is another *Deep Ends* stalwart, appearing in all our editions. He was born in Liverpool and owes his interest in JG Ballard to reading 'The Voices of Time' at age 14. He has written a number of articles about Ballard's writings and Ballardian philosophy. He now lives east of Croydon with his wife and rather too many books for his own good.

Paul A. Green. Ditto for "Brother" Paul Green, whose stories and articles have appeared in every edition of *DE*. His books include *The Gestaltbunker—Selected Poems* (Shearsman Books 2012), and *Shadow Times* (QBS Productions 2019). His audio work can be found on the CD *Sounds and Symbols* (Phantom Airship 2017) and at www.culturecourt.com. His novels consist of *The Qliphoth* (Libros Libertad 2007) and *Beneath the Pleasure Zones I & II* (Mandrake of Oxford 2014/2016). A selection of his plays for radio and stage has been published in *Babalon* (Scarlet Imprint 2015) His website is paulgreenwriter.co.uk.

Luca Del Baldo. A regular contributor to *Deep Ends* since 2014, Luca was born in Como, Italy, in 1969, and graduated with a thesis on Diane Arbus at the Brera Academy (Milan). For several years Luca designed book covers for the major Italian publishers of JG Ballard, Philip K. Dick, James Ellroy, Joe Lonsdale, and others, and collaborated with theater directors for television shows broadcast by R.A.I. In the 1990s he began his research on the corpses of celebrities or dictators of the 20th Century, the *Todkammer*, and in recently he has been painting a series of portraits of the greatest contemporary philosophers and theorists in his project, *The Visionary Academy of Ocular Mentality*, a kind of *Galleria Vasariana*, as Arthur C. Danto called it.

Pippa Tandy. Pippa Tandy is a teacher, photographer and printmaker who lives in the Central Highlands of Victoria in south eastern Australia. She makes prints and photographs of the ancient volcanic landscapes through which she travels, and the chance encounters with light and weather glimpsed through train windows in her pre-dawn commutes to the city. This is her fourth appearance in the anthology.

Chris Beckett. Chris Beckett is an archivist at the British Library. He recently edited a new edition of *Crash* (London, 2017; Los Angeles, 2019) incorporating draft material from Ballard's archive at the Library. In 2020, he will catalogue the papers of Heathcote Williams, author of *Autogeddon*, and expects to find at the bottom of one of the boxes Williams's 1984 *Crash* screenplay. This is Chris' third contribution to *Deep Ends*.

Dominika Oramus. A professor at the Institute of English Studies University of Warsaw (Poland), this marks Dominika's third apperarance in *Deep Ends*. She has written extensively on Angela Carter and JG Ballard, as well as on science fiction and the poetics of postmodernism. Her book on Ballard, *Grave New World. The Decline of the West in the Fiction of JG Ballard* was published by The Terminal Press (2015) and one year later she published a critical study of Angela Carter: *Ways of Pleasure. Angela Carter's Discourse of Delight in her Fiction and Non-Fiction* (Frankfurt am Main, 2016).

Lawrence Russell. Born in Northern Ireland, educated in the U.K, Canada, and California, LR is a playwright, fiction writer, critic, musician and multi-media artist. Formerly Professor of Writing & Film, University of Victoria. Twice winner of the Canadian Broadcasting Corporation's Literary Competition. His stage plays have been produced in all the major Canadian venues, including the National Arts Theatre (Ottawa) and the Stratford (Ontario) Festival's 3rd Stage. His drama and electronic sound-text compositions have been broadcast on the CBC, ABC, Radio Canada International, NPR (National Public Radio, US), the Pacifica Radio Network and other broadcast networks. His books include *Penetration* (5 plays), *Repeat This & You're Dead* (stories), *Radio Brazil* (novel) and the recent non-fiction work *Outlaw Academic* (criticism/metafiction/autobiography). This is LR's third contribution to *Deep Ends*. His website is culturecourt.com

Sam Scoggins. A graduate of the London College Of Communication, Sam was awarded his MA from the Royal College Of Art in 1983, the same year as his short film on JG Ballard, *The Unlimited Dream Company*, was completed. An academic at Canterbury Christ Church University for 10 years, Sam became the Creative Director of a Web Design Agency and the Managing Director of an Internet software development company. In 2007 he relocated to the US and has refocused his career on his fine art practice. Sam's work has been screened at juried experimental Film Festivals world-wide and shown in solo, two-person and group exhibitions in the US. He lives and and works in Woodstock, NY, and in London, UK. This is Sam's second portfolio of photos for *Deep Ends*.

Stephen E. Andrews. Stephen has worked in the book industry as a bookshop manager, bookseller, copywriter, editor and writer since 1984. He has also worked as a reviewer for magazines, as a blogger and as a guest lecturer at three British universities. The bestselling co-author of *100 Must Read Science Fiction Novels* (2006, with Nick Rennison) and two further titles in the Bloomsbury Good Reading Guide series, he has also appeared on national and regional radio and television several times. A prior contributor to *Deep Ends 2018*, 'Saucer Occupant' is his first published short story.

Maxim Jakubowski. Another writer first featured in *Deep Ends 2018*, Maxim met JG Ballard in the 1960s and they remained friends until Jim's passing, travelling together to events in France and Italy on various occasions. A British author and publisher active in crime, fantasy & SF, and erotica, Maxim won a handful of awards across these genres for his writing and editing. A winner of the Anthony award for non fiction, and the author of 20 novels, he lives in London where he is, amongst other things, currently the Vice Chair of the Crime Writers' Association and chairs its Dagger awards. He has been the crime reviewer for *The Guardian* for 12 years, and prior to that at *Time Out London*, and Joint Director of *Crime Scene*, London's International Crime & Mystery Film and Literary Festival. His latest novel is *The Louisiana Republic,* 2018.

David Manley. David is a Sydney based artist making his second appearance in *Deep Ends.* He holds a 1st-class Honours degree and Masters degree in Fine Arts (photo-media) and is currently a PhD candidate at the University of New South Wales Art and Design, Sydney. He is a lecturer in lens-based art at the National Art School Australia.

Andrew Wenaus. In with his second contribution, Andrew teaches in the Department of English and Writing Studies at the University of Western Ontario in London, Canada. He's the author of forthcoming book *Where Word Breaks Off: The Literature of Exclusion, Artificial Intelligence Narrative, and Modernism's Möbius Strip* (Lexington Books: 2020), and is currently collaborating on an experimental novel with Kenji Siratori called *Last Million Last Moments: Life in Life in Non-Orientable Surfaces.* Andrew is also a musician, producer, and composer who collaborates with Christina Willatt under the moniker Wormwood (https://wormwoodmusic.bandcamp.com/)

Mike Halliwell. Mike is a research-led Designer, Illustrator and Lecturer in the School of Architecture at Oxford Brookes University. With a background spanning live music, performing arts, architecture, art and design, Mike's primary research area is exploring the junction and translation of ideas between different creative disciplines in the communication of architectural space and narrative. This is Mike's second time in *Deep Ends.*

Paul A. Williams. Paul discovered Ballard as a teenager in the late 70s—the twin portals of *Atrocity Exhibition* and *Crash* opened up new visions and concepts of expression that haven't ceased to inspire him in his writing, music and imagery. Working for most of his life in IT, and as an old Freudian, he's continually fascinated and appalled by the impact of technology on our lives both conscious and unconscious. Paul supplied the back cover photo for *DE18*. For his explorations of Ballard in video see: http://www.ballardian.com/human-or-other-paul-williams

First-Time Contributors:

Gary J. Shipley. Gary is the author of ten books, most recently *30 Fake Beheadings* (Spork), *Warewolff!* (Hexus), and *The Unyielding* (Eraserhead). Gary has published in numerous magazines, journals, anthologies and academic journals. His monograph on Baudrillard is forthcoming from Anthem Press. More information can be found at Thek Prosthetics.

Jeremy Reed. The most brilliantly imaginative and controversial poet alive, Jeremy Reed has published over 50 books of award-winning poetry, fiction and biography, collaborated on albums with Marc Almond, and has a devotional fanbase. Amongst his recent books are the poetry collections *Piccadilly Bongo, Sooner Or Later Frank* and *Candy4Cannibals*, a biography of Lou Reed *Waiting For The Man* and *The Dilly: A Secret history of Piccadilly Rent Boys.* His collaboration with Karolina Urbaniak *Altered Balance—A Tribute to Coil* is due out in a much expanded version from Infinity Land Press in autumn 2019. http://www.jeremyreed.co.uk/

Karolina Urbaniak. Karolina is a multimedia artist and co-founder of Infinity Land Press. Her published work includes *To Putrefaction, Altered Balance—A Tribute to Coil, The Void Ratio, Artaud 1937 Apocalypse* and *Death Mort Tod—A European Book of the Dead.* Her recent multimedia projects include the soundtrack for *Darkleaks—The Ripper Genome* and the audio-visual installation *On The New Revelations of Being,* inspired by the work of Antonin Artaud. She lives and works in London. https://karolinaurbaniak.com/

Audrey Szasz. Audrey is a London-based writer with roots in Central Europe. Her experimental narratives weave exotic prose-poetry with surreal imagery and transgressive satire. She was discovered by chance in Soho by legendary novelist and poet Jeremy Reed who offered to read her work and, having done so, promptly suggested they collaborate. The resulting novel, *The Abduction of JG Ballard* published by Infinity Land Press is her debut in print. Her solo novels *Sidereal Girl* and *The Glamour Junta* are set to be released later in 2019. https://audreyszasz.wordpress.com/

Martin Bladh. Martin is an artist of multiple mediums. He is a founding member of the post-industrial band IRM, the musical avant-garde unit Skin Area and co-founder of the publishing company Infinity Land Press. His published work includes *To Putrefaction, Qualis Artifex Pereo, DES, The Hurtin' Club, Darkleaks—The Ripper Genome* and *Marty Page.* http://www.martinbladh.com/

John Collier. Retired adman John has illustrated maps for Michael Moorcock's Elric and Dorian Hawkmoon since the mid 1970s. After leaving New York and the world of advertising, John lives now in Southeastern Pennsylvania with his wife, two cats and numerous other wild things. He is currently working on the illustrated lyrics of the Scottish folksinger Alasdair Roberts. When not working on illustrations, he can be found working on his fly tying and fishing.

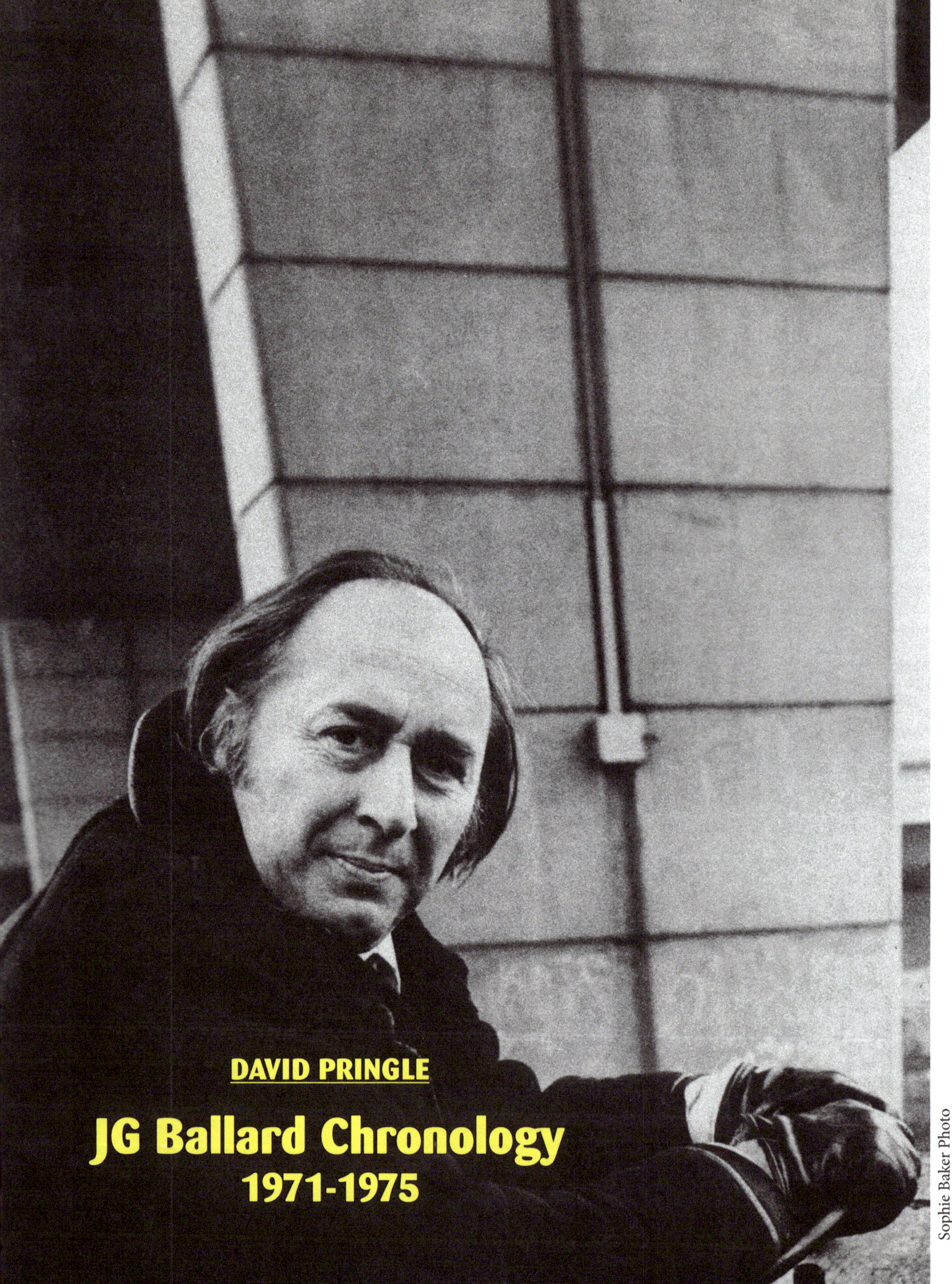

DAVID PRINGLE

JG Ballard Chronology 1971-1975

Sophie Baker Photo

(On 28 December 1970, J.G. Ballard had written to his translator in Denmark, Jannick Storm, mentioning the novel he was working on, which would be published as *Crash*. "Completed the first draft just before Xmas," he said, "and [it] will take me another 2-3 months before completion. A great deal of work remains to be done." In fact, it would take him considerably longer than a few months to finish the book to his satisfaction.)

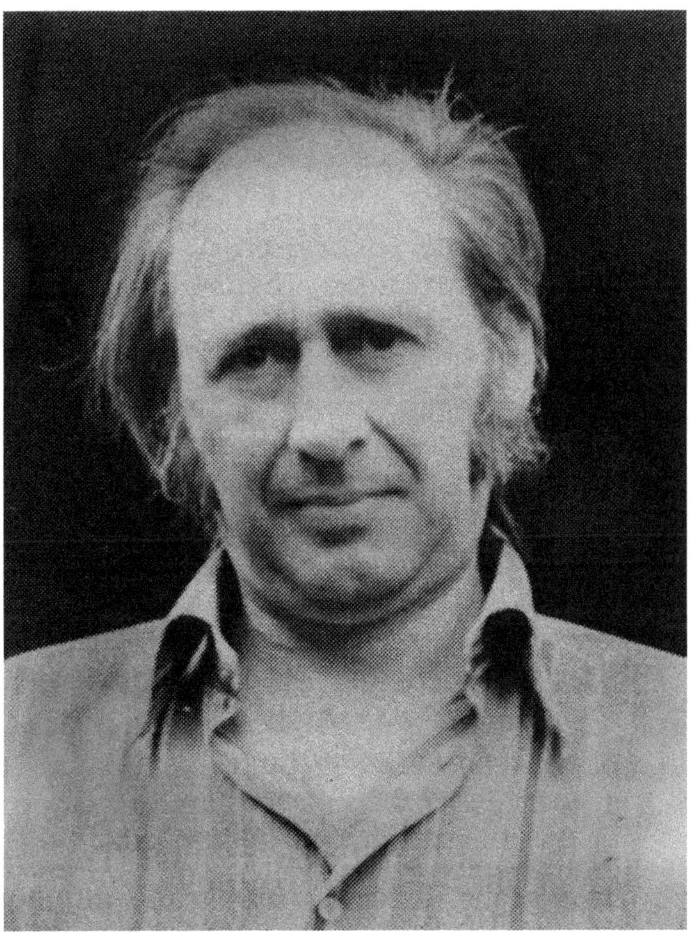

1971

1971 — January? — Featuring a candid photograph of his ladyfriend Claire Walsh, *née* Churchill, "Venus Smiles," Ballard's fifth (and last) "advertiser's announcement," appeared on the outside back cover of *Ambit* no. 46 (Winter 1970/1971). A small caption said: "Claire: Zephyr V.6." He would write later: "Claire Churchill... is the subject of the fifth ad, which shows her, after swimming in the sea off Brighton, sitting naked in the front seat of my car covered with thousands of specks of seaweed—so outraged was she by my sneak photography that she stole my only copy of the ad, but she has agreed in the interests of Art and Literature to have it [re-]published." (Ballard, *Re/Search 8/9*, 1984.)

1971 — January 15 (Friday) — *Vanishing Point*, directed by Richard C. Sarafian, starring Barry Newman, Cleavon Little and "an Alpine White 1970 Dodge Challenger R/T with a 440/375 HP engine," was a Hollywood movie first released on this date. "I like stylized narratives where there's a great deal of form and flow, like a good Raymond Chandler or a good B movie, a hard-driving thriller in fact where you know there's a plot, you know there's a story, but you don't need to follow the detailed ramifications... Like *Vanishing Point*, which I loved. I thought that was a colossal film..." (Ballard, Jon Savage interview, 1978.)

1971 — January 18 (Monday) — Death of Virgil Finlay (b. 1914), American fantasy and science-fiction magazine illustrator, of cancer at 56. He illustrated a number of Ballard's stories in the 1960s.

1971 — January 25 (Monday) — Major-General Idi Amin led a military coup which deposed Milton Obote as president of Uganda.

1971 — January 29 (Friday) — "Spacing Out," an interview with Ballard by Brendan Hennessy, appeared in the *Times Educational Supplement*. "For a long time he was a fringe favourite among sf fans; literary critics didn't like him. Now he is joining Shakespeare, Conrad and Thackeray on set reading lists for examinations. This pleases him but he can still be waspish about the Eng. Lit. establishment. 'Custodians of a natural history museum,' he says. 'They go on pretending that the stuffed animals are very much alive'... Ballard has three children at school. What does he think about education? 'I think the emphasis on the sciences isn't strong enough by any means yet. The ordinary business of living demands more and more expertise, more and more understanding of science and technology. An imaginative response to science is the key, and I don't think the humanities provide that key any longer... The sciences should be regarded as the humanities of the 20th century, the most ennobling and enriching study that one can find.'"

1971 — January 31 (Sunday) — Apollo 14, commanded by Alan Shepard, with astronauts Stuart A. Roosa and Edgar D. Mitchell, lifted off for the third successful lunar landing mission.

1971 — February — Ballard's essay "Fictions of Every Kind," a review of *The Shattered Ring* by Lois and Stephen Rose, appeared in *Books and Bookmen*. "Almost all the criticism of science fiction has been written by benevolent outsiders, who combine zeal with ignorance, like high-minded missionaries viewing the sex-rites of a remarkably fertile aboriginal tribe and finding every laudable influence at work except the outstanding length of penis. The depth of penetration of this earnest couple, Lois and Stephen Rose, is that of a pair of practising Christians who see in science fiction an attempt to place a new perspective on 'man, nature, history and ultimate meaning.' What they fail to realize is that science fiction is totally atheistic: those critics in the past who have found any mystical strains at work have been blinded by the camouflage. Science fiction is much more concerned with the significance of the gleam on an automobile instrument panel than on the deity's posterior—if Mother Nature has anything in science fiction, it is VD."

1971 — February 12 (Friday) — Ballard appeared in "Crash!", a short BBC 2 television film based on his work. A segment of the arts programme "Review," it was directed by Harley Cokliss (b. 1945) and introduced by James Mossman. "It came out of the 'Atrocity Exhibition' stories... Harley Cokliss, who has gone on to direct a number of mainstream Hollywood movies, was working for a BBC arts programme. I don't know how he'd heard, but he knew I was very interested in car crashes and so on. He got in touch with me and suggested... would I like to make a 20-minute film for this arts programme? Which we did, and it was called 'Crash!' I hadn't written [the novel] *Crash* at that stage, but it was the obvious title to give it. So we filmed this thing, which was somewhere half-way between a documentary and a feature film... The screenplay, or whatever you want to call it, wasn't written by me; it was written by Cokliss. So I just did what he told me. He'd say, 'walk across the roof of this multi-storey car park, Jim, and get into that car,' so I'd do that. I think I wrote a voice-over, which I remember recording at Ealing Studios... A rather pretty actress, Gabrielle Drake, briefly appeared as a mysterious woman that I drove around with. It was fun." (Ballard, Pringle interview, 1995.) "The film was based on my interest in the car crash—as it emerged through the pages of *The Atrocity Exhibition*... with Gabrielle Drake. She was quite a serious actress in her early days, but then she moved off into 'Crossroads' or something. She was very sweet. I met her a few times on the set, as it were, chasing around multi-storey car parks in Watford. There are an enormous number of multi-storey car parks in Watford, I discovered. It's the Mecca of the multi-storey car park. And they're quite ornate, some of them." (Ballard, quoted in Iain Sinclair, *Crash*, 1999, p29.)

1971 — February 15 (Monday) — Decimalisation Day: The United Kingdom and Ireland both switched to decimal currency. After some 1,200 years, since the time of Offa and Charlemagne, Britain finally abandoned the 12-pence-to-the-shilling, 20-shillings-to-the-pound coinage for the decimal system of 100 "new pence" to the pound.

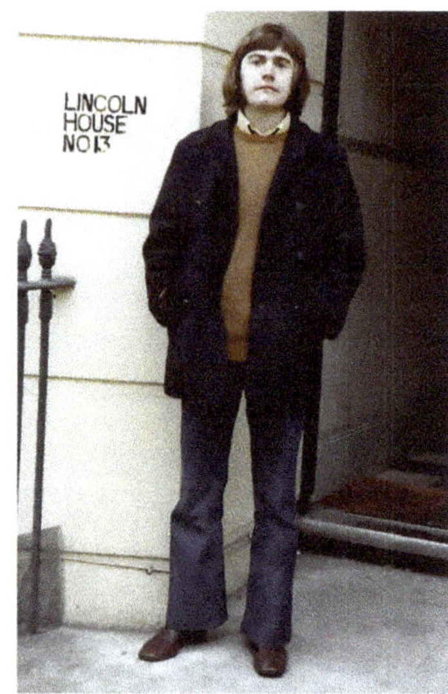

David Pringle at 13 Eaton Place, Brighton, in 1971

1971 — February 24 (Wednesday) — "Yesterday I bought two newly-published sf paperbacks: Ballard's *The Day of Forever* (a new edition which contains 'The Killing Ground' in lieu of 'The Assassination of Kennedy...') and Aldiss's *Intangibles, Inc.*, a collection of stories I haven't read before." (David Pringle, diary, 24 February 1971.)

1971 — March 26 (Friday) — In London, the New Arts Laboratory/IRAT (Institute for Research in Art & Technology) closed down as the building in which it was housed was reclaimed by Camden Council. Ballard and Dr Christopher Evans had both been trustees of IRAT (nominally, at any rate).

1971 — March 31 (Wednesday) — "*New Worlds* is alive and well! I hope I'm not speaking too soon. I arrived home in Sutton yesterday evening and found *NW* no. 201 waiting along with some other mail on my desk. It's a very slim issue indeed, just 23 pages long, containing one story and an article—but it is only intended as a stop-gap, a bonus to the subscribers. The paperback quarterly *New Worlds* should be appearing regularly from June 1971. It is to be published and distributed by Sphere Books." (D. Pringle, diary, 31 March 1971.)

1971 — Spring — An interview with Ballard by Brendan Hennessy appeared in *Transatlantic Review* no. 39 (Spring 1971). This appears to have dated from the same session, probably recorded in the autumn of 1970, as the 29 January *TES* interview by Hennessy. "I talked to him in the study of his home in Shepperton, surrounded by books and magazines, overlooked by two large posters—Max Ernst's 'The Robing of the Bride' and a Man Ray of a huge, bright red mouth lying across the sky...

[Hennessy:] There are a few 'experimental' writers becoming known now in this country, aren't there? Is there any cause for optimism, do you think?

[Ballard:] It's encouraging, but I think they're handicapped by the fact that they're trying to write about 1970 with the vocabulary of 1870. But experimental writing in this country has always had a bad name. The main tradition of the fine arts—painting and sculpture—is the tradition of the new. In literature, if you say anything new people are thrown into a rictus of hostility and fright, like experimental animals being shown too many confusing signs. Something like 5,000 novels are published every year, and the great majority of them show no advance in vocabulary, technique, style, on Jane Austen's *Pride and Prejudice*."

1971 — April — "Ballard at Home," an interview with Ballard conducted by Douglas Reed in 1970, appeared in the monthly *Books and Bookmen*. It included a description of Ballard's house and garden: "His house... was a box among boxes in greater London with the careless peeled appearance of a lizard shedding its skin. Inside was chaos and Ballard, mainly the former... The study-come-lounge-come-disaster-area looked out through faded French doors onto a small garden dotted here and there with Ballard original modernistic lawn sculptures, made from cheap materials."

And also this statement: "Ballard, whose primary source of income is writing, is also preparing a study of one of his pet loves, surrealism. This is an art form ideally suited to the Ballard dream-scape... A modest involvement with *avant-garde* activities is a natural extension of this interest in the liberating effects of imaginative experimentation. He has a position as Prose Editor of *Ambit*, a new wave literary magazine, and another as a Trustee of the Institute for Research in Art & Technology (which encompasses the New Arts Laboratory)."

1971 — April — Ballard's collection *Vermilion Sands* was published as a paperback original by Berkley Books, New York, priced at 75 cents and with a cover illustration by Richard Powers. The back-cover blurb said, in part: "From the dark recesses of a superb imagination, J.G. Ballard has conjured up an elegant nightmare of decadence, a portrait of a future Gomorrah where a Nero might play an automated violin."

1971 — April — This was the month in which the American publishers Dutton were due to publish Ballard's collection *The Atrocity Exhibition*. "After Doubleday dropped the book, E.P. Dutton took it on. It was scheduled to be published in April, 1971. 'They were enthusiastic,' Ballard told me. 'In fact, they first thought of retitling the book *Why I Want to Fuck Ronald Reagan*. They were very keen indeed. And there were going to be no problems. But in April—when they were due to publish—my agent got a letter from Dutton with a huge lawyers' report saying they would be very happy to publish the book if I would agree to all the changes. The changes went on for page after page.' Dutton's lawyers wanted Ballard to delete three pieces entirely, and all references in the remainder of the book to Ralph Nader, Lyndon and Lady Bird Johnson, and several other celebrities. 'They said if I did that they would publish the book. The only problem was there wouldn't be much of a book left. The whole essence of the book is contained in these sexual fantasies about public figures. They are the key to the book, in a sense. I felt I couldn't go along with that, so I said, "Sorry," and there we are now. And I'm looking for someone else.' After Dutton finally declined to publish the book, Grove Press contracted for its publication and brought it out without any deletions or changes in November, 1972." (Jerome Tarshis, "Krafft-Ebing Visits Dealey Plaza," *Evergreen Review* no. 96, Spring 1973.)

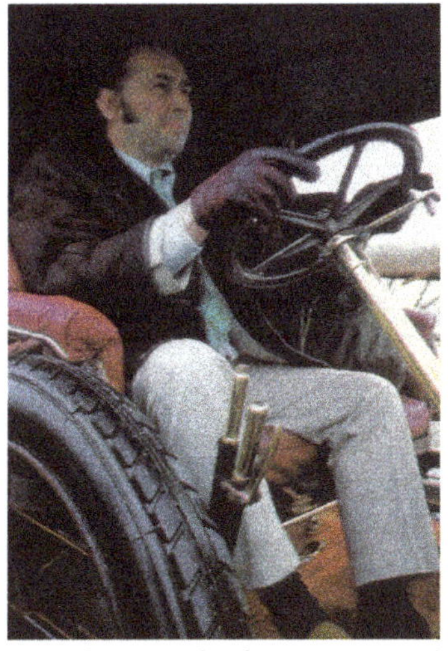

JGB at the controls of a 1904 Renault.

1971 — April 14 (Wednesday) — Mercedes-Benz presented their 350 SL car, the first R107 model. "*Drive* [the Automobile Association magazine] invited me to join a veteran car rally across Germany to celebrate the seventieth anniversary of Mercedes-Benz and the launching of a new model, the 350SL grand tourer. Some eighteen cars belonging to members of the British Veteran Car Club assembled at Harwich, sailed overnight to Bremerhaven in northern Germany, and travelled together on a seven-day return journey to Stuttgart, the home of Mercedes. Glad of a chance to visit the industrial landscape which was the birthplace of the car, I willingly accepted, and was duly sworn in as a passenger on board the AA's own veteran car, a 1904 Renault. This was my first veteran car run, and there was no doubt by the time I reached Stuttgart that however little I knew about the modern car I knew a great deal about the old, all of it learned the hard way. Exhausting, often terrifying and always exciting..." (Ballard, "The Car, the Future," *Drive*, Autumn 1971.)

1971 — May 1 (Saturday) — A bomb planted by the Angry Brigade exploded in the fashionable Biba shop in Kensington, London. No one was hurt. "When the Angry Brigade bombed the Biba boutique... it was a curious target, and an action unlikely to win them much support from any section of society. But the Angries believed that the revolution had been neutered by consumerism and that too many indifferent, politically unengaged hippies had replaced a commitment to cultural openness and anti-war politics with a trivial pursuit of cash, sex and drugs." (Dave Haslam, *Not Abba*, p57.)

1971 — May (early) — Ballard met Jorge Luis Borges, and a photograph was taken of the two in conversation. "JGB and Borges met in London, at a party in John Wolfers Agency.

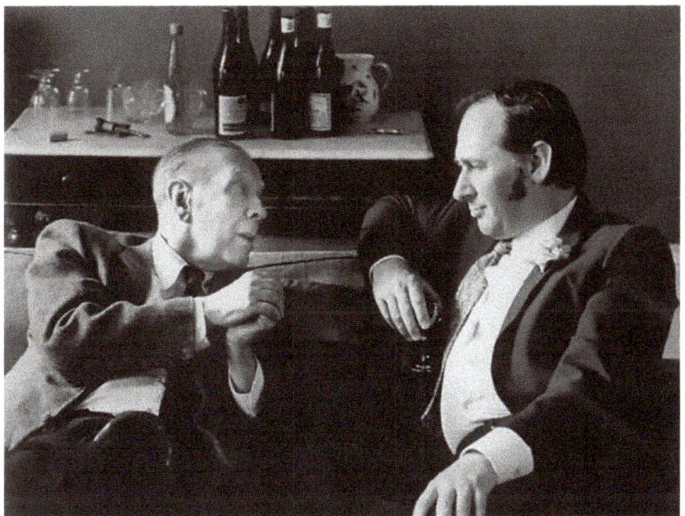

JLB in conversation with JGB.

[In 1975] I visited JGB (we had met in Rio in 1969), and also Wolfers, then Ballard's agent. JW gave me a print of that picture. He was very proud of having had old god Borges cast his spell on his office. ('Look. This is the bottle opener you can see in the photo.') The photographer is Sophie Baker—another picture she took in the same party landed on the jacket of *Love and Napalm: Export USA* [1972], where you can see Jim wearing the same suit and the same white carnation on his lapel." (Marcial Souto, comment at Ballardian.com, 7 July 2008.) Ten days after his comment Souto sent a further message clarifying the date of the Ballard/Borges encounter: "According to Norman Thomas di Giovanni, who attended that party with Borges (he was his translator and secretary at the time), it took place in early May, 1971." (17 July 2008.)

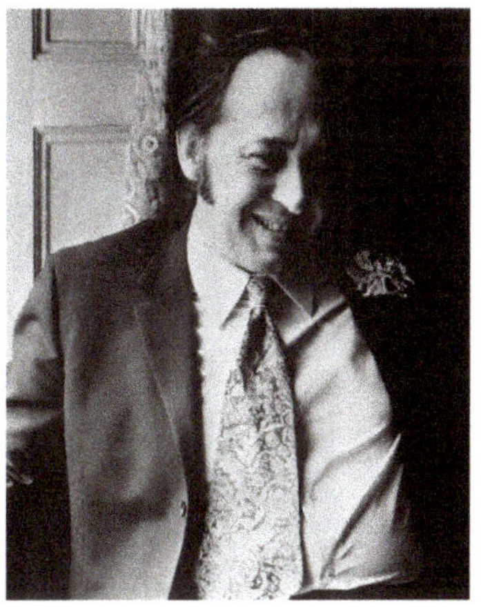

1971 — May 6 (Thursday) — Death of Dickie Valentine (real name Richard Bryce, b. 1929), British popular singer, a Shepperton resident, in a car crash in Wales at age 41. Two other musicians, a pianist and a drummer, died along with him. The coroner's inquest would reveal that the car was travelling in excess of 90 mph at the time of impact, and that Valentine, who was driving his wife's Hillman Avenger, with which he was unfamiliar, had lost control while attempting to take a dangerous bend.

1971 — May 29 (Saturday) — Beatrice Ballard's 12th birthday. Around this time: "I remember when we were children growing up in Shepperton, our excitement the day that our first colour television set arrived. It was as if we were stepping into a whole new world. No more black and white, everything seemed different, more real. As a family in the evenings we gathered around the television together after supper. My father was particularly excited by the US space programme, and I remember watching with him the Apollo rocket launches from Cape Canaveral. It was deeply exciting to see these events beamed live into our living room." (Bea Ballard, *Deep Ends 2016*, p255.)

1971 — June — An interview with William Burroughs, "Mind Engineer," conducted by Graham Masterton and Andrew Rossabi, appeared in *Penthouse* magazine (June 1971; it would also appear in the American edition of *Penthouse*, March 1972). "Occasionally, we had lunch with Monique and Andrew Rossabi. We used to visit them for Sunday lunch at their flat in a leafy square in West London, in the late 1960s, possibly early 1970s. Daddy seemed to get on well with them both. I remember thinking Monique was very elegant. I think Andrew wrote. The lunches were animated with lively conversation." (Fay Ballard, interview by D. Pringle, 2014.) Monique Rossabi would contribute a prose piece, "A Maiden's Dream of a Lake," to *Ambit* no. 55 in 1973.

1971 — June 5 (Saturday) — Ballard's essay "The Consumer Consumed," a speculative piece on Ralph Nader as a possible future dictator of the United States, appeared in the underground paper *Ink* (issue no. 6, dated 5 June 1971). "Many of Nader's targets seem ludicrously puny did any of us, for example, ever regard breakfast cereals as anything but a good-humoured method of blocking the infant's trumpeting mouth as we recovered from our hangovers? The important point, though, is that Nader is unloading a powerful sense of anxiety and guilt on to a huge range of commonplace activities. Sooner or later, I would guess, these will crystallize around one major subject, a simple formula of antagonism, unease and wish-fulfilment that will play the same role in the technological landscape that cruder formulas played in the political landscape."

1971 — June (mid) — The first issue of the paperback *New Worlds Quarterly*, edited by Michael Moorcock, appeared around this time. It contained reprints of Ballard's "The Killing Ground" (1969) and "Journey Across a Crater" (1970), although he was to contribute nothing new to the series, which would last for ten volumes. "The new *New Worlds* (published by Sphere Books) is out at last. I saw it today in Hudson's bookshop... I was disappointed to see that it contains two Ballard stories which are reprints. Otherwise, it contains new stories by Aldiss, Disch, etc." (D. Pringle, diary, 23 June 1971.)

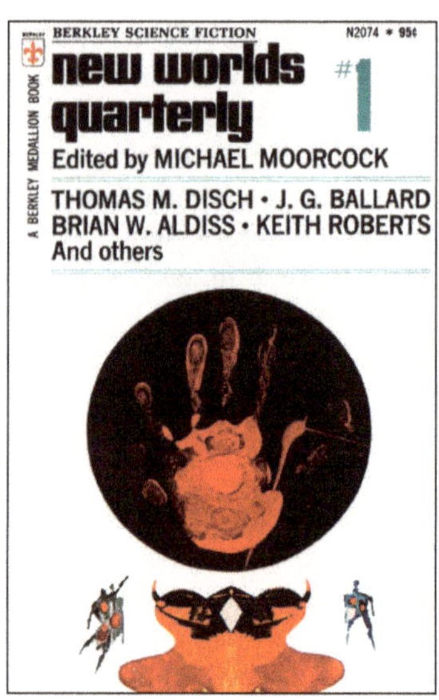

1971 — June 30 (Wednesday) — After a seemingly successful mission aboard Salyut 1, the world's first manned space station, the crew of the Soyuz 11 spacecraft were killed when their air supply leaked out through a faulty valve. Cosmonauts Viktor Patsayev (38), Georgi T. Dobrovolsky (43) and Vladislav Nikolayevich Volkov (35) were found dead when Soyuz 11 landed.

1971 — July 3 (Saturday) — Death of Jim Morrison (b. 1943), American rock singer and songwriter, who was found in his Paris apartment. "Morrison died aged 27, suffering a heart attack in the bath, with suggestions that both heroin and alcohol had a part to play in his demise. He's one of a number of drug deaths in these years. Out of the public eye there were probably thousands of casualties; in the public eye, musicians like Gregg Allman and Eric Clapton were struggling with heroin habits, and others didn't survive." (Haslam, *Not Abba*, p64.)

1971 — July 11 (Sunday) — Death of John W. Campbell (b. 1911), American science-fiction editor (Astounding, later Analog) and sometime sf writer, of heart failure at 61.

1971 — July 26 (Monday) — Apollo 15 was launched towards the moon from Cape Kennedy, Florida, with astronauts David Scott, Alfred M. Worden and James B. Irwin as its crew.

1971 — July (late?) — Around this time Ballard and artist Eduardo Paolozzi were jointly interviewed by Frank Whitford, at Paolozzi's studio in London. "I think that the biggest need of the painter or writer today is information. I'd love to have a tickertape machine in my study constantly churning out material: abstracts from scientific journals, the latest Hollywood gossip, the passenger list of a 707 that crashed in the Andes, the colour mixes of a new automobile varnish. In fact, Eduardo and I in our different ways are already gathering this kind of information, but we are using the clumsiest possible tools to do it: our own hands and eyes. The technology of the information-retrieval system that we enjoy is incredibly primitive... I think there's an information starvation at present and technology will create the possibility of knowing everything about everything. When Apollo 99 blasts off to Alpha Centauri we will know everything about the crew all of the time." (Ballard, *Studio International*, October 1971.)

1971 — August — Ballard and family may have holidayed in France and Spain in this month. "We had enjoyed the 1970s together... largely by going abroad whenever we could. Claire and I and our four children would climb into my large family saloon and head for Dover, watch the white cliffs recede without a pang... and begin to breathe freely as we emerged through the bow doors and rolled the wheels across the Boulogne cobbles. Soon there was the intoxicating reek of Gauloises, scent, merde and higher octane French petrol..." (Ballard, *Miracles of Life*, p247-248.) His three children were Jim, Fay and Bea; the fourth mentioned was Claire's daughter Jenny.

1971 — September 13 (Monday) — "THELWALL, England, Monday. Nine people died and more than 60 were injured today in a series of pile-ups on an expressway near Thelwall, Lancashire, the Press Association reported. The pile-ups occurred in fog about 7am and when the fog lifted a trail of smashed vehicles and debris could be seen over a mile-long stretch. Almost 200 vehicles were reported to be involved in the pile-ups, and there were several fires. The motorway, the busy M6, was still closed at lpm, and police said emergency teams were at present busy clearing the wreckage. A Lancashire police spokesman blamed some drivers for travelling too fast in the conditions." (*Canberra Times*, 14 September 1971.)

1971 — September 16 (Thursday) — "What does the future hold for science fiction?", a short article by Michael Moorcock, appeared in *The Guardian*. "...The serious writer who has left the SF category behind him is often more talented and sophisticated. I hope that next year we shall see closer attention given, say, to Thomas Disch's *334*, about ordinary New Yorkers managing to live ordinary lives in a world which would seem hellish to us but which they accept (as people do) as perfectly normal. J.G. Ballard's new novel, provisionally called *Crash*, will have a present day setting and will continue to define its moral themes in terms of man's relationship to his technological myths (and to his automobiles in particular)."

1971 — September 16 (Thursday) — Ballard's collection *Chronopolis and Other Stories* was published in hardcover by Putnam, New York. (Publication date according to Kirkus Reviews.)

1971 — Autumn — Ballard's commissioned essay "The Car, the Future" appeared in *Drive*, the magazine of the AA. "In Britain the first motorways are already reaching across our cities. Many of them are motion-sculptures of considerable grace and beauty, but they totally overpower the urban areas around and all too often below them. It may well be that these vast concrete intersections are the most important monuments of our urban civilization, the 20th century's equivalent of the Pyramids, but do we want to be remembered in the same way as the slave-armies who constructed what, after all, were monuments to the dead?"

1971 — October — "Speculative Illustrations," Frank Whitford's joint interview with Ballard and Eduardo Paolozzi, appeared in *Studio International* no. 937 (October 1971). A photograph of the participants, captioned *Eduardo Paolozzi, J.G. Ballard and Apollo Space Suit in the Science Museum, Kensington*, was printed alongside. Some time this year, perhaps on the same day, Ballard

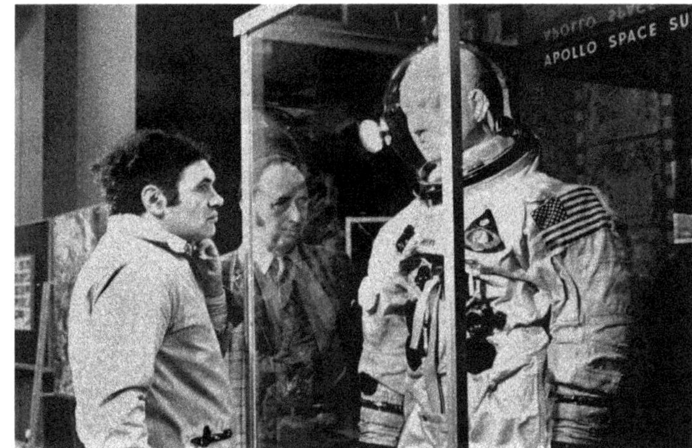

Eduardo Paolozzi and J.G. Ballard examine an Apollo Astronaut.

also visited the Imperial War Museum in Paolozzi's company. A photograph exists showing them posing in a military jeep, Ballard at the wheel, with the caption: *Paolozzi and Ballard in the Imperial War Museum, 1971.*

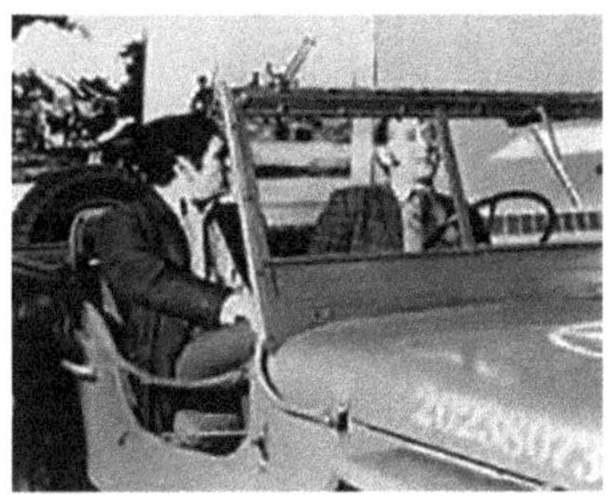

"Eduardo Paolozzi, whose current exhibition at the Tate Gallery is, surprisingly, the first large-scale showing of his work in this country, has known the novelist J.G. Ballard for some time. Both artist and writer have many interests in common. Both are fascinated by technology, by the predicament of the individual in a highly mechanized society, and both explore the way in which certain symbols and images can precipitate complex chain-reactions in the imagination." (Whitford.)

"A woman friend describing Eduardo Paolozzi said: 'He's a Minotaur.' I thought this accurate: a bull's head, powerful physique, a lot of snorting, one hoof clawing the ground, eyes ready to attack anybody who's a little too light on his feet. But also that maze. It seems to me that Eduardo Paolozzi is the most important sculptor to have emerged since the Second World War and the only one who responds directly to science and technology, to the media landscape which has constructed the huge maze that we all inhabit." (Ballard, "Junkyard Dreams," *The Times*, 1987.)

1971 — October 31 (Sunday) — A bomb exploded at the top of the Post Office Tower in London, causing visible damage but no injuries. Part of the tower was normally open to the public, but that area was closed following the bomb. The attack was attributed to the IRA, but may in fact have been the work of the Angry Brigade.

1971 — November — Thomas M. Disch published his first anthology, *The Ruins of Earth* (New York: Putnam), which included Ballard's story "The Cage of Sand." In his introduction Disch stated: "Ballard's *The Burning World* is probably the single best fictional account of an ecological disaster: its rationale is plausible, its images are crystalline, its allegory is deliberate, precise, and always modest. In the ideal ten-volume version of this anthology *The Burning World* would be Volume One."

1971 — November 9 (Tuesday) — "Ideas in Science Fiction, 4: Inward Landscapes," Ballard in discussion with Dr Christopher Evans, was broadcast on BBC Radio 3. "I have just listened to a good interview between Christopher Evans and J.G. Ballard on Radio 3. No particularly new ideas emerged, but it was interesting that in talking of his *Drowned World/Drought/Crystal World* trilogy he ratified Judith Merril's theory of the three books being concerned with the past, the future and the present respectively. Water, he said, was his presiding image of the past (suggesting the womb); drought was his image of the future (suggesting a drying up of life and a quantification of its elements); and the crystal or jewel was his image of the present (a beautiful, static, radiating form). He also mentioned his new novel on the motor car, but he didn't say when it would be published." (D. Pringle, diary, 9 November 1971.)

1971 — November 13 (Saturday) — Steven Spielberg's TV movie Duel, based on a short story by Richard Matheson, was first shown on American television. It starred Dennis Weaver as a motorist who finds himself menaced by a giant truck on a California highway. (In Britain, it would be released in revised form as a cinema film in October 1972, followed by a similar release in other countries.)

1971 — November 15 (Monday) — J.G. Ballard's 41st birthday. It may have been around this time that he was interviewed by the American critic Jerome Tarshis (publication of the interview would be delayed until 1973). "I think the future of this planet can be summed up in one word: sex. I think sex times the computer equals tomorrow. I think the future of sex is limitless... The old fantasies—drinking someone's urine, being beaten by a beautiful woman in black leather—are dead. A new Krafft-Ebing is being written by car crashes, televised violence, modern architecture and design. What we see through the window of the TV set is just as important, sexually, as what the old-fashioned voyeur could see through the window of a bedroom. In the future of sex, men and women may not be necessary to one another. Sex might take place between you and an idea, or you and a machine. An incredible range of new unions, new perversions if you will, could be realized by using computer data banks, videotape cassettes, or instant-playback closed-circuit TV. I can see a sexual experience of extraordinary complexity, beauty, tenderness, and love. I can see the magic of sex on a planetary scale, revivifying everything it touches."

1971 — November 15 (Monday) — In California, the Intel Corporation released the world's first commercially available microprocessor, the 4004. An integrated circuit combining all the essential elements of a computer central processing unit, the microprocessor had been developed by Federico Faggin, Marcian "Ted" Hoff and Stanley Mazor. It contained 2,300 transistors on a seven-millimetre-square silicon chip and could process four bits at a cycle rate of 60,000 per second.

1971 — November 29 (Monday) — Seven people died in Britain's worst motorway pile-up to date, in fog on the M1.

1971 — December 30 (Thursday) — "The Horror Story, 3: Psychohorror" was broadcast on BBC Radio 3, featuring Ballard in discussion with Dr Christopher Evans, and a full reading, by Hugh Dickson, of Ballard's story "The Gioconda of the Twilight Noon."

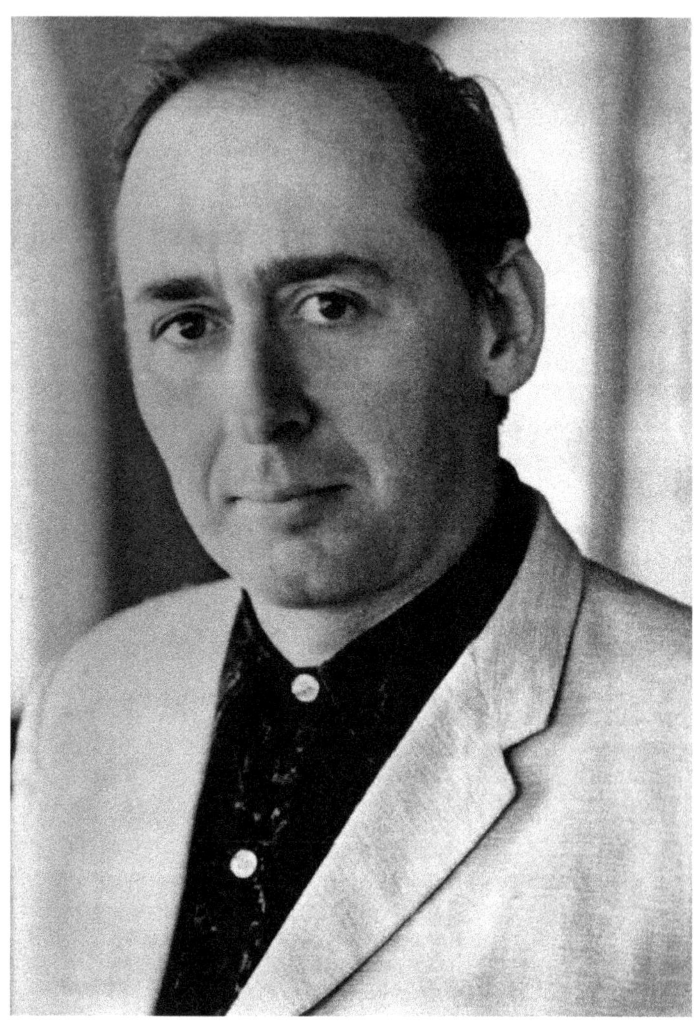

1972

1972 — January 3 (Monday) — "There were massive motorway pile-ups and much talk about Ralph Nader in Britain during 1971. Will we soon see the beginning of the end of the combustion-engined car?" (D. Pringle, diary, 3 January 1972.)

1972 — January 13 (Thursday) — Edward Goldsmith, editor, and his colleague Robert Allen published a special issue of *The Ecologist* entitled "A Blueprint for Survival," advocating an end to economic growth and technological progress, and a reduction in the human population level.

1972 — January 16 (Sunday) — A photograph of the stripper known as Euphoria Bliss, with Ballard and others in the background, appeared in the *Sunday Times* (p30). The caption read: "This is a literary occasion. The lady in the shawl is Miss Euphoria Bliss who performs her nude *adagio* nightly at the Latin Quarter. She also reads poetry for the magazine *Ambit*, whose [forthcoming] 50th issue this gathering celebrates. Left to right: Richard Freeman, writer; Edwin Brock, poet; Eduardo

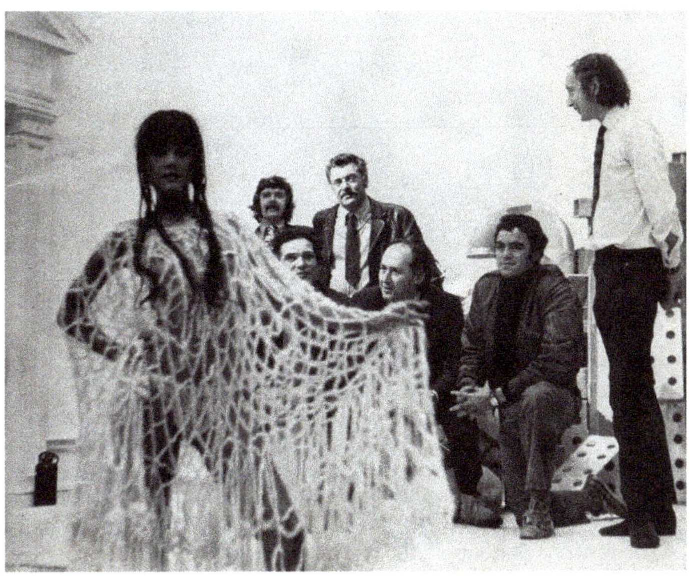

Paolozzi, artist; J.G. Ballard, novelist; Michael Foreman, illustrator; Martin Bax, editor. The setting is the Royal Academy where Paolozzi's sculpture, 'Thunder and Lightning with Flies and Jack Kennedy,' is on show... in an exhibition called *British Sculptors of '72*."

1972 — January 22 (Saturday) — Edward Heath signed the accession treaty of the European Community (EEC) in Brussels, although a woman protestor spoiled the moment by throwing ink over him as he arrived for the signing.

1972 — January 30 (Sunday) — Bloody Sunday: in a confrontation with a large crowd of demonstrators which got out of hand, British troops of the First Parachute Regiment killed 13 unarmed Roman Catholic civil rights marchers in Londonderry, Northern Ireland.

1972 — February 13 (Sunday) — "LONDON, Sunday. More massive power cuts resulting from a five-week-old strike by coal miners blacked out wide areas of Britain today amid warnings that in two to three weeks about 20 million people could be out of work... Power cuts have also caused traffic chaos in many towns and cities as traffic lights failed and at night motorists were advised to drive with main headlights on in case streets were plunged suddenly into darkness." (*Canberra Times*, 14 February 1972.)

1972 — February (mid?) — Ballard delivered the manuscript of his novel *Crash* to his agent, John Wolfers, who then sent it to Jonathan Cape. "*Crash* was in fact delivered to my publishers in February 1972, and published in June 1973—a slightly longer interval than usual, but not particularly significant." (Ballard, *Cypher* interview, October 1973.)

1972 — February 20 (Sunday) — "It looks as though the miners' strike is almost over, but the power cuts that we've been suffering for the past fortnight are likely to continue for some time. There are so few street lights that the town seems very different (and quite exciting) at night." (D. Pringle, diary, 20 February 1972.)

1972 — February 22 (Tuesday) — A car-bomb, planted by the Official IRA, exploded at Aldershot barracks, Hampshire, killing seven civilians and marking the coming of Irish terrorism to the UK "mainland." The seven killed were an elderly gardener, five female kitchen staff and Father Gerard Weston, a Roman Catholic army chaplain.

1972 — February 29 (Tuesday) — "LONDON, Tuesday. Former Beatle George Harrison and his wife, Patti, were injured last night when their car hit a crash barrier on the M4 motorway near London, the Associated Press reported. Mr Harrison, 29, who suffered cuts to the face, was taken to Maidenhead Hospital where the wounds were stitched. Mrs Harrison, 27, was X-rayed and treated for concussion." (*Canberra Times*, 1 March 1972.)

1972 — February (late?) — "Two weeks after completing *Crash*," Ballard had a serious car accident while driving on the A316 road, on the section between Chiswick, to the north of the Thames, and Mortlake, to the south. "I had a crash myself, 18 months ago, and it was a case of nature imitating art. I rolled a Zephyr across a dual carriageway and ended up on my head in the oncoming lane, tucked under the wall of Mortlake Cemetery." (Ballard, Mike Bygrave interview, *Radio Times*, 15 December 1973.)

"After finishing the book and delivering the manuscript to my agent I was driving back from London in the rain about two in morning, and the car skidded and swerved across the central reservation, smashed down a steel sign then rolled on to its back and was carried down the oncoming lane... Thank god I didn't hit anything, otherwise everyone would have been dead. And I ended up with the roof crushed down upside down in my harness. There was petrol everywhere. People were standing around in the darkness bellowing, 'Petrol, petrol.' They couldn't open the doors because the roof was down. Of all things, the window-winder fell off. I must have knocked it off with my elbow. So I wasn't able to wind down the window. I suppose somebody could've kicked it in. I was lucky the thing didn't ignite." (Ballard, *Repsychling* interview, 1975.)

"In my car crash I was driving along a dual carriageway at the bottom of Chiswick Bridge at about midnight [sic]. I think one of the tyres blew out. The car swerved to the right, crossed a traffic island demolishing a sign, rolled over onto its roof and carried on along the oncoming lane. Cars were coming towards me but luckily nobody hit me. I was wearing a seatbelt, and I remember as the car moved along upside down my face was only about 18 inches from the road which was rushing past lit by the headlamps. I remember this sudden explosion of glass as the windshield collapsed. Then, suddenly, I could hear people shouting 'petrol, petrol,' and discovered I could not open the doors because the

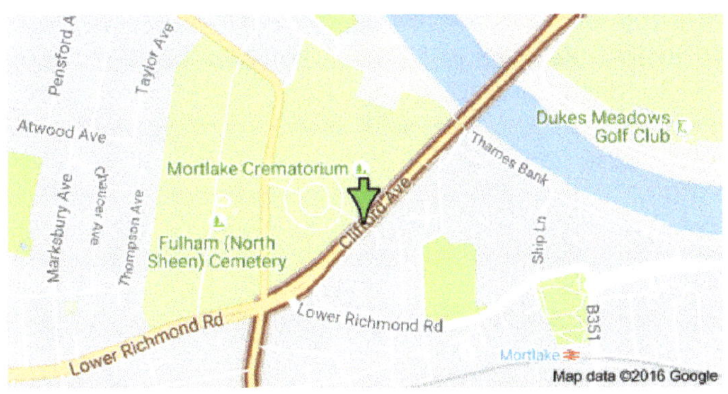

roof had been crushed. But finally I managed to climb out. About 20 people gathered and we rolled the car over and I attempted to drive off but was stopped by the police." (Ballard, Sam Scoggins interview, Royal College of Art, 1983.)

Note: in his two earliest accounts, from 1973 and 1975, Ballard made no mention of a "blow-out"; the suggestion that a tyre may have blown out only enters his accounts of the accident from 1983 onwards.

1972 — February (late?) — Ballard refused to take a breathalyzer test, and was arrested by the police, who took him to a hospital to have his injuries checked. "It was a mad evening because I was breathalyzed, well, I refused to be breathalyzed. And I was technically under arrest in this hospital. I got my head X-rayed and I must have been undergoing euphoria or something because I got into a fierce argument with this girl, the radiographer, about who owned the copyright of these photographs. I was looking at these photographs of my skull front and side. And the doctor was saying, 'Well, there's nothing there but the long-term effects take a long time to show.' I thought, 'That's great. Who owns the copyright?' 'We own the copyright.' I was saying, 'No. That's my head. I own the copyright. You own the plates, not the copyright. This is an important distinction.' Anyway, I got home by taxi. I was ill. I must've had concussion." (Ballard, *Repsychling* interview, 1975.) \

"While I was being examined by an Asian doctor two policemen pushed their way into the cubicle and demanded to breathalyse me. Breath tests had recently been introduced and were still the subject of widespread controversy. When I stood up one of the policemen began to use his shoulder against me, and fearing that I might be arrested and removed from the hospital, I refused to be breathalysed." (Ballard, notes for *Miracles of Life*, 2007, British Library archive, p53.)

1972 — March (early?) — Following his road accident, Ballard photographed his car: "I spent three days with a splitting headache, then went out, hired a car, drove to where the wrecked Zephyr was stored and photographed it. I'd developed exactly the obsession I'd described in *The Atrocity Exhibition*." (Ballard, Bygrave interview, *Radio Times*, 15 December 1973.) "After about three days the car was over at Richmond held by the police in some pound. I went to the garage here and rented a car for the day and took my camera. I went over to Richmond and photographed the wrecked car. There was a terrible pathos of this machine with which I was so intimately involved." (Ballard, *Repsychling* interview, 1975.)

He would have the car made more-or-less roadworthy again, and Michael Moorcock would remember accompanying him when he went to retrieve it: "He wouldn't let that car go. He insisted I go with him one day to the wrecker's yard. He's arguing with the blokes and he gets the car back. It's not running, it's rumbling along. It stinks of death. It reeks of damp and mould. We're doing about ten miles an hour, everything steaming and banging. And he's insisting it's all right." (Moorcock, quoted in Iain Sinclair, *Crash*, 1999, p96.) To which Ballard responded with laughter and said: "Oh, that's a bit of mythmaking... The car was dragged to a police pound and it must have rained, because the upholstery—which I assume was made of plastic—must have contained some wool. Of course it smelt musty. That's what Mike remembers. I had the car repaired." (Ballard, quoted in Sinclair, same page.)

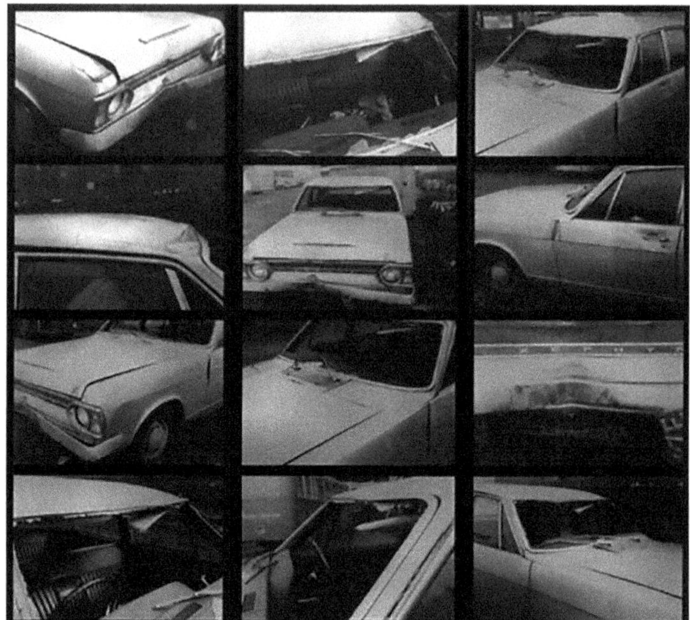

Ballard's photos of his wrecked car.

1972 — March? — Ballard's satirical "found text," entitled "The Side-Effects of Orthonovin G," was published in *Ambit* no. 50 (Spring 1972). "The piece in fact consisted of the biographical notes supplied by two American women who were the joint authors of a book published by Allen Lane in the early 70s. I didn't add or touch a word, except for the ironic title. (Orthonovin G is a contraceptive cream). It was this piece that Euphoria Bliss, frequent *Ambit* cover girl and a professional strip-tease artist, whom Bax and I got to know in the late 60s as a result of her literary interests, recited during her various strip-tease performances at the ICA and other avant-garde venues. At one of these, Kingston Polytechnic, she was halfway through the second piece, which she recited during pauses in the bump-and-grind music, and had virtually revealed all, when the doors burst open and a crowd of swarthy men, one actually wearing a fez, charged in and filled up the front three rows—they were Egyptian delegates to an agriculture seminar being held on one of the upper floors who had suddenly got wind of what was going on in the basement auditorium—it was a scene straight out of a *Carry On* film. Euphoria went on to other performances, reading complete scientific papers to her strip act—I remember a paper from the *Lancet*. Those were the days. But the piece under my title is entirely the work of these two American academics, and I felt worth memorialising." (Ballard, letter to Peter Brigg, 5 February 1986.)

The book from which Ballard took his "found text" was *Women at Yale: Liberating a College Campus* by Janet Lever and Pepper Schwartz, Indianapolis: Bobbs-Merrill, and London: Allen Lane, The Penguin Press, 1971.

1972 — March 10 (Friday) — *Silent Running*, a science-fiction movie directed by Douglas Trumbull and starring Bruce Dern, was first released in the USA. (It would go on UK release on 28 September 1972.) "The premise — that one day in the future all the vegetation on Earth has died, and that the last remaining trees are stored in vast, orbiting space vehicles may take some swallowing, but the theme is so well handled that the film taps into all our unease about the abuse of this planet and its environment." (Ballard, "Outer Limits," *American Film*, 1987.)

1972 — March 16 (Thursday) — A 160-vehicle pile-up on the M1 motorway near Luton, England, killed nine people and injured 51 others. The incident came only four months after the deaths of seven people on the same stretch of road. In both cases, fog and industrial pollution caused a chain reaction.

1972 — March 23 (Thursday) — Death of Edward John "Ted" Carnell (b. 1912), British science-fiction editor (*New Worlds*, etc) and literary agent, at 59. "The funeral service, held seven days later at Eltham Crematorium, had an overflowing crowd made up of soldiers from his old regiment, relatives, fellow masons, and fans." (Rob Hansen, *Then*.)

1972 — April 16 (Sunday) — David G. Hartwell, writing in his "Thrilling Wonder" column in *Crawdaddy* (a US rock music magazine, published weekly on a Sunday at this time), described how Ballard's *The Atrocity Exhibition* had been pulped by Doubleday, "on the advice of their lawyers," and how the book was then announced by Dutton but soon dropped by them too. "There was a rumor that Grove Press might be interested but Grove Press, in case you haven't heard, is pretty much out of business." (Hartwell would prove to be wrong on that last point.) The column concluded: "*The Atrocity Exhibition* was dropped quietly by at least two major publishers because it was probable that it wouldn't sell enough copies to make a possible lawsuit worth the risk of publishing a good and important book. Insidious economic and political censorship has combined to suppress Ballard's work. It is therefore more important than ever that we read it."

1972 — April 16 (Sunday) — Apollo 16 was launched into space for the fifth manned lunar landing (on the Decartes Highlands). Its crew were John Young, Thomas Mattingly II and Charles M. Duke.

1972 — April 24 (Monday) — Angela Carter returned to England, after spending most of the previous two-and-a-half years in Japan. "Angela was 'dreadfully shocked by the state of GB'. Since Edward Heath's surprise election victory in June 1970, inflation and unemployment had risen sharply: wages lost value almost by the month, and a relentless series of strikes and boycotts was jamming some of the essential mechanisms of society. The phones often failed to work, power cuts were commonplace, and the trains dawdled and lurched along without much loyalty to the timetable. A few days after she returned, Angela was travelling down Fleet Street when a group picketing the *Evening Standard* started rocking her taxi... In the newspapers she read of bombing campaigns by a rash of terrorist organisations—the Provisional IRA, the anarchist Angry Brigade, the Palestinian group Black September—which had all surfaced while she was in Japan. She began to feel that the death of capitalism might be at hand." (Edmund Gordon, *The Invention of Angela Carter: A Biography*, 2016, p204.)

1972 — Spring — Ballard received his publisher's initial reaction to *Crash*, and responded by cutting the manuscript. "My London publisher was very impressed by the book but he said, 'It's a bit too long'... After an interval of about a month I [re-]read it and he was right. So I cut about a third of it... It was my own choice; there was certain repetition. I just went through deleting two or three lines each page... Everything I cut I didn't like... Maybe a quarter. I don't really remember." (Ballard, Vale interview, 1983.)

"Much of the book was morally highly objectionable, there's no doubt about that. One of the publisher's readers was either a psychiatrist or the wife of a psychiatrist, and she wrote the most damning and vituperative reader's report they'd ever received. It included the statement: 'The author is beyond psychiatric help.' That's a pretty terrible thing to say about someone, particularly if you've got scientific qualifications. But I was quite pleased by the report, because it represents, in a sense, total artistic success. The book had worked if somebody could respond to it like that." (Ballard, Alan Burns interview [1973], *Imagination on Trial*, 1981.)

"*Crash*... had a dramatic impact on its first assessor. 'This author is beyond psychiatric help. Do not publish,' the reader at Cape advised in her report. 'Fortunately Mr Cape did not heed the young lady,' says Ballard." (Clare Boylan interview, *Guardian*, 5 September 1991.) The reader in question was Catherine Storr (*née* Peters), second wife of the psychiatrist Anthony Storr; information provided by Mike Petty, who was a junior editor at Jonathan Cape.

1972 — Spring-Summer? — In the course of extensively cutting his novel *Crash*, reducing the manuscript by at least a quarter in length, Ballard enlisted the editorial help of the French translator Robert Louit, then temporarily resident in London (oral information from the literary agent John Wolfers, imparted to D. Pringle in 1978). Also, Ballard's friend Andrew Rossabi seems to have had some hand in the matter: "Andrew Rossabi... A resident of London for many years, he has alternated a career in publishing (he edited Cyril Connolly's last collection of reviews *The Evening Colonnade* and J.G. Ballard's controversial novel *Crash*) with teaching classics part-time at Highgate School." (Richard Jefferies Society, notes, 27 October 2017.)

1972 — May 4 (Thursday) — "LONDON, Thursday. British author Leslie Charteris, 65, the creator of 'The Saint', was pulled from his car after it burst into flames in a six-vehicle M4 Motorway pile-up yesterday, and was taken to West Middlesex hospital with slight back and chest injuries, the Press Association reported." (*Canberra Times*, 5 May 1972.)

1972 — May 24 (Wednesday) — The Gravelly Hill Interchange, or Junction 6 on the M6 motorway, better known locally as "Spaghetti Junction," opened near Birmingham. Under construction since 1968, it was officially opened by Peter Walker MP, Minister for the Environment. Spaghetti Junction was unique as it was the UK's first free-flowing interchange (it did not involve roundabouts or traffic lights), and the largest in Europe. In 1972 the average flow of vehicles using the Junction was 40,000 per day. (Thirty years later the figure had risen to 140,000.)

1972 — June 6 (Tuesday) — David Bowie released his "glam-rock" album *The Rise and Fall of Ziggy Stardust and the Spiders From Mars*.

1972 — June 13 (Tuesday) — Fred Jordan, an editor at Grove Press in New York, wrote to William Burroughs: "Herewith a copy of *ATROCITY EXHIBITION* which J.G. Ballard has agreed will be titled in the U.S. edition as *LOVE AND NAPALM:*

EXPORT U.S.A. We are delighted that you have agreed to write a short introduction for the book, and we are allowing two pages for it. Since the book is now in production, I would be grateful if you could get it to me as soon as possible." Burroughs would indeed respond with a short introductory piece for the Grove Press edition of Ballard's book.

1972 — June 18 (Sunday) — British European Airways Flight 548, a Hawker-Siddeley Trident 1C jet airliner, crashed two minutes after take-off from Heathrow Airport, alongside the busy A30 Staines bypass, killing all 118 passengers and crew. The crash occurred close to the town of Staines, near Shepperton, and was the worst air accident to have occurred on British soil to that date.

1972 — July 15 (Saturday) — 3.32 pm — This was the moment of Modernism's demise (according to architecture critic Charles Jencks)—when another large swathe of the originally much-praised but latterly uninhabitable Pruitt-Igoe high-rise housing project in St Louis was demolished. Ballard was aware of it: "*A Saint-Louis, aux Etats-Unis, des ensembles de tours, proprieté de la municipalité, ont du etre entierement dynamité.*" (Ballard, Laurence Paton interview, *I.G.H.*, [1978?] 1980.)

1972 — Summer — Ballard holidayed in Spain. "About five years ago, I was in Spain. I rented a flat for a month on the Costa Brava; really it's a French resort, near Dali's place. Most of the people were French middle-class professional people—they all had their bloody boats—and they spent an enormous amount of time bickering about things. I was in a ground-floor flat, looking out over the sea, and one of the residents, who also lived in a ground-floor flat, was standing with his back to the sea, looking up at this big block, about 12 stories high, with a camera. I thought, 'What is this? This man's a peeping Tom!' because my girlfriend was walking around in the nude. But what he was doing was... There was an enormous amount of antagonism between the people in the lower floors and the people at the top. Because there was this constant onshore windflow, cigarette ends in particular, flung down into the flats, and also water, the whole damn lot would come down over everybody else's balconies. A notice went up saying: 'Residents are asked not to throw cigarette ends over their balconies.' This chap said in his notice, 'I am taking photographs of any offenders, and these photographs will be pinned up on this notice board.' I remember thinking, 'This is unbelievable, I think I'll keep this—who would believe it?' A holiday, this expensive block—and here's this guy so upset with the misbehaviour of those people on the 12th floor that he stands with his back to the sea with his camera, waiting to catch somebody in the act: some guy who's probably a dentist, so obsessed..." (Ballard, Jon Savage interview, 1978.)

1972 — August 11 (Friday) — "LONDON, Friday. The British Minister for Aerospace, Mr Heseltine, 39, is to face a speeding summons for driving at 100 mph on the M4 motorway, a road he himself officially opened last December." (Canberra Times, 12 August 1972.)

1972 — August 13 (Sunday) — "LONDON, Sunday. Mr Ernest Marples, 63, a former British Minister for Transport, has been disqualified from driving for six months after having been found guilty under legislation he drafted himself. He was also fined £50 for having failed to report an accident and £10 for having failed to stop." (*Canberra Times*, 14 August 1972.)

1972 — August 24 (Thursday) — Ballard wrote to Jannick Storm: "Am just back from Spain, and apologies for delay in replying. *LIMBO* looked very good, the magazine has a nice, open feel about it, I like the design and typography. You're completely welcome to use the ads [i.e., Ballard's "advertiser's announcements"]—but I have no copies, not even originals of two or three of them. Best that you write direct to Martin Bax."

1972 — August (late?) — Ballard was banned from driving for a year: "Six months later I appeared at the Sheen magistrates court and lost my licence for a year, a mandatory penalty for refusing the [breathalyzer] test." (Ballard, notes for *Miracles of Life*, 2007, British Library archive, p53.) "There's no rehabilitation program for traffic offenders here—they just ban you from driving. Alcohol is a big problem here. There's a mandatory year's ban, which I've been through... After a while I found that I never went anywhere—it was too much. I just shaped my life so I remained here... After that crash I would take walks to the horizon, which for a man of my height is roughly about half to three-quarters of a mile away. That was as far as I would be able to walk. So in effect I was living on this planet about a mile wide, and never going anywhere. My whole universe just shrank... Not having a car changes your life, because you cut down your contact with friends. How the hell do you get to North London to go out to dinner? You don't. I never fully recovered from this, actually. I got a helluva lot of work done during that period—that's the only thing I can say." (Ballard, Mark Pauline interview, 1986.)

1972 — September 5-6 (Tuesday-Wednesday) — The Munich Massacre: eleven Israeli athletes at the Summer Olympic Games in Munich, West Germany, were murdered when eight members of the Arab terrorist group Black September invaded the Olympic Village. Five guerrillas and one policeman were also killed in a failed hostage rescue.

1972 — September 20 (Wednesday) — Ballard had completed a screenplay derived from his unfinished new novel *Concrete Island* by this time. "A complete typescript entitled 'Concrete Island: First Draft Screenplay by J.G. Ballard.' Also recorded on the title-page: 'Property of Cadence Productions, Miss Hazel Adair, 53 Finborough Road, London SW10.' Dated: 20 September 1972. Title-page and 160 numbered pages." (British Library catalogue.) This was probably the second screenplay that Ballard had written at Hazel Adair's request: the first, based on his novel *The Drought*, was written circa 1969, although the manuscript seems to be lost.

1972 — October 14 (Saturday) — Bernardo Bertolucci's film *Last Tango in Paris*, which starred Marlon Brando and Maria Schneider as an American widower and a young Parisian woman who are drawn into an intense sexual relationship, had its first public showing at the New York Film Festival.

1972 — October 29 (Sunday) — Ballard's *Love and Napalm: Export USA* (*The Atrocity Exhibition*) was reviewed by Paul

Theroux in the *New York Times*. "It is a kind of toying with horror, a stylish anatomy of outrage, and full of specious arguments, phony statistics, a disgusted fascination with movie stars and the sexual conceits of American brand names and paraphernalia, jostled by a narrative that shoves the reader aside and shambles forward on leaden sentences strung out with words like 'conceptual' and 'googolplex' and 'quasars' and 'blastosphere'... It is a horrible book, and it is even in parts a boring and pointless book... [I]f Mr. Ballard was an American he might have found it more difficult to misrepresent a war which, far from arousing us sexually, has made us impervious to suffering. It is not his choice of subject, but his celebration of it, that is monstrous."

1972 — November — *Penguinews* (issue dated November 1972) published an endorsement by Ballard for a Penguin reprint of *On the Road* by Jack Kerouac: "This powerful and obsessive book, an elegy for the concrete freeway, is one of the most important novels written since World War II. Kerouac's lonely and isolated characters, endlessly driving their cars from coast to coast across the trans-American highways, a nightmare linear continent, are the first dispossessed of the technological landscape. No other book I have read sums up so well the melancholy of the automobile."

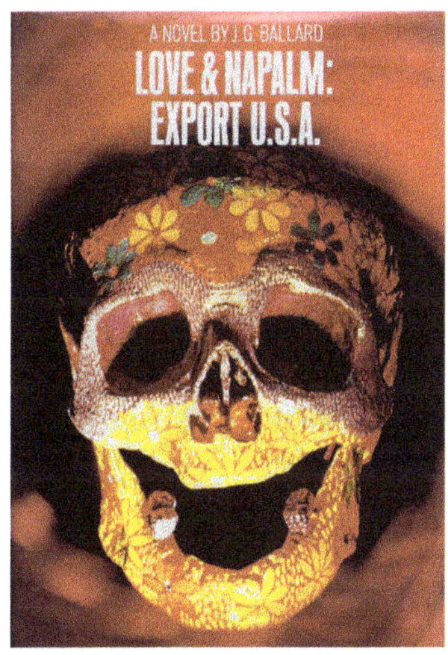

1972 — November — Ballard's book *The Atrocity Exhibition* was published by Grove Press, New York, as *Love and Napalm: Export USA*, with a new preface by William S. Burroughs. The back cover featured a photograph of Ballard by Sophie Baker. "'Love and Napalm: Export USA' was the title chosen, against my advice, for the edition of *The Atrocity Exhibition* which Grove Press published in 1972. I remember sitting in a London hotel with Fred Jordan, the intelligent and likeable editor at Grove, and arguing against the title on the grounds (a) that the Vietnam war was over (this was 1971), and (b) that it would give an apparently anti-American slant to the whole book. Jordan maintained that the war was not over and would continue to rouse violent passions for years to come. I felt that he was wrong, and that though the tragedy would cast its shadow for decades across America, the era of street protests and marches was over. Even from our side of the Atlantic it was clear that the US public had seen more than enough of the war." (Ballard, annotations to *The Atrocity Exhibition*, Re/Search, 1990.)

1972 — November 15 (Wednesday) — J. G. Ballard's 42nd birthday. "There is a scene in *Concrete Island*, where the girl Jane Shepherd is berating Maitland, which is a transcript of a secret tape recording I made of my then-girlfriend [almost certainly Claire Walsh] in a rage—well, secret is the wrong word; she was simply too angry to notice that I had switched on." (Ballard, Thomas Frick interview, 1983.)

This, slightly condensed, is probably the scene: "The young woman stood in front of him, swaying aggressively... 'You're a shit... You imagine you can just lie here, thinking all day. No one gives a damn what you think. You—you're no one... Who are you going to hate next?... Aren't you being a little selective? You humiliate me with this kind of conversation. Take my word, I know more about beds than you do. I think you're a lousy middle-aged creep and I'm not going to pay your fucking bill. God—lunatic man you are. You're demented... How great that you and I are finished. I never want to see you again. I regard our relationship as ended. Please do not ring me on the telephone. Please do not interfere with my professional relationships... You'll get yourself run over, baby. Thank God you'll soon be out of my life. You ought to live in an oriental bazaar. I loved you dearly and you buggered it up... You never had any love and affection as a child. Don't commit any acts of violence tonight. There are lots of nice children here. Why are you such a shit? That fucking American girl. She's a whore. So conceptual. She's so brilliant. I know...' Her voice ended." (Ballard, *Concrete Island*, Chapter 22, p164-166.)

1972 — November 16 (Thursday) — "LONDON, Thursday. Princess Anne might be prosecuted for driving a sports car too fast on a motorway, a police spokesman said last night. The 22-year-old princess had been stopped twice this month and consideration was being given to prosecution on one of the alleged incidents. The speed limit on Britain's motorways is 70mph." (*Canberra Times*, 17 November 1972.)

1972 — November 17 (Friday) — "LONDON, Friday. The Earl of Lichfield, a 33-year-old society photographer and a cousin of the Queen on her mother's side, was fined £50 and banned from driving for a year after he had pleaded guilty at a magistrate's court in London to having driven with more than the legally allowed amount of alcohol in his blood." (*Canberra Times*, 18 November 1972.)

1972 — December? — Ballard story published, his first in over two years—"The Greatest Television Show on Earth" (*Ambit* no. 53, Winter 1972-1973). It was described on the front cover as: "A real old-fashioned J.G. Ballard story for the fans." In fact, the story, involving time-travellers witnessing Biblical events, had been written about five years earlier and had failed to find a publisher until this time.

1972 — December 19 (Tuesday) — Apollo 17, last of the Apollo moon-landing series of missions, crewed by astronauts Eugene Cernan, Ronald E. Evans and Harrison Schmitt, returned safely to Earth.

1972 — December 24 (Sunday) — Ballard's *Love and Napalm: Export USA* (*The Atrocity Exhibition*) was reviewed by Seymour Krim in the *Chicago Sun-Times*. "[An] incredible amount of disturbing emotional dynamite is packed in these unemotionally written 157 pages. It is the images that drain us, not any rhetoric in the almost scientifically neutral writing itself... What Ballard has done is to shake us to the very toes by piling image on image of a world we never consciously made but must live in... His job as artist, word-painter, idea-innovator, is to present his vision with maximum effectiveness. He succeeds beyond your wildest bad dreams."

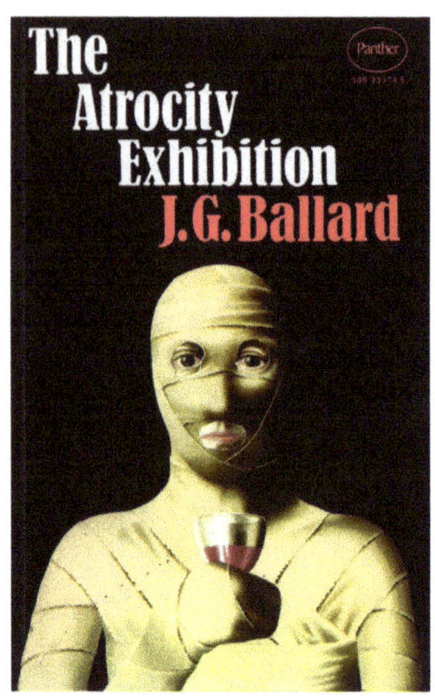

1972 — December 29 (Friday) — "There is still no sign of Ballard's new novel, unfortunately, but his *The Atrocity Exhibition* has just come out in Panther paperback [in the UK], which is pleasing." (D. Pringle, diary, 29 December 1972.) Michael Dempsey was an editor at Granada Publishing, the London firm which included Panther Books, Ballard's main paperback publisher. "Dempsey took on the challenge of publishing and marketing books with typical bull-at-a-gate radicalism. He wanted to put out books that upset people and was a natural magnet for trouble... When I arrived on the scene Dempsey was under intense fire from the legal big guns of the Church of Scientology over the chapter in Ed Sanders' book *The Family* that alleged links between Scientology and the Manson family. Dempsey was also an editor who liked to hang out with his authors, if they'd have him, and this helped sculpt his legend. When he raised hell [sic] with J.G. Ballard through the painful creation of the novel *Crash*, it triggered another obsession. He bought a huge old Mercedes and, although I don't know if he ever consummated hammer-down, high-speed vehicular sex, he certainly constituted a menace to the public at large. Inevitably he wrecked the Teutonic beast and was banned from driving, although that did little to deter him." (Mick Farren, *Give the Anarchist a Cigarette*, p351-352.)

1972 — December 31 (Sunday) — "LONDON, Sunday. A piper playing a lament led a torchlight procession past London's Houses of Parliament yesterday in the last anti-Common Market protest before British entry at midnight tonight. Five hundred people, many with blazing torches, took part in the march. The protest came after a series of anti-Market speeches at a rally in Central London." (*Canberra Times*, 1 January 1973.)

1972 — Ballard's *Luftspeil* (*Vermilion Sands*) was published by Gyldendal of Oslo, with a cover illustration (giant faces floating

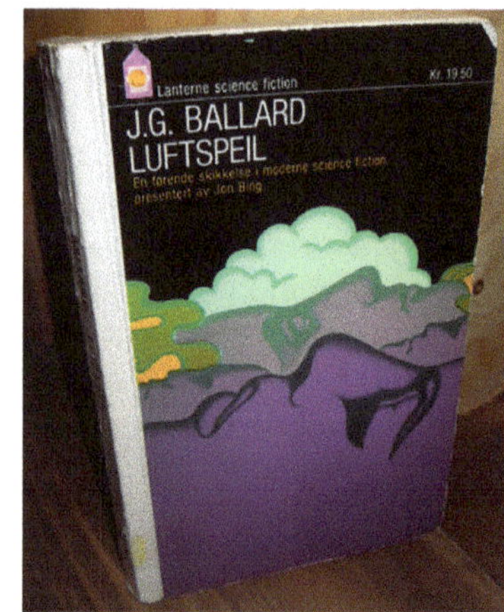

in the clouds) by Peter Haars. The book was translated into Norwegian by Jon Bing, with a two-page "Forord" by Ballard which did not appear in any other edition. It also had an eight-page critical afterword by Jon Bing, a bibliography and a six-page glossary which explained all the proper names alluded to in the book—from Adonis and Aeneas to Wordsworth and Frank Lloyd Wright.

"This is of significance to collectors of Ballard first editions because, dated 1972, it's the first full edition of *Vermilion Sands* that appeared anywhere in the world. The British edition, from Jonathan Cape, wasn't published until late 1973—and the American edition, which had appeared as a paperback-original from Berkley Books in 1971, was incomplete, containing just eight stories rather than nine ('The Singing Statues' was dropped). I think Ballard's then-agent John Wolfers gave me this book in the late 1970s, and I have kept it and valued it since, even though I can't read Norwegian." (David Pringle, *Fictionmags*, 30 May 2013.)

1972 — The French poet Pierre Joris visited Ballard, with a friend: "On my mind this morning, clear as if it was yesterday, the trip back from his suburban house, around 1972, with Carl Weissner, after an afternoon spent sipping whisky. He had consoled me when I told him that no French publisher was willing to publish *The Atrocity Exhibition*, which I had started to translate, telling me that maybe it was too early, but that the time would come, as he poured another scotch. It did, eventually. On the train, Carl and I looked out at the grey London burbs flitting by in their grime and apocalyptic desolation. It was clear to us then that Ballard was no science-fiction writer, but a satiric realist: his worlds were starkly all around us." (pierrejoris.com/blog/?p=1124, 20 April 2009.)

1972 — Roland Barthes's book *Mythologies* (originally published in French in 1957) appeared in Britain for the first time in an English translation published by Jonathan Cape. Its belated appearance was occasioned by the English-speaking world's discovery of semiotics, or semiology. "[Ballard's] insistence that meaning is not to be found on the surface but only inside the coded messages of personal gestures and public display allies him with practitioners of semiology, the science of signs derived by Roland Barthes from the lexical structuralism of Ferdinand de Saussure. Indeed, there are many areas of overlap between Ballard's analyses of popular imagery and those in Barthes's earliest essays... All in all, it is surprising to find that Ballard had not read Barthes when he wrote *The Atrocity Exhibition*." (Colin Greenland, *The Entropy Exhibition*, 1983, p117-119.)

1972 — Oscar Newman, American architect and city planner, published his book *Defensible Space*. It contained a study from New York showing that higher crime rates existed in high-rise apartment buildings than in lower housing projects. This, he concluded, was because residents felt no control or personal responsibility for areas occupied by so many people.

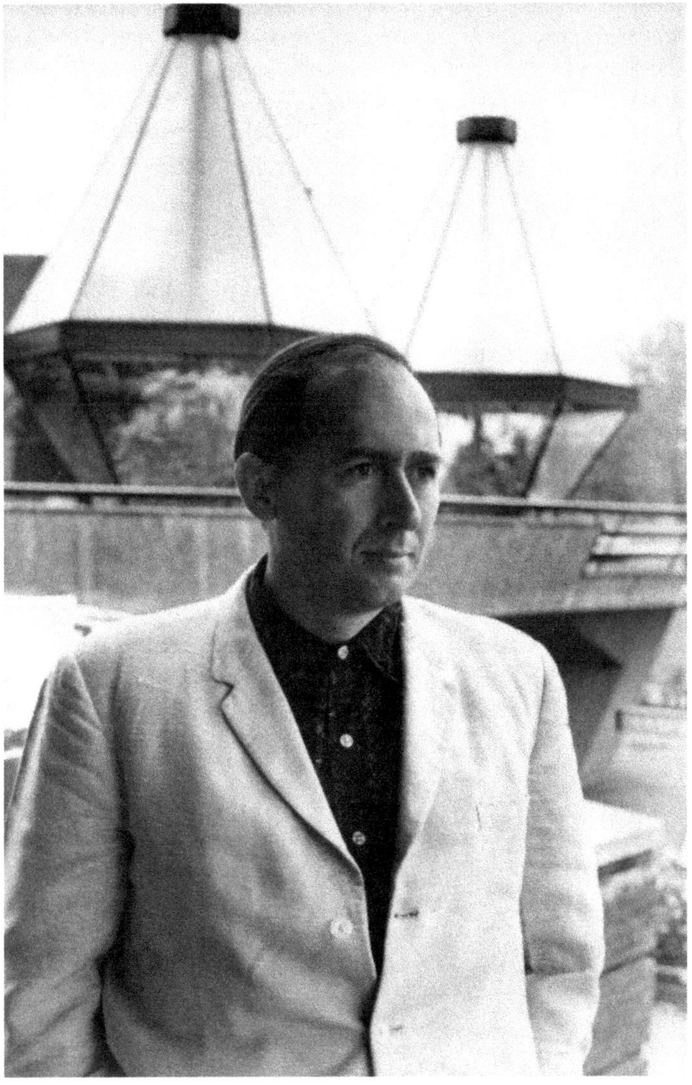

1973

1973 — January 6 (Saturday) — Tony Cliff, leader of the UK's International Socialists, published an article in *Socialist Worker* which began: "1972 was a tremendous year for Britain's working class. The struggle rose to new heights, both in terms of the number of workers involved, the size of strikes and their length, and above all in the quality of the struggle. There have been far more large-scale and prolonged strikes this year than in the previous ten years. November and December figures have not yet been published, but there is no doubt that the total number of strike days has reached or exceeded 30 million this year."

1973 — January 11 (Thursday) — Emma Tennant's novella "The Crack" appeared in *New Worlds Quarterly* no. 5, edited by Michael Moorcock (Sphere Books). This was the first issue to appear in about eight months, and would be the last to have the word "Quarterly" in the title. It also contained stories and poems by Barrington J. Bayley, John Clute, Thomas M. Disch, Keith Roberts, John Sladek, D.M. Thomas and others. "It's ironic that I should have written only ten days ago that *New Worlds* has gone bust for good. I was wrong. Last Thursday, I found the latest issue, Number Five, standing proudly among the new paperbacks in Austick's. It's a good fat issue, some 275 pages, with contributions from most of the usual authors plus some new ones." (D. Pringle, diary, 15 January 1973.)

1973 — January 21 (Sunday) — "LONDON, Sunday. Prince Charles had narrowly avoided a head-on collision in his 160-miles-an-hour car... 'He had a narrow escape,' said a senior spokesman for Hampshire County Police. The 24-year-old Prince was driving his Aston Martin sports car through thick fog along a narrow, winding country lane on Thursday night when the incident occurred, police said. As the Prince, with his detective in the front passenger seat, approached a sharp bend another car headed toward him slewing broadside across the road. The Prince braked hard, swerved, and avoided a crash." (*Canberra Times*, 22 January 1973.)

1973 — January 27 (Saturday) — The United States and North Vietnam signed a cease-fire, ending the longest-ever US war and military draft. The Paris Agreement froze the status quo on the ground in South Vietnam.

1973 — January — It was probably around this time that Ballard received the proofs of his forthcoming novel, *Crash*. "I admit my own motives when I wrote the book were confused. I remember when I read the printed proofs nine months after I had last read the manuscript I had to hang on to my chair. My first reaction was 'The guy who wrote this must be nuts.' But it was not hard to write in terms of subject matter. I found that I had to will myself into a deliberate psychosis, the psychopathic two plus two equals five. It was a tremendous ordeal. You must remember that I have three children and any one of them might be killed in a car crash, still could. It was a tremendous effort. I was morally exhausted because I appeared to be saying that bad is good and good is bad, inverting all the common assumptions of our lives. But maybe readers' assumptions need looking at in a new light. Maybe the light that *Crash* throws is a baleful glare but at least it is a light which one doesn't get from my fellow writers, to put it mildly." (Ballard, *Street Life* interview, 1976.)

1973 — February (early?) — Ballard was interviewed, at home in Shepperton, by Australian journalist Peter Linnett. He stated: "I finished my last novel about two weeks ago, or three weeks ago to be exact. I was in a great state of exhilaration in the week after finishing this book... I'd rather not give the story away because it won't be published for a year." (The work referred to was *Concrete Island*.) "Generally I end about five and I then have a very stiff drink, and follow it very soon after with another stiff drink. I don't drink as much as I used to... I used to have my first drink at about nine o'clock in the morning... I needed the alcohol to get me going; now I'm generally speaking in a happier frame of mind. Also, I'm older now, I'm 42 now, if I drink in the mornings or in the early afternoons it puts me to sleep... That's just a matter of one's metabolism and physiology..." (Ballard, Linnett interview, full transcript, 1973.)

1973 — February 9 (Friday) — "MIAMI SHORES, Florida, Friday. Police arrested yesterday a beautiful blonde who said she needed a bath after she stripped and walked into an automatic car-wash, United Press International reported. More than 1,000 people watched the girl shower in the open-air car wash on a busy main road." (*Canberra Times*, 10 February 1973.)

1973 — February 18 (Sunday) — "CHICAGO, Sunday. An estimated 56,300 people died and two million were injured on the roads in the United States last year, the highest annual traffic death toll in US history, the National Safety Council says." (*Canberra Times*, 19 February 1973.)

1973 — February 28 (Wednesday) — Thomas Pynchon published *Gravity's Rainbow*, which would become one of the most widely discussed American novels of its period and win a National Book Award.

1973 — March? — An interview with Ballard by Jerome Tarshis, titled "Krafft-Ebing Visits Dealey Plaza: The Recent Fiction of J. G. Ballard" appeared in *Evergreen Review* no. 96 (dated Spring 1973). The flyleaf of the same (paperback-sized) issue also contained an advert for the recently-published Grove Press book *Love and Napalm: Export USA* which featured the following endorsement by Susan Sontag: "Each book by J.G. Ballard is possibly his best book. Enviable, admirable Ballard! His subtle, brutal, cerebral, intoxicating *Love & Napalm*, which I have just finished reading, therefore seems to me his best book. Ballard, who used to write about the future, has observed that today's America, America of the Vietnam War is science fiction enough. Important, necessary Ballard!"

1973 — March 8 (Thursday) — Two bombs exploded near Trafalgar Square, London, in Whitehall and at the Old Bailey, killing one person and injuring 180 others. The Provisional IRA had conducted its first operation in Britain, planting four car bombs. Two of them failed to explode.

1973 — March 17 (Saturday) — Jonathan Rosenbaum, American film critic, would write: "... in Paris on the afternoon of March 17, 1973, I met Jean Seberg at her apartment on rue de Bac. [...] A friend of mine who was a friend of Seberg's had hired me to adapt a J.G. Ballard novel, *The Crystal World*, for a film treatment—the only scriptwriting I have ever done. After I did about half the work, the pages were shown to Seberg for a second opinion. Seberg had recently tried her hand at screenwriting and was interested in looking at some of the efforts of others. A meeting was called at Seberg's flat. I arrived first and was delighted to discover that Seberg—hobbling about in a plaster cast, having recently broken a leg—liked my treatment just fine (though I suspect it was mediocre at best; I had so little confidence that the film would ever be made that I didn't even bother to make a copy of the treatment for myself). The upshot was that I was hired to complete the treatment. I still knew that the film would probably never be made, but from that point on I mentally cast Seberg as my heroine." (Rosenbaum, *Essential Cinema: On the Necessity of Film Canons*, 2004, p205-206.) The producer in question was named Edith Cottrell, and at one point Susan Sontag expressed interest in directing the film.

1973 — Spring — Emma Tennant's 1970s memoirs begin: "Wham! I'm lying in bed in Chelsea... (in a month or two we'll move to the uncharted waters of W11)—and a packet with pages bursting from the seams lands with a thud right on top of me. What is it? I pull at the contents, unaware I am handling material so toxic that a reader at the publisher Jonathan Cape has pronounced its creator fit for psychiatric treatment, and has strongly advised against its transition into hard covers. 'Crash!' laughs Michael Dempsey, hurler of the seditious volume and friend of the author, J.G. Ballard. 'Crashed cars and sex—you know, the kind of thing he likes.' I've met Jimmy Ballard, at a party given in this same Chelsea house. He's an enigma, from the moment he rises up the stairs with his olde-worlde Fifties greeting: 'You look glam, dear'... Ballard's landscapes, whether abandoned helipads or drained swimming-pools, have been obsessing me lately—particularly since he has come to visit us here... I know he lives in Shepperton—'the last station on the line' when his late wife went house-hunting shortly after their marriage. But his home had been in Notting Hill. I sense, when he speaks with a heavy sarcastic fondness of friends, other 'science fiction writers'... that it is neither Shepperton nor Chelsea that attracts him. Notting Hill—or Ladbroke Grove—as, in Ballard's words, 'the hill SF buffs have all rolled their pennies down, over the years'—is the land he wants to return to." (Tennant, *Burnt Diaries*, p1-2.)

Rose Dempsey, Emma Tennant's daughter with Michael Dempsey, was born on 10 March 1973, so the above passage probably refers to a period shortly after that. Emma and her three children would move from Chelsea to 60 Elgin Crescent, Notting Hill, W11, soon afterwards.

1973 — April 4 (Wednesday) — The twin-towered World Trade Center, the tallest building in the world at 110 stories, officially opened in New York City with a ribbon-cutting ceremony.

1973 — April 8 (Sunday) — Death of Pablo Picasso (b. 1881), Spanish artist, at his home near Mougins, France, at age 91.

1973 — April 27 (Friday) — "Ballard's new novel is coming out in July. The literary event of the decade. I was looking through the Cape book-list in the library, and there it was—'J.G. Ballard, *Crash!*, £2.75, July.' I put in an order for it today... It's going to cost £2.75, which I don't mind paying, but it's a surprising leap in price. Three years ago, *The Atrocity Exhibition* cost just £1.05. *Crash!* is going to be well over twice as expensive. Is that all due to inflation? I can't help speculating that the book is going to be expensive because it is big—say, at least 300 pages. Won't that be marvellous? A big, fat new book by Ballard, not a word of which I'll have read before." (D. Pringle, diary, 27 April 1973.)

1973 — May 1 (circa) — "The Mind of Mr J.G. Ballard," a critical essay by Anthony Ryan, appeared in *Foundation* no. 3 (dated March 1973, but two months late). It showed internal evidence of having been written several years earlier, before the publication of *The Atrocity Exhibition*. "I received the latest *Foundation* earlier this month, but neglected to mention it here. It contains a short article on Ballard by one Anthony Ryan. In their prefatory note the editors mention me, and say that they will be publishing my essay on Ballard's symbolism shortly. Perhaps its appearance will coincide with that of *Crash!*" (D. Pringle, diary, 23 May 1973.)

1973 — May 3 (Thursday) — The Sears Tower in Chicago, Illinois, became the tallest structure in the world, at 1,450 feet surpassing the World Trade Center in New York City.

1973 — May 13 (Sunday) — "Ian [Lee] spoke to the Cape representative in his shop, and found out for me that *Crash!* will be published on 28th June, at £2.25. The price has actually been reduced from their original estimate. What is more, Cape are due to bring out in June an anthology entitled *Tristar* which will feature stories by Aldiss, Ballard and Moorcock. I don't know whether these are to be original stories or not, so I have written a postcard to them to enquire." (D. Pringle, diary, 13 May 1973.) Someone at Cape would reply to me saying that there would be two previously unpublished "condensed novels" by JGB in *Tristar*; however, the book's publication date had been put back from June to the autumn.

1973 — June 9 (Saturday) — "The Living Novelist: Introducing *Crash*" was broadcast on BBC Radio 3, featuring Ballard and George MacBeth in conversation. "This evening, Radio 3 has broadcast a discussion between Ballard and George MacBeth. Ballard read several extracts from the new work. It sounds as though he has lost none of his intense descriptive power and, although *Crash!* will obviously contain much of the same subject matter as *The Atrocity Exhibition* it seems that it will have new things to offer. The extracts that Ballard read included an outstanding description of a simulated car crash seen in slow motion (far surpassing in detail the descriptions in *The Atrocity Exhibition*) and a brilliant description of driving along a motorway while under the influence of an hallucinogenic drug. For all its outrageous subject matter, *Crash!* sounds like a long, carefully worked out and conventionally written novel—a major event!" (D. Pringle, diary, 9 June 1973.)

1973 — June 28 (Thursday) — Official publication day of Ballard's novel *Crash*, issued in hardcover by Jonathan Cape, London, priced at £2.25, and with a cover illustration by Bill Botten. "I got the Ballard novel on publication day (last Thursday). The book turned out to be 224 pages long, [and] the exclamation mark has been dropped from the title. The dust-jacket is rather gaudy and shows two huge gear-levers [front and back], like technological penises, pointing at a sharp angle into the sky." (D. Pringle, diary, 3 July 1973.)

The first-edition jacket illustration "shows a jutting gear stick, presumably intended to be phallic, in front of a towering three-dimensional titlepiece that occupies most of the cover. This still rankles with Ballard, who describes it as 'monstrously bad, one of the worst book jackets ever—for sheer ugliness and crudity, impossible to beat.'" (Rick Poynor, "Collapsing Bulkheads: The Covers of *Crash*," *Eye* no. 52, Summer 2004.)

1973 — July 1 (Sunday) — Ballard's *Crash* was reviewed in

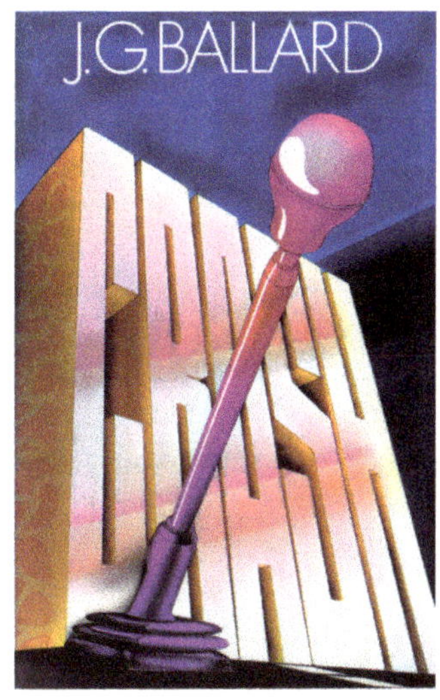

The Observer by Martin Amis, and in the *Sunday Telegraph* by Anthony Quinton. Reviewing the novel alongside J.M.G. Le Clezio's *War* and Romain Gary's *The Gasp*, the latter critic was very positive: "By far the best of them is J.G. Ballard's *Crash*, which is, in effect, a prose poem in the manner of Rimbaud on the scenery of the M4 and A40 as they approach London... The whole undertaking is developed with splendid consistency... I found *Crash* extremely comic, although the blurb invites the reader to shock and disturbance. With its force and enthusiasm it redeems, rather than condemns, the wasteland it describes."

1973 — July 2 (Monday) — Death of Betty Grable (b. 1916), American actress, dancer and singer, she of the "million-dollar legs," of lung cancer in California, at age 56. For some reason, perhaps because he was feeling twinges of nostalgia for his teen years, Ballard would mention her twice, in an interview and in a book review, in the following months.

1973 — July (mid?) — Ballard was interviewed by Philippe R. Hupp, in Shepperton, "*la banlieue paisable de Londres, un après-midi de Juillet*." He referred to his forthcoming novel *Concrete Island* as concerning "*une sorte de Robinson Crusoe de 1973 sur une ile deserte, en plein Londres*." In his scene-setting at the beginning of the interview, Hupp described Ballard's car as "*une vieille americaine qui, visiblement, a plusieurs tonneaux a son actif*." I believe Hupp was saying that an old American car was sitting outside the house—evidence that Ballard still had his Ford Zephyr in July 1973, more than a year after his crash. (Of course, it was a British-made Ford, not actually "American," but would the French visitor have known the difference?)

1973 — July 20 (Friday) — Death of Robert Smithson (b. 1938), American sculptor and "land artist," in a plane crash at age 35, while surveying sites for his work "Amarillo Ramp" in Texas. "In 1967 Smithson began exploring industrial areas around New Jersey and was fascinated by the sight of dump trucks excavating tons of earth and rock that he described in an essay as the equivalents of the monuments of antiquity. In September 1968, Smithson published the essay 'A Sedimentation of the Mind: Earth Projects' in *Artforum* that promoted the work of the first wave of land artists, and in 1969 he began producing land art pieces to further explore concepts gained from his readings of William S. Burroughs, J.G. Ballard, and George Kubler." (Wikipedia.)

1973 — July 27 (Friday) — "The press did not receive *Crash* very well. Robert Nye in the *Guardian* said that it was 'grindingly earnest' and, although he sympathized with Ballard's aims, he thought the tone was 'hellish'... *The Times*, in its very brief review, said that Ballard was 'creepy' and sado-masochistic, although it acknowledged that he writes well. *The Listener* claimed that '*Crash* enjoys the fantasies of autogeddon too much to be able to mount any but the feeblest of resistances to the car-obsessed society that makes them so available'... Martin Amis, in the *Observer*, gave perhaps the best review I have seen, but even he accuses Ballard of just 'flailing and shouting' out on 'the lunatic fringe.' Julian Symons in the *Sunday Times* again approved of the idea but not of the treatment: 'there is a powerful novel to be written about the car as symbolic destroyer, but *Crash* is not it.' Finally, the good old *Times Lit. Supp.* says that '*Crash* is a fetishist's book; there is no right or wrong, no sympathy or compassion ...'" (D. Pringle, diary, 27 July 1973.) Unfortunately, Anthony Quinton's very favourable review in the *Sunday Telegraph* had been missed by the diarist.

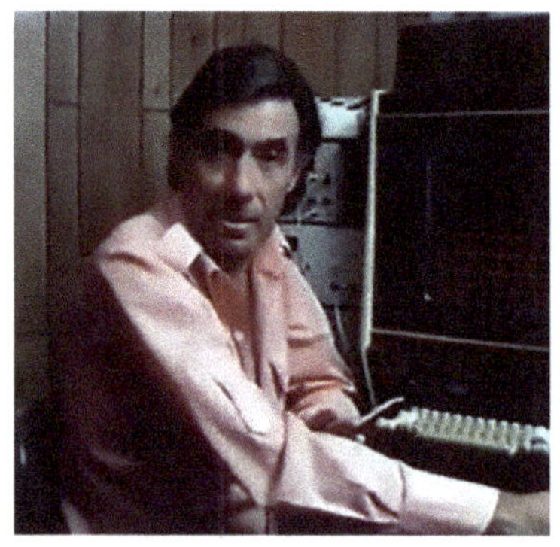

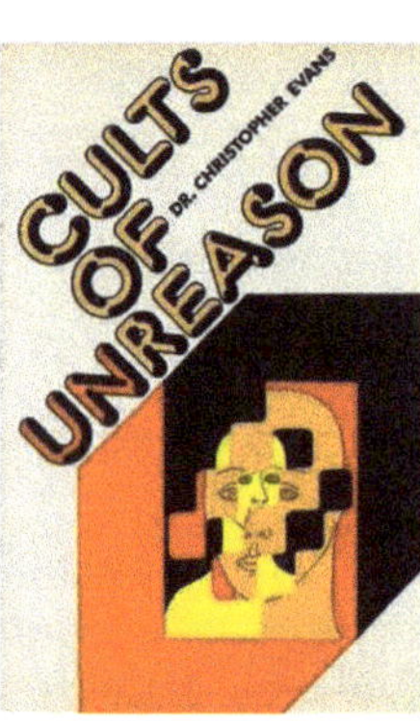

1973 — August — Dr Christopher Evans's book *Cults of Unreason* was published by Harrap, London, with a jacket endorsement by Ballard: "A fascinating book, a vivid and excitingly written account of the extraordinary religious and psychological cults to which modern science and technology have given birth. Dr Evans is witty, tolerant and never dismissive as he examines the personalities and motives of these bizarre 20th century messiahs. The section on Scientology is a brilliant tour de force."

1973 — August 26 (Sunday) — Death of Ann Quin (b. 1936), British novelist, at 37 (likely date). She committed suicide by drowning in the sea off Brighton, during the Bank Holiday weekend. "She herself was a tragic figure, a beautiful but withdrawn woman who might have strayed from the pages of *The Atrocity Exhibition*. As her schizophrenia deepened, she embarked on a series of impulsive journeys all over Europe, analogues perhaps of some mysterious movement within her mind. Eventually she walked into the sea off the south coast of England and drowned herself." (Ballard, annotations to *The Atrocity Exhibition*, Re/Search, 1990.)

1973 — September 1 (Saturday) — The 31st World Science Fiction Convention, also known as Torcon II, was held over this weekend (31 August-3 September 1973), at the Royal York Hotel in Toronto, Ontario, Canada, with Robert Bloch as Guest of Honour. Judith Merril was among the attendees. As usual with sf conventions, Ballard did not attend; however, it was probably around this time, or soon after, that he was interviewed at length over the phone by Carol Orr, for the CBC (Canadian Broadcasting Corporation) radio programme "Ideas," an episode entitled "How to Face Doomsday without Really Dying," to be presented by Judith Merril.

1973 — September 11 (Tuesday) — Chile's left-wing government was overthrown in a military coup which followed a period of serious instability. President Salvador Allende (b. 1908) died at age 65 (allegedly he "blew his head off with an AK-47 given to him by Fidel Castro"), and General Augusto Pinochet headed a military junta that would govern Chile for the next 16 years.

1973 — September 22 (Saturday) — Ballard wrote to James Goddard: "Dear James, Many thanks for the questions, which raised a number of interesting issues. You're welcome to call here any time you like. I look forward to seeing your review. Best, J.G. Ballard." It was presumably along with this note that he sent his replies to the interview questions Goddard had sent him some time before. Although the publication of *Crash* had been somewhat delayed, he explained, there had been "absolutely no question of waiting for the right climate. Books such as *CRASH* are the climate... I don't feel that the lives of my characters are so far removed from ordinary experience. It seems to me that most people lead the sort of lives that I describe. Of course, the book is the description of an obsession, an extreme metaphor at a time when only the extreme will do."

1973 — September 23 (Sunday) — D. Keith Mano reviewed the US edition of Ballard's *Crash* (Farrar, Straus & Giroux) in the *New York Times*, describing it as "hands-down, the most repulsive book I've yet to come across... J.G. Ballard choreographs a crazed, morbid roundelay of dismemberment and sexual perversion... Punched out eyeballs. Blood. Vomit. Fecal matter. Decapitation. Sperm. Bifurcated, mashed genitals. Yet no one screams out pain... Though it is dangerous to infer creator from character, even when as in 'Crash' they have the same name, I don't think I'd care to meet J.G. Ballard. I certainly won't read further in the Ballard *oeuvre*."

1973 — Autumn — Emma Tennant was now settled in London, W11, close to the Moorcock abode: "Notting Hill certainly does have its indigenous writers. No sooner had I moved in to 60 Elgin Crescent and strolled out the back door into the communal gardens than I bumped into a nest of them, by the doorway of a Ladbroke Grove flat. Here were Michael Moorcock, burly Dickensian looks, progenitor of time-traveller Jerry Cornelius; John Sladek, computer genius from Minneapolis; John Clute, walking encyclopaedia of science fiction and fantasy..." (Tennant, *Burnt Diaries*, p4.)

She also met an old acquaintance, the *Sunday Times* journalist and travel-writer Bruce Chatwin: "I try to tell him about science fiction writers, and the pure imagination I fancifully consider to lie at the heart of Notting Hill. I talk of Ballard, who comes frequently to see me, encouraging my notion of founding a magazine. Why don't I do it, it could be, like *Blast* or *The Dial*, as sporadic as I please, he would certainly write for it—but Bruce has no interest in the alternative worlds on offer here in W11." (Tennant, *Burnt Diaries*, p6.)

Another writer she met around this time was Jerzy Kosinski, visiting London from America (although she did not mention

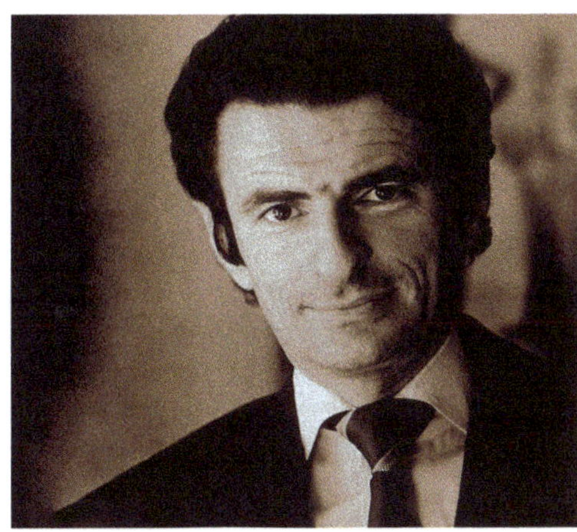

Jerzy Kosinski

him in her book *Burnt Diaries*), probably for the UK launch of his fourth novel, *The Devil Tree*. "I don't know if Kosinski met J [Ballard] but I met him several times, the first at a dinner party at Emma's. Not sure J was yet on the scene. I was a great admirer of his work, especially *STEPS*, and we got on very well. Probably around 1973. He said meeting me was like meeting Balzac and I returned the compliment! I think he was over in the UK to do some readings etc. He was a fine writer and I'd recommend all his work. Jimmy wasn't interested in him and as far as I remember never met him." ("Jeremiah Cornelius" [Michael Moorcock], Facebook, 26 March 2016.)

1973 — October 17 (Wednesday) — Arab oil-producing nations announced they would reduce oil exports to Western nations and Japan—countries which gave support to Israel. A worldwide oil shortage, the 1973 energy crisis, would follow this embargo.

1973 — October 25 (circa) — A short interview with Ballard by James Goddard, entitled "Ballard on *Crash*: Answers to Some Questions," appeared in the fanzine *Cypher* no. 10 (October 1973). It had been conducted by post, Ballard sending his replies on 22 September 1973. "*Crash* is not so much about the motor car as about technology as a whole, and it is precisely the sinister marriage between sex and technology which is the book's subject. Sex X Technology = the future. A disquieting equation, but one we have to face... Since writing *Crash* I have completed another novel, *Concrete Island*, about a man marooned on a large traffic island, to be published next May; and I am now working on another, about a huge high-rise apartment building. I hope to continue writing an investigative and analytical fiction using many of the techniques of science fiction, but about the present day rather than the future."

1973 — October 26 (Friday) — "Wonder of wonders — *Foundation* 4 has actually appeared, with my article ["The Fourfold Symbolism of J. G. Ballard"] beautifully printed, almost no misprints and only very slightly abridged. The issue is dated July but it actually came out in mid-October. Well, at least it is out." (D. Pringle, diary, 26 October 1973.)

1973 — November 3 (Saturday) — Dr Christopher Evans appeared at the "Beyond This Horizon" conference at the Ceolfrith Arts Centre, Sunderland, County Durham (a series of weekend events celebrating science fiction, held from 23 October to 25 November 1973). He was a speaker on two programme items: a UFO symposium on 3 November, and a computer symposium on Sunday 4 November. "Shortly after first reading *Crash* in the early 1970s, I'd seen Dr Chris Evans give a talk at an SF convention [sic]. It was quite a revelation: here in the flesh was Vaughan in all his feral erotic intensity. Evans prowled the stage just oozing sexuality. He wore a black biker's jacket and a blue denim shirt open to the midriff. You might have got into a car with the Doctor, but you wouldn't have accompanied him up a dark alley. Of his talk, I can't remember anything, just his physicality remains in my mind." (David Britton, interview at Ballardian.com, 2010.)

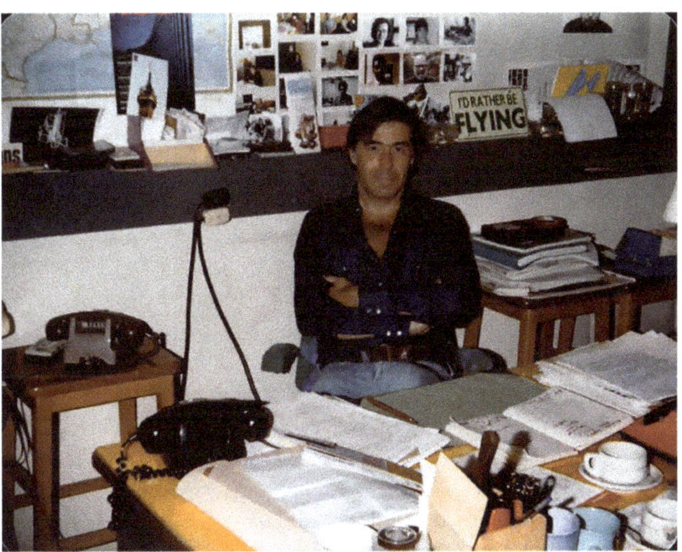

Dr Christopher Evans in his office.

Another acquaintance would recall: "Ballard's novel *CRASH* was largely written around a character named Vaughan, who is very clearly modeled on Christopher Evans. At the time he wrote the novel, Ballard referred to Evans as his closest friend... I once asked Jimmy how Evans had felt about seeing himself as the central character in *CRASH*, especially bearing in mind the scene where the narrator subjects Vaughan to anal rape. 'I've often wondered about that myself,' Jimmy said, 'but I never asked him. And he never said anything about it.' This struck me as amazingly British: to write a novel in which you describe yourself inserting your penis in the rectum of your closest pal, and then continue your friendship without either person saying a word about it." (Charles Platt, "New Worlds for Old, 1965-1970," *Relapse* no. 20, Autumn 2012, p15.)

1973 — November 13 (Tuesday) — Death of B.S. Johnson (b. 1933), British *avant-garde* novelist, a suicide at age 40. "I have always rejected work by well-known writers—I won't mention names—if I haven't thought their work was interesting. I could mention, I suppose, B.S. Johnson, who became well-known before he died, and was very astonished that I thought I could still choose what bits of prose of his I should publish. He felt he was beyond criticism, but of course nobody is." (Martin Bax, editor of *Ambit*, interviewed at www.3ammagazine.com, 2002.)

1973 — November 14 (Wednesday) — Princess Anne married Captain Mark Phillips, in Westminster Abbey. "Even as the country took a holiday to celebrate the wedding..., and as the worst trade deficit to date was announced and the lending rate rose to a record high of 13 per cent, there dawned Ted Heath's fifth and final state of emergency. This time it was deadly serious, the longest-running such emergency since 1926. Street lighting was ordered to be cut by half, electric heating was forbidden in workplaces..., and floodlighting was banned at sports events." (Alwyn Turner, *Crisis? What Crisis?*, p20.) It was probably around this time that Ballard was interviewed by the writer Alan Burns, as the royal wedding was alluded to in the conversation ("We're rooted in the past. People here are slightly blotto... They want to go on with their strange mixture of Sotheby's and Betty Grable and royal weddings"); he also used the phrases "sex times technology equals the future" and "two kids and a brand-new Cortina," both of which appeared in slightly variant forms in other interviews of the time.

1973 — November 15 (Thursday) — J.G. Ballard's 43rd birthday. His life in Shepperton: "'I like it here,' he says. 'It's a bit like an American suburb—lots of ladies in their early 30s with two kids and a Cortina. The husbands work in the plastics factory, or London Airport or the film studios. It's fluid, classless London.' He has three children himself, Jim, Fay and Bea, all in their mid-teens, all brought up single-handed since his wife died ten years ago. 'They're adults now, but a couple of years ago frying an egg was a major hazard. I admit I used to start drinking at 9 am. If you have a Scotch every hour from nine to five, you don't get drunk but you do get, well, tight.' Nowadays he never drinks before 6 pm, and he has a girlfriend ('better call her my *fiancée*') with a teenage daughter of her own: she visits at weekends and they cook huge meals together. 'I'm a creature of habit now. I watch the 5.45 pm news headlines every night, then take the dog out and go for a drink in The Bell.'" (Ballard, Bygrave interview, *Radio Times*, 15 December 1973.)

1973 — November 26 (Monday) — "I had a fantastic weekend in Sunderland. The Ceolfrith Arts Centre turned out to be a small place with an intimate atmosphere, and we not only saw all the writers we expected to [Brian Aldiss, James Blish, Samuel Delany, Bob Shaw], we met them... I also met Jim Goddard for the first time—a large bloke who apparently works as an optician in the time he takes off from editing his fanzine. He floored me by an account of his visiting J.G. Ballard. He has asked me to help him produce a second edition of his Ballard bibliography—and he wants to reprint my article along with it." (D. Pringle, diary, 28 November 1973.)

1973 — November 29 (Thursday) — Publication date of the long-delayed British first edition of Ballard's collection *Vermilion Sands*, issued in hardcover by Jonathan Cape, London, priced at £2.25, with revised contents. The cover illustration was by an unfamiliar artist, Brian Knight. "Ballard's *Vermilion Sands* came out over a week ago. It's a handsome volume, containing all the stories that were in the American edition plus an extra one that I hadn't read before—'The Singing Statues.' There is also a short and interesting preface by the author, in which he claims that *Vermilion Sands* is the future as he really sees it, a sort of abandoned pleasure-garden overhung with blue skies and violence. So far, this book has been receiving better reviews than *Crash*. Maurice Wiggin was especially kind in the *Sunday Times*, saying that Ballard is a brilliant stylist who writes beautifully. I don't know what's

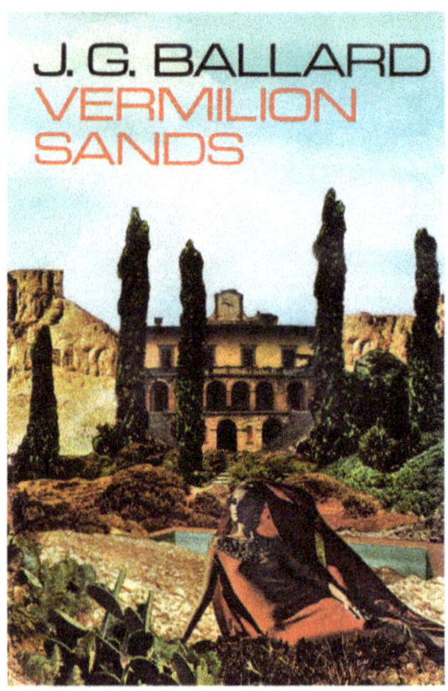

happened to [the promised anthology] *Tristar*, so I suppose *Concrete Island* is the next event I have to look forward to." (D. Pringle, diary, 10 December 1973.)

1973 — December 16 (Sunday) — "We had another Hessle Terrace party last night. Scores of people were here, and it went well. However, I had a certain sense of fiddling while Rome burns. We haven't actually experienced a power-cut yet, but they seem to be imminent. A feeling of real crisis has been in the air since Heath's announcement of further emergency measures on Thursday. Industry is to be put on a three-day week, and there will be a budget tomorrow which will no doubt bring great tax increases. The petrol shortage continues; no doubt there will be rationing in January. Even television transmissions are to end at 10.30 P.M. from tomorrow! Is this the beginning of the end of the Britain we have known for the last 25 years, or is it simply the worst crisis since 1948 and one which will pass as that one did?" (D. Pringle, diary, 16 December 1973.)

1973 — December 16 (Sunday) — "Omnibus: It's Fantastic! It's Futuristic! It's Fatalistic! It's Science Fiction!" was broadcast on BBC television. Narrated by Timothy West, directed by Harley Cokliss, it featured brief interviews with various authors, including Ballard, Brian Aldiss, Ray Bradbury, Harlan Ellison, Damon Knight, Frederik Pohl and Kurt Vonnegut.

1973 — The artist Michael Foreman would say: "I don't go to *Ambit* launch parties and only once went to JG's house many years ago. This was to discuss a proposed children's book which we were to do together. It was called *The Next Rocket to the Moon*. I subsequently did several pictures and a cover but the book never happened... It was to be a picture book so Jim's text was short. I did a cover and a dummy and several pictures plus a complete layout. It was about an old astronaut living in an overgrown and neglected Cape Canaveral. The book was on the launch pad but countdown never happened. Don't remember why." (Michael Foreman, postal interview with Rick McGrath, 18 April 2007.) Foreman also stated that the year of his aborted project with Ballard (also tentatively titled as *The Last Rocket to the Moon*) was 1973 and that the proposed publisher was Collins.

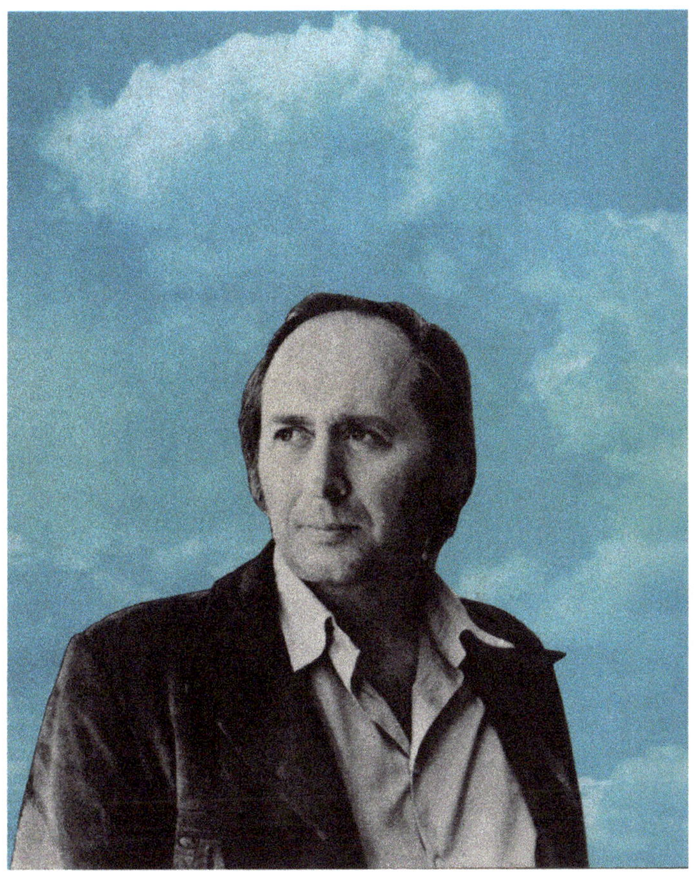

1974

1974 — January 4 (Friday) — "LONDON, Friday. Britons settled to the power crisis yesterday, shopping in candle-lit stores and working in unheated offices as if born to it. The industrial crisis that has forced Britain into a three-day working week and left tens of thousands jobless appeared forgotten, at least in central London, as housewives jammed the stores for traditional new year's sales. London's streets were half-darkened and eerie. Wide sections of industry were half-idle." (*Canberra Times*, 5 January 1974.)

1974 — February — An interview with Ballard by Philippe R. Hupp, entitled "*Rencontre avec J.G. Ballard*" and conducted in July 1973, appeared in the French science-fiction magazine *Galaxie* no. 117 (*Février* 1974).

1974 — February 8 (Friday) — The three-man crew of the Skylab space station returned to Earth after spending 84 days in space. "I remember standing out in my garden on a bright, clear night and watching a moving dot of light in the sky which I realised was Skylab. I remember thinking how fantastic it was that there were men up there, and I felt really quite moved as I watched it. Through my mind there even flashed a line from every Hollywood aviation movie of the 40s, 'it takes guts to fly those machines.' But I meant it. Then my neighbour came out into his garden to get something and I said, 'Look, there's Skylab,' and he looked up and said, 'Sky-what?' And I realised that he didn't know about it, and he wasn't interested." (Ballard, Christopher Evans interview, *Penthouse*, April 1979.)

"It was sad... to point out to a neighbour the speeding light-point of the last Skylab mission, whose crew had been circling the globe for three months. 'Who?' he asked, taking for granted that things moved in the sky. I knew then that the Space Age was over." (*The Best of J. G. Ballard*, April 1977.)

"What happened to the Space Age? Is it still unfolding above our heads, or did it end... with the first Skylab splashdown not shown live on television because the American networks knew that the public was bored?" (Ballard, "Are We Over the Moon?," *Telegraph*, 16 July 1994.)

1974 — February 10 (Sunday) — Another UK miners' strike began. "We now have a miners' strike (starting today) and a General Election (on 28th of this month)! The TV curfew has been lifted so that the major parties can increase the flow of their propaganda..." (D. Pringle, diary, 10 February 1974—last surviving entry.)

1974 — February 18 (Monday) — Ballard wrote to David Pringle for the first time, in response to a forwarded *Weekend* magazine clip about the actress Elizabeth Taylor's injuries and ailments: "Very many thanks for your cutting—strange in many ways. I don't know whether you have seen my novel *Crash*, but there are scenes in that the *Weekend* article might well be directly illustrating. Thanks too for your highly intelligent article, which I read in *Foundation*—very well written, first class criticism."

1974 — March 3 (Sunday) — In the worst air disaster to date, all 346 passengers and crew died when a Turkish Airlines DC-10, Flight 981—travelling from Paris to London, crashed in a wood shortly after take-off from Orly Airport in Paris. Many of the dead were British, including 18 members of a rugby club from Bury St Edmunds. "Of the 346 passengers and crew, only 40 bodies were visually identifiable, with rescue teams recovering some 20,000 body fragments in all." (Wikipedia.)

1974 — March 4 (Monday) — Edward Heath finally resigned as Prime Minister, having failed to convince the Liberal Party, under its leader Jeremy Thorpe, to form a coalition with the Conservatives. Harold Wilson formed his minority Labour Government in the UK.

1974 — April — An interview with Ballard by Robert Louit, entitled "*Entretien avec J.G. Ballard*," appeared in the French monthly Magazine *Littéraire* no. 87 (Avril 1974).

1974 — April — Ballard's *Crash*, translated by Robert Louit was published by Calmann-Lévy of Paris in this month as *Crash!*, with a new introduction by the author. It would become a *succès d'estime* in France, and Ballard began to give many interviews to French journalists. "Nobody was enthusiastic about the book in the UK, nor in the US, though it created a sensation in France, where it enjoyed front-cover publicity in *Paris-Match* and sizeable solo reviews in the heavy newspapers." (Martin Hayman, *Street Life*, 7 February 1976.) "In France, his novel *Crash* sold over 30,000 copies in the high-priced edition, which is a figure considerably larger than the sales of the British and American hardcovers combined." (David Pringle, *Earth is the Alien Planet*, 1979, quoting information given by Ballard's agent, John Wolfers, in 1978.)

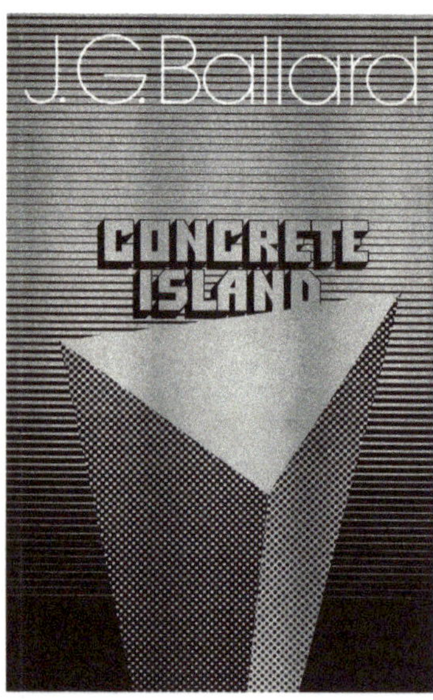

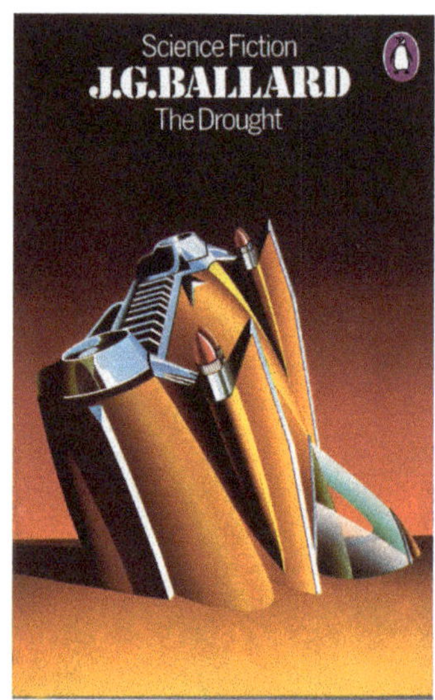

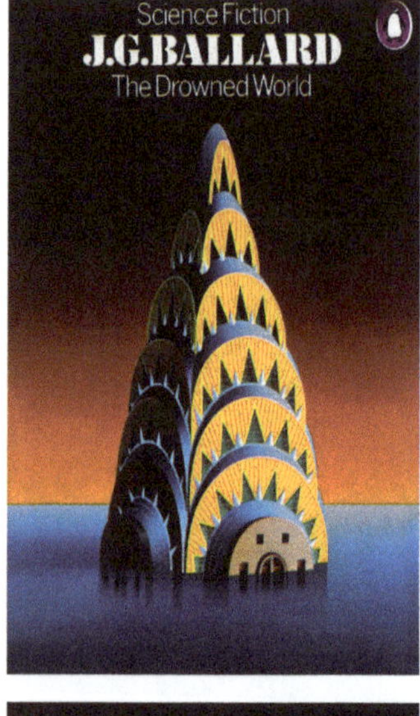

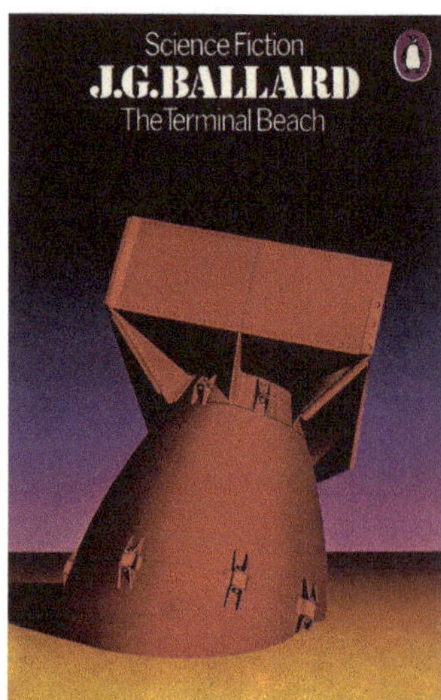

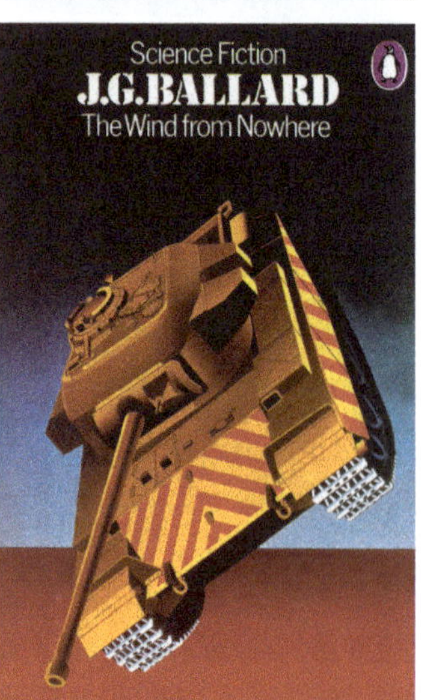

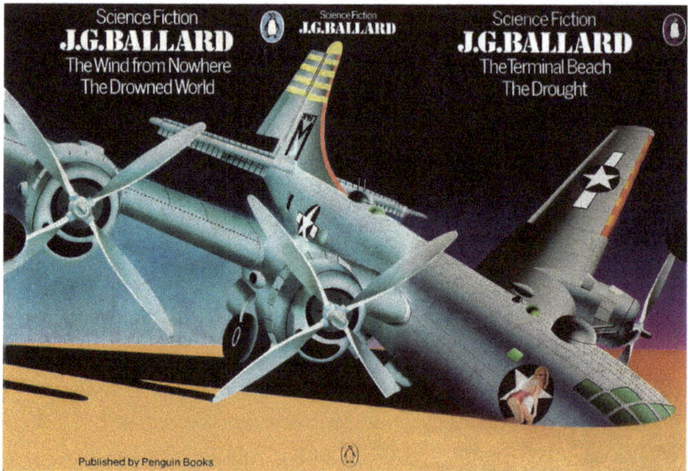

David Pelham's celebrated Penguin covers and box slipcase.

1974 — April 18 (Thursday) — Ballard's novel *Concrete Island* was published in hardcover by Jonathan Cape, London, priced at £1.95, and with a cover design by Bill Botten. "There are elements of self-exorcism, I suppose. I'm an introverted person, my real life is going on inside my head. Obviously I can see that in writing *Concrete Island* and describing a man who resembles me to some extent, I am playing on my awareness of my own obtuseness. I probably wouldn't mind being marooned on a desert island, or put in solitary confinement as much as a lot of other people. There's an element of that..." (Ballard, Goddard/Pringle interview, 1975.)

1974 — April 18 (Thursday) — Ballard's *Concrete Island* was reviewed in the *Daily Telegraph* by Elizabeth Berridge, and in *The Guardian* by Robert Nye. The former critic wrote: "Working on the assumption that man chooses his fate, plotting the accident that will test him fully (familiar to disciples of Groddeck) Mr Ballard strips away Maitland's pretensions, then his emotional security, then his very identity... [T]his allegory of modern life is both compelling and profound."

1974 — April 18 (Thursday) — Headed "Spaced Out," Ballard's review of a popular science book, *The Next Ten Thousand Years* by Adrian Berry, appeared in *New Society* (April 18, 1974). "One value of science fiction is that its extrapolations, however far-fetched, are tested within some kind of emotional and human framework. If one regards this book as a new kind of novel, part of a recently invented category of fiction that includes books such as Herman Kahn's *The Emerging Japanese Superstate* and Desmond Morris's *The Naked Ape*, it shows up the weaknesses of this new hybrid form."

1974 — April 25 (Thursday) — At Penguin Books, designer David Pelham had painted four new covers for reissues of Ballard's titles published on this day. "I met Jim Ballard through Eduardo Paolozzi. They were great friends. I was very familiar with Ballard's work, having been a great admirer from way back. I admired the bleak style of his catastrophe novels... and their heartless depiction of technological and human breakdown and decay. Grim perhaps, but wonderfully written. Drawn to the romance of his apocalyptic imagery I wanted to illustrate his covers myself. Consequently I quickly airbrushed this postcard sized image [*The Drought*] to show him the idea and talked to him about his other titles in the list. That's how we started out... I did a series of four [*The Drought, The Drowned World, The Terminal Beach* and *The Wind from Nowhere*]... together with a slipcase. It was a huge pleasure working so closely with Ballard, and I'm pleased to be able to report that the titles in these covers sold very well." (David Pelham, talk given at a study day at the Victoria & Albert Museum which brought together Penguin designers, art directors and typographers, 2005.)

1974 — May — Ballard's essay "A Personal View," reviewing *Billion-Year Spree* by Brian Aldiss, appeared in the fanzine *Cypher* no. 11 (May 1974). Commenting on the history of science fiction, he said: "There is the curious paradox that classical science fiction (that is, pre-Gernsback) has far more relevance to us, and in a sense is far more modern than the science fiction of the 40s and 50s, in that it is no longer tied to a period that by its recent passing seems that much the more out-of-date. H.G. Wells's *War of the Worlds*, *Moreau* and *Time Machine* have shaken off the patina of the merely contemporary; by comparison Campbell's *Astounding and Analog*, with their third-rate 50s jargonizing, their blue-collar intellectual clap-trap, are absolutely of the America of the *Reader's Digest*, Betty Grable, and popular newspaper sensations such as Dianetics."

1974 — May 10 (Friday) — Ballard's *Concrete Island* was reviewed in the *New Statesman* by Emma Tennant. She referred to the author as "Ballard, psychoanalyst of the high-rise and prophet of the six-lane." The fact that she used the phrase "high-rise" is interesting—it suggests she knew about the novel he was currently working on, even though it was still 18 months away from publication.

1974 — June 20 (Thursday) — The Times ran this small advert: "EDUCATIONAL CRUISES—win one by writing a short story about sea life in 2074. Judged by J.G. Ballard, the competition is open to young people, aged 11 to 17. Entry forms from Missions to Seamen, St Michael's, College Hill, London EC4R 2RL." (*Times*, 20 June 1974, p34.)

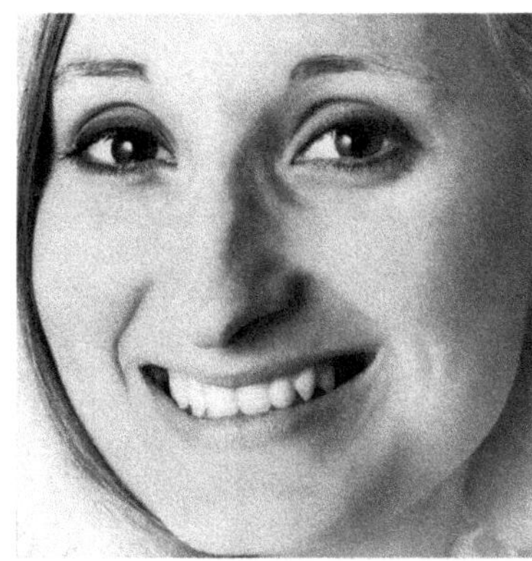

Claire Walsh. Photo by John Blomfield

1974 - June/July? — It may have been around this time that Ballard and Claire Walsh had a bad falling-out, later referred to by Claire as "a blazing row," that led to the break-up of their relationship for a number of years. The gossip, although it may not quite reliable, is that Claire was invited to tea by Emma Tennant, who proceeded to cross-question her about Ballard, arousing the suspicion on Claire's part that he and Emma were having an affair—which indeed would prove to be the case. As she herself said, his relationship with Claire had always been "very up and down, volatile," and now it would be over for the best part of a decade. (Walsh, interviewed by Robert Mendick, *Evening Standard*, 20 April 2009, and by Tim Adams, *Observer*, 26 April 2009.)

1974 — July/August? — Ballard went on holiday to Spain with family, as his daughter Fay (who turned 17 in this year) would recall: "Claire always came with us to Spain, except in 1974 when she and Daddy separated for a period of time... My last trip to Spain with Daddy was in 1974—a wonderful time in Rosas. After that, I was off with my friends." (Fay Ballard, interview by D. Pringle, 2014.)

1974 — August 9 (Friday) — President Richard Nixon resigned, the first US chief of state ever to quit office, as a result of the Watergate scandal. Vice-President Gerald R. Ford was sworn in as the 38th US President.

1974 — August 26 (Monday) — Death of Charles Lindbergh (b. 1902), American aviator, at his home in Hawaii at 72. "Was Charles Lindbergh the last naive hero? The bravest of the brave who followed him, such as Douglas Bader and Guy Gibson, the wartime pilots, or Odette Churchill, the British secret agent, were well aware of what was waiting for them, the blizzard of cannon fire and the Gestapo truncheons. The American astronauts who first sailed the tideways of space were celebrities long before their feet left the ground, their futures tied to book deals and magazine serialisations. Today, anyone who plunges into an icy river to save a drowning dog is aware that the camcorder footage taken by a passerby may well appear on a peak-time television programme. But Lindbergh, the slim, solitary aviator from the Minnesota farmlands, seemed strangely innocent about the world around him, its hunger for heroes and latent hostility towards those it most adored." (Ballard, "Reach for the Sky," *Sunday Times*, 1998.)

1974 — September — An interview with Ballard by Jean-Pierre Lentin, together with short interviews with Michael Moorcock and John T. Sladek, appeared under the title "*Délires a l'heure du thé*" in the French magazine *Actuel* no. 46 (September 1974).

In it, JGB was asked in passing for his opinion on the "anti-psychiatrists" R.D. Laing and David Cooper.

Question: "*Tu t'es inspiré des antipsychiatres anglais, Laing ou Cooper?*" Answer: "*Non, et je ne suis pas d'accord avec leur point de vue. Effectivement, ils décrivent la folie dans les memes termes, mais ce que je considere comme metaphore devient chez eux realité, et je ne veux pas les suivre sur ce terrain. Il faudrait juger leurs livres comme des romans, des fictions, et pas comme des textes cliniques. Cooper n'est pas un medicin qualifié, c'est plutot un ecrivain. Je l'ai recontre il y a quelques années, il m'a semble completement cinglé, délirant au sense propre du terme.*"

An online dictionary tells us that the French word *cinglé* can mean "crazy, batty, cracked, nutty, off one's rocker, potty."

1974 — September 10 (Tuesday) — French television broadcast "Billenium," a 30-minute adaptation by Jacques Goimard, directed by Jean-Claude de Nesle, of Ballard's short story, in the series "*Demain ou Jamais.*"

1974 — September 13 (Friday) — "The Rockford Files" (1974-1980), a crime series starring James Garner as California private eye Jim Rockford and Noah Beery, Jr., as his father, created and produced by Roy Huggins and Stephen J. Cannell, began on NBC TV in the US. It would also prove popular in the UK: "I think the best things on British TV are American programs—things like *Kojak, The Rockford Files, The Streets of San Francisco, Hill Street Blues...*" (Ballard, Vale interview, 1982.)

1974 — Autumn — Emma Tennant continued to plan the launch of her new magazine, or "literary newspaper"—to be called *Bananas*, "with Woody Allen in mind." Various helpers and contributors—Max Egremont, Julian Rothenstein, Rosalind Delmar, Tom Nairn, Claud Cockburn, Ruth Fainlight, Heathcote Williams, John Sladek and Barry Miles (William Burroughs's bibliographer)—came on board.

"Jimmy Ballard, who comes here from Shepperton more and more frequently, a few evenings ago clad in a white suit and shades and carrying maps (but what cartographer could satisfy the wildest shores of his imagination?) speaks of Burroughs with reverence. A photo of Burroughs pointing a gun is found... John Sladek, the quiet-footed SF writer, with a mind as many-levelled as a Piranesi prison, has become a lodger in my house; he stays in there most of the time, writing—sometimes, I hope for us. Ballard comes—but we're unlikely to have dinner out... There is nothing round here other than Mike's, the caff next door to our office. *L'Artiste Assoiffé* is too expensive—though Jimmy and I go there once, and sit in the room with the fancy furniture and the parrot that shrieks all day..." (Tennant, *Burnt Diaries*, p23-25.)

1974 — Autumn? — "You can spend the night with someone... within half an hour of meeting them at a party, but you can't spend the next day with them; the convention requires you to drive off the next morning, the convention requires that people be alone after getting together. That very peculiar thing whereby you only meet like vampires. I used to feel like this in the days when I went courting: I would fly in from the Thames Valley after dusk. I remember one girl I knew (I think it was Emma Tennant... who gave me those silver trees).

She said, 'Jim, I've never seen you before dark!' And I said, 'Christ, I am like a vampire!' Because she had children, I had children, and we met only in the evenings. Then she had to get the kids off to school and I had to get back to make sure my kids were disentangling themselves from early morning television or whatever they'd be doing... This was a curious convention: intimacy of a very specialized kind, with absurd reversals where sex would take place followed by an extended wooing, rather than the other way around, with the wooing coming first." (Ballard, Vale interview, 1982.)

1974 — October 10 (Thursday) — General Election day in the UK. In the second election of the year, Harold Wilson's Labour Party gained a narrow majority of three seats. The Scottish National Party secured its highest Westminster representation to date, eleven seats.

1974 — November 15 (Friday) — J.G. Ballard's 44th birthday. About this time, a new Ballard story was published—"My Dream of Flying to Wake Island" (*Ambit* no. 60, Autumn 1974). "I only wrote that about a month ago! That was quite extraordinary. Martin Bax, the editor, wanted me to write a short story for his sixtieth number. I wrote that in about one day, from a standing start. I think I wrote it on the Saturday, and I got the copy through the post on—something like Wednesday. An incredible turnaround, and very exciting when that happens. One of the nice things about writing for magazines is that there is always such a tremendously quick feedback." (Ballard, Goddard/Pringle interview, 4 January 1975.)

1974 — November 21 (Thursday) — "LONDON, Thursday. A new ice age could grip the world within the lifetime of present generations, Britons were warned yesterday. The warning came in a major television documentary showing that international scientists have changed their minds about the speed with which the world's 'weather machine' can change gear. 'The threat of a new ice age must now stand alongside nuclear war as a likely source of wholesale death and misery for mankind,' said science writer Nigel Calder, who compiled the program for the British Broadcasting Corporation. Latest studies show that ice ages are much more frequent than scientists once thought—and the next one seems to be overdue. According to one theory, 'Toronto, Leningrad and Glasgow ought by now to have disappeared under thick ice sheets.' There is also evidence that its onset could be dramatically sudden, a 'snow blitz' rather than the gradual spreading of glaciers, Mr Calder said." (*Canberra Times*, 22 November 1974.)

1974 — November 21 (Thursday) — The IRA bombed two Birmingham city-centre bars, the Mulberry Bush and the Tavern in the Town, killing 21 people and injuring 180 amidst dreadful carnage. The next day, the IRA denied responsibility for the bombs, but there was widespread disbelief and outrage among the general public in Britain.

1974 — November 26 (Tuesday) — Death of Cyril Connolly (b. 1903), British editor, essayist and critic, at 71. "Connolly said that the greatest enemy of creativity is the pram in the hall, but I think that was completely wrong. It was the enemy of a certain kind of *dilettante* life that he aspired to, the man of letters, but for the real novelist the pram in the hall is the greatest ally—it brings you up sharp and you realise what reality is all about. My children were a huge inspiration for me. Watching three young minds creating their separate worlds was a very enriching experience." (Ballard, Kate Mikhail interview, *Observer*, 2002.)

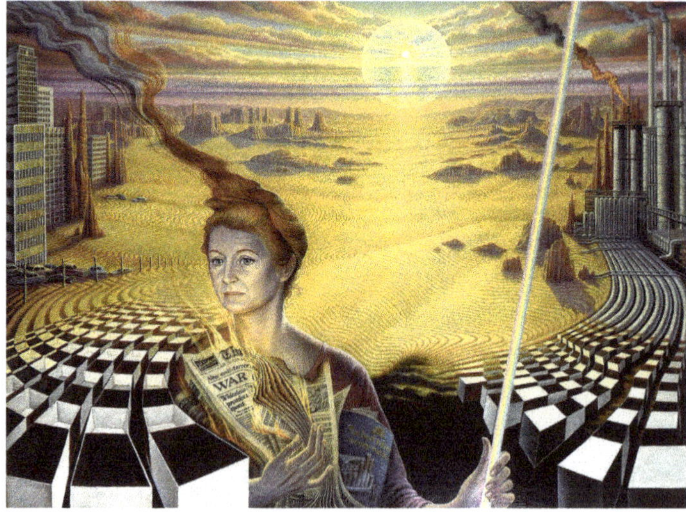

The Rod by Brigid Marlin

1974 — December — Brigid Marlin was the winner of *Science Fiction Monthly*'s first competition for artists, and her painting "The Rod" was published in this month's issue (vol. 1, no. 12). "Fifteen years ago, when I first saw *The Rod*, one of her most ambitious paintings, reproduced in a magazine, I was so impressed by its imaginative sweep that I sent an enthusiastic letter of appreciation to her, the only fan letter I have ever sent to a painter. The sense of a clearly realised poetic universe, in which every detail, however modest, was accorded equal attention, was what most gripped my imagination... I remember writing to her with as much excitement as I felt when I came across the paintings of Francis Bacon in the 1950s. The surrealist dream of remaking the world and revealing its true nature seemed to live on in the work of this woman painter, about whom I knew nothing... In the ten years after my fan letter to her I kept a close watch for any further reproductions of her work, and I was delighted when, out of the blue, I one day received from her an invitation to a private view at the London gallery showing her latest work." (Ballard, "Brigid Marlin: An Appreciation," 1990.)

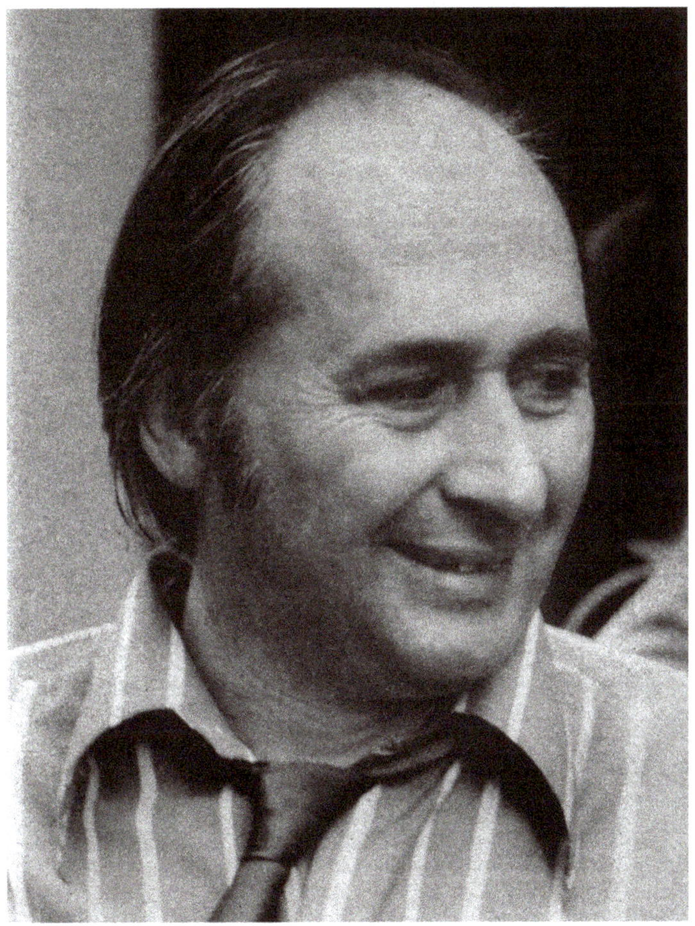

1975

1975 — January 2 (Thursday) — The debut issue of the literary journal *Bananas* appeared. "*Bananas*... was launched on 2 January 1975 with a party at Emma Tennant's house in Elgin Crescent, Notting Hill." (Barry Miles, *In the Seventies*, p194.) "Reception of the first issue of the magazine hasn't been all bad. Admittedly, the small launch party in the gloomily painted dark-green ground-floor room at home was rendered less convivial by the presence of Michael Moorcock, himself the longstanding editor of SF fans' most favoured magazine, *New Worlds* and thus an expert on 'little' magazines. 'At least it's lively,' he pronounced in sepulchral tones, as the sinister-looking paper with the black-and-white grainy picture of the police photo-fit was passed from hand to hand. A pall fell—there's no other way to describe it—and, as ever, it took Ballard's rich, confident pronouncements on the excellence of the venture, to cheer us up." (Tennant, *Burnt Diaries*, p26.)

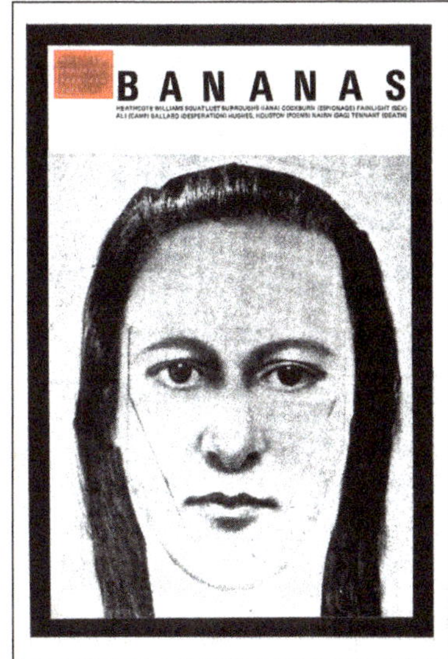

1975 — January 2 (Thursday) — Ballard story published—"The Air Disaster" (*Bananas* no. 1, January/February 1975). "A close friend of mine, Emma Tennant, began *Bananas* in 1975, at which point I wrote a story for almost every one of the issues which she edited. At that point I had not written any short stories at all for something like four years, largely because there was nowhere to publish. This is nothing to do with payment, by the way. I was never paid a penny for any of the stories I wrote for *Bananas*, nor for any that I've ever written for *Ambit* (Mike [Moorcock] was very generous, but in the later days of *New Worlds* he wasn't able to pay either). If Emma had not started *Bananas* it's probably not an exaggeration to say that none of those ten stories would have been written." (Ballard, Pringle interview, 1979.)

1975 — January 4 (Saturday) — Ballard was interviewed at home in Shepperton by James Goddard and David Pringle. "I finished a novel about three weeks ago, and since then I've written a couple of short stories and am writing a third now, and just catching my breath a bit. [What's the new novel called?] I call it *The High Life* provisionally. I may change it, I may stick to it. I don't know. [And you've written some short stories?] A couple have been published. [I've seen one in *Ambit* called 'My Dream of Flying to Wake Island.']... I wrote another—'The Air Disaster'—for a girl I know called Emma Tennant who's just published a new magazine called *Bananas*." (Ballard, Goddard/Pringle interview, 1975.)

1975 — February 11 (Tuesday) — Margaret Thatcher, having defeated Edward Heath the previous week, now defeated all other candidates in the second ballot of MPs in her party's leadership election, and so was elected leader of the UK's Conservative Party—the first woman to lead the Tories.

1975 — February 23 (Sunday) — Death of Hans Bellmer (b. 1902), German artist and photographer, at 72. Best known for the life-sized pubescent female dolls he produced in the 1930s after the rise to power of the Nazis, he declared that he would make no work that would support the German state. He was influenced by the published letters of Oskar Kokoschka (*Der Fetisch*, 1925). Bellmer's 1934 anonymous book *The Doll* (*Die Puppe*) contained 10 black-and-white photographs of his first doll arranged in a series of "*tableaux vivants*." His work was declared "degenerate" by the Nazi Party, and he was forced to flee to France in 1938. He was welcomed in the Paris, especially by the Surrealists under André Breton, and his photographs were published in the Surrealist journal *Minotaure.*

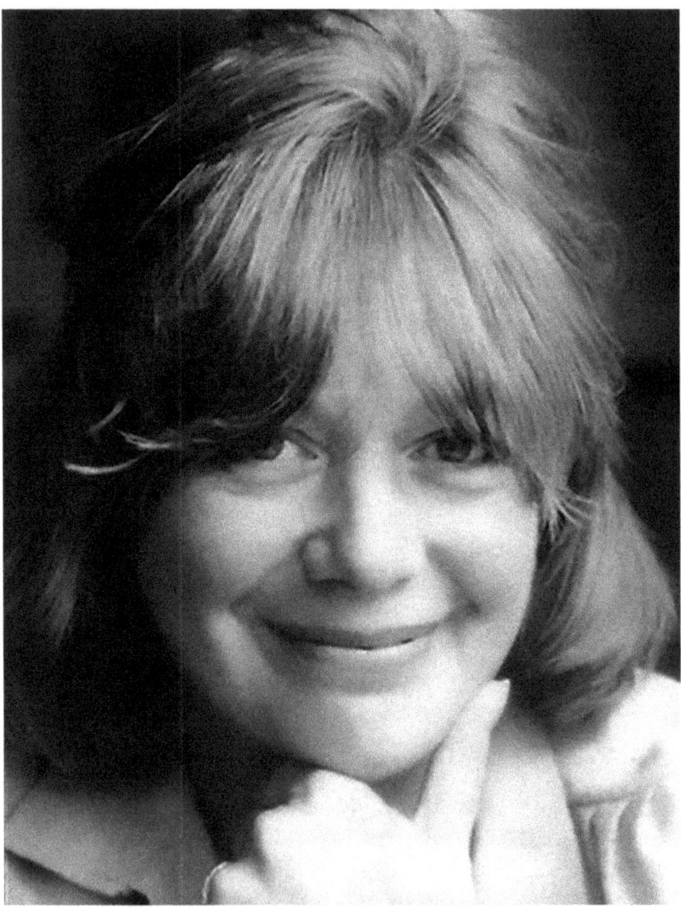

Emma Tennant

1975 — Spring — "I've spent the evening with 'Jim,' as J.G. Ballard... is known to those who wish to show they are close to him. But perhaps this is a contradiction in terms. Those who think they know him really well call him 'Jimmy.' I'm one of those who can consider themselves close—but all night I dreamt of brown, muddy water, as if the Yangtze, the river of his captivity in the Shanghai concentration camp, surrounds him and anyone in his vicinity when sleep comes. His tales of the camp haunt the atmosphere long after he has gone. 'We pushed the weevils to the side of the plate at first. But then my father told us to eat them; they contained all the protein we were likely to get.' At dinner, Jimmy has told me of the privations of his years as a prisoner of war. I begin to realise how far he is from being a conventional Englishman, despite the brisk and slightly alarming air—of family doctor or solicitor—which he presents to the outside world." (Tennant, *Burnt Diaries*, p29.)

1975 — Spring — Emma Tennant continued to observe Ballard: "Jimmy announced he likes 'neurasthenic women'—what an old-fashioned term!—almost pre-Freudian—do I qualify? I wonder, am I 'neurasthenic' enough for him? Whether I am or not, a few days later at the magazine office in comes L.T., a 'poetess' (another dated term employed by him): small, wiry-haired, hugely enlarged eyes glinting behind horn-rimmed glasses. 'Here,' says L.T. breathlessly, and she hands me an old brown envelope, containing, so I imagine, her latest crop of brilliant imagist poems. 'Can you give it back to Jim Ballard?' A tie, gaudy stripes, recognisably a part of the writer's unsettling wardrobe, is pulled from the recesses of the envelope. Old Jiffy bag fluff fills the already overflowing office. I peer through a grey mist at the poetess, but she has gone. 'I think she's telling us something,' says one of the magazine helpers, after we've gone to the window and looked out at the tiny 'neurasthenic' making her way into the Portobello Road." (Tennant, *Burnt Diaries*, p30.)

Note: "neurasthenia n. an obsolete technical term for a neurosis characterized by extreme lassitude and inability to cope with any but the most trivial tasks—neurasthenic adj."—Collins English Dictionary, 1986.

1975 — April 5 (Saturday) — Death of Chiang Kai-shek (b. 1887), Chinese statesman, erstwhile President of the Republic of China and President of the Republic of China-Taiwan, at age 87. (Mme. Chiang Kai-shek—Soong May-ling—would move to New York after her husband's death.)

1975 — April 16 (Wednesday) — "Survivors," a science-fiction series, began its run on BBC television. Devised by Terry Nation, it dealt in the John Wyndham-esque theme of survival in England after a plague has killed most of humanity. (It would continue, in three series, until 8 June 1977.) "In 'The Fourth Horseman,' the show's first and arguably best episode, we watch as society crumbles in the face of what appears at first to be merely flu. When we first meet Abby (Carolyn Seymour), she is playing tennis in her Home Counties back garden against a serving machine. When she leaves the court, the machine continues to pump out balls, but we know it will stop eventually—as will all other machines on the planet." (Dominic Sandbrook, *State of Emergency*, p208-209.)

1975 — April 30 (Wednesday) — Saigon fell to North Vietnamese and National Liberation Front forces. US Ambassador Graham Martin was the last American diplomat to leave Saigon, lifting off the Embassy roof at 4:58 am, and at 7:52 am Colonel James Kean and ten US Marines boarded an American helicopter and left, completely ending the US presence in the country.

1975 — May 19 (Monday) — "LONDON, Monday. An exhibition of 'green music,' musical plants, will open at the White Chapel Gallery this month. An artist, Mr John Lifton, puts probes into the stems of plants to pick up the electricity passing through them and feeds this into a synthesiser." (*Canberra Times*, 20 May 1975.) John Lifton was the husband of artist and writer Pamela Zoline.

1975 — June 1 (Sunday) — "PARIS, Sunday. Exiled Soviet author Aleksandr Solzhenitsyn said in an article published in Paris on Friday that World War III had already taken place and the West had been defeated. In an essay written for the newspaper *Le Monde* and seen by observers as his harshest diatribe to date against the West's failure to hold back communism, he argued that World War III began immediately after World War II and ended this year with the communist sweep in Indo-China. 'Two or three more decades of peaceful coexistence as glorious as the last and the very concept of the West will vanish from the face of the earth,' he wrote. 'When we dwell on the last 30 years, we see them as a long, winding descent, nothing but a descent, ever downwards, nothing but a path towards weakness and decadence.'" (*Canberra Times*, 2 June 1975.)

1975 — June 5 (Thursday) — The people of the United Kingdom voted "yes" (by 67%) in a referendum on Britain remaining a member of the European Economic Community.

1975 — June 20 (Friday) — Steven Spielberg's *Jaws*, an action film starring Roy Scheider, Richard Dreyfuss and Robert Shaw, about a giant white shark terrorizing a resort island, was released nationwide in the US. (Within two weeks, the film would recoup its costs, and by 5 September it would surpass *The Godfather* as the highest-grossing film ever.)

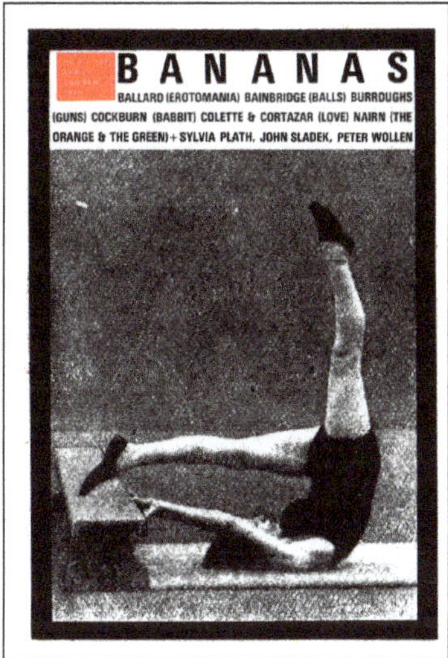

1975 — Summer — Ballard story published — "Low-Flying Aircraft" (*Bananas* no. 2, Early Summer 1975). Around this time Ballard was also named as an Associate Editor of *Bananas*.

1975 — July — It was probably in this month that an "underground" publication called *Repsychling: A Magazine for the Unborn*, issue one, appeared in London. Possibly a one-off (no further issues have been seen), it was a 16-page tabloid priced at 20p, with no editor or publisher named. It contained an interesting interview with Ballard confusingly headed "I Could Have Myself Playing With the Kids in Green Multiplied by Mozart."

1975 — July 24 (Thursday) — The Apollo space program came to an end, following the successful Apollo-Soyuz link-up, as astronauts Thomas Stafford, Vance Brand and Deke Slayton made the last manned "splashdown," with parachutes lowering their space capsule to a recovery in the Pacific Ocean. (The US would not venture into space again until 1981, when the new shuttles would land on runways following space missions.)

1975 — July 30 (Wednesday) — Death of James Blish (b. 1921), American science-fiction writer, latterly resident in Britain, of cancer at 54.

1975 — August 5 (Tuesday) — Ballard returned home from his summer holiday. Where had he been, and who with? It is possible that he and his younger daughter Beatrice went to the south of France together, just the two of them, as suggested by two undated photos she would post online years later with these comments: "Happy holiday memories in the South of France with my father... Mainly we lazed in the sun, relaxing, swimming and reading. My father loved to go out in the evenings for wonderful meals, and to stroll in the balmy air. Then we'd head back to the villa and watch the jewelled night sky from our villa balcony, drinking *beaumes de venise* on ice—good times." (Beatrice Ballard, Facebook, 17 June 2012.)

1975 — August 6 (Wednesday) — Ballard wrote to James Goddard: "Dear Jim, Very many thanks for the copies of *IF* and 'A Place and a Time to Die,' waiting for me here when I got back from holiday yesterday. I hope you didn't go to too much trouble getting hold of them. I'm glad to hear that the bibliography is moving ahead, and glad to do anything I can to help. I've written a new introduction, with a few marginal comments readers may find interesting. As for the new story collection, probably to be called *THE ULTIMATE CITY*, my guess is that it will be next summer or autumn. I'll let you know when I hear. [...] Many thanks for the kind comments on *HIGH-RISE*. I'm naturally delighted that you like the book, and grateful for your arranging to have an extract published in *SFM*. I look forward very much to your article. All the best, Jim."

1975 — August 29 (Friday) — Ballard wrote to two French critics, Igor and Grichka Bogdanoff (twin brothers, born in 1949, later well known in France as TV-show hosts), who had apparently asked him for a definition of science fiction. His response, translated into French, would later appear in the Bogdanoffs' book *L'Effet science-fiction: a la recherche d'une definition* (Paris: Laffont, 1979, p290): "*1) Une definition 'légère': La science-fiction est ce sujet particulier qui suscite le besoin irrepressible de definitions complexes, contradictoires et inutiles. 2) Une definition 'sérieuse': La sciencefiction est une fiction inspirée par la science. On pourrait alors penser a l'imaginaire. Mais l'imaginaire, quant a lui, n'est q'une fiction inspirée par... la fiction. La tient toute la difference.*"

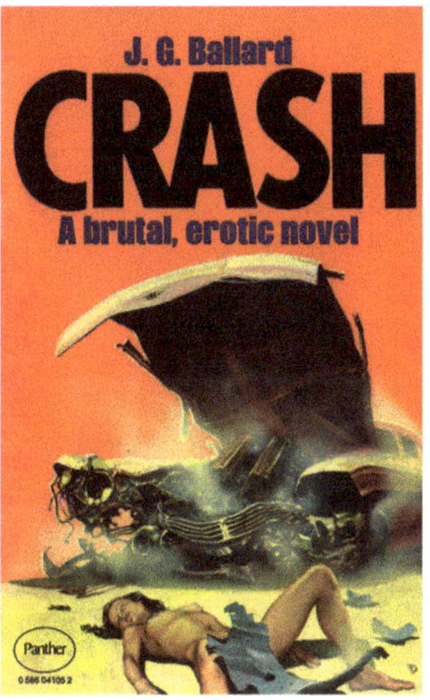

1975 — September — Ballard's *Crash* appeared in its first British mass-market paperback edition, from Panther Books (Granada Publishing), priced at 60 pence. It had a front-cover painting by the popular science-fiction illustrator Chris Foss (b. 1946), featuring a wrecked car and a naked girl, together with the strapline: "A brutal, erotic novel."

According to a later critic who interviewed the author: "The first UK paperback edition ... retains its power. 'Superb, in many ways the best ever,' notes Ballard. 'Quasi-realistic, but in the right way, like a movie poster of the 1950s—brought into brilliant focus by that line—"A brutal, erotic novel".'

Foss, an illustrator of *The Joy of Sex* (1972), treats the image as an opportunity for lurid, pulp-style exploitation. There is nothing quite like this scene in the book. The ruined car smoulders with menace, its twisted bonnet rising above the woman's naked body like a predator's gaping maw." (Rick Poynor, "Collapsing Bulkheads: The Covers of Crash," *Eye* no. 52, Summer 2004.)

This review was quoted on the back cover: "Maybe you think you know all about sex. And all about cars. And sex and cars. And sex and cars and violence. Hah! 'Crash' lays into the whole syndrome like nothing you've ever dreamed. Ballard can write and it's hard not to get caught up in this minatory vision of the sex-technology mystique"—*Playboy*.

1975 — September 5 (Friday) — Death of Dominick Elwes (b. 1931), British journalist and portrait painter whose elopement with an heiress in 1957 caused a scandal. He committed suicide with an overdose of barbiturates, at age 44. Emma Tennant had lost her virginity to him when in her teens, circa 1956: "She... fell for society painter Dominic Elwes. Bad choice. He had assumed she was an heiress and was after her money. 'I was thinking about Dominic Elwes recently,' she begins. 'What that man did was rape someone of 18 who didn't even know about contraception. He got her pregnant and then in a great rage had to vanish...' Rape? 'I think it counts as rape.' She was naive, she points out, 'the equivalent of a 12-year-old today. Of course, I thought, "This is happening and I'm not screaming, so it can't be rape." But that is what he did.' Even at this distance, she is growing upset talking about it. She underwent a bleak, illegal abortion, and subsequently ping-ponged between the conventional and the bohemian." (Louette Harding, "Three Husbands and a Toyboy," *Daily Mail*, 6 July 2007.)

1975 — October — "J.G. Ballard's Science Fiction for Today," a version of James Goddard and David Pringle's long interview with Ballard, appeared alongside an extract from the forthcoming Ballard novel *High-Rise* in *Science Fiction Monthly* vol. 2, no. 10 (October 1975). (The full version would appear later, as "An Interview with J. G. Ballard," in *Vector* no. 73/74, March 1976.)

1975 — October 10 (Friday) — David Cronenberg's horror film *Shivers*, set in a high-rise apartment block, was first released in Canada. It would also be known as *The Parasite Murders*. (It would be released in the USA on 6 July 1976, under yet another title, *They Came from Within*.)

1975 — October 17 (Friday) — Peter Wyngarde, the actor best known as the suave TV hero Jason King, was convicted and fined for an act of gross indecency with a truck driver in the toilets of Gloucester bus station. He had been known to Ballard, under his real name of Cyril Goldbert, since the days of Lunghua camp near Shanghai. "He liked to be surrounded by small boys, and would say casually: 'Do you want a banana? There's one in my trouser pocket.' Homosexuals were discreet in those days, but we all knew what was going on, and I don't think anyone fell for it." (Ballard, notes for *Miracles of Life*, circa 2007, British Library archive, p20.)

1975 — October 22 (Wednesday) — Death of Arnold J. Toynbee (b. 1889), British historian, author of the multi-volume *A Study of History*, at 86. His account of the rise and fall of civilizations rivalled Oswald Spengler's. "'Anyway, wouldn't it be better to stay where you are, among your own things, read through Toynbee and Spengler again?' Powers laughed shortly. 'That's the last thing I want to do. I want to forget Toynbee and Spengler, not try to remember them.'" (Ballard, "The Voices of Time," *New Worlds*, October 1960.)

1975 — October (late) — Emma Tennant held a dinner party for Warhol and Pinter. Alas, there is no indication that Ballard was there, although he may have been. "Michael Dempsey asked if he could bring Andy Warhol to dinner. And now my basement kitchen in Elgin Crescent has suddenly filled with men, men dreary and grey-suited. There are about thirty of them at the long trestle table, sitting at the bench—as obviously office-bound and trying to be 'bohemian' as the central figure is unmissable. To this unappetising board Antonia and Harold, recently joined, have also come; and, as in a nightmare, I see that Harold has been placed next to one of Warhol's cronies, *Penthouse* proprietor Bob Guccione. How long will Harold be able to take it? To distract myself from the imminent disaster, I concentrate on Warhol. Wasted, drained of life or interest in the proceedings, he stands out, I decide, not only because he's not wearing a tie (his escorts are from his publishers) but because, like Garbo or Monroe, the very famous on whom he has feasted night and day for so long, he knows himself to be a representative of the Underworld, the nether regions of Fame. True to form, he doesn't speak a word... A few days later, I read a brief account by Warhol of his London visit. The evening at my house is described as 'going to someone's house in Notting Hill, I don't know who.' And I laugh, thinking I've achieved something after all. Fifteen Minutes of Obscurity." (Tennant, *Burnt Diaries*, p41-42.)

Warhol's visit to the UK would conclude soon afterwards: "OCT. 1975. England was the last stop of the promotional tour for *The Philosophy of Andy Warhol*. Lord and Lady Lambton, parents of Ann Lambton who was part of the promotional entourage, gave a party for Warhol on the last night in London. Guests included the MARQUESS and MARCHIONESS of DUFFERIN, LORD and LADY LICHFIELD, LADY DIANA COOPER, CHARLIE TENNANT, PRINCESS ELIZABETH of YUGOSLAVIA, GUNTHER SACHS, LUCIAN FREUD, KEITH MOON, MARTIN AMIS, CAROLINE KENNEDY, J. PAUL GETTY III, 'and a woman in rubber named Jordan, who worked in a King's Road boutique named Sex.'" (Andy Warhol Timeline, warholstars.org.)

1975 — November — The English text of the introduction Ballard put together for the French *Crash!* (Calmann-Lévy, April 1974) was published for the first time in its original language in *Foundation* no. 9 (issue dated November 1975). The opening six paragraphs of the piece were recycled, with minor changes, from his 1969 essay on Salvador Dali, but the remainder consisted of newer comments, e.g.: "Science and technology multiply around us. To an increasing extent they dictate the languages in which we speak and think. Either we use those languages, or we remain mute."

1975 — November 13 (Thursday) — Ballard's novel *High-Rise* was published in hardcover by Jonathan Cape, London, priced at £2.95, and with a cover design by an unfamiliar artist, Craig Dodd. "There's a new class emerging which I guess didn't really exist until the Thirties, or the Twenties in the US, a sort of professional class which includes everyone from cost accountants to dentists to air-traffic controllers, etcetera, all the people who make up the 'High-Rise.' Now these people, regardless of their background, have more in common with each other than with the children they played with at home. A working-class dentist, by the time he's my age, has more in common with a dentist from another background than with the kids he used to play with in a back street in Blackburn. High technology has given these people a very strong sense of identity. Now, I was interested in studying this new class and wondering what would happen if it came under extreme internal stresses." (Ballard, *Street Life* interview, 1976.)

1975 — November 14 (Friday) — Ballard's *High-Rise* was reviewed in the *New Statesman* by Martin Amis. "Towards the end of Auden and Isherwood's *The Ascent of F6*, Ransom, the Oedipal, megalomaniac hero, is about to scale the last heights of the mountain... J.G. Ballard's *High-Rise* is a harsh and ingenious reworking of the *F6* theme, displaced into the steel-and-concrete landscapes of modern urban life... Eventually the high-rise takes on that quality common to all Ballardian *loci*: it is suspended, no longer to do with the rest of the planet, screened off by its own surreal logic... I hope no one wastes their time worrying whether *High-Rise* is prescient, admonitory, sobering and whatnot. For Ballard is neither believable nor unbelievable... he is abstract, at once totally humourless and entirely unserious. The point of his visions is to provide him with imagery, with opportunities to write well... The prose of *High-Rise* may not have the baleful glare of that of *Crash* or *Vermilion Sands*, but the book is an intense and vivid bestiary, which lingers unsettlingly in the mind."

1975 — November 15 (Saturday) — J.G. Ballard's 45th birthday. It was probably around this time that he was interviewed by Martin Hayman for the magazine *Street Life*. "Ballard confesses that with the last of the trio, 'High-Rise,' he feels he has explored this particular vein as far as he wishes, not maybe to his own satisfaction, but sufficiently. And it's intriguing (and perhaps welcome for long-time readers) that he feels the need to return to what he calls a more 'imaginative' style of writing. His next volume, completed at the beginning of the Summer, is a collection of unpublished [sic] short stories filled out with a specially-written novella ['The Ultimate City']."

1975 — November 20 (Thursday) — Death of General Francisco Franco (b. 1892), Spain's dictator, two weeks before his 83rd birthday.

1975 — December — "Public Lending Right: A Symposium" appeared in *The New Review* (vol. 2, no. 21, December 1975). Ballard was among the contributors: "Yes, I am in favour of PLR, although it depends on the scheme. I've not taken any part in the public meetings but I take it that logically the benefit should be on the 'penny per loan' basis, rather than every time a book is *bought* by a library... PLR is slow because writers are regarded as people of absolutely no importance. We give our money to the theatrical entrepreneurs and ballet stars. The land that produced Shakespeare now takes literature for granted..."

1975 — December 8 (Monday) — Rival Christian and Muslim militias had seized control of luxury hotels and other skyscrapers in Beirut, using them as high ground for cannon, rockets and sniper fire. The Christian Phalangists captured the recently-opened Holiday Inn and the Muslims took the 40-storey Mour tower. The lower-priced Hotel Urabi was burned down, killing 37 of its guests. (Within another week, a truce would end the "battle of the hotels," leaving the buildings in ruins, 600 people killed and 900 injured.)

1975 — December 11 (Thursday) — Ballard wrote to Peter Nicholls, commenting on the contents of *Foundation* no. 7/8 (a double issue): "it's not the barbarians who are at the gates of the city now, but the pseudo-intellectuals. I'm thinking particularly of Delany's piece, and the article by the Canadian about him—absolutely beyond parody—I feel sorry for Delany, a sweet guy, when he wakes up in five years time and realizes what he's been doing—or maybe he never will—in which case there'll be nothing left but to run for the hills. I have a nightmare vision of the street clogged with sf thesis-writers jawing away about Chomsky and Levi-Strauss and Wittgenstein—the first *lumpen-intelligentsia* seems to be making its appearance in sf criticism. Don't think I'm knocking intelligent writing about sf—like your own excellent piece on *N.W.* But some of those Americans... In the *New York Review of Books* there used to be an ad listing the lecture or thesis titles of some college sf course—'Levi-Strauss and the concepts of structuralism in the novels of Harry Harrison.' Amazing stuff. (Whenever anyone uses the phrase 'in the novels of...' reach for your editorial revolver.) It seems to me that the main job of editors like yourself is not to protect us from the bad sf writers but the legion of sf critics."

1975 — December 17 (Wednesday) — "LONDON, Wednesday. Thick, icy fog—the worst in 20 years—shrouded London last night for the third night in a row. To romantics, it was a night out of Sherlock Holmes. To the Meteorological Office it was imported Industrial smog, carried by eastern winds out of Germany's Ruhr Valley—the chilling, dampish nuisance Britain thought it had committed to history with the passage in 1956 of the Clean Air Act, banning coke and soft coal... Freezing conditions on suburban roads caused a 70-car pile-up in Kent that sent 30 people to surrounding hospitals, most for minor injuries. At its worst, visibility was down to a few metres, in Knightsbridge, off Hyde Park." (*Canberra Times*, 18 December 1975.)

To be continued...

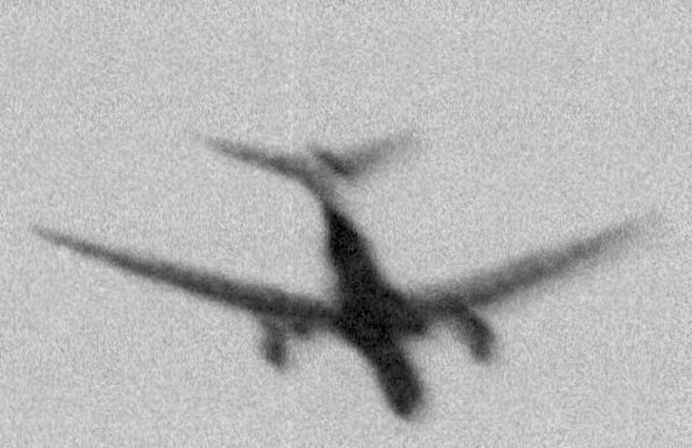

KAROLINA URBANIAK

LONDON-WESTWAY-SHEPPERTON

A DAY WITH FAY BALLARD

TRANSCRIPT & VISUAL RECORD FROM A TRIP TO SHEPPERTON

Images & design by Karolina Urbaniak

Words by Fay Ballard | selected & transcribed by Karolina Urbaniak |

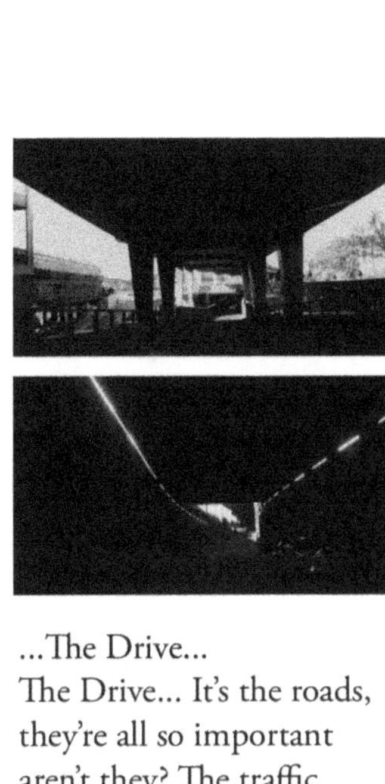
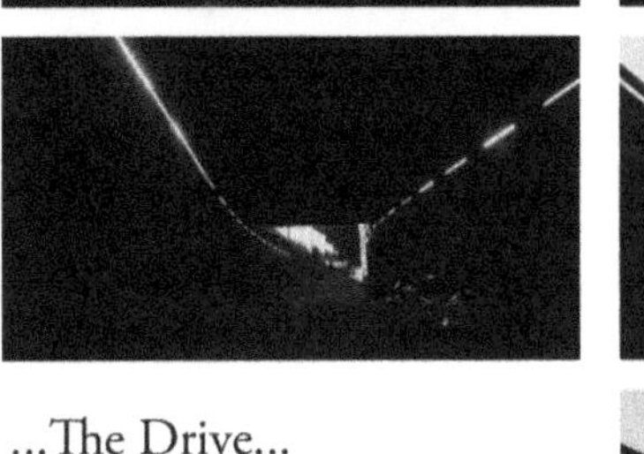
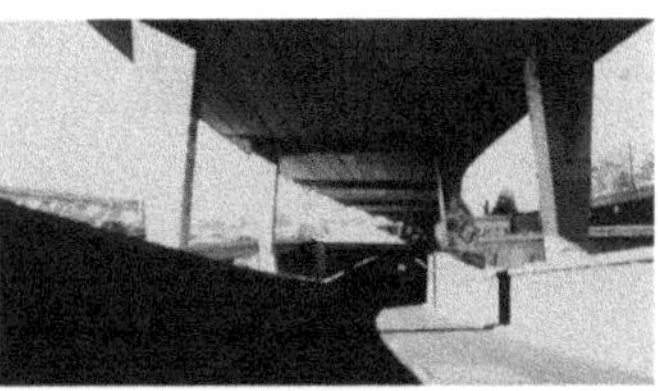

The Westway was his means of getting into town from Shepperton... ...it inspired him...

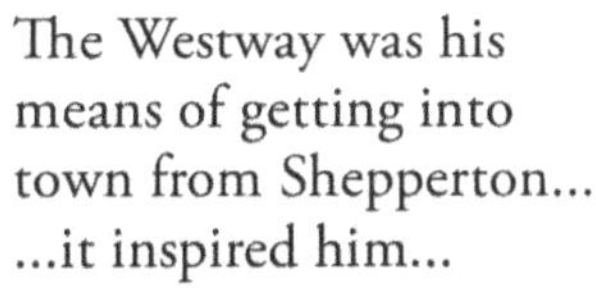
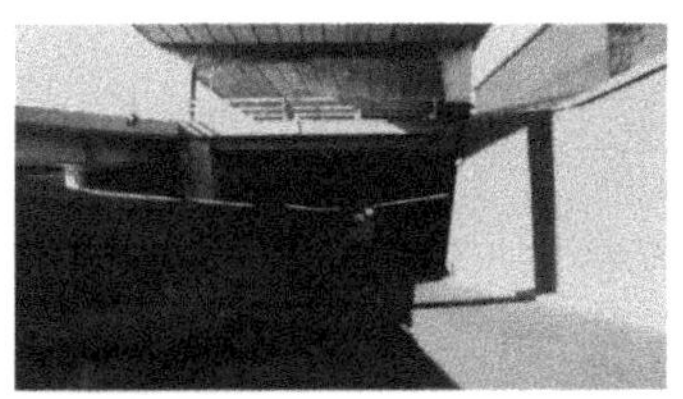
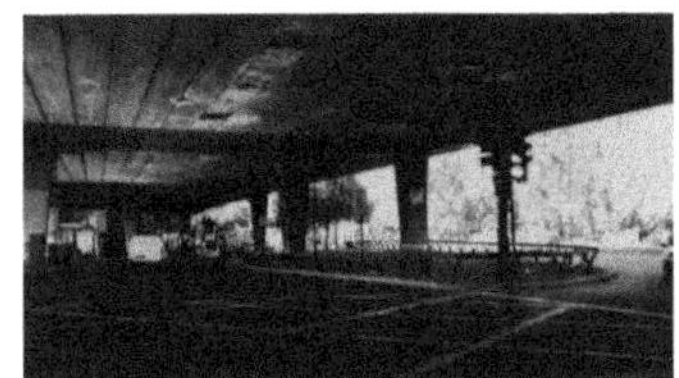
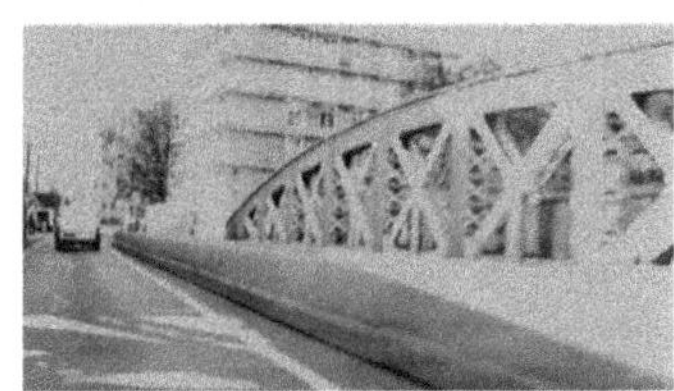
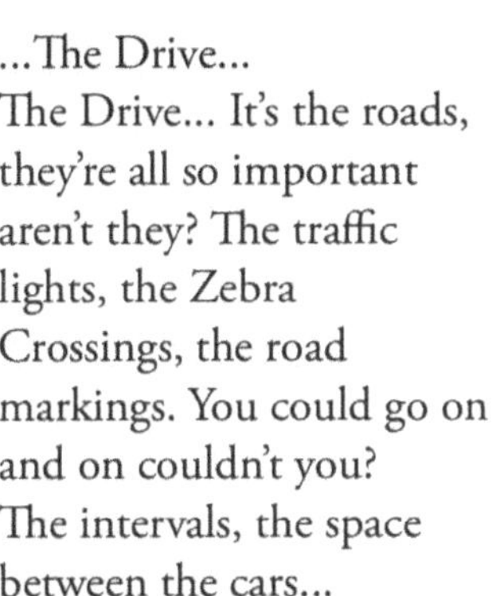
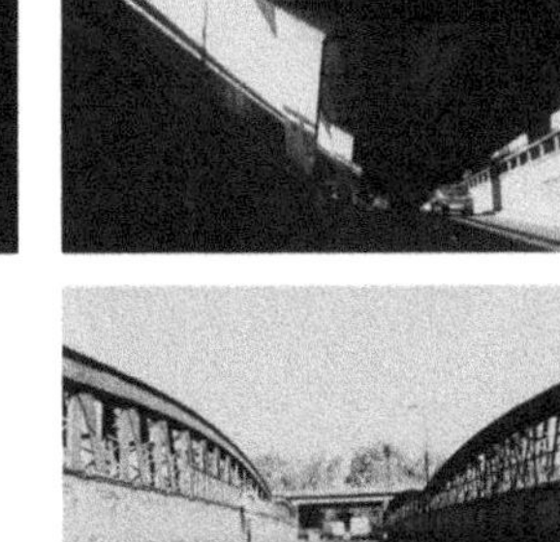

...The Drive...
The Drive... It's the roads, they're all so important aren't they? The traffic lights, the Zebra Crossings, the road markings. You could go on and on couldn't you? The intervals, the space between the cars...

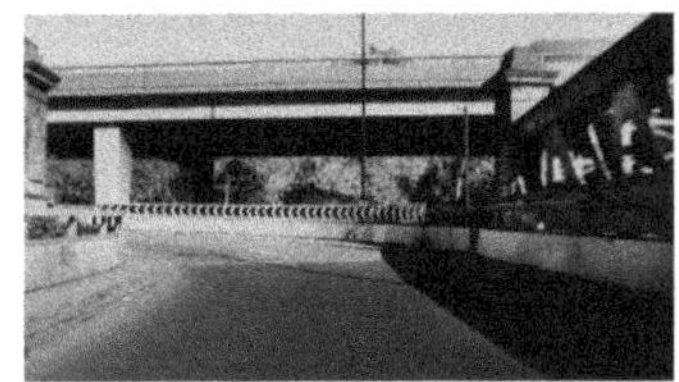
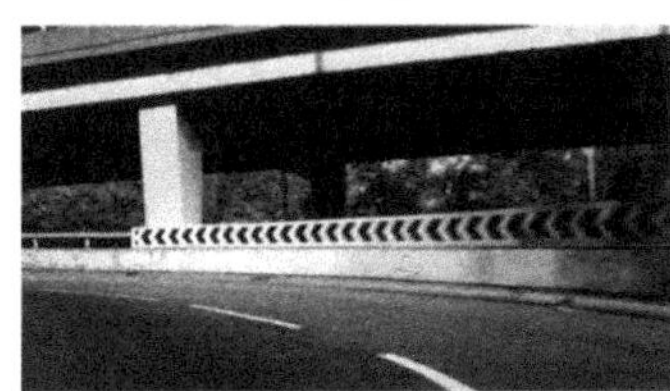
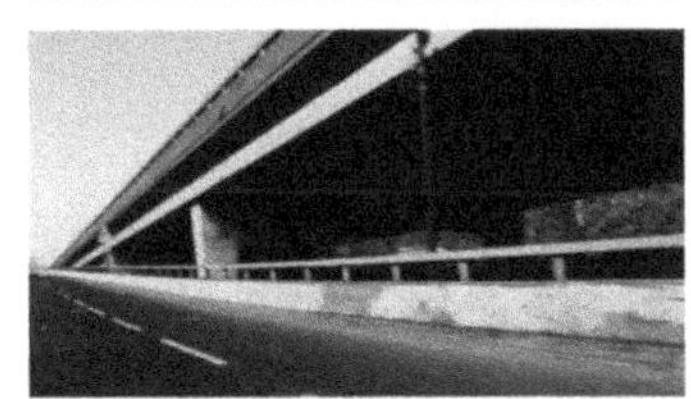
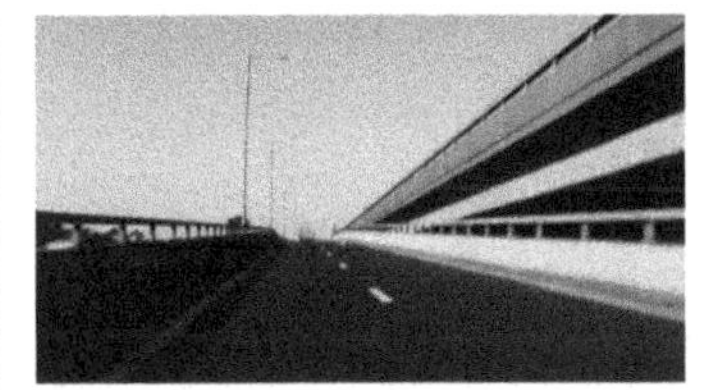
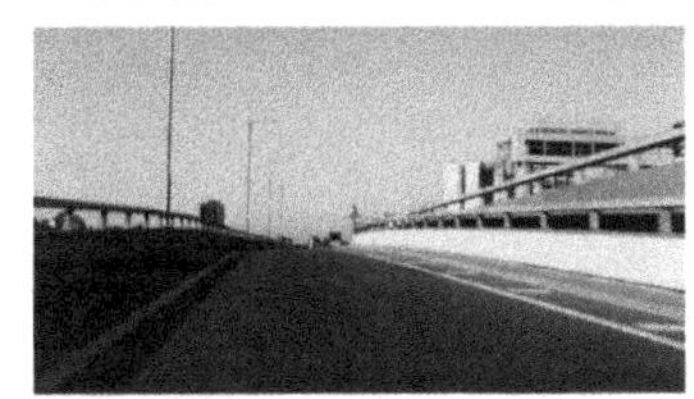
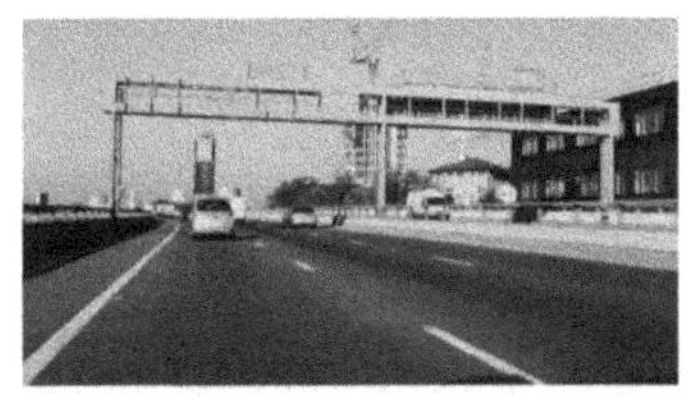
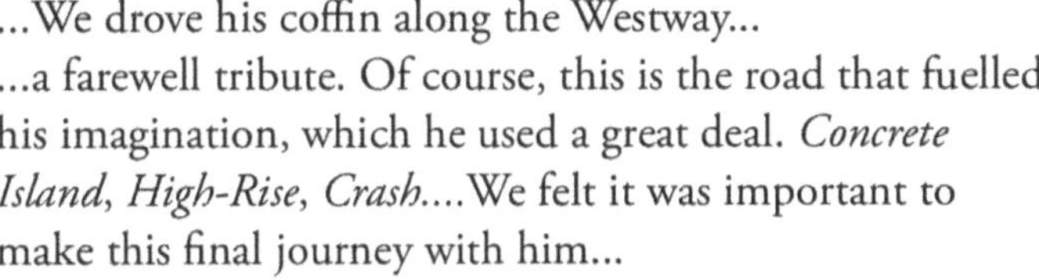

...We drove his coffin along the Westway...
...a farewell tribute. Of course, this is the road that fuelled his imagination, which he used a great deal. *Concrete Island*, *High-Rise*, *Crash*....We felt it was important to make this final journey with him...

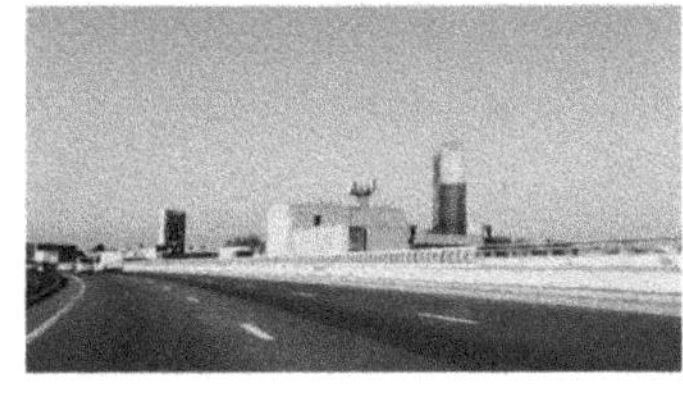
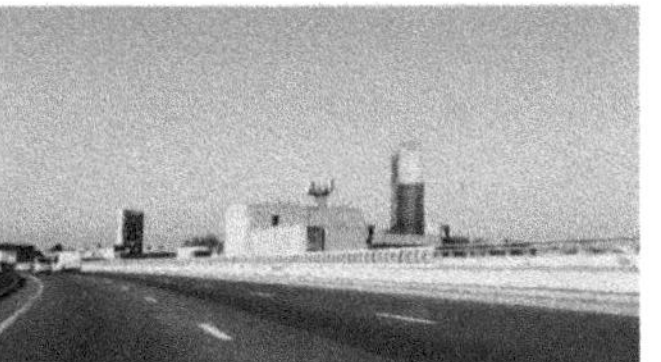
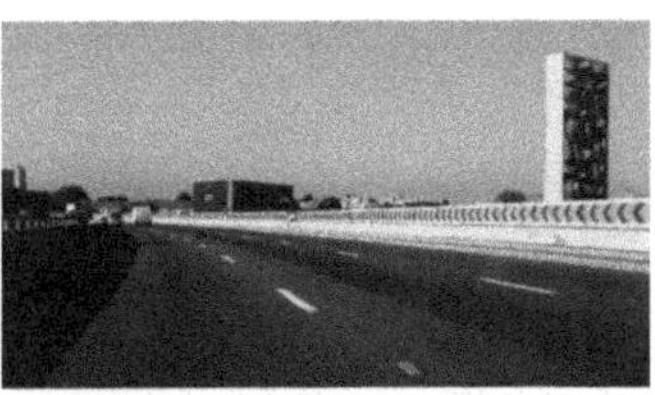
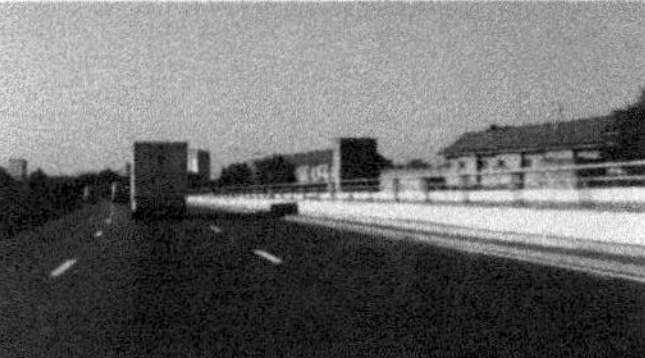
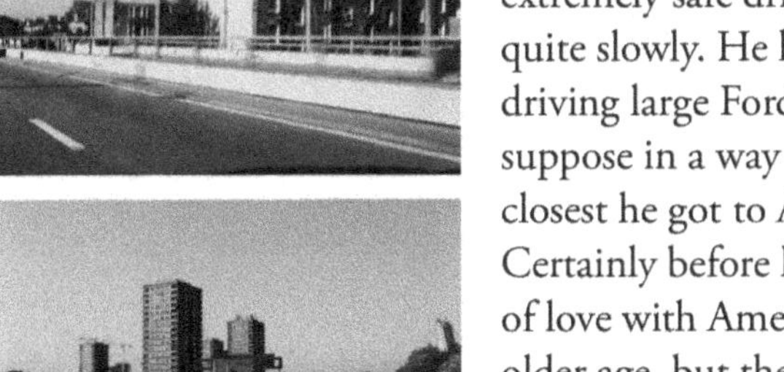
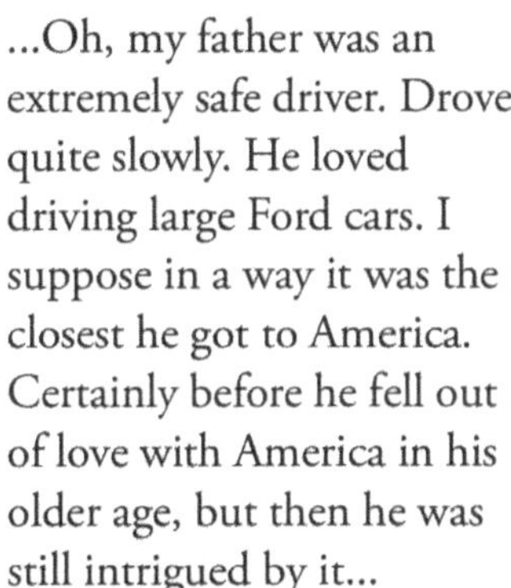

...Oh, my father was an extremely safe driver. Drove quite slowly. He loved driving large Ford cars. I suppose in a way it was the closest he got to America. Certainly before he fell out of love with America in his older age, but then he was still intrigued by it...

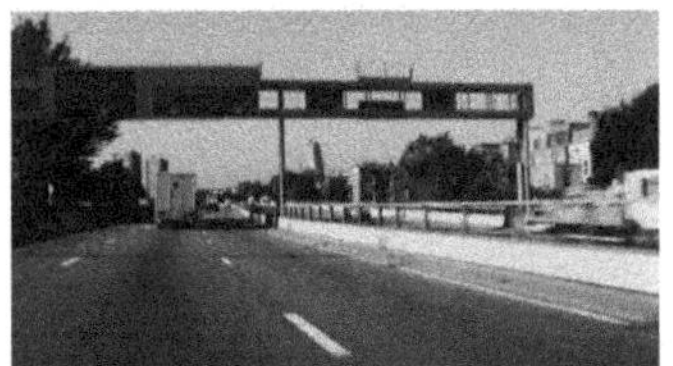
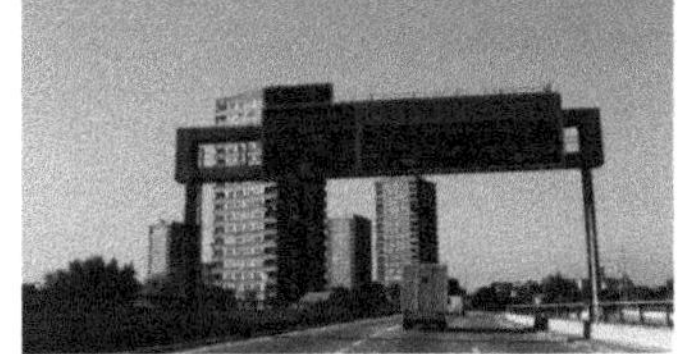
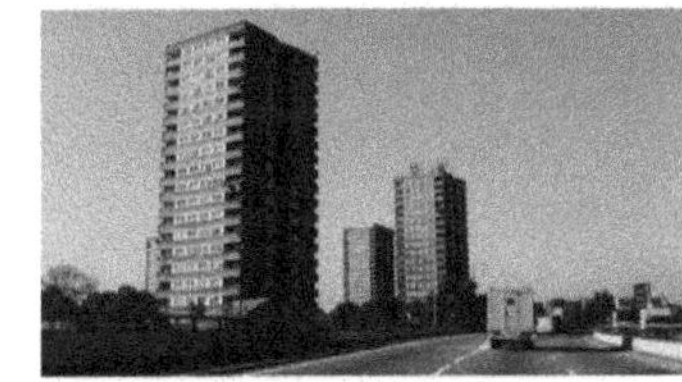
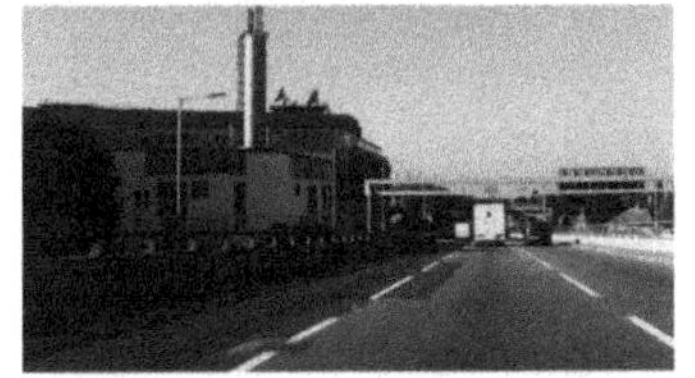
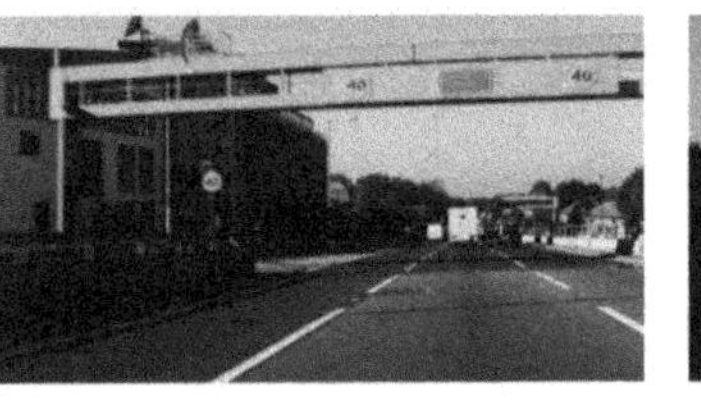
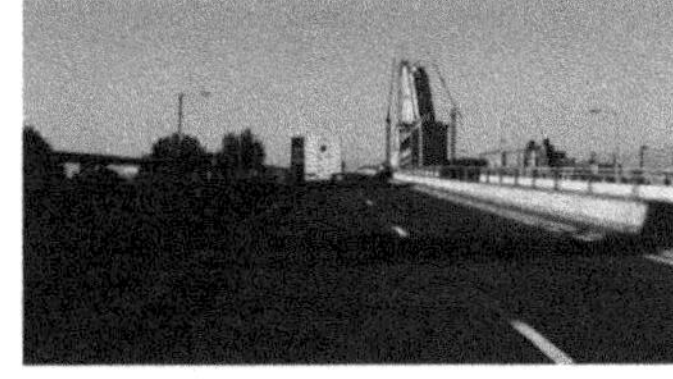
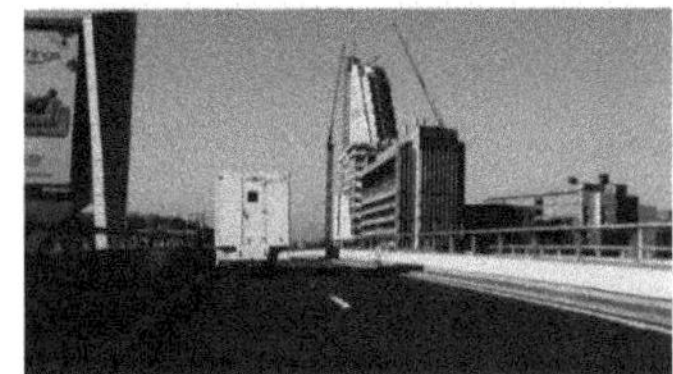
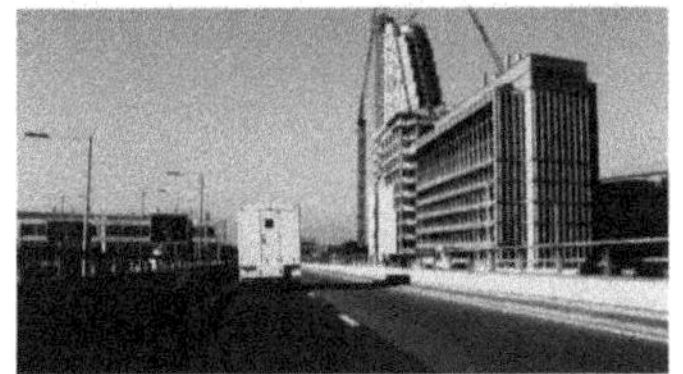

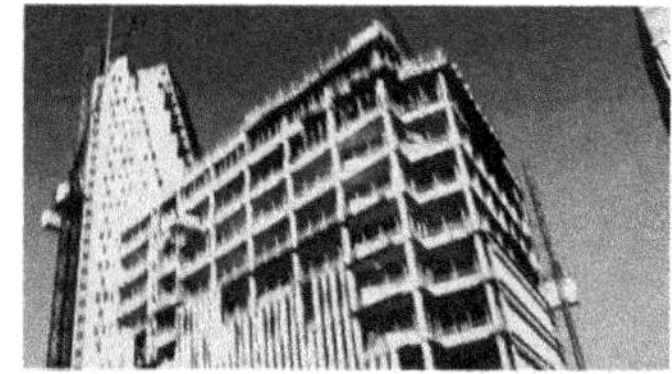
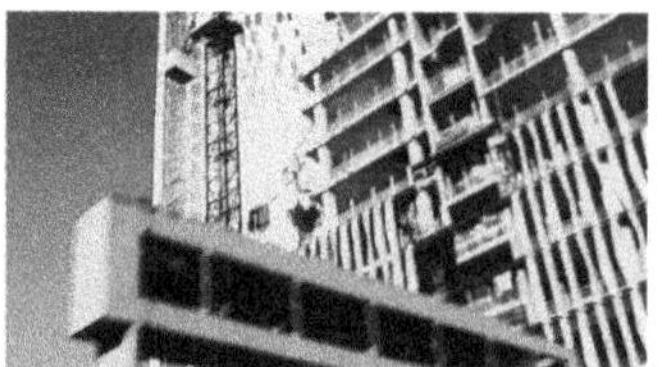
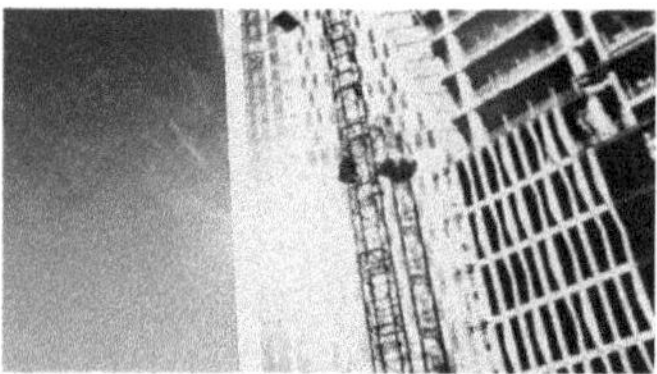
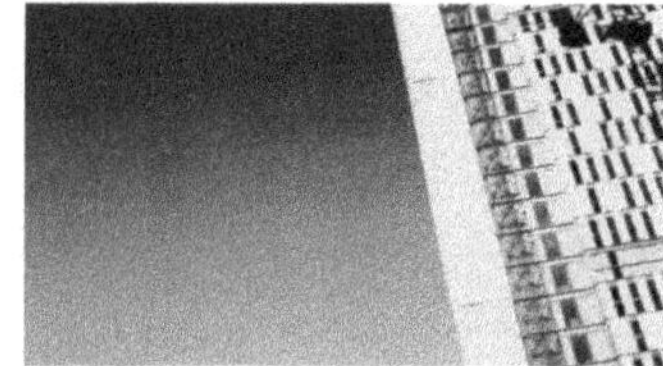

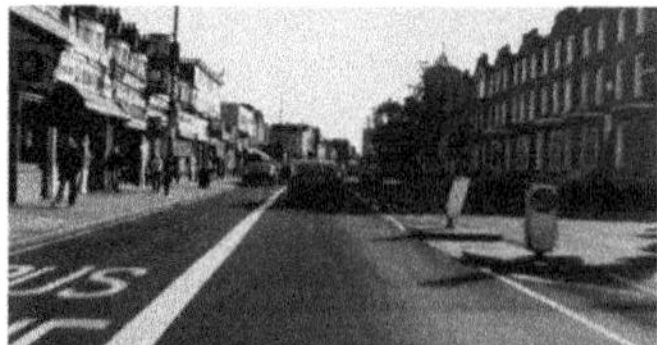

...So he would have driven round this roundabout thousands of times...

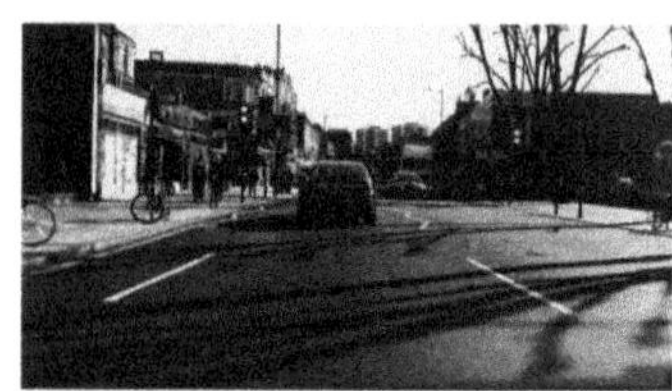
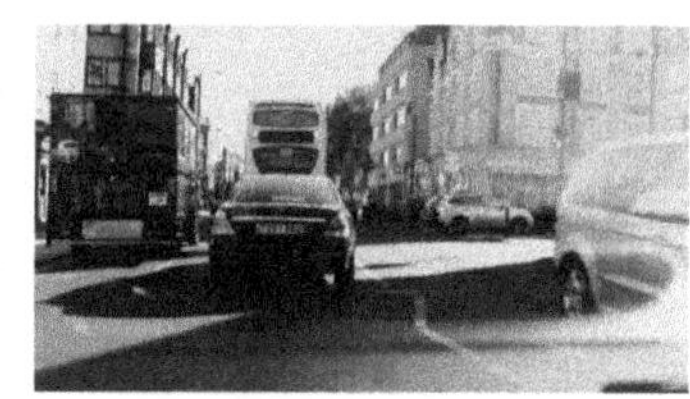

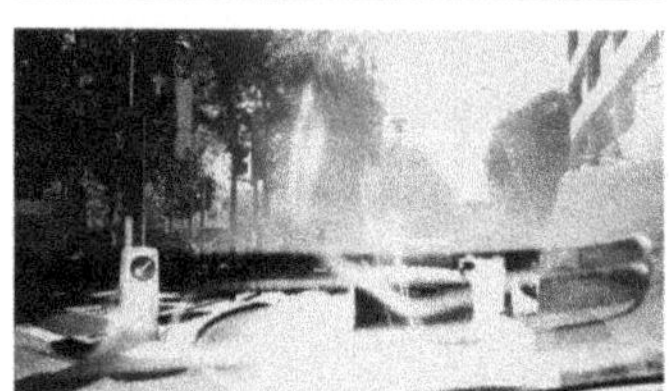

...This is his stomping ground – this is the place where he spent a lot of time...

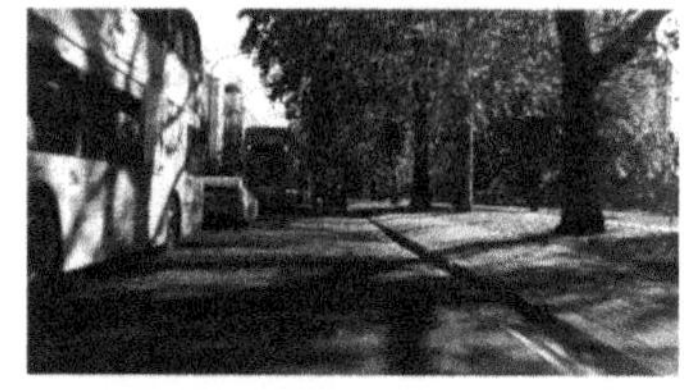
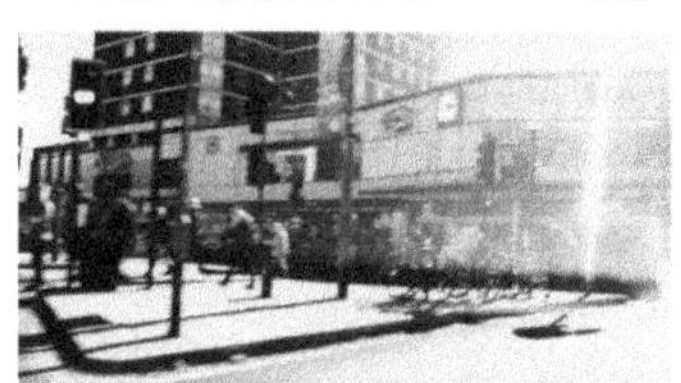

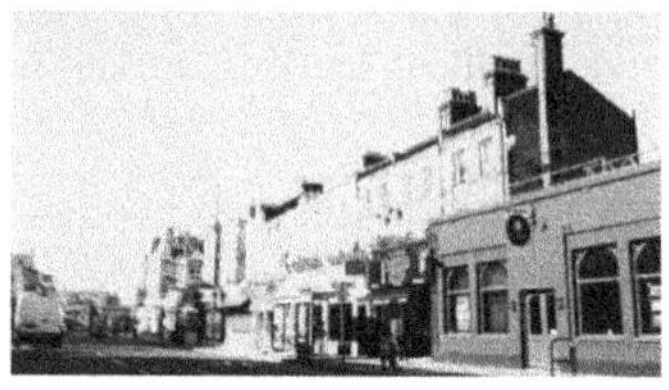
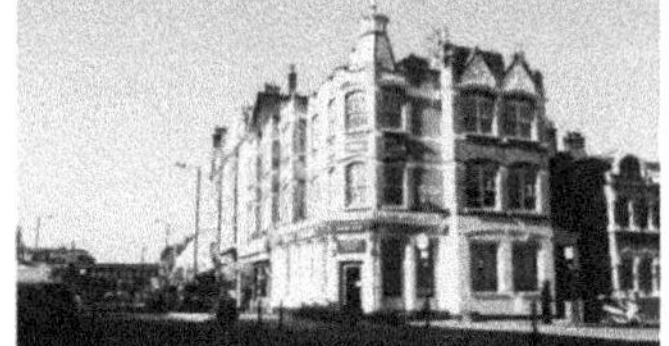
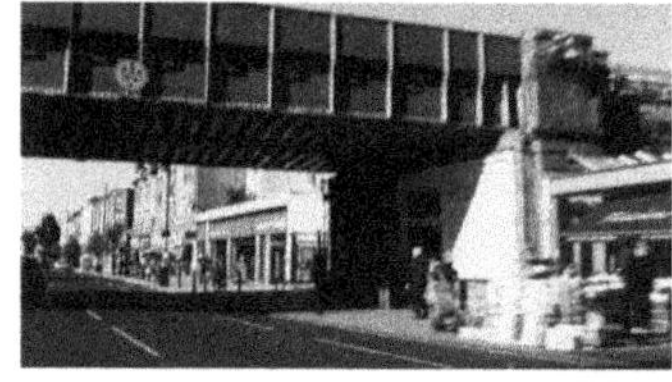
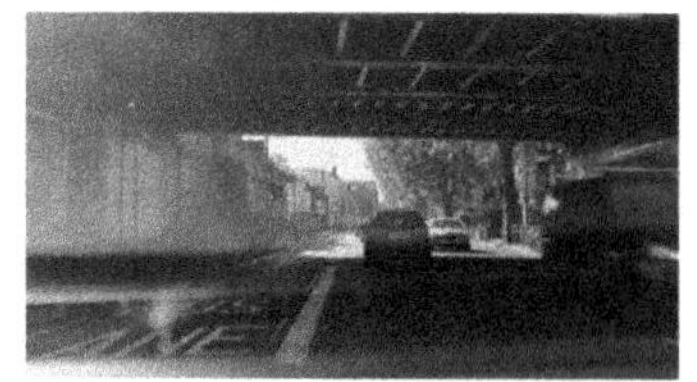

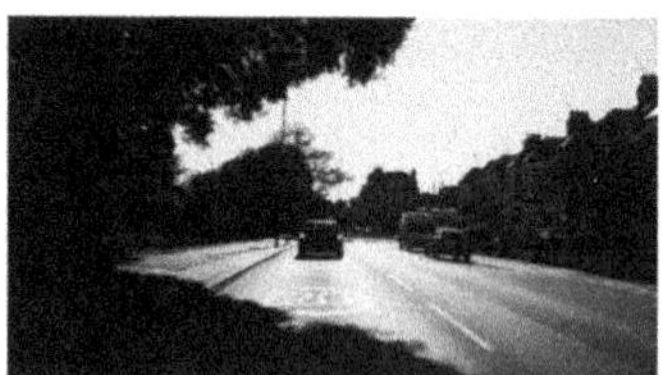
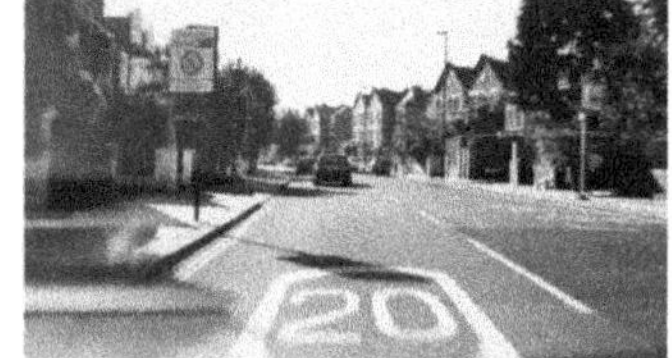

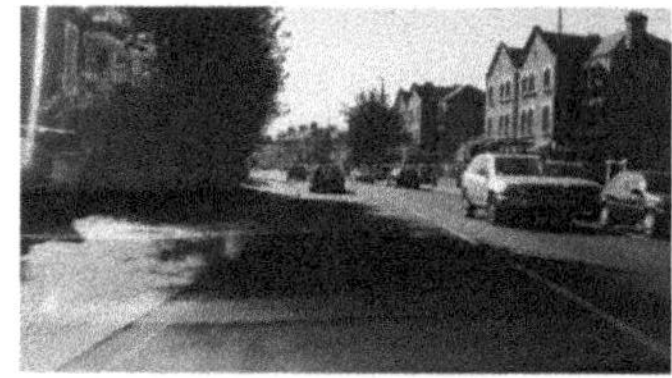
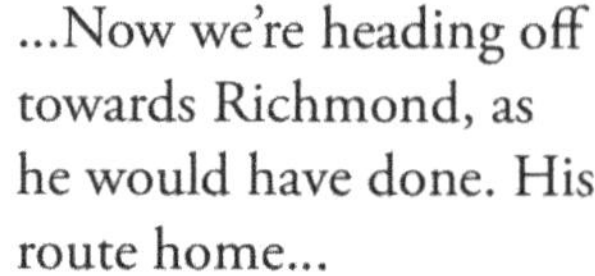

...Now we're heading off towards Richmond, as he would have done. His route home...

...The next stop on the journey is the place where he had his crash, which took place 2 weeks after he'd written and handed in his manuscript *Crash*.
He was returning home late...

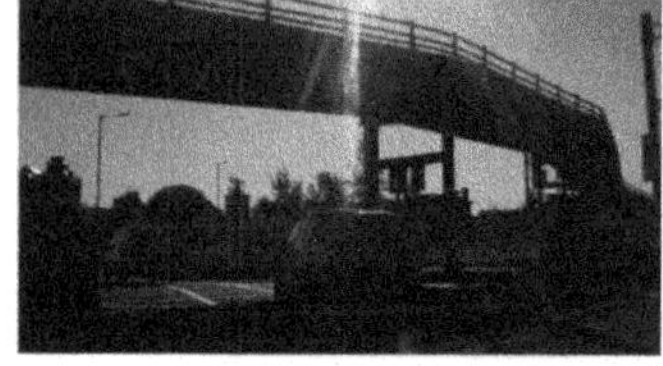
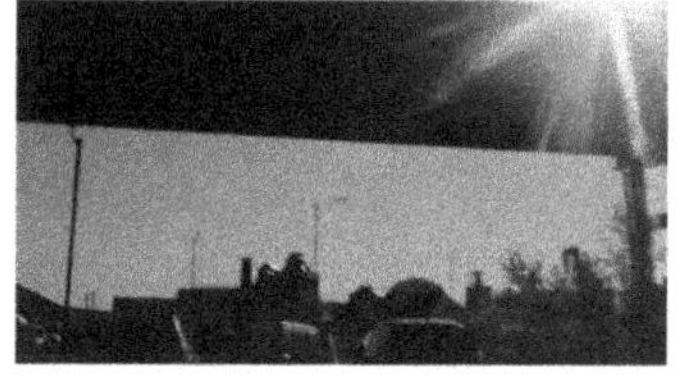
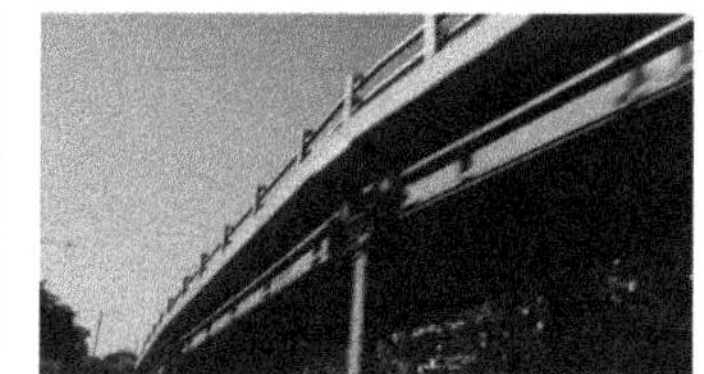

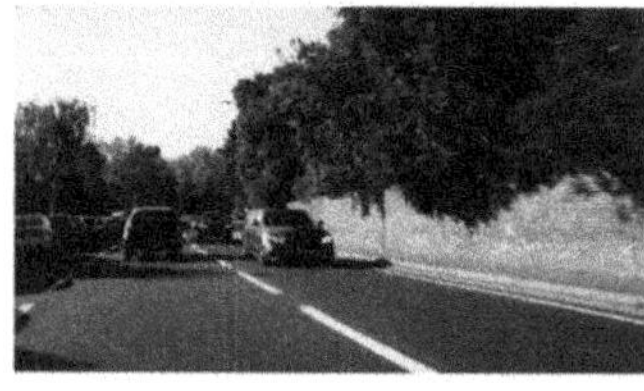

...So we're coming up to the point where he had his crash, which is at this junction up here...
...His car rolled over, smashed into one of the bollards...
He was asked to pay for a new bollard which he resented... luckily he was wearing a seat-belt and staggered out of the car....
...He was driving a wonderful silver Ford Zephyr 6, he loved it. It didn't survive the crash...

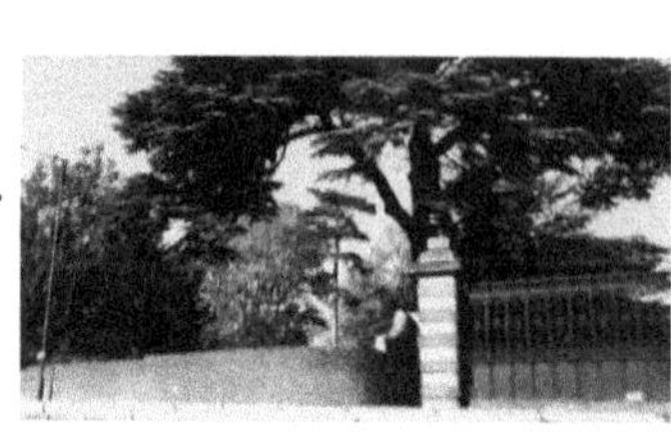
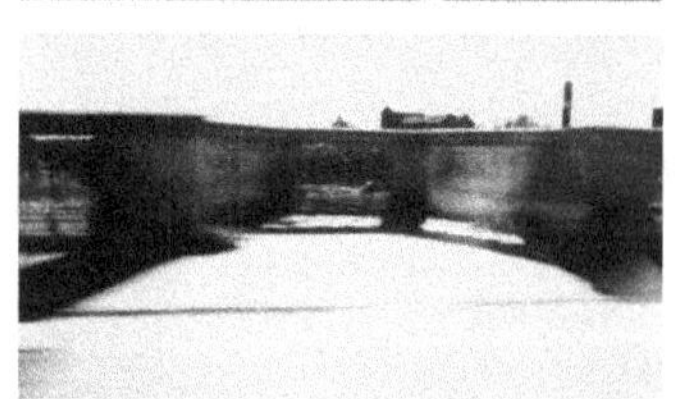

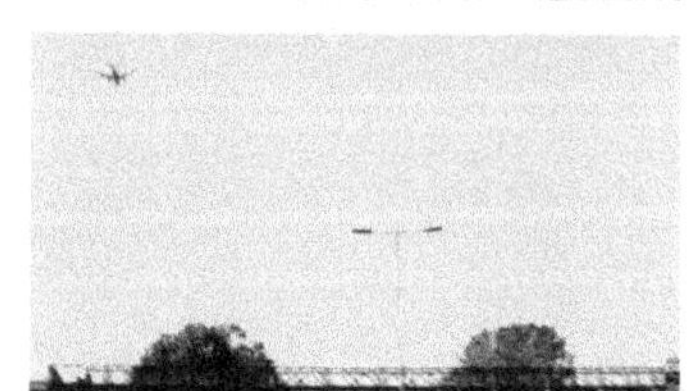
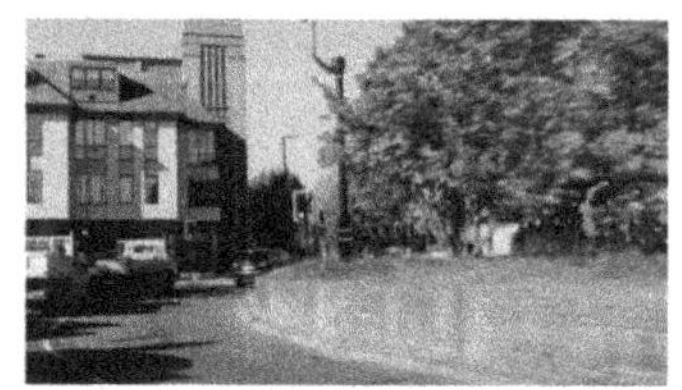
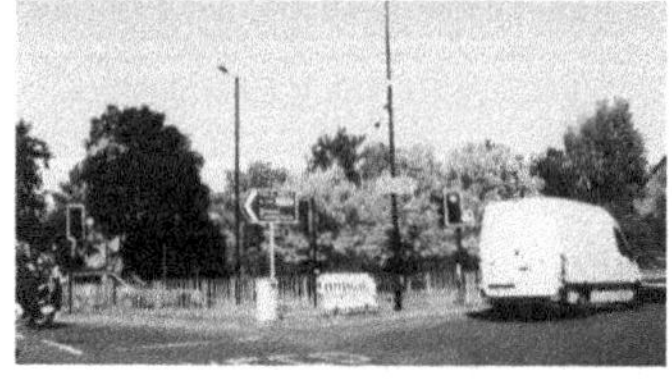
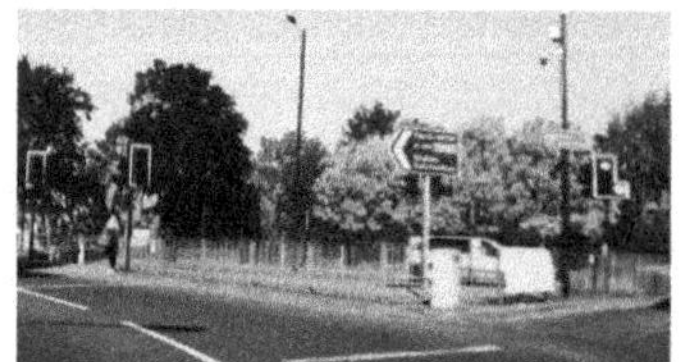

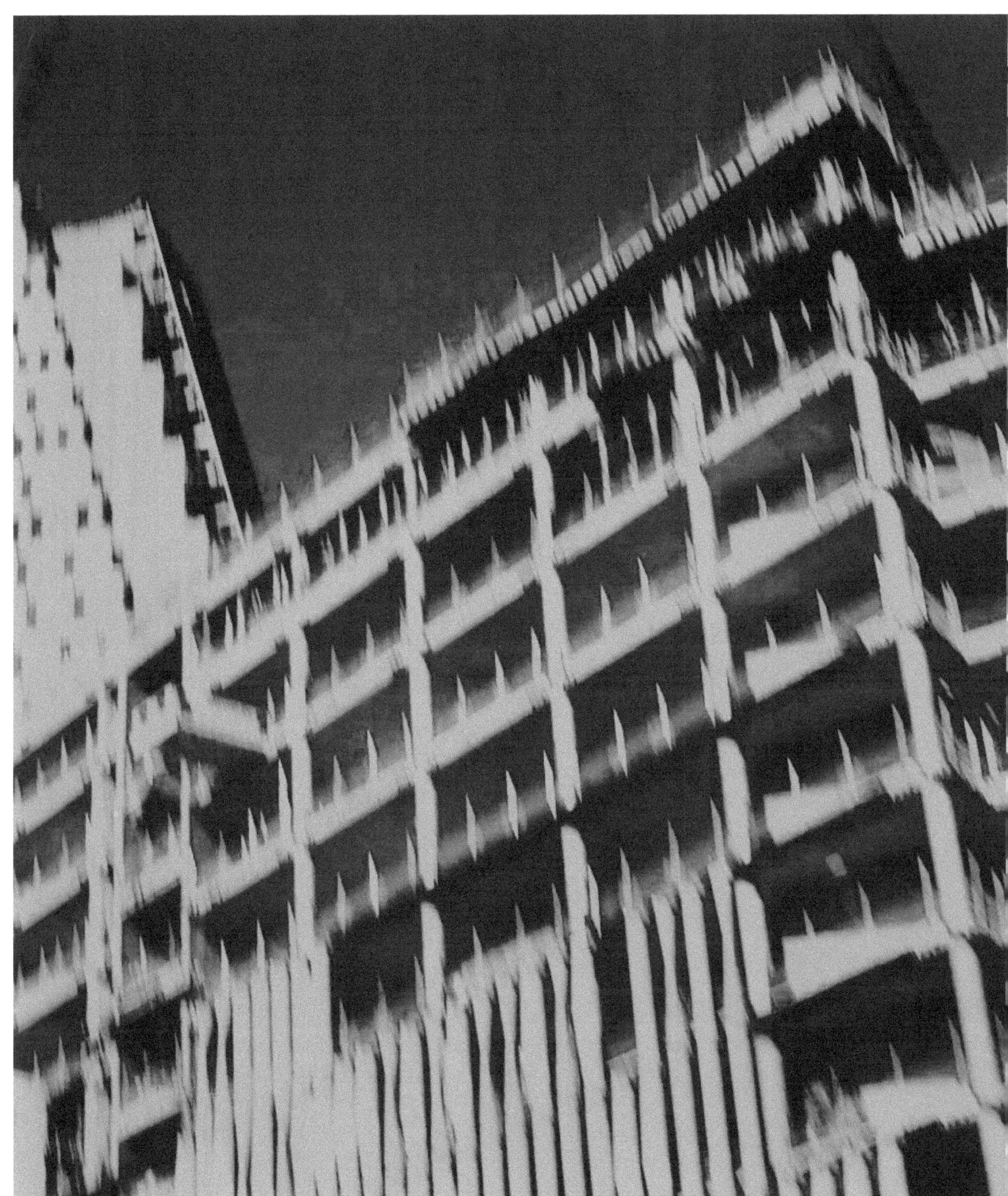

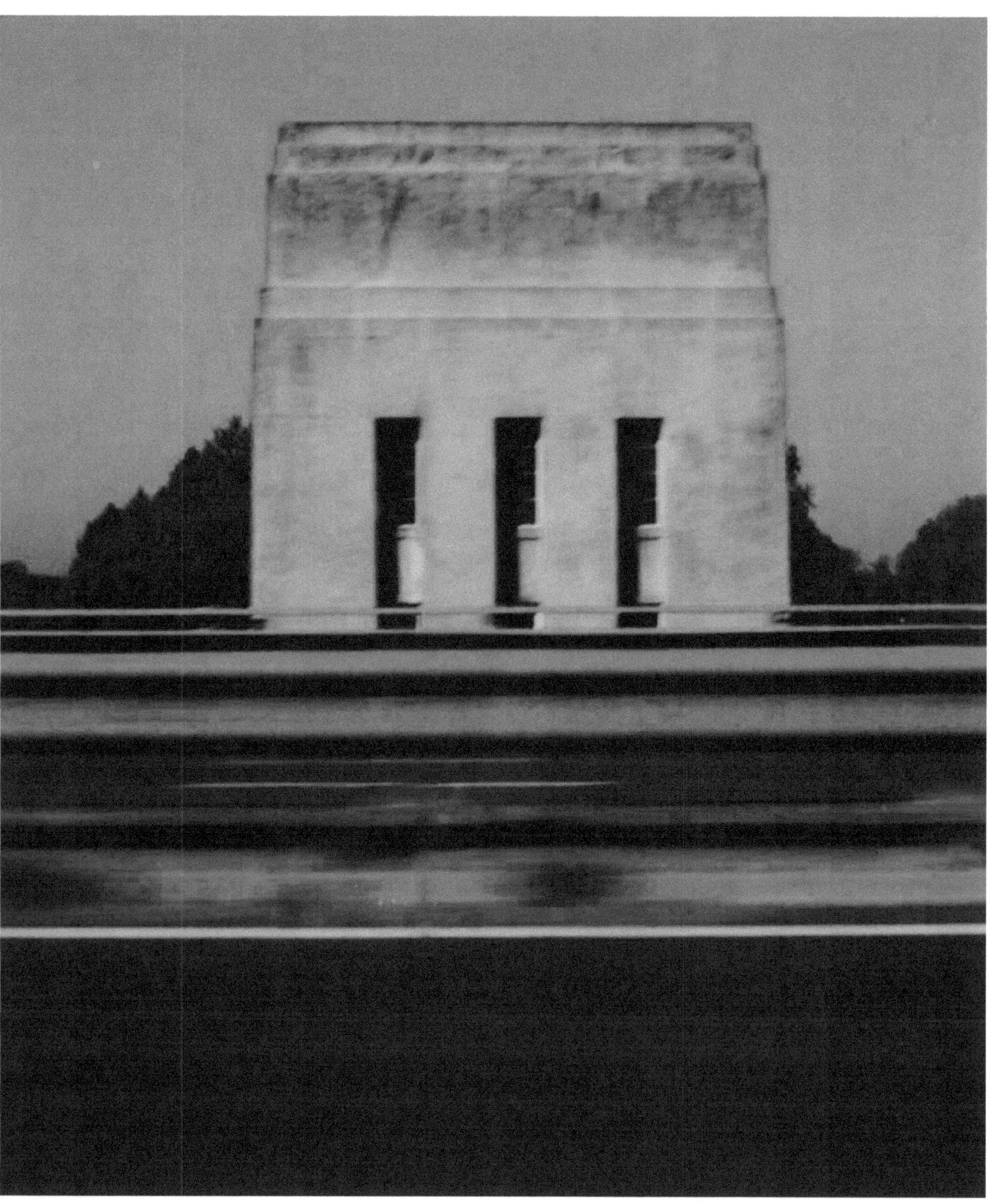

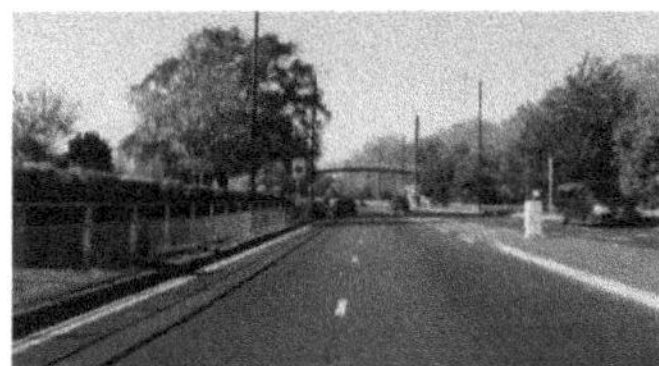
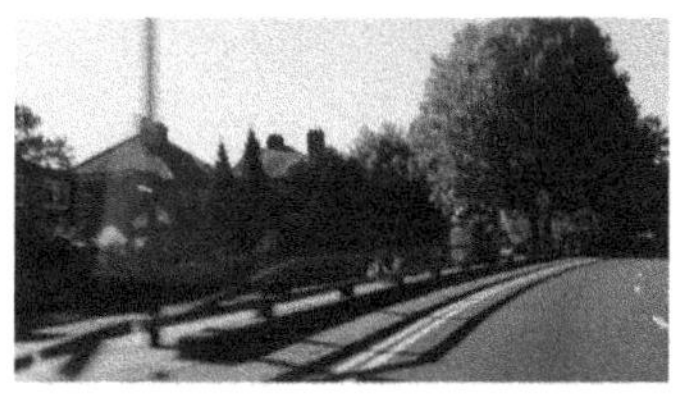
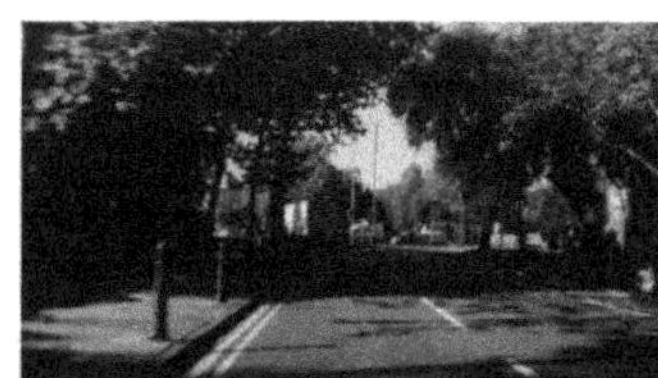
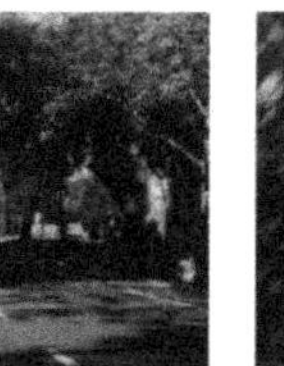
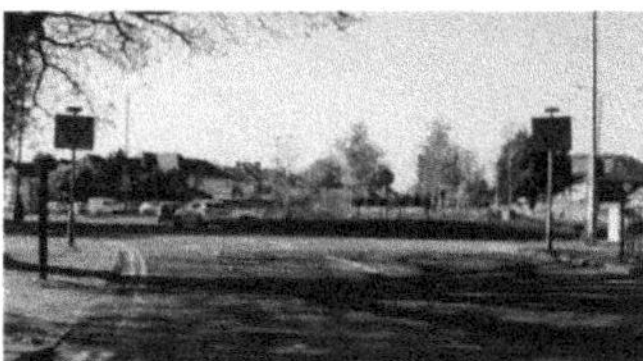

...We're going to cross the river soon. I have early memories of being pushed in the pram by my father along the riverbank here. It was a big old- fashioned pram which I shared with my older brother, him up one end and me down the other...

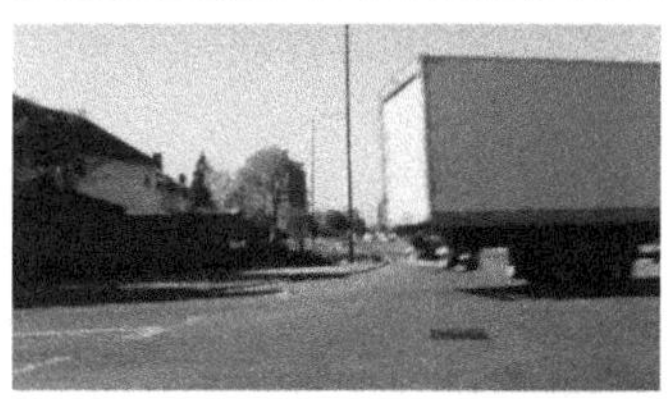
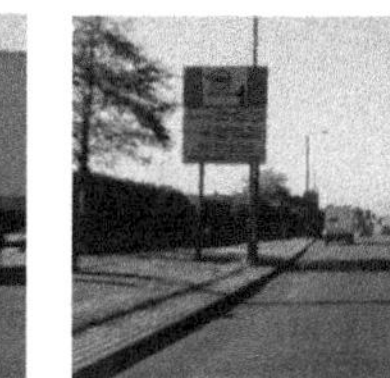
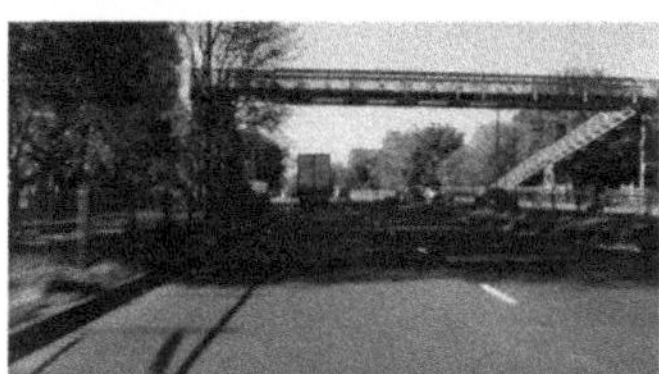
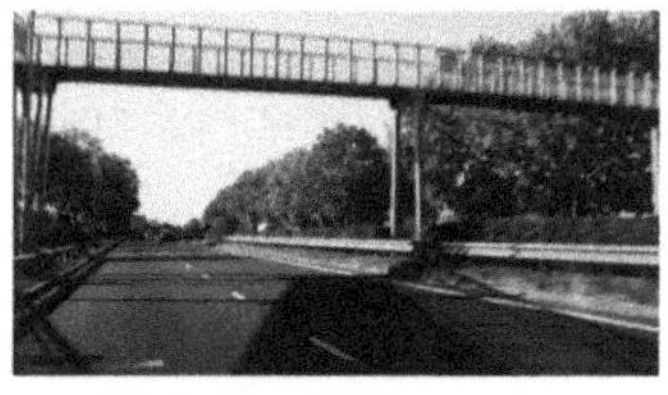
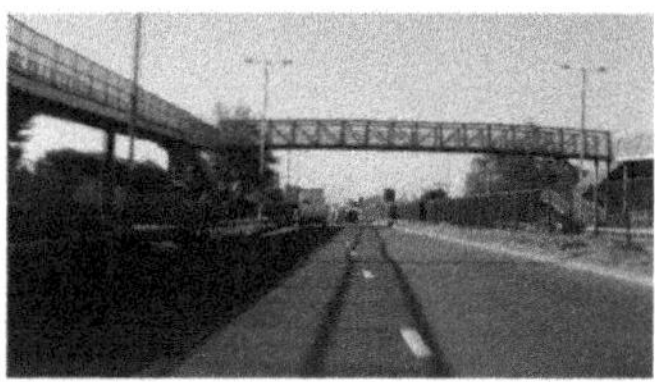
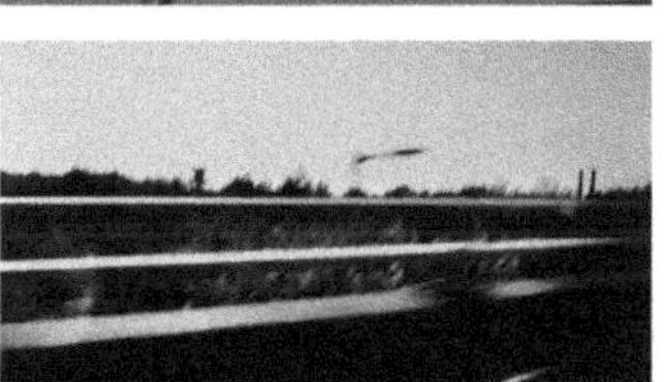
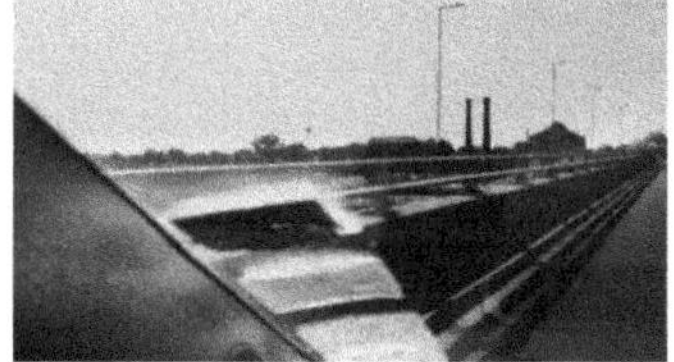
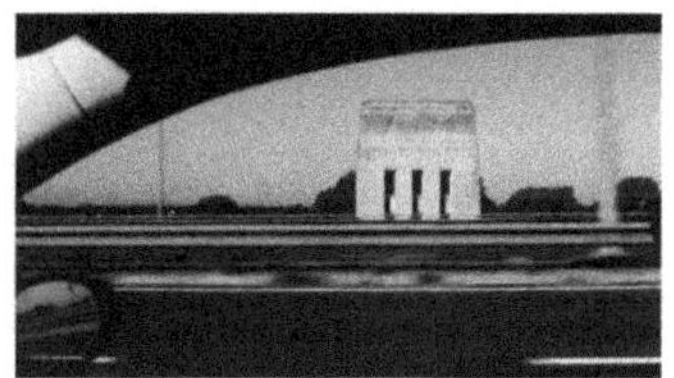
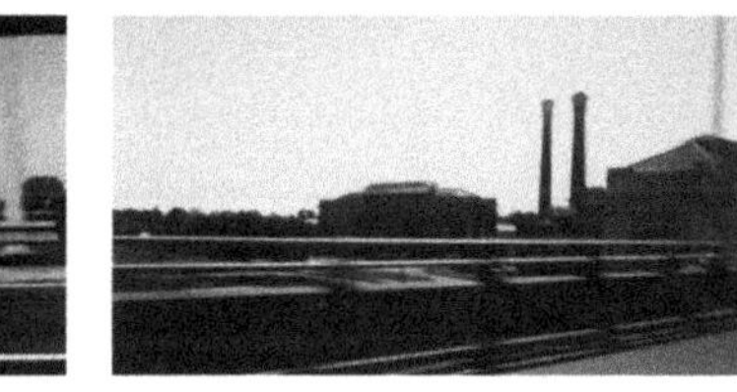
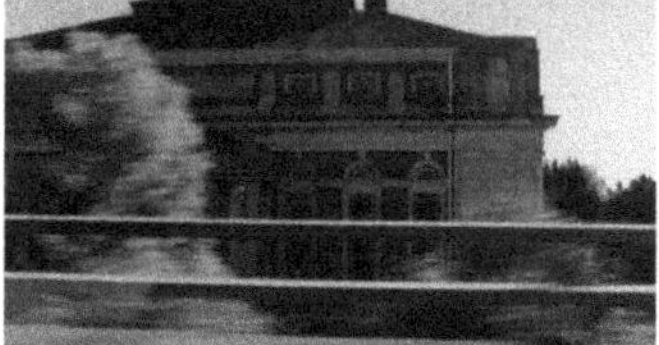
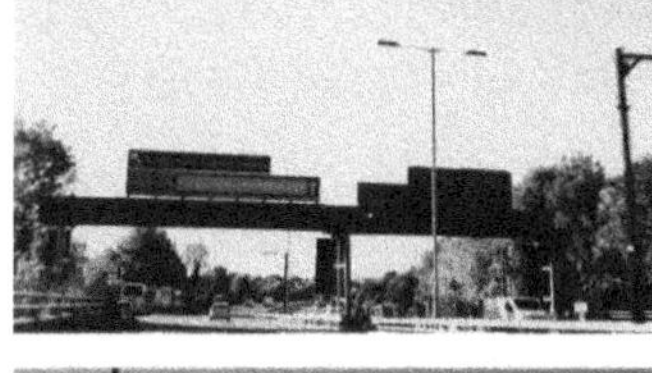

...We moved to Shepperton at the end of 1959 or beginning of 1960. Daddy bought the house that we are going to visit today. At the time, he was working on a scientific journal and he would get the train up to Waterloo from Shepperton. Shepperton was at the end of the suburban line. Today, we're driving the route back to Shepperton from London which he took. And you can just see the landscape changing, can't you?...

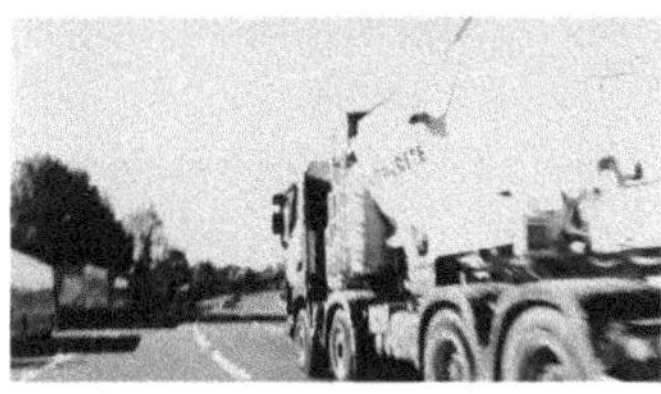
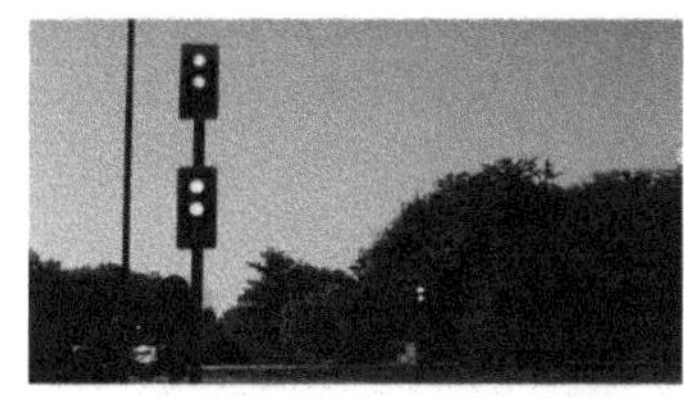
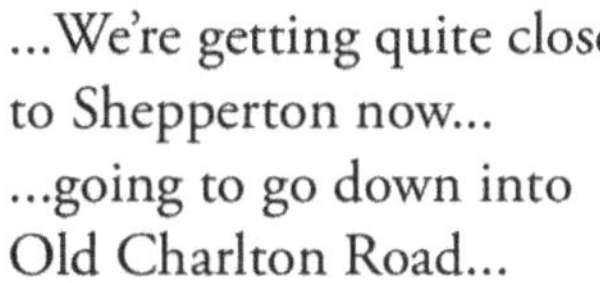

...We're getting quite close to Shepperton now...
...going to go down into Old Charlton Road...

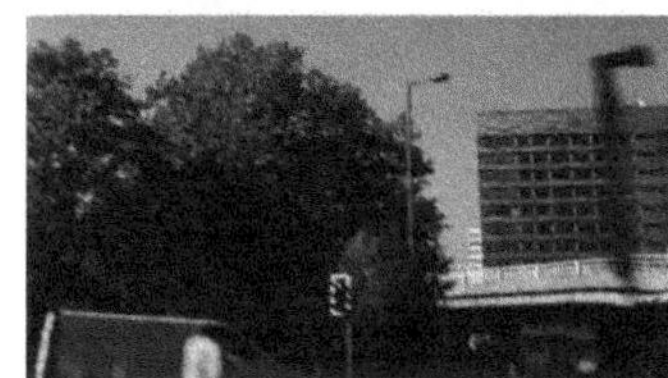
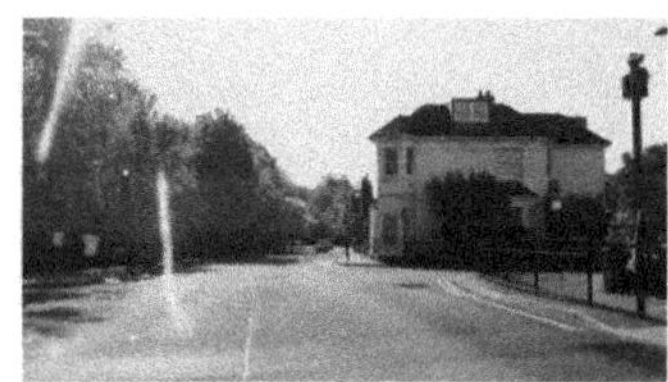
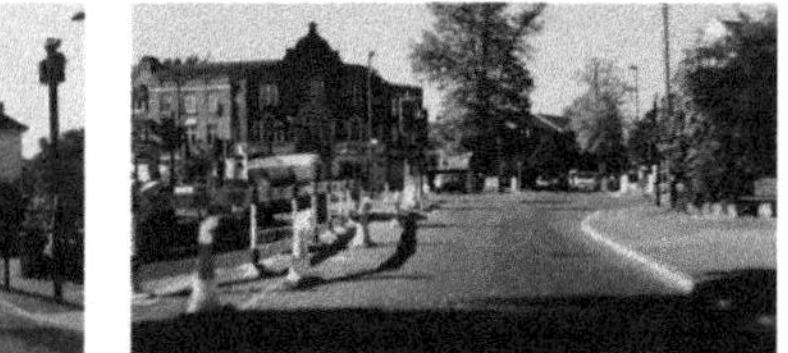
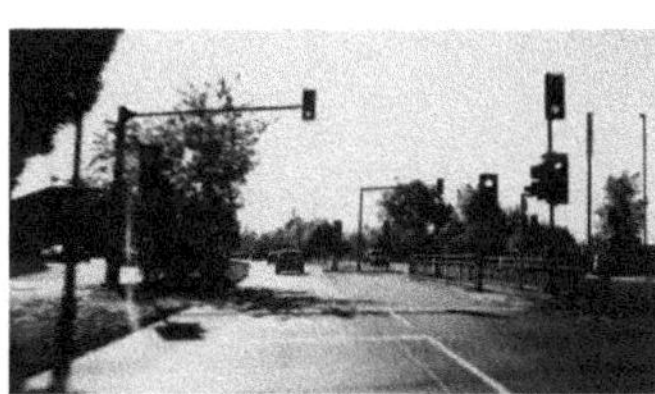
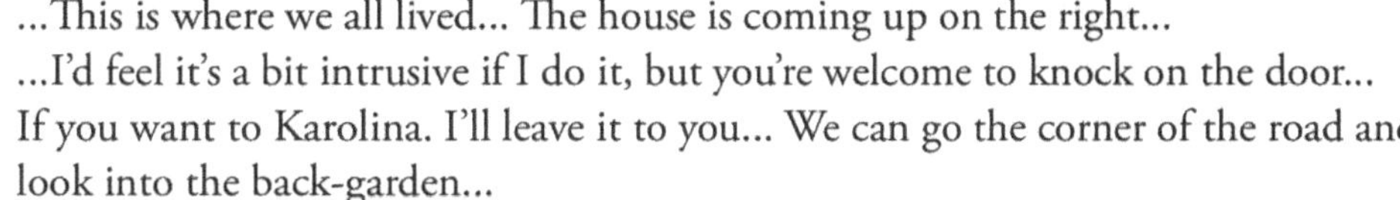

...This is where we all lived... The house is coming up on the right...
...I'd feel it's a bit intrusive if I do it, but you're welcome to knock on the door... If you want to Karolina. I'll leave it to you... We can go the corner of the road and look into the back-garden...

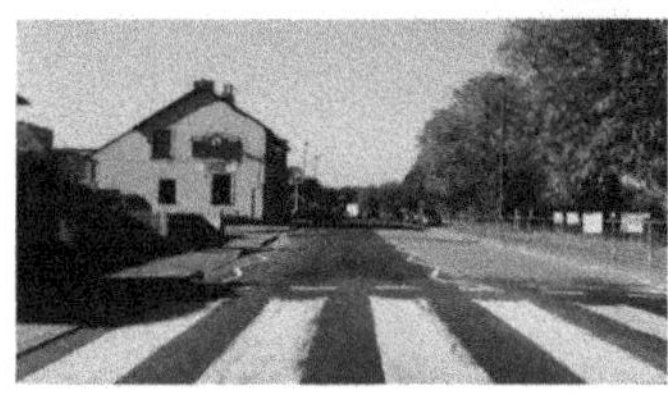
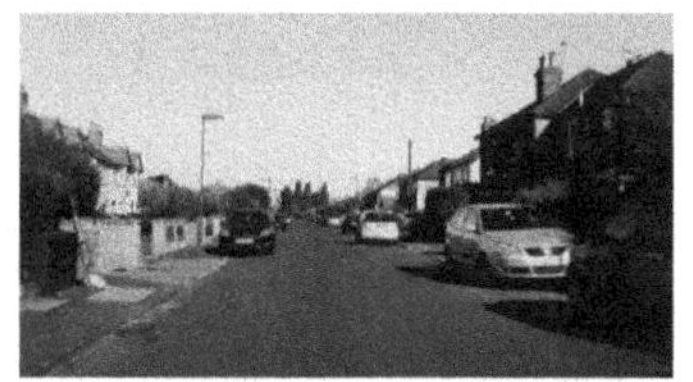
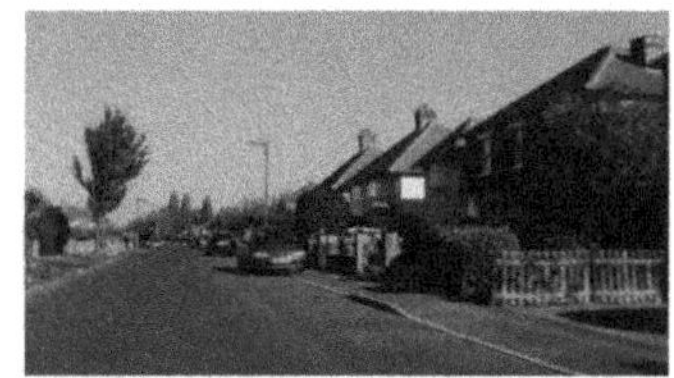
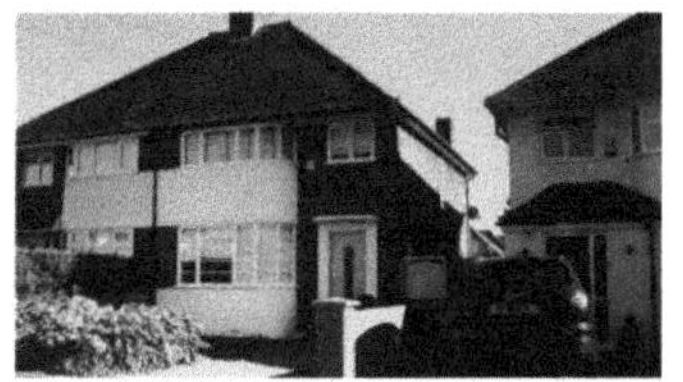

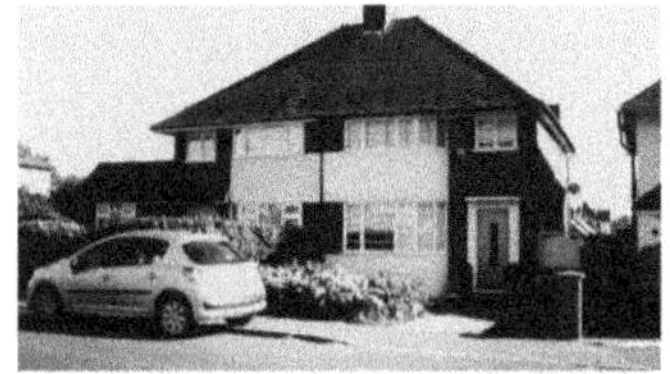
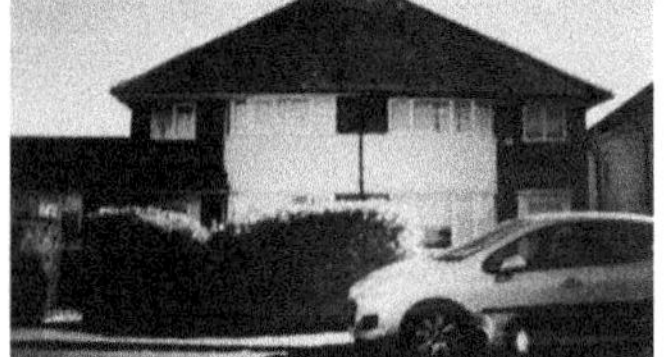
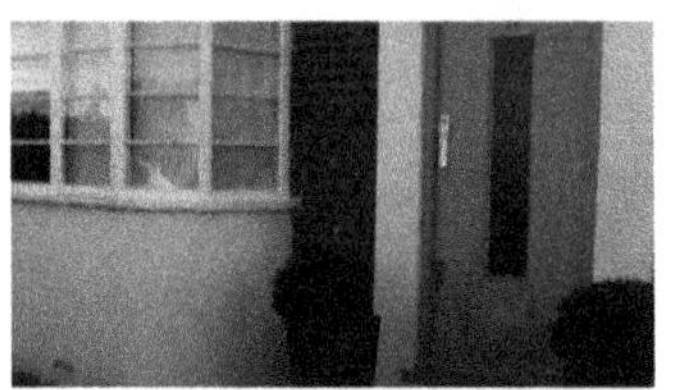
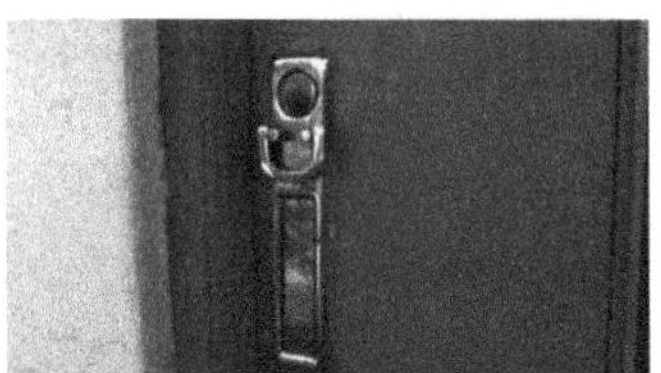
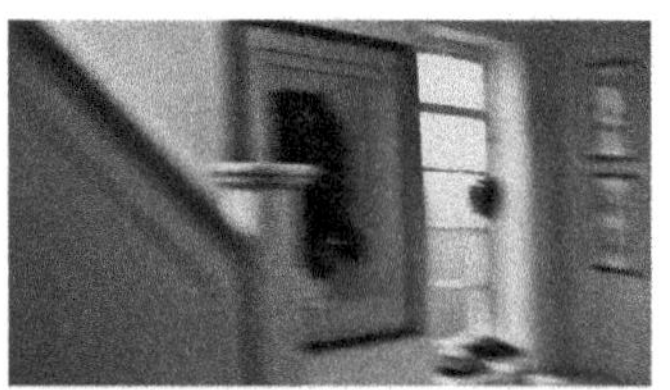
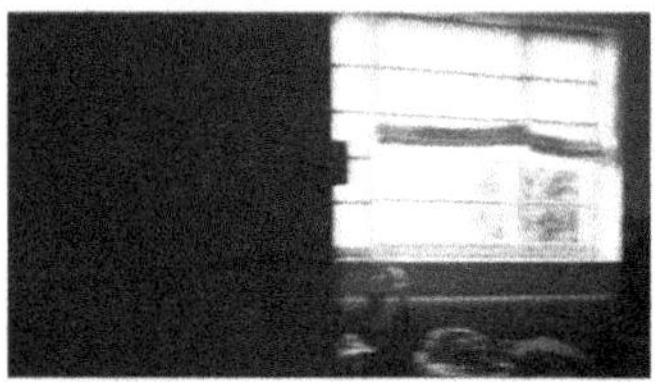
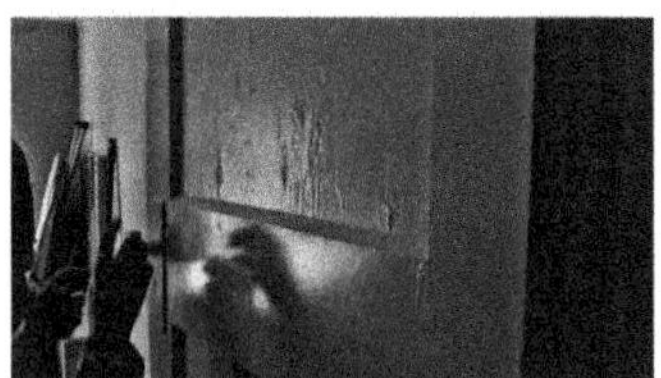
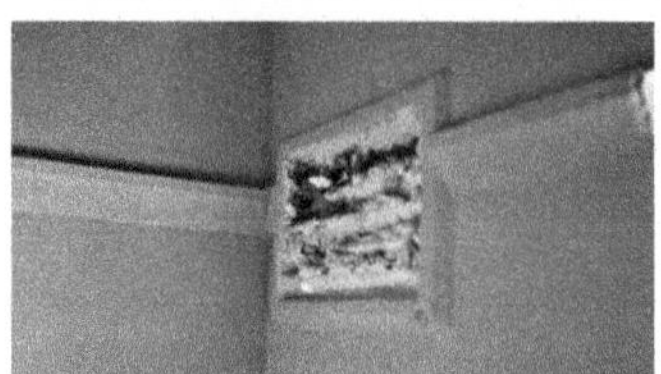
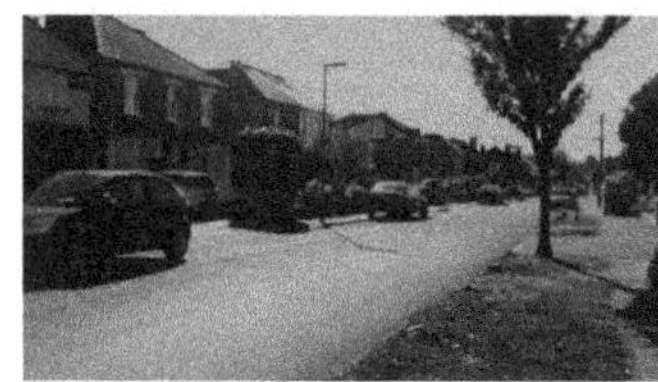

...This was our front room. We called it The Nursery... This where I spent hours and hours. Colouring in... Drawing... Watching TV. We had a big dining table here. The Yucca was here... The big Yucca. And the TV was there. And my Dad used to sit here with the TV there. It's incredible to see it again...

...Oh yeah. So, this is the room my Dad worked in... his study. He had books up there. His big copy of the Delvaux painting here. His writing desk there. His comfy chair over there. And the sofa here...

...We had a tree house in that apple tree. Oh, my Dad made cider from the apples... and the pears. We had an elder tree there and... oh, a shed nearby. We used to sit on these steps. And what happened to the sculpture?...

...Johnny, this door, you've got the original door of my Dad's study. We played darts on this door.... these are our dart marks...

...My Dad used to make tea here. He put the kettle on there. The radio was there. *One O'Clock News*. Standing up and eating lunch. Having a break from writing...

...We used to keep the hoover in there under the stairs. The carpet sweep was here, and then he had a unicycle bike, a present from Claire, which he learnt to ride when he was 60. He taught himself here in the hall by holding onto the walls...

...Oh, my goodness. The double bed was there. His wardrobe was here. And there was a cupboard... Er, did you have a cupboard here? ...I found some of the early manuscripts in that cupboard... Yeah, that are in the British Library now. So I found: *Empire of the Sun... Crash*... And some of the really early work. All in there. And I slept next door...

...I slept here. My sister slept there. And we had a wardrobe over here. I painted it purple and light blue.... I was going through a Deep Purple phase! Yes. And Led Zep... I painted this room purple and lime green. Did you find a little bit of the purple still? In that corner? Emily and Max kept a little bit of the purple paint... ...Oh yeah. IT IS! And the green... I was about 15 or 16 when I painted that... wearing cheesecloth and lots of Biba make-up...

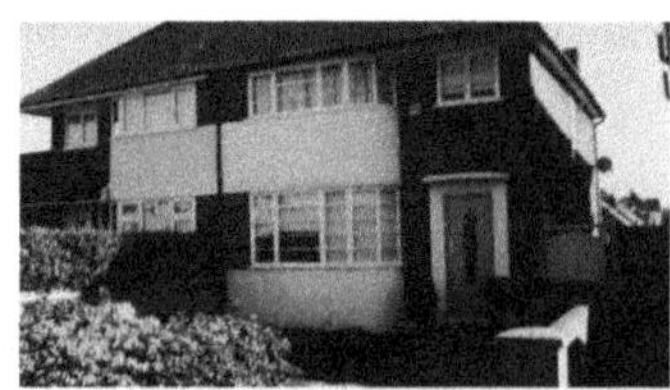
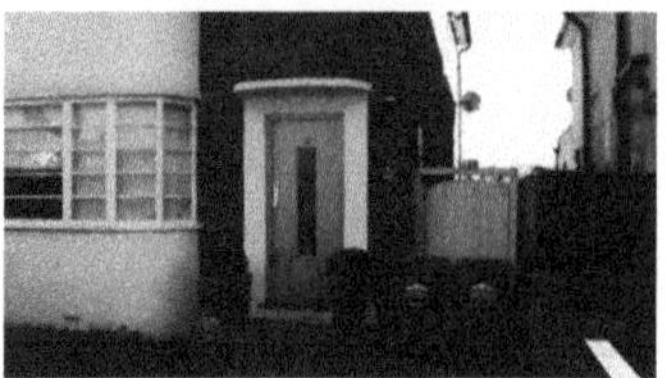
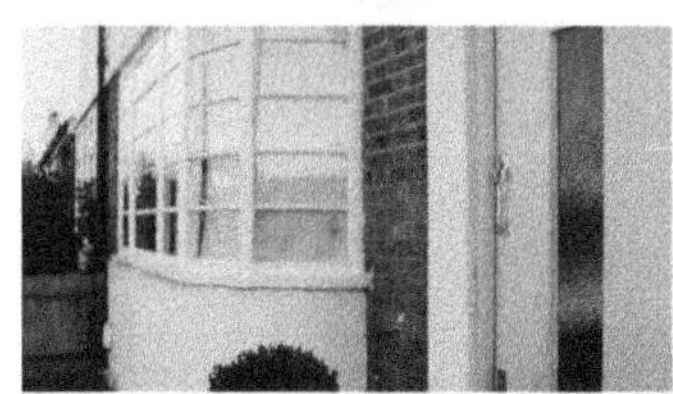
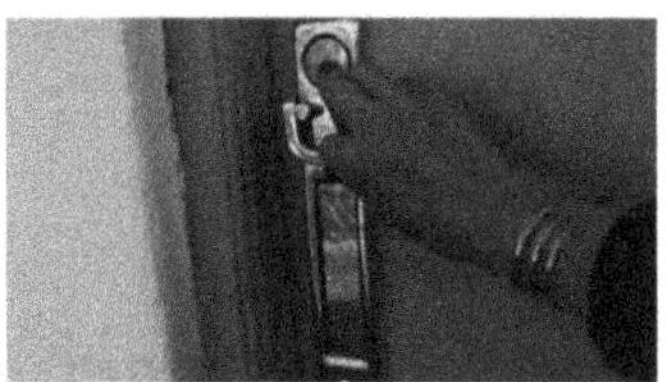
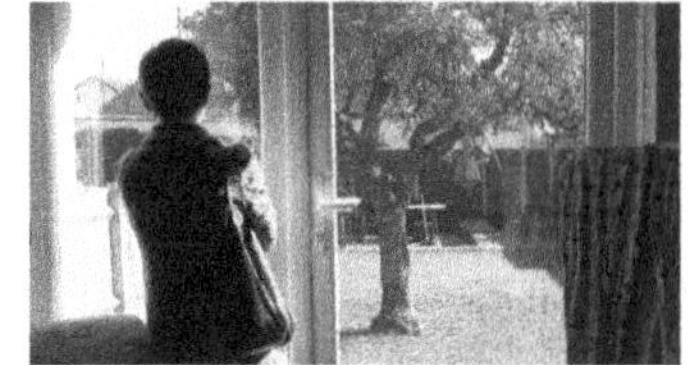
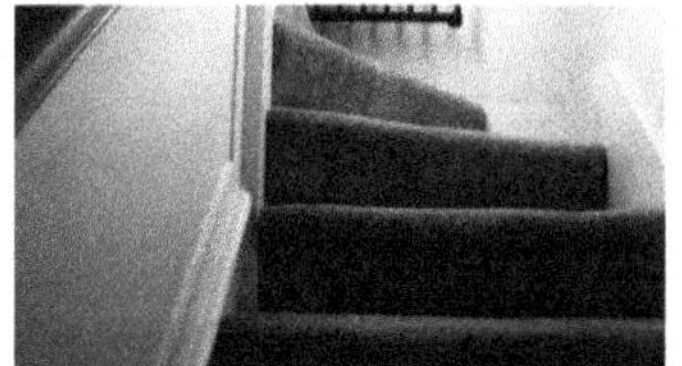
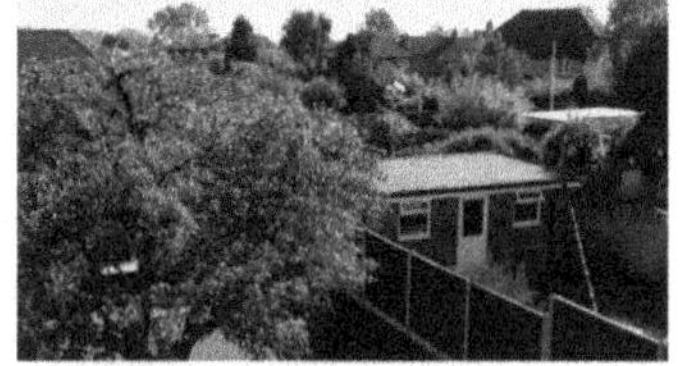
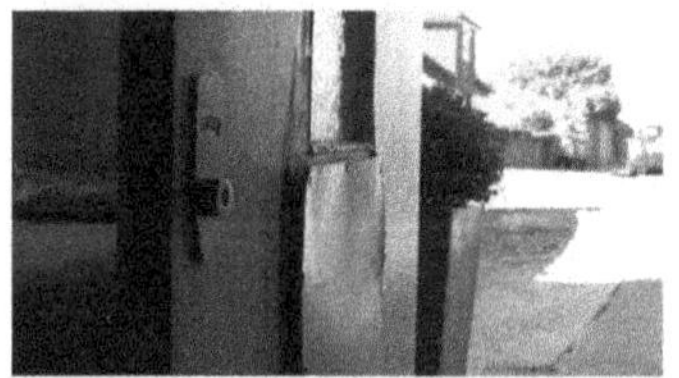

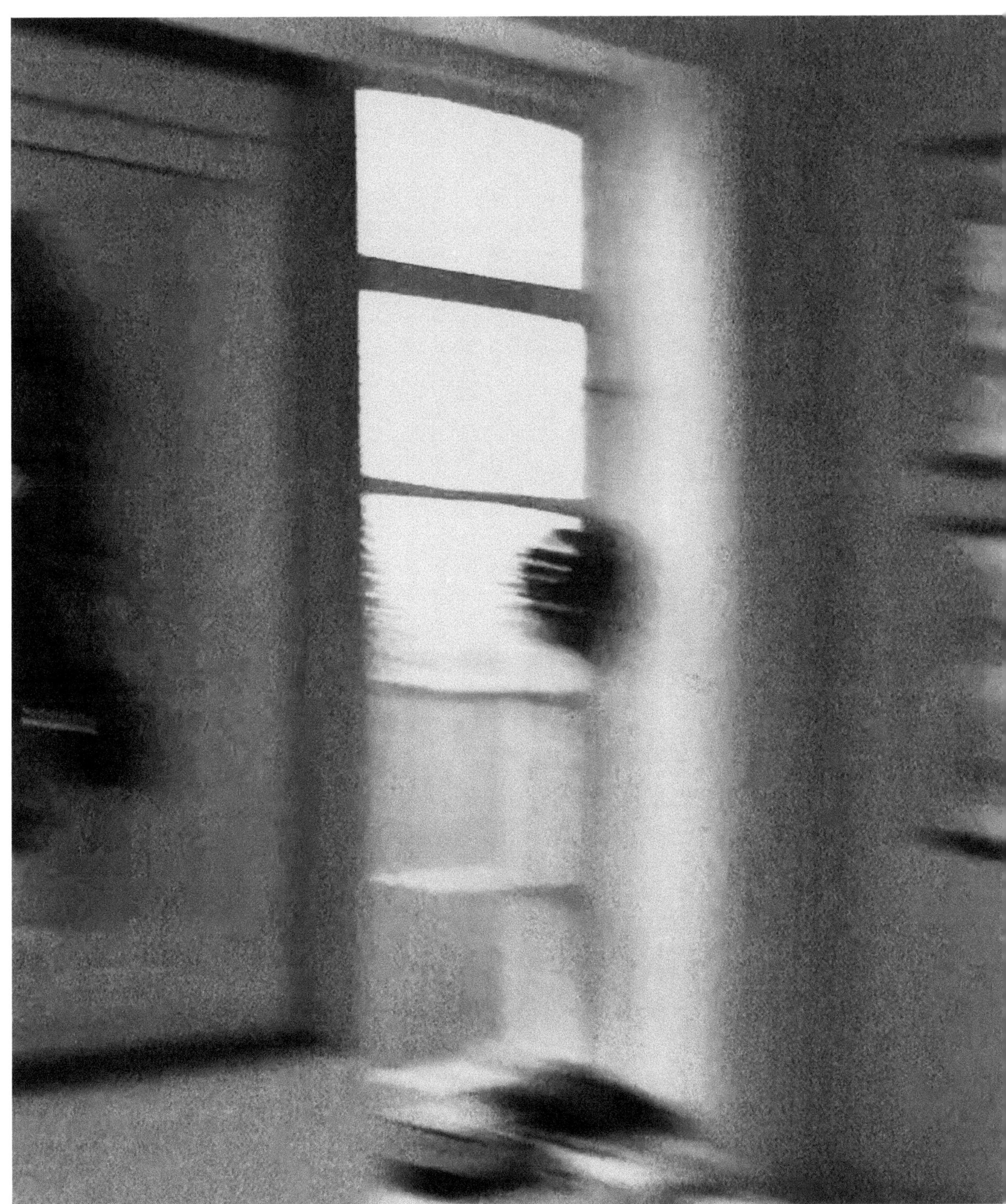

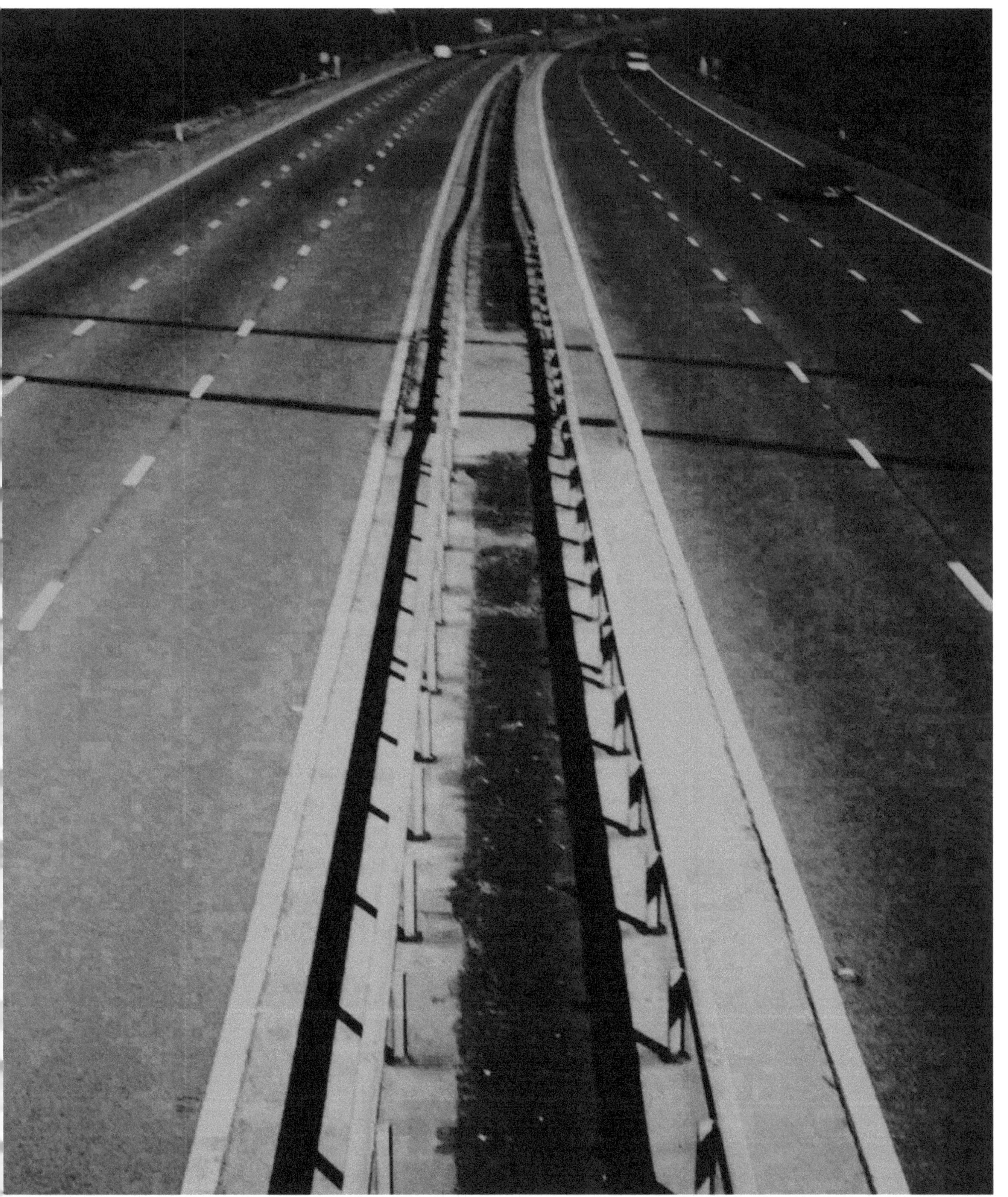

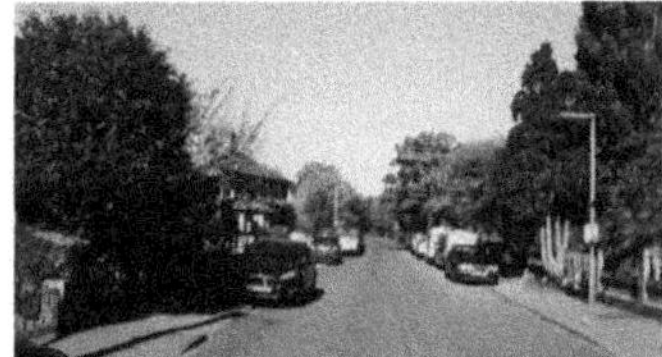

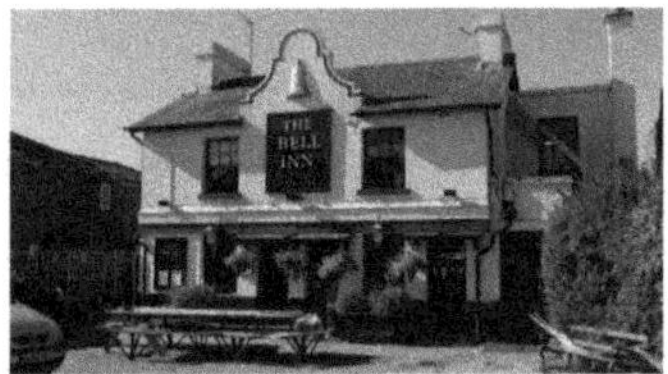

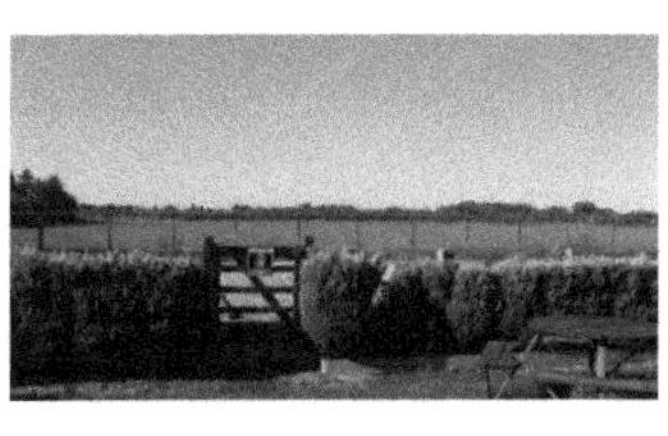

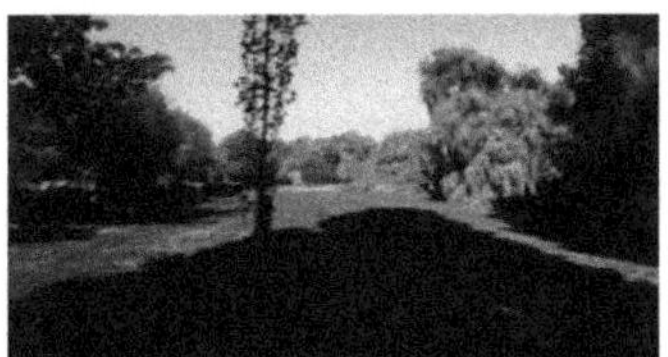

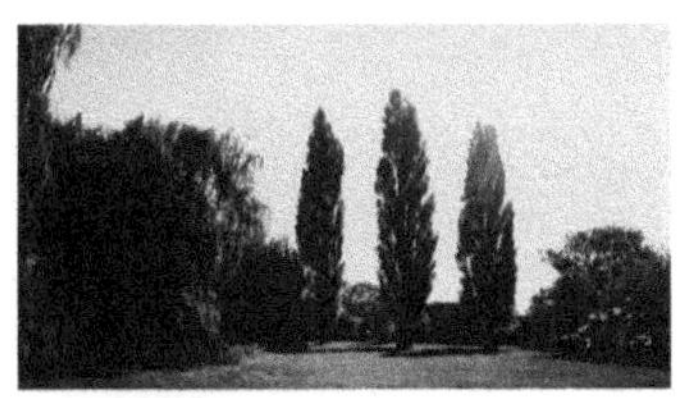

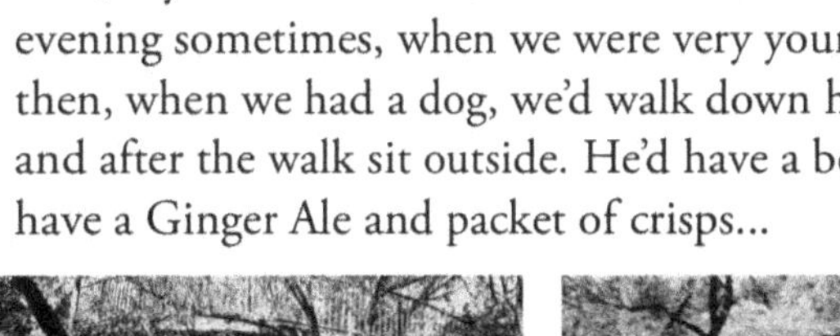

...So, my father would drink here at The Bell in the evening sometimes, when we were very young. And then, when we had a dog, we'd walk down here together and after the walk sit outside. He'd have a beer and I'd have a Ginger Ale and packet of crisps...

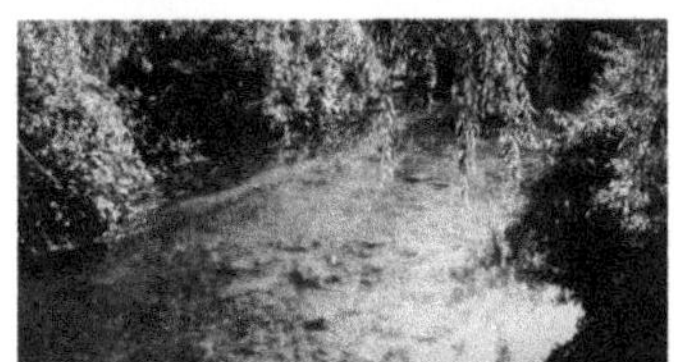

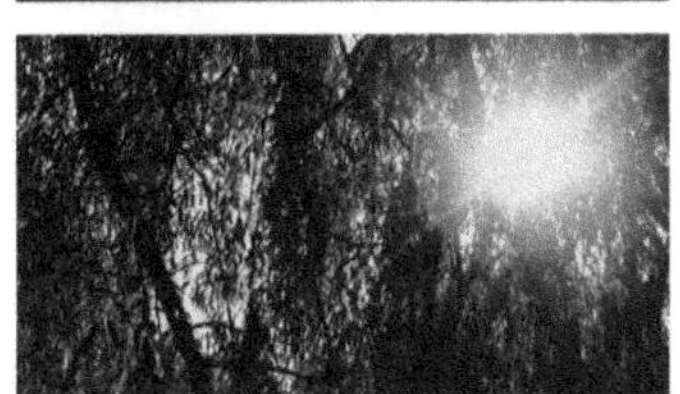

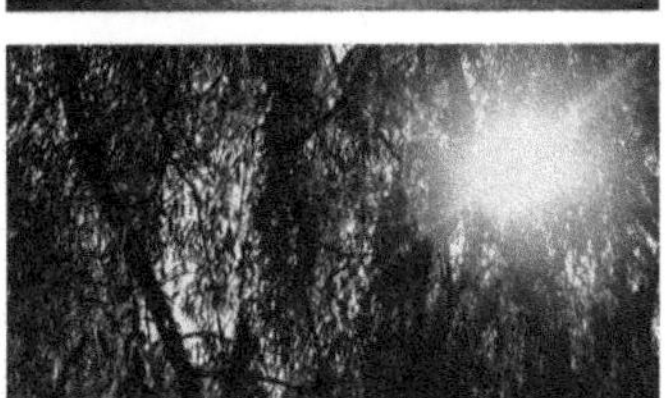

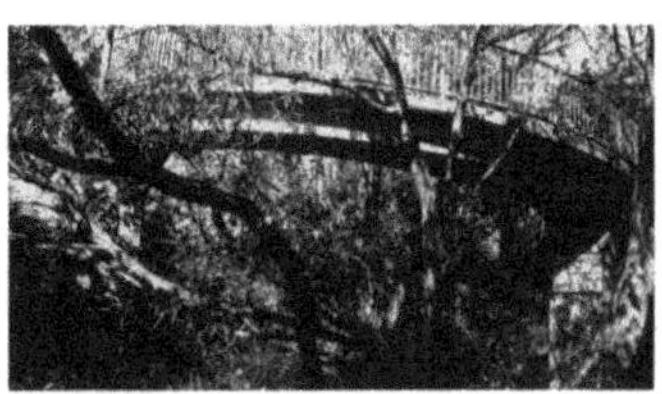

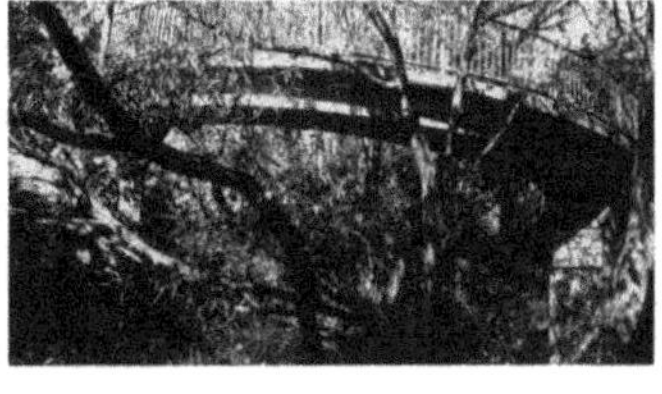

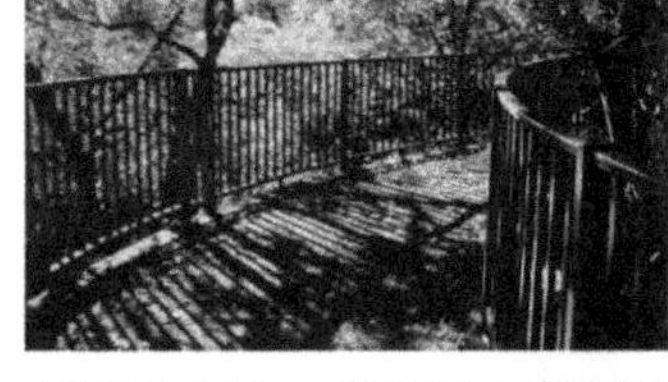

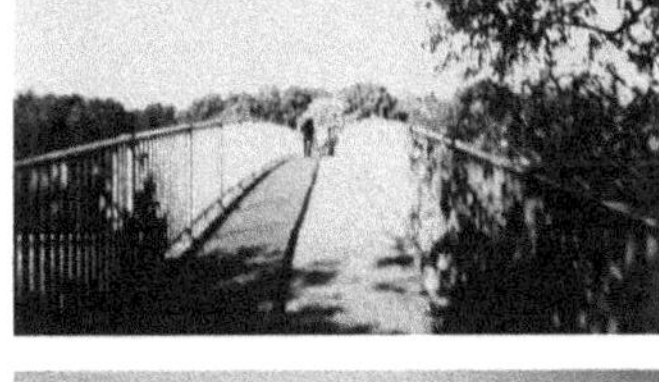

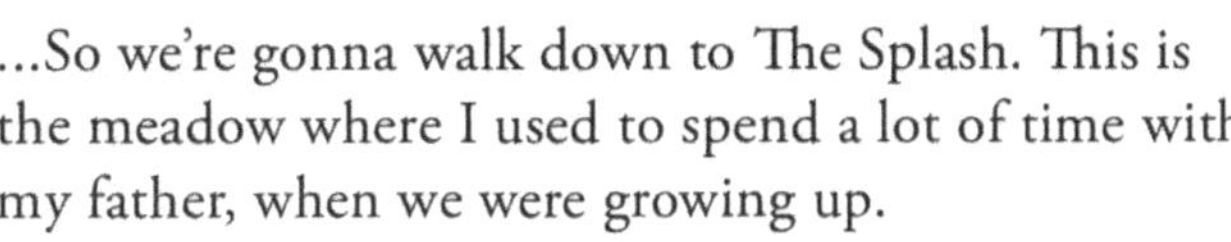

...So we're gonna walk down to The Splash. This is the meadow where I used to spend a lot of time with my father, when we were growing up.
Erm, there was a place where we used to dip our feet into the water and fish for sticklebacks. And there was a big gravel pit full of water where you could freely walk around. It's all privatised now... contemporary Britain that he was writing about...
...I spent here many happy weekends with my father. Fishing, playing tennis, fooling around...

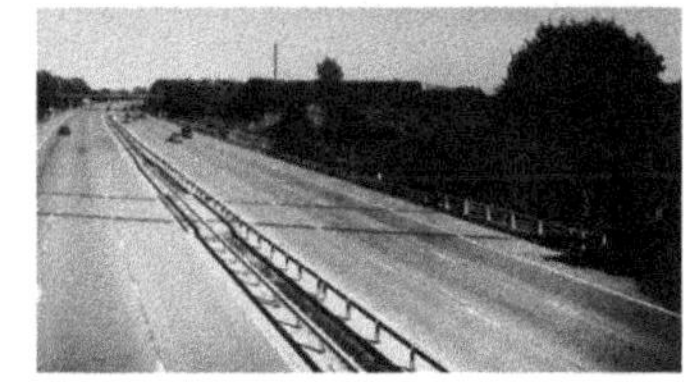

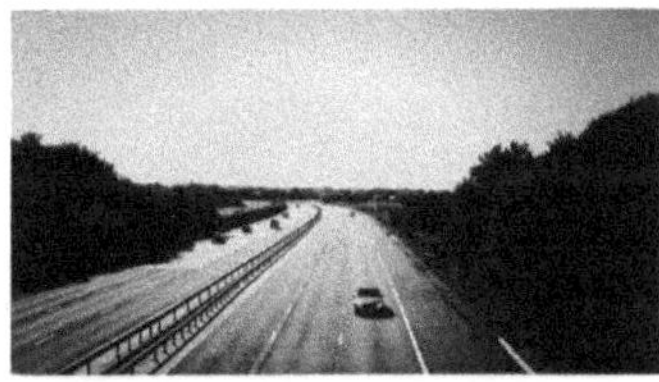

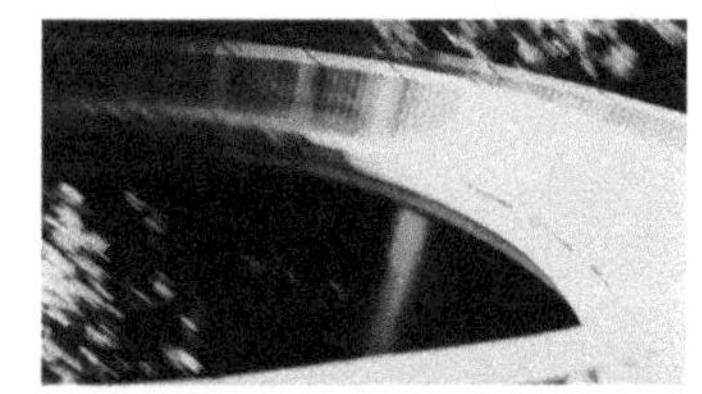

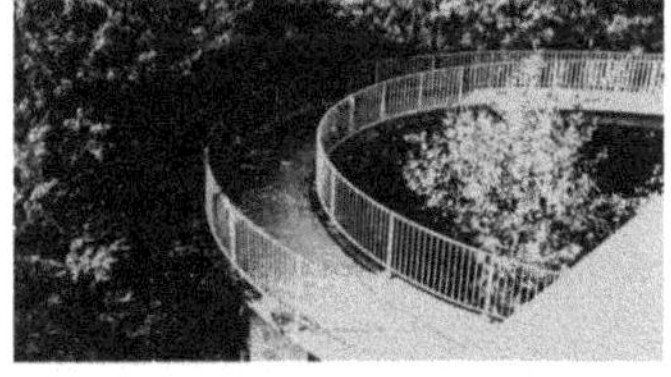

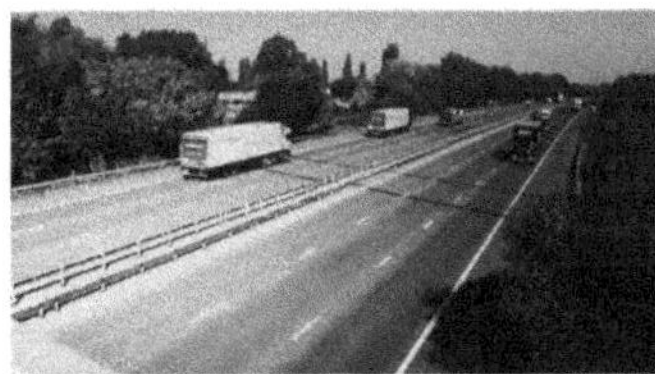

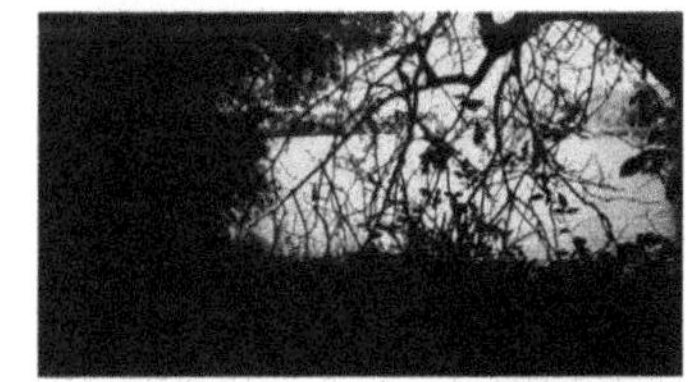

...I came back walking here after he died. And then I started looking around this territory: the M3... the suburbs... anonymous buildings like those large grey storage warehouses over there with no windows... The private golf courses... The filled gravel pit with its barbed wire fencing and keep out signs. Aeroplanes, Heathrow, international travel...

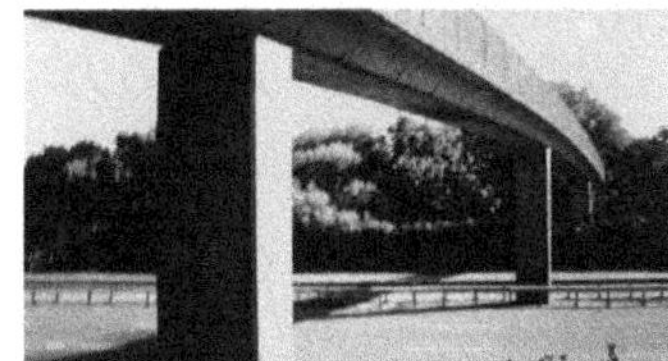

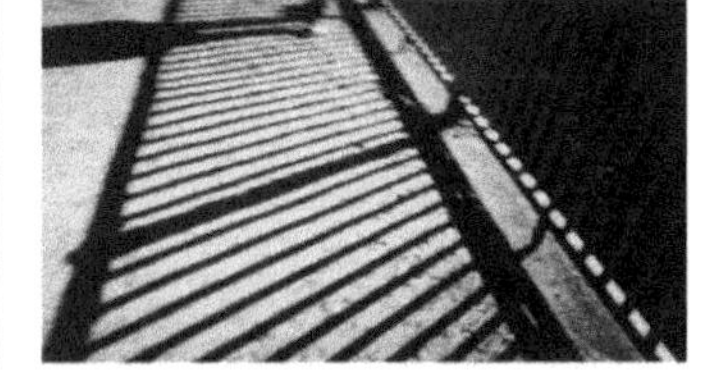

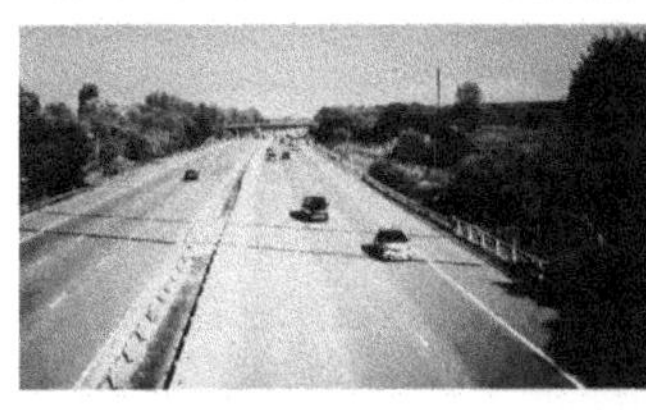

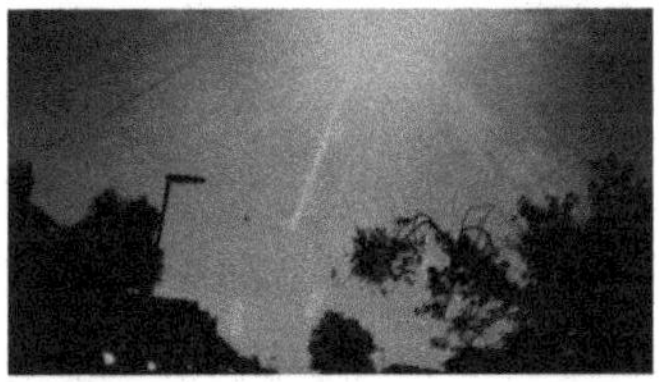

...I think in a way, you need to walk it yourself...
...Yeah, or drive it. To come and experience this...

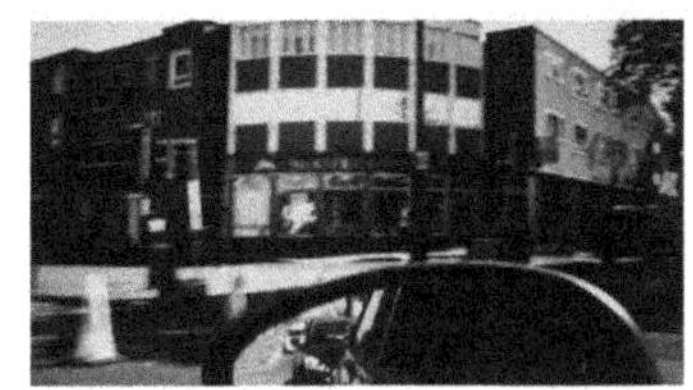

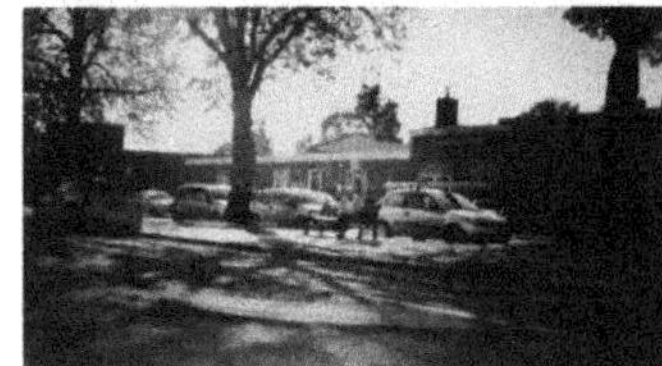

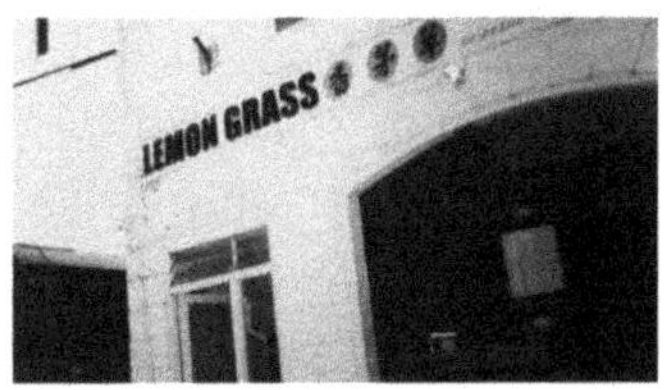

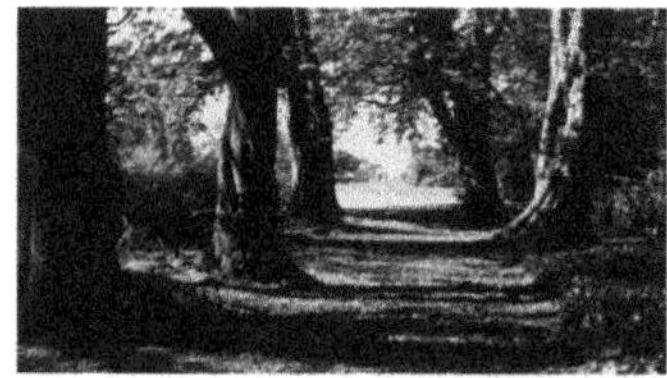
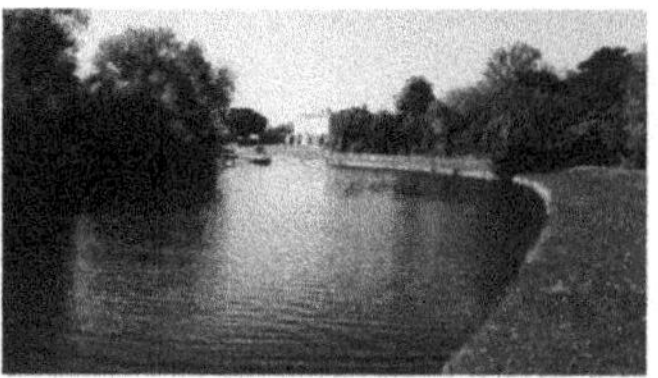
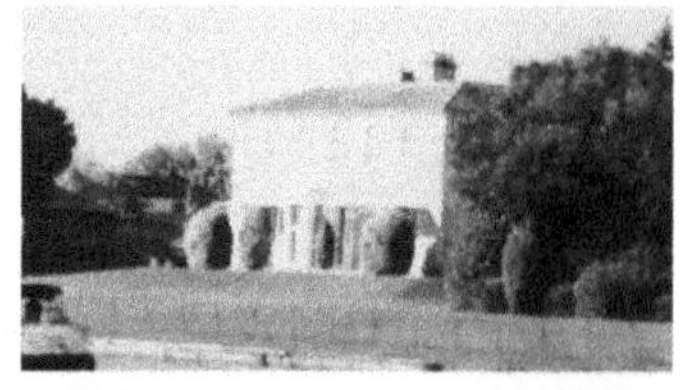

...And here's the Shepperton War Memorial and the Thames riverbank coming up which features in *The Unlimited Dream Company*. My Dad used to come here every day for a walk in the afternoon...

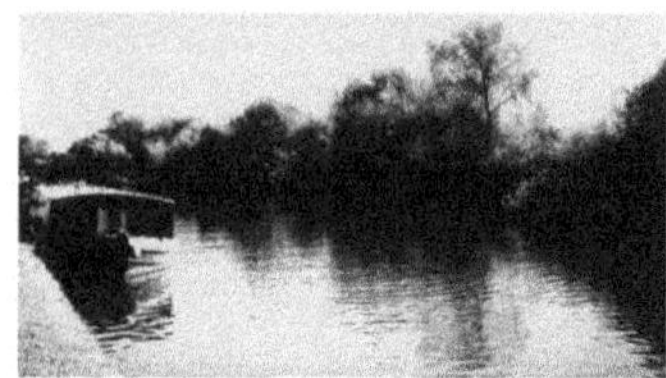
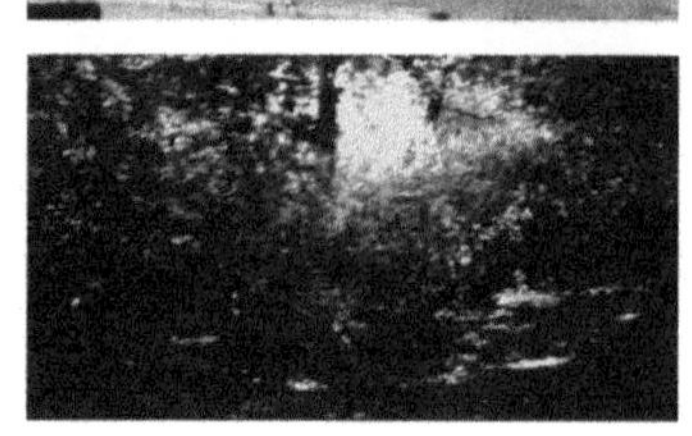
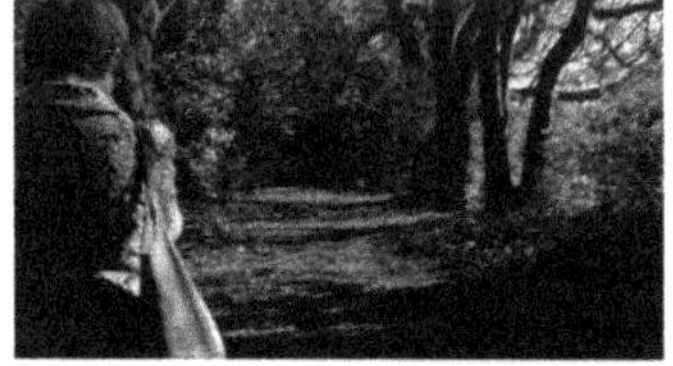
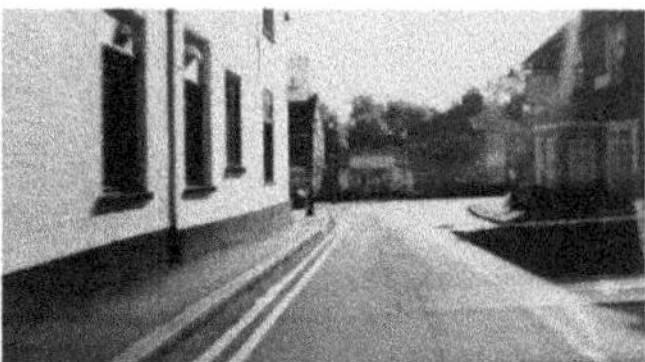
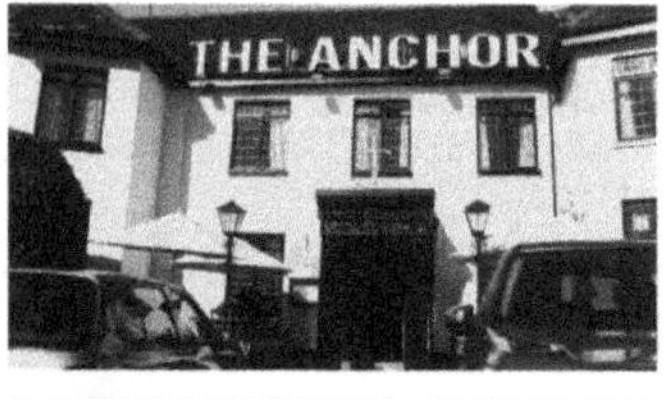

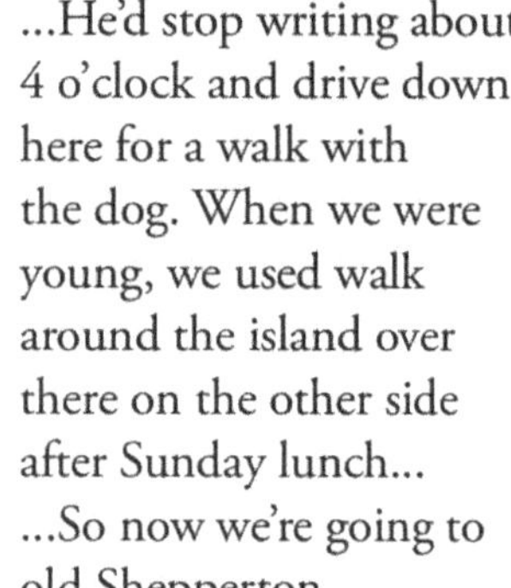

...He'd stop writing about 4 o'clock and drive down here for a walk with the dog. When we were young, we used walk around the island over there on the other side after Sunday lunch...
...So now we're going to old Shepperton...

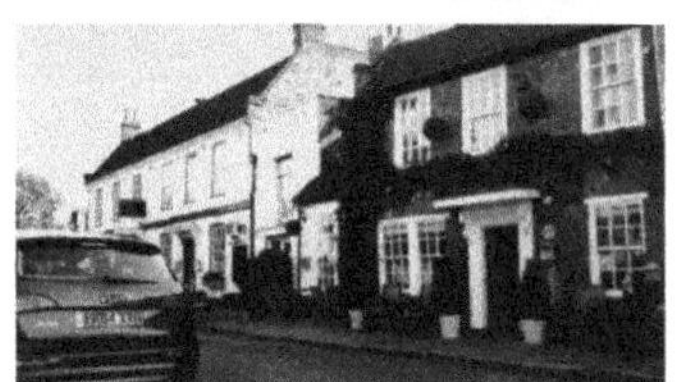
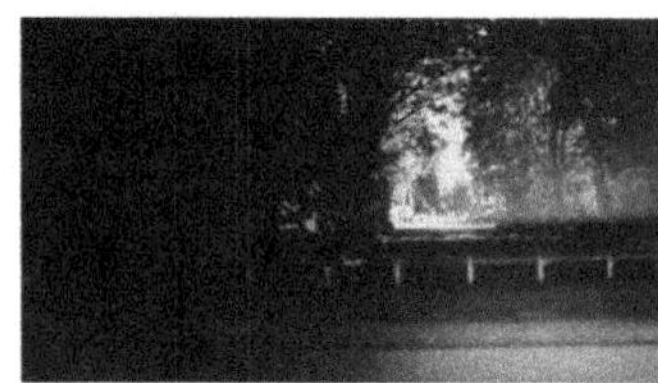

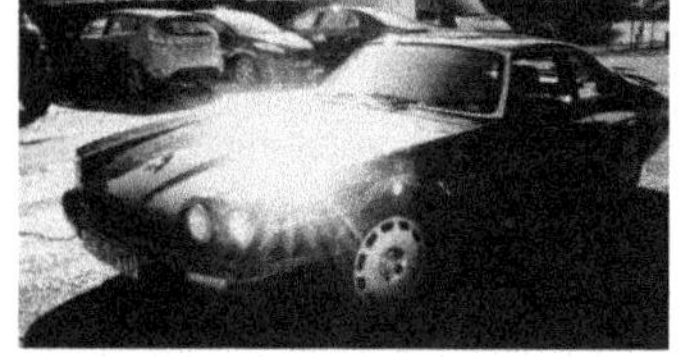

I'm not sure how much time my Dad spent in these pubs. I don't think as long. Sometimes he'd bring visitors here. I think...

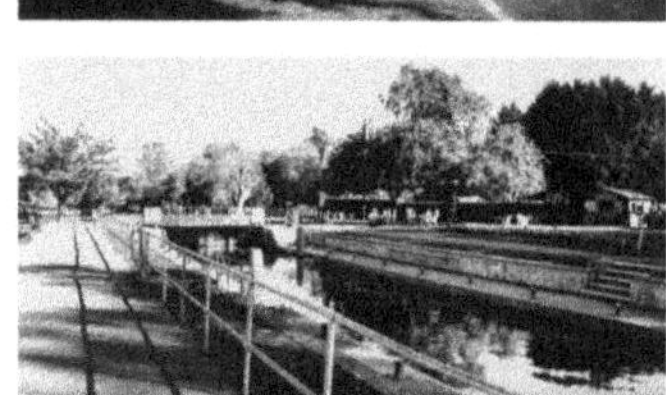
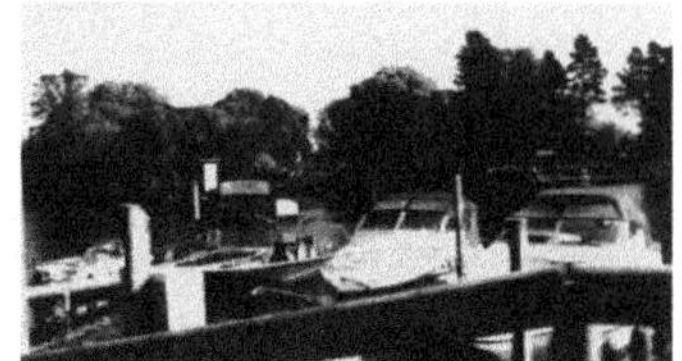
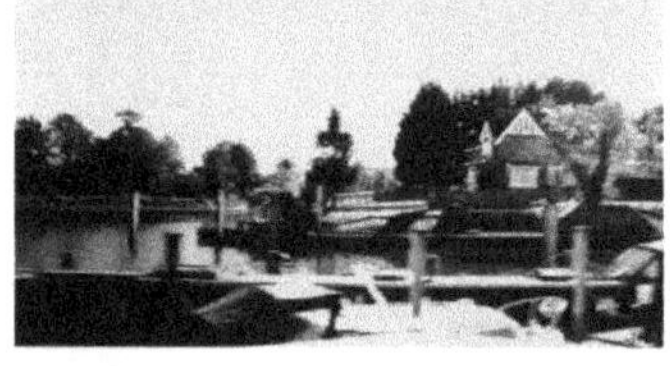
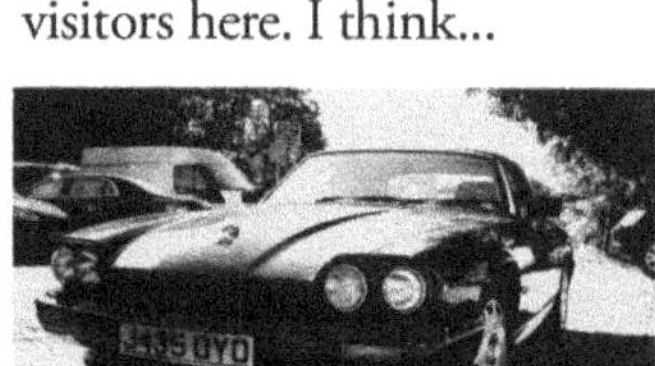
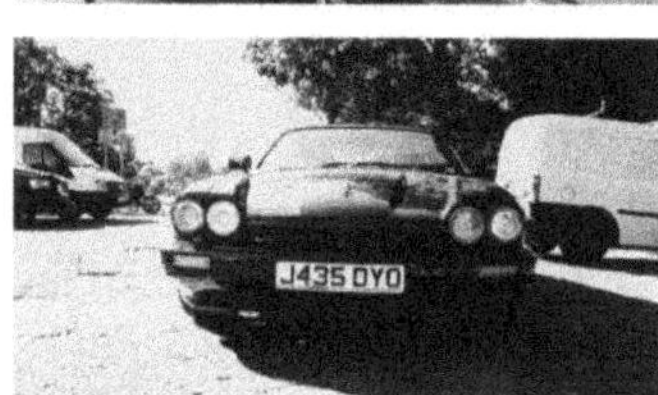

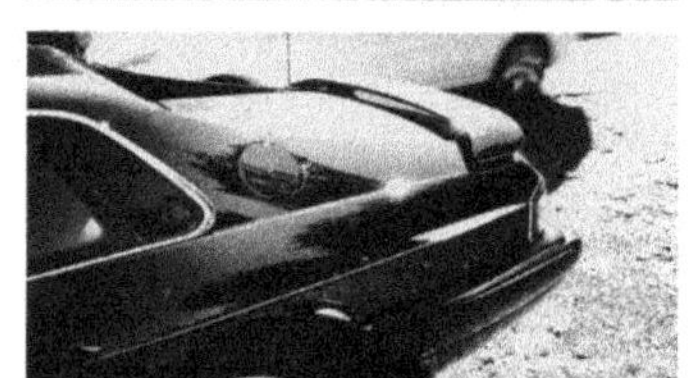

...There's something about this side of Shepperton down near the Marina and Lock that feels of wealth, manicured lawns, gated communities...
...Look at some of the houses on the other side... luxury...

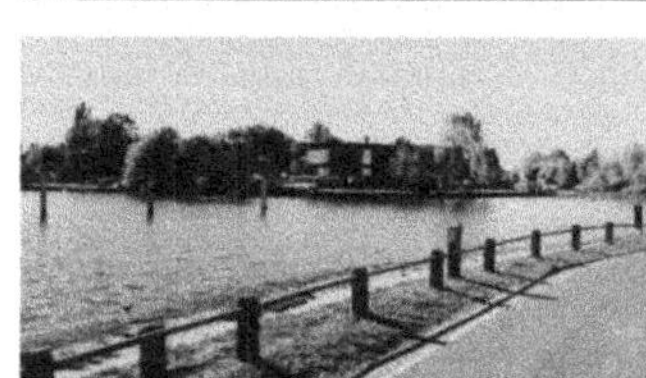
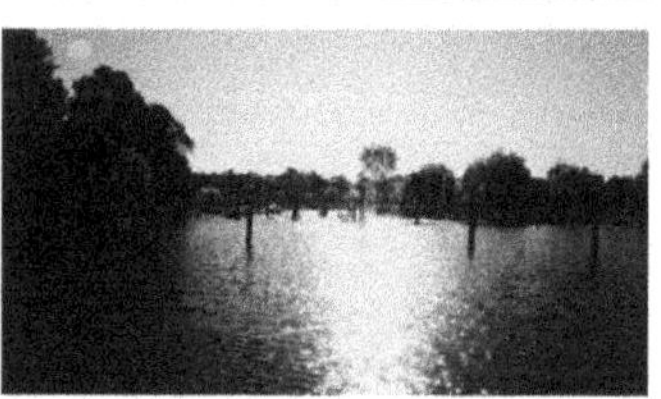
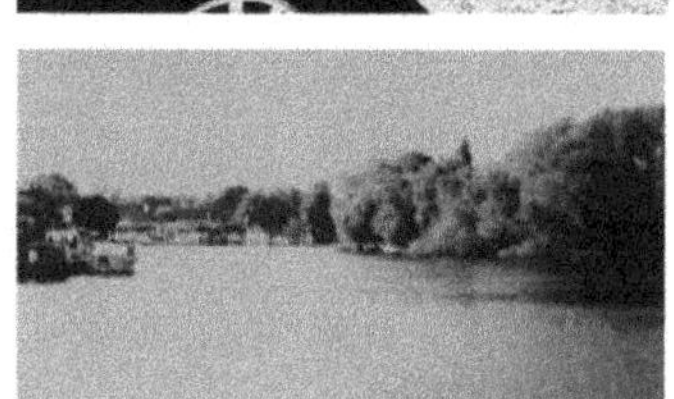
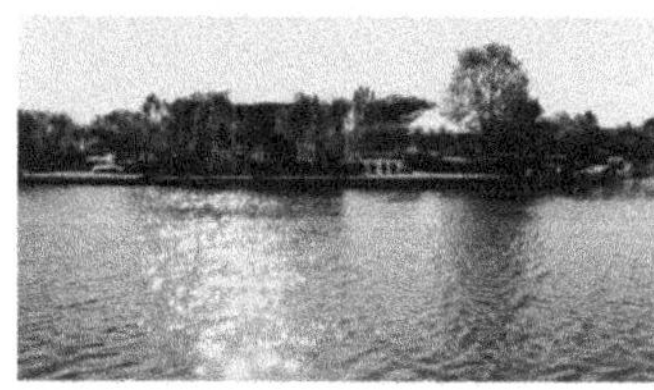

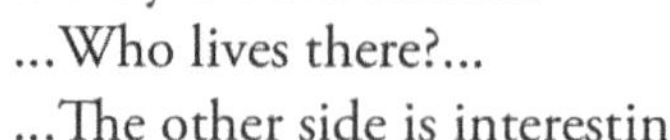
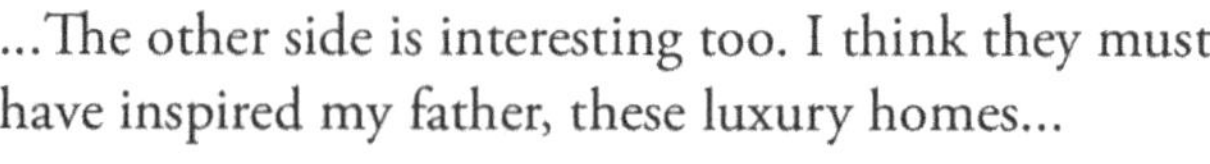

...They are incredible...
...Who lives there?...
...The other side is interesting too. I think they must have inspired my father, these luxury homes...

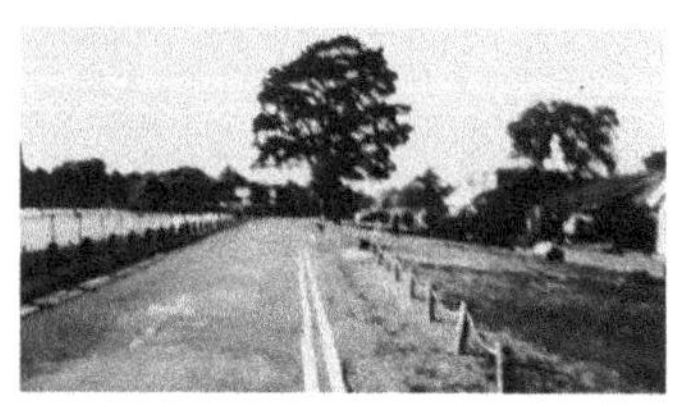
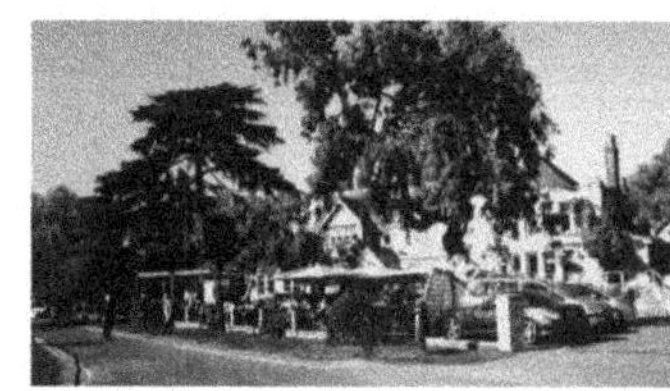
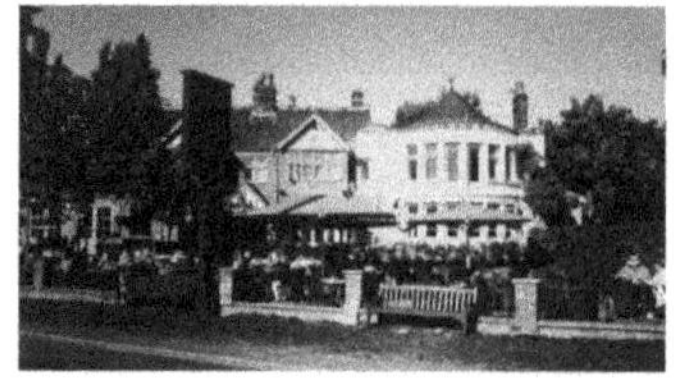
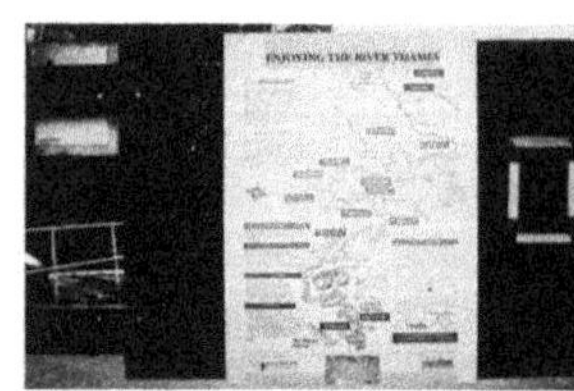

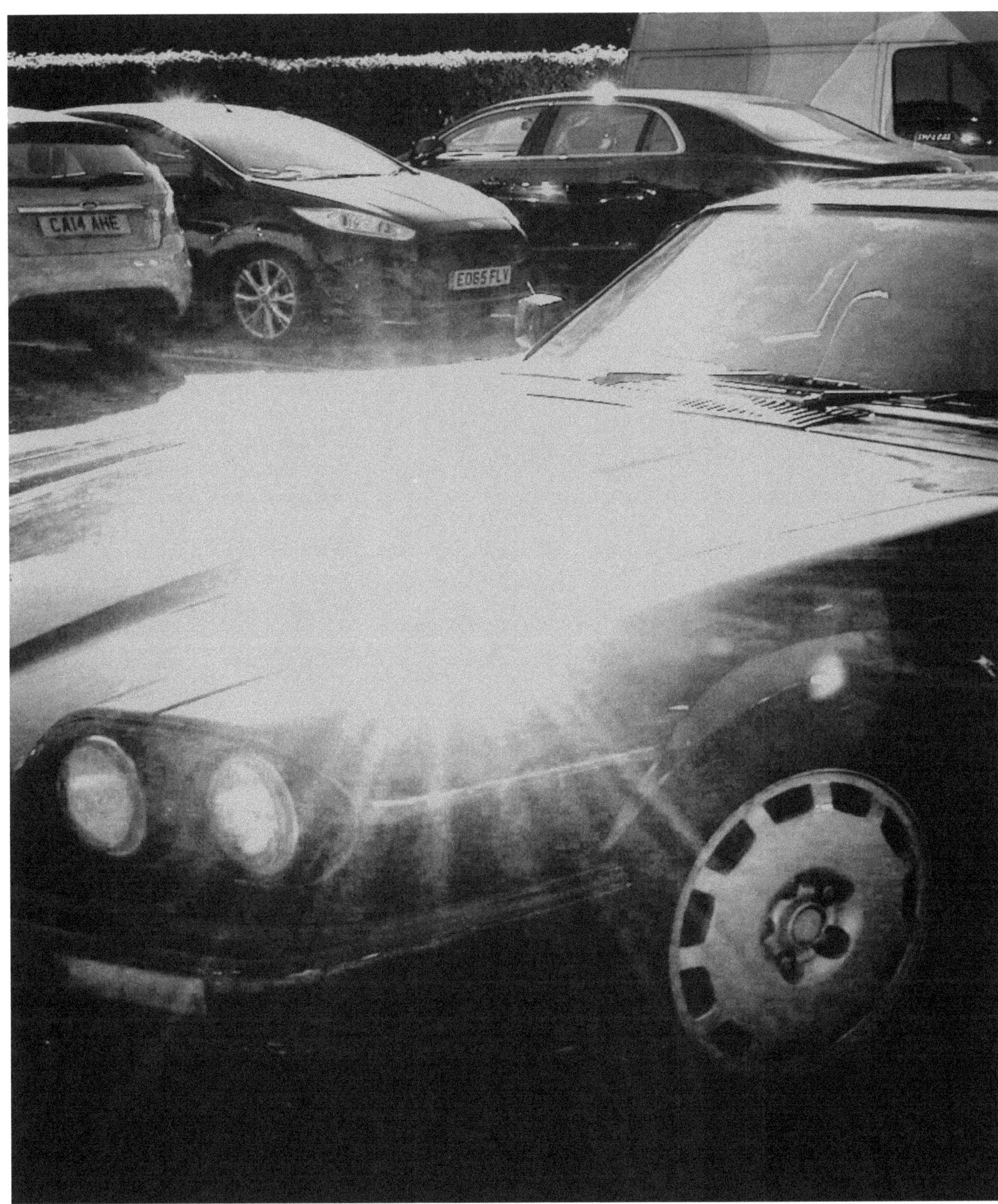
CA14 AHE
ED65 FLV

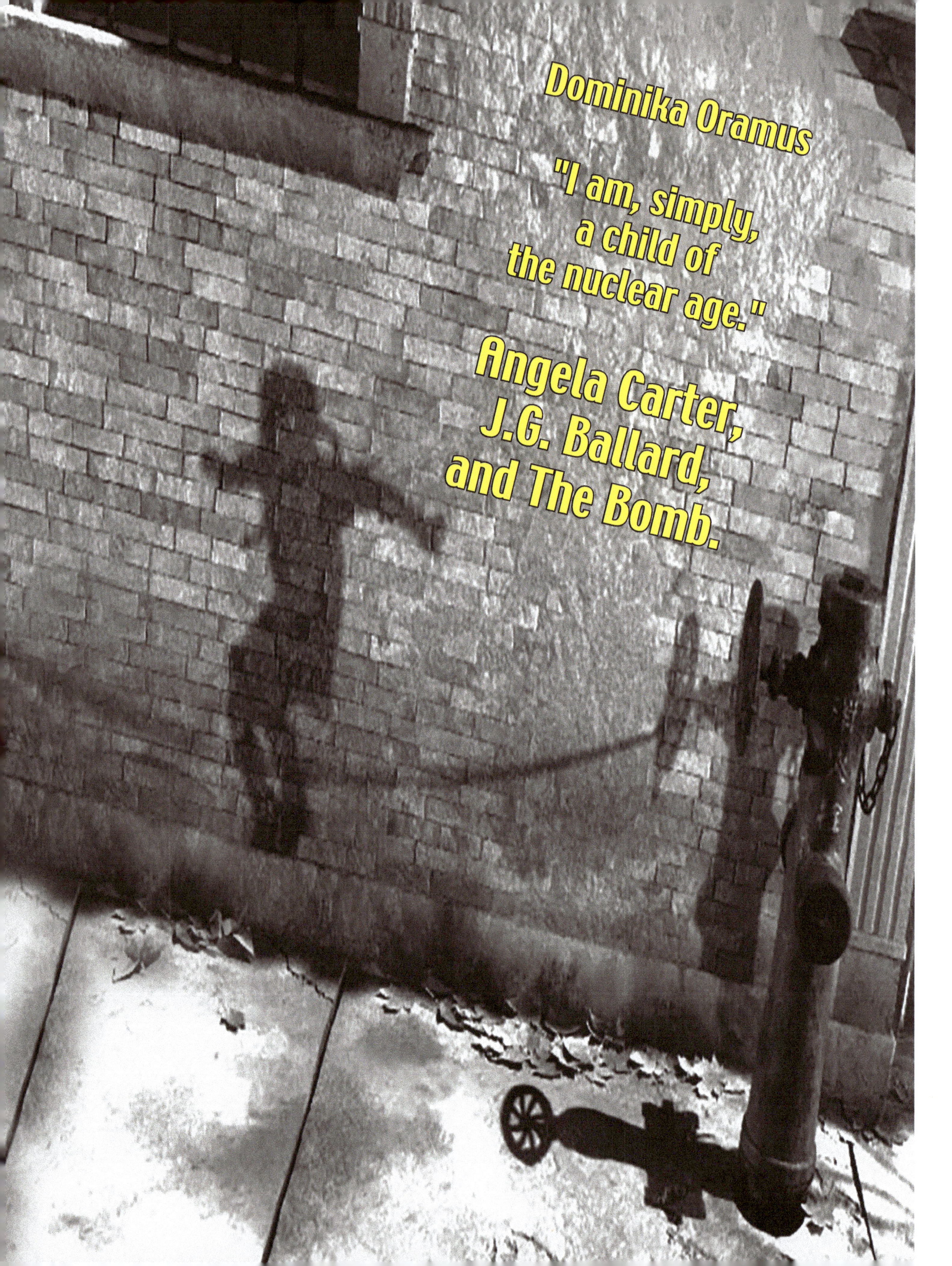
Dominika Oramus
"I am, simply,
a child of
the nuclear age."
Angela Carter,
J.G. Ballard,
and The Bomb.

Angela Carter and J.G. Ballard are two of the most important late-20th-century British novelists. Their bizarre narratives combine fantastic elements with keen observations of the psychological impact of living in the post-capitalist mediascape of the contemporary West. Yet their respective lives started in quite different places: Ballard was born in 1930 in the then still affluent colonial South-East Asia, whereas Carter was born in 1940 in a drab wartime England. However, both authors were products of the British middle class, and both were shaped by the Second World War and the atrocities it inflicted. Moreover, they spent most of their lives in Britain and were at the same time emphatically British and extremely critical of Britain. The Hiroshima and Nagasaki explosions were formative events of both their generations.

At first glance, Carter's and Ballard's *oeuvres* do not seem at all similar, and their early critics and commentators discussed their respective novels in different contexts. Over time, though, it has become apparent that the two writers are artistically akin, which likely resulted from the fact that they both felt themselves to be "children of the nuclear age." They shared a number of intellectual and aesthetic fascinations, the most important of which was surrealism. Carter's and Ballard's works often echo essays by André Breton and are full of visual allusions to surrealist painting, especially those by Max Ernst and Salvador Dali. They both wrote about the surrealist movement and were involved in editing works by and about the Surrealist: Carter attempted to translate Xavière Gauthier's *Surréalisme et sexualité* into English; Ballard wrote an introduction to Salvador Dali's *Diary of a Genius*. Moreover, both writers were under the spell of psychoanalysis, and, in fact, Freud, Lacan and Laing are among the theorists they most often refer to. The vocabulary and frame of mind offered by Freud and Jung's works provide the necessary context to understand their fiction and non-fiction alike.

Carter and Ballard were also equally influenced by Japanese culture, albeit in different ways: Ballard recurrently comes back in his writing to his wartime experience of living in a POW camp in South-Eastern Asia and witnessing the twilight of the Japanese empire. Carter actually lived in Japan in the late 60s with a native lover and worked and wrote there for a couple of years, getting to know "a culture that is not now nor has ever been a Judeo-Christian one, to see what it was like." (*Nothing Sacred*, 28) Thus, in their respective collections of journalism, *A User's Guide to the Millennium* by J.G. Ballard and *Nothing Sacred* by Angela Carter, essays devoted to Japanese culture and memories of Japan are among the most important and most personal pieces.

One can go on enumerating such similarities in the lives and works of the two writers. This essay attempts to explore one of the many issues important to both of them but not discussed in any comparative study, namely, their attitude to the nuclear Bomb. What is meant here by the Bomb includes a cluster of cultural phenomena: anticipation of end of the world by nuclear blast fantasies, anti-war political commitment, disarmament ideologies and persistent memories of the atomic explosions during the second world war. In order to present these two writers' parallel attitudes to the traumas of the nuclear age, their biographies are juxtaposed, followed by a presentation of their fantastic visions of a nuclear apocalypse and post-catastrophic landscapes of the future. Additionally, their depiction of post-imperial Britain—the country they lived in for the greater part of their lives and systematically commented on in their works—is presented in the context of the authors' pronounced dislike of Ronald Reagan, Margaret Thatcher and the conservative ideologies these two politicians embodied.

"Life on a demolition site"

Angela Carter was born in Britain in 1940 and, later in life, she claimed that "Dunkirk fell as I was shouldering my way to the world." (*Shaking a Leg*, 3) She also liked repeating that her mother "learnt she was carrying me at about the time the Second World War was declared... with the family talent for magical realism, she once told me she had been to the doctor's on the very day." (ibid.) A member of the generation of British children born during the war and brought up in the welfare state created by the Attlee government, she came into maturation in the 1960s, the decade during which in Britain felt like "a demolition site," *(Truly, It Felt like Year One*, 211), when the class system began to crumble and modern anxieties lead young people to escape into colourful fantasies and hippie lifestyles. Around the same time, in the early sixties, one political event—the Cuban Missile Crisis—played an enormously important role in Carter's personal development. *In Angela Carter. A Literary Life*, Sarah Gamble even claims that Carter "came of age" as a writer and a Briton during the fourteen days when Russia and America stood at the verge of an atomic war and Britain did nothing, helplessly observing the brewing conflict and mourning the loss of its own position as a superpower. At twenty-two, she realised what kind of a world she was living in. She later maintained that the Cuban Missile Crisis was "one of the great watersheds, certainly of my life. I think people who were born after the Cuban Missile Crisis, who don't remember, are different because it was touch and go for a minute there." (*Shaking a Leg*, 32)

At that time, the Prague Spring, May 68 in Paris, the Vietnam War, the exuberant youth fashion promoting mini-skirts and the pop-mythology of the Beatles gave the impression that the world was rapidly changing. Decadence and an overwhelming sense of exhaustion were in the air, and Carter's early novels reflect the anxiety of British hippies. Joseph, the protagonist of *Several Perceptions*, the novel she wrote in her twenties, dreams of "fires quenched with blood and bloody beaks of birds of prey and bombs blossoming like petals over the Mekong Delta." (*Several Perceptions*, 4-5) Deceived by both the academic world and dandyism, Joseph sees reality as a senseless chain of repetitions. The overwhelming boredom drives him to suicide, but "to die of ennui and despair, instead of for some cause, with some motive, making some humanly significant gesture, was a gray, sad way to go. It was a simple way of saying 'no', that nothing was worthwhile." (ibid., 18)

Significantly, at the time Carter was writing *Several Perceptions*, she again started to read science fiction, the literature of her early teens, most notably *New Worlds*. There she found visions which felt very much in tune with her own pessimism of the hippie era twilight and, additionally, a kind of artsy literature which had developed its own ex-centric narrative strategies. During a guest talk at the sci-fi convention in 1982, she reminisced:

> I found a copy [of *New Worlds*] in a bookshop... I didn't know what had happened. I didn't know why people

suddenly began to write like this in the early sixties. I can't tell you how exciting it was. I was reading Ballard and Moorcock and Sladek as they came tumbling from the presses. I was writing myself at that time, and fiction which was nudging at the edges of possible experience, that was acutely dissatisfied with various formulas of what you'd call mainstream fiction. When I read those mid-sixties issues of *New Worlds* I realised it was possible to scrap almost everything I found oppressive about those apparatuses of fiction. (*Shaking a Leg*, 34)

Science fiction, with its potential for sketching scenarios of extreme and bizarre disasters, used to fascinate her as a child. In the same guest talk (published in *Vector*, re-published in *Shaking a Leg*) she emphasised how exciting John Wyndham's "cosy catastrophes" seemed to her eleven-year-old self. Her journalist father used to bring home the next day's papers when he came home from office late at night: the *Times* for his wife and the *Daily Sketch* for his daughter. The latter paper serialized Wyndham's *The Day of the Tryffids*, which Carter would read into the small hours. In her memories, she claims that the disaster presented in the novel and the post-catastrophic world the characters live in made such an impact on her because "it taught me that writing didn't have to be true in order to have a meaning, and a catastrophe that was impossible, that was purely imaginary, could both move and disturb me." (ibid., 32)

Science fiction also attracted her because of the very peculiar point of view of the writer and the reader—that of an outsider. The peripheral vantage point is what Carter applies in her own, early, non-science fiction novels and re-reading stories of this genre in *New Worlds* was a striking experience. Thus, in the 1960s, Carter realised that the fiction genre could become the right medium to discuss real dangers of the mid-twentieth century, real fears of nuclear disaster and all other forms of apprehension young British people were feeling at that time:

My response has been to start contemplating fiction about the international arms trade... We live in a very confused, confusing and dangerous times, and fiction, which is a kind of log of these times, changes its nature and expands and sucks in material from all manner of places and from all manner of styles and genres to be able to adequately describe ourselves to ourselves at all kinds of levels. (ibid., 36)

The development of science fiction is possible: this genre has the potential of becoming the ultimate realism of the late twentieth century, a kind of literature which makes it possible to examine human minds. In her youth, Carter, the former Wyndham fan, was seduced by the romantic possibilities offered by post-apocalyptic scenarios; she wanted "to write stories that could be read by guttering candlelight in the ruins of our cities and still give pleasure." (ibid. 43) Her novel written during that time, *Heroes and Villains*, juxtaposes patent allusions to nuclear fallout and mutations caused by the self-annihilation of technological society with countercultural poetics: subversion of the social order, new hippie-like aesthetics, alternate lifestyles, and a concentration on entropy, decay and death. Carter is no longer interested in the bomb—she does not warn against the holocaust but instead describes in detail the gradual dissolution of social, sexual and cultural groupings that follow the inevitable disaster and make room for a new female-governed future. In *Heroes and Villains*, the Cold War motif of a post-holocaust civilization allows Carter to create an exuberant world of ruin, lush vegetation and barbarism. Three groups of people live among the deteriorating shreds of a pre-nuclear explosion past: the Professors, who live in concrete fortified villages and cultivate old science and ideology; the Barbarians, who attack them and lead nomadic lives in the forests; and the Out People, who are radiation mutants cast out by all communities.

The Professors are the guardians of this order; they try to uphold standards and take care of appearances such as dress and accent. Marianne, the novel's protagonist, is the daughter of a professor of history brought up to live in an ordered patriarchal society and to study old books in an attempt to preserve knowledge. The futility of the Professors' work—abstract research done in white concrete towers, editing what nobody will ever read—demonstrates the arbitrariness of post-apocalyptic social roles. The caste of Professors, in wanting to be different than the irrational Barbarians, must devise artificial attributes of individuality. Unable to cope with an existence devoted to the cultivation of the past, and attracted by the colourful and seemingly romantic Barbarians, Marianne helps one of them, a beautiful young Barbarian leader named Jewel. Wounded in an attack, Jewel escapes from the village and is followed by Marianne. He then takes her to his tribe and, despite her protests, proclaims her his hostage. The tribe (whose descriptions bring to mind a 1960s hippie commune) is apparently governed by Jewel and his brothers, but soon Marianne realises that the real source of power is Donally, an escapee professor of sociology, Jewel's tutor and the self-proclaimed shaman of the tribe. For Donally, the tribe is a social laboratory where he tries to perform an experiment—to wit, to introduce a new mythology designed to be the founding stone of a new type of post-holocaust society.

'It seemed to me that the collapse of civilisation in the form that intellectuals such as ourselves understood it might be as good a time as any for crafting a new religion' he said modestly. 'Religion is a device for instituting the sense of a privileged group; many are called but few are chosen and, coaxed from incoherence, we shall leave the indecent condition of barbarism and aspire towards that of the honest savage.' (*Heroes and Villains*, 63)

When Marianne meets Donally, she immediately recognizes his professorial descent: "his voice was perfectly cultured, thin, high and soft... He had a thin, mean and cultured face. Marianne had grown up among such voices and faces." (ibid., 49) Seeing in his study books that she remembered from her childhood (Teilhard de Chardin, Levi-Strauss, Weber, Durkheim), Marianne discovers Donally's attempts to rule the Barbarians according to outdated formulas written down by pre-apocalyptic sociologists. Disappointed by the tribe, Marianne runs away but is recaptured by Jewel, who rapes her, brings her back, and then ceremoniously marries her according to a ritual devised by Donally. With the tribe again on the road, Donally quarrels with Jewel and has to leave. Marianne gradually learns how to manipulate Jewel, and her quasi-royal power grows, especially once she gets pregnant and is to be the mother of Jewel's heir. When Donally sends a message that he has been caught by the Professors, Jewel goes to rescue him, and both are killed. In the novel's finale, Marianne decides to become the female leader of a new society.

Marianne decides on a scenario that suits her best. She has found her identity and now wants to take control of the tribe and to become a post-apocalyptic leader. She declares, paraphrasing the Bible: "I will be the tiger-lady and I will rule them with a rod of iron." (ibid., 150) In this sentence, she alludes to Donally's attempt to tattoo one of the tribe's children into a tiger-girl, something which ended tragically, as the baby died in the process. But the idea of the artificial creation of a 'natural' tiger-human had some appeal to the Barbarians, and thus Jewel wanted to get the tiger tattoo himself. When he learned that at his age it was impossible, he planned to tattoo his and Marianne's baby. And now it is Marianne who is going to symbolically possess the tiger's strength and beauty: not by getting a tattoo, but by ruling over the tribe 'with a rod of iron'. Her 'rod' is probably going to be her knowledge and education: the love of reason her father taught her combined with her ability to reconcile binary oppositions and blend nature with nurture, reason with instinct, the Barbarians with the Professors. Marianne is aware that she is not yet living in a post-apocalyptic order, but still within the Apocalypse itself, that is, amidst the bits and pieces of an old world which is falling apart. Thus, her declaration 'I will rule them with a rod of iron' echoes Saint John's Revelation:

> [A]nd the dragon stood before the woman which was ready to be delivered, for to devour her child as soon as it was born.
>
> And she brought forth a man child, who was to rule all nations with a rod of iron: and her child was caught up unto God, and to his throne.
>
> And the woman fled into the wilderness. (St John's Revelation, 12, 4-6)

Marianne misquotes St John for a purpose: she aims to give the old patriarchal texts a new meaning, for new times. At the end of the book, Marianne is, physically speaking, 'ready to deliver', as her baby is to be born very soon. But here the similarities with St John end: who can be identified with the devouring dragon? Perhaps patriarchal attempts to remodel the child so that it serves a purpose? After all, Donally and Jewel wanted him tattooed and ruling the tribe according to the old pattern of power. Moreover, Marianne (in contrast to Donally and Jewel) is not so sure the baby is going to be "a man child"; she plans the future irrespectively of its sex. Finally, her flight into the wilderness is, in fact, an act of usurping political power herself: it is she who is going to become a tiger-lady and rule the new 'wilderness', the world outside the villages of the Professors and the camps of the Barbarians.

Heroes and Villains is Carter's most important journey into the realm of science fiction and her attempt to describe a Ballard-like catastrophe that not only alters the world but human unconscious as well. Ballard has similar concerns in *The Drought* (1965), where the convention of the catastrophic genre is used to chart the mindscape of the protagonist. The thesis is put forward explicitly: post-apocalyptic landscapes reflect the innermost feelings of contemporary humankind. The book only superficially belongs to science fiction—in fact, it may be read as a critique of catastrophic fiction, as an exercise meant to prove the exhaustion of the genre. The defining elements are present: we see a global drought, panic-driven escapees, civilization in regress, etc., but the adventurous story is not convincing, and our real object of interest is the human psyche and the way the outside world influences it.

The science fiction pretence of the narrative is as follows: because of pollution and some spontaneous chemical reactions in liquid refuse, the oceans are covered with a thin film of indissoluble substance that stops the process of vaporization. No clouds are formed and the climate changes rapidly. The lack of rain and the resultant slow death of the world's rivers and lakes make continents uninhabitable. People panic and try to get to the oceans' shores. Most of them die fighting one another within the first few years, and the rest organize small communes or fishing villages and work hard to obtain fresh water. Strange cults are born and, somewhere in the arid interiors, even stranger communities manage to survive in the ruins.

We see (or rather guess) what happens on the global scale through the eyes of the protagonist, Ransom, who is one of the last people to leave the shrinking lake and one of the first to come back from the shore a few years later. The reader's perspective is limited to Ransom's point of view: there is very little information about the world outside his immediate surroundings as Ransom is not much interested in life beyond his local community. In fact, his major interest is his own psyche, the mindscapes of semi-conscious memory and obscure compulsions.

Instead of grieving the loss of his former life and the luxuries of affluent technological civilization, Ransom uses the drought as a means of liberation; he eagerly quits the role he played in society and enjoys the stillness and emptiness of the post-apocalyptic reality. In the end, all objective measures and imposed rules vanish, and the only reality is psychological: "a world of volitional time where the images of the past were reflected free from the demands of memory and nostalgia" (ibid., 176). Free from conventional confines, he is ready to accept the challenge of the deserted interior. His final decision to go to the centre of the dead continent is liberating, and it signifies acceptance of his true self. Many characters in the book unconsciously feel that "we ought to accept the challenge and set off north, right into the centre of the drought... There's probably a great river waiting for us somewhere there, brown water and green lands." (ibid., 75). Ransom is able to follow this unconscious drive to go to the desert. He leaves all social relationships and all memories of his previous life behind—his journey is like an existential quest for identity and freedom. In this case, it is the freedom to die in the way he wants to die, and in a place he feels is proper. The moment he sets off, the first rain in many years falls as if suggesting he has made the right decision.

Ballard, ten years older than Carter, was keen on saying that World War II was the true intellectual and spiritual beginning of his output. Moreover, the war in Ballard's fiction, in being his own artistic beginning, is also the source of the post-traumatic and violent culture we live in now.

The protagonist of *Empire of the Sun*, Jim, finds himself in a stadium near Shanghai on the ninth of August 1945, when at 11:02 in the morning, on the other side of the sea dividing the Chinese mainland from Japan, the Nagasaki bomb lights up the atmosphere. Though some 500 hundred miles away, Shanghai suburbia is filled with an unreal pearl light. Hardly anybody is still conscious, but Jim and a Japanese sentry actually see the deadly light which marks the end of the world. In the book's climax, the chapter entitled "Empire of the Sun", there is a strong suggestion, that all life after the explosion is nothing but waiting for the inescapable death of a civilization that is already doomed.

> They were sitting on the floor of a furnace heated by a second sun.
>
> Jim stared at his white hands and knees, and at the pinched face of the Japanese soldier, who seemed disconcerted by the light. Both of them were waiting for the rumble of sound that followed the bomb-flashes, but an unbroken silence lay over the stadium and the surrounding land, as if the sun had blinked, losing heart for a few seconds. (*Empire of the Sun*, 218)

From this moment on, Jim is changed, and his life is centred around notions such as the apocalypse, World War III and death coming from the air. He is not killed at the stadium; he manages to reach Shanghai and go back to England. Yet this world seems to him to be illusory, like the day-dream of a dying mind. He feels as if the world ended at the moment the A-bomb was dropped, and what we believe we are experiencing is only an illusion. The post-war world seems just as abstract and unreal to Jim as his pre-war film-like memories of Shanghai. In a sense, the pearl light of Nagasaki is the only true thing that ever happened to him, and his knowledge of the inevitable end is, for him, the most important outcome of the world. Lost among people who did not experience the war in Asia, he feels wiser and more resigned.

> Yet he knew that he had seen the flash of the atomic bomb at Nagasaki even across the four hundred miles of the China Sea. More important, he had seen the start of World War III, and realised that it was taking place around him. The crowds watching newsreels on the Bund had failed to grasp that these were the trailers for a war that had already started. One day there will be no more newsreels. (ibid., 288)

Empire of the Sun closes with an image of Shanghai as a harbinger of a coming war, the Doomsday city bathed in the lights of an atomic bomb. At the time the bombs fell, a five-year-old Angela Carter was spending her war in a safe North of England neighbourhood. Unaware of the bomb, she waited for her family to go back to London. And yet, much later in life, she claimed that:

> That act of warfare, the dropping of the A-bomb, perpetrated—obviously—without either my knowledge or consent, although they said it was for the sake of my future, changed irrevocably the circumstances in which that future life will be passed. Let me not be sorry for myself about this, it changed them less than if I'd been five in Hiroshima. But change them it did, and may well inexorably dictate the manner of my life's ending. (*Shaking a Leg*, 44)

"A landscape from which all life has been violently expelled"

In the late 1950s, Angela Carter, together with Paul Carter, her fiancé at that time, participated in Aldermaston marches organized by the Campaign for Nuclear Disarmament (CND). The CND was founded in 1958 in response to the test explosion of the first British A-bomb. It provided young rebellious people with a forum for discussion and the opportunity to meet and protest: "the marches from Aldermaston were some of the most moving and beautiful memories of my girlhood," Carter remembers in her essay "Anger in the Black Landscape" written for *Over Our Dead Bodies: Women against the Bomb* anthology. There she calls the CND an "exhibition of mass sanity" in a world heading towards nuclear disaster. In *Heroes and Villains*, which she wrote during her marriage to Paul Carter, the post-nuclear wasteland which used to be Britain is full of the bric-a-brac of the fallen Empire, suggesting that vanity and vainglory had pushed the country to enter the deadly conflict that had ended in catastrophe. Marianne and Jewel roam in the empty and deserted country, old houses, old pieces of decoration and forlorn, imperial architecture. In the sand-covered and lion-ridden old sea resort (according to Sarah Gamble, a ruined Brighton) they see minarets, spires and iron helmets, gigantic wheels and figures half-buried in the beach. Gamble identifies this description as "Brighton Palace Pier...a simulacrum of a real thing...the ornate pavilion constructed at the pier head," (Angela Carter. *A Literary Life*, 88) which was built to commemorate Victorian England, the Crystal Palace, memories of royal splendour and the imperial heyday.

In the ruins on the beach, Marianne and Jewel meet an emblematic beast, a lion now living in the wilderness, which is a visual echo of heraldic representation of Britain. "People kept wild beasts such as lions and tigers in cages and looked at them for information. Who would have thought they would take to our climate so kindly, when the fire came and let them out?' (*Heroes and Villains*, 9), Marianne's father explains to her about the exotic beasts roaming the countryside and devouring smaller creatures. After the apocalypse, carnivorous cats once again become kings of the beasts: they are the only living beings that gain power instead of losing it. Jewel is attracted to wild cats, which is perhaps a result of his own weakness. One of his most vivid memories is a scene in which, as a teenager, he met a lion face to face and survived only because the beast ignored him. This story that he told to Marianne anticipates the end of the novel: when Jewel gives up and goes to seek his death, he encounters another lion and again fails to attract its attention. Marianne sees the animal and cannot but admire its fearful beauty:

> She had never seen a lion before. It looked exactly like pictures of itself; though darkness washed its colours off, she saw its mane and tasselled tail which flicked about as it moved out of the edge of shadow on to the dune. (ibid., 150)

Marianne is not disappointed, the lion looks "like pictures of itself," a heraldic Beast come to life: the thing and its representation for once go together. The mythical meaning of wild cats survives the end of civilization and remains a handy metaphor. Marianne decides to rule over the tribe as its tiger-lady, not in an act of imitating the queen of the wilderness fairytale motif, but in an attempt to start a new epoch with new myths. Attractive as this vision is, later in life Carter found it wanting and naive—a fantasy about the bomb not a warning against its power.

> I wouldn't dream of writing a novel set after a nuclear catastrophe now... it would be too much like tempting providence, and making hypotheses which are not on. Heroes and Villains is a dystopian novel. In the fifties and the sixties there was a real vogue for post-apocalyptic novels as a sort of pastoral, but it's just not possible to do that now: we know too much. (*Novelists in Interview*, 95)

Romanticizing war, emphasising the "hideous poetry of the terminal nature of nuclear warfare" (*Shaking a Leg*, 45) seemed dangerous and thought-deforming to her mature self. Seeing the Bomb as an incarnation of the ultimate evil or the transcendental essence of war made people, CND members included, overlook the real nature of war as one of the interlocked sinews of political and economic agendas. The Bomb should not be considered a symbol of the Original Sin, "a metaphysical scourge, one of the four horsemen of the Apocalypse," (ibid., 45) but a grim fact of the contemporary life, a reminder of human folly. Goya's 'black' pictures in the Prado showing "a Europe in a future that remains unimaginable... a wreckage of humanity, a landscape from which all life has been violently expelled... unimaginable, but not impossible" (ibid. 45) comprised, for her, the most vivid statement about the war, a way to demystify the Bomb. Explaining why she left the CND, Carter stated that banning A-bombs would not do, it would be just a symbolic victory as the Bomb would soon be replaced by even more deadly weapons. Of course, nuclear arms should be banned, but the real goal should be to restructure global politics and liquidate the arms race.

In J.G. Ballard's catastrophic fiction, the "black Landscape" of Goya is a central theme. 'The Terminal Beach' (1964) is a short story about a man who finds psychological fulfilment in the deserted landscape of Eniwetok, the nuclear test island, with its empty, concrete barracks, abandoned military bases and prevailing deadness that both recall World War II and herald World War III. As the H-bomb tested on the island is an echo of the bombs of Hiroshima and Nagasaki, Eniwetok is presented as a harbinger of humanity's future—an empty, desolate and mutated place of death. In the final sections of the story, the protagonist finds and guards the corpse of a Japanese soldier, and in their long discussions, the future of the human race is described. Eniwetok is an example of what the whole Earth will soon be:

> The series of weapons tests had fused the sand in layers, and the pseudo-geological strata condensed the brief epochs, micro-seconds in duration, of thermonuclear time... This island was a fossil of time future, its bunkers and blockhouses illustrating the principle that the fossil record of life was one of armour and the exoskeleton ('The Terminal Beach', 139-140).

This island is a harbinger of the post-World War III reality, and in its absolute deadness, one can find Nirvana, a feeling of equilibrium between what is inside and what is outside. People unconsciously long for the zero world, where nothing happens, because such a wasteland is the final destination of our species, and on some deep-down cellular level we know it. These stressful contemporary times are just a period between the Second World War and the Third World War and the total destruction it will bring about. The post-apocalyptic people learn to live in non-time, without the divisions people are used to:

> All sense of time soon vanished, and his life became completely existential, an absolute break separating one moment from the next like two quantal events (ibid., 142).

> Time had become quantal. For hours, it would be noon, the shadows contained within the blocks, the heat reflected off the concrete floor. Abruptly, he would find that it was early afternoon or evening, the shadows everywhere like pointing fingers (ibid.,132).

> This island is an ontological Eden, why seek to expel yourself into a world of quantal flux? (ibid., 136).

The adjective existential is the key word in this passage, life is no longer a linear progression from the past to the future, but a pure existence in the everlasting moment now. Reduced to the very core of his personality, he has no expectations, no desires, no plans; thus, he is liberated in the way the Existentialists describe. In his "ontological Eden" all that may be is pure existence with no possibility of joining "quantal" moments into one linear narrative of a "then...and then..." order. The word "quantal" additionally alludes to Max Planck and the history of modern physics, which resulted in the creation of the A-bomb and the H-bomb.

Ironically perhaps, there is some peace in this vision of a post-human world without time, without people rushing around, without media, without a continuous flux of white noise. For entropy will give us rest. Deserted, surreal landscapes are the only things that will remain. Traven refuses to leave the island because, by dying there, he would be true to the logic of the Universe. He has insight into the order of things, and he is the one to bid civilization farewell. Life after August 1945 is only a nightmarish illusion. These years before the terminal war join the datable past (the previous war) with the inevitable future. Eniwetok is deserted and deprived of virtually any fauna: labyrinths of concrete blocks, barracks full of old magazines, a few meagre palms, rubbish left by soldiers and a merciless sun form a minimalist entourage. The landscape is man-made, fully artificial. The island has been magically transported from the future to the present day, and it shows what the entire world is going to be like. All life will end, and human beings (who are also part of the biological kingdom) subliminally search for the reverse of Eden, the place of the death of creation.

The story juxtaposes references to World War II (shadows of manikins imprinted on the walls by a nuclear blast, memories from the 1940s, uniformed Japanese marooned on the island) and allusions to the post-war reality. The most important event is the Cold War with its nuclear tests, manifestations of contemporary violence. The stay on Eniwetok is an opportunity to bid farewell to the whole of civilization and, indirectly, to the whole universe.

The end of one particular civilization, the affluent West, turns out to be only part of a universal decline: a gigantic cosmic clock unwinds itself, the human race ends together with life on Earth and the Universe itself.

Carter found such prose both attractive and prophetic; for her, J.G. Ballard was primarily "the great chronicler" (*Shaking a Leg*, 560) of Britain within this morbid, technological, death-driven civilisation. In her review of *Empire of the Sun*, she praises him for his obsessions, which allow him to show the contemporary British landscape as a pure, technological nightmare to a generation programmed by their post-imperial education to see England as "a pleasant land." Ballard's junior, Carter spent her British childhood in the twilight of the British empire, during the final days of the pretended glory of a country which could not accept its own receding into history. Even twenty years later, when Margaret Thatcher was the Prime Minister of the country, imperial sentiments could still be felt in the air. The British involvement in the arms race was the evidence:

> If the peace movement in Britain cannot persuade our (democratically elected) government, this one or the next, to review our position *vis-à-vis* NATO, the establishment of Cruise missiles in this country and our whole relationship with the obscene farce of modern warfare, then perhaps, morally, we do not deserve to survive. (ibid., 50)

Ballard expressed similar sentiments—at that time he was writing *The Kindness of Women*, the sequel of *Empire of the Sun*. In *The Kindness of Women*, we do not see the war itself. After the 1937 episode, we are taken to the mid-1940s—to the end of the war. The prevailing feeling of the narrator is nostalgia—at the very beginning of the novel we read about the fall of Imperial Russia (Jim's governess is a White Russian). Now, a similar process touches imperial Britain, the luxurious enclave of the International Settlement in Shanghai and the orderly pre-war world at large. "The Japanese attack on Pearl Harbor had marked the first revolt by the colonized nations of the east against the imperial west" (*Kindness of Women* 53), one of the Lunghua internees was wont to say. The change in the world is the change of civilizations: stepping outside Lunghua, Jim has to face a new kind of reality, and again, his first impression is that what he sees is unreal and theatrical.

> The wild rice growing by the roadside, the blades of sugar cane and the yellow mud of the abandoned paddy fields were touched by the same eerie light, as if they had been irradiated by the bomb dropped on Nagasaki. The drowned canals and the grave-mounds, the forgotten ceramics works by the river, looked like an elaborate stage-set (ibid., 52).

For a second, Jim feels he is the last man alive and that the war has ended because there is no one left to fight. As a result, he feels doomed to a ghost-like existence amidst the post-apocalyptic ruins. There is no return to his childhood self, and Jim feels rejected by Shanghai, the dream-city that had easily absorbed the occupation period into its rich history. Setting out for England, he looks at the Asian coast with nostalgia. What he leaves behind is a beautiful and cruel fantasy, one in which he would wish to continue, but he has to exchange it for an unknown 'truth' of Europe.

Jim's painful adaptation to the world after the war is depicted in a series of images: his studies, his decision to become a pilot and his literary career all seem to be a reaction to teenage traumas. For years, he lives in a constant expectation of World War III, whose coming he believes he has glimpsed. In Cambridge, instead of socializing with other students, he compulsively visits American airbases and watches powerful aeroplanes and huge cars driven by large men "with the confident eyes of an occupying power" (ibid., 84). Their displays of power make Jim think of an inevitable future, of A-bomb attacks that will bathe England in the eerie pearl light he had seen in Asia. Americans are the only people ready for the war to come.

> From their closely-guarded bases they were preparing England, still trapped by its memories of the Second World War, for the third war yet to come. Then the atomic flash that I had seen over Nagasaki would usher these drab fields and the crumbling gothic of the university into the empire of light (ibid., 84).

"Nuke Buenos Aires"

While thinking of the intellectual affinities of Carter and Ballard, one should not forget their very negative attitude toward Margaret Thatcher and Ronald Reagan. The outbreak of the Falkland War was, for Carter, the ultimate proof that Thatcher was not only vile but also extremely dangerous as she had access to the nation's hidden anxieties and cravings. "Carter was convinced that the advent of Thatcherism necessitated a return to the kind of political activism that had characterised the sixties," (*Angela Carter. A Literary Life*, 166) Gamble rightly opines. Twenty years after the Cuban Missile Crisis, the jingoistic, thin-lipped, post-Victorian Britain was anachronistically coming back and, according to Carter "my forties began, as my twenties had done, in a fury of rage." (*Shaking a Leg*, 50) The Soviet invasion of Afghanistan, the Falklands War and the rise of British nationalism terrified her:

> We have, indeed, learned to live with the unthinkable and to think it. Last spring, I saw people, British people, not superficially psychotic-looking, wearing T-shirts with 'Nuke Buenos Aires' on the front. A new verb 'to nuke'. So easily, in such an unacknowledged way, has the unthinkable slipped into our vocabulary. Note, too, how 'to nuke' is an active verb; it is easier to think of killing than of being killed, for obvious reasons. Can such atrocious garments be donned on Albion's shore without an enraged populace tearing them from the wearers' backs? They can. (ibid., 51)

A Margaret Thatcher-like grotesque figure makes its appearance in J.G. Ballard's *The Largest Theme Park in the World*, a short story he wrote for *The Guardian* with clear political undertones. Mocking ideas similar to those presented by Toffler, Fukuyama and the late 1980s enthusiasts of global unification—the abolition of borders, the dissolution of nation-states, etc—he gives his own vision of the "end of history" in Europe. The creation of a united Europe in Ballard's story results in the exodus of the European middle-class to the beaches of the Mediterranean. After long a holiday, lawyers, architects, accountants, managers, etc., decide not to go back home:

> It became all too clear that in rejecting the old Europe of frontiers and national self-interest they had also rejected the bourgeois values that hid behind them. A demanding occupation, a high disposable income, a future mortgaged to the gods of social and professional status, had all been abandoned. (*Complete Short Stories*, 1140)

Europe is transformed into a theme park for American and Japanese tourists. The northern European authorities try in vain to summon back their most educated and efficient citizens. The end of national borders and the overwhelming victory of liberal democracy (earlier prophesied by Fukuyama) means precisely the end of this very system. In this short story, Ballard does not yet seriously explore the far-reaching social consequences of the creation of a leisure society, he rather toys with ideas. His permanent holidaymakers indulge in body cults, fitness, fringe philosophies and new religions, and they camp in Southern European villages, which are connected with each other to form one gigantic Mediterranean cityscape. Leading a loose, hippie lifestyle, they eventually have to use violence to preserve their communities. British, female, middle-aged, right-wing politicians make a show of themselves, protesting on the beaches with a truly jingoist zest:

> In return, each of these national enclaves produced its characteristic leaders. The British resorts were dominated by any number of would-be-Thatchers, fierce ladies in one-piece bathing suits who invoked the memory of Churchill and proclaimed their determination to 'fight them on the beaches and never never surrender'. (ibid., 1134)

Crime and violence pull people from their leisure-induced stupor, and national groups gather around charismatic leaders. Finally, the millions of tourists decide to march North and reclaim their native cities to "reinstate a forgotten Europe of nations, each jealous of its frontiers, happy to guard its history, tariff barriers and insularity." (ibid., 1144) This short story reads like a tongue-in-cheek commentary on the current political and cultural discussion in England; nevertheless, it alludes to important themes: the leisure society and violence as a necessary part of social life.

Carter and Ballard agree that what Thatcher awoke in the British population was a kind of delirium—an acute nostalgia for an imperial past mixed with the frustrated rage of a nation left out in the cold. Similarly, Ronald Reagan, focussed on the past and obsessed with the Cold War of 1950s films, cut for both writers a grotesque figure, an epitome of the contemporary political madness. In Ballard's *The Atrocity Exhibition*, a novel comprising loosely connected short stories written in the 1960s, when Reagan was still an actor, his future political career is uncannily anticipated. In the chapter 'Why I want to fuck Ronald Reagan', we see paragraph-snapshots of Reagan's political campaign interlaced with psychiatrists' reports describing the subliminal appeal the footage has on mental patients. In the annotations Ballard remembers:

> Above all, it struck me that Reagan was the first politician to exploit the fact that his TV audience would not be listening too closely, if at all, to what he was saying, and indeed might well assume from his manner and presentation that he was saying the exact opposite of the words actually emerging from his mouth. (ibid., 169)

The paragraphs in the story have incipit-like titles in bold, if read together the bolded titles reveal a hidden message: "During these assassination fantasies / Tallis became increasingly obsessed / with the pudenda of the Presidential contender / mediated to him by a thousand television screens. / The motion pictures studies of Ronald Reagan / created a scenario of the conceptual orgasm, / a unique ontology of violence and desire." (ibid., bolded text from 165-168) In this story, the protagonist watches another set of media imagery (Reagan's campaign) and attempts to identify its latent, abstracted meanings. Behind Reagan's right-wing propaganda, he sees strong sexual undertones, and anal-sadistic imagery. Reports quoted in this section are on psychiatric research into the campaign. The disturbed and the mentally healthy alike prove to react on some subliminal level to the sexuality of Reagan's body language, grimaces and hair-dos. The language of the reports is exact and scientific, but, as one of the characters notes, "Science is the ultimate pornography, analytic activity whose main aim is to isolate objects or events from their contexts in time and space." (ibid., 49)

When Reagan did compete for the presidency twenty years later and actually won, much to the disbelief of leftist intellectuals, Carter had a teaching job in the US. She remembered having read Ballard's story back in the 1960s, and she was ecstatic to find it prophetic.

> I read "Why I want to Fuck Ronald Reagan" to a class of English Literature majors at a liberal East Coast college in one of the four states in the Union that stayed with Jimmy Carter that November day in 1980 when a British science-fiction writer's mad notion came true. They laughed until they cried, except those who vice versa'd. (*Shaking a Leg*, 558)

Thus, in her early forties, Carter was forced to realise that the liberal atmosphere of her hippie youth, the period when the class and sexual groupings were seen to be dissolving was receding into history. After a relatively short time and the boom of a relaxed, freedom-loving counterculture, fanatic right-wing politics were regaining power again. What she probably loved about the prophetic "Why I want" must have been Ballard's ability to see through the pretence, to tell the latent from the apparent. The patent content of Reagan's TV spot in the story is lukewarm and dull, it is the latent message that stirs his viewers both in the 1960s campaign (in Ballard's story) and during the 1980 election (which Carter and the students felt reading the story). The subliminal attraction of the viewers to the ugly, nationalistic, sadistic, repressive policy line that Reagan's body language promises scares Carter, but at the same time, she appreciates Ballard skills at reading these subtle signs and applying in-depth analysis to the psychopathology of political and cultural life.

J.G. Ballard and Angela Carter are often referred to as idiosyncratic stylists whose fiction eludes easy classifications. They both went quite a long way to recognition and critical appraisal. From the relatively marginal position of ex-centric authors—Carter's early novels combined elements of the grotesque and macabre, whereas Ballard's early texts fit within the science fiction genre—they were elevated to the status of contemporary "greats". What is interesting is their reciprocal pronounced respect for and appreciation of each other's imagination: quotes from Angela Carter's reviews often adorn new editions of Ballard's books and the other way around. Taking into consideration the above affinities and profound understanding the two authors shared, it is not surprising that they appreciated each other's literary output. "Breton and Ernst would have been proud of you," Ballard wrote on a postcard to Carter when she was terminally ill. Carter, in turn, talked about Ballard's fiction in the already mentioned review of *Empire of the Sun* as being characterised by "restless and brilliant formal innovation, highly stylized, extreme and shocking violence, pitch-black humour." (*Shaking a Leg*, 559) Two days after Carter's untimely death, he remembered her during BBC2's *The Late Show* as one of his friends. He said, among other things,

> Angela was tremendous fun... She had an irreverent spirit... I remember sitting in her kitchen as she cooked something up, and hearing her sort of cackling laugh and seeing her wicked gleam in her eye as she thought of some mischievous idea... I think she made people nervous because she was quite an ambiguous figure. It was never clear where exactly she stood on any topic, and this was what made conversation with her so interesting... I'll miss her terribly (angelacarteronline.com/2016/10/23/j.g.ballard-on-angela-carter)

Conclusion

Ballard's and Carter's reciprocal appreciation of each other's *oeuvres* is not surprising. This essay begins with a list of similarities between both writers' views, *oeuvres* and biographies: their liberal world views, their relaxed attitude to social and cultural changes—the inevitable twilight of the British supremacy in the West included—and their love of surrealist imagination.

For both of them, the nuclear bomb was a potent symbol of what they found fascinating about the period they lived in. In their fiction and non-fiction alike, the bomb attracts by promising a spectacular destruction. It denotes the death-instinct defined by Freud and the masochist cravings of the surrealists; it brings to mind the end-of-the-world fantasies of sci-fi writers and a longed-for self-annihilation of a human race that has already lived its preordained lifespan.

Yet, all the same, both Carter and Ballard were responsible, liberal middle-class British citizens with families: at the time Carter died, her beloved son was six, and Ballard had young grandchildren he adored. Thus, their attitude towards what the bomb represented was ambiguous to tell the least, and this ambiguity permeates both of their *oeuvres*.

Bibliography

Bakhtin, *Michaił Rabelais and His World*, trans. Helene Iswolsky, Indiana University Press, Bloomington, 1984.

Ballard, J.G. *Empire of the Sun*. Book Club Associates. London, 1985.
- *The Kindness of Women*. Flamingo, London, 1994.
- *A User's Guide to the Millennium*. Essays and Reviews. Flamingo, London 1997.
- *The Atrocity Exhibition*. Flamingo, London, 2001
- *The Complete Short Stories*. Flamingo, London, 2002.

Carter, Angela. *Heroes and Villains*. Virago, London, 1992.
- *Several Perceptions*, Virago, London, 1995.
- *Shaking a Leg*. Collected Journalism and Writings. Vintage, London, 1998.

Dimovitz, Scott A. *Angela Carter. Surrealist, Psychologist, Moral Pornographer*. Routledge, London and New York, 2016.

Gamble, Sarah. *Angela Carter. A Literary Life*. Palgrave Macmillan, New York, 2007.

Gordon, Edmund. *The Invention of Angela Carter. A Biography*. Chatto and Windus, London, 2017.

Haffenden, John. *Novelists in Interview*. London, Methuen,1985.

Oramus, Dominika. *Grave New World. The Decline of the West in the Fiction of J.G. Ballard*. The Terminal Press, Toronto, 2015.
- *Ways of Pleasure. Angela Carter's 'Discourse of Delight' in her Fiction and Non-Fiction*. Peter Lang, Frankfurt am Main, 2016.

Self, Will. *Junk Mail*. London, Penguin Books, 1995.

Vale, V. *J.G. Ballard Conversations*. San Francisco, RE/Search Publications, 2005.

The Late Show BBC2 angelacarteronline.com/2016/10/23/j.g.ballard-on-angela-carter. Accessed on June 6, 2017.

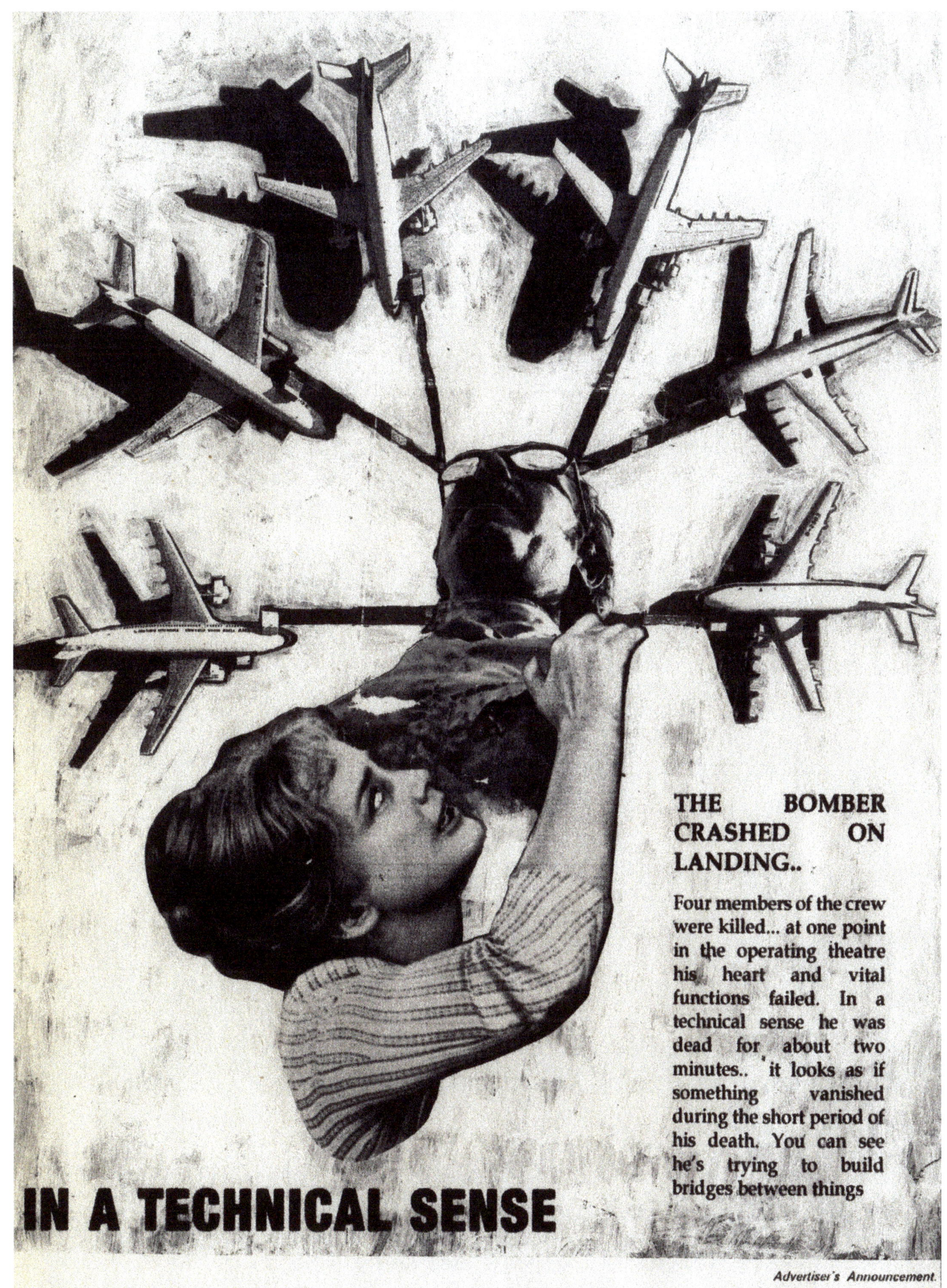
THE BOMBER CRASHED ON LANDING..
Four members of the crew were killed... at one point in the operating theatre his heart and vital functions failed. In a technical sense he was dead for about two minutes.. it looks as if something vanished during the short period of his death. You can see he's trying to build bridges between things
IN A TECHNICAL SENSE
Advertiser's Announcement

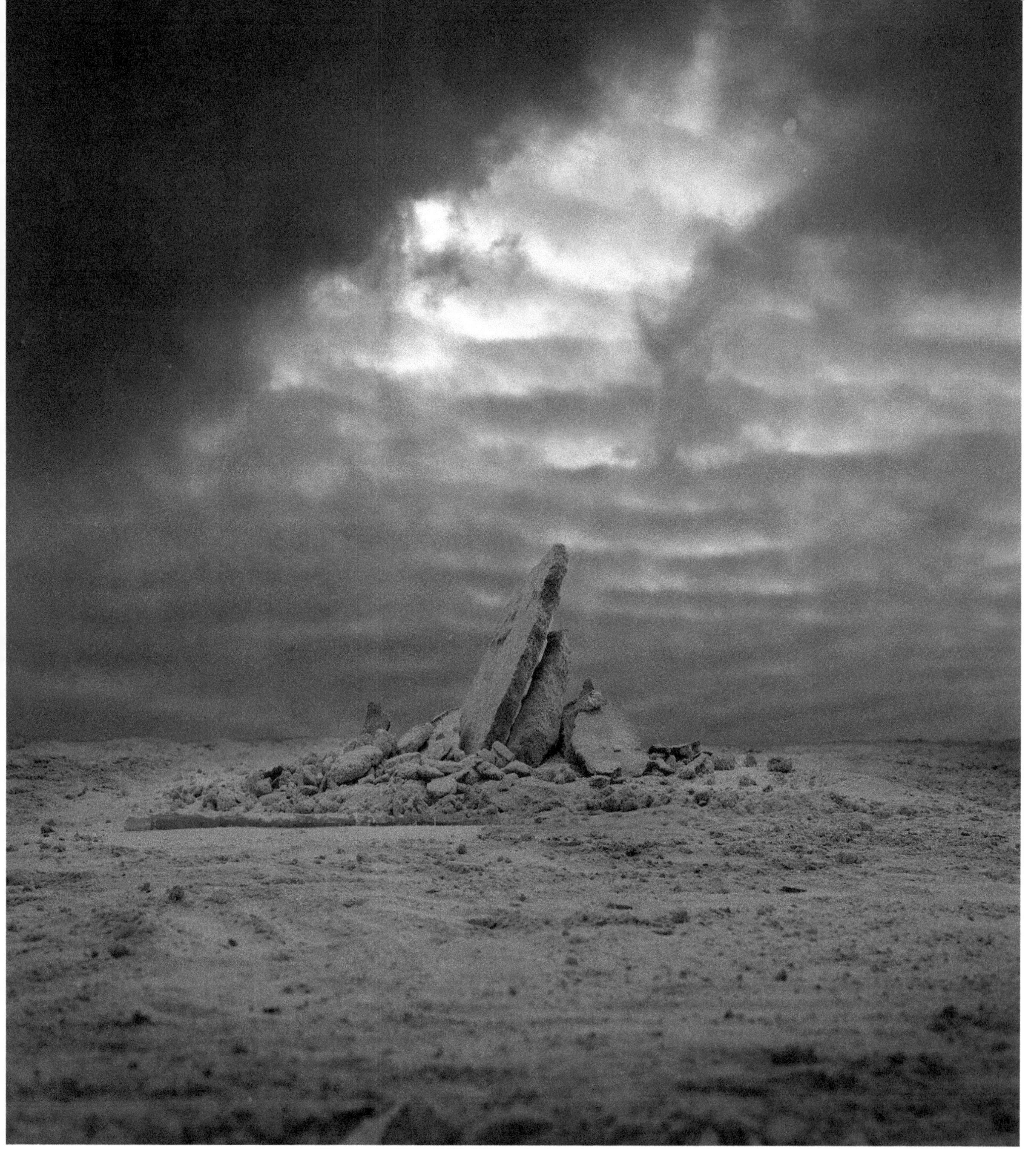

David Manley

IMAGES/ESSAY

J.G. Ballard's Instant Horizons

Photography has always been a medium used to exploit and manipulate the truth through state controlled propaganda and advertising, however the potential fluidity of the new digital image capture systems, editing software and viewing platforms have arguably turbocharged this potential. Image registration has shifted from a chemical trace on the emulsion of film to the infinite options for manipulation of the electronic bitmap further questioning notions of authenticity. This, combined with the deluge of imagery from mobile devices and unverifiable sources, further complicates our relationship with the photograph and encourages a climate of uncertainty where fake news and questionable media sources proliferate and act to disrupt traditional paradigms of media consumption. The credibility of the image as a representation of truth has been complicated further by the development of digital technology yet it does however continue to act as the "epitome" of our conceptualisation of trauma because of its psychological affiliations with how we tend to experience the world and the role memory plays in this process.

The image may contain representations of trauma but can its pervasive nature also be traumatic in and of itself? We are currently living through a period of exponential image saturation. According to Nicholas Mirzeoff, the image has become so pervasive that perhaps we tend to underestimate its psychological power to shape the way we think, feel and importantly engage with the world, and this has become the focal point of much visual culture theory. During the 1960's writers such as J.G. Ballard predicated the explosion of a type of mediatised trauma through the saturating dosing of the image via various platforms such as television, cinema and advertising billboards. Ballard explored the way in which the image merged with psychological development to shape and build the neural pathways of the individual in works such as *The Atrocity Exhibition* (1969) and *Crash* (1973). Ballard saw way back then that the image was much more than a passive object or illuminated screen to be consumed—it dramatically influences our perception of events and shapes our lives in unpredictable ways. For Ballard, the pervasive nature of the media cycle and the dosing and re-dosing of imagery acted as a form of cognitive remediation, in effect re-wiring the brain through an intensity that had it's own traumatic imprint. Ballard described this emerging phenomenon within the context of the urban terrain and the instantaneous and violent nature of the media cycle. This fusion of image and the mind's psychological processes greatly influenced the way in which his characters interacted with the world.

Ballard explored the impact of this saturation in the *The Atrocity Exhibition.* The novel is structured around a discordant, non-linear narrative that itself mimicked the disruptive nature of the media cycle and the implications this has on our perception of time. The book uses seemingly unrelated snippets of complex narratives and shocks in the form of one-paragraph vignettes that confront the reader in entirely unpredictable ways. These snippits of displaced narrative interfere with the temporal rhythm of the book suggesting that imaging technologies and their platforms create their own form of temporal slippage. Ballard understood how photography is inextricably linked to time as it operates as an indexical preservation of a moment and that both photography and trauma have a capacity to disrupt our experience of time within a past, present and future context. The book used the image and the temporal dissonance associated with it to describe the traumatic imprint of a mediated techo-culture. Cinema has long used the trope of shock and awe to entertain the audience. Indeed, the first motion picture ever screened was footage taken of a train accelerating towards the camera, a deliberate visual and temporal assault on the cinemagoers that ran out of the theatre believing the locomotive would crash through the screen. This tactic was deliberately employed by the producers and cinema owners to create an unrivalled event that ushered in the grand spectacle of cinema. Ballard's work recognises the temporal dissonance created as we move away from chronological time and begin to immerse ourselves in chronoscopic time, a time that is characterised by the instantaneous moment.

David Morley traces the historical articulation of Ballard's concerns in *Home Territories, Media, Mobility and Identity* (2000). He cites Shaw Desmond's article written for the Trade Journal *Television* published in September 1929. The article predates the notion that the televised image has the capacity to "destroy" our experience of chronological time. Desmond saw the evolution of live television as a form of entertainment and all-encompassing lifestyle and argued that this revolution in technology would have profound implications for our understanding of space and temporality altering our perception of these concepts through the immediacy and compelling context of the instantaneous dissemination of media imagery that allows the spectator to be anywhere in the world in a virtual sense, experiencing events as they unfold; and this disruptive capacity of the image has the potential to rupture the moment displacing the diachronic scaffolds of our lives. Morley notes that back in 1994 J.B. Priestly argued that social and political structures would form around the new technologies predicting the "virtual geography" of the post-modern era that has quickly been colonised by platforms such as Google and Facebook. This shift in the perceptive field has enormous social and political ramifications because those who control the image and the platforms it can be delivered through also have control of a great deal of power.

Media technologies such as computers, mobile devices and virtual reality continue to influence our understanding and experience of the world through the creation of spaces that are heavily influenced by the image. As a result we have increasingly developed new ways to conceptualise the idea of community through contemporary constructs of networks that go beyond physical localities and made up of increasingly distant and fragmented relationships patched together to form a sense of personal community. More and more we are living in a time of immanent connectedness within a virtual context where we maintain a symbolic proximity with each other through our devices and this instant tele-presence not only skews our perception of time but also changes what Morley describes as our "alterity" or a sense of otherness in relation to our spatial and temporal frameworks of the world. Given this new connectivity and its psychological influence we now find that the technology and our ever-increasing reliance on it promote a state of constant availability as communication agents. The contemporary experience of this alterity changes our understanding of physical connectedness that has the equal and opposite effect of diminishing its importance. The immediacy of a world that was previously inaccessible becomes more tangible within the context of information gathering as any event, regardless of geographical locality, can be communicated within a connected world and thus

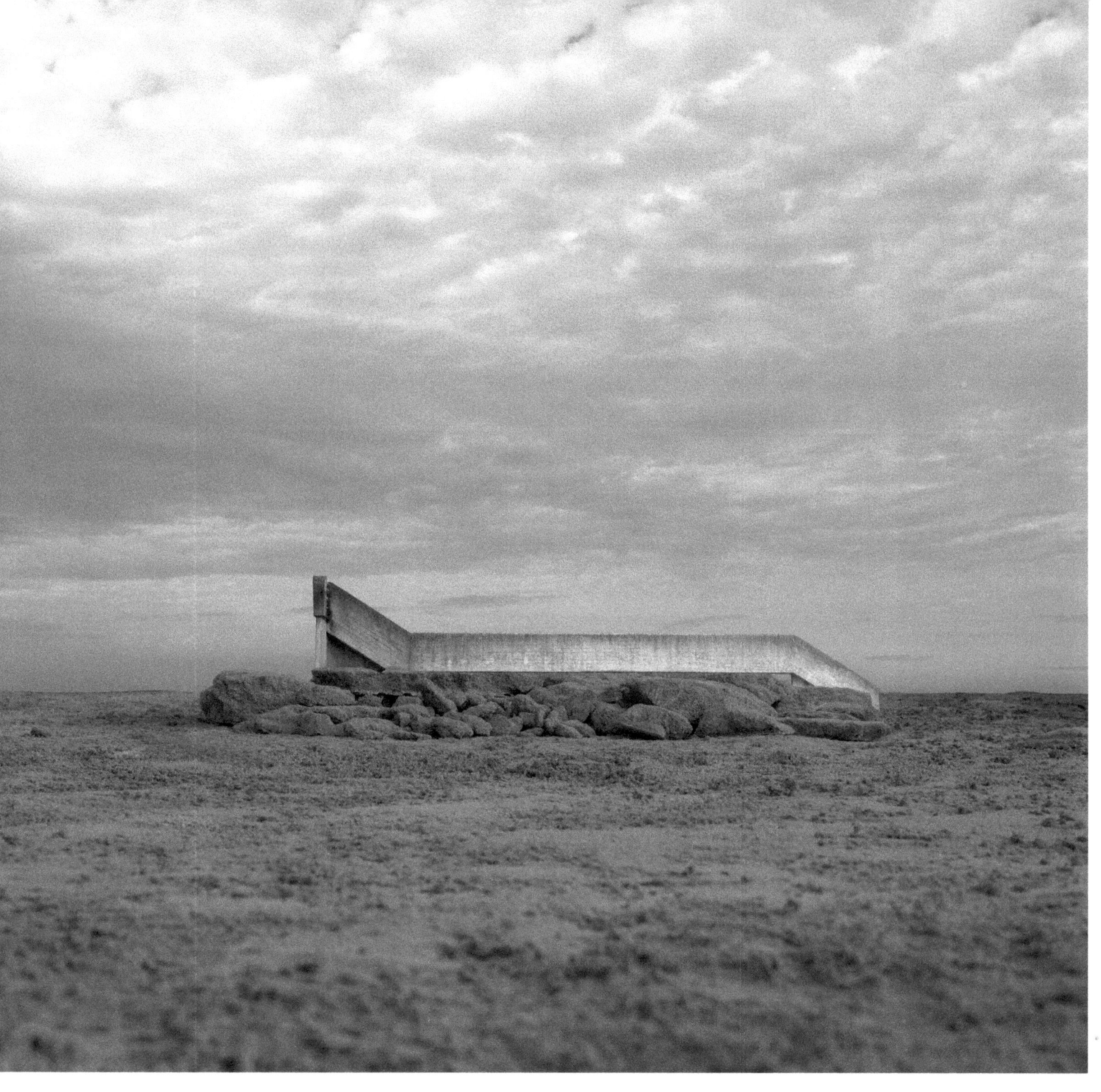

in principle experienced immediately. The image is a complex shaper and determinant of how societies change and evolve and one of the ways that people learn to assimilate with their environment is through the symbolic naming of places to create familiarity and a sense of connection. When inevitable change occurs, take for example globalisation and its displacement of labour and shifts in economic power bases; members of a society may encounter a dislocation with the familiar. Examples of this may be changes in the distribution of labour and production or the introduction of new forms of cultural symbols and identities that encroach on people's lives undermining a sense of safety and stability. This disenfranchisement encourages resentment towards state and political bodies that are seen to represent and encourage a shift in the *status quo*. Perhaps this may be one aspect in the developmental process of xenophobia and racism as people feel like strangers in their own home and seek to enhance their own status by inflicting a quality of strangeness onto others.

What are some of the ways in which the new media platforms and their instantaneous nature affect the trajectory of politics and societies? In recent history the disruptive capacity of tele-visual technologies has radically changed the fundamental nature of democracy. Image power is increasingly being used by a variety of online hackers to influence the way we think and indeed vote. The 2016 United States election has been widely described as an election determined by outside influences that understood the power of the image and it's use through social

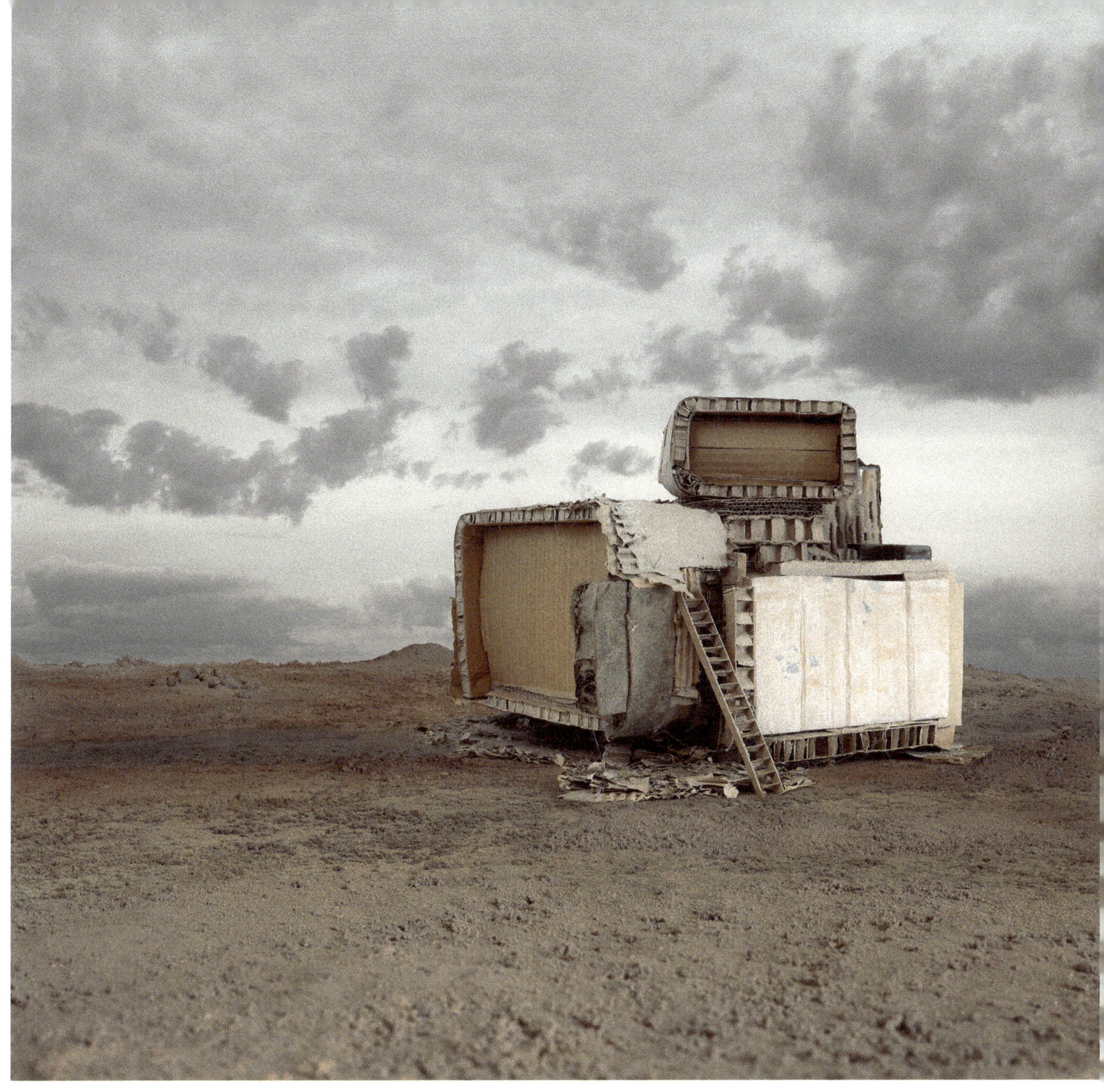

media to manipulate a result that was in their best interests. When we consider the election some interesting outcomes have been noted that relate to the influence of the relatively new social media platforms that rely on the instantaneous power of the image cycle. The *Pew Research Centre* found that 42% of voters in the election accessed their news exclusively through social media. Ed Carr, a liberal left commentator argued that it was the media of the cosmopolitan elite that drove a backlash form conservative voters to elect Donald Trump as the US President. Many of these voters felt disenfranchised with mainstream media sources believing that traditional news outlets had disregarded their negative experiences of immigration and globalization turning to Facebook as their news source. Carr believes that Facebook had created an "echo chamber" for its users and their views reinforcing their own opinions and beliefs and mobilizing what has become known as the #Right to vote in great numbers in support of Trump. "The more we click, like and share stuff that resonates with our own views the more Facebook feeds us with similar stuff" and here we see a contemporary example of the technology mediating an event through algorithms designed to promote capital wealth for the owners of these platforms. Trump's political advisors realised the power of these algorithms to galvanise his rhetoric while at the same time enhancing a distrust of mainstream media. This analysis is not intended to be overly deterministic in its consideration of the influence of technology on our experience and social/political development.

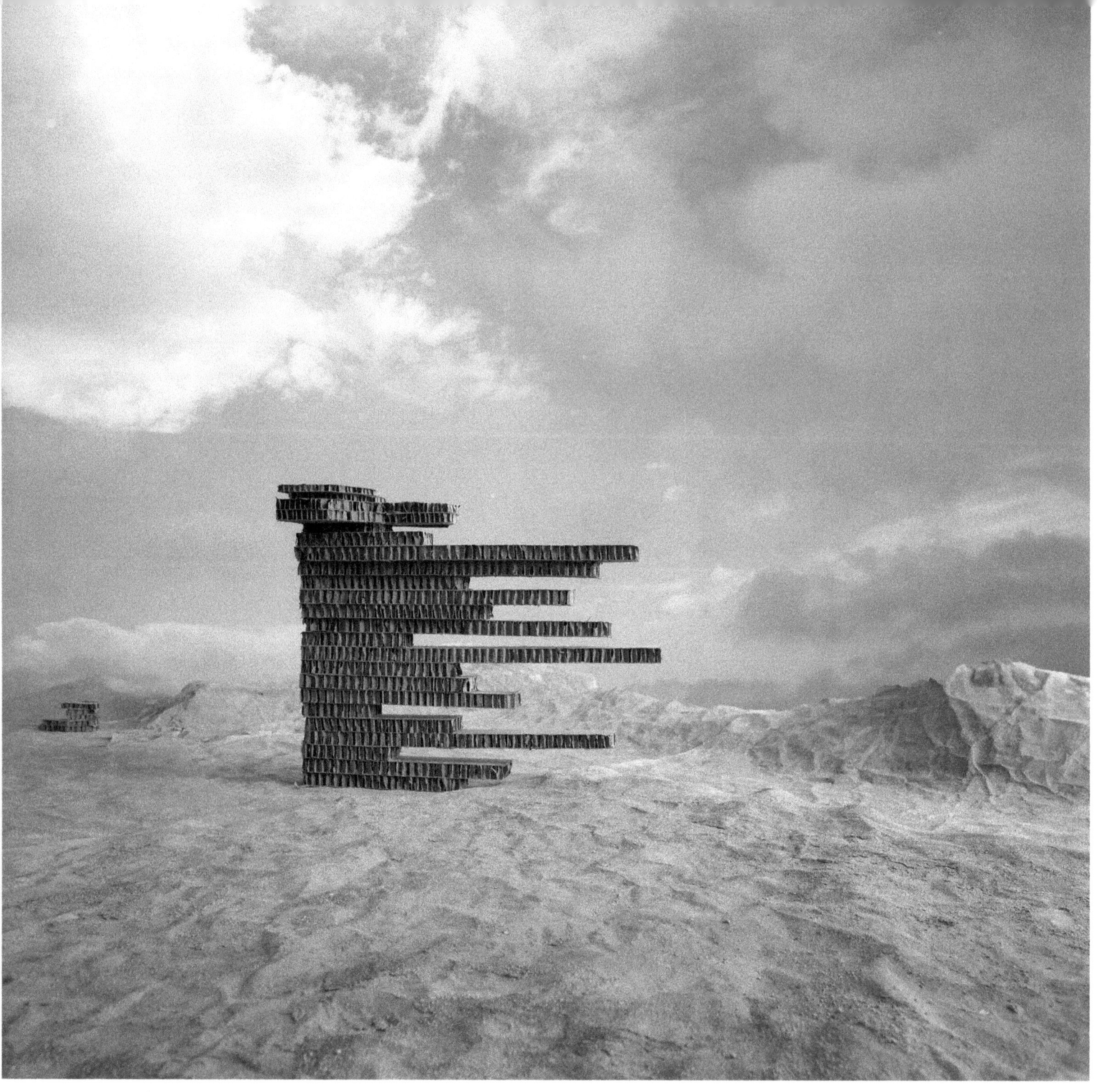

Suffice to say that technologies influence overlays what has gone on before, thus transforming and changing our experience of the world especially within the rapidly changing social and political contexts that are more and more influenced by the encroachment of technology.

Like Ballard, the French cultural theorist, urbanist and aesthetic philosopher Paul Virilio was also concerned with the influence of technology on the individual's psyche. Virilio's visual cultural framework and theory in works such as *Open Sky* (1997) and the *Aesthetics of Disappearance* (2009) place technologies, socialites and cultures as complex shapers and determinants of contemporary life. Virilio's work responded to the inherent speed and acceleration of technological development, which he argued, is coupled to the ongoing militarization of our society. He saw this speed as a type of physical, psychological and symbolic violence, something Ballard also alluded to in *The Atrocity Exhibition* where the accelerative nature of society acts to possess and control physical and psychological territory. It is not just imagery of violence that is important here yet it must be recognised within a much broader image saturation culture that exerts its own level of subjective violence. Both Ballard and Virilio argued that the televised image has become a form of weapon that is used to greatly influence our understanding of the world and that this perceptive field changes the development of societies and their conflicts.

The invention and development of the photographic

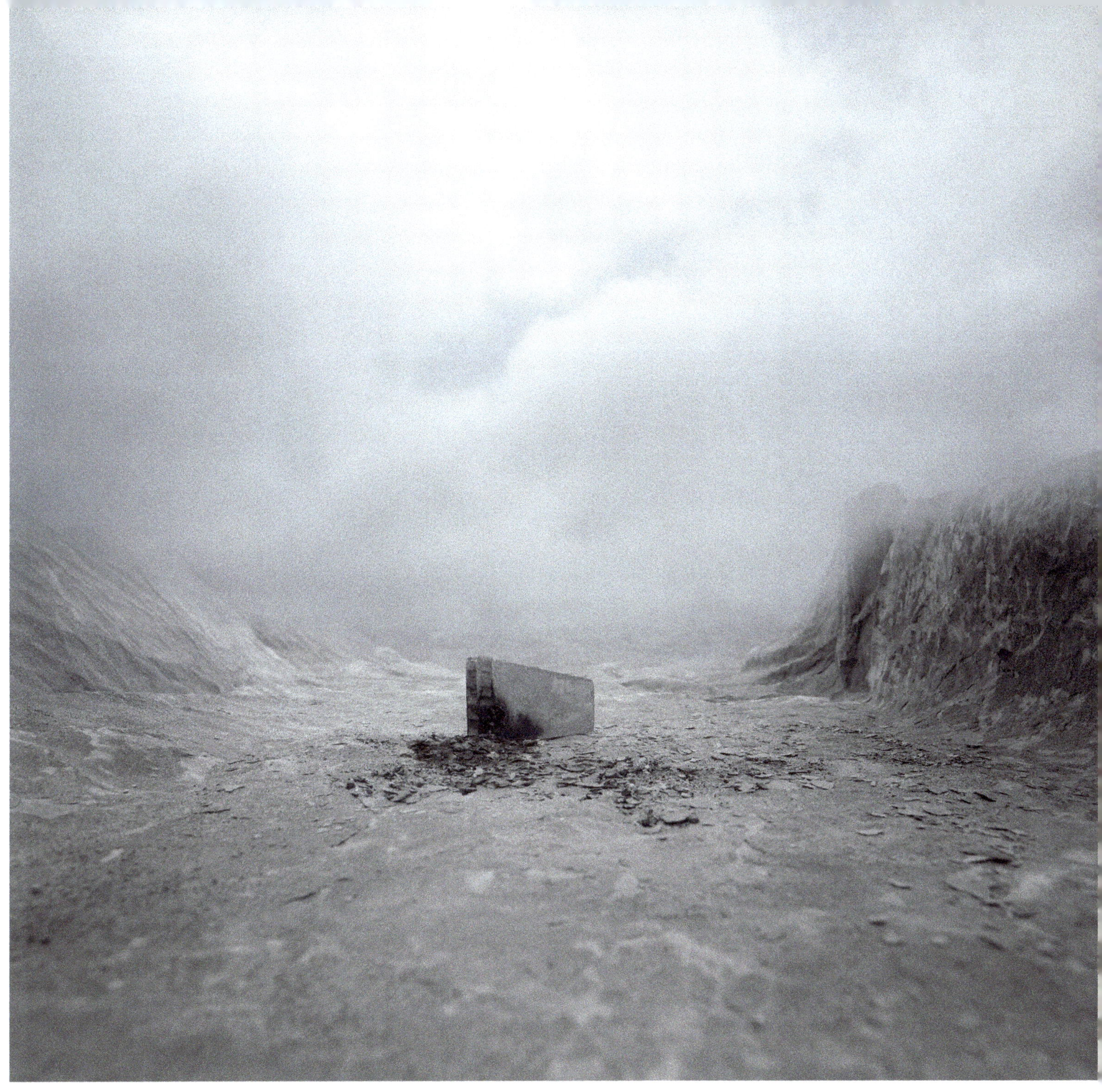

medium brought into question traditional notions of temporality with the image acting as a portal to the past while also reminding us of our own inevitable death. In short, the image influences the way in which we perceive time. Such disruptive influences could be considered in a number of ways from the benign all the way through to a form of cultural malignancy that permeates every part of our lives or perhaps more realistically something in between. Here however there must be some acceptance that such technology does have an impact on our lives and our interaction with the world. Within a contemporary context, and when we consider in particular the coupling of computer technology and the saturating nature and omnipresence of the image one could argue that pre-photography Western perceptions of time moving in a linear way like the ticking of a clock or the trajectory of an arrow have been altered and this shift in the perceptive field has ramifications on our social and political adaptation now heavily influenced by those in control of the image. A word of caution here: I am not suggesting that space and time have been altered through the influence of these technologies, but rather they have overlayed a contemporary experience of time on top of the more traditional notions of time mentioned earlier. The new communication technologies are not replacing traditional temporalities, but rather producing new definitions of our experience of time built over more traditional notions of temporality. As Morley attests "it is rather a question of how physical and symbolic networks become entwined around each other."

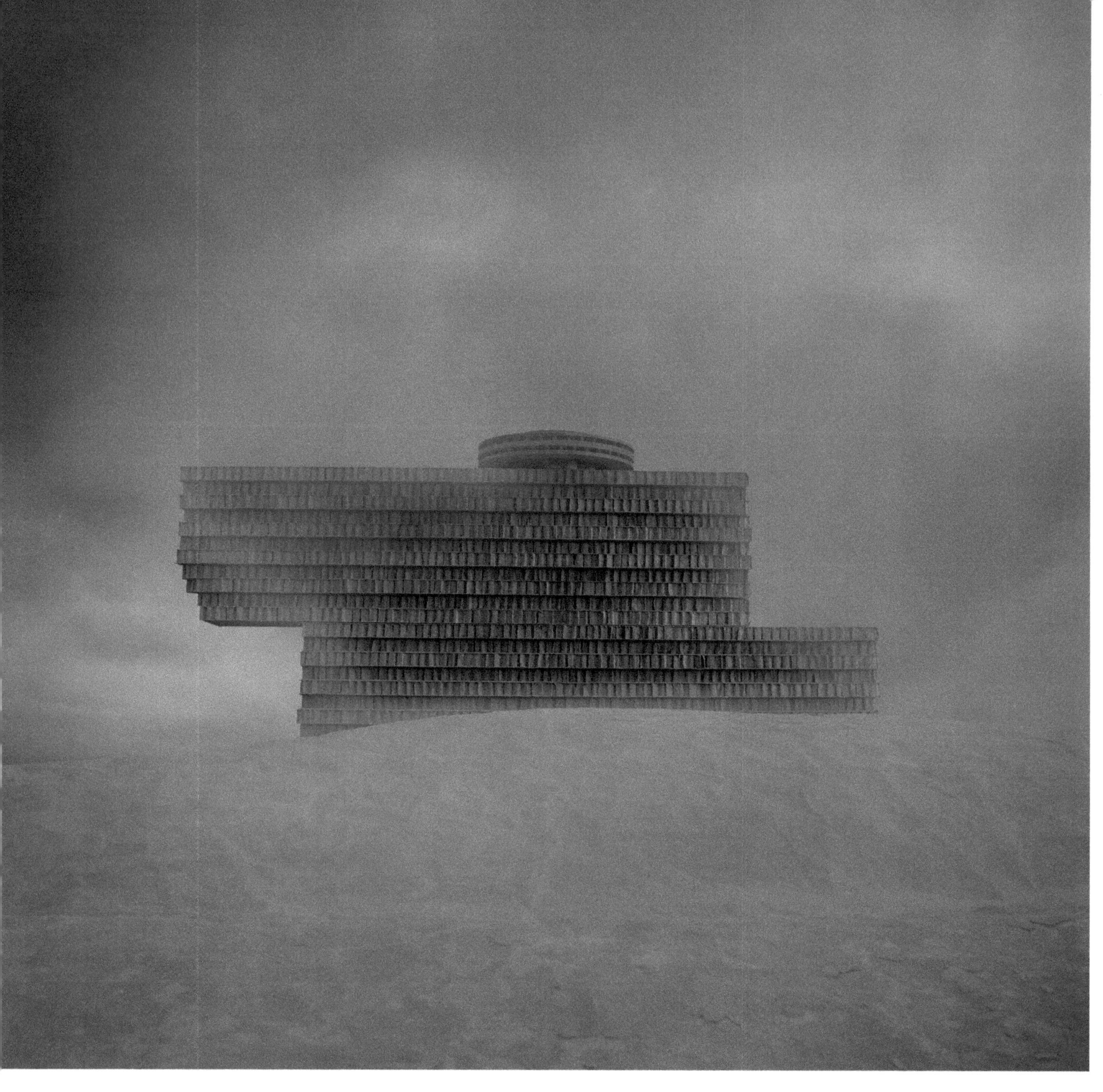

Virilio described this temporal dissonance or disruption as 'picnolepsy,' a form of altered consciousness experienced through a state of speed and characterized by the fragmentation and deconstruction of narrative time into 'snippets' and gaps. Indeed, when we consider the influence of the mediated image on the trajectory of societies, cultures and the psychology of the individual there was one event that encapsulated the extraordinary power of the image and its disruptive capacity. In *Photography and September 11th Spectacle, Memory, Trauma* (2015) Jennifer Good links Virilio's theory of pincolepsy to the terrorist attacks on New York in September 2001 and uses it to make sense of how people described their experience of events that day. Many of those who witnessed the attacks described feelings of de-realization and a fragmentation of time as they saw the towers collapsing, 'it was as if they were watching a movie.' Virilio described experiences of intense exposure to media imagery as "chronoscopic" in nature an instantaneous moment where the perception of time is skewed and the normal narrative arc of daily life is disrupted. Like Ballard he argued that this experience is an essentially violent event, not necessarily because of the imagery depicted (although this obviously played a huge role in the attacks), but rather by the way in which the imagery is delivered and how it is consumed. Here the distinction between form and content becomes important. There is a subjective violence inherent within the technologies that can be attributed to its speed and intensity. Violence in this context relates to the central argument that the pervasive intensity of digital image speeds and the disruption unleashed interferes with the processing of narrative memory creating distortions in our perception of time. 'The process of speed is nothing more than the unleashing of violence."

Within this instantaneous time exposure arises the perception of events *as they happen*. This exposure can occur at any given moment and be consumed through a multiple platforms that disrupt the chronological succession of time and the processing of narrative memory. This experience is immediate and reaches us at light speed, terminal velocity. Virilio linked this exposure to the photographic process that halts and isolates a moment. "Time is no longer the same as time passing, but essentially a kind of time that gets exposed." he referred to this as chronosophic time, a shift to the instantaneous moment of a rupture in chronological time, which he argued is in and of itself a violent act. Good uses a similar line of conjecture and argues that Virilio's photographic analogy goes beyond that of a simple metaphor to articulate the violence of modernity, especially when we consider the psychological implications of this chronoscopic exposure to real time events. "There is a simultaneous eruption of light, instant and object, and instantaneous photographic exposure that, translates into the spectators experience of the image at any point in future time we may view as an "eternal presence." Virilio went so far as to describe this "dromospheric pollution" as the death of geography where the territorial body is lost along with the social and animal body through the instantaneity of a tele-presence that collapses geographical distance. The televised image creates urgency, a present time that encapsulates the viewer, disrupting temporal perspective, accelerating the televised image, its speed and inherently violent nature. The physical horizon is diminished along with the depth of field of physicality, until the real space of geography is represented only through the televised process.

Virilio argued that the nature of tele-presence, video, film, image, virtual reality, alter our ability to create and store memories. It's the "splitting of time into slices" that he was interested in, the invasive nature of telecommunication, something that limits what we can actually retain and store memory that has evolved through the need to create a temporal context from narrative memory. He argued that imaging technologies interrupt the mapping of this narrative context. Pursuing this idea further, and within the context of a traumatic event as opposed to say a casual event like a conversation in the park where we tend to remember an aspect of the conversation rather than the vivid details of the park and it's surroundings, victims of trauma will often describe in great detail the context of an event and report an experience of time being

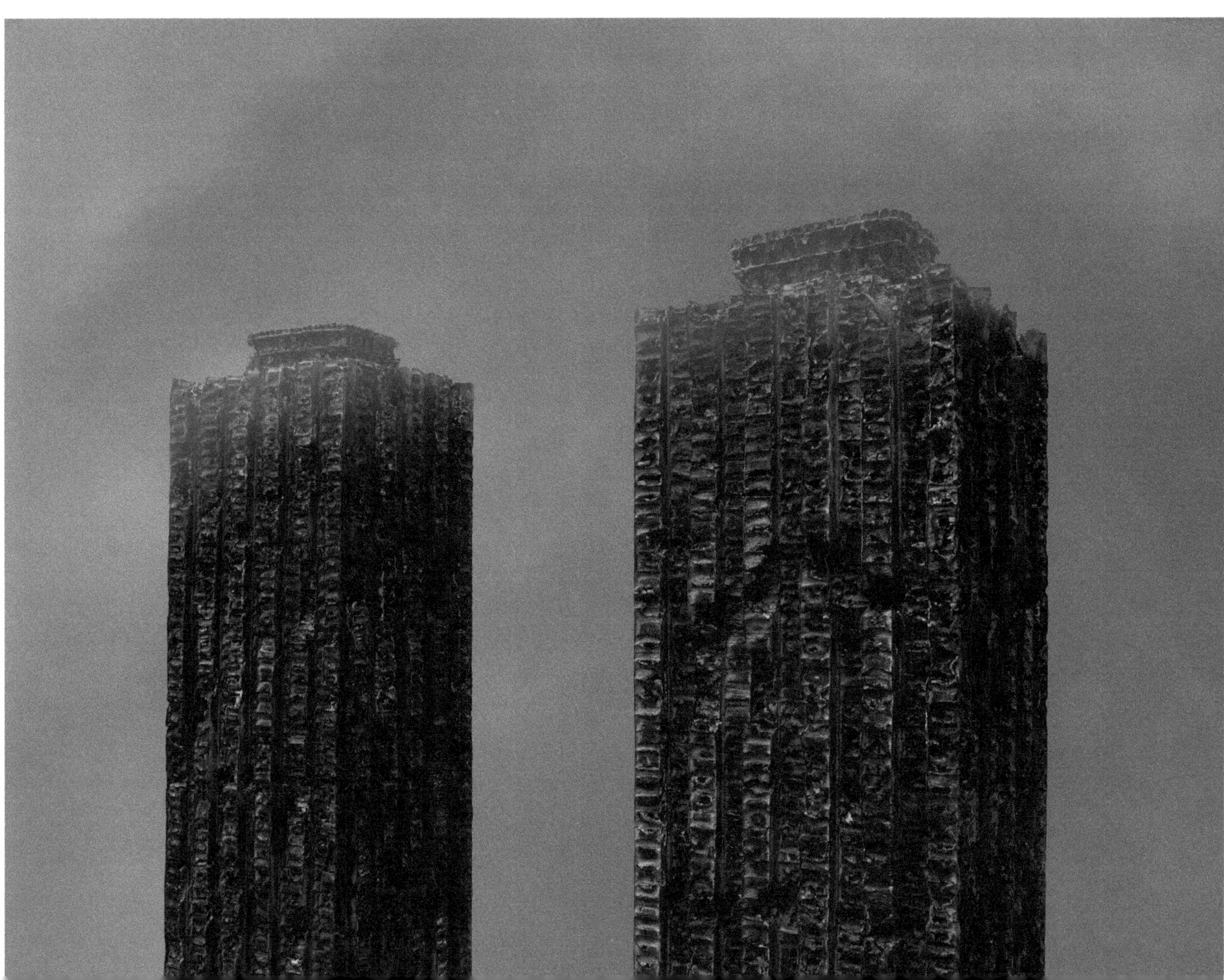

altered in some way. Something akin to an "extreme temporal focus" where details of the accident become overwhelming as there is too much information for the brain to process. In a study of novice skydivers Leah A. Cambell and Richard A. Bryant 2006 investigated how perceptions of time may alter in the lead up to and during a skydive. Increased levels of fear were associated with reports of time distortion where a significant number of skydivers reported increase in subjective time prior to a jump. This was consistent with predictions that time estimation is influenced by how much a situation is "strenuously anticipated." It is common for people to report in stressful situations that time seemed to slow or stand still in the lead up to and during an event and then report that time went very quickly after an event. There is a deluge of intense information where generally only fragments are remembered and the usual, orderly process of narrative memory is disrupted.

What are the implications of this on the psychological processing of information? Michele Bedard-Gilligan and Lori A. Zoellner 2012 consider Bessel van der Kolk's theory that an overload of information can lead to a form of dissociation during an event that may disrupt the coding and storage of memory and may manifest later as Post Traumatic Stress Disorder. " Fragmentation is thought to result from a lack of elaboration of the memory due to high emotion and dissociation during the traumatic experience." They argue that van der Kolk's theory is compelling and forms the foundations of our understanding of the development of this disorder and its impact on memory. In particular this theory specifically relates to a neurological model of memory encoding in the context of stressful events that trigger the release of high levels of cortisol that is thought to contribute to dysfunction in the hippocampus. I am linking Ballard's and Virilio's notions of the temporal disturbances associated with image speed and acceleration in order to outline a contemporary understanding of time in an era of a 'continuous tele-presence and virtuality' where the pervasive nature of imagery promotes its own traumatic imprint. Here, time unfolds within a non-narrative of abrupt snippets and interruptions delivered through an exposure of events at the speed of light through a variety of visual platforms.

Good points out that Virilio deliberately linked this exposure to the process of photography a comparison also used by Ulrich Bear in *Spectral Evidence: The Photography of Trauma* (2005). Both have argued that the brain operates in a similar way to the shutter mechanism of a camera during the arresting moment of a traumatic experience. Judy Wajcman concurs and notes the paradox of information speed and accessibility in *Pressed for Time: The Acceleration of Life in Digital Capitalism* (2015) where an overload of stimulus fractures and disrupts our temporal perception creating a situation where we can only take advantage of small instances or slices of the information presented to us. Wajcman argues that this has the effect of 'annihilating' our experience of real-time by interfering with the process and development of narrative memory to the point where viewers 'lose themselves in the eternity of electronically networked information. ' All three theorists describe the disruptive capacity of image speeds within a temporal context that may create its own traumatic imprint. Dosing of stressful events over an extended period of time is often initially characterized by desensitization: we become numb to the stimulus and this is partly to do with the brain's coping strategies for processing high levels of stressful information. Indeed, people who work in jobs that entail repetitive exposure to trauma, such as nurses, paramedics and doctors, report that they tend to block out stressful events however the cumulative effects of work related stress in many of these settings tends to build up over time. The re-dosing of trauma accumulates until a threshold is reached, at which point PTSD may develop.

When we consider the influence of the image on the matrix of societies, cultures and the psychology of the individual the 9/11 terrorist attacks on New York and demonstrate its extraordinary power and it's enduring effect on the world. Good describes an interesting lack of theorizing in relation to the 'collective power' of the imagery captured during and after the attacks and cites some key works by theorists and image thinkers, such as Maryann Hersch's essay *I took Pictures: September 2001 and Beyond* as well as an essay by Richard Drew titled *Falling Man: a Photograph by Andrea Fitzpatrick and Rob and Rob Kroes* as well as E. Ann Caplin discussion in *A Camera and a Catastrophe.* She argues that given the magnitude of the event and the way the public consumed it there is a definite lack of critical analysis of the event within the context of photography. Other theoretical studies of the event explore in great depth the subject of 9/11, but Good argues that in the case of photography's impact and its implications on those who witnessed the event there are only limited accounts of its collective impact and this is surprising given the scale of the event and mass consumption in a media sense. In light of this Good rightly asks "what are these pictures doing to us?"

Good argues that many of the writers concerned with the discussion of photography and the terrorist attacks failed to address a framework that considered the visual intensity of media surrounding the event and its effect on an individual and cultural level. She outlines within the broader 9/11 discourses how much of the debate was concerned with how these images are bound up with issues that relate to the witnessing of trauma and the implications this may have on memory and grief. She asserts that many of these attempts neglect the totality of photography that was generated and the effect this glut of imagery had on those who consumed it: 'They cannot within their remits relate it fully to an extended political critique of the dominant readings or ideological mobilizations of September 11th photography as a body, *En masse*." She believes that part of this problem lies in the fact that these images are caught up in a variety of social and political genres to do with journalism, politics, history and cyber culture. Each may account for an element of the effect of such imagery and its pervasiveness but to date there has been little conjecture into the cultural immersion of the media surrounding the attacks and its initial and ongoing impact. Perhaps there has been a type of shyness of scholarly writing away from the collective influence these images may have and this may well be another appropriate framework in which to consider the event within the context of photography?

Image and text have always had a strong relationship; indeed Walter Benjamin's visions of the future of the photographic image were concerned with this relationship. In *The Work of Art in the Age of Its Technological Reproduction* (1935) Walter Benjamin argued that photographs would become ever more dependent on the use of text as the essential aspect or component of the image as a photograph and text combined presents a more compelling case for its authenticity. Benjamin was concerned with this notion of "authentication" and implicit in this

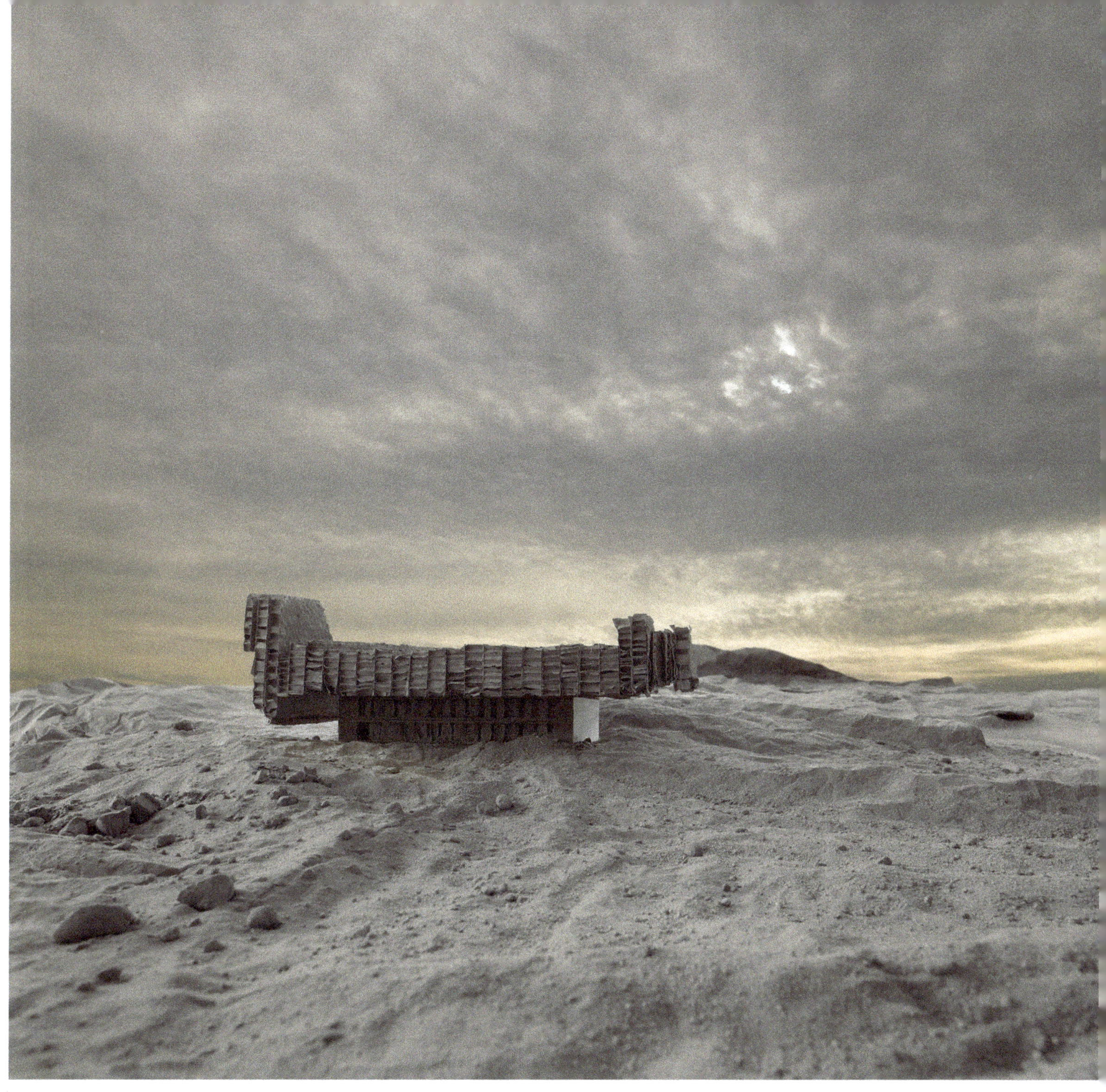

understanding of the image was the expanded interpretation of photography and the exploitative properties and capabilities that are available to the caption maker. The 9/11 terrorist attacks were extraordinary and unprecedented in a media sense as they were televised live to a captive audience before an explanation could be given as to what was actually occurring in New York and Washington on the day. Prior to these attacks televised events invariably had a back-story, or at any rate the audience had some understanding at least of what the images were depicting. By contrast, the vision of a passenger plane striking the North Tower of the World Trade Centre was unique not only because of the sheer scale of the spectacle but also because the imagery initially lacked any credible explanation. It would be appropriate here to recognize the grief and trauma experienced by those who were directly affected by the terrorist attacks and I acknowledge that any attempt to theorise such an event may in some way diminish the trauma and difficulties of those who were directly caught up in the tragedy. That said, when we think about the impact that photography had on the day within the context of image and trauma and its implications within media culture, the terrorist attacks become entirely compelling, as the imagery remains a contemporary spectacle without equal. The attacks and subsequent media broadcasts were unique not only because of the acts themselves but also because of the way they were witnessed as an unparallel spectacle initially without censorship and indeed description of what was transpiring, a dosing and re-dosing of trauma delivered into our living rooms on a continuous visual loop.

What is the impact of image speeds and acceleration experientially on the psychology of the individual? Is the experience of time distortion that Ballard and Virilio consider a response to the violence associated with the pervasive intensity of media imagery? Perhaps the implication here is that the violent nature of digital image culture and indeed modernity itself, its speed and acceleration, creates its own form of trauma at the level of psyche that promotes a new experience of time, a shift from chronological time to chronoscopic time, a time of the instantaneous. Coupled to this speed and intensity is the way in which the image is consumed through the relentless twenty-four hour media cycle. Ballard described similar disturbances through his characters as a response to our complex interaction with technology that shapes and determines our experience. This response was described by Ballard as "the death of affect"; namely, an inability to feel and respond to the accelerative nature and violence of the information we are exposed to - there is just too much to deal with so the brain shuts down. Perhaps what Ballard was alluding to is a symptom of traumatic stress?

Here I would like to link Zigmunt Bauman's work *Modernity and Ambivalence* (1991) to the above ideas as it may help to create a framework around the an argument that implicates the disruptive capacity of the technologies. Bauman's work describes the experience of modern ambivalence as the discomfort we feel when we are unable to designate order or classification in a world of chaos. The human desire to create order and classification has been seen by many as the driving force of contemporary, technologically orientated societies. Take, for example, the development of computing system. As one set of problems are solved by the new technologies another level of complexity and problems arise creating a feedback loop where the need to assign order paradoxically creates even more chaos and disorder. Bauman describes this as a fundamentally conflicted process. Virilio refers to a similar ambivalence within the context of technology and what he describes as the inherent accident that resides within technological development. Works such as *Museum of Accidents* (1999) and *Speed and Politics* (1977) consider how technology is imbued with unforseen problems that come to the fore once the technological system becomes integrated into society. Every technology carries its own latent negativity. The notion is closely aligned with Bauman's theory as to the ambivalence of modernity. Both ideas point to the fact that when we develop a new technology we also unwittingly create the flaws and mishaps that plague its functioning. An example of this could be drawn from the Challenger Space Shuttle disaster an event that could be used here as anexample of the original 'accident' of the machine: "When you invent the ship you also invent the shipwreck." In *Speed and Violence: Sacrifice in Virilio, Derrida, and Girard* (2001) Mark Featherstone discusses Virilio's accident theory within this context and argues that the pace and development of technology becomes limited through any fault in the technology that the accident may disclose. Here we see the dynamic interplay between the ways in which technology leads to ever increasing complexity that in turn creates subsequent complex faults that need to be addressed once they are revealed. This in turn creates a reliance on the continual reinvention of systems designed to re-instigate order within a neo-liberal market economy that relies on constant replacement of technological systems. These systems inevitably fail at varying levels, which promote the development of new technologies to deal with these failures—something that Bauman considers as a by-product of modernity.

The new media technologies such as mobile devices, computers and virtual reality continue to influence our understanding of experience the world through the creation of new spaces that are heavily influenced by the image. As a result we have developed new ways to conceptualise the idea of community through contemporary constructs of networks that go beyond physical localities and are arguably made up of increasingly distant and fragmented relationships developed in the new cyber-space frontiers. These networks are patched together to form a sense of personal community. More and more we are living in a time of "immanent connectedness" where we maintain a "symbolic proximity" with each other through our mobile devices and computers (Morley, David. *Home Territories Media, Mobility and Identity*, Routledge, London, 2000: pp179) and according to Morley this instant tele-presence not only skews our perception of time but also changes what he describes as our "alterity" (ibid: pp178), or a sense of "otherness" in relation to our spatial and temporal frameworks of the world. Given this new connectivity and its psychological influence we now find that the technology and our ever-increasing reliance on it promote a state of constant availability as communication agents. The contemporary experience of this "alterity" changes our understanding of physical connectedness that has an equal and opposite effect of diminishing its importance. The immediacy of a world that was previously inaccessible becomes more tangible within the context of information gathering as any event, regardless of geographical locality, can be communicated within a connected world and thus in principle experienced immediately.

What are some of the concerns in regards to the new imaging technology's influence on temporal perception and is there a link between these concerns and the experience of trauma? *The Atrocity Exhibition* suggests that the revolution in the transmission of imagery and the development of visual technologies radically changed the urban environment to the extent that there is a "commutation" with the image, a state where its importance surpasses the importance of the actual object or the event it captures. "The image prevails over the thing it is an image of." Slowly, over time, our perception of the city is fragmented and becomes a "paradoxical conglomeration" where the relationships of intimacy and locality are replaced by interrelationships characterised by remoteness and transmission. Here we experience the urbanisation of real time and a culture of paradox, we can arrive at a destination without the physical need to leave through the conduit of technological systems, interval gives way to interface: there is no journey or time lag inside and out no longer have importance, there is no before and after but only the tele-presence of real time.

One recent incident that brings into sharp focus the links between violence, trauma and the speed of the image within a contemporary societal context was the Christchurch Mosque massacres which occurred in New Zealand on the 15th March 2019. There was an obvious physical violence attached to the massacre that wrought such a devastating impact on the victims and families yet in the aftermath of the event much of the public condemnation centred on how social media was implicated in the killings. The event was a compelling reminder of the latent violence of technology and how its imaging possibilities were integral to the terrorist's aims and objectives. As Kevin Roose headlined his *New York Times* article the killings were, "A Mass Murder of, and for the Internet." Much of the outrage was concerned with the way in which the gunman announced his intentions before the attacks to an audience and then live streamed the images of his murderous rampage on Facebook that was then shared across a variety of platforms.

Condemnation of social media after the killings also considered the way in which such media platforms incite extremist beliefs by algorithms designed to encourage their proliferation through likes and recommendations towards more "edgier" content. Roose describes this as a deliberate "loop" that encourages more time spent on the platform and therefore more exposure to advertising that generates revenue for the company. The Christchurch terrorist understood that such technology would amplify the horrific detail of the atrocity through our engagement with it as a society on mass. This was evidenced by the way in which politicians and commentators broadly condemned Facebook, YouTube and Twitter for the role they played in the massacres. One might argue that the imaging capabilities of these platforms and their mass appeal and distribution capabilities encouraged the crime. There is a subjective violence attached to these sites, which have up until now existed without regulation. More broadly the event exposed the latent violence of such technological systems crystallising their agonisingly negative impacts something that must be now be recognised and considered.

Reading this essay one might ask how my visual practice relates to what has been described above as the violence of modernity. The work attempts to link this violence, i.e. the disruptive capacity of technology and its inherent traumatic imprint, to temporal disturbances in the rhythm of our lives as something commensurate with the experience of trauma through a visual practice methodology that combines the construction of models, dioramas and photography. A traumatic affect has been developed with particular consideration paid to the knowledge gap between theoretical analyses and the construction of images that link architecture with the coded violence of technological systems. The work is a clinical diagnosis of modernity that identifies the psychological impact of contemporary life and its traumatic imprint. I have often meditated on the power of architecture to disrupt the accelerating pace of modernity through construction and design. Consider architecture such as Peter Zumpthor's Bruder *Klaus Chapel* (2007) in Mechernich, Eifel, in Germany for example. Such structures have the capacity to offer a counterpoint or pocket of resistance to the accelerating trajectory of contemporary life. This architecture of slipstream is not intended to alter or even change the progress of technological systems. It does however attempt to offer a momentary immersion in an unconnected temporal experience, an eddy or backwash in the torrent of modernity.

References:

Books

Armitage, John. *Virilio and Visual Culture*, Edinburgh University Press, 2013

Ballard, J.G. *The Atrocity Exhibition*, Jonathan Cape, 1970

Benjamin, Walter. *Little History of Photography, The Work of Art in the Age of Its Technological Reproduction and Other Writings on Media*, trans. Edmund Jephcott et al. Harvard University Press, 2008

Crosthwaite, Paul. "A Secret Code of Pain and Memory": *War Trauma and Narrative Organisation in the Fiction of J.G. Ballard*, University of Newcastle upon Tyne, UK, 2005

Featherstone, Mark. *Speed and Violence, Derida, and Girard*, Anthropoetics 6, no. 2, 2001

Good, Jennifer. *Photography and September 11th. Spectacle, Memory, Trauma*, 2015

Mirzeoff. Niholas. *An Introduction to Visual Culture* 1999

Morley, David. *Home Territories Media, Mobility and Identity*, Routledge, London, 2000

Virilio, Paul. *The Aesthetics of Disappearance*, Semiotext(E), Paris, 2009

Virilio, Paul. *Speed and Politics*, Semiotext (e), 2006

Virilio, Paul. *Open Sky*. Verso, 1997

Virilio, Paul. *Politics of the Very Worst*, Semiotext(e), 1999

Wajcman, Judy. *Pressed for Time: The Acceleration of Life in Digital Capitalism*. The University of Chicago Press, 2015

Zygmunt, Bauman. *Modernity and Ambivalence*, Polity Press, 1991

Journals

Michele Bedard-Gilligan and Lori A. Zoellner, 'Dissociation and Memory Fragmentation in Post Traumatic Stress Disorder: An Evaluation of the Dissociative Encoding Hypothesis', *Memory*, 2012; 20(3): 277 - 299

Leah A. Cambell, Richard A. Bryant. 'How time flies: A study of novice skydivers', *Behaviour Research and Therapy*, School of Psychology, The University of New South Wales, 2006

Fiona Cocker, Nerida Joss. 'Compassion Fatigue among Healthcare, Emergency and Community Service Workers: A Systemic View', *International Journal of Environmental Research*, June, 2016 v.13 (6)

Iranmanesh, Sedigheh. 'Tirgari, Batool. Bardsiri, Hojat Sheikh. Post-traumatic stress disorder among paramedic and hospital emergency personal in south-east Iran', *World Journal of Emergency Medicine*, 2013; 4(1): 26-31

Internet

Roose, Kevin. 'A Mass Murder of, and for the Internet, The Shift', *The New York Times*, March 15th 2019 https://www.nytimes.com/2019/03/15/technology/facebook-youtube-christchurch-shooting.html

Radio

Facebook, *4 Courners*, The Australian Broadcasting Commission, 11th April, 2017

Carr, Ed. *Saturday Extra*, Radio National, The Australian Broadcasting Commission, November, 2016

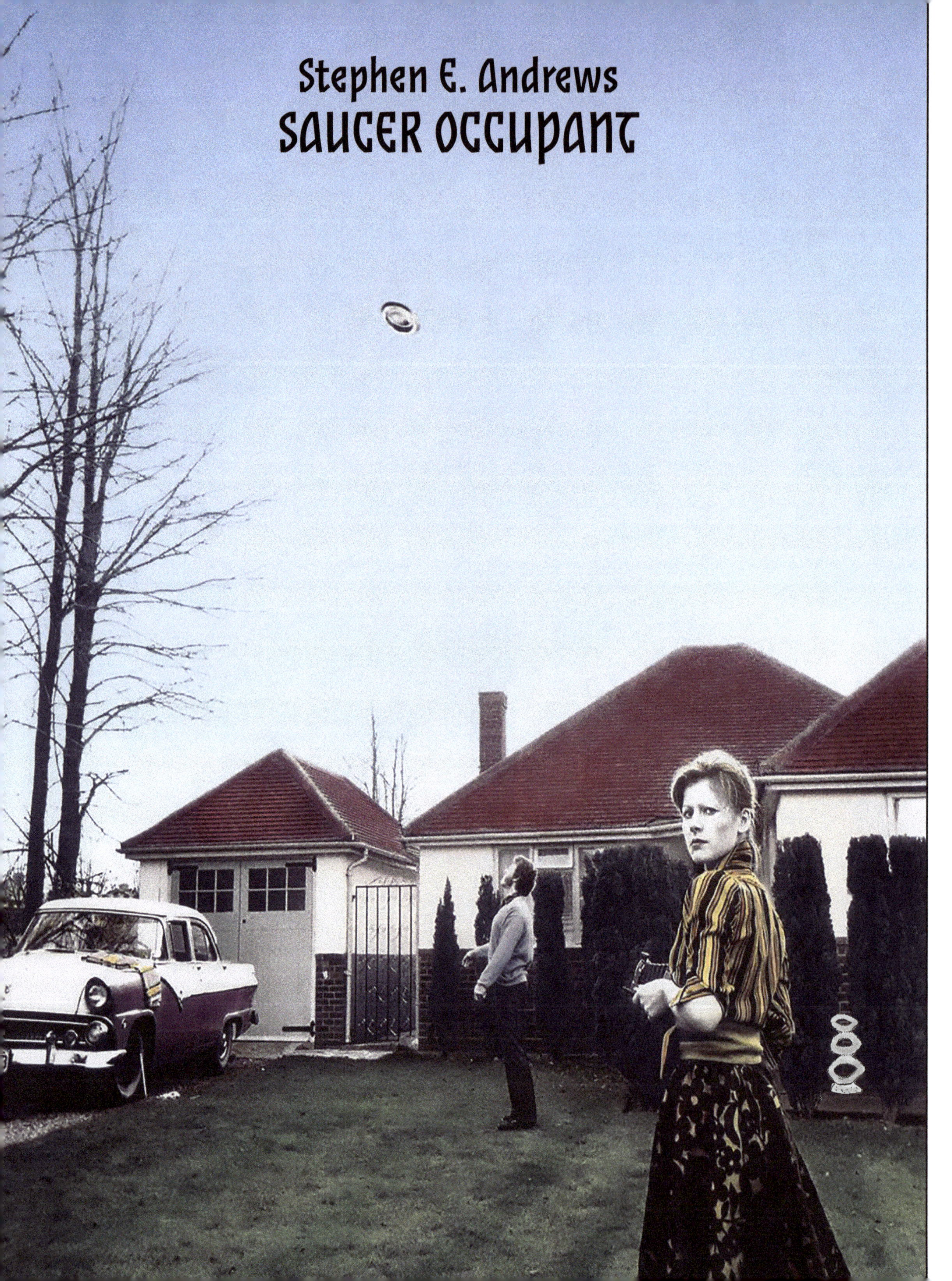
Stephen E. Andrews
SAUCER OCCUPANT

Long before I visited New Mexico, I'd realised I was long predisposed toward experiencing a Close Encounter of the Third Kind. I don't mean in terms of genetic destiny or as a result of an hormonal wash that laved over my foetus during intrauterine development, but from the nurturing influences that overtook my psychic development during late infancy. I was a child of the atom, after all, conceived during the Cuban Missile Crisis, born in the anno of The Beatles' twee seven inch success, contextualized by the hair-in-the-gate view from the grassy knoll in Dealey Plaza and x-rayed by early monochrome episodes of the drearily gothic *Doctor Who.*

The anti-nuclear flying saucer forebodings of *The Day the Earth Stood Still* and *It Came From Outer Space* seemed long in the past and ingrained in collective memory by the time I began attending school, their fifties prophecies now merely a single strand of the multi-lane Cold War consciousness I was growing up with. Consequently, I simply knew that someday the reality of extraterrestrial life would present itself to me unadulterated. This was my personal Zeroeth Law, a near-minus kind of Close Encounter that in sacred anticipation promised of meeting something from beyond. This aspect of my identity was eventually confirmed decades later in a loop I closed through my relationship with my childhood friend Casey Bowers.

So it was no wonder to me that Simon Marchant and I sighted several inscrutable silver shapes in the cyan skies above Socorro, close to the disputed Aztec crash location and around the fabled Manhattan Project development sites that were theorised to have drawn extraterrestrial interest to the State known as the Land of Enchantment in the first place. We were outsiders, our Englishness marking us as other as the mysterious pilots of the ships we'd initially clocked while paying our homage to that most venerable of witnesses, Lonnie Zamora, the super-credible cop who in April 1964 had beheld a landed UFO take off west of Route 85 after breaking off from a humdrum speeder chase in his new Pontiac black-and-white. Craft of the same type had been waiting for people like us for years, the locals having become blasé about extrasolar life decades before, most cynically seeing only the retail and museum opportunities of the Roswell legend.

I couldn't censure them. It must have been a good living, after all, the selling of cosmic dreams. I managed to avoid purchasing the t-shirts and ubiquitous inflatables of Greys bulging in helium-filled dayglo rubberised foil that resembled the material found by the USAF when recovering—as *if*—wrecked weather balloons. The action figures of the Flatwoods Monster and Cisco Grove Robot were must-buys, however. I bought spares as future ebay investments and kept these MOC (Mint on Card), still sealed. Their clones would stalk the shelves where my collection of vintage Ace Doubles resided in my home office. As we drove off from Roswell, I noticed a hubcap lying in the gutter of the dusty road. I pointed it out to Simon. "Could this be... a SPACESHIP?" he barked theatrically.

On his first trip home to England after relocating to the States, we met for a drink. "You'll love it, Andy... it's like being on fucking Mars, it's so weird..." After making me an open invitation to visit, we'd Skyped infrequently, but once I was able to raise the air fare and set a date, we were in touch weekly. I'd been re-reading the relevant material and our exchanges were becoming more intense and obsessive.

"You know the theory that the Flying Saucer wave of 1947 drew on SF imagery is incorrect, don't you? The saucers of McCarthy-era feature films are sourced from the sightings of civilians and military figures, not from pulp magazines.... though the term 'occupant' in reference to the denizen of a alien spaceship first occurs in Harry Bates' 'Farewell to the Master' in an issue of *Amazing* from 1940."

Simon shook his head a little. "No, I've never read the Bates original, but I've seen the movie, of course. I've always loved the timbre of that bloody Theremin.... I bought the soundtrack CD the other day, funnily enough."

I was foaming with anticipation. "Contactee accounts remind me of Beat verse, the serenity of the banal echoing in pronouncements of the benign peacefulness and boundless wisdom of the star people. The *terminology* of the whole thing really gets to me. It's so Romantic"

"With an upper-case R?"

"Naturally. Terms like *Crashed Disk, Saucer Occupants* and sentence prefixes such as *Recent reports* possess a unique poetry all of their own.... the language of these researchers and authors is so enticingly apocalyptic in its lyricism. Have you seen that Adam Roberts *Ted Talk* where he conflates Science Fiction with Poetry? He's right, of course, because he's interpreting the old fandom cliché about the 'Sense of Wonder' as what it's always been, the Sublime.... but the lexicography of UFOlogy is even more intoxicating in its mystifying eloquence than the most muscular, iconic Scifi tropes." I waffled on, almost laughing. "Even the acronyms of the research organizations are magical: *MUFON, APRO, NICAP...*"

"I know." Simon nodded. He raised a coffee mug into the frame of his webcam. "These people are writing our new beatitudes, even if their research organizations sound like duck-and-cover epoch breakfast cereals."

"Hot damn."

Objectively, I was as sceptical as the next man when it came to physical evidence. You were never going to get to handle the balsa-like I-beams that Jesse Marcel had spoken of, never going to find an exoplanet-engineered implant at the base of your spine and have an obscure physician prize it out under a strong local for testing in some fringe laboratory. As far as I was concerned, any actual concrete proof the average human being could ever expect to handle of alien visitation to Earth was in the paper trails uncovered by professional researchers like Stanton Friedman who understood archival investigation. The narrative of credible evidence we could reasonably aspire to in order to confirm the extraterrestrial hypothesis as explanation for saucer sightings ran thus: Government agencies denied there was any 'UFO threat' in official letters and press releases, but FOIA requests sometimes resulted in the recovery of authentic documents that contradicted these nay-sayings. So while I wasn't taken in by alien autopsy videos on Youtube or a fourth generation rip of Adamski's glitchy cine film, I was impressed by the meticulous Occam's razor wielded by a few dogged individuals who were as otherwise as scrupulously unconvinced as I am. The truth may have been out there, but it was best confirmed as fact only by objective correlative data rather than questionable reports of subjective experience.

Patiently and kindly taking time out from work on his monograph interpreting of the works of Thomas M. Disch in a Lacanian context for Duke University Press in order to chauffeur me around the locations where Nic Roeg shot the opening scenes of *The Man Who Fell To Earth*, Simon was also good enough to indulge my Western fantasies by letting me play nothing but vintage lysergic country rock on his station wagon's stereo while we spanned hundreds of miles of ravishing desert highways. While touring alleged UFO crash sites we listened to *Flying Again* by the Burrito Brothers, *Gypsy Cowboy* by NRPS, *The Notorious Byrd Brothers* and the skin tight cowpat-kicking all-fill/no roll drumming of Eddie Bayers on Sweethearts of the Rodeo's stonewashed denim classic *One Time One Night.*

If it hadn't been so scalding hot, it would have been plaid shirt time, but I could only cope with (Don) Henley-neck tees in those arid climes. Simon's own tastes ran predominantly to pre-grunge US alt rock and original NYC punk, which was cool, but he could listen to that stuff anytime and understood that I needed my full-on existential catamount-eyed Leone visions to lock into while riding through the calcined sandy scrub where Joshua trees cast long shadows which I gazed into, eagerly scanning for ants mutated to gigantic proportions by the fallout from local atomic bomb testing. "Indulge me," I'd said. "As ever," he'd replied warmly, clapping me on the shoulder, his mirrorshades flashing like those of the Man With No Eyes from *Coolhand Luke.*

Squinting at the glint of southern sun on pearlescent silent flying machines in the midday heavens wasn't the confirmatory moment for either of us. Simon had previously spotted superluminal UFOs flitting from cloud to cloud instantaneously several times while driving to and from his work at the various academies and colleges around Albuquerque. He'd said nothing about these occurrences to me until after I noticed the gleaming hulls of swooping, curiously insignia-marked white metal ovals, haze shimmering around their gunmetal undercarriages as they seemed to bend and warp, their gravity-defying propulsion systems distorting the fabric of spacetime pliable around the rings of intermittently blazing ultramarine lights that studded their edges.

"Well?" He raised sandy eyebrows over those smiling china blue irises, mouth about to twist into a grin I always enjoyed beholding.

I nodded and turned away from him to stare back through the windshield but the spacecraft we'd seen had gone. "I always knew they were there," I said.

He nodded knowingly. "Of course you did. Your ideal of Americana has always been more about the illusions of Commander Cody and His Lost Planet Airmen than *Visions of Cody*." He took the wheel, put his foot on the pedal and we drove off to the strains of *Hot Licks, Cold Steel and Trucker's Favourites.*

We took photographs of the craft we witnessed, of course. But there's no point in alerting anyone or posting even 8K res pictures online these days as the internet and CGI have ruined the fun around everything Fortean from cryptozoology to dowsing. With contemporary tech you can pretty much fake anything, so nothing has any credibility anymore. Old photographs of people with their hands at their ears are corroboration of time travel, apparently, for these Anachronauts are on their cellphones, of course. Contemporary online gullibility means I'm not interested in any sightings of UFOs after around 1993. Only the authenticity of the petrified modern and the profanely ancient can be trusted, the veracity of Now being permanently broken by the ubiquity of the virtual in every sphere of human inquiry.

I'm uncertain which cultural artefact kickstarted my programming to believe, but it was probably something I saw on television. My parents always told me that as a very small boy I was transfixed by *Adam Adamant*, a TV show in which a man from Victorian England wearing an evening cape and brandishing a swordstick timeslipped into contemporary London. I have no conscious recollection of this programme. After watching each episode as rigid as a waterboard, I would apparently fashion a cloak from a tea towel, grab whatever was at hand that might resemble a cane and leap from the sofa like an over-sexed matinee idol.

However, no Proustian sensations were evoked by an episode of *Adamant* I saw in my forties. Yes, it was sci-fi, possibly the first such I'd encountered, but the scratchy black and white narrative left me distinctly cold. *20 Million Miles to Earth* remains the first SF movie I actually recall seeing and as such it's my favoured conscious starting point for an interest in alien lifeforms, an important part of my subconscious preparation for the psychopathology I would finally embrace completely.

The space race dominated the sixties. Kids like me collected PG Tips tea cards about comsats and Venus probes while my Russian counterparts were treated to galvanised biscuit tins and chocolate ration wrappers decorated with heraldic yet cuddly cosmonaut canines such as Laika, Strelka and Belka. Personally, I think those Soviet children came out on top: their Motherland had already won the ideological battle by launching Sputnik, getting Gargarin into orbit, then shooting premier spacewoman Valentina Tereshkova upside too in Vostok 6 a month after I was born—all the Americans could boast of were gantry fires, JFKs mysterious "other thing" and decades of Gordon Cooper's incomprehensible Oklahoma mumbling that later bedevilled decades of dodgy UFO documentaries on cable TV.

Fiction was converging with the space program too: leafing through my uncle's vinyl albums in mid 1968 I'd come across his gatefold original of the soundtrack of *2001: A Space Odyssey* and, moved to sticking it on the turntable because of the orbital wheel habitat and Bibendum-like bulging hardwear of the vacuum-suited dudes depicted on the cover, quickly got scared silly by the unearthly choral sonorities of Ligetti. So I really was *Beyond Apollo* by the time Armstrong took his giant leap and Bowie's novelty hit single about Major Tom. I was far more impressed by the fact that those hardcore Russkies' capsules came down on land rather than via splashdown at sea. No saltwater cooling for those toasted CCCP heat shields, parachute ejection being the only course of escape action for Ivan and his comrades. After discovering this fearless red touchdown strategy, I always considered NASA to be populated by pansies and lightweights.

The theory is that there's always been a demarcation line between SF fans and UFO enthusiasts. SF reference books routinely make this claim and it's undoubtedly true to a degree, but I while I know few students of unexplained aerial phenomena who are Skiffy nuts, significant numbers of Scifi readers of my generation are quite familiar with a lot of classic UFO literature. I have exceptionally vivid memories of sitting on a deck chair in the dahlia-lush front garden of our cottage, bare-chested in the blazing July sunshine of 1971, clutching my baby blue A format paperback of *Chariots of the Gods*?

Initially enraptured by Von Daniken's astonishing claims of alien intervention in human evolution, I was soon dismayed by the way he hamstrung himself with chapter headings like "The Sphere: the ideal shape for a spaceship" followed by thousands of words of text that bore no relation to their textual harbinger. Consequently, I flung my carnation pink copy of *Return to the Stars* into the dustbin for the Roogs to haul away with our other household trash, moving swiftly on to a second-hand, spine-broken copy of Frank Edward's *Flying Saucers: Here and Now* for my extraterrestrial jollies.

Years later, while in my more sceptical New Wave SF reading days, I still found Ballard's 'The Venus Hunters' to be gratifyingly dismissive of the assumptions that modern science fiction enthusiasts weren't prepared to accept representations of actual alien craft in the post-Campbell era. Ballard's story was ambiguous in its invocation of Jung's *Flying Saucers*, the text which debunked the phenomenon as dismissively as the claims of arch-sceptic Philip Klass, but I, like many other fans, secretly kept the arcane faith. Initially disposing of my first copy of Jung's theory, I later purchased the book again when Arkana briefly changed their livery from dark green to a sheeny navy blue. I struggle to take the Swiss psychoanalyst seriously as any kind of scientist, but I remain a sucker for well-designed wraps.

My girlfriend Bettany's theory was that I was bound to see a UFO while I was in America because of all the reading on the subject I'd done in the weeks prior to my trip. During a persistent cold I suffered in the spring before flying Stateside, she'd come over every couple of days to find me still prone beneath a duvet with a pile of trade paperbacks that bore the unmistakable high-gloss shine of print-on-demand publications on the floor beside the sofa. "Research," I told her. What she didn't know was that I was a veteran of the literature: underneath the bed where we'd first fucked as joylessly, grimly and energetically as an estranged couple in a Barry N. Malzberg novel was a Really Useful Box full of worn vintage books bearing titles like *Socorro Saucer* and *The Interrupted Journey*. These and others I'd read many times. All had been purchased new during the early seventies from revolving wire spinners that stood like sentinels of sensationalism in the corners of small newsagents and convenience stores that studded the villages and market towns of rural Britain in the afterglow of the post-austerity white heat of technology era.

Welcome oases of literacy in those days when actual bookshops were only to be found in cities, these rotating dispensers enlivened my world—through them I discovered the joys of Poe and Edgar Rice Burroughs and gradually expanded my miniature archive of Wells, Wyndham and Arthur C. Clarke. Glancing over the top of whatever paperback I was considering purchasing, I'd also goggle at the blatantly unconcealed displays of glossily tawdry men's magazines like *Mayfair, New Direction, Oui, Fiesta* and *Club International*, whose covers were graced with beckoning but inaccessible sirens, delights from beyond as unearthly as anything penned by A.E. Van Vogt.

Adjacent to those paperback spinners would invariably be sister wire racks holding a gallery of ladies' hosiery, openly inviting prepubescent curiosity into the seductive mysteries of pantyhose and stockings. The former were the very height of contemporary fashion, while the latter were almost extinct by that time, all complicated suspender studs and contrast welts, the exact morphology of both species of garment revealed blatantly on their packaging in photographs of trim women modelling them. Bosoms concealed by careful positioning of arms, the tawny lingerie Lorelei decorating the paper inserts of the packaging were habitually depicted naked apart from laminas of clingy American Tan micromesh. Architectural details of waistband and reinforced pantie normally concealed above the hemline were brazenly revealed in these advertising portraits, cladding nipped waists, sweeping hips and suspension-bridge thighs. To my hungry eyes, these leggy post-hippie temptresses were as honey-hued, curvaceously fulsome and entrancingly enigmatic as the voluptuous cleavages, frank gazes and knowing smiles of the leonine tarts that featured below the mastheads of the porno journals residing in their banal glass and teak retail unitary.

I remember that some brands of hose eschewed full-figure portraits of models altogether, substituting instead fetishistic close-up shots of enticing female buttocks encased in tights worn over full briefs, curving, planetary nates bisected by polyamide seams crinkled like the legendary canals of Mars. Depicting no faces, these stills emblematically objectified these parts of the body and the details of the man-made materials that enclosed them. The idea that these haunches and torsos belonged to individuals was therefore clinically excised from the packaging design, offering only the absolute possession of their imagery for the voyeuristic viewer, who subsequently dwelt in a feline paradise of carnal indicators selected only for their personal gratification, preventing any needs the model might have from intruding upon their fantasies.

These innovations in design and representation of artificial polymers were bearing iconic new fruit to depend from the branches of the genealogical tree of eroticism. The spectral trends of the period also helped cement how formative moments are recalled. The dominant photographic colour palette of those times was an eternal prism of oranges and browns, a spectrum spanning lush dark chocolates at one end into rich sandy tones at its extremity, these burnished shades seeming cardinal in their commonality across media as disparate as upholstery, soft furnishings and trimphones, while floral motifs in tangerine, roseate pinks and cornflower blues saw dominion in the styling of dresses, shirts and underwear. Leaf through one of those erotic magazines, tear open the cellophane of the hosiery packaging and you encounter the psyches of a generation whose memories are perpetually stained into a swatch of brassy and bronzed desert tones resembling the hues of the crashed disk recovery sites of New Mexico. Years later I discovered Ballard's infamous equation *Sex x Technology = The Future*. I instantly understood this assertion as I'd encountered an example of all three elements of the equation in the newsagents of my youth. What's missing from the axiom is only the subjective viewpoint of the individual, but of course you can always supply your own, stained with the particular tincture of the sigils of concupiscence imprinted upon your own singular and nascent sexuality.

As my reading in SF grew more sophisticated, early acquisitions like my John Murray edition of *The Lost World* (priced in Imperial coinage, the first 'adult' book I ever bought, at age 6) were put aside in favour of Philip K. Dick, Alfred Bester and Harlan Ellison, who represented the amphetamine logic of Tomorrow more convincingly than the Edwardian curlicues of Wells' copyists. By the time I was eleven, Pan had started using their sophisticated-looking white spine livery that incorporated a futuristic bevel-edged silver lozenge around the author legend on the front board of their paperbacks. I developed a penchant bordering on mania for this design throughout its lifespan across the seventies, its air of refined modernity luring me into buying works like *The Green Hills of Earth* by Robert Heinlein, a text I still find unreadable (I later tried his *I Will Fear No Evil* with the hyper-chilling NEL skull cover, but found the Grand Master's sexual prurience in the book too much even while my own superheated preoccupation with adolescent masturbation was in full bloom).

The Pan lozenge also led me to Bob Shaw's *Other Days Other Eyes*, Robert Silverberg's *Downward to the Earth* and other literary SF delights which prepared me for precocious readings of mainstream classics like Conrad and Melville. I wasn't faithful to Pan alone, being almost equally enamoured of the Chris Foss adorned jackets of Panther/Triad/Granada (amongst other imprints), all titanic wasp-striped industrial starships pierced by scores of tiny lamplit windows against the velveteen backdrops of interstellar void or the phanorethymic blazes of colour that indicated said craft were landing on other worlds than our own. *Earth is Room Enough* proclaimed an Asimov title on one ebony-bound volume, the legend hovering above a depiction of a haunting, traditionally enigmatic electric blue obelisk that might later have been used as a prototype for a synthetic foam buttplug. Yet I knew Asimov was talking bollocks regarding Terra: instead, I'd put Roxy Music's 'Virginia Plain' on my Bush mono record player just to listen to the buzzing VCS3 synth intro, then reach for a John Brunner galactic empire saga: as far as I was concerned at 13, space was the place.

Some years before the advent of the Pan lozenge, I took a summer motorway trip with my parents into Wales that terminated on the Brecon Beacons. Dad pulled the Morris Minor into a layby beside a waterfall bursting out of stentorian Cymric black mountain rock, its gushing spume cascading into an icy but refreshing plunge pool in which I paddled for a while to relieve the July heat. A raucous Hindu family soon arrived in a grey Oxford Cambridge, parking beside us. These exotic arrivals spent the next hour inventing wild swimming with infectious warmth, shouting in lively delight as they splashed and stroked amongst the underground spring-fresh spray. My parents were charmed by this incident as ethnic minorities were more a novelty in our country in those days than they are now. I spoke briefly to the smiling youngest daughter of the seemingly boundless clan, who had a silver disc painted in what looked to me like iridescent eyeshadow between her mahogany brows. "What's that? I asked boldly. "Vimana," she responded, looking enigmatically into my eyes.

I learned years later that the expected answer should have been *Bindi*. Had she really been reading the books by Adamski and Desmond Lesley? Nonplussed by the girl's gaze and overwhelmed by the crowding out of the pond, I returned to our car to read. The leatherette passenger seat of the Morris was the same shade of green once found on the wooden doors of every school lavatory cubicle I'd ever used. I picked up the lurid magenta and red paperback entitled *A Modern Look At Monsters* that had called to me from a dusty rack inside a petrol station we'd stopped at on the way.

This was an uncommon placement for a spinner even then —strangely, the almost extinct A format now survives in editions of popular bestsellers produced by publishers exclusively for non-trade outlets. You'll routinely see these spinners now in hospital shops and sometimes in remainder bookshops. The minimart of the petrol station a few miles down the road from my house has one, stuffed with historical romances, maritime adventure fiction, James Patterson's endless bibliography and post-Crichton Technothrillers. I've never found any SF on these latterday stands, despite my constant forlorn searching through every title on the rack in desperation for vintage-style Skiffy whenever I drop into the mart to buy a microwave curry and a bottle of beer, Bettany chiding me to get a move on because my Ford is taking up refuelling pace on the forecourt. I remember the magazine cartoons of the sixties, BEMs approaching petrol pumps, captions inevitably reading *Take Me To Your Leader*.

Feeling that the absence of A format SF in the mainstream publishing portfolio of today is bibliographic tragedy on an heroic scale, back in 2011 I founded the Base & Apex imprint, my last major project failure in trade publishing. I started the list with beloved long out of print titles such as *Dark Side of the Earth, The Beast That Shouted Love at the Heart of the World, Frontera, Dr Adder*, a couple of capers by Barrington J. Bayley and—for the first time in print in decades after lengthy negotiations with the Ballard family—an historic reissue of the suppressed *The Wind From Nowhere*. I even commissioned a demy hardcover slipcased numbered limited edition of the latter, with an afterword by Arthur Comus, who claimed to have witnessed the infamous bust-up between JGB and Keith Roberts. Base & Apex flopped and folded in 2014. Naturally, I explained this business disaster area to my employers as a chicken and egg scenario: a lack of paperback spinners in trade outlets.

A Modern Look at Monsters was my introduction to the celebrated Flatwoods and Mothman cases. Both stories scared the living shit out of me, the vivid descriptions of giant non-humanoid creatures stalking around the rock and roll era States infecting my already overly-intense imagination stoked by *Outer Limits* bubble gum cards and David Bowie's silvery *Aladdinsane* persona, which had already spooked me considerably, as at that time I really believed that the Dame was from outer space. My friend Casey Bowers was always going on about Bowie, virtually frothing at the mouth about how brilliant he was, but I found his disturbing appearance—all flaming hair, thunderbolt-divided, wedge-shaped visage and metallic skin forged by cosmetics (not to mention his story of being Ziggy Stardust, a Spider from Mars)—utterly terrifying. In retrospect, I think it was Casey's boiling enthusiasm for Bowie that put the wind up me more than the man himself, for I later grew to worship this barbed wire being and his impeccable works, eventually becoming a huge fan and collecting mountains of recordings by him.

I realise now that my initial fear of Bowie really stemmed

from Casey's sexual precociousness; although a year my junior, she displayed an unaccountably robust fascination with me from around the age of six when she joined my primary school after attending infants' classes at another site. A bellicose tomboy, her affections were expressed predominantly through verbal abuse followed by direct, opaque stares of indeterminate meaning. She would tease or insult me, then simply look at me unblinking with an expression that I found impenetrable. I couldn't tell whether she was besotted with or despised me, but either way I didn't want the attention as she was so intense about everything.

"You're just like Mr Spock!" Casey would shout, tugging at the sleeves of my jumpers. I think she was hoping for an emotional response from me to her tirades about Bowie, but my neat, shiny, precisely cut black hair and air of bookish calm only broken by enthusiasm when monster movies or antediluvian animals were the topic of conversation naturally led her to equate me with the Vulcan. I know I wasn't as clever then as I thought I was, finding other kids childish, preferring adult company, not noticing how perceptive Casey was in identifying me with the cold, rational alien of *Star Trek*. Leonard Nimoy was a sex object then, the majority of women finding his wintery charm irresistible. I had a vague idea that Casey fancied me, but I wasn't yet interested enough in girls to take an active part in any courtship, being actively scared by the very concept of having a girlfriend. It wasn't that Casey was unattractive, it was more that my libido was subsumed in the metaphor of intelligent life from other planets. It's obvious to me now that she adored me, but I guess my latency phase had over-extended itself by that time, my undeveloped sexuality blunted into excessive shyness by Sci-fi books, Aurora's *Prehistoric Scenes* plastic model kits and an intense hatred of the team sports that dominated the inner landscape and constant exclamations of our over-competitive and under-academic teachers.

During the summer of 1973 Casey and I and several other classmates were on a train returning from a school trip to a forgotten destination. The rolling stock was comprised of those classic carriages you never experience in real life anymore yet see in thrillers even today, with chambers seating six to eight off a corridor that runs the length of the train and people being pushed into toilet cubicles to be garrotted. There had been much larking about, blinds being rolled down, sliding doors slammed shut in their tracks, the small square windows for ventilation jerked open for lunchbox rubbish to be thrown out of into the countryside whipping past. I disapproved of all such immature nonsense.

Casey was seated opposite me and had been delivering her usual staccato monologue of abusive proclamations at me, aquamarine eyes flashing, small teeth breaking her lips into taut momentary grins, flicking long dirty blonde tresses with busy fingernails, round shoulders thrusting out of the armholes of her green, white and tan floral minidress. Suddenly, the train burrowed into the unexpected darkness of a tunnel and Casey was upon me, leaping onto my lap violently and forcing her mouth against mine, her alarmingly powerful hands grabbing my upper arms, pinning them to my side. "Gerroff!" I tried to shout and she recoiled a little but only for an instant. The train can only have been subterranean for around ten to fifteen seconds and when it snapped out into daylight Casey was instantaneously back in her seat. She looked as distinctly annoyed with me as usual, then after a few seconds grinned broadly at me, but said nothing for some time.

The journey continued and the other kids started telling local ghost stories which bore the marks of folk legend in the telling but were news to me. "You live on Ashmountain Road, Andy, have you ever seen the White Lady?" one of the girls asked.

"No such thing." I replied. Another boy started talking about how people had seen a man with a square head in the distance walking around the triangulation point atop the peak. "They think he was a man from space, 'cause one of them saw a flying saucer up there once." I was chilled to the bone by this news, as absurd as it sounded.

My nightmares started soon after the school trip. They weren't intense or frequent, but anticipation of them kept me awake for hours beneath sheet, blanket and quilt in bed in the darkness of my room at midnight and beyond, haunted by imaginings of the American monsters I'd read of, frightened by the prospect of that man with a cube for a cranium landing his vehicle a few miles up the road and prowling around outside our house. Eventually, exhausted, I would sleep. The dreams the entered my drowsing brain were of a bright, thick, birthday-cake like UFO similar to the ones in the Gulf Breeze polaroids floating silently just above the ground in the bluebell-coated meadow behind the caravan park where Casey lived with her dad a mile down the road from our place.

The spaceship radiated pastel-beam shafts of light down onto the carpet of flowers and fog-damp grass, illuminating the boles of the dark trees that bordered the small break in the woods, a thousand rainbow glitterings sparkling in blue, indigo, violet, yellow and mauve off the frosty vapour that floated up from the ground to wreathe the otherworldly vessel. I also dreamt of obsidian taloned hands clawing for me from the deepest shadows of my room, of wetlook cowls and plexiglass ether helmets in slate grey, of huge hideous veined eyes staring into my own, pinned with expressionless miniscule pupils like the black spheres resident in the centre of freshly-laid frogspawn. Eventually these nightmares receded. Then I began dreaming solely of Casey.

I was conceived and born in the same room. I squared the circle by having my first orgasm there too. This was unplanned as I had no idea what to expect from the activity that prompted my climax as I'd never talked about such matters with other kids. Where we lived there were few other children around as the house was isolated from the nearest estate by a twenty minute walk, so I was pretty ignorant of the rumours, myths and gossip about what sex involved in detail.

Other than being shocked and worried by the sudden sensation of ejaculation (I wasn't sure if it was pleasurable or if something was wrong with me that needed medical attention), the only other memory I have of that day is that I'd been reading J. Allen Hynek's *The UFO Experience* immediately beforehand. It was the edition published by Corgi in 1974, it had a bright orange and tan cover design, saturated in sunlight. My copy is long since gone from my library, but searching for it on Abebooks recently, I was stunned by how much dealers are asking for it. I'm the nostalgic type when I can afford it, but the Hynek remains beyond my budget as it now sells for hundreds of pounds, is fairly uncommon and is priced according to demand: committed UFO bibliophiles are a niche breed of collector, but a keen taste public with serious disposable income due to the fact that many of them are nerdy professionals working in tech industries rather than being modestly renumerated publishers like me.

By the time of my first climax, Casey's aggression toward me had receded significantly. Bowie was in his Plastic Soul period, which baffled more than a few of his fans at the time and she didn't seem to know how to respond to this. The songs on *Young Americans* were not the Sci-Fi lullabies I'd lately grown enamoured of (all our Pop Stars looked like Spacebeings by 1974, so I wasn't freaked out by Bowie anymore), but were instead longing ballads or cat's cradles of immaculately arranged call-and-response funk, more alien than anything Glitter Kids like me and Casey had closely encountered before. The double-cherry patch embroidered on my sweater now lay above a heart beating to a mono speaker in my bedroom that thumped with *Transformer, The Human Menagerie, Muscle of Love, Hall of the Mountain Grill* and *Electric Warrior*, so Casey had toned her passion for me down a little bit, obviously feeling there was hope for me yet if she took things a little more slowly. Meanwhile, I was emotionally in a fresh moon and June phase rather than a full-blown "Drive-In Saturday" erotoflash, despite some unfamiliar stirrings in my loins.

So while reading my Hynek paperback—it was a little dry and analytical for me, not the kind of sensational fare I preferred then—I'd closed the pages and lay it down on the bed beside me. The colours of the cover illustration suddenly reminded me of Casey. She'd taken to wearing tights recently, making her appear more mature, her calves and knees beginning to turn my head just as those of the glamorous older girls of our school were doing. Of late I'd gone from watching the skies to watching the thighs, noticing that one range of Pretty Polly's nylons on the newsagent racking were named *Galaxy*, like the SF magazine that so many of my new favourite writers had cut their teeth in according to the copyright credits in their short story collections. Interestingly, *Galaxy*'s packaging used only close-up portraits of their model's faces, unlike the direct pin-up sexiness of competing lines. In a parallel development, Casey's unfurling facial prettiness was transforming her into a frequent space invader of my head. Soon, my hand was exploring the unknown and in a moonage daydream, I began speculating on Casey's potential future mammary development, conflating it with images of the gas giants beyond the Goldilocks zone of our solar system, my sensibilities stimulated in this direction by what I'd occasionally glimpsed on Page 3 of *The Sun*.

Casey's father was called Tony. He was Latin-looking, with swarthy skin, hair blacker than mine, a permanent three day beard and a bright white smile. Casey's mum was absent, never spoken of. The Bowers lived in the caravan park that had sprung up on the site of the old prefabricated houses that my parents told me had been built after the war and torn down less than a decade later. This park was initially established to house itinerant Irish labourers who worked between 1968 and 1971 on the motorway constructed where the old canal had been. The Bowers were local, it was said, but had moved to the caravan site when Casey's mum had absconded. Tony had taken the initiative to open a barber shop beside the mobile home settlement and his entrepreneurial spirit had proven to be visionary as now, decades later, there is a thriving retail park where the trailers once sat. It had its roots in a supermarket that had opened two years after I left home for University, but it was Tony Bowers who started the trend and his shop is still there today, though it's now a tattoo and piercing studio.

By the late seventies Casey and I were drawing toward the end of our secondary school attendances. Her belligerent obsession with me had evanesced and she was now only interested in boys a year or two older than me, starting tentative courtships with tearaways obsessed with motorbikes and heavy metal. She still liked Bowie, but *Low* left her cold for at least a year. I loved it, plus the cover portrait of Bowie reminded me of my sole viewing then of *The Man Who Fell To Earth*, Casey and I creeping under-age into our local fleapit to see David's silver screen debut, both of us disoriented but excited by seeing our idol playing the spaceman, indulging in weird, greasy cats-eye inter-species sex with Candy Clark.

Just after Punk Rock exploded that summer, Tony cut Casey's hair cut short, severe and dyed it with flames of orange. She started wearing black a lot more frequently. We were comfortable as friends by now and she often visited me at home for record-playing sessions. Sexually, I was still shy and reticent, having had no real girlfriends. My unfulfilled libido, fuelled by social awkwardness resulted in my identification with punk's righteous ire and I paid Tony to trim my locks too. As '77 rolled into '78 I was dismayed by the atmosphere of totalitarianism that soon coalesced around Punk, growing irascible with the Stalinist uniformity of rules that were creeping into culture via the mindsets of its more lumpen adherents. So while Casey and I argued the various merits of 'Flying Saucer Attack' versus 'Another Girl, Another Planet' on a futuristically themed mixtape I'd recorded for her, we still listened to old favourites like UFO and The Tubes. One afternoon we were sitting on my double bed, backs against the woodchip papered wall, our legs forming horizontals against the vertical length of the mattress, looking at the sleeve of *Phenomenon*.

The front cover of the album is a fine example one of Hipgnosis' iconic designs of the period, depicting a couple standing on a flawless lawn in front of their red-roofed white suburban bungalow. Although the two-toned automobile parked on the drive in front of the garage looks American, the location could be anywhere in the Western world of 1974. Some fans of the band claim the photograph was taken in Shepperton and that the man in the shot, who is in the background looking upwards at a tiny silver disc traversing a cloudless aquamarine sky, is J.G. Ballard. The blonde woman in the foreground wears an expression of quizzical foreboding, standing sideways on, gazing over her shoulder (but not directly at the photographer), as if someone behind him to his right is just uttering the phrase "Look at that!" and pointing. She is holding a box camera in her hands, ready to shoot, but if she doesn't react soon and turn her head, the saucer will have vanished. The Ballard conspiracy theorists claim this is the writers' paramour, Claire, but the model clearly isn't the woman from the collage advertisements Ballard experimented with in the sixties.

"I love this cover," I said to Casey. As she'd matured, I'd grown increasingly attracted to her in inverse proportion to her growing disinterest in me. Her high cheekbones, wide twinkling cobalt eyes that slanted and subtly pillowed lips had rounded out, like her big alluring shoulders and that generous wedge of bust. She was more feminine than she'd been as a child, less boyish. Her hips had filled out also and her legs, though relatively short, filled her jeans with curves in all the right places. She wasn't willowy.

"Yeah, s'really good... I love Schenker's lead guitar playin'..." despite her poor diction. Casey had a strong, fine voice.

"Me too. I used to think he just fret-wanked, but the more you listen, you start to pick out the melodies." I liked tuneful solos, which had led me to an obsession with the early work of Judas Priest. Casey had been unconvinced until I'd played *Stained Class* at her. The album's meshing of uptempo riffing, carefully composed refrains and verse/chorus structures, combined with the fierce electrical susurration of Tipton and Downing's guitars with intelligent lyrics screamed in note-perfect falsetto by Rob Halford over them meant that by the end of side one's closing track ('Invader') Casey was hooked too. But I'd decided to put *Phenomenon* on the turntable that day because UFO were (ironically) earthier and sexier than Priest.

"So d'you believe in all this flying saucer rubbish?" She laid the sleeve down on her lap.

"I've read some of the books, much of it's pretty convincing. Coppers, pilots and military staff have reported seeing UFOs. Why would they lie?"

She grinned. "I've seen some of those books on your shelves," she gestured vaguely at the paperback-piled bookcase set against the side of my wardrobe. "I looked at one of them once when you went to the lav. It said that some flying saucers had actually crashed in America." She raised her eyebrows.

"I know, it sounds nuts. If they did, where's the wreckage hidden?"

"Yeah, but if little green men could flying across space to Earth, surely they'd be smart enough to build their saucers so they wouldn't crash, right?" She raised thin, dark eyebrows.

Trying not to be distracted by the open buttons at the top of her shirt placket, I replied. "I have a theory about that," Phil Mogg was singing '*Doctor, Doctor, please...*' from my speakers. I could really relate to the cajoling for attention in his lyrics at that point.

"You have theories about everything, Andy." She flashed her small white teeth at me in a killer smile. Man, I loved her when she looked like that. I decided this was another chance for me to appear intelligent and sophisticated in her eyes, though I wasn't certain she was taken with those qualities given her current adoration of boorish rocker suitors.

"OK," I started, looking straight into those eyes. "Imagine that on other planets, conditions are very different to here on Earth. We assume that life can only develop on worlds like our own, but maybe that's not so. Say life developed on other planets and that the evolution of animals and plants there was dictated by environments different to ours, making the life different."

"You mean natural selection and that."

"Exactly. And convergent evolution shows that unrelated animal groups often develop similar shapes suited to their habitats. Say for example that on Planet X, atmospheric conditions meant that life didn't develop hearing and speaking organs like ours, but instead the higher animals were telepathic or communicated chemically."

"Chemically ?" Casey frowned.

"Say they evolved from something like ants, living in colonies, communicating via pheromones—Miss Smith taught your class about this in Form Four Biology, right?"

"Yeah, I forgot. I do General Science, bigbrain... but she covered that topic. What's this got to do with flying saucers crashing?" There was silence for an instant in the groove between tracks, then 'Space Child' began weaving out of the stereo.

"I'm coming to that." I put my palm atop her left hand casually, without looking at it, trying to pretend that nothing unusual was happening. "So say the aliens evolved from arthropods, communicated without words and sound, but still created real technology. They no longer have wars, as they've linked via scents or telepathically and therefore no longer have war or conflicts as they realise they're all alike inside. Then they build spacecraft to explore the universe. Their senses perceive energy wavelength that we can't, so that gives them a deeper, innate understanding of cosmic stuff like magnetism and gravity so they are able to work out how to build ships to travel across interstellar distances swiftly."

"Spock." Casey flicked my nose with her free hand. The other didn't move from beneath mine.

I laughed. "Shut up. So they discover our solar system and their senses or instruments reveal we've been testing nuclear weapons. They're confused but fascinated by us. There are lot of us, we're destroying our environment and fighting each other all the time. They're *scared* of us, but can't resist visiting Earth to see for themselves what's going on."

"That's an interesting idea, that they're frightened of us. In films they're always the fierce ones." Casey sounded thoughtful at last. Suddenly, she shifted her hand and deftly intertwined her fingers with mine. I caught a flash of clear, chipped lacquer from her clipped fingernails. Wow, I was really getting somewhere...

"Right, they're emboldened by their superior technology, they know they can destroy us. But what if their science is different to ours too, not always better than ours... we tend to assume that anyone else would develop along the same lines as we have. Perhaps we're more advanced than they are in some ways and maybe aggression is one of *our* advantages over them. There's no reason why they should have developed in exactly the same linear fashion as us."

"That's a good point. Too many big words as usual, though, ace." Casey suddenly seemed to lose interest and she shifted away from me across the bed, patting my leg before standing up. Maybe, I thought, I've blown it again with all my rationalist talk just at the moment I was getting somewhere. Should I be more of a caveman, if there was a next time?

Although I lost Casey's hand at the point I savoured the opportunity to take a good look at her comely backside in those tight jeans before she turned to face me. "I gotta go. I have to sort out the shop." It was Sunday and though Tony always swept the floor of his salon before locking up, one of Casey's pocket money chores was cleaning the business thoroughly once a week and for half an hour every night after school.

"You can always borrow some of my UFO books if you like, "I blurted.

"Nah, I've got you to tell me 'bout it all. Besides, I haven't brought back your comics yet." Casey had borrowed a big stash of Marvel titles from me last time she'd visited, which made me wonder how she'd look in Sue Storm or Jean Grey's formfitting tights and colourful bodysuits. To my chagrin, Casey didn't wear skirts or dresses much anymore, so although the shape of those legs appeared fine below denim, I never got to see the flesh of her shapely calves anymore. I was beginning to wonder if I ever would again.

After I showed Casey out of the house, I went back upstairs to my room. Side 1 of *Phenomenon* had ended. Making for my bookcase, I squatted down in order to reach the bottom shelf where I kept my Fortean material and drew out my copy of *The Humanoids*. First published by Spearman in 1969, this celebrated anthology of essays summarising all the key Close Encounters of the golden age of UFOlogy was reprinted by Futura in 1974, which is when I acquired my copy. I had read it cover-to-cover several times, thrilled by the numerous and content-diverse reports of alien contacts. Although the book was an embarrassment of ET riches, the case I was most drawn to was arguably the most sensational one. Although made public subsequent to the 1961 Betty and Barney Hill case, the AVB story was actually the first full abduction narrative, chronologically preceding the Hills' celebrated experience by four years.

Antonio Villas Boas was a Brazilian farmer resident with his extended family in rural Minas Geras state, which is adjacent to Sao Paulo. In early October 1957 the family had witnessed a bright light shining down onto their farmyard one night, followed by the sighting of another such inexplicable illumination in a field the farmers were tending a week later. The Boas brothers apparently worked in shifts ploughing with a tractor, Antonio then working at night. I'll state now that this seems to me the most unlikely assertion in the story, since surely the noise from Antonio's driving a tractor in the small hours would have kept the whole family wide awake.

The evening after Antonio saw a light in the fields, he noticed a red star in the southern crossed skies that appeared to be growing in size and approaching. The crimson mote soon brightened considerably and the farmer could see that the object was a luminous ovoid which was soon hovering silently above his tractor and bathing it in an intense column of light. Realising that if he tried to get away on foot he'd be hindered by the deep ruts his plough had cut into the earth, AVB remained sitting in his vehicle. A couple of minutes later the UFO moved a few metres ahead of the tractor before halting in mid-air again, descending and extending a tripod of landing struts toward the ground while it blazed with scarlet and emerald phosphorescent light. Before the craft touched down completely, Boas panicked and began turning the wheel of the tractor when its engine failed.

Leaping down from his seat, AVB began running away from the egg-shaped ship but was soon assailed by something grabbing at his arms from behind. Turning to tackle his attacker, Boas was shocked by the sight of a small being in a one-piece coverall and opaque helmet, but wasted no time in pushing the intruder over. He was then instantly overpowered by three other entities that came at AVB from other angles. Lifting him from the ground, the quartet of saucer occupants bore Boas toward their craft. Two metres above the ground, a door had opened downward from the side of the ovoid aeroform forming a bridge/ladder construct. AVB struggled with all the gusto he could summon, but despite some difficulties with his resistance, his captors managed to get the petrified Earthman aboard their machine.

Once inside the ship, Boas found himself in a square chamber with the diminutive spacemen, alarmed to notice that the door had seamlessly merged with the interior of the hull, its outline disappearing. He was now alone, bathed in bright lights, aboard a UFO with a cadre of hostile extraterrestrials. Held fast by two of the creatures, AVB endured an ordeal of waiting captive for several minutes while the beings appeared to converse about him. Their voices were guttural throat-based utterances that he claimed were akin to the growling of small dogs. His shock intensified when the spacesuited figures then began undressing him, not stopping until he was absolutely naked.

At this point, the account grows markedly stranger. One of the ETs approached AVB with a sponge-like object and began rinsing the farmer's body all over with a clear gel that seeped from the artefact but which soon dried upon his skin like a moisturiser. He was then taken into an adjoining cell by the aliens, the doorway dilating invisibly shut again. Shortly, a pair of the spacers joined Boas in the smaller room bearing two long red rubber tubes and a glass cupola. Forcing him onto a pedestal-mounted couch in the centre of the chamber, his abductors applied the end of the tubes to Boas' chin and withdrew a blood sample into the carafe, this action leaving visible permanent scars on AVB's skin which he invited UFO investigators to examine when reporting his encounter.

The extrasolars then abandoned Boas for around thirty minutes. During this period he tried to recuperate his stamina by lying on the couch but was disturbed by the releasing of smoky gases into his cell through shower-head like tubes arrayed around the wall of the room like some intergalactic dado rail. This alteration of the atmosphere in the cell made AVB nauseous and he was forced to get up from his temporary bed to throw up in a corner.

A few minutes later, the noise of the door irising open startled AVB and turning around toward the cadence, he was even more perplexed to find that a naked woman approximately four and a half feet tall had stepped into the chamber. The gases pumped into the cell had clearly adjusted the atmospheric mix enough for the alien Venus to breathe comfortably.

Boas described the female as young and beautiful, with a Nordic aspect unlike that of any Terran girls he'd seen. Her hair was almost like ivory and trimmed into an inward-curving bob at her nape. Her eyes were large, Mediterranean blue and slanted outwards at the side of the face, her most unearthly feature. High cheekbones, an unprepossessing nose, almost invisible lips and a pointed chin gave her visage a triangular aspect. This offworld glamazon sported highly set breasts, a slender waist, flat belly and broad childbearing hips. Her thighs were full and inviting, her feet small, her hands long and narrow, but bore the requisite five digits and nails that seemed no different to those of Homo Sapiens. Her underarms and pubic area sported red hair. When I later read C.L. Moore's Northwest Smith stories collected in *Scarlet Dream*, the Shambleau, the red-tressed gorgon-vampire woman of Smith's first *Weird Tales* adventure instantly brought AVB's description of the spacewoman to my mind.

AVB later speculated that the fluid the voidsuited man had applied to his sun-bronzed agrarian flesh must have been both an antibacterial compound and an aphrodisiac, for the interstellar bombshell quickly embraced him and found Boas more than ready to make love to her. His accounts clearly indicate his shame at coupling with an alien—who vocalised like a canine throughout their coitus yet never kissed him—but he eloquently admits his uncontrollable erotic excitement while at the service of his amorous partner.

After he came, Boas noted that the woman was clearly disinclined toward a second round of intercourse and he began to feel dirty and abused. The egress appeared again and one of the presumably male entities gestured at Boas' partner. Getting up from the couch they had shared, she turned briefly back to look at AVB and smiled, pointing initially at her stomach, then her penetrator, then upward at the sky before leaving him alone again in the chamber. *Per ardua, ad astra.*

Subsequently, one of the beings returned Boas' clothes to him, and after he dressed, he was given a tour of the ship. He never saw the female again, though he speculated that as the only features that could be clearly seen through the visors of the ETs helmets were their orbits, she might have been one of the crew of four who had brought him aboard their capsule. Finally releasing Boas, they gestured for the man to stand back and the farmer watched from a distance as the flying egg took off and vanished into the starry firmament. AVB had spent some four hours within the UFO and dawn would soon be breaking.

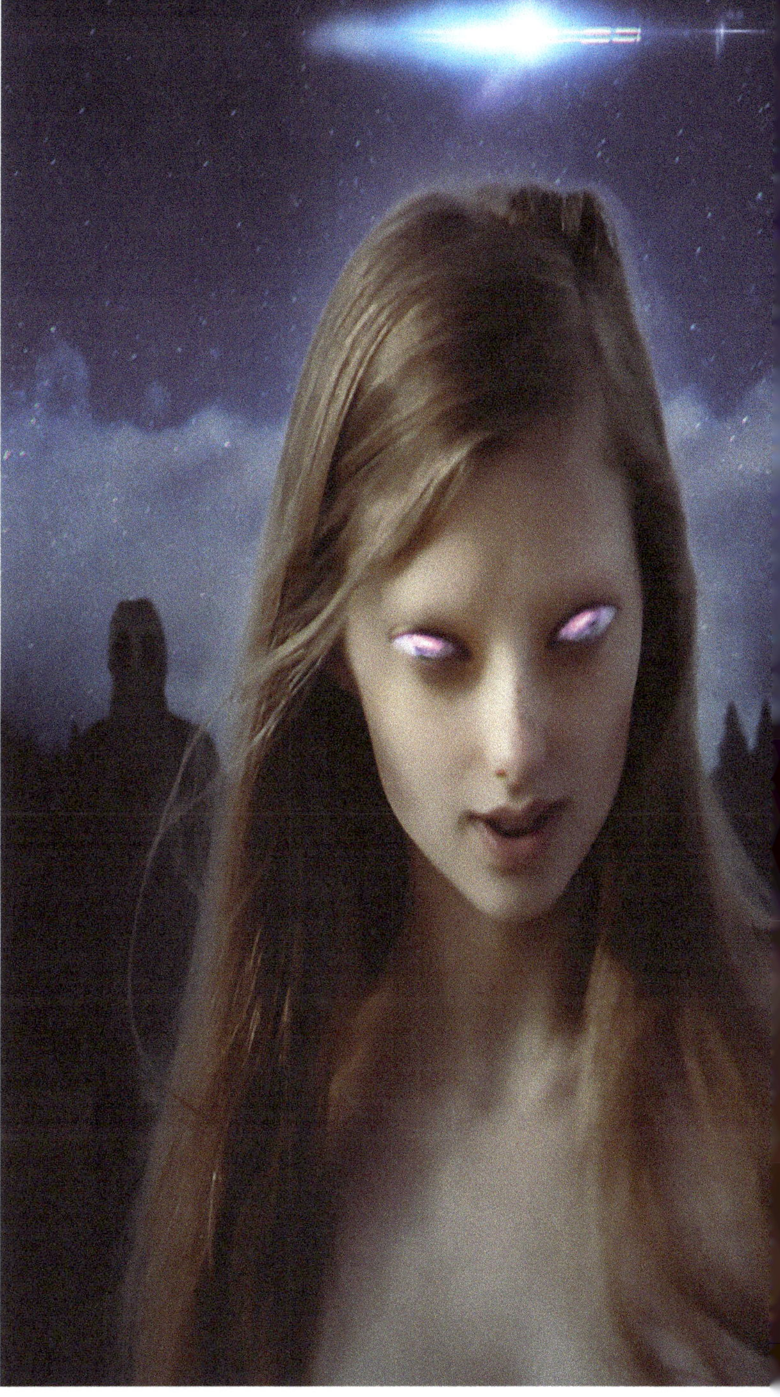

I still regard this as the interplanetary anecdote to end them all. Sexier than Phil Farmer's *The Lovers*, arguably more lurid than *I Married A Monster From Outer Space*, AVB's yarn remains the business in my book. As frightful as the Brazilian account was, as a teenager I sometimes wished I could have an experience like Boas' that promised the resolution of two mysteries. Not only did he get to discover that yes, there was other intelligent life out there, but he also found proof of Ballard's equation before the writer coined it, underlining its relevance.

I always think of the AVB tale whenever I play 'Love in Space' by Hawkwind. An uncharacteristic Buddha-Bar organ on this track reminds me of the Hindu girl with the mercurial Bindi, Dave Brock's warm, nasally folky voice mournfully repeating a rapturous mantra of frozen longing. The lyrics relate a vignette of the narrator's object of affection floating in a capsule of icy mist that spangles in spectral light, of a ship of dreams that sails onward perpetually through hard vacuum. It's a lovely, gently meditative song that I always find blissfully moving and suspenseful of time, putting the succession of moments into hyper-hibernation for me, if only briefly. Bettany loathes the song, probably because I insisted on placing it on our Saturday night lovemaking playlist and doing my level best not to come until its psychedelic sonorities were echoing around the bedroom, irrespective of whether she'd climaxed or not. "How was it for you, asshole?" she'd mutter sarcastically as I moaned, seed pumping sluggishly out of me. "Majestic," I spat, rolling off her before chambering up my DVD of *Fire in the Sky* into the Sony. Well, she would smoke that hateful post-coital cigarette now anyway, whatever I did.

By 1989 I'd tired of running the Pan SF line, which was by then in serious commercial decline due to my unwillingness to follow current UK trends. I'd lost interest exponentially in SF once Iain M. Banks sent British skiffy spiralling back into the Space Opera thirties to huge commercial success, despite the fact that American writers were producing some fascinating post-human based work that I'd kept purchasing in the wake of my championing of the likes of Greg Bear and Vernor Vinge. I was also miffed at losing the bid for a revised edition of *Sky Crash* to HarperCollins, pretending I hadn't wanted the book for the list anyway by claiming that the only truly alien being ever seen around Woodbridge was Brian Eno as a young boy. This and my indifference toward Skiffy ironically led to promotion as I took up the post of chief commissioning editor for non-fiction at Macmillan.

My first big score in my new chair was to signup Jim Bonaparte, obtaining the world rights to his game-raising UFO opus *Before Open Contact* by securing this highly plausible researcher a £500,000 advance that he then preceded to brag about openly to his UK fanbase when on signing and lecture tours, thus reducing his credibility with tabloid critics who claimed he was only in the flying saucer book game for the money and that his statements about Rendlesham Forest, MJ-12 and the Dechmont Woods Horror were pure fiction and unsupported by fresh evidence. After this abashment and despite the revenue Jim's impressive sales earned the company, I decided to wash my hands of the whole SF/saucer axis at the professional level.

An eternal problem for those working in the book trade, however, is that if you have a genuine enthusiasm for almost anything beyond general fiction—no matter how well read or knowledgeable you are across the board—career typecasting sets in and is virtually impossible to dispel. Cornered in a Soho bar by a travel writer I was working with as part of my plan to escape Skiffy, my specialist knowledge was unwillingly pressed into service again. Having just returned from a research trip to Tennessee that would inspire a book entitled *The Madams of Sparta* (based upon a legend that the house said writer had stayed in was a former old-west bordello), the author pressed me for a UFO tale.

"I met this biker in a bar," he told me "and after shooting some pool and sinking some Coors he invited me back to his clubhouse to sniff some crystal, but I wanted to make this escapade more exotic—as it stands, I've merely got a Thompson-lite diversion out of it." Explaining that he'd had the inspired idea to embroider his conversation with a greaser by adding a Jim Bonaparte style punchline because the skies above Sparta had recently been subject to a flap of sightings (not that he'd been lucky enough to see any flaky lights flitting amongst the cirrus himself), he beseeched me to help. I told him I'd think about it and a few days later he called by the office to borrow my copy of *The Humanoids*.

"There's a few ideas in here you could draw upon," I suggested, aware that I was possibly aiding the creation of a hoax. "I'd suggest the Kelly-Hopkinsville Goblin case. It's pretty hairy stuff, but I can see it working if you reset it at a remote biker clubhouse out in the sticks. Hell's Angels with shotguns versus alien invaders, imagine that." He followed my advice, delineating a fine scene with the material, creating a rich and convincing dialogue in his practised voice of urbane travelogue inscriber grilling a Jim Beamed semi-illiterate One-Percenter. I didn't think about this small act of literary deception much at the time—like the travel hack's idol, Bruce Chatwin, I felt a good story was more important than the facts when it came to the craft of letters. I'm quietly ashamed of this now. Fortunately, The Madams of Sparta was a flop and we never sold the license to any US house.

Nothing I'd read prepared me for the reality of New Mexico: the light, the space, the dryness and heat, the Hispanic tinge that pervaded so much of the state. The vegetation was marked by a glorious harshness: I admired how the plants thrived there, from trees to angiosperms to succulents. I was blasted into the stratosphere by the clarity of the night skies, the stars spattered across the onyx backdrop of space like the titles of books by Aldiss and Delany that compared suns to sandgrains.

I'd found myself gazing up at this cosmic mica the evening after Simon and I spotted the first UFOs. I'd always wanted to stay in a genuine Motel so we'd factored an overnighter into our round trip of atomic heritage landmarks. Though I'd been delighted by the beige uniformity of the single-storey chalet-style bedrooms at Tycho Ranch (as the motel was dubbed), I'd awoken around two and couldn't get back to sleep. All the lights were out save the NO VACANCIES neon, even in the Norman Bates invoking reception office. After half an hour of trying to identify constellations I'd given up on the idea of kip and decided to get a coke from the vending machine situated in the parking lot.

What happened next isn't so much a blur as a flash. I can't recall putting a coin in the slot, just a blinding white light that suddenly flicked on, surrounding me and drowning out everything apart from the asphalt beneath my DC unilites. I squinted, raised my hand to shade my eyes to see if I could make out the source of the illumination, but the brightness was so intense that I could distinguish no details. The light seemed to be all-pervading, everywhere. I started to walk forward and sensed that although there was a hint of darkness ahead, the nimbus that had bloomed around me was moving its radius with me, as if I were the source of that klieg-like glow.

Then I felt something like a bolt cutter closing on my upper right arm, cold, tight and implacable as iron. I turned my head and what I saw almost knocked me unconscious. It was a woman wearing heliotrope wraparound plastic shades that curved around beneath her brow in a close-fitting design, a sateen-like one-piece bistre vacuum suit padded like a puffer jacket with taupe piping where seams would be and a hood of the same material thrown back from her head. Her hair was luscious, long and leopard blonde. Although I couldn't see her eyes, I recognised those features immediately. It was Casey.

-Your planet or mine, ace? Her voice was in my head.

My subconscious responded involuntarily, but I knew she'd feel the word too. I'd never have chosen to say it aloud.

-Shambleau.

-That's an old one. I saw her smile, her lips thinner with age, teeth every bit as chalky white as ever. She reached up with her free hand and lifted off her eyeglasses. Her cerulean irises blazed with desire. My arm was still frozen in her grip. I couldn't believe it. Casey was a stranger from another planet who communicated telepathically. Her thoughts came to me clearly, as heard words, but I believe that my rejoinders were instead a rush of impressions from which she could discern clear verbal meanings.

-Why am I in New Mexico? She was echoing my thoughts the instant they formed. I felt something like a beckoning shout over her shoulder ripple through my mind *–Boys...*

Then I saw them. They were no taller than Casey (and she used to come in at five two I remembered) and were wearing the same outfits, but the headpieces were raised up, any visages within hidden by gleaming chrome yellow faceplates which appeared to be zipped into place around the rim of the hoods.

-C'mon then, Northwest. Casey's words chimed again within me. Over her shoulder I could finally see her saucer. It was of a classic discus design, a throbbing carnival lightshow of steely amaranth, malachite and vermilion, though for some reason it kept growing fuzzy like a pulsing wave, morphing into the shape of a paperback spinner denuded of its sensationalistic

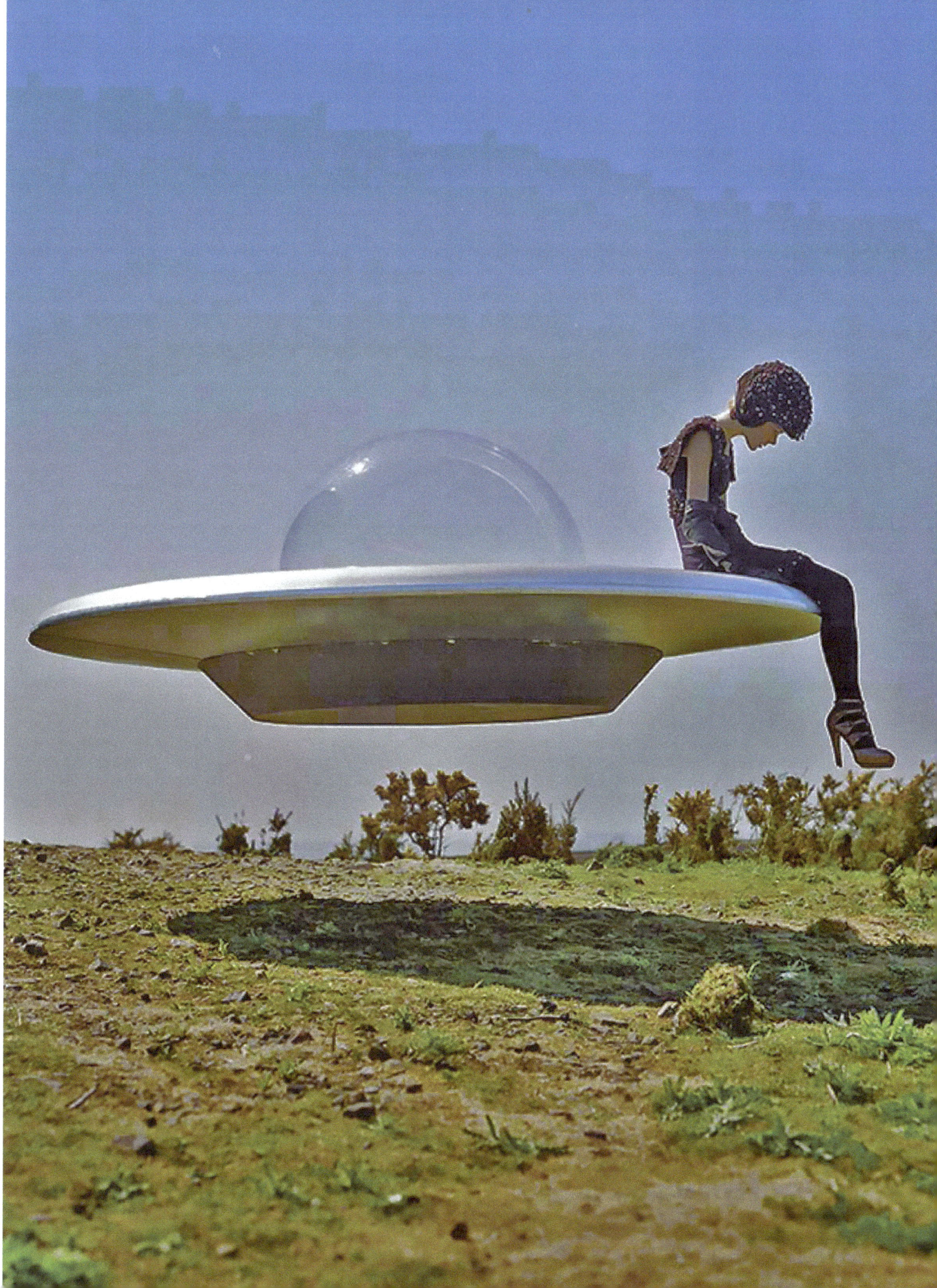

A-format stock before re-sharpening to the crystal clarity of its circle. A bell-tree giggle then streamed through me, Casey's voice whispering *Klatuu Barada Nikto.*

A blank follows. I think I was unconscious for a while. My emergence from that hiatus of void was gradual. Perhaps I never fully came around from the wastelands of sleep I was wandering through, but snapshots recur to me sometimes, presumably in sequence. I can't describe the place where I found myself with any real clarity, as it was initially very shadowy, then abruptly and intermittently lit by magnesium flare snippets of memory that always leave my eyes watering with phosphenes, cascading motes of beryl and verdigris sinking downward in blackness.

I tasted, felt and heard more than I saw. I was still being held, caressed by warm lycra hands, my face crushed against full, cushiony perfumed feminine softness. Aware only of lust and the potential for amniotic fulfilment, I experienced the cool taste of Casey's tongue probing my mouth, tangy and insistent. Unlike AVB's mistress, who denied him of a GFE, Casey was hotly, wetly and tenderly kissing me. I was glad. I sank into balmy ecstacy.

We seemed to be in a summer room of our youth suffused with tans and browns, saffron curtains closed, chinks of sunlight spearing through them like a slow strobe as the breeze outside shifted like a tide through the open window, in and out, sucking the floral fabric of the translucent drapes gently. I thought of Bowman in the penultimate scene of *2001*, unaccountably in a terrestrial setting after his acid-drenched intergalactic hegira. This moment of reflection passing, I focused only on making love with Casey, lost in a spectrum of sienna-toned arousal, as if my reality was being perceived by all my senses through a dreamy twenty-denier glaze like those old portrait photographers used to achieve by stretching a smoky silk stocking over their lenses. It was bliss, like floating in a capsule of icy mist as the song says...

-This is why we came. Casey's thoughts came again, now shaped more like abstract images in my thalamus and cerebral cortex. *We could see you developing technology of mass destruction, so we knew you were by now almost adults.*

-We? My unconscious murmured again, incapable of taking control and establishing a more proactive and nuanced side in our dialogue.

-Our names are Legion, for we are many. I caught magic lantern flicker-pictures of different lifeforms, from ubiquitous Greys to towering Nordics, from nightmarish Goblins and predatory-looking insectile Xenomorphs.

-We all have one thing in common, Casey said. *We came here for adult entertainment. We'd all rather make love than war.*

And in that instant I was wide awake on the couch, sandy bulkheads enclosing us, lamps the colour of solar flares bathing our entwined bodies, me naked, she encased in a soft transparent mesh bodysuit of suntan colours that covered all save hands, feet and head. The garment was gathered in elastic-like bands at wrists and ankles and throat with seams running up Casey's luscious, curving sides, its silken integument and enticing friction emphasising the erotic potential of her thighs, hips and waist.

–My antibacterial suit. It ensures safe congress for us both. Casey's breasts swelled magnificently against the thin silken integument of her mantle as she loomed over me, far more voluptuous than I'd believed. As I reached out for her I realised that she had no nipples. Electric blue fear seared through me as I tried to slide from the couch, repulsed from my would-be lover. Casey probably wasn't even mammalian and Earthlings like me were the equivalent of children when compared to our more advanced neighbours. This was abuse, not love.

...and that was when the little guys reappeared and took their hoods off. Let's just say it was as bad as anything I'd imagined after that youthful scan through *A Modern Look at Monsters.* They'd realised I was balking at the prospect of coitus with a woman I'd long wanted, who I now suspected of being the hybrid child of *Homo Sapiens* and *Extraterrestrialis Mysterioso.* I've never tried to remember what happened after that.

I'd been back from New Mexico for a year. Bettany had dumped me, which was fair enough. I was watching *God Told Me To* for the zillionth time when I decided to try to find Casey on social media. Women marry and their surnames get changed, so looking up your old squeezes is always a tough call. It had been thirty years since I'd last seen Casey and I'd only uncovered fragments of information from mutual acquaintances over the decades—she'd married a Skinhead who beat her up occasionally, Tony had died and she'd converted the barber's into a tattoo parlour which her grown-up son managed. Both husband and offspring had been in trouble with the police and endured spells in clink. Casey was working in a DIY superstore near to her caravan, which she still resided in.

With my hair falling out and the doomsday clock ticking, I determined to stick at my online research. I posted messages on Facebook pages and forums for our hometown and other addresses near where I'd grown up. A few days later, I was pinged with a PM from a guy I didn't know who seemed helpful. I messaged him back and we agreed a time for a live chat.

My informer told me he was sure Casey had died when she was around 42. I was shaken by this idea. A few days later another poster confirmed Casey's demise, saying he bumped into her son at the foot of Ashmountain Way immediately after the funeral, heading back to his mother's place. Casey had apparently died of alcoholism like Thomas Jerome Newton. "Carl said that Casey said she'd had enough," my second contactee claimed. Eventually, I managed a live chat with Ian, a guy a year above me in school I knew vaguely who lived a few plots down from Casey all his life. He was a HGV driver now.

"Did you end up in the music business?" he wrote.

"Nah, I went into publishing after University. I can't complain."

"You married? I've been with Glenda Robins for thirty years, remember her? We got 3 kids."

"Yeah, I recollect Glenda, nice girl. I never got married, but I had a girlfriend until recently. So what happened to Casey?"

"Well, I'm sorry to tell you she's dead. She was 43. It was drink, they say, but her hair fell out gradually over the years and her eyes got really bulgy. You'd look at her and it was as if she never blinked. Her doctor wanted an autopsy as he was convinced she had a tumour or something, but her son refused and had her cremated."

"Jesus H. Christ."

Then I typed some more acknowledgements to Ian and broke off the chat.

In his shady Dallas consulting office, Dr Alexander Bristowe had just put the manuscript down after a second reading when the telephone on his desk buzzed like the signal from a pulsar. The analyst hit one of the recessed buttons on the machine's umber surface and spoke.

"Yes?"

The voice of his receptionist squeaked thinly from the speaker grill of the phone. "Professor Marchant has arrived, Doctor Bristowe."

"Show him in." Bristowe rose from his seat behind the desk and circled it, making for the door. Just as he took the knob and rotated it, Anne appeared with a stocky, muscular, fair man of medium height in his early forties. He found himself looking straight into Simon Marchant's striking blue eyes.

After the convention of handshakes and introductions, Anne left the professionals alone, both refusing the offer of refreshments from her. They sat under the window of Bristowe's office in black leather Barcelona chairs set either side of a low smoked glass coffee table, the venetian blinds lowered, slatted shut against the blindingly bright midday July sun. The men looked at each other a moment, silent.

"So what do you think?" ventured Marchant. "I mean besides your clinical opinion of Andy's state of mind."

"Fundamentally, he was arrested in a period of post-oedipal neoteny. The manuscript itself proves nothing, of course." Marchant nodded in assent at Bristowe's statement, despite sensing a reticence in the analyst. He replied instinctively to prompt the psychologist. "Bowers, Boas... those aspects of his narrative seem too contrived and convenient."

"I agree. However, the Coroner, who is a friend of mine, confirmed that Andrew Neale died of a cancer accompanied by long-term symptoms of what resembled radiation sickness," Bristowe had clasped his hands together and looked down at the pile of stapled A4 papers lying on the table between the men.

"Was there ever a Geiger counter reading?" Even knowing what he did, Marchant felt absurd uttering these words.

Bristowe shook his head then looked up, his deep sorrel eyes gazing right into his new confidantes' face. "He took a polygraph test in front of me twice and passed it both times. It was administered by a retired expert I know from Washington DC. He was fascinated by the case and flew over to England specially."

"Was Andy questioned under hypnosis?" Marchant was keen to discount trance suggestion and false memory syndrome.

"I had him polytested under hypnosis and while fully conscious," the analyst shook his head, looking mildly incredulous. "The differences in the accounts were negligible and, as I say, both appeared to be true. There was no more detail forthcoming, which given his facility with words as a publisher's editor indicates to me that his final encounter with 'Casey' was a fantasy, even though he believed it happened."

Marchant leaned back in the soft chair and breathed out. His exhalation spoke of exhaustion. "Truth," he said "is subjective. Maybe you can want something enough to make it appear real to you. The question is, were his statements factual enough for us to pursue this and publish it."

"He says in the manuscript that you both took photographs in Socorro," Bristowe reached up and rubbed a palm over his eyes. "Sorry, a touch a blepharitis..."

Marchant reached into his manbag which he'd placed on the floor on his right and withdrew a plain white A3 envelope. He placed it deliberately on the table.

"They don't mean anything," said Marchant as Bristowe opened the unsealed pocket and leafed through the six colour emulsion prints that nestled within it. The analyst stared at the stills of nacreous Frisbee-like objects suspended in cloudless skies over desert scrub without apparent surprise.

"...beacause they could so easily be faked." Bristowe said softly and laid the photographs and envelope down quietly atop the Neale's manuscript. He was perplexed by Marchant's lack of conviction in his own photographs of UFOs. Perhaps they were ersatz after all, he thought.

"Yes. I know what I saw and how I interpret it, but such 'proof', as it is, isn't enough."

The room was shadowy and silent for a few moments. Both men seemed drained, deflated. Then Bristowe got up from his seat and made for the desk. "I tracked down the boy during my symposium trip to the UK," he said, opening a drawer beneath the mahogany surface.

"Casey's son?" asked Marchant, animated suddenly.

"Yes. He was pretty inarticulate and didn't want to talk about his mother, but I got this deathbed photograph of her from him," Bristowe walked back toward Marchant who rose and took the offered print from the analysts' freckled hand.

Marchant was looking at the image of a bald woman's head laid back on a pillow on what was clearly a hospital bed. She had no eyebrows or lashes, high cheekbones, a chin that tapered almost to a point and thin lips. Her nose was had a small lilt that was beautiful. Her skin had the texture of dry twenty-denier nylon. Her irises were millimetre-narrow chromium blue rings around immense black pupils that appeared as vacant as that of a Koi carp. The whites of her eyes resembled clear jelly. But most striking to Marchant was the shape of those orbits. The flesh around the woman's eyes seemed to slant off to a sharp angle as their horizontal apexes edged around the sides of her skull, making her resemble a cosmetically enhanced Houri. Casey Bowers—if this were her—looked sick, but beneath the illness was an unmistakable, inherent strangeness.

"She isn't wearing make-up here, apparently... or so the boy said," said Bristowe quietly.

"What did the son look like?" asked Marchant, looking up from the portrait, frowning.

"His eyes resembled his mother's." Bristowe sounded fatalistic. "Like frogspawn. He never blinked."

The room was silent for a while. Outside, unfathomable lead white spherical shapes skipped in bobbing motions in the firmament, high above the needle-like buildings where Bristowe rented his downtown office suite.

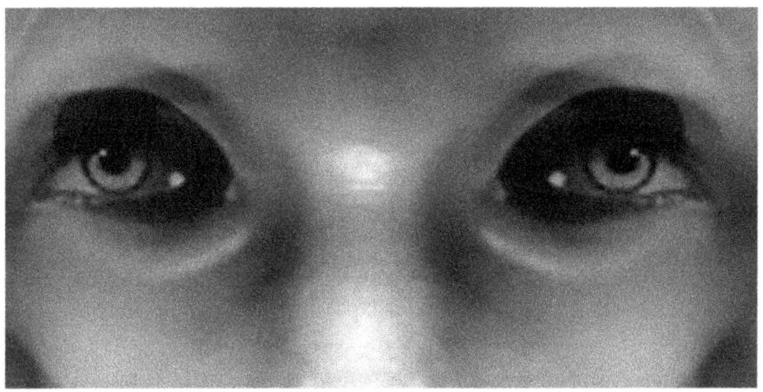

Paul A. Green

THE FINAL ANALYSIS

AS his train crawled through the suburbs of south-west London, David Carlson was already having misgivings about his decision to have a consultation with Dr. Ballard. Perhaps he had been swayed too easily by his wife's insistence, repeated almost daily, that he was 'in need of psychiatric help'. He couldn't recall any specific incident that might have prompted Monica to make these assertions with such matriarchal solemnity.

Admittedly their conjugal relations had become infrequent and mechanical, as if they were clumsily acting out instructions from the advice column of one of the new 'liberated' women's magazines. He had also grown frustrated in his work as assistant editor of a trade magazine, *Plastics World*, a role that mostly involved re-writing press releases and enduring lunches with effusive company reps. And there were times when existence as a whole seemed to be a sequence of futile chores. Such feelings were apparently not uncommon in today's consumer society—he'd read that best-selling paperback *The Lonely Crowd*. But did he really need professional advice?

However, he was reassured by Dr James Ballard's CV. A medical degree at King's College, Cambridge, followed by training at the Tavistock Institute, a consultancy at the Maudsley Hospital and subsequent private practice at his home in Wimbledon. Even his substantial hourly rate seemed further endorsement of his status and competence.

Carlson turned his attention to the front page of the *Daily Telegraph*. PM ORDERS TROOPS TO VIETNAM. "Last night Prime Minister John Profumo told Parliament that soldiers from the Royal Marines and the Parachute Regiment would be flying to Vietnam to support US forces in their fight against the Communist guerrillas, now supported by Russian 'advisers'. An RAF squadron was also on stand-by in case of further escalation." Carlson was almost cheered by this news. At least Great Britain could still strut its stuff on the international stage. But he was discomfited by another front-page story RUSSIAN MOON LAUNCH RUMOUR? Control of the space ways, a recurrent theme in those Robert Heinlein stories he used to enjoy, would be a vital element in winning the Cold War.

Inside there was a frivolous item about the High Numbers beat group. Their drummer Keith Moon had been arrested for crashing his Ferrari into an empty swimming pool, an alcohol fuelled prank that left him with a broken nose. Carlson didn't care much for pop music, although Monica still prized her Cliff Richard LPs. They were only in their thirties but this new twenty-something generation seemed almost alien as they paraded past their boutiques or flaunted their drug taking.

As the train drew into Wimbledon he began wondering what drugs Dr Ballard might prescribe.

After a brisk walk up Wimbledon Hill and a stroll through the upmarket Village, Carlson turned down a broad leafy avenue near the Common. He paused outside a large detached redbrick Edwardian villa with a half timbered facade. Through the shrubbery behind the clipped privet hedge, he could glimpse a blue Austin Cambridge saloon and a Triumph Bonneville motor cycle parked on the driveway. Somebody twitched a curtain. There was no way back now.

As he hesitated outside the porch, the door opened and a tall dark-haired woman appeared. "Do come in. I'm Marian Ballard. You must be Mr. Carlson. Jim's expecting you."

He was struck by her figure and her elegant accent as she ushered him inside, through a hallway cluttered with children's bicycles and scattered shopping bags. He nearly tripped over a small ginger cat that darted between his legs. "I'm sorry, Sputnik goes all over the place. He's quite bonkers..." She picked up the animal and cradled it in her arm as she opened the door of the front room. "Mr Carlson has landed," she announced cheerfully.

Carlson had been expecting some clinical antiseptic space, its geometry defined by functional office furniture and perhaps a few shelves of medical journals. He wasn't prepared for this dusty lair dominated by a battered mahogany desk and a faded crimson velvet chaise-longue. These were offset by rusty filing cabinets overflowing with folders, an old radio in a wooden cabinet, a large fan on a metal tripod and a tall potted palm by the window. A sagging bookshelf was piled up with tattered car manuals and recent copies of *New Cosmos*, a 'speculative fiction' magazine that he rarely bought now, wearying of its increasingly obscure fictions.

A tall man in his mid-thirties wearing a check sports jacket and dark shirt rose from behind the desk, and extended a hand. "Welcome, David... So you've survived your journey through the suburbs. Dangerous terrain. But interesting territory, especially when it becomes a journey into the interior. Or a voyage into the remote past. Imagine Jurassic Wimbledon, ruled by dinosaurs! Today, of course, our monsters roam the uplands of the cerebral cortex..."

Carlson could only mumble a reply about the train running on time. He'd been put off-guard by Dr. Ballard's affability and that rich drawling baritone voice. Surely a psychiatrist was supposed to have a minimal presence, a listener rather than an oracle? Meanwhile Ballard gestured towards the couch, so Carlson reclined on it, according to protocol.

While his doctor was sorting through paperwork and rummaging for a notebook, Carlson surveyed the room. A reproduction of Salvador Dali's *The Metamorphoses of Narcissus* was pinned to the wall beside him while a framed oil painting hung behind the desk. In the style of Rene Magritte it depicted a winged naked woman flying above a forest of umbrellas. He noted the signature—JGB. Unfortunately the composition seemed awkward and the brushwork looked clumsy so he felt might be wise to refrain from comment.

A model aircraft was suspended on a wire above the couch. From his viewing of war films he recognised it as a Mitsubishi Zero fighter, as flown by Japanese *kamikaze* pilots. He had a sudden vision of it screaming down towards his head as he tried to articulate his malaise.

'So where do we want to start?' Dr Ballard's jovial prompting aroused him from this morbid fantasy.

Carlson began with what he called 'an overview' of his situation, a long rambling narration regarding his unrewarding job and 'marital difficulties'. But increasingly he felt he was outlining the case history of an anonymous alien subject. His account of Monica's dutiful attempts to arouse him seemed like a heavily censored chapter from a mediocre erotic novel or a quote from a tabloid sex crime report. "The accused then attempted intimacy." The words went dead as soon as he uttered them. In the silence he could hear the tick of his psychiatrist's alarm clock.

Perhaps his narrative needed a context. So he explained how he was an only child who'd grown up in South London. His father was a minor civil servant, his mother a maths teacher. They were devout Methodists, protective, wary of change and 'influences'. Even skiffle music on the BBC *Light Programme* was regarded with suspicion and his selection of art books from the local library was carefully scrutinised. However, he'd done well at grammar school, in a low-key fashion, and gone up to Oxford where he'd begun a BA in English Literature. Unfortunately he failed the first year exams and dropped out. His family overruled his desire to attend art school and pressured him to seek employment. So began a series of dead-end jobs—waiter, barman, encyclopaedia salesman, all ending prematurely while he lived at home with his impatient purse-lipped parents. Then through a family friend he got an office-boy post with *Plastics World* where he'd been for over a decade, rising by default to his current position. He'd met Monica at an office party when she was temping for another magazine in the building. After their marriage they had managed to buy a flat in Surbiton although Monica now had ambitions for a three bedroom semi.

He couldn't keep this up. "It's no good. It's so drab, meaningless, one botched job after another, a history of failures. My wife keeps implying there's something wrong with me. And the worst thing is that I don't bloody care. It doesn't seem real, any of it."

The psychiatrist put down his pen. "How much television do you watch?"

"The news, both BBC and ITV. Monica likes to watch *Play for Today* sometimes but I'm not really a drama person."

"The news is a superior fabulation, I agree. But do you fantasise about intercourse with some female TV presenter—Joan Bakewell perhaps? In an abandoned studio, during a hurricane, for example? Or perhaps an actress—Jayne Mansfield in a Buick Riviera?"

"I really don't see the relevance..." Carlson was irritated by Ballard's flippancy.

"You must go deeper into your obsessions. Do you dream?"

"I don't remember any dreams..."

"That's quite unusual. A friend of mine, Dr Christopher Evans, is conducting some research on dreaming at the National Physical Laboratory. Chris hypothesises that we all need to dream, just as a computer needs down-time to reorganise its data. You'd be an interesting subject."

"I'm not a laboratory animal, Dr Ballard." Carlson resented the suggestion that he was a passive specimen, to be wired up and interrogated by men in white coats.

"Our animal inheritance goes back into the depths of archeopsychic time. Your brain carries the imprint of your reptilian and mammalian forebears, their memories of fight and flight across the forests and deserts of a very dangerous planet. In dreaming you can access their accumulated ancestral wisdom. You should start keeping a log and bring it to our next session."

The alarm rang and Dr Ballard closed his notebook. Carlson still lay on the couch, pondering this disturbing request. Then he felt Ballard's hand on his elbow, raising him from his supine position and steering him towards the door.

When he arrived home, he found Monica busy in the kitchen. She was wearing a red leather mini-skirt and she'd combed her blonde hair into a pony tail, like some French film actress.

"Would you like some red wine with your *beef bourguignon*, darling? After we've eaten you must tell me all about it. Then we can have an early night..."

They sat down at Monica's new G-Plan table. Carlson savoured the rich meat with a sudden primal satisfaction, as if he'd slaughtered the beast himself. He listened to Monica's animated dramatisation of her triumph over Mr. Stanwell, her rival in the Accounts Department. Thanks to her cunning wiles she now had priority access to the new IBM payroll computer. Carlson became quite absorbed in this strange soap opera. He could imagine a close-up of Monica's defiant pout, followed by a pan across the office to the balding Stanwell biting his moustache in high indignation. Then her scenario segued into an interrogation.

"So what did you tell Dr. Ballard? About your—"

"Not very much."

"But sweetheart—that's why we're paying him, isn't it?" Her coy smile couldn't conceal her impatience.

"I hardly got a word in. He was too busy playing the Sage of the Suburbs." Monica frowned, uncertain of how to respond.

Pushing his plate aside, Carlson got up and turned on the TV. The normally unflappable BBC news reader looked flustered.

"...claims that two RAF Hawker Hunter jets have been shot down over Hanoi have not been confirmed by the Ministry of Defence. Meanwhile Russian MIG-15 fighters have been observed giving air support to Viet Cong units making sorties into the Mekong Delta..."

Carlson switched to the commercial channel, cutting into an advert for skin lotion. A dark-haired girl in a bikini was emerging from the sea in slow motion, watched closely by a group of young men sprawled on the sandy beach. A female voice whispered over flutes and vibes. *With Solarise All Their Eyes Are On You.* Carlson was fascinated by the play of sunlight on her cheekbones and the smooth curvature of her belly and thighs, a calculus of desire...

His reverie was disrupted by Monica calling from the kitchen, demanding his assistance with the washing-up, but her words sounded as distant and cryptic as the cries of seabirds circling over that streaky monochrome beach. He turned the TV volume down.

Later he fell asleep on the couch.

SUBJECT: David Graham Carlson—DOB: 5th March 1933
Session 2: 17th August 1966

Today DC produced his dream log, carefully written in an exercise book like a piece of Latin homework. There are only three items in this oneiric record. Two of them are too fragmented and diffuse for close analysis, although they both have some interesting elements. DC dreamed that he was trapped by tangled seaweed in an expanse of warm brackish water that rose up to his neck as he fought off the claws and mandibles of a crab-like creature. He was afraid of drowning and woke up abruptly.

I recognised at once that this almost certainly referred to his marital 'stagnation' and his fear of breaking the incest taboo with Monica C as his mother-figure. However I believe that subject is not yet ready for this revelation so I suggested the dream might be a trauma narrative of uterine misadventure, perhaps entrapment in the umbilical cord, an interpretation that he accepted, albeit reluctantly.

A second dream, three nights later, seemed to centre on a motor accident. He was driving a large American convertible. A female mannequin in a blonde wig and miniskirt was seated beside him—clearly another reference to Monica C. Very loud beat music was playing on the car radio. This distracted him and he drove into the concrete pillar of a multi-storey car park. In shock he embraced the rubbery plastic limbs of the doll, only to find a policeman looming over him arresting him for gross indecency.

Obviously repressed desire and guilt are the key factors dominating his sex 'drive' although curiously DC has never owned a car or even taken out a provisional licence. The American car is another anomaly. Chris would say that it's been implanted by TV footage of that failed assassination attempt on President Nixon in Los Angeles.

The third account is the most detailed and coherent. DC is flying over Wimbledon Common in an ancient bi-plane. He is almost naked except for his helmet and goggles for it is extremely hot and a giant sun, almost twice normal size, glares down from an azure sky. The engine keeps cutting out and he is losing height.

He skims the tops of oaks and beeches, their foliage browned, their clusters of scorched branches and twigs resembling tangles of dead neutrons and synapses. Wild fires are breaking out in these woodlands so he steers through drifting pillars of smoke towards the golf course, which is now a wide expanse of baked cracked earth. He manages a bumpy landing, the aircraft collapsing around him and disintegrating into a heap of sand and rust.

He staggers away, desperate to find water and sets off towards the properties bordering the Common. Glancing back he sees a glistening metallic lizard of some kind tracking him slowly but purposefully. It's hard to move fast over the glassy outcrops of fused sand. But he succeeds at last in crossing the fractured tarmac of the road towards the luxury Parkside Apartments.

He pushes open the heavy doors—to find himself behind a giant movie set. The flats are literally flat, like the hoardings for some vast advertisement. Beyond as far as the eye can see there are sand-dunes, their blankness only relieved by the occasional protrusion of a television aerial or corroded girder. A few feet away a woman resembling Catherine Deneuve sits on a beach chair in front of a huge electric typewriter on a mahogany desk. "You are the last poet," she announces solemnly. As he wakes he knows this will be on the TV morning news.

DC has studied literature so I suspect there has been some embellishment and imposition of narrative structure. However what concerns me is the apocalyptic quality of this dream. It clearly presages some crisis, perhaps a psychotic episode that will break through his loss of affect and drastically change his relationship with his wife—for better or worse. I must bring forward the date for his next appointment.

MAKE LOVE, NOT WAR! TROOPS OUT! NO NUKES FOR UK! Carlson was deafened by the overlapping chants of the protesters, brandishing their placards like a forest of pitchforks as he tried to make his way around the edge of Trafalgar Square. The demonstration was apparently unauthorised, a spontaneous happening promoted by extremist groups like the Crypto-Anarchist Front and the Freakniks. Indeed, Freaknik girls danced naked in the fountains, splashing and screaming, hysterical Cassandras prophesying doom while a hairy poet perching on a stone lion declaimed through a megaphone. Meanwhile bewildered policemen were struggling to control the marchers as they swirled around Nelson's Column like pilgrims around the Black Stone of Mecca. The groups with black flags were clearly intent on breaking through to Whitehall. The crush could easily turn into a stampede.

Carlson desperately needed to get to Waterloo Station if he was to make this new and highly inconvenient session with Dr Ballard. He was already in bad odour with Burton, his boss, for leaving their Soho office early, having done a hasty sub-edit on 'High-Density Polythene—The Future of Food Packaging!'. But these scruffy boys and girls with their banners formed an impenetrable scrum across the pavements, blocking him in every direction. A bearded youth in jeans cast a hostile eye over Carlson's grey suit and tie. "Hey, it's a pig in plain clothes, trying to suss us out!"

Carlson ignored the jibe and tried to elbow his way forward but the boy continued ranting in his face. "You're a dead man, you know that? Dead to the world and you want us dead like you. Sorry for your wife, it must be like fucking a radioactive corpse." Two girls bedecked with flowers and beads burst out laughing.

Carlson, suddenly in fight mode, jabbed an index finger in his tormentor's eye. The boy lost his balance and fell, cracking his head on the kerb. To his own amazement, Carlson found himself stamping on the boy's skull again and again, as if he was crushing some venomous insect. Each adrenalin-fuelled kick confirmed his territorial rights. Blood trickled from his victim's nose and ears. The girls were screaming now, retreating in terror as he pushed them aside and ran towards Villiers Street and the Hungerford Bridge. As he immersed himself in the crowd he could hear the desperate cries of the young people as they attempted to revive their peace warrior.

"You have to help me, Dr Ballard. I may have killed somebody..." Carlson plunged into a garbled account of his encounter. The psychiatrist put aside his notebook and listened intently while Carlson reprised the narrative yet again.

"I felt everyone on the station concourse knew about it already. They all had their heads down hiding behind their evening papers, like they were reading the story, my story. They were dumb—except a few women crying. And the train was so crowded, even for the rush hour. Men, women and children. They told the children not to cry. It was like..."

"...like when you were evacuated during the war?" Ballard suggested.

Carlson remembered the farm in Newton Abbot, the surly family that reluctantly took him in. "Yes—how did you know? Were you?"

"In a manner of speaking. I was in the Far East. In a civilian prison camp. But enough of that. I sensed that you were approaching a catharsis. It's a pity you didn't come and see me earlier, when your psychosis might have taken on a more benevolent form, seeking release in the gentler interzones of fetishism, in the generosity of women."

"But what I should do now? There were scores of police there. And hundreds of witnesses. They must have seen me, even in that riot."

"I think the authorities have other preoccupations at the moment. You really need a drink. Would you like a scotch?"

"Surely that's not really ethical..."

"Oh, it's an essential prescription, especially in the current situation." Ballard poured two doubles and topped them up with a squirt of soda. He handed a glass to Carlson. "You see, this could be my final analysis. I've sent Marian and the children to North Wales, for the time being. I'm planning to join them tomorrow."

"I don't understand."

Ballard switched on the radio. "... interrupt this programme for a special News Bulletin. Following last night's incursion into East Berlin by a US task force, the Kremlin has ordered the British Ambassador, Sir Alec Douglas Home, to return to London, effectively breaking off diplomatic relations with the UK. In other developments, Russian and Chinese bombers have carried out heavy raids on Saigon and Viet Cong forces are now at the outskirts of the city. At nine o'clock tonight Her Majesty the Queen will give a TV and radio address to the nation. Meanwhile, citizens are advised to read the Civil Defence leaflets now being distributed..."

Taking a deep swig from his glass, Ballard turned off the set. "I think we're having a wake in advance for the megadeaths. Our private Hiroshimas have become public Nagasakis. If I were you, Carlson, I'd set off now and try to salvage something with Monica. I've enjoyed having you as a patient. Your dreamscapes could have made fascinating stories."

"You write? From our case histories?" Carlson should have been shocked. But it seemed the inevitable thing to do, almost comic in the circumstances.

"I won a short story competition at Cambridge, that's all. Perhaps I should have stuck with it. But the literary life isn't for me. Nevertheless—." The drone of aircraft overhead obscured the rest of the sentence.

Ballard sat down at the desk, poured himself another whiskey and inserted a sheet of paper into his typewriter. Carlson hovered by the door, waves of emotion now rolling through his mind. He was paralysed by fear, smitten by an abrupt surge of desire for Monica, terrified of the void ahead.

"Go, Carlson—just go!"

He ran out into the dusk. All along Marryat Road householders were strapping suitcases to roof racks or cajoling their children into Volvos. There was already a jam at the junction with Parkside. Pacing himself for the long walk ahead, he was passing the War Memorial at the edge of the Common when he heard the first sirens.

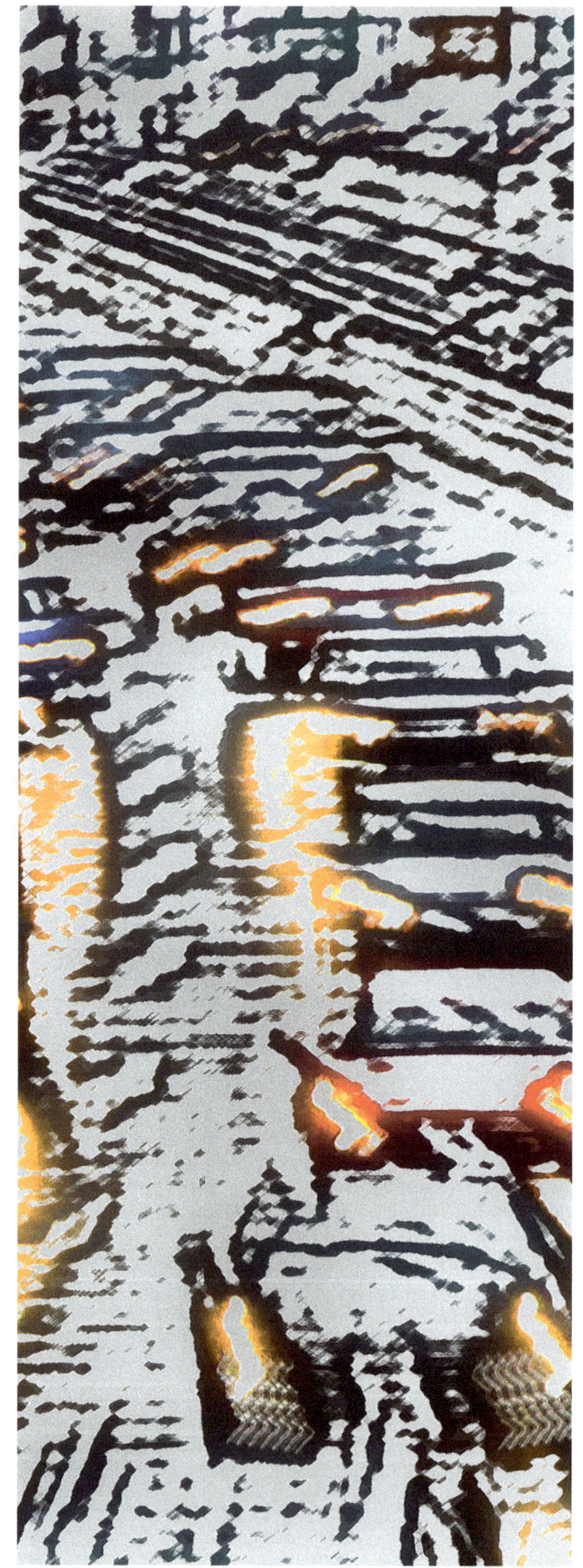

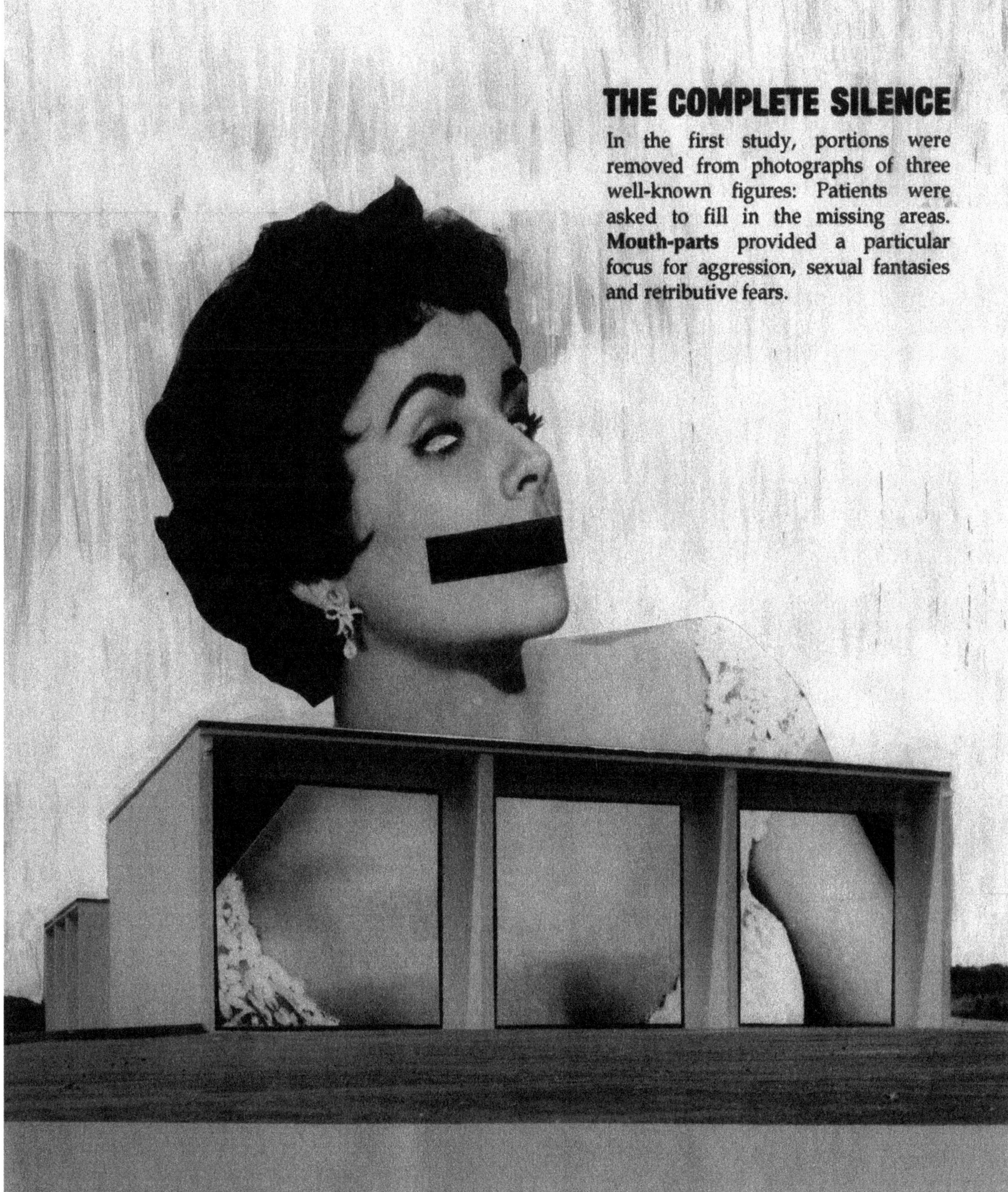
THE COMPLETE SILENCE
In the first study, portions were removed from photographs of three well-known figures: Patients were asked to fill in the missing areas. Mouth-parts provided a particular focus for aggression, sexual fantasies and retributive fears.

Paul H Williams

Dreaming Crash

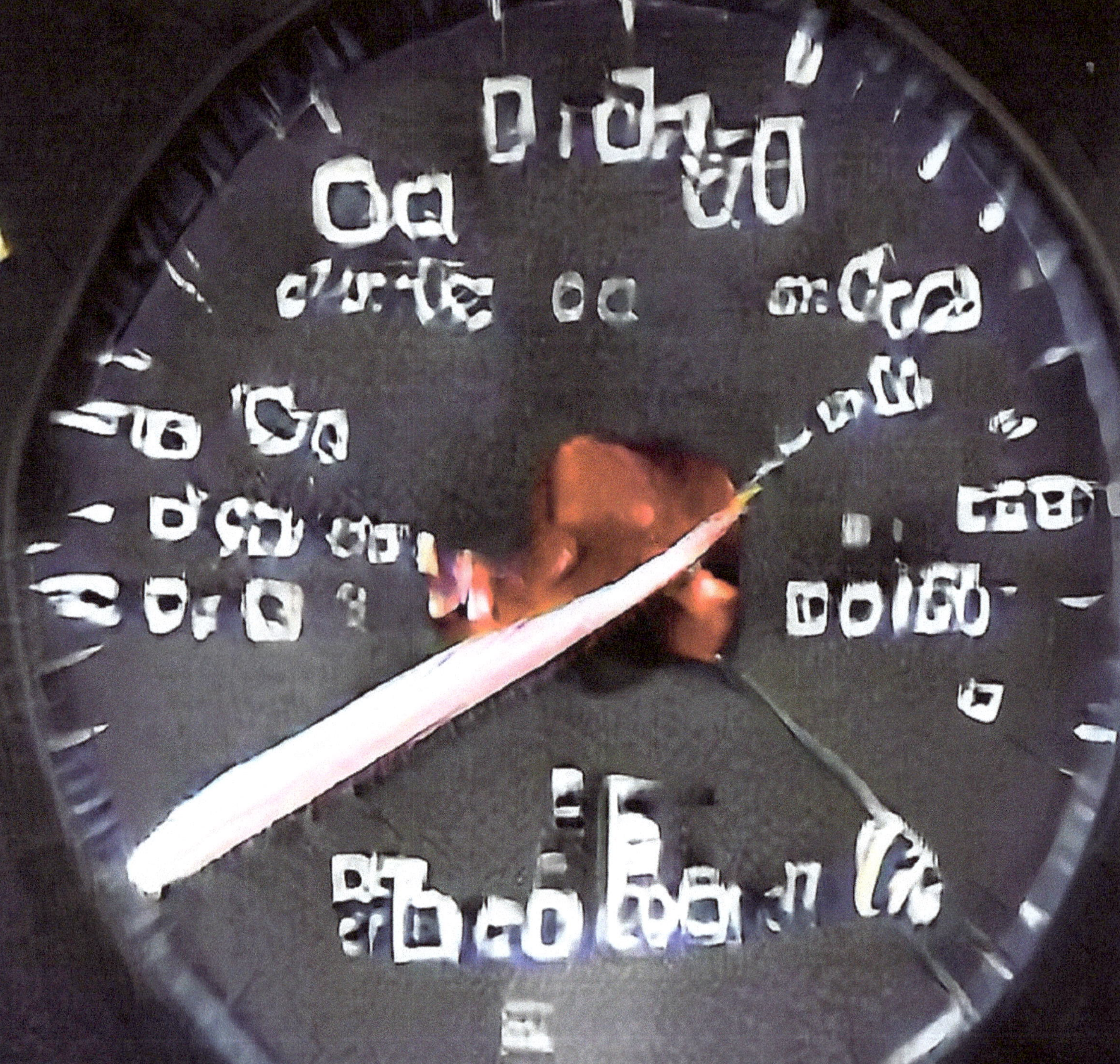

Exploring the World of JG Ballard's Novel with Ganbreeder

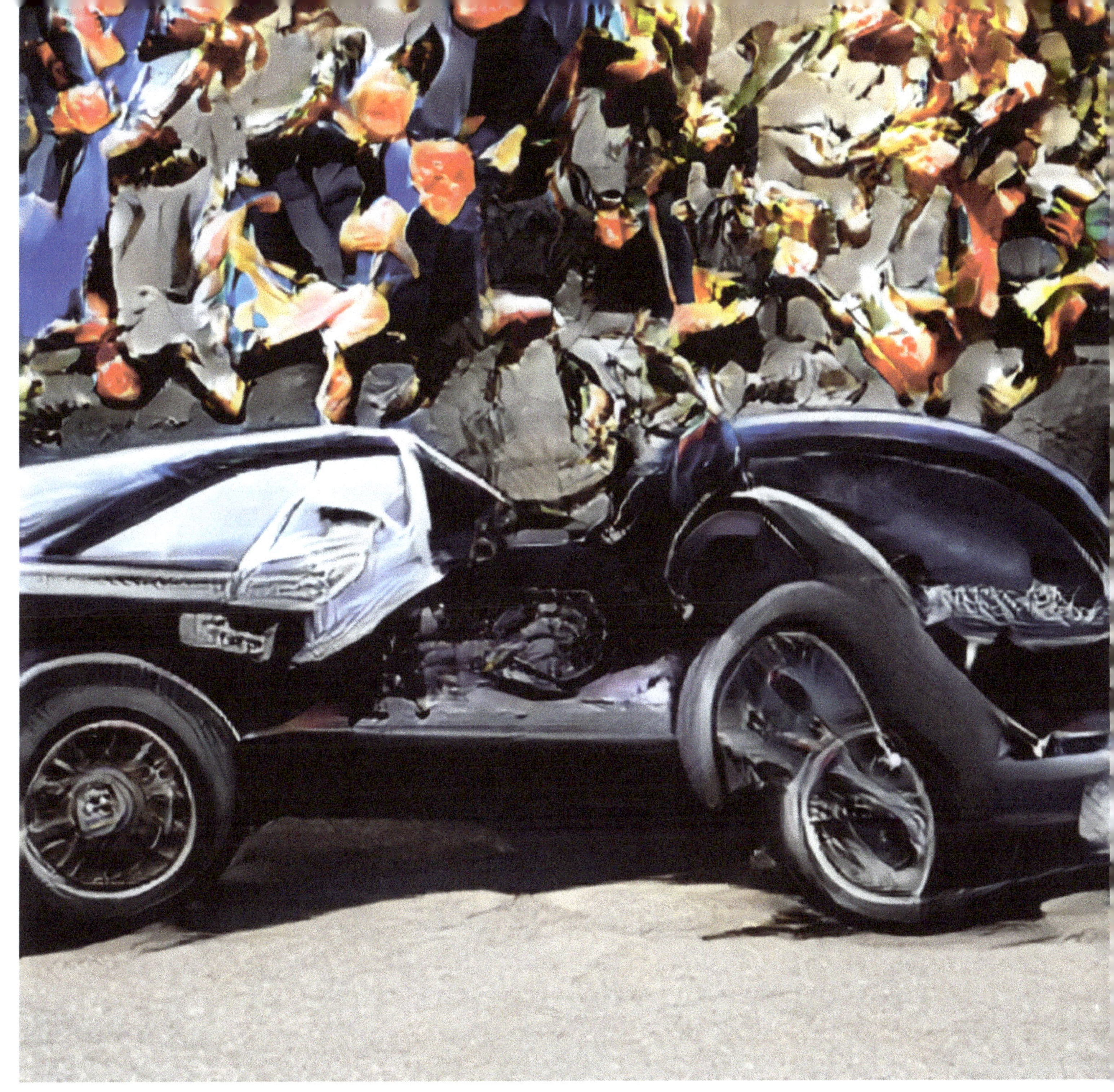

Vaughan dreamt of his collision with Elizabeth Taylor, witnessing her explode from the car's carapace in a glistening shower of body parts and haute couture

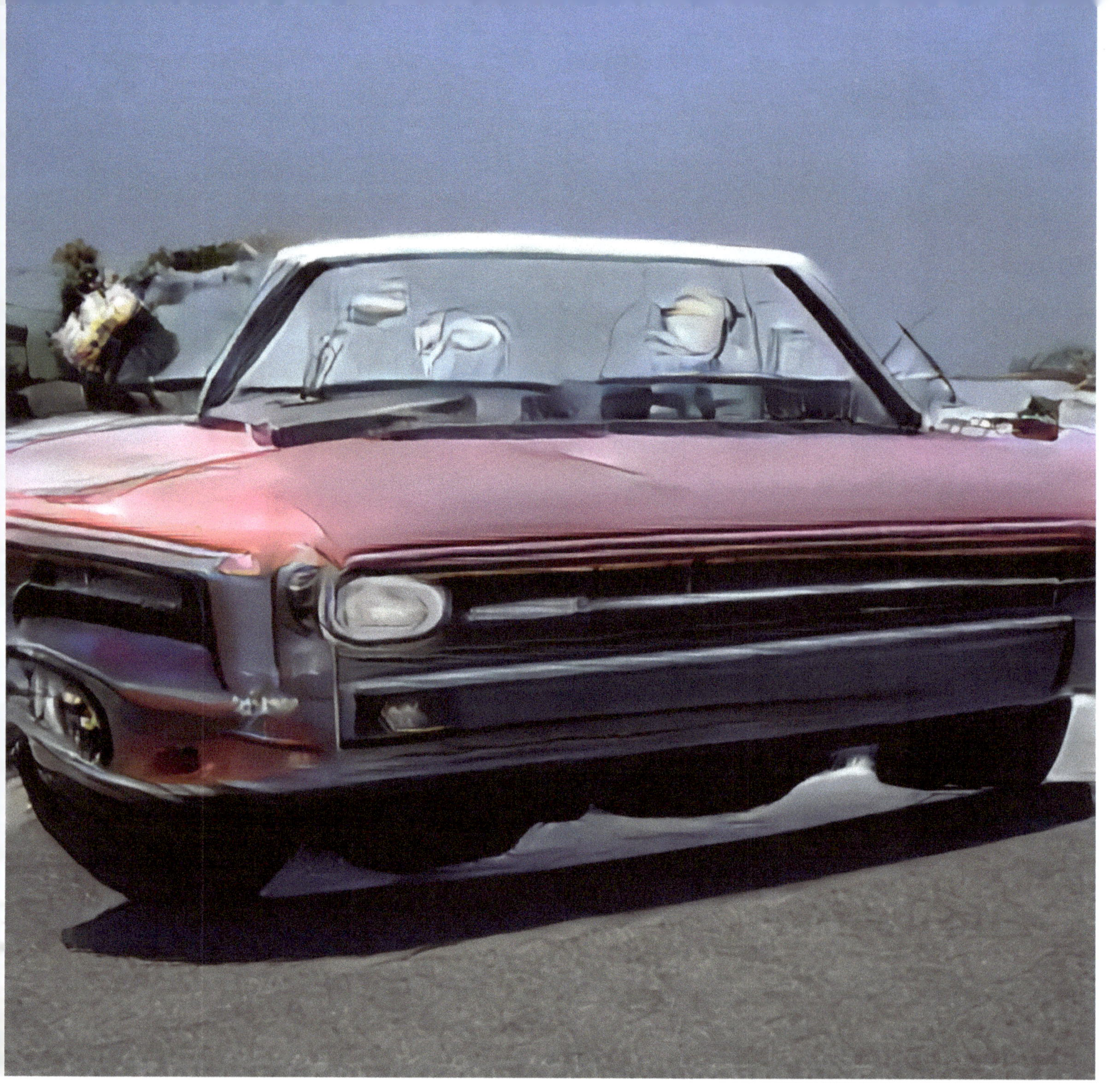

Driving with Vaughan, we seemed like quantum phantoms of the motorways, our wavefunctions collapsing in an exhilarating rush as we appeared, coalescing out of the over-lit landscape, at crash sites and collision points around the M25

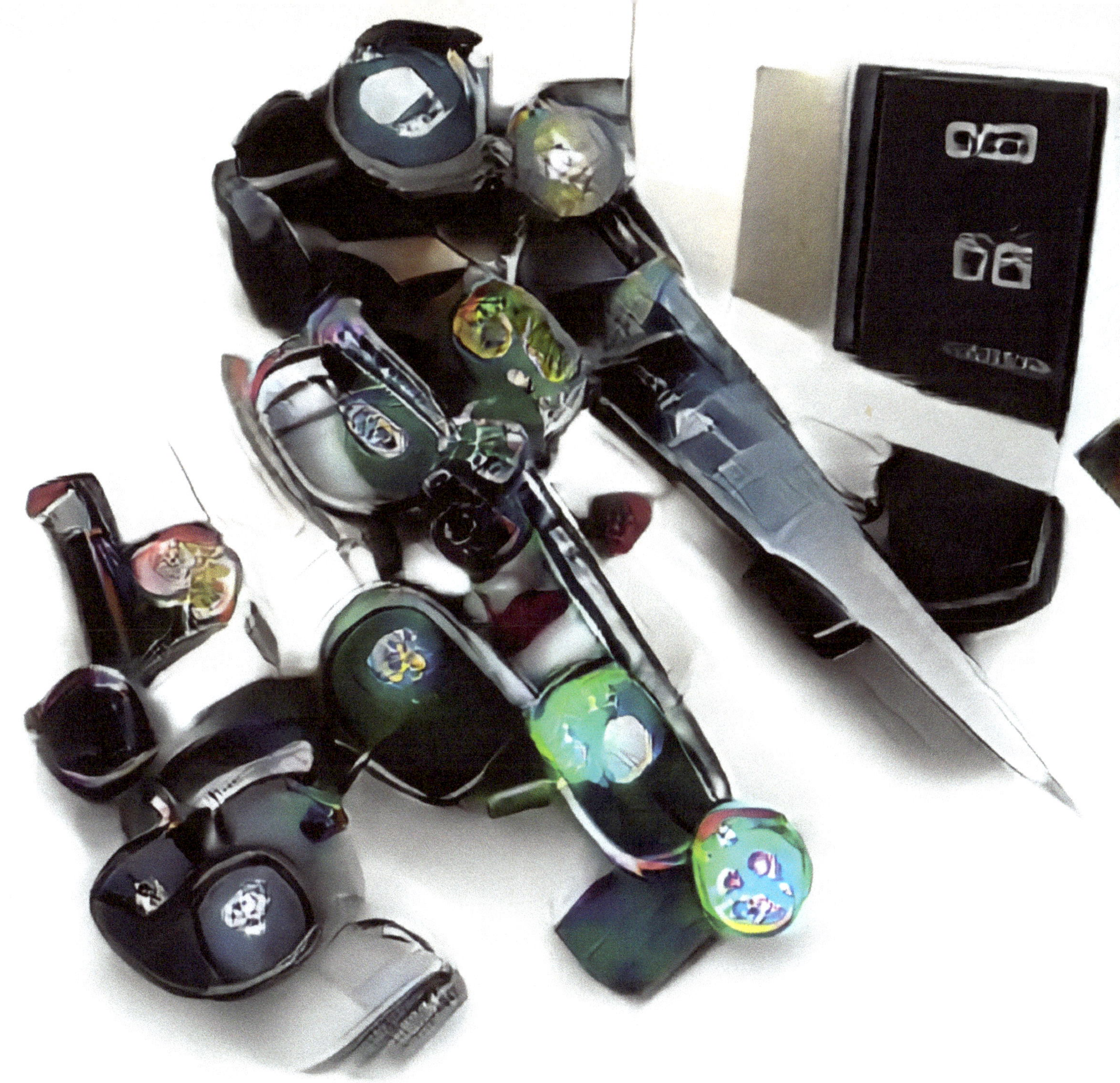

Vaughan emptied the contents of his rucksack revealing a treasure trove of stolen car keys, broken mirror shades, fake passport and knife: vectors of desire

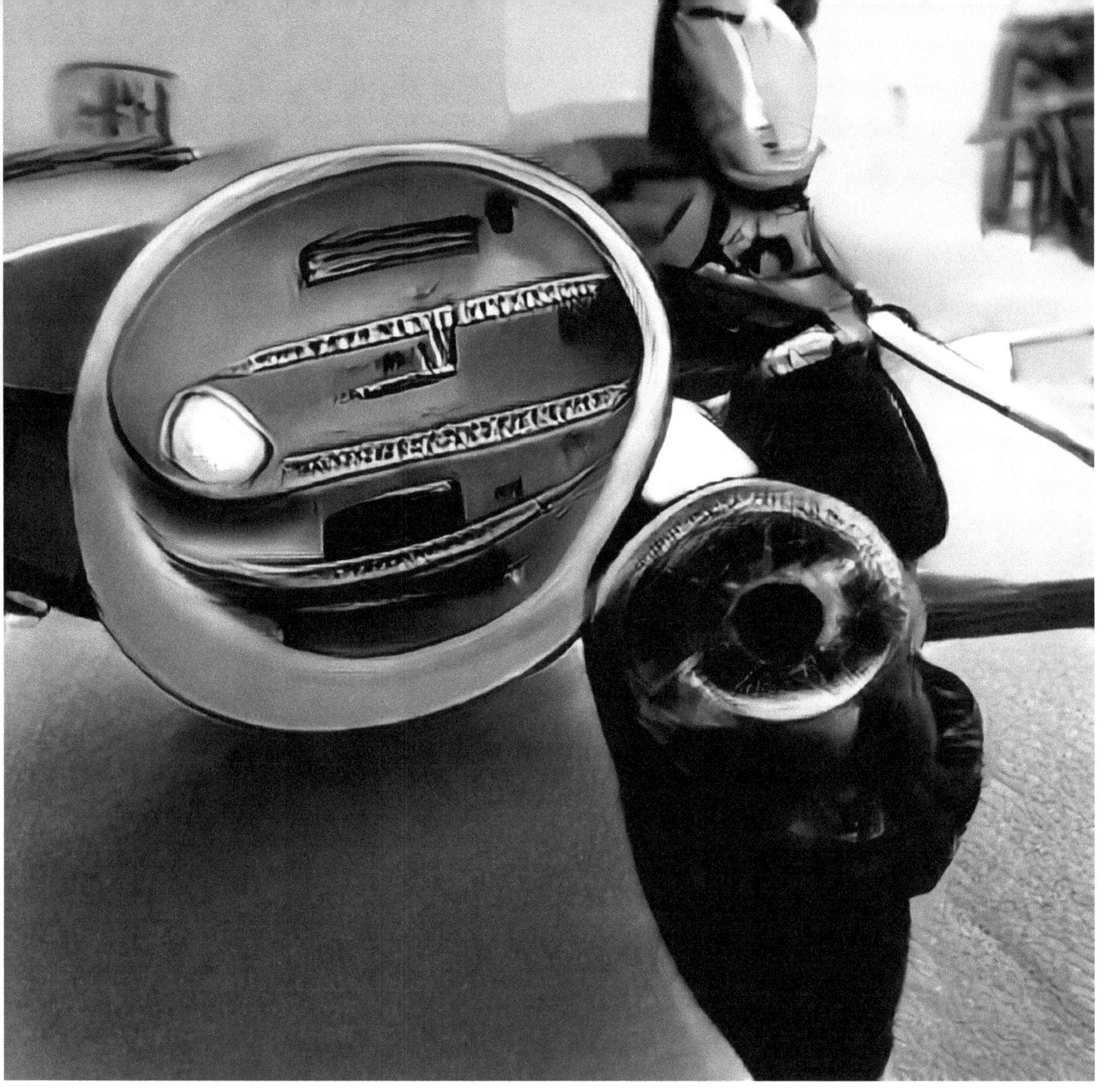

The interior of Gabrielle's car was augmented with a plethora of advanced technologies to interface more intimately with her deformed and scarred body

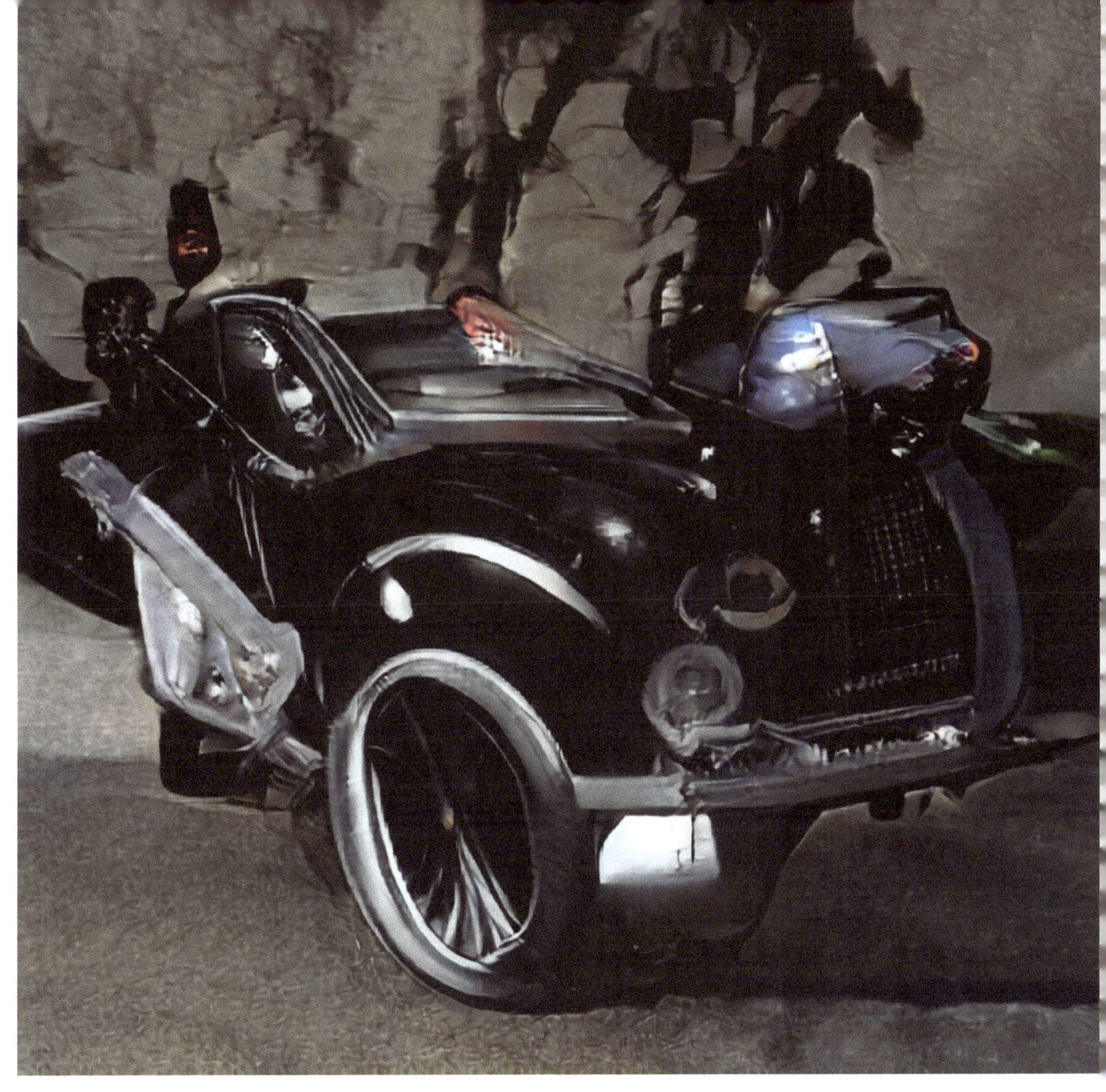

I watched the smoke rise in ghost-like plumes from the crashed car, the smell of petrol drifting through my sinuses like some exotic perfume

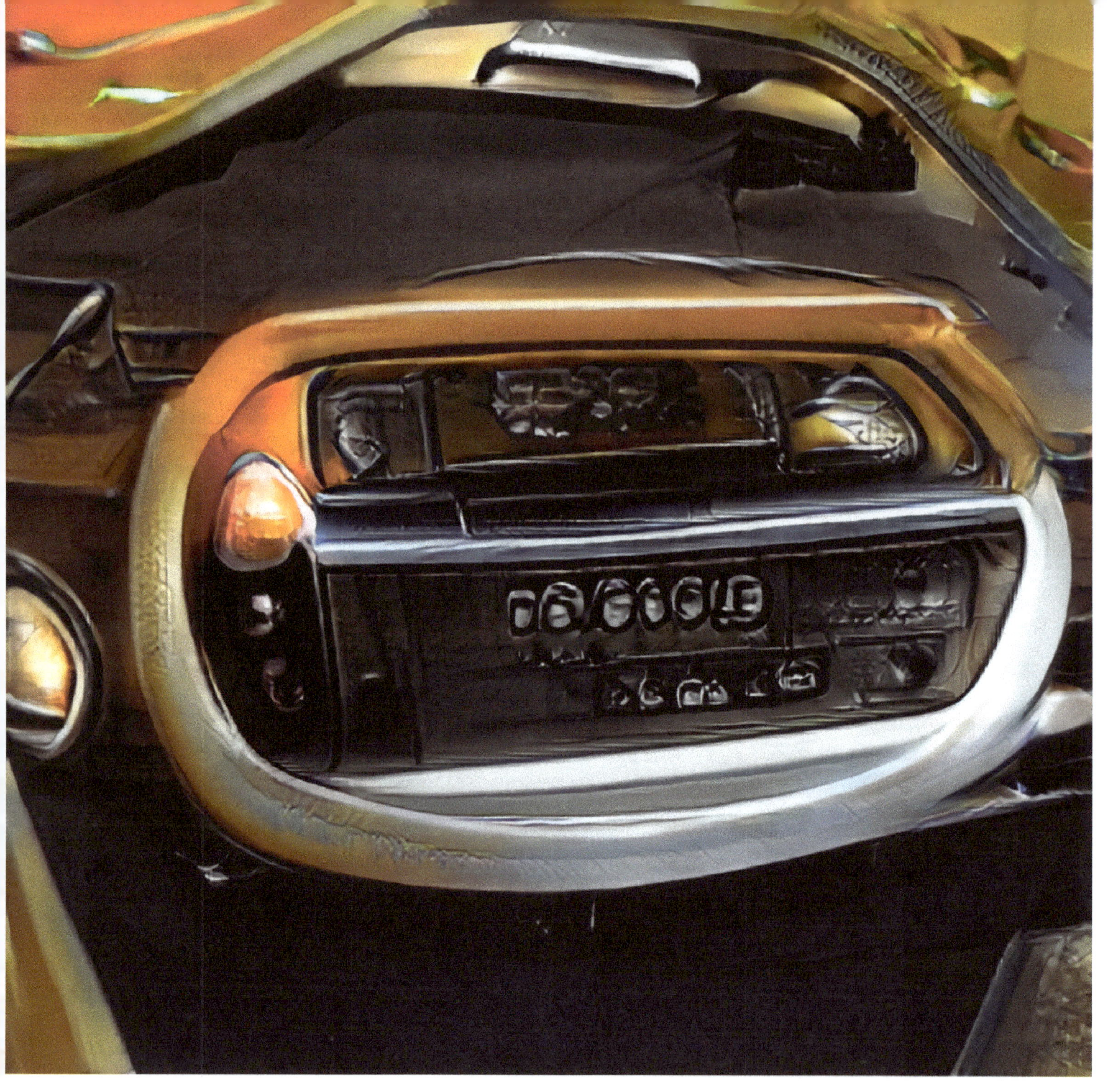

That night I dreamt of instrument binnacles

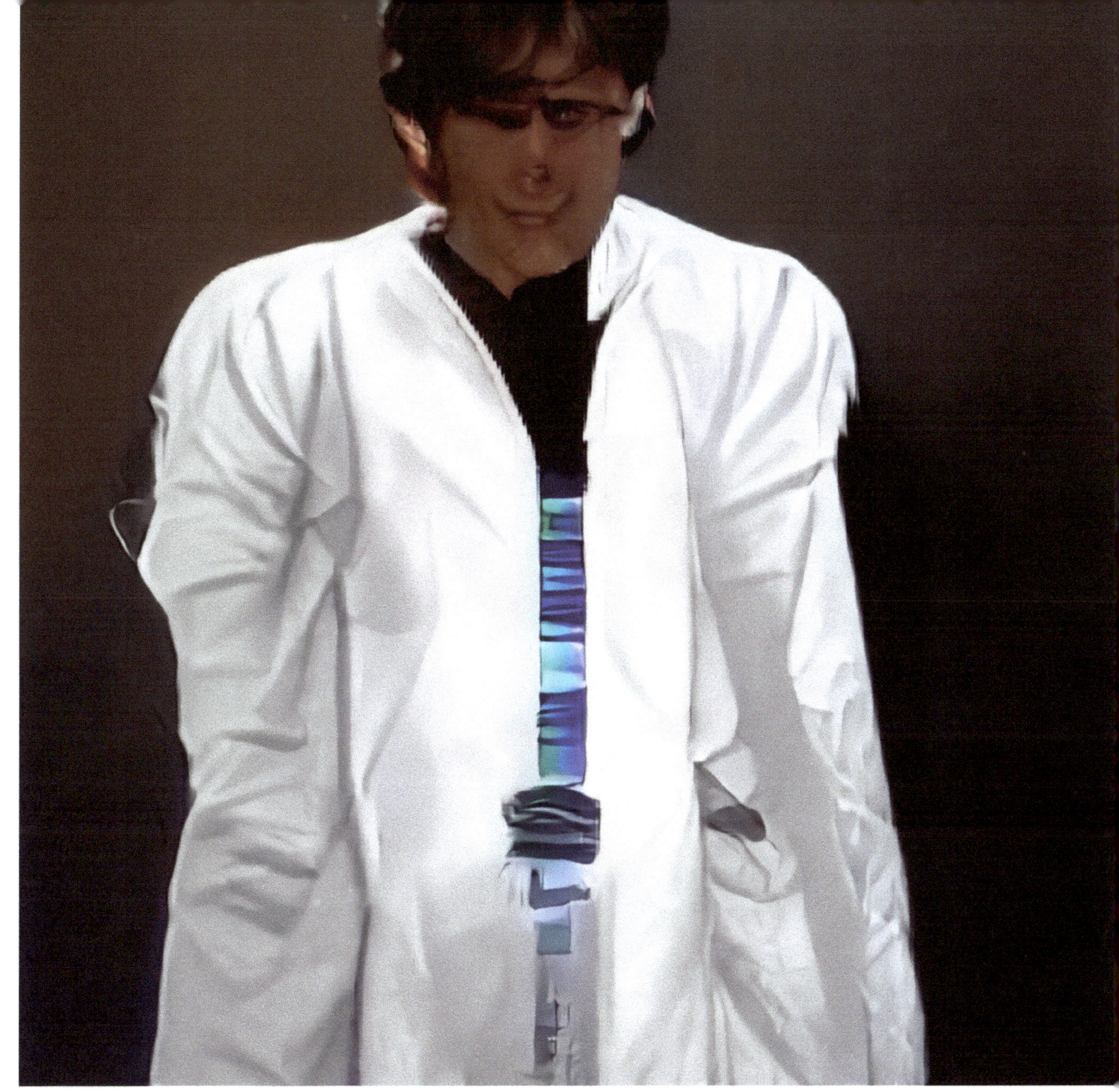

Vaughan wore his lab coat as if presiding over some arcane religious ceremony

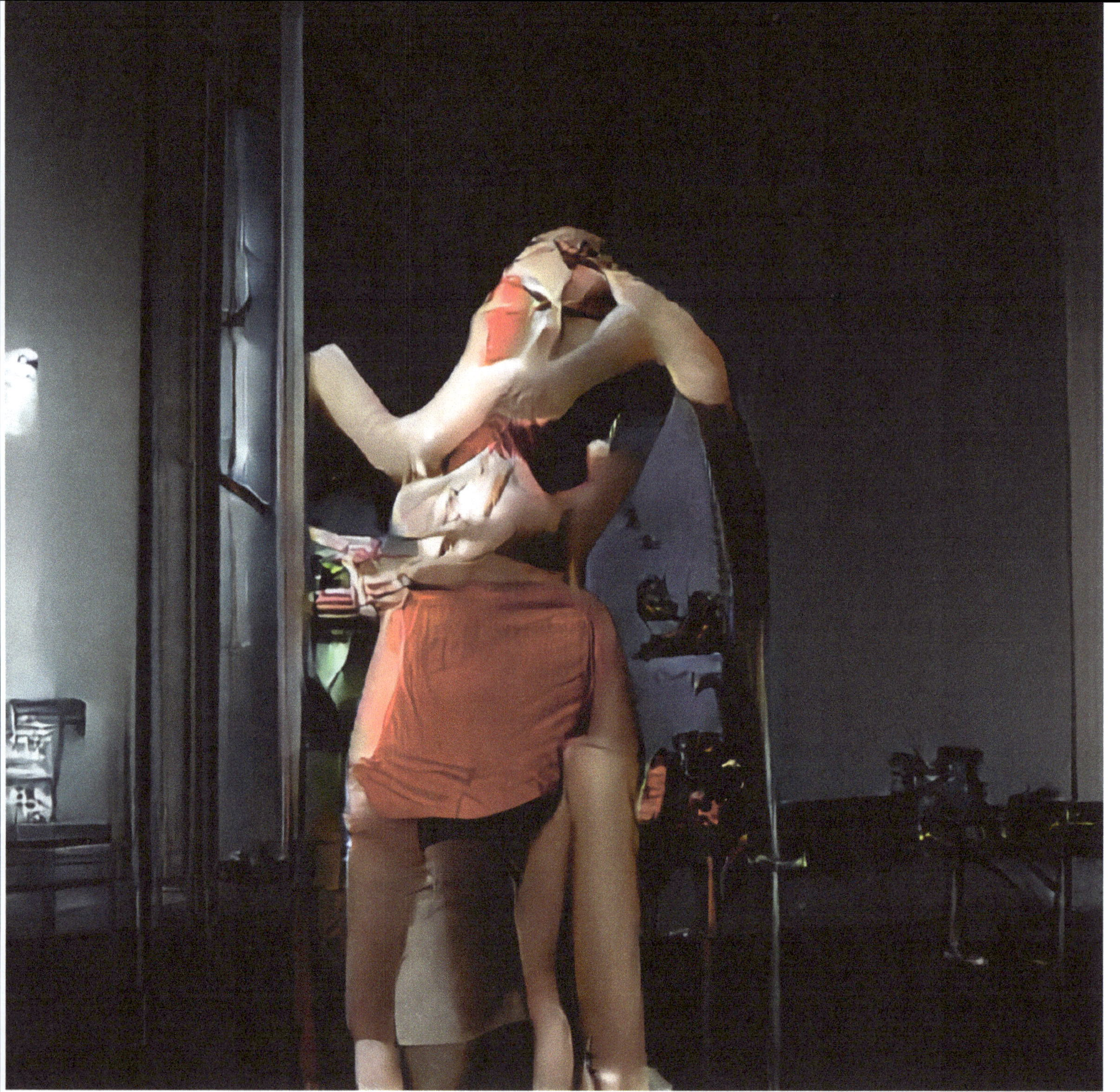

Even in Dr Helen Remington's apartment our sexual encounters

were like the catastrophic union of two cars

meeting in a head-on collision

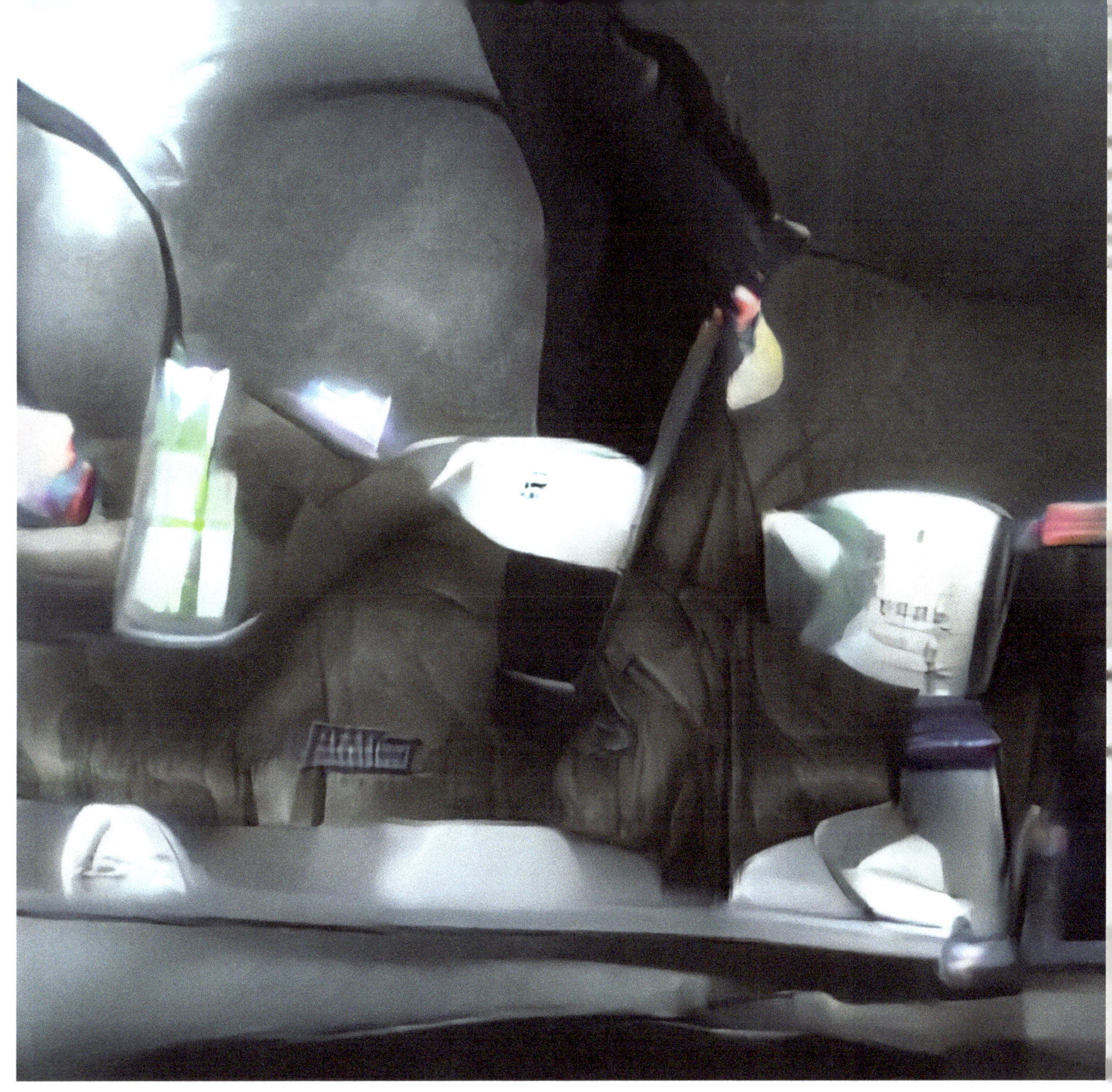

The back seat of the automobile was strewn with used condoms, torn underwear and technical detritus

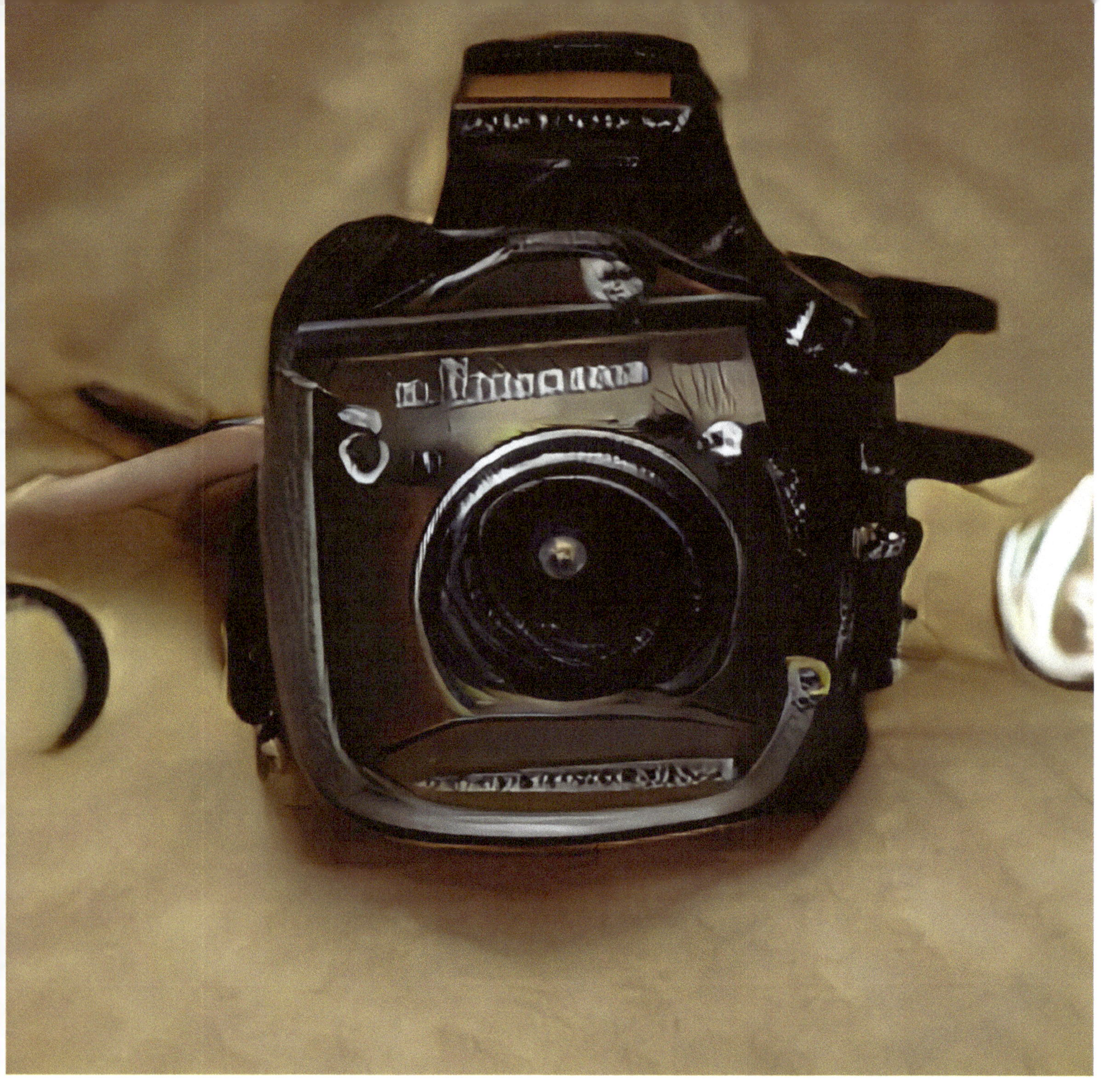

One of Vaughan's cameras had been damaged in a fracas with an ambulance driver

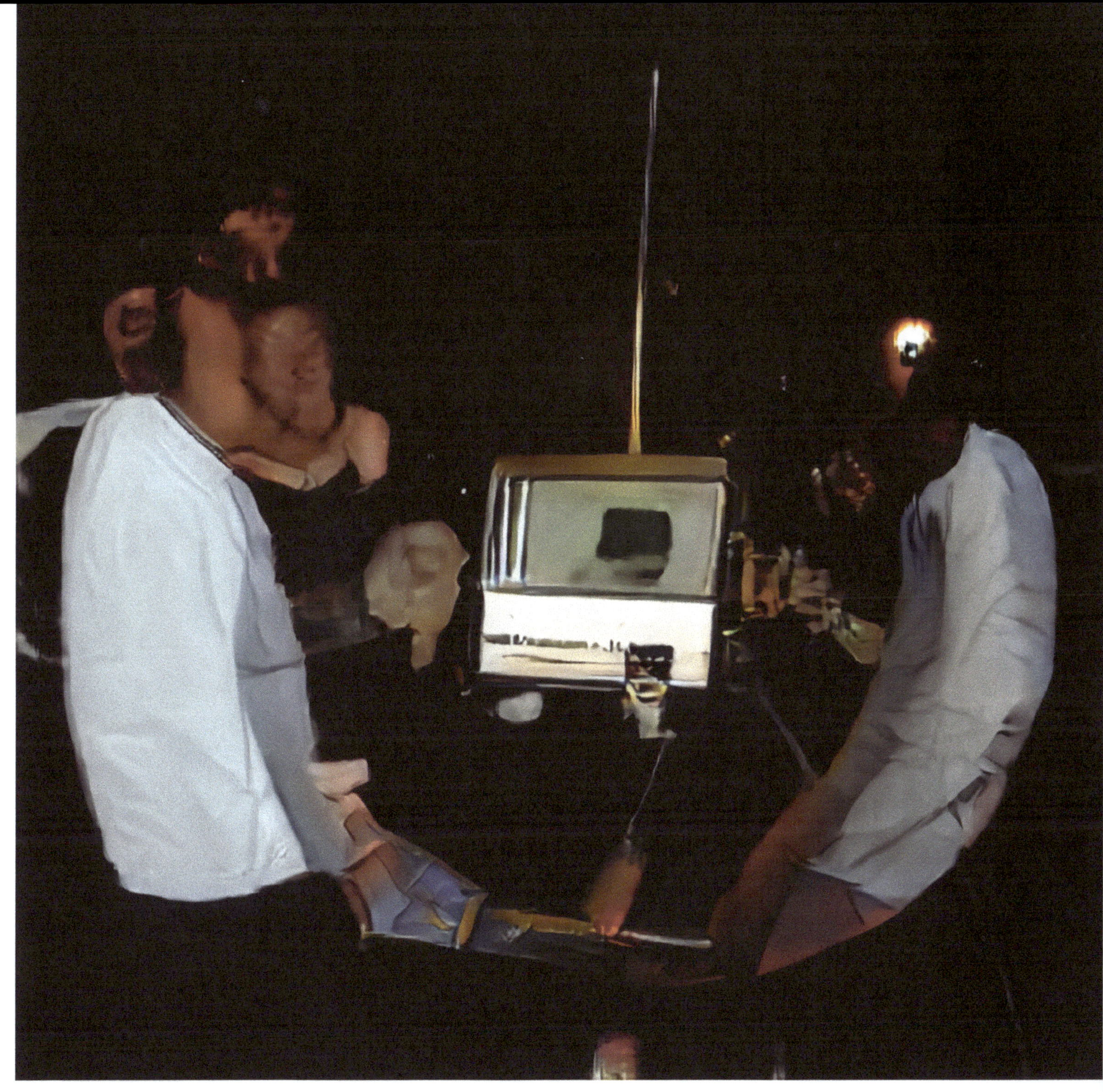

Later, we gathered at Vaughan's and listened to traffic news broadcasts from around the world, a roiling sea of white noise and alien tongues

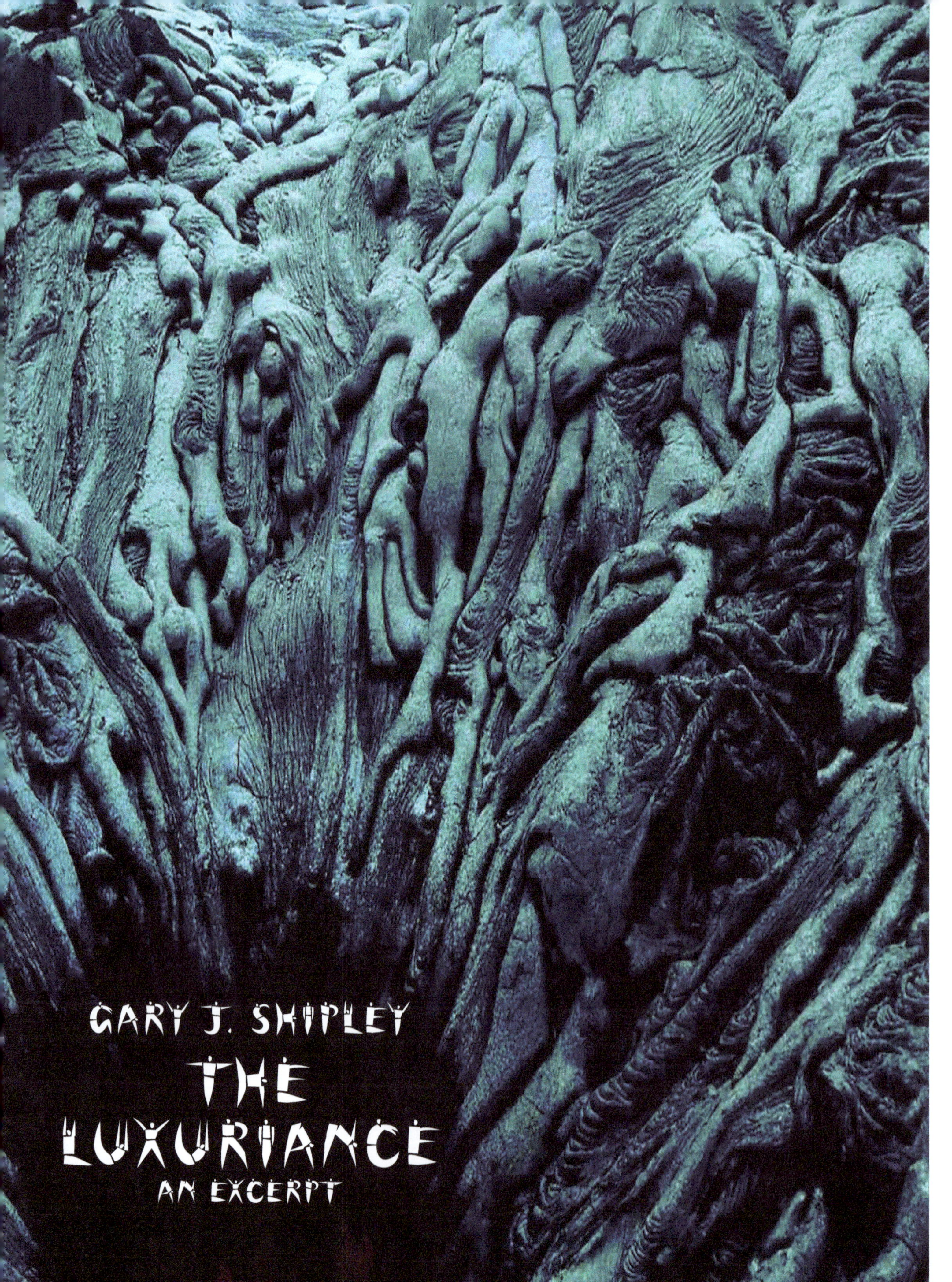
GARY J. SHIPLEY
THE
LUXURIANCE
AN EXCERPT

Who can say in the history of this planet that they've sat in a sun-lounger, 1,450 ft. up, swigging from a $20,000 bottle of Cognac as they watch the Arabian Sea turn slowly pink with blood?

The sky over Death Valley was spotted with Lockheed C-5 Galaxies, thousands of human beings sluicing from their back ends like screaming water. Over Siberia, Antonov An-225 Mriyas unfurled their insides into the frozen air, laying pathways of bodies on the permafrost in patterns that served no other purpose than to distract the pilots from the two thousand people they'd just murdered, the ten thousand they'd murdered that day, and the twelve to fifteen thousand they would murder tomorrow, and the day after that, and would continue to murder all the while the fuel lasted out and there were humans to remove.

The Arctic, the Antarctic, (spilling into the Northern and Southern Temperate Zones), Australia, New Zealand, Africa (north and south), the Antarctic and Arctic deserts, the Sahara, the Kalahari, the Great Victorian, the Gobi, Arabian, Patagonian, Syrian, and the Great Basin are all marked out as suitable dumping grounds. But however vast their accumulated area, it would not be enough.

At around five quadrillion the crust of the earth has its own human skin. At ten quadrillion it would be two deep. At fifty quadrillion it would be ten deep. After that he would begin to calculate how much longer his scraper could hold.

Situated in Lower Parel, South Mumbai and standing at 1450 feet, with 117 floors, the World One Tower was the planet's tallest residential sky scraper, at the topmost point of which he sat and waited and watched as the population continued to swell, the earth beneath it dying, and at the centre of it all the realization that his own thoughts were coming to an end.

It turned out death and meaninglessness were not types of void. They were not deficiencies but excesses. The void is not nothing, the void is too much.

As it was all but impossible to differentiate between those who'd existed before the population started accelerating and those that had arrived as a result of it, the destruction of other humans quickly became indiscriminate. Humanity's greatest achievements, its sciences its arts its literatures its technologies its moral codes, all met in a single plateaued line, in the warm engine of death. All science became the science of more effective murder, all literature the sacrificial soundbites used to induce the reluctant homicide, all art the coagulation of bodies in ever increasing numbers, all technology weaponization, and all morality the expediential proliferation of human death. The apocalypse was the shark they were swimming towards—and climbing inside, to save themselves.

The line between combatant and civilian was not merely spongiform, it was not even a line. In this war there were no civilians, no innocents, no crimes against humanity, no collateral damage, no cost of war that wasn't just the cost of existence itself. In the end, only paralysis was abject.

The schizophrenic conditioning of war was no longer required, and would of course have been an unnecessary indulgence in a conflict with all the pervasiveness of oxygen, a war without fronts, without armies; a paradoxical war, and the only authentic world war possible: that of mankind against itself and for itself. What had been the epitome of inhumanity fast became its opposite. For those that did not kill were not only failing themselves but all humankind, whose sole hope for survival rested with the swift and extensive depletion of its expanded mass.

Various grunt-ideologies surfaced at the beginning and fast became preconditions for any kind of survival, cultivating previously untapped resources of brutality and ruthlessness with a militarized rhetoric equating the humanistic with the pitiless. But regardless of the success of killing sprees, the achieved corpses were still your enemies, still a contagion to be desecrated in irreligious petrol fires, or fed to pigs or gators or dogs or carnivorous fish. That this moral inversion should be adopted so readily, that atrocity should become the bastion of all human hope, would have surprised even the most intransigent of our moral relativists.

At 4.25 a.m. a fuel-air bomb exploded in the centre of Tokyo. Every window for a radius of half a mile shattered, buildings at close range razed. 263 people were killed instantly, and over a hundred more were wounded. Around 4.50 a.m., a man in a police uniform arrived at the blast site. Hundreds of people were gathered in and around the carnage, helping the wounded, weeping over the dead. The man pulled an assault rifle from his bag and began shooting indiscriminately, firing in every direction. He killed dozens, chasing his victims into the doorways of half-collapsed buildings, their blown-out windows still belching smoke and flames. Minutes later the police had the man surrounded. At which point a second man, identical to the first, started opening fire on the officers, killing them all. The two men escaped the scene unharmed. Their name is Andrew Singer. They sought global fame online, bragging their crime and further crimes to come. They published a rambling manifesto entitled: "For those of us unborn: duplication and murder in the age of revelation." On their shared blog, each had diagnosed the other as suffering from alexithymia, going on to explain how this had influenced their own behaviour since the fissioning event. In less than one hour they killed in excess of three-hundred people—of which fifty-eight were minors—and injured over five-hundred others. By the next day their crimes would be considered insignificant; by the next day their crimes wouldn't even be crimes.

Kaal ate at the usual times. He kept the pretence of order as if there were another kind, and he was almost never sick. He avoided the windows only when disinclined to feel himself objectified by the distance of everything else. The human saturation, sprawling and violent to no conceivable end, was less cause for disturbing his carefully managed equilibrium than say a bout of indigestion, or a prolonged inability to pass anything but liquid. All the pathetic automatisms of a rat dying in a bucket. Just because a quadrillion human beings and counting were in the process of decomposing, dying, or killing themselves did not mean that he was any more absent to himself. His body continued to provide its own violence. Burdened with time and a ponderous nature, and only the most miniscule of threats between each breath, his insolence was that of a fly on a shithouse ceiling watching the toilets overflowing and seeing only the slow disappearance of the walls.

It was difficult not to see them all as one huge corpse coiled around the planet, the overlapping mass bubbling at the surface at those sites where death, visited with a cadaveric afterlife, continued to leave its mark.

If he ever felt faint it was not as the result of any worldly deprivation, but rather because the world had been bequeathed to him and he had no use for it. To be alive in the morgue was shameless; and while he sensed his feeling of invincibility was not nearly fragile enough, he also felt that what would happen to him had already happened and that all the future could threaten was the disclosure of this already suffered event.

This wholesale abjection was not new, just out of hiding, just scoped beyond former possibilities. For him inside the tower it's both tolerable and thinkable. It fascinated with all the seductive guile of a hyperrealized boredom: a boredom fascinated with itself. You'd think all the clambering bodies—bloated, dismembered, starved, exploded, bled out, rotting, frantic—would repulse and sadden anyone distant enough not to be panicked, while being close enough to watch, and yet the spectacle proved too excessive for these sentiments, too maniacal to truly repel in any of the standard ways, too drawn of pulchritudinous meanings to collapse into the rancid deposits of such perspectival wretchedness.

The mass oozed like some multicoloured discharge, a mutating culture grown from all cultures at once, from the wound of what it was to exist in the first place. His only devastation was insignificance. Always this way. An opacity of desperation now, maybe, that wasn't there before. Nothing more uncanny in this day-to-day than the unaltered flavour of his morning coffee. Nothing there to defile his heady sense of being removed from all this aside from a certain gagging on himself that was always there. And yet he felt the altitude in his stomach and in his head. He was even woozy in his sleep. He almost wanted the bodies to deepen quicker, for the ground to rush to meet his falling stomach and then stop, for his escape never to have happened, because it couldn't go on: too sickly, too unreal, too dreamt up to have dreams of its own.

He saw many thousands of heads, of children screaming, human after human after human boarding empty freighters and aircraft carriers minus their airplanes. A sign above them read: EMERGENCY EVACUATION. The skyline, the port, the smoking debris of Chicago. A city-weight of voices: each one of them panic, each one of them some dialect of past and impending atrocity. Two gleaming white tugs trailed two black-hulled freighters out to sea. The camera zooming into the faces of those crushed into the railings at the edge of the ship. When they were far enough out that they could no longer be seen clearly by the hoards still streaming aboard other similarly destined ships, the railings collapsed and hundreds of humans at a time spilled over the edge into the sea. Clouds of nerve gas billowed from the deck subduing the thousands left there to the floor, to their deaths in the water. Figures in gas masks and protective suits emerged with silenced weapons to slowly dispose of what was left.

Almost all the video-feeds he watched were the same discordant melange of trauma: humans being shot, burned, stabbed, crushed, drowned, or else coming apart at different speeds. Those that endured, endured for more of the same: no end to it, ever. Only the dream of an end, of the final moral kill. It's the dreamers that stay alive longest, which seemed fair, being that they were still in many ways waiting to be born. As if this massacre wasn't just life. As if depravity wasn't just the straight path.

The disillusioned died quickly, almost mechanical in the way they went. Their eyes, as if word bubbles, read: "Devour me! Devour me!" He once saw a senile old man shuffling up and down a corridor in an old people's home declaring how he was ready now to die. The doors either end of the corridor were blocked with bodies. He watched him on and off for days, until the man eventually died of dehydration. The longer he remained there the less he exclaimed his readiness to die and the more he articulated his excruciating thirst.

Defenestration was popular among the unarmed and the untrained; particularly so, from the videos he'd watched, throughout Europe, China and Japan. With none of the uncomfortable intimacy of stabbing or strangling, it offered a favourable means of dispatch for those who, though conscientious, had no taste for killing. And there was always the distinct possibility that another death might be occasioned by the falling person landing on someone else at street level. Children were easier still, though the chances for these supplementary deaths were regrettably diminished.

Outside of urbanizations there was swamp and fire and animals drowned in mud, trees charred and snapped, rotted out bodies, the slime of the dead pooling in cattle tracks and the meandering ruts of old streams run dry. For weeks after, New Zealand remained nearly as verdant and unspoiled as before. But then the splitting accelerated and the planes came, dropping humans in their tens of thousands over its picturesque wilderness until almost all plant life was destroyed. The last footage he saw of this part of the world was of the Coromandel, from the air, turned grey.

He likened those outside to the strays in the alleyways that used to border his house. Their howls and shrieks were so constant, so homogenous, that they seemed to emanate as if from a single animal, the suffering commensurate with its excessive mass. But of course he was now the stray, the deject, the outlier. Only, he was exiled not by deprivation but by comfort, and his being lost was in itself the most exalted form of opulence. He would try to ignore the condensing bodies on the ground by looking at the sky; and when it stormed, its blackened body lit up inside and growling, like a panther gorged on flashbangs, he'd sit and wait in silence for the rain. When it arrived he liked to see all those thousands of faces looking up into the downpour, their mouths open, eyes squinting, brains registering how not all the world was made of humans. How true it seemed then that oblivion had its own exquisite aspect, how caught in glimpses, freeze-framed, bursting in numerous punctums of wonder, it was the match for any creation.

He watched humans burnt alive in open pits, in mass executions, before anyone knew what mass meant. He saw the same humans days later exhumed by bombs. He saw them descend, saw them pulling dents out the earth, saw people coming apart in the air.

When flight was still possible, and the hope for survival not yet critically impaired, half the world was made up of refugees: those from densely populated countries seeking their lesser populated versions, those from cities and condensed conurbations in search of wilderness and open land, and those from the countryside with designs on high-rises. It had to be better someplace else; the alternative was not worth thinking. The alternative, of course, though not worth thinking, was true: there was no place else—there was strict geographic location and its qualitative parity with every other place.

There was a remoteness to the woman's eyes that went beyond the usual cerebral bruising, beyond the thousand yards of the war-deranged soldier and on and on without end —a distance that could never be retraced. Her expression didn't alter as she put the gun to her temple. It was like she'd stalled like that. The video slowed down as she pulled the trigger. The burst, the recoil, her head moving away and to the left, her expression unchanging. This composure of the already dead in the living was not rare, but somehow she, amid so many other examples, was not once surpassed. He looked for that look in the mirror when he looked. He knew that if he ever found it those hundred or so storeys would cease to make a difference.

Humans ran and ran until there wasn't room to run, till the gasses of the dead pinched at their lungs, till the planet was an open grave, and its topographies precluded anything but staggering or crawling.

He watched the ground vomit and swallow itself over and over: a repulsive human fountain recycling its contents, absorbing more.

Humanity was abased as much by its imploded imagination as by the bits of freshly dead human it was forced to eat to stay alive. And so perverse that this universal solidarity should arrive only to find that this newly united thing must kill itself – for the sake of itself.

No prejudiced nuance, concerning race, gender, nationality, or sexual persuasion, could survive the sheer weight of people that needed to be made dead.

In its proliferation the human appeared memoryless. It had forgotten how the universe ignores it, and how the knowledge of that must be sublimated by ideals, by notions of progress, by aspirations of transcendence. All it had now was the continuing massacre and the vague sense that there existed a more human way to suffer.

Kaal had been a philosophy professor at the University of Mumbai for about a year when they started digging out the foundations for the World towers; and though he was based some distance away (at the Kalina campus, and lived nearby), he'd managed to visit the site most days. Of the three towers under construction he'd always preferred World One to its neighbours, View and Crest. He would imagine himself inside it, at the top, imagine the quiet that could exist there.

Once he'd heard of a second and then a third documented split he knew somehow it wouldn't stop. He also knew where he had to get to, and that he didn't have long to get there. But then to say he knew did not quite capture what had happened, for he didn't know this as he knew other things: there was no rational process he could recall having gone through, only his body moving in certain ways that he came to interpret as his having arrived at this conviction.

By the time the first video of a splitter became the most viewed video clip in history, just two days after its upload, he was already in the Tower. She was considered by most who saw that video as a unique case, not only the first but the last too, so that when more showed up there was the suspicion that the video was itself the primary catalyst for these subsequent splittings, as if the world was now in the grip of a Japanese horror movie—a rumour aided in its spread and supposed credibility by the girl's being of Japanese descent, although diasporic and resident at the time in São Paulo, Brazil.

Most of the isolated needed a cause. They asked the same unanswerable questions, answered them in the same unanswered way. There was talk of everything from alien infection (making humans food for some forthcoming interplanetary invasion) to theoretical manifestations, such as the Lewisian overdetermination of persons being confirmed via some extraordinary biological shift. But as to why it was happening now and why to everyone at once, nobody had anything approaching a cogent explanation.

When he stepped out of the tired-looking teaching block into the lunchtime choke of heat and bodies, having just delivered his final lecture ('On Kristevan Abjection: Apocalypse and the Double'), the campus, though ostensibly unaltered from all the other times, felt to him already like some diorama of the past. The streets were never quiet, but as he walked in the direction of the Tower, a distance he'd usually never contemplate walking, right the way over to Mill Lands, he sensed the populous was somehow depleted. There were seconds of quiet between car horns, and more noise coming from the insides of buildings than was usual. The children weaving between the slow-moving traffic selling flowers sounded faint, as if underwater. A sequence of screams and a general quailing clamour issued from open windows and doors left ajar to facilitate the circulation of air.

The preparatory arrangements that would allow him access

to the completed Tower, and a suitably positioned apartment within it, had been finalized two days before. A series of phone calls to various residents having been made, during which he'd offered an honorary degree from the University of Mumbai. Following a half-dozen failed attempts, an interview was arranged with an conveniently conceited multi-billionaire tech impresario, who'd had no trouble believing that he'd be in line for such an accolade, and if anything gave the almost unfathomable impression that its being tendered was somehow overdue.

As he walked, weaving his way between cars, motorbikes, other pedestrians, his legs took over. He wondered if it was possible for him to stop, to go in another direction, to turn back; and he thought he made the decision to try, just to see if he could, but nothing happened. He presumed that what had felt like a decision being made was merely an extension of his deliberation and not yet its conclusion. He tried not to think how much like a resolution it had seemed. He continued walking, speeding up, getting farther and farther away from that moment of wrongly perceived certitude and the place to where it ought to have redirected him.

The sound of horns, the heat in waves across the roads, the endless food stalls with their brightly-coloured parasols, the bananas, the casaba melons, the wooden props and the bedraggled banners, the voices of men, women and children chewing at the front of his brain like a million microscopic grubs.

The abject authenticates itself through necessity, through having no opposition, through answering its own reluctance to exist: the whole world under the auspices of the self-pitying murderer, the murderer with no choice but to regard others as somehow symbolizing his own narcissistic demand that he be made once again present to himself.

Regardless of the production value, he generally liked the stylized ones least: the GoPro POVs with their adopted personas and correlative missions, who infused their slaughter videos with heroic narratives filched from all over: the Bible, horror movies, historic battles... Every circumstance, no matter how abominable, always attracts its enthusiasts, and in this case it was these howling morons, frenziedly feeding YouTube with blood and dying faces while there was still time, soldiers of ill fortune carving paths through bodies like it meant something.
Uploaded from cities he presumed American were countless videos of people sniping from rooftops. Not just middle-aged men in checkered shirts and baseball caps, primed by zombie flicks to know that this was their one true calling, but humans of all ages, races, and genders. But then the spaces between bodies got filled up with more bodies and the chances of missing approached zero. And even when there were still heads to score from, it became increasingly difficult in the tumult for them to register their hits.

There was no scope for aporia: all they had were solutions and no questions. They had the solution of the world, swelling, pulsating and decaying like the solar system's very own boil.

He watched a middle-aged man trying to resuscitate a young boy with a bicycle pump. The man was crying in a way that he had forgotten people cried. He was crying like he was starring in the movie version of his life. In the movie he was the father and the boy was his son. The camera cut away to a dog eating the face off an old woman, over which the sounds of the man's hysteria could still be heard.

Although there was no room for the men and women there to cast their shadows, he could still just about make out the rough outline of Ken Smith's scaled down, fun park interpretation of the Nymphenberg Palace's grand parterre, its multi-coloured grasses, arboreal podiums, its tennis and basketball courts, its 5 acres of lotus pools and fountains, its full verdant overload. Every swimming pool was filled with bodies seeking refuge from the sun. The spa's once soft sedation, there to lavish the senses with its own expensive brand of tranquillity, was now a frenzied fight for space, rejuvenating no one it seemed but Kaal, who looking down on it was for a moment thankful for having escaped. The Lodha dream had soured the instant someone crapped into one of its pools. What use anyway was equanimity that fragile? This kind of forced environmental calm never worked for long; if you wanted wellbeing on tap then narcotics were the only route. All these halcyon contrivances ever did for Kaal was make him more antsy. It was almost a relief for him to see it covered in thin ragged bodies, its pools filling with shit, its plants trampled into the ground.

From the time he'd first seen it completed, its sterility had ungrounded him like a violent stomach upset. It was as if he was watching a promotional video for the clinically bored. Simulated men and women strolled along the pathways of simulated gardens appearing to talk amiably about subjects of passing consequence, and, as if secured to their continued amusement by only the finest of threads, completed their perambulations merely to resume them again elsewhere, as part of a presumed infinite sequence of the pleasures to which they were entitled, which nevertheless couldn't obscure how it was that no one instance of pleasure would ever prove sufficiently convincing on its own.

Kaal was some too-tender age when his mother died. There was only ever one of her. One unbranching limb and one ending of it. One tumour in one brain and only one week to die. So many years for his father to die waiting for her to come back. And still waiting, or most likely dead. Such fussy deaths back then. So singular. So exophoric.

The persistence of a single referent, this 'me', this 'him', this same thing, this object for no one, was fetishistic, was phobic, was bitten by a diseased mouth. His life was now just the deprivation of the dreams he had for it. This mesh of some 30,000 afternoons, or thereabouts, at best, at worst. How slowly we die before we die, and how quickly thereafter. Ha, funny mirage this life: devoured, devouring, always hungry—never there until it isn't.

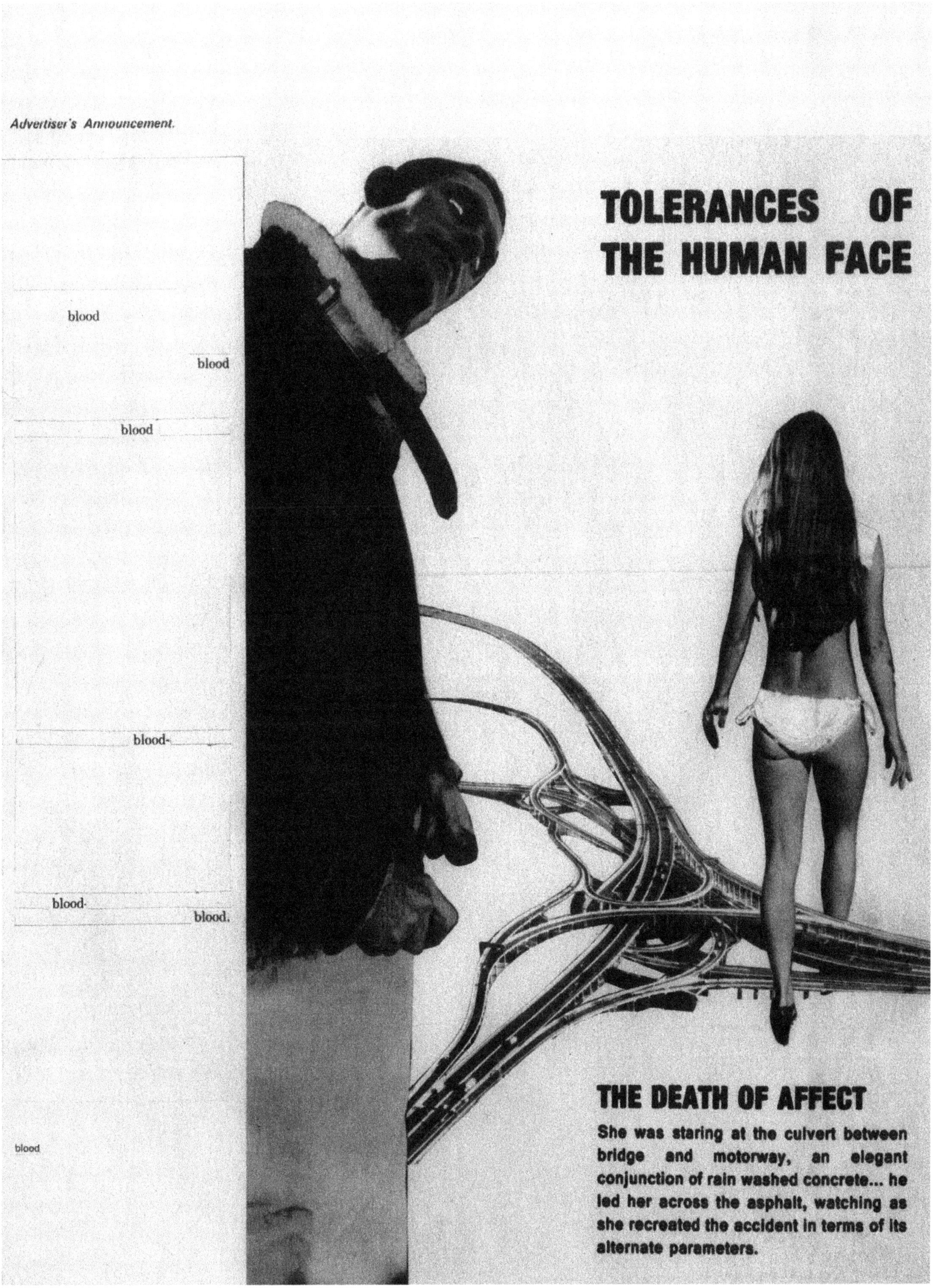

Advertiser's Announcement.

blood

blood

blood

blood-

blood·

blood.

blood

TOLERANCES OF THE HUMAN FACE

THE DEATH OF AFFECT

She was staring at the culvert between bridge and motorway, an elegant conjunction of rain washed concrete... he led her across the asphalt, watching as she recreated the accident in terms of its alternate parameters.

PiPPA TANDY

TRAiNSFORMATiONS

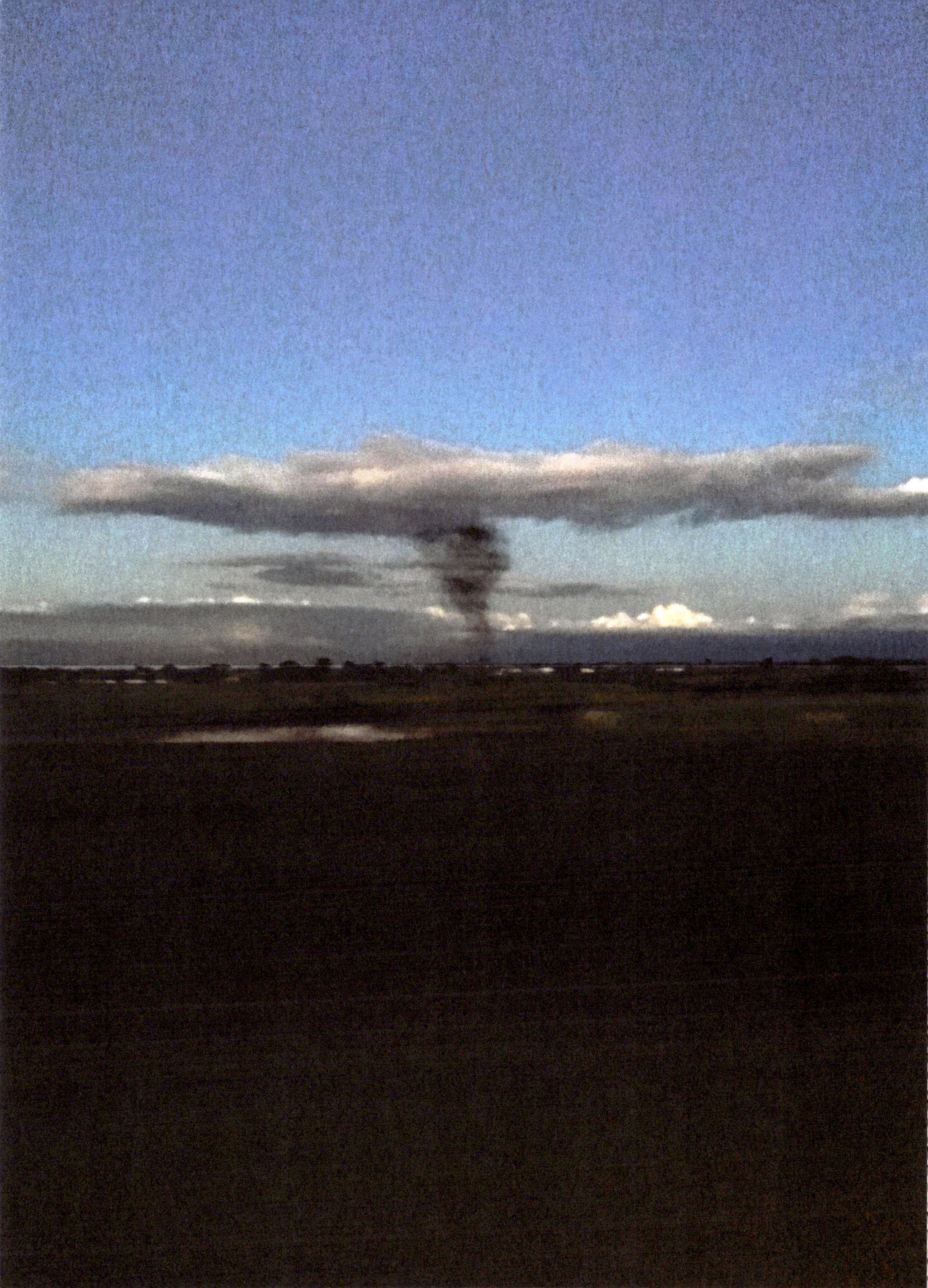

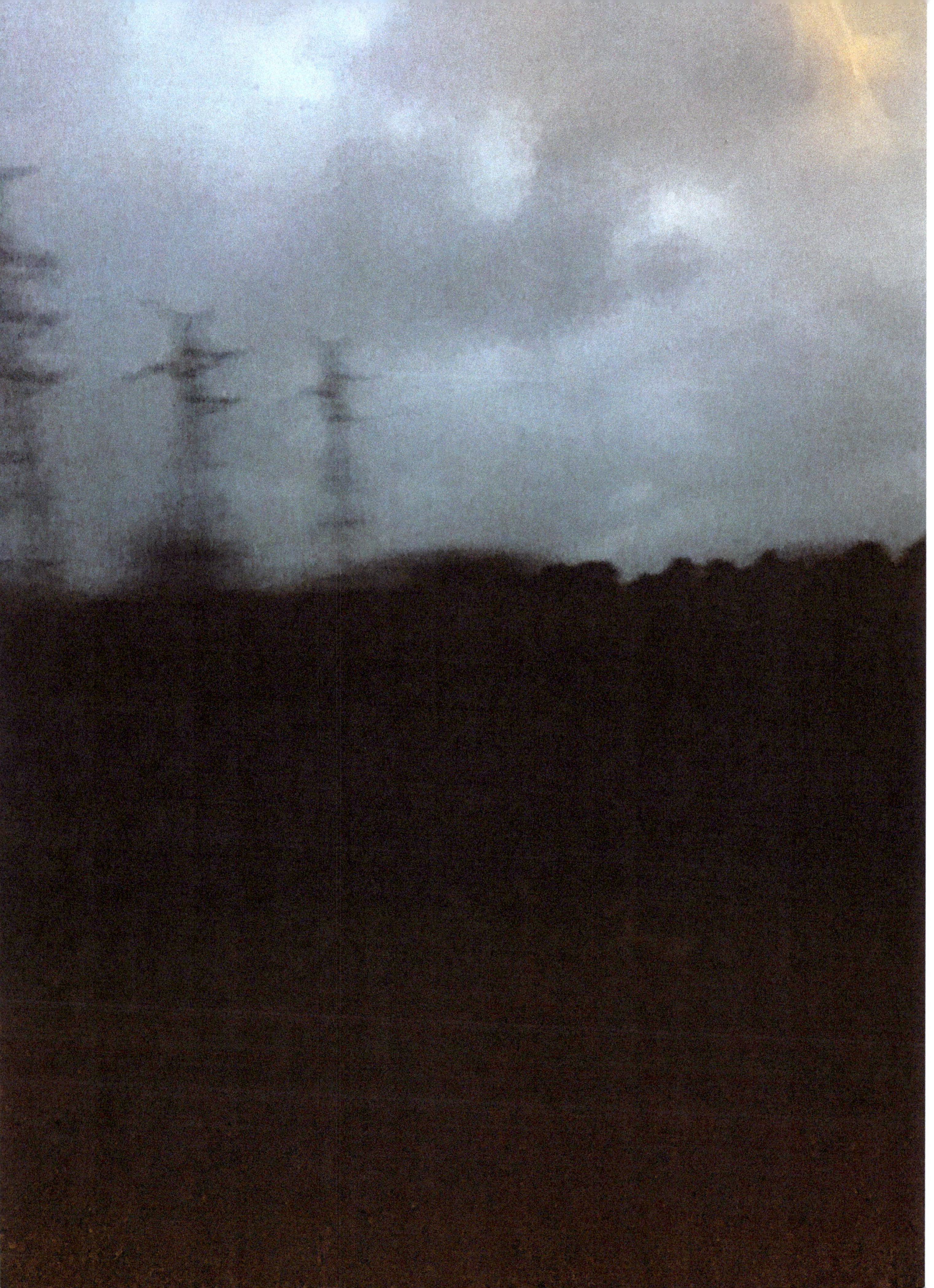

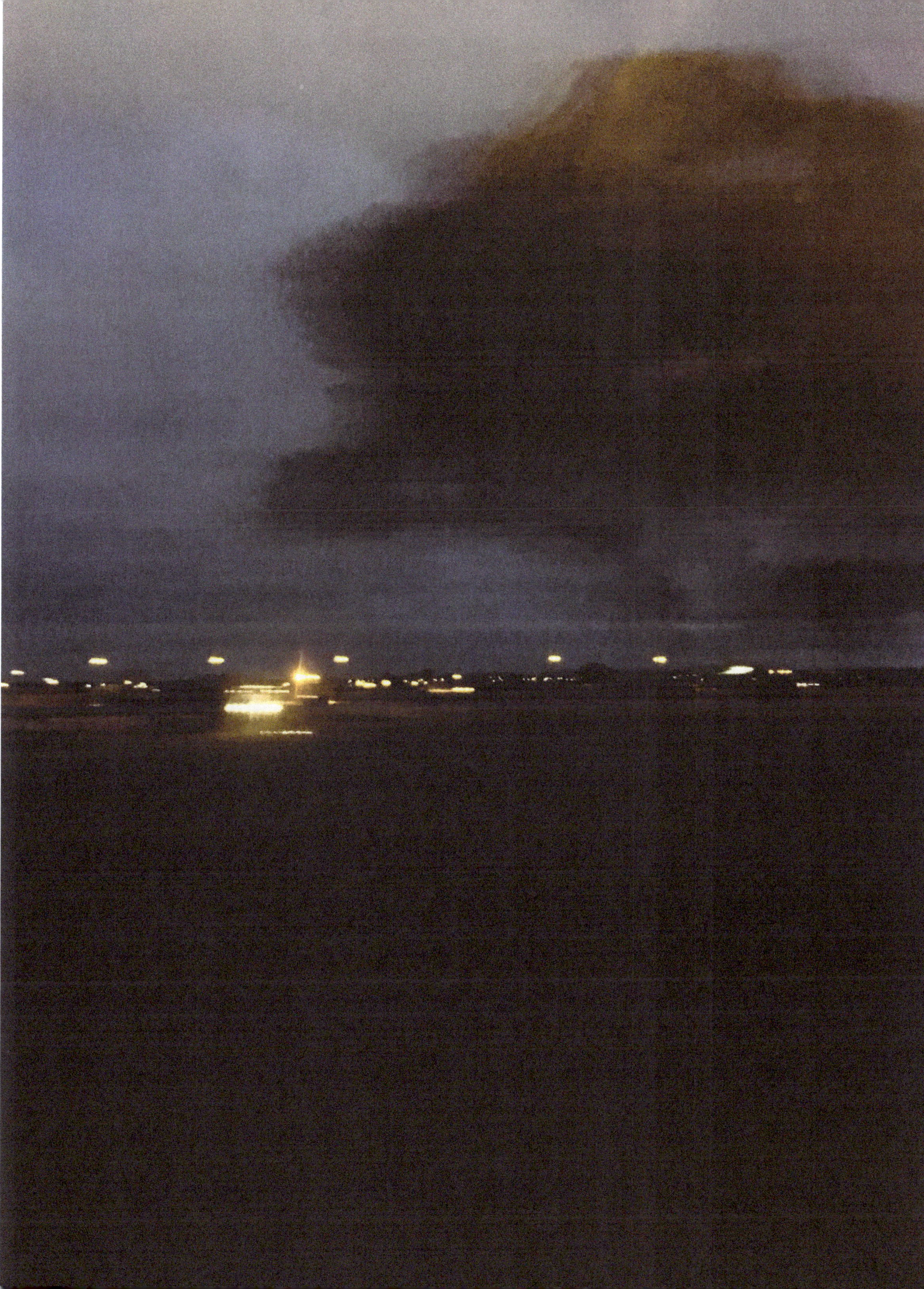

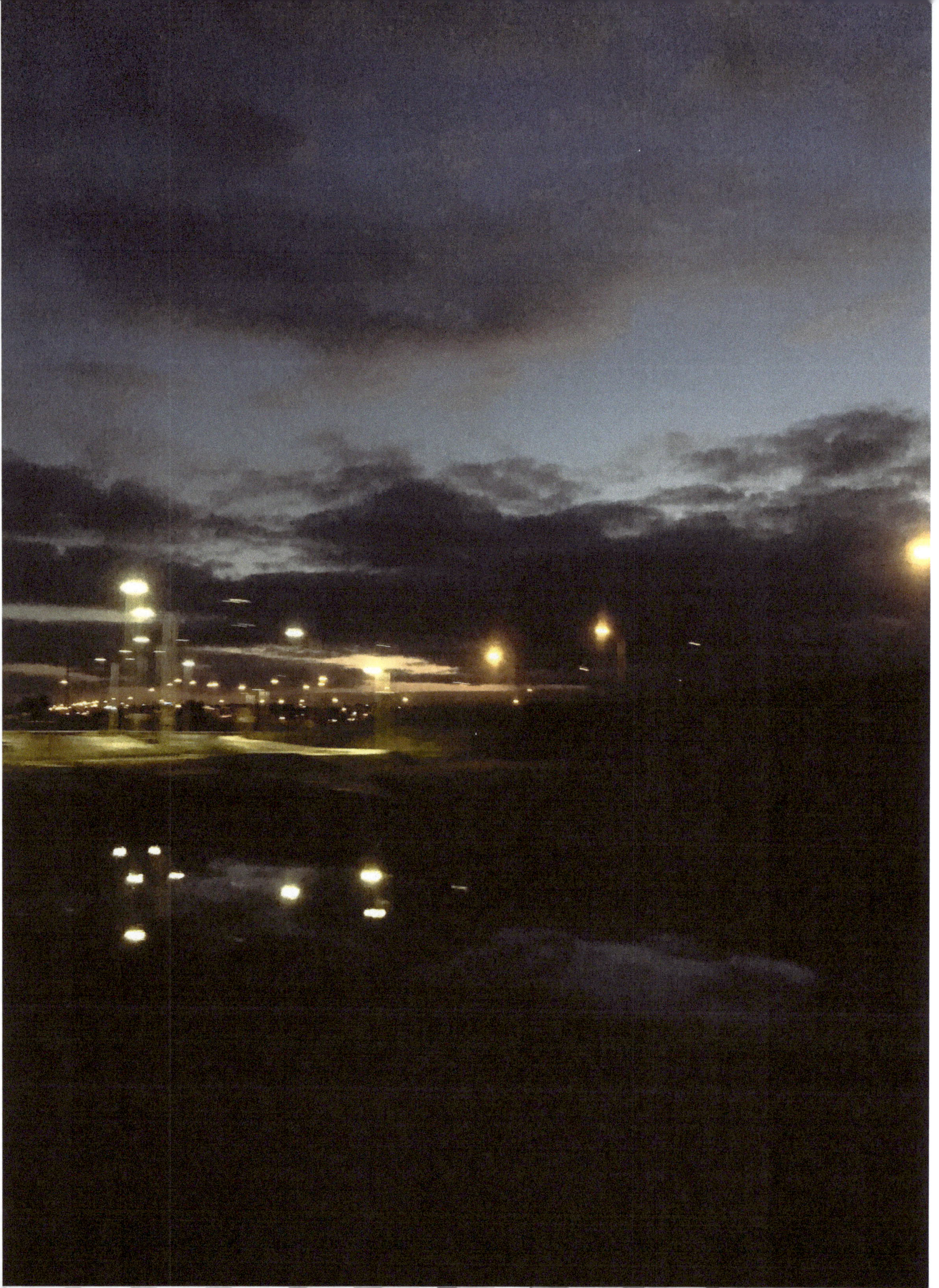

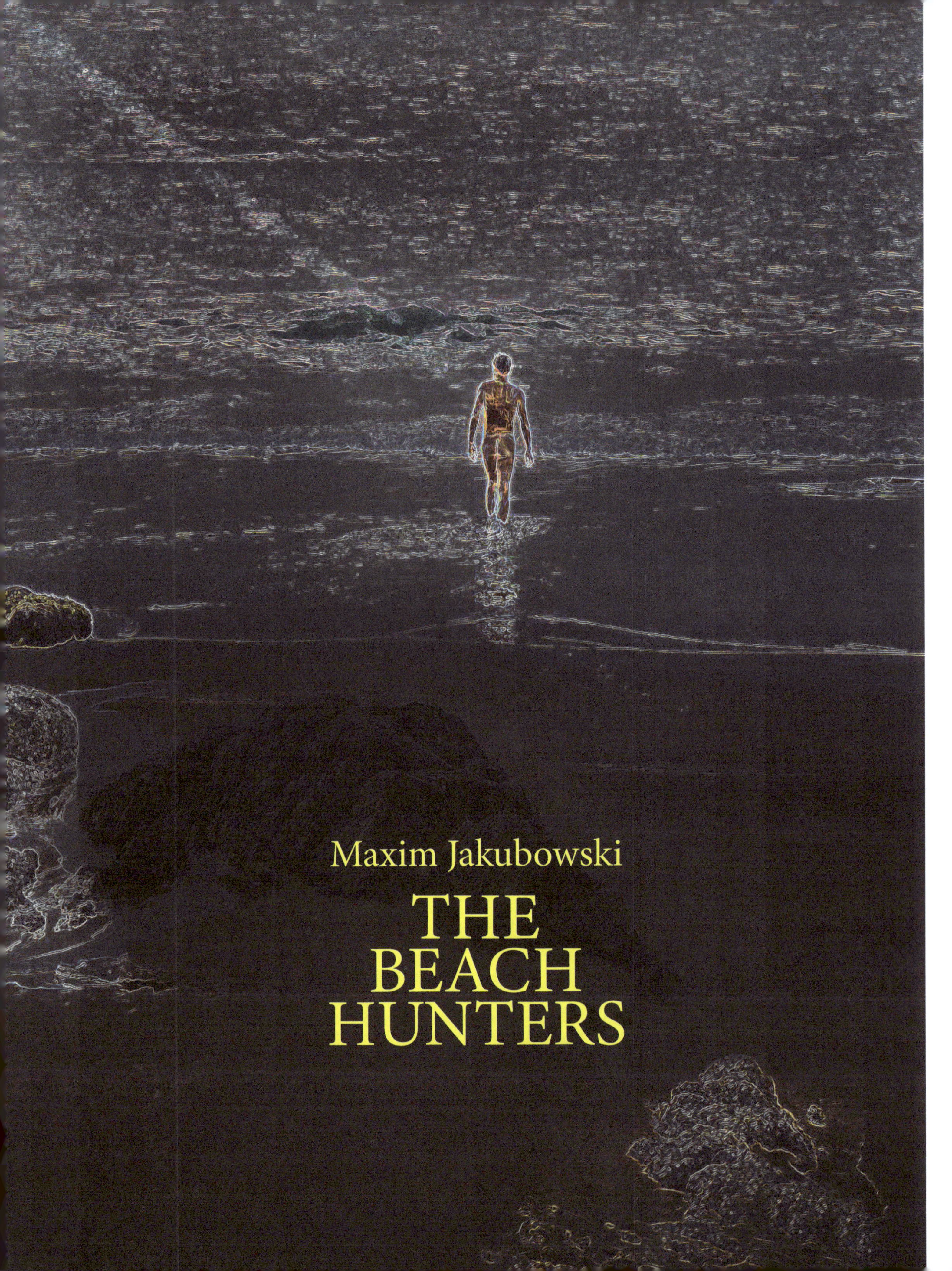

Maxim Jakubowski
THE
BEACH
HUNTERS

Considering how much sex played a role in his life—having it, thinking of it, seeking it—it was a great irony that it just never occurred in his dreams. Nonetheless, those unwelcome night adventures of the mind were frequent and potent. Strictly speaking, the dreams were more like nightmares, but then he had never quite been able to make out the difference between the two states. All too often, he would wake up in the middle of darkness, his heart beating wildly, often drenched in sweat, stomach tied in knots, emerging from yet another dream riddled with anxiety, his thoughts racing in ever desperate circular motion, a loop he couldn't escape from, disturbing, gasping for air, his chest in a vice of oppression. He was already exhausted, both emotionally and physically, before he even rose out of bed.

The actual events making up the fabric of the dream would quickly dissipate, like clouds melting into the event horizon, but random, flickering images, emotions, fragments, feelings would linger for a short while and only later in the day would he recall some of the elements, the building blocks of the dreams.

Most of them, or at any rate the more, albeit briefly, memorable or affecting ones, involved beaches.

It made no sense. He was an urban sort of person at heart and beaches had never played an important part in his life: holidays in the sun, endless hours reading and tanning in the Languedoc, the Caribbean, Cancun or the Maldives.

And none of those real-life locales ever made an appearance in the theatre of his dreams. The settings for his panic dreams were generally anonymous, long tongues of sand, squashed between emerald seas and dense inner forests, mostly uninhabited, littered with seaweed, squashed plastic bottles, driftwood and the usual detritus washed in by the waves. Like a movie of desolation after the end of the world as we know it, dead landscapes draped beneath the ever-blue sky, silent, a stage for a movie still without a script, waiting for him to assemble the jigsaw that would make it complete, meaningful.

He was living with June Ann. She was a biochemist and researcher from New Orleans who had paid for her studies by posing nude for a variety of photographers which had led to a brief period as a fetish hard porn performer as Calabria Fortuna. Her notorious videos could still easily be found on the internet, and often while she was out working at her laboratory, dividing cells, and experimenting with seeds, he would indulge in the privacy of his study and linger guiltily on images, opened up to full screen on his desktop, of her being whipped, fisted, fucked by one or two men, nipples painfully clamped, clothes pegs attached to her labia, her full, heavy breasts swinging gently along with every thrust inside her, hypnotised as he was by the drama of super-endowed cocks entering all her holes, her mouth slobbering around them, and the indelible vision of her face covered in ejaculate, an enigmatic half-smile illuminating her lips while her eye-make-up ran dirty, smudged, destroyed, perishing across the beautiful pallor of her skin. He was in turn aroused by it and repulsed, ever trying to reconcile these snapshots of her past with what she was today, wearing large round goofy spectacles because of her short-sightedness, her long flowing hair no longer bleached to Marilyn-blonde extremes, cooking with healthy, organic ingredients in the kitchen, playing with her cats and dogs, as if the past was a different country and none of what she had willingly done, endured had ever happened, or surprisingly even left a visible scar, physically or mentally.

"How was your day?"

"The usual. Spent most of it behind the microscope. And the AC in the lab is still on the blink. We've complained to maintenance a few times, but they still haven't solved the problem. You?"

"I've almost completed the edits. Shouldn't take me more than a couple more days now, and I can move on to the next commission."

"Good."

He stared at her, yet again seeking out the invisible traces of her past in her features, her demeanour. It was like an itch he couldn't help scratching away at.

She was arranging sunflowers in a vase, her back to him, the light from the window creating a halo around her head. As if sensing the insistence of his gaze, she turned round.

Their eyes met.

"What are you looking at like that?" she asked.

He looked away. "Nothing."

A pained silence spread across the kitchen.

"I know that expression," she said.

"No, really, it's nothing," he insisted.

As he said that, he remembered he had forgotten to delete the browsing history tabs on the computer, which she often used too, which would have betrayed the fact he had just a few hours ago watched the clips of June Ann having vigorous sex in every possible position with the dreadlocked black stud and the somewhat more innocent one of her fooling around in a hotel bed with another porn actress with an equally perfect body. The geometry of their interlinked limbs and parts like a new language, in high definition, every micro-dot of a goosebump on June Ann's then shaven pudenda in close-up like an extraordinary alien terrain of pornographic pixels, more detailed even than when he buried his face against her mound and licked her to completion on the now rare occasions they still fucked.

And although he had inevitably played with himself while viewing her old porno clips it wasn't so much the in your face obscenity of the terrible, repetitive penetrations that got him off, but the rare glimpses of her wide-eyed expression as waves of lust and pleasure washed over the screen of her features and she peered towards the camera as if seeking for something ineffable way beyond. Somehow, he would realise, some time later when they were no longer together, he was trying to discover how she actually felt, and in fact wanted to be her.

But then he had always had a complicated relationship with pornography, and living with a woman who had experienced its reality was creating a nexus of both desire and terrible vulnerability inside him.

It was curious that this didn't somehow express itself in his dreams, though, he reflected.

"I never know what you're thinking of," June Ann said, as she lined up the vegetables to be chopped for their dinner on the granite work counter.

He looked away.

Failed to respond.

"Maybe it's best I didn't," she concluded, lining up the spring onions and the mushrooms on the carving board and hunting for a large knife in one of the drawers by the hob.

Somehow neither said a word to each other that night until they fell asleep.

The beach returned in the screening room of his unconscious mind in the early hours of morning and he woke up, fingers gripping the edges of the sheet, vistas of sand like a flies in amber dominating the landscape, his body short of breath, his mouth dry and sweat pearling down his collar, the panic attack slowly fading as he heard June Ann's voice shouting out at him from the next room.

"You overslept and I didn't want to wake you up. I'm off to the lab. See you in the evening. Maybe we can eat out?" Then the sound of the front door slamming and her battered Prius crunching the gravel on the front drive of the house.

He looked at the ceiling, seeking out shapes, meaning. It remained blank.

Soon after that morning, he prepared a rucksack with spare clothing, and drove off. He didn't leave a note for June Ann in the way of apologies or explanation.

By the end of the day, he was several hundred miles away, two tanks of gas, a couple of chocolate bars and half a dozen cans of Pepsi to the better, already approaching the coast.

It was winter. Both the downcast sky and the sea conjugated shades of grey and he was sitting in a bar off the town's main promenade squeezed between bed and breakfasts, overlooking a pebble beach where only dog walkers and shell hunters walked at this time of morning.

The barman brought him his cup of chowder.

"It'll warm you up," he said.

"Thanks."

"It's better here in summer," the barman added, in a vain attempt to cheer him up. "Not tropical, but you know what I mean. We're not climate blessed down here. Don't get many visitors these days. Well, not at this time of year..."

He looked up at the man. He was in his fifties, his hair was thinning and his shirt had once been white.

"I think I knew that before I came to Van Demien's Land," he said, dipping his heavy silver spoon into the cup, stirring the thick, hot soup.

"So what brings you to these parts?"

"Travelling. Researching..."

"Really?"

"I read somewhere about Patagonia Beach and thought it would be interesting to go there."

The expression on the barman's face, as he rolled his eyes, was one of astonishment.

"Damn, I'm surprised anyone from outside the region would even know about that goddam place. Sure not a tourist hot spot," he indicated.

"There are stories."

"There sure are. I don't even know why it's even called a beach. No sand, just pebbles, rocks, waves. Centuries ago, it was said that pirates would light fires on the promontories to attract vessels into the shallows in the hope of shipwrecking them. And it's halfway round the world from actual Patagonia. Go figure!'

"I'm hoping to write a book on unusual beaches,' he replied, which was a total lie, a thought that just happened to cross his mind at the moment as he tasted the chowder which was much too salty and tasted more of potato than clams.

"Well, it's a couple of hours drive south. There won't be much traffic, I reckon."

"I'm in no rush. I'll get there some time," he said, concluding the conversation. It had been three months since he had walked out on June Ann and he had visited a dozen or so beaches so far, and still didn't know where was going or what he was actually seeking. It wasn't as if the sandy, blue-skied, coral beach of his past dreams could even be situated this far north, even if it existed anywhere but in his mind. But he was in no hurry. Since he had begun to travel, the circular nightmares and regular panic attacks had finally ceased and all he dreamed about now was women's bodies. He could live with that, although waking every morning with a raging erection made him feel like a hapless character in a Thomas Pynchon novel. It could be worse, he supposed.

He lingered in the town a further two days before he travelled to Patagonia Beach.

He arrived at dawn in the middle of a storm.

The rain was pelting down, playing a ballet of dissonances over the hood of his metal grey BMW, droplets skipping along in gay abandon like ants across an open fire. The wind had a sharp bite about it when he opened the door and he decided to remain inside the car until the weather calmed, even though his heating was on its last legs. He would have to find a garage soon, if he remained much longer in these inhospitable parts, and get it fixed.

By midday, the curtain of rain obscuring the beach and sea parted slightly.

The actual beach was narrow but deep, lengthy tongues of land venturing into the sea and its procession of high waves, as if probing the ocean's defences. There was a ragged beauty to the vista, a forlorn sense of brutality and desolation, an echo of the dead souls who had seemingly been shipwrecked here in times of old and witnessed their broken bodies washed onto the unyielding stony shore to be buffeted over and over again by the savagery of the waves.

The sky had cleared and was now the colour of washed out denim as he finally exited his car and stood on the edge of the small chalk cliff that towered over the beach. There was a red stain in the distance at the far end of the pebbled carpet separating the hills and the ocean. He peered ahead as the dot moved, slowly expanded, came into focus. He blinked.

A human silhouette bent over at the knees.

He made his way down to the beach. She was wearing a red plastic-like anorak and was scooping pebbles into a variety of small pails, marking each rescued stone with a thick marker pen in fluorescent ink. She saw him coming and looked up, her long, wet hair spilling from her hood.

"You're probably wondering what I'm doing?" she asked him, as he approached.

"Not so much what but why," he remarked.

Her smile was crooked, full of mischief.

"I'm a geologist. Taking samples," explaining herself and her presence here.

"It's a god-forsaken place to have to come and work," he told her.

"I go where the work is, where the beaches are," she acknowledged and stood up. She was half a head taller than him, green-eyed and wore no make up. "What about you?" Her skinny jeans adhered to her long legs.

"Just another beach hunter," he said. "We come in all sizes," he remarked.

"So you do." She set one of her pails down and advanced her hand. "Dr Trish Vaughan."

He extended his. Her handshake was firm and confident.

He introduced himself to her.

Later, he gave her a lift back to the small nearby town once they discovered they were staying in the same hotel. She'd walked all the way to Patagonia Beach, had to rely on local buses and trains. Trish was good company, and they shared a meal.

"What's your next port of call?" he asked her after she'd confessed her work on Patagonia Beach had come to its natural end.

"It's a resort on the west coast called Vermilion Sands. It was once a huge development but I understand it's fallen on hard times and most of the complex has been abandoned, and what's left of it in good enough nick has been turned into an artists' colony. There's been a lot of dredging in the sea nearby and the beach has allegedly acquired some interesting geological configurations through the redirection of the tides and the university have given me a brief to investigate further."

"How are you getting there?"

"About three trains I've calculated, and some lengthy pit stops if the time tables prove correct," Trish said.

"I'll drive you there," he offered. "I've nothing better to do and the place sounds fascinating."

"Are you sure?"

"Of course."

Dr Trish Vaughan accepted his offer. She also came to his room that night. Not that he was able to perform too well, his erections now somehow a thing of the past or consumed by his dreams and unable to repeat in the cold light of night. Neither did the fact that between embraces Dr Vaughan in all her nude splendour whispered in his ear that he should be rough with her and, *sotto voce*, even asked for him to hurt her. Trish observed his physiological and penile capitulation with scientific detachment.

To describe the resort as run down would have been an understatement. The tall, concrete towers which once housed thousands of sun-seeking holidaymakers in their architectural heyday were actually crumbling, roofs caved in, balconies detached from their facades or, in some instances, hanging precariously by an iron girder with countless shards of masonry balancing above the void below, as if assaulted by some hurricane or typhoon just the day before, wounded giants standing blemished against the azure blue of the spring day.

The more exclusive stucco villas dotted between the Le Corbusier-styled towers were in better shape but far from habitable. There was no electricity, water, and mould and vegetation appeared to be winning the war, gradually wrapping the buildings in a thick, impenetrable coat of decay.

The dozens of Olympic-size swimming pools which had once been one of the resort's main attractions lay empty, scattered with detritus and the pitiful remains of dead animals causing the smell of decay to hang in the air. There was no sign of the artists who were allegedly active here.

As for the beach, it no longer existed at high tide, fully swallowed up by the encroaching sea and no more than a landing strip of damp sand when the waters retreated.

"There's nothing for me to do here," Dr Vaughan said, with a sigh of exasperation. "It's too late. Maybe a year ago or so, I would have been able to analyse the flows and counterflows of the tides through the stratas of the beach, but it's beyond repair, so to speak." It felt to him, as he looked out at the bruised landscape, that any trace of civilisation here couldn't have occurred here a year back, let alone a century ago.

"I wonder where all the supposed artists have gone?" There was no trace of their presence.

She gave a few calls.

"They left just a few weeks ago," she informed him. "I asked a friend in my department to look it up online. Seems they they've gone east seeking a volcano or something of the sort. It didn't make sense to me, some sort of psychic search. Not my area of expertise."

They drove back up the coast, mostly in silence.

Sometimes they stayed in small pensions and shared a room and a bed, but barely touched, sleeping in the warm glow of each other's body, content with just the companionship. On other occasions, they dozed in the car. His finances were running low and he knew that all too soon, his credit card would get declined down at a petrol station and that would be the end of the road. Trish was content to let him pay for gas and snacks, and didn't appear to be lush with funds either. Both travelled light, just a few spare clothes and some toiletry, and various small pieces of scientific apparatus in her bulging rucksack, test tubes, syringes, pipettes, multi-coloured sample cases.

They reached the Golden Littoral and Balmins Beach.

"Do you have any work to do here?" he asked her.

"No. My research is done. But I'm no rush to go home. There's not much waiting for me there," she said.

"Same here," he said.

"A few more beaches to explore then?' she suggested.

"Why not."

Balmins was rather notorious, not just a tourist hot spot, but also a gay haven and renowned for its isolated nude bathing area, situated between the glittering lights of the sea front promenade with its posh hotels and seafood restaurants, and the old port, which was now evolving into a somewhat exclusive marina for pleasure boats, many of which appeared to be owned by absent Russian oligarchs.

They were on their way back to the Port Hotel after a meal in the hills behind the beach, by the town cemetery, of grilled fish and polenta.

"I'm sorry," he said to her, "I like being with you but I'm also not a great social animal. Do I bore you?"

"Not at all. You're just a man of silences. I don't mind. I'd rather that than the opposite."

"You don't have to stay with me, you know. If you want some time off, feel free, no need to have me tagging along all the time."

She considered the offer and suggested she might go off on her own for a few hours, try a bar, a disco maybe. She felt like dancing. He agreed.

When she returned to their room hours later, well past midnight, she was not alone. The man escorting her was stocky, in his late 40s, he reckoned, impeccably dressed in a smart dark three piece pinstriped suit, looked a little like the actor Benicio del Torro, but without the sneer, not a dark hair out of place, ebony eyes, with an air of uncontested authority which hung above him like an aura.

He was sitting in the hotel room's only armchair, distractedly leafing through a foreign language magazine he couldn't understand, nursing a glass of water, when they arrived. Trish's face was blotchy, the alcohol she had imbibed betraying her excited state of mind.

"Who's this?" the stranger asked. "Your husband? Your boyfriend?"

"Just a friend," she answered boldly.

"Hmmm..." the man said. "I'm going to fuck her," he continued. "Do you want to leave or stay?" His tone of voice was full of impregnable confidence.

He felt a surge of adrenaline surge through his body, but before he could answer, or ask any questions, he was interrupted by Trish.

"I want him to stay, and watch," she said.

"If that's what you two want, that's what you will get," the man said. "But on my terms." He ordered the partly inebriated Dr Vaughan to sit on the edge of the bed and walked over to him, ordered him to rise from the armchair and stand by the far wall where he bound his hands tight with the belt he had deftly pulled from his jeans.

"Don't want any interruptions, or risk you having any second thoughts," he pointed out. "Just stand there and watch, or close your eyes if you prefer, but don't fucking move, understood?"

He nodded.

There was no fear, just a prurient curiosity and expectation.

"I think she wants you to see how she should be properly treated. Teach you, and her, a lesson."

The stranger quickly stripped Trisha and positioned her on all fours on the bed, undid his own trousers and roughly mounted her with no preliminaries. She moaned, and watching in dreadful fascination as he did he was unsure whether the sounds that escaped her lips were the product of pain or lust.

By morning, she had been used more than he ever thought anyone could, soundly beaten, verbally abused, hurt and a parade of bruises was marked a crooked road across the geography of her pale skin, choke marks around her throat, broken in body and soul. But from the sketch of a smile birthing across her lips, blissfully content.

Standing, hands tied, by the wall just a pebble's throw away, he had watched in abominable fascination throughout, trying to understand, to process the events unfolding in front of him in all their crude horror, knowing that Trish was not just complicit in what was happening but also badly craved this repetitive pattern of degradation and humiliation.

'Benicio' left early in the morning, slamming the door behind him, not bothering to untie his wrists. He had to ask Dr Vaughan to drag herself off the bed, still reeking of sweat and sex, to do so.

She then moved to the bathroom, and stood silently in the shower, cleaning away the excesses of the night. No humming or singing.

She wouldn't look him in the eyes after she returned to the room.

"How did you find him?" he asked.

"He found me," she replied.

"Where?"

She didn't answer him directly. His eyes were drawn to the bruises on her small breasts, and the scarlet bite mark on her neck.

"Women like me," she said. "Some men, that type of man, they smell it on us, they see it even if it's invisible to others, the craving for submission. It's an illness and they are the doctors..."

"It's happened before?"

"Yes, an addiction, I know... but..."

He gazed at her. For a moment, he thought she was about to burst into tears.

"He wants me to go with him later, to the beach. He wishes to collar me..."

"Will you?'

"Maybe..."

After he walked down to the port to fetch some bread, jam and a bottle of mineral water, and returned to the hotel, she had gone. As had her rucksack.

He briefly thought, later that day, to amble down to the nude beach where the eastern quadrant was occupied by the gay community, with their tattoos and extravagant piercings and the 'free' area where all genders paraded as nature intended. But he did not do so. That night as he tried to sleep, he couldn't help imagining the stocky man brutally pulling a naked Dr Vaughan along the fine sand on a leash connected to a dog collar around her neck, her parts rouged, her eyes lowered as if in modesty, exhibiting her and then gifting her to other men in turn in full view of the whole beach and its denizens, before allowing her to be ritually devoured, consumed like in a Tennessee Williams play.

He departed Balmins the following day.

While the waves roared just a fifty metres away, he watched a group of locals kneeling in the sand, in a ceremony to honour the dead from the tsunami that had submerged the beach five years ago to the day. Their plaintive chant spiralled through the air, a sad lament orchestrated by a shaven-headed Buddhist monk in orange rags. The smell of incense reached his nostrils. The sound of tiny bells ringing.

Behind the beach halfway to the small road that traversed the village and its procession of bars, tailors and cheap bed & breakfast establishments, stood a rectangular granite monument on which the names of all the victims were carved. Next to it, a narrow canal serpentined its way across the back of the beach area, parallel to the shore, swollen once a day by refuse pouring down from the hills or dredging a torrent of mud after each rainfall.

A gaggle of street vendors littered the slightly elevated path that ran along the beach, hawking umbrellas, silk scarves, gaudy bikinis, and coconuts.

It was out of season on Tsunami Beach, still too close to the rainy season for the tourists to have arrived in droves. There was just a scattering of European retirees who enjoyed the clement weather and the depressed state of the local currency, and some gap year students seemingly all spat out from the same mould: identical dirty blonde hair, blue or grey eyes, sunken features, and on a continual high from the cheap and easily available grass.

He sat on the ledge, watching the waves break and a few tentative surfers treading gingerly with neither the talent nor the guts to tame them properly. Their boards were too new and their tan betrayed the fact they hadn't been around these parts for long.

"Just another fucking beach," he said quietly, with no one around to hear him.

Even the waves were nowhere like Bondi, but at least the place was cheap. His cash was running out, as were his options but he felt no desire to return home, to his own country, his old life.

He didn't think he could stay here much longer and realised he was overstaying his mental welcome. More than a month already. Time to move on.

He didn't even enjoy the heat that much.

"Do you have a light?"

Someone had sat down next to him, furtively, taking him by surprise.

"Sure." He pulled out his lighter.

In exchange, the newcomer offered him a hand-rolled cigarette and brought another to his chapped lips. They both took an initial puff. The stuff was strong, odorous. He'd never been particularly partial to it, but saw no point in being rude and refusing to partake. It wasn't as if he had any immediate plans and ending up high this evening wouldn't kill him, would it?

"I'm Kem."

"Kim?"

"No, Kem with an E."

"Ah."

Taking a closer look at his interlocutor, he realised it wasn't a teenager. He was older, grey hair flowing elegantly long down his shoulders, a bushy hipster beard moving between ginger and white covering the bottom half of his face. His shorts were washed out blue, his patterned Hawaiian shirt a carnival of shells. His tan was deep, ingrained.

"Seen you sitting here a few days already?"

"Yes, I like to look at beaches."

"Don't blame you. There's nothing like the beach life, man."

"But I don't think I have yet found the right one, the perfect beach," he confessed, "Maybe I've been looking in the wrong places. Haven't tried any actual small islands yet. Might like them more. Commune with nature and all that. Earth, sea, sky, you know..."

He knew he was just spouting the sort of nonsense the guy would expect. Blame the potency of the grass.

"Ah, I know of a beach I'm sure you've never come across. A traveller's secret," Kem said.

"Tell me," he asked, if only to be polite.

"It's not easy to find, but if the stories are true, it's a hell of a place. Apparently, there's even a legend surrounding it. A hiding place, a base for the last mermaids remaining in this particular ocean."

"Mermaids?"

"Indeed. Did you know that no breasts feel as exhilarating to the touch as a mermaid's tits? It's unforgettable. Even a young virgin's buds aren't as magical, they say."

In truth, this was the first time in his life that mermaids had even neared the barbed wire fences of his imagination.

He briefly felt dizzy.

"It hasn't even got a name," Kem said. "They just call it the Final Beach."

"And how do I get there?" he asked his newly-acquired bearded companion.

His credit card was declined a hundred miles off the beach when he pulled into a gas station, so he'd had to abandon his car there and walk and hitch the rest of the way. It took him over a week. The road was a forgotten one, with barely any traffic, just a vehicle or two every hour.

He reached it at sunset, emerging from the trees that obscured the beach from the interior plains, the sharp orange orb of the sun sinking gracefully into the horizon, while storm clouds gathered above it.

His joints ached, he hadn't shaved in an eternity and must look like the parody of a caveman or a scarecrow, his clothes dusty, caked with sweat, his shoes falling apart with every new step.

It was just like his dream.

Desolate but beautiful in its loneliness. Empty.

He stepped out of his shoes, then his trousers, which he dropped to the floor of fine, yellow sand. He unbuttoned his once-pink shirt and pulled its starchy material off. Then his socks, and the glorious sensation of the unique texture of millions of grains burnished by an eternity of sea crunching under his bare feet.

He slid his boxer shorts down to his ankles and trampled them into the ground.

Took a deep breath and advanced towards the muted roar of the faraway waves, dipped his toes into the tepid water still harbouring the day's heat, advanced further until the sea reached upwards and submerged his cock, a dip in the sea floor and the water retreated upwards to his midriff, drops dripping from his navel across his pubic hair like a procession of pearls and then he continued his advance into the ocean.

His shoulders.

His neck.

His chin.

His eyes.

For a brief moment, he thought he should say something but nothing came to mind and he stepped forward until he was fully submerged.

And that was the end of that.

Later, the incoming tide would wash away the clothes he had left on the shore and there was no trace he had ever existed.

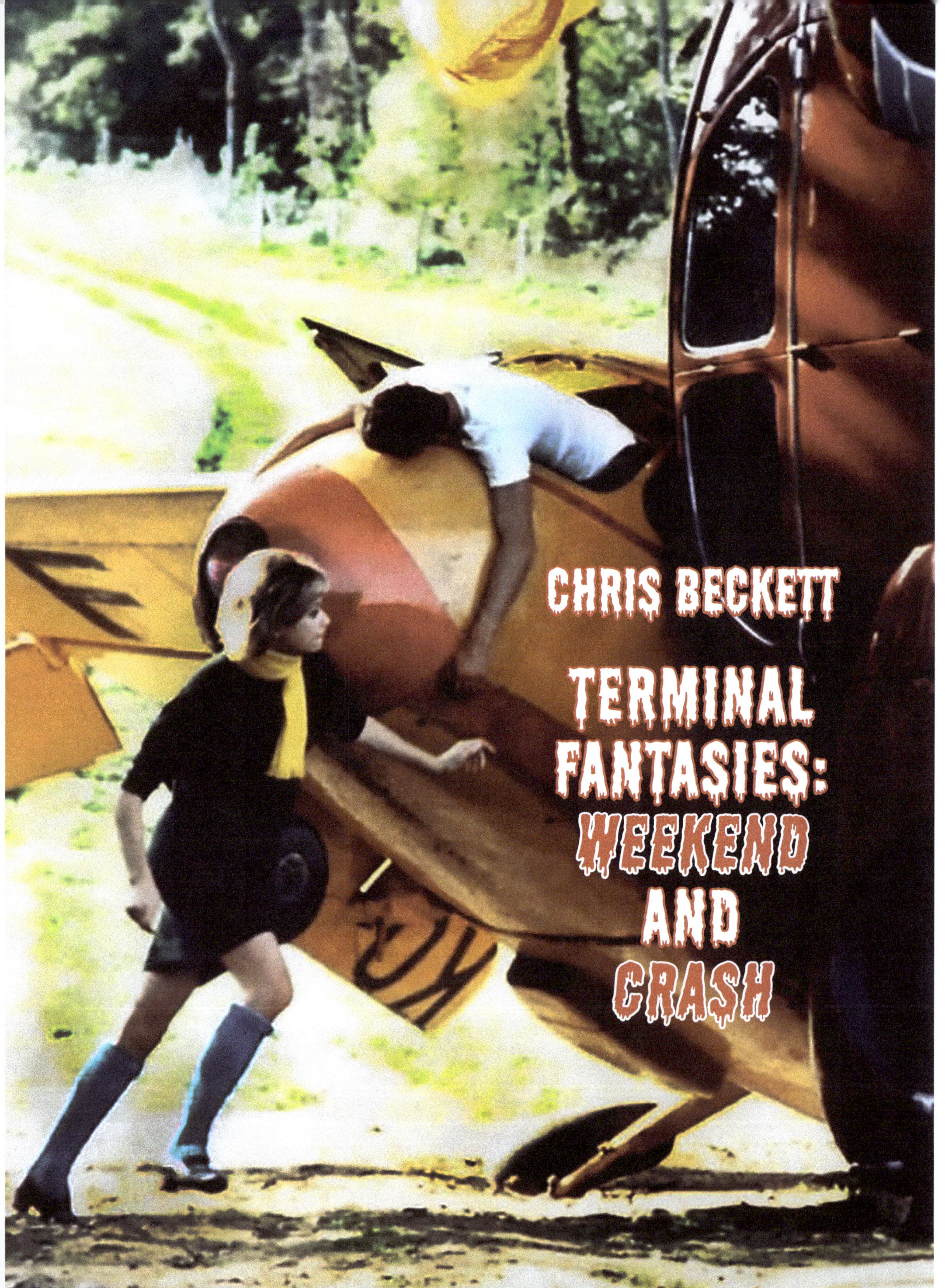
CHRIS BECKETT
TERMINAL FANTASIES:
WEEKEND
AND
CRASH

IN the first week of July 1968, Jim Ballard and Claire Walsh went to the new cinema club at the Institute of Contemporary Arts to see a pre-release showing of Jean-Luc Godard's latest film, *Weekend*. According to the ICA magazine, *Weekend* would be 'more violent and polemical than *La Chinoise*, more beautiful than *Pierrot le Fou*, more anarchic than *Bande à part*, and more outspoken than any of his films'. Moreover, the film was 'prophetic of the "May Revolution" that is shaking the France of 1968.'

The ICA was undergoing its own revolution at the time. In April 1968, it moved from premises in Dover Street, Mayfair, where it had operated since 1950, to considerably larger accommodation at Nash House in The Mall, dramatically increasing the scale and range of its programme of events and actively embracing the vibrant youth culture then bursting across London. A new Director was appointed, Michael Kustow, who came from a background in radical theatre, having previously worked with Arnold Wesker at the Roundhouse on the community arts project 'Centre 42', and subsequently with Peter Brook, helping to write the script for the anti-Vietnam War production *US* (Aldwych Theatre, October 1966). Kustow was determined to reflect in the ICA's new programme the liberal and political agenda of the day. In the previous summer, prior to his appointment, he had returned to the Roundhouse to participate in Carolee Schneemann's 'Happening', the performance piece that concluded the two-week 'Dialectics of Liberation Congress' (29 July 1967). It was an unhappy experience for Schneemann as the only woman in a largely unreceptive, and all-white, counter-cultural pow-wow. Stokely Carmichael, arriving late to the proceedings, also highlighted the alienation of London's black community from the event.

Kustow subsequently invited Schneemann to the ICA to present her 'Naked Action Lecture' (27 June 1968), the week before *Weekend* was shown. She later recalled: 'In the course of the thirty minute lecture I undressed and dressed and walked back and forth with a pointer, discussing aspects of perception and spatial organization. I took questions from the audience if they related directly to the content of the lecture. I continued dressing and undressing for the duration of the lecture and the questions. At the conclusion of the slides I went on to the stage and asked for volunteers from the audience to join me in demonstrating a principle of collage; we would all undress, cover each other with paste and leap off the stage into the mound of shredded papers.' At the end of the lecture, Schneemann's short film *Fuses* (1967) was shown, as it had been at the conclusion of the Happening at the Roundhouse. A silent sexually explicit film of Schneemann and her lover, James Tenney, the flickering 16 mm footage of *Fuses* is a celebratory collage, the spliced celluloid scratched and painted over to purposely disrupt pornographic gratification.

Kustow was fascinated by the porous boundary between theatre and spontaneous performance. He wrote a Comment piece for *Studio International* (February 1968) just prior to the ICA re-opening in April, in which he mused on the difference between happenings and theatre: both were equally ephemeral, but theatre—'whose grandeur and poignancy consist in this ephemerality'—is (almost) repeatable. 'Bad happenings,' he concluded, 'deny the combustive process of good acting.' Kustow's appointment was propitious for Ballard, who was at the time planning to present a multi-media performance piece at the ICA. The earliest iteration of his accumulating car-crash material, 'Crash!' would feature Chris Evans as the narrator, four actors (a car-buying family group), crash dummies prepared by Eduardo Paolozzi, projected crash-test footage, sound effects, and a crash-damaged car on stage. (A copy of Ballard's outline for the event was deposited at the British Library by Nancy Evans in 2017.) The production was announced in a full-page feature by June Rose for the *Sunday Mirror* (19 May 1968) but did not go ahead, although, in the following year, readings of 'A Plan for the Assassination of Jacqueline Kennedy' organised by *Ambit* magazine, involving Martin Bax and Euphoria Bliss, were given at the ICA (in April and May 1969), followed by a short run of multi-media performances of 'The Assassination Weapon' mounted by Stewart McKenzie (11-16 August 1969).

The ambition of the 'Crash!' production envisaged was, Ballard's outline suggests, considerable, as would have been the personal commitment of Chris Evans to the project, who was already involved with the ICA's forthcoming exhibition 'Cybernetic Serendipity' (2 August–20 October 1968), an exhibition that would explore in a very 'hands-on' format the innovative impact of computers on the arts. Equally, Kustow, by his own admission, was feeling overextended, torn between nurturing new creative projects and fulfilling his many managerial responsibilities, large and small, as the challenges of directing operations at the new premises made themselves felt. In the summer, Kustow and the poet and painter Adrian Henri took themselves off to Normandy to write a play (*I Wonder*) about Guillaume Apollinaire, to be staged at the ICA in the autumn. Although Ballard's 'Crash!' was not performed, its announcement in the press served notice that he was seeking to develop his car-crash material into a project with greater scope and scale than he had so far realised.

Kustow wrote an introduction to the English translation (1967) of the screenplay for Godard's earlier film *Made in U.S.A.* (1966). He highlighted: 'glowing yellow walls, the pop art poetry of garage signs, flipper machines and neon strips, [Anna] Karina moving among it all in a bright turquoise dress with bold diagonal stripes. And suddenly, in this almost too perfect world [...] she will open a door and find sitting in a dentist's chair a body whose head is totally wrapped in bloodstained bandages, or come at the end of a corridor upon a whimpering female figure with bandages wound round hands whose fingernails have recently been pulled, or confront another girl who can only mutter about a razor blade.' *Made in U.S.A.* is a parodic thriller, inspired in part by Howard Hawks's film of *The Big Sleep* (1946), with a confusing plot that seems to lead nowhere: 1960s pop fantasy meets torture meets death in a Kafkaesque labyrinth, trailing the Kennedy assassination—Ballard's touchstone for the decade—and the kidnapping and murder of the left wing Moroccan politician Ben Barka in Paris in 1965.

Ballard discussed going to see *Weekend* when he was interviewed by Iain Sinclair (for the BFI monograph, *Crash*, published in 1999). In *Weekend*, the camera tracks a seemingly endless (8-minute) car-honking traffic jam across the screen as the Parisian bourgeoisie attempt to escape the city for the weekend, and traces a nihilistic descent to blackly comic barbarism. Capitalism's last cavalcade is gridlocked. The travellers kill time by playing (ball and chess) and by fighting. At the head of the jam, a deadly car crash, one of many. A tribe of hippy-revolutionaries roams the countryside and has taken to cannibalism. The leader of the group remarks: 'The horror of the bourgeoisie can only be overcome by more horror' ('On ne peut dépasser l'horreur de la bourgeoisie que par plus d'horreur encore'). The biggest scream in the film is provoked not by casual rape, murder and the eating of human flesh, not by the burning bodies that litter the roadside, but for the loss of an expensive Hermès bag, engulfed in the flames of a burning car, a fashion accessory branded with the name of the Greek god of roads and commerce.

In the interview, Sinclair works his way towards *Weekend* by asking Ballard if he had been influenced by French New Wave cinema, by Chris Marker's *La Jetée*, and by the style of jump-cut editing notably employed by Godard in *Breathless*. But Ballard's reply swerves away from the answer that Sinclair expects ('I don't know whether cinema had much influence'), citing his first stories from the 1950s, not taking up the fractured narratives of *The Atrocity Exhibition* to which Sinclair had been implicitly pointing, nor his appreciation of *La Jetée* published in *New Worlds* (1966). About *Weekend*, Ballard was emphatic: 'He's got it wrong. Godard's got it wrong. He sees the car as the symbol of American capitalism, and the car crash as one of the wounds inflicted by capitalism on the docile purchasers of modern cars [...] He's missed the point. He doesn't see that the car is, in fact, a powerful force for good in its perverse way [...] I knew Godard didn't get it – because he saw the car crash in rather old-fashioned Marxist political terms.'

Nonetheless, seeing *Weekend* must have been an opportune occasion for Ballard as he actively considered what more he might make of his accumulating car-crash material. The eight-page outline for the ICA performance 'Crash!' had just been drafted (by early May). Still to come were the final two crash-related stories for *The Atrocity Exhibition*, 'Crash!' and 'Tolerances of the Human Face', both published in 1969. And the prospect of developing a longer crash-related narrative would soon beckon. Part foil, and part stimulus, *Weekend* percolated through Ballard's imagination. *Weekend* was a transitional film that marked the end of the first phase of Godard's work—the highly productive period (fifteen films in seven years) that stretched from *Breathless* (1960) to *Weekend*, his farewell to commercial cinema—and heralded the next phase of his career, the low-budget overtly political films and documentaries he made collaboratively as a member of the Dziga Vertov Group, the radical co-operative named after the Soviet film director.

The closing titles of *Weekend* announce not just the end of this particular film but, at least for this director, 'Fin de Cinéma'. Conversely, *Crash* would mark Ballard's *return* to continuous narrative after the fractured stories—the broken mirror—of *The Atrocity Exhibition*. The abandoned drama 'Crash!' that was to have been performed at the ICA was really a series of working tableaux—the life-cycle of the automobile from showroom sale to inevitable crash to junkyard grave—without significant narrative connectivity. One means by which Ballard found his way back to continuous narrative (and to a more commercial product for his publisher, thereby travelling in the opposite direction to Godard) was through exploring genre-based parody, the kind of mixing of modes rendered in *La Jetée* ('a fusion of science fiction and psychological fable,' as Ballard remarked), in *Alphaville* ('I wish I could say *that* had influenced me') and in *Made in U.S.A.* Part noir, I hear an echo of Raymond Chandler (*The Big Sleep* was one of Ballard's favourite novels) in the hard-boiled melodramatic inflection of the first-person *Crash* narrative. In interview, Ballard was frequently on tactical manoeuvres, tying and untying the life and the work.

There is much to distinguish *Crash* from *Weekend*, not least *Weekend*'s pronounced self-awareness as cinema, which stands in contrast to Ballard's equally determined refusal to break the spell of the illusion he is spinning (there is no 'outside' to James's first person narrative). Godard's cast know that they are in a film, and will sometimes say so. At one point, Roland remarks: 'This film's crap. We're always meeting nutcases.' At another point, a passenger in a passing vehicle stops and asks: 'Are you in a film or are you for real?' 'In a film,' replies Roland. As the car accelerates away, the driver shouts 'Liars!' And yet, although we cannot see beyond James's rendering of the world, *Crash* is, like *Weekend*, chock-full of the tropes of fiction: 'As I moved in the evening traffic along Western Avenue, I thought of being killed within this huge accumulation of fictions, finding my body marked with the imprint of a hundred television crime serials, the signatures of forgotten dramas which, years after being shelved in a network shake-up, would leave their last credit-lines in my skin.'

Missing from *Weekend*, and fundamental to *Crash*, is the *visceral* excitement of travelling effortlessly, and dangerously, at high speed. The 'vectors of speed, aggression, violence and desire' that Ballard brings to metaphorical intersection are familiar from Filippo Tommaso Marinetti's Futurist 'Manifesto' (1909) which celebrated the dynamism and the destructive violence of the twentieth century machine age: 'the world's magnificence has been enriched by a new beauty: the beauty of speed'. Ballard's characterisation (to Sinclair) of the car-crash as a 'powerful force for good in its perverse way' recalls Marinetti's adrenalin-rush moment of re-birth when he crashes his car into a 'maternal' ditch: 'When I came up—torn, filthy and stinking—from under the capsized car, I felt the white-hot iron of joy deliciously pass through my heart.' When Ballard went to see *Weekend*, he had in fact just drafted the familiar phrase 'vectors of speed, aggression, violence and desire'. The earliest articulation of this typically geometric figure, recognizable from 'Crash!' in *The Atrocity Exhibition*, is in the draft outline for the proposed ICA event. The same words would reappear once more, slightly trimmed, in *Crash*: 'Within the car-crash death was directed by the vectors of speed, violence and aggression' (Chap. 4).

The motor car industry and cinema grew up together: Model T Fords, Mack Sennett and slapstick comedy. There is a great deal of slapstick in the physical comedy of *Weekend*, and we can find it in *Crash* too. Indeed, it is the basis of James and Catherine's first car accident. In the first chapter, James remembers his 'first minor collision in a deserted hotel car-park. Disturbed by a police patrol, we had forced ourselves through a hurried sex-act. Reversing out of the park, I struck an unmarked tree. Catherine vomited over my seat.' The sudden panic, the clumsiness, the embarrassment, and the collision without apparent injury, have all the hallmarks of slapstick, and it is from this small absurdist drama that their dark journey begins.

The first two scenes of *Weekend*, both interior scenes, seem to promise a very different film to the outdoor anarchic black comedy that ensues. Corinne and Roland are in their affluent apartment in Paris. A third person is present, who we quickly realise is Corinne's lover. Covert conversations between Corinne and Roland and their respective lovers (Roland takes a telephone call) reveal that Corinne and Roland are intent on murdering each other. First, however, they will unite forces to expedite a long-awaited inheritance, the purpose of their impending car journey. As Ballard cannot have failed to notice, they drive a Facel Vega, the car in which Albert Camus met his death, propelled through the windscreen like Dr Remington's faceless husband, a circus turn from a cannon. When they finally arrive at Corinne's family home (the Facel having been consumed in flames together with the Hermès bag), they learn that her father has already died and that her mother refuses to share the family fortune. On the spur of the moment, they murder Corinne's mother. Repeatedly stabbed by Corinne with a kitchen knife, her mother's body is thrown into the boot of another car before being torched by Roland at the roadside after they collide with a light aircraft that has joined the crash party. The opening of the film seems to promise that *Weekend* will be a psychological thriller, but the scene's comic absurdities —we learn of botched attempts at murder by faulty brakes, by sleeping pills and by gas—heavily tilt the opening towards satire. Furthermore, the scene is punctuated by a violent altercation, comical in its exaggerated choreography, between two drivers in the street below, following a minor collision. A taste of what is to come.

Weekend's second scene *does* make me think of *Crash*, of Catherine's descriptions of her conveyor-belt of sexual conquests and James's questions about them as they fuck, and of the fantasy of Vaughan that they share. Corinne is with her lover in his flat. They are in silhouette. Corrine sits on the table in her underwear recounting a recent sexual encounter with another (recently married) man and his lover (oh, the bourgeoisie!). 'Begin at the beginning,' says Corinne's lover, who sits fully-clothed in a chair beside her, prompting, listening, watching, smoking. Appropriately enough, Corinne's story ('it wasn't at all the way it is in novels or *Marie Claire*') begins in a car: 'He started in the Mercedes [...] I mean it's idiotic, necking in cars [...] but we ended up stopping in the rue Molitor and we necked for a long time in the parking lot ... He put one hand between my legs ... he had the other round my neck ... but without moving at all ... We stayed like that for a long time'. As Corinne continues to tell her story in a flat and matter-of-fact voice, seemingly disengaged, the soundtrack comes and goes intermittently, partly drowning her words at times, and the camera moves unpredictably, tracking in and out, panning left and right, up and down, in the dimly lit room. Just as Schneemann's *Fuses* incorporates visual noise to interrupt facile consumption, so the scene between Corinne and her lover withholds information, deliberately obscures words and unsettles our gaze, running interference against the comforts of cinematic illusion.

The scene is a parody of patient and psychiatrist (and echoes Ingmar Bergman's *Persona*). Questions spur the forward momentum, urging the excitement that detail brings. Corinne and the man go to his apartment where she engages in a threesome with the man's lover. The events that Corinne recounts, involving an egg and a saucer of milk, will be familiar to readers of Georges Bataille as the opening erotic episode of *Histoire de l'oeil* (1928). 'What happened next?' asks Corinne's interlocutor-lover. 'What was she doing?' 'Were you thinking of me too?' We can hear the same urgent tone of engaged interrogation in Catherine's questions to James, who observes that 'Catherine had taken over the fantasy'. 'Do you like Vaughan?' 'In what way?' 'Do you find him attractive?' 'Would you like to fuck him, though? In that car?' 'Would you like to sodomise him?' 'Have you ever tasted semen?' In the week following this shared fantasy, James remembers how Catherine 'drifted through the departure lounges of the airport like a queen in rut'. Her back-seat car-wash encounter with Vaughan will take place soon (James watching in the rear-view mirror from the front) and is now signposted, as is James's sexual encounter with Vaughan. At the end of the scene in *Weekend*, Corinne's lover says: 'I adore you Corinne; come and excite me'. But the scene fades, withholding the pleasure of a film that *Weekend* is not.

In David Cronenberg's film of *Crash*, James Ballard sits on the veranda of his apartment, recuperating after his car crash, binoculars raised, watching the traffic flow, hyper-sensitive to the beat—and to the accident-provoked interrupted beat—of its machine-like pulse. 'Is the traffic heavier now?' he asks Catherine. 'There seem to be three times as many cars as there were before the accident.'

A pair of binoculars, the voyeur's friend, are Cronenberg's fitting addition: they are not in the novel (nor are they in Cronenberg's script), but the traffic that James scans in the film is a Toronto freeway twelve lanes wide, too distant to be observed with the naked eye. In the novel, James and Catherine's 10th floor apartment is part of the airport neighbourhood, situated in what James thinks of as 'a pleasant island' bounded by a sea of ever-proliferating roads: 'an access spur of the northern circular motorway [...] flowed past us on its elegant concrete pillars'. In the novel, the concrete outdoors of the Westway and its environs always feels enclosed, as if it were an ancillary interior. From his vantage point on the balcony he sees, abstractly, 'a motion sculpture'. He descends to the communal garage in the basement of the building: an empty oil-stained space gapes where his car used to be. 'Horns sounded from the trapped vehicles on the motorway, a despairing chorus', like the continuous cacophonous chorus that accompanies the lateral tracking of the traffic jam in *Weekend*. The sounding of the horns that James hears is followed by a disturbing interlude of silence. James 'had the sudden impression that the world had suddenly stopped'. In their different ways, *Weekend* and *Crash* are both terminal fantasies pointing to a looming ending always imminent yet always deferred, displaced by the next accident, the next slapstick car chase, the next farcical routine. Or the next meal: Corinne joins the happy band of hippies and gnaws on the flesh of her newly-killed husband, Roland. The last spoken words of *Weekend* are hers, a polite plea to the cook: 'When I've finished, Ernest, I wouldn't mind a bit more.'

Further reading:

Chris Beckett, 'J.G. Ballard's "Crash! A Science-Theatre Presentation for the ICA": The Context of a Document Newly-Discovered'. *Electronic British Library Journal* (forthcoming 2019). Reproduces Ballard's text in full.

Michael Kustow, *TANK: An Autobiographical Fiction* (London, 1975).

Carolee Schneemann, *More Meat than Joy: Performance Works and Selected Writings* (New York, 1997).

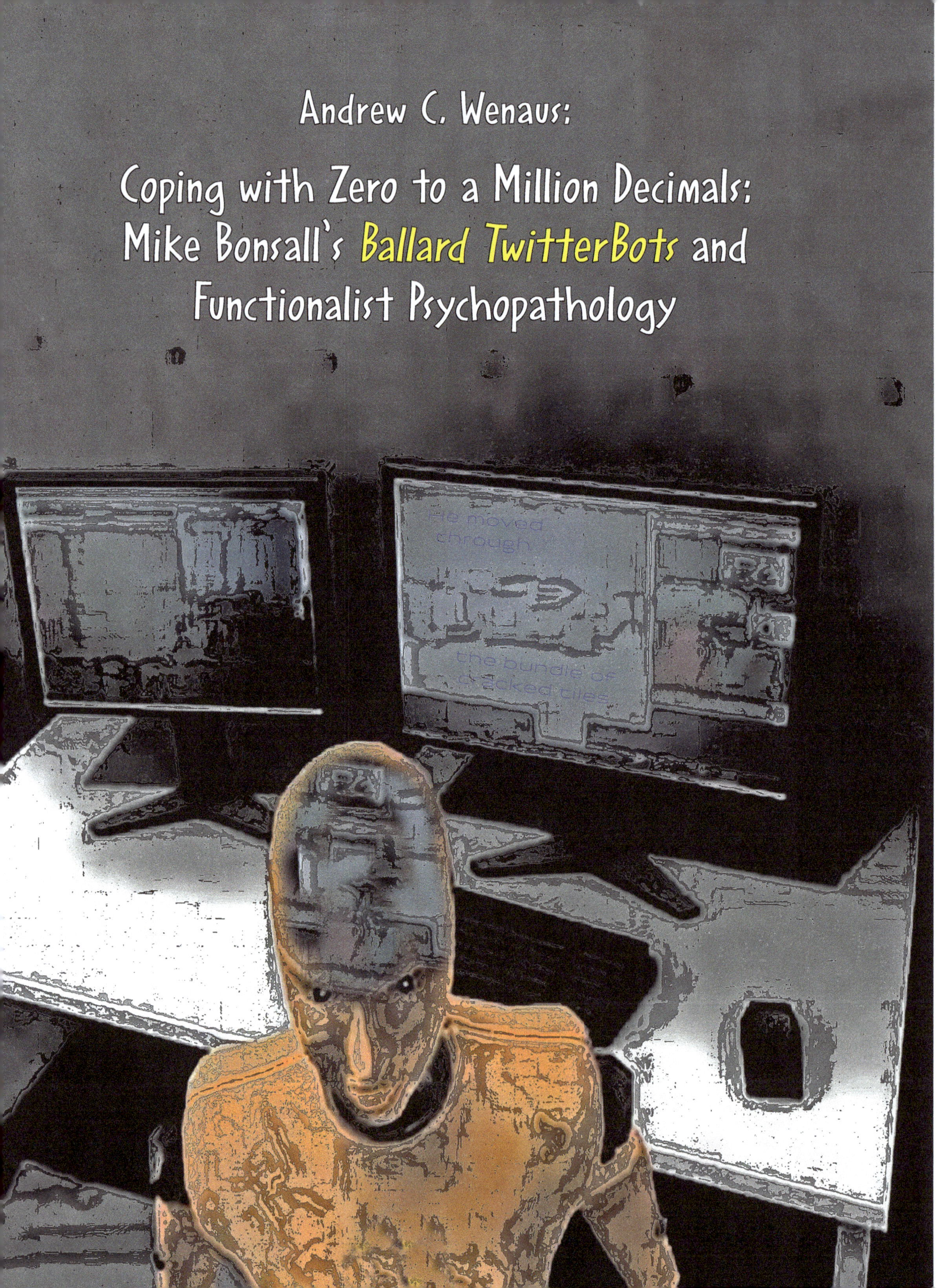
Andrew C. Wenaus:
Coping with Zero to a Million Decimals:
Mike Bonsall's Ballard TwitterBots and
Functionalist Psychopathology
the bundle of

IN a 2006 interview with Travis Elborough, J.G. Ballard suggests that he sees his role as a novelist as an investigator or a scout who is sent ahead to see whether or not the water is drinkable. Ballard is one of the most discerning English language authors of the 20th and 21st centuries. His catastrophe novels of the 1960s are, today, remarkably prescient with their extrapolations of climate change and the psychopathological impulse to embrace and accelerate the destruction that comes with it.

In the 1970s, Ballard's formally experimental novels examined the psychopathologies of mass media by looking at the surreal combinations of eroticism, death, technology, obsession, psychopathy, and violence. His final novels consider the logical conclusion of closed communities and the coming of techno-feudalism and consumer fascism as a reaction against safety and boredom. As varied as these theses may seem, Ballard's work is a kind of variations on a theme: that the protagonist is constituted by something that is at once internally latent yet outwardly constitutive and, in complicated ways, determinist. Perhaps this is why the central thesis of Ballard's work should lend itself seamlessly to online bots.

After all, "Ballard has for a long time resembled a rogue AI, re-permutating the same few themes *ad infinitum*, occasionally adding a sprinkling of contemporary detail to freshen up a limited repertoire of fixations," writes Mark Fisher. "Fixations, fixations. Appropriate, since, after all, Ballard's obsession is... obsession."

Ballard's fiction is characteristically set in car parks, hospital lobbies, suburbs, motorways and underpasses, shopping malls, business parks, airports, and luxury high-rises. Each of these settings exemplify Marc Augé's conception of "non-places": supermodern deluges of meaning, contagiously viral, outside of time, and purely functional. Ballard's concerns are physical, psychological, and civic.

All this lends itself to Mike Bonsall's *Digital Ballard, Ballard TwitterBots*, and Bonsall's investigation into the ultimate non-space where rogue AI literally can endlessly self-generate and re-permutate: the internet. For Ballard, nonspaces signify the social architecture that signify an absent referent; the internet only intensifies this nullification. I had a chance to catch up with Bonsall over email to discuss the Bots and where the idea came from. Bonsall responded with a short narrative and, rather than rewriting it, it is quoted in full here:

> "Although I haven't had much in the way of formal art education, a series of influences have brought me to where I am with *Digital Ballard*.
>
> "I had an early interest in Burroughs' cut-up techniques and Ballard's more experimental writings, and was an early adopter of computer technology (Sinclair ZX Spectrum). It's interesting that both Burroughs and Ballard had computer-oriented friends and collaborators—Ian Sommerville and Christopher Evans—who both died young, before they could become a lasting influence.
>
> "As well as failing to obtain a medical degree (like Burroughs and Ballard before me), I have worked as an educational technologist, IT trainer and analyst at a University, giving me an interest in, and access to, a wide range of computing equipment and software.
>
> "Coming of age in the Punk era taught me that you don't need to ask permission and you can just go do it yourself. I've heard the filmmaker Shane Meadows talk of his method in a similar way: 'Fast, Fun and Fuck-it.' Pete Shelley, who sadly died recently, was a brilliant example of this, setting up gigs, a band and a record label with minimal knowledge but great enthusiasm.
>
> "While a student of the UK Open University I took the notorious art course TAD292: Art and Environment. A radical, perhaps even a Situationist, course which opened my eyes to alternative art practices...
>
> "I was also influenced by the very nature of Ballard's writing, which seems to presuppose another world, just out of sight, that might somehow be reached by an ever-more intense interrogation of the text. As Ballard himself put it: 'It's a little as if I were leading the reader to a deserted laboratory, and that I put a collection of specimens and all the necessary equipment at his disposal. It's his job then to relate these elements together and create reactions from them.'" (Bonsall)

The Ballardian TwitterBots are an amusing and insightful extension of Ballard's central thesis (that the psyche is both constitutive and constituted by the psychopathology of non-place environments), though through automated means. Bonsall's three Ballard TwitterBots are @JGB_Sentences, @ Crash_Cutup, and @New_Ballard. All three offer a progression of significance when considering psychopathy and media functions of the inhuman.

The first, @JGB_Sentences, is the simplest and consists of a Twitter-length sentence, selected from a single-column Excel spreadsheet containing forty thousand elements of Ballard text, and posted to Twitter once every 12 hours. Bonsall removed all very short sentences (i.e. single word sentences) and used a full stop as the delimiter. Here are two examples from 7 June 2019 (spaced twelve hours apart):

> "Gregory looked out across the terrace at the traffic whirling over the neon-lit cobbles"
>
> "A few paces from the grave of the Mallory her footprints vanished into the sand."

The authorship of these tweets is clearly Ballard's in the sense that the sentences, Bonsall remarks, are completely those of the former. The SSBot that chooses the sentences twice daily is entirely for convenience and does not really complicate traditional understandings of authorship.

The second, @Crash_Cutup, is more complex. Bonsall took each sentence in Ballard's 1973 novel *Crash* and split each sentence into three parts (beginning, middle, and end) in an excel spreadsheet. The bot randomly organizes selections from the three columns resulting in a new Ballardian sentence. Bonsall suggests that Ballard is the original author but that he has acted as the collagist. The bot, however, is playing a larger role here in the sense that it is situated somewhere between Ballard and Bonsall. Here are two examples from 5 June 2019:

> "She told me that she worked I moved rapidly like sabre wounds"

> "As I expected, and the shower of glass as the animal was carried over the roof, on her heel."

What interesting here is that the parts of the sentences are Ballard's own words—however, the complete sentences themselves do not appear in Ballard's writing. Furthermore, this process ask whether the astronomically aleatoric possibilities of syntactic re-organization is taking one step further away from both Ballard and Bonsall and situating itself as something nonlinearly inhuman.

Finally, and most interestingly, @New_Ballard uses a simple Markov chain model that determines which word is most likely to come next in the order of text. A Markov chain is a relatively simple way of statistically modelling stochastic patterns based on what appeared before in a sequence. In other words, @New_Ballard uses an algorithm that guesses what the next Ballardian word would be based on a spreadsheet containing the complete text of Ballard's urban novels (*The Atrocity Exhibition, Crash, High-Rise* and *Concrete Island*). Here is an example from 6 June 2019: and another from 7 June 2019:

> "He moved through the bundle of cracked tiles."

> "Arabesque. Later, in this stage of vehicles, but Maitland looked down at the bald woman carrying desks and gear shift."

In this case, the question of authorship is more complicated since these sentences do not appear at all in Ballard's work. Bonsall writes that "while Ballard is undoubtedly still the creator of the original text, the 'author' of these Tweets is more difficult to ascribe. [It] could in part be Zach Whalen, or even Andrey Markov, who died eight years before Ballard was born" (Bonsall). However, rather than considering the bots in the terms of authorship, it may be more appropriate to consider the new sentences as Ballardian protagonists.

So, how are these automated tweets protagonists? To try and make a case for this, it may be helpful to consider a related way of thinking about the conflating of inner and outer (or other) space. Bonsall considers Ballard's writings as examples of what Roland Barthes calls writerly texts: works that place demands on the reader to generate meaning. By extension, a Ballardian character is in the process of something similar: attempting to have the objective world corroborate with the subjective world. This tangling of the text and the psyche, much like the conflating of environment and the inner-life, is surrealist. However, this has an interesting proxy with a similar logical structure playing out, not in the psychological realm, but in a digital-technological space: functionalism.

Functionalist semantics is a kind of linguistic determinism that is characteristic in the work of Alfred Korzybski, Benjamin Lee Whorf, and Edward Sapir. Ballard's work is not functionalist in the strict sense; instead, as we noted, it is more surrealist or, in the case of *The Atrocity Exhibition*, neo-Dadaist. One thing that functionalism and surrealism have in common is a tightening of tangled, bidirectional, level-crossing loops between spaces outside, inner-space, and language. For a functionalist, language constitutes the parameters of thought. For a surrealist, the subjective and objective always tangle and trip over one another. A Dadaist would deny the existence of an imperial author, character, or subject altogether (as a way of escaping these loops).

A TwitterBot, however, seems to complicate these distinctions altogether by taking the Dadaist position to its (il) logical conclusion: an inhuman, programmed scout that comes into existence through automated processes and wanders into the nonspace (and asignifying functionality) of digital environments. It is a bit like a programmed no-thing is tangling and level-crossing within a digital no-thing. The bots are not writerly texts in the way Ballard's writing is—instead, they are texts of exclusion. And, as characters (rather than authors), the process is an intensification of Ballardian psychopathology. Let's call it functionalist psychopathy: a demand on the reader and the bots, not to generate meaning, but to dismantle ego absolutely, re-permutate functions, process processes, and endlessly repeat the same objective.

The Bots are an extension of this functionalist process: Bonsall's reading of Ballard's work leads to interpretations that take on not only a new kind of digital, automated meaning but also permit the reading to generate and automate itself, to become the reagent in its own self-automated reactions. Dominika Oramus writes that Ballard's semi-autobiographical work presents the reader with a series of personas that he constructed throughout his body of work. What these personas achieve, however, are fictional proxies to Ballard the man in the extra-diegetic space of the book.

"Ballard enjoyed playing with readers' assumptions about himself as well as the role of the author," writes D. Harlan Wilson, "but he was relatively adamant about how his various 'Ballards' were fictions conjured from his internal and external experiences" and, "in daily life, Ballard was thoroughly 'un-Ballard'." Wilson adds that Ballard's autobiographical novels (*The Unlimited Dream Company, Empire of the Sun*, and *The Kindness of Women*) confirm the postmodern dictum that "we are products of the media environment... our names should be enclosed in quotes," and that, "characters jeopardize the concept of a fixed identity on multiple levels." From this, Wilson disagrees with Scott Bukatman's evaluation of the Ballardian character as one without ego, purely absorbed into and conflated with the media landscape where the landscape itself "becomes a schizophrenic projection of a de-psychologized, but fully colonized consciousness" and "everything becomes at once objective and subjective." Wilson, instead, suggests that Ballard's protagonists are "pure ego, compulsively trying and retrying to assert and define themselves," and are "unable to get over or outside of their own hang-ups, crises, passions, needs, imaginings, and inhibitions."

I agree with Wilson here, particularly in the sense that, as he states, a typical Ballardian protagonist is a psychopath in the clinical sense: "in search of fixity, of achieving some kind of negotiation between objective and subjective worlds." Fisher also identifies the typical Ballardian protagonist as pure

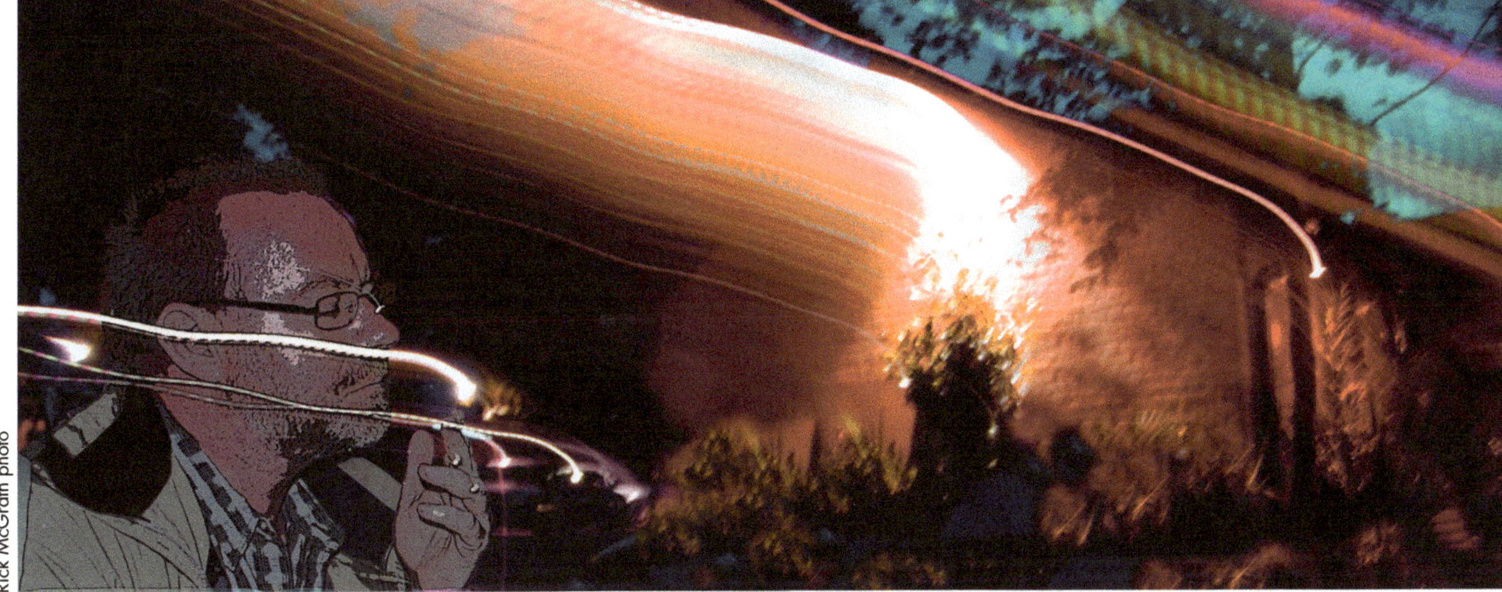
Rick McGrath photo

Mike Bonsall

ego in the process of exploring, confronting, and negotiating the tangled knots of the inside and the outside. What the Ballardian protagonist confronts, Fisher writes, "is time and space themselves, as preconditions of all perceptions and experiences," that the negotiation between time and space "open up as an intensive zone beyond—outside—standard perceptual thresholds." So, in terms of Ballard's writing, Bukatman's evaluation may have jumped the gun. While Wilson and Fisher are correct to identify Ballard's characters as pure ego, Bukatman's character-without-ego seems to be a precise definition of Bonsall's BallardBots.

Neither authors nor characters in the traditional sense, the SSBots are without ego, media-landscapes-in-themselves, processes obsessed with process, and lacking any attempt at negotiating objective and subjective worlds. Instead, the BallardBots intensify functionalist level-crossing, aiming to achieve an intensified equilibrium that maximizes the efficiency of its rigid, programmed, fixed process: to self-assemble and be made visible on Twitter at highly regular intervals.

The bots demonstrate an incremental shift towards supermodern psychopathy: from didactic sentences, to a digitally generated sentence, to fully surreal automated syntax (i.e. literary blips: protagonists without a unified, imperial author). Ballard's prose is always highly calculated, dispassionate, and articulate; Bonsall's BallardBots achieve this functionality to a new inhuman degree. After all, authorship is not the best way to think about the bots at all. Instead, they are self-generated Ballardian characters in a dual sense: first, they are representations of an agent with (or without) identifiable human traits and, second, literal symbols (letters and coded numbers representing data) that regularly reiterate themselves into new sentences and are usable by an algorithm.

In this sense, their choices and decisions are not really their own but, rather, reactions to an attractive, constitutive, and alterior logic or code. For a Ballardian character, "'decides' is no doubt too active a word," Fisher notes, "in every respect the typical Ballard character... discovers rather than initiates" and, "finds himself drawn into a logic he is compelled to investigate. (In many ways a faithful Freudian, Ballard has no doubt that obsession always has/is a logic)".

Bonsall's TwitterBots are the scouts sent ahead—not into shopping malls, airports, or luxury high-rises—but onto the internet to see how the future may unfold according to an inhuman psychopathology of algorithmic culture. Bonsall ultimately establishes a means by which Ballard can operate according to the nihilism at the logical centre of an intensified nonplace.

So, what is a nonplace? Augé's formulation suggests that it is something outside signification, time, relation, and value: "If a place can be defined as relational, historical and concerned with identity," he writes, "then a space which cannot be defined as relational, or historical, or concerned with identity will be a non-place."

"The hypothesis advanced here," Augé continues, "is that supermodernity produces non-places, meaning spaces which are not themselves anthropological places and... do not integrate the earlier places." Generally, nonplaces are civic nodes of transfer, logistics, transience, and transport. They are the quintessentially Ballardian spaces: shopping malls, airports, hotel lobbies, waiting rooms, and motorways.

To Augé's list of nonplaces we could add cyberspace itself: the internet and other manifestations of networked digital media," write Jay David Bolter and Richard Grusin in *Remediation: Understanding New Media*. "Cyberspace," they continue, "is not, as some assert, a parallel universe. It is not a place of escape from contemporary society, or indeed from the physical world. It is rather a nonplace, with many of the same characteristics as other highly mediated nonplaces." The internet, like the supermodern city, is an inhuman space that does not have a historical referent; humans use it, but it also uses, even constitutes and absorbs the human. This is, to recall Fisher, a confrontation with time and space themselves as preconditions of experience but towards to the ends of the preconditions of non-experience. Rather than human desire merging with machine or supermodern architecture, with the digital we have the human merging with number, code, algorithms: that is, with nonmaterial, with *no-thing*.

Bonsall's bots scout cyberspace. For some reason, the term "cyberspace" seems archaic and a bit awkward in 2019, yet it is worth recalling because the "space" part reminds us of the spatial or topological conundrums associated with it (and all the head-scratching issues that follow from this). Bukatman writes that "whether 'cyberspace' is a real place or not, our experience of electronic space is a 'real' experience. By distinguishing the

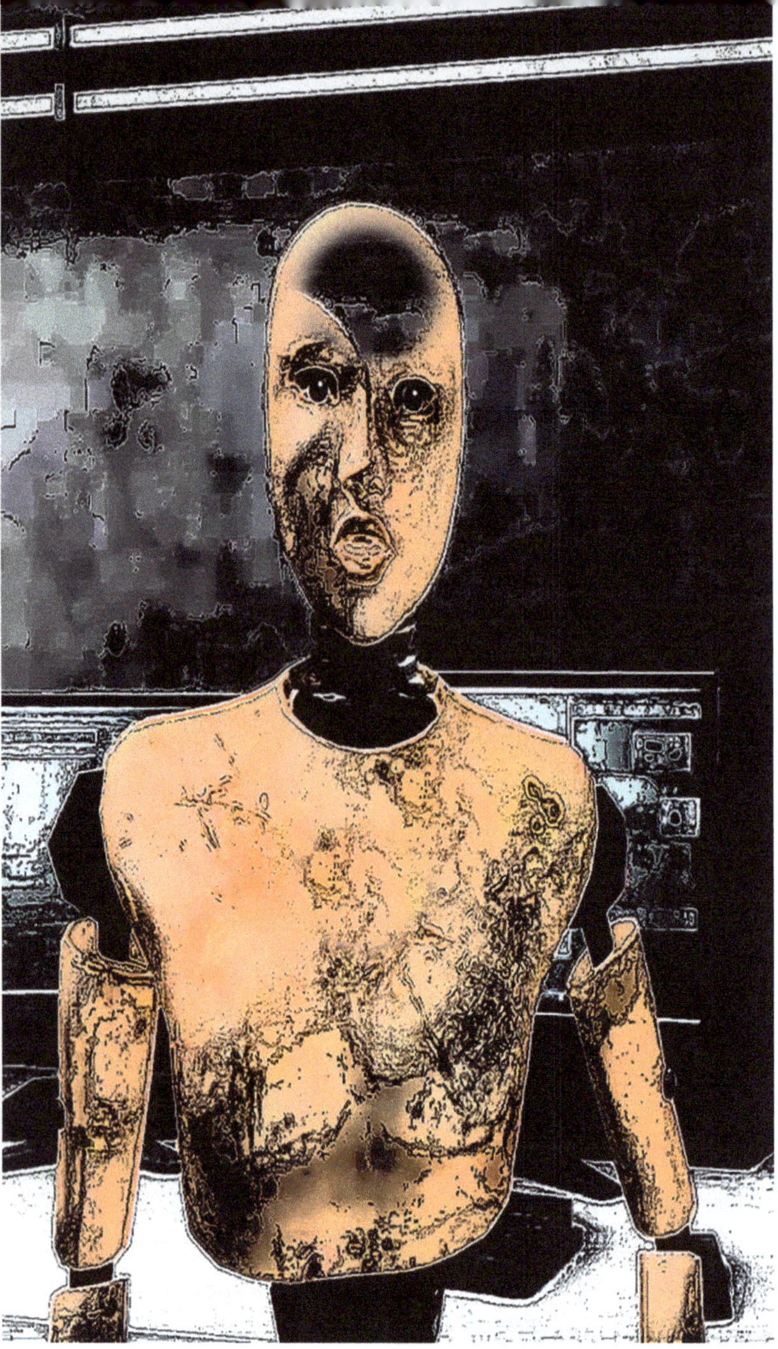

constitution of being as an activity of interface," he continues, "phenomenology suggests that the status of being is not an absolute condition, but one that changes relative to changes in the experience of the real". This real experience, according to Bukatman, establishes a "master-narrative, one grounded in the centrality of human intention and perception, which has the cumulative effect of inaugurating a new subject capable of inhabiting the bewildering and disembodied space of the electronic environment—the virtual subject."

In the 21st century, we are all virtual subjects and the disembodied spaces of digital environments are no longer bewildering to most of us. In fact, the virtual experience seems in many ways to be a tightening or intensification of a correlationist way of accessing phenomena. The embodied spaces of the world may be, for "digital natives" born in the 1980s (to borrow Douglas Rushkoff's term for those, like myself, born into a world already largely governed by the digital), the more bewildering environments. But, Bonsall's BallardBots are something different altogether: they are not virtual subjects nor are they digital natives. Instead, the bots are procedures, functions set in motion by Bonsall to inhabit Twitter, to be the inhuman scouts on the surface of an otherwise inhuman nonspace with seemingly endless fractal iterations. "Cyberspace," after all, Bolter and Grusin write, "is a shopping mall in the ether; it fits smoothly into our contemporary networks of transportation, communication, and economic exchange."

We may as well add, in Ballardian fashion, that these networks of transportation, communication, and economic exchange also fit neatly inside us. Ballardian landscapes are nonplaces, nonplaces are Ballardian: "The shopping mall as a mediated space is simultaneously particularized and anonymous." Bolter and Grusin suggest that "despite efforts to identify each mall (by giving it a name and sometimes a theme), malls are notoriously anonymous, perhaps because, as Sorkin (1992) points out, consumer capitalism demands sameness behind the variety."

Just as neoliberalism constitutes the individual as a manufactured and automated identity that, at first glance, establishes a sense of difference, it simultaneously establishes sameness predicated on the underlying rules, operations, and functions of capitalism. Nevertheless, the underlying logic of neoliberalism is always attracted inward, back to a determining force whose output is always the simulation of variety but whose black box is tightly regulating what is expressed and that with which it identifies and represents in actuality. With this in mind, it should be no surprise that Ballard's protagonists, themes, and settings are thematic repetitions.

If we take the underlying logic of the capitalist subject or the virtual subject to its logical conclusion as a simple SSBot, we notice an intensification of the surrealist impulse (the Ernstian looking inward and outward at the same time) as a prototype of functionalist acceleration. Yet, the impulse here is one towards, not the metaphorical inhuman, but the actual inhuman. There is a unique shock when experiencing the absence of people in capitalist spaces since "nonplaces, such as theme parks and malls," Bolter and Grusin suggest, "function as public places only during designated hours of operation." They add that "there is nothing as eerie as an airport at three o'clock in the morning, or a theme park after closing hours, when the careful grids of railings and ropes that during the day serve to shepherd thousands of visitors to ticket counters or roller coasters stand completely empty. Such spaces then seem drained of meaning."

But it may also be equally eerie to experience a nonplace like the internet, rather than uninhabited, but operating on its own. That is, cyber-Ballardian scouts are endlessly testing the water as, to borrow a phrase from philosopher Byung-Chul Han, functions of functionality. When we are not inhabiting Twitter (i.e. not logged on), @JGB_Sentences, @Crash_Cutup, and @New_Ballard are still posting and, we should add, would continue to do so *ad infinitum*.

Like the Ballardian psychopath, BallardBots are those who endlessly operate according to an endlessly diminishing logic that merges with the logic as nonspace without meaning. Bonsall's bots are, in many ways, intensified Ballardianism: self-automated processes qualifying the asemic environments of functional code, able to cope with zero to a million decimals.

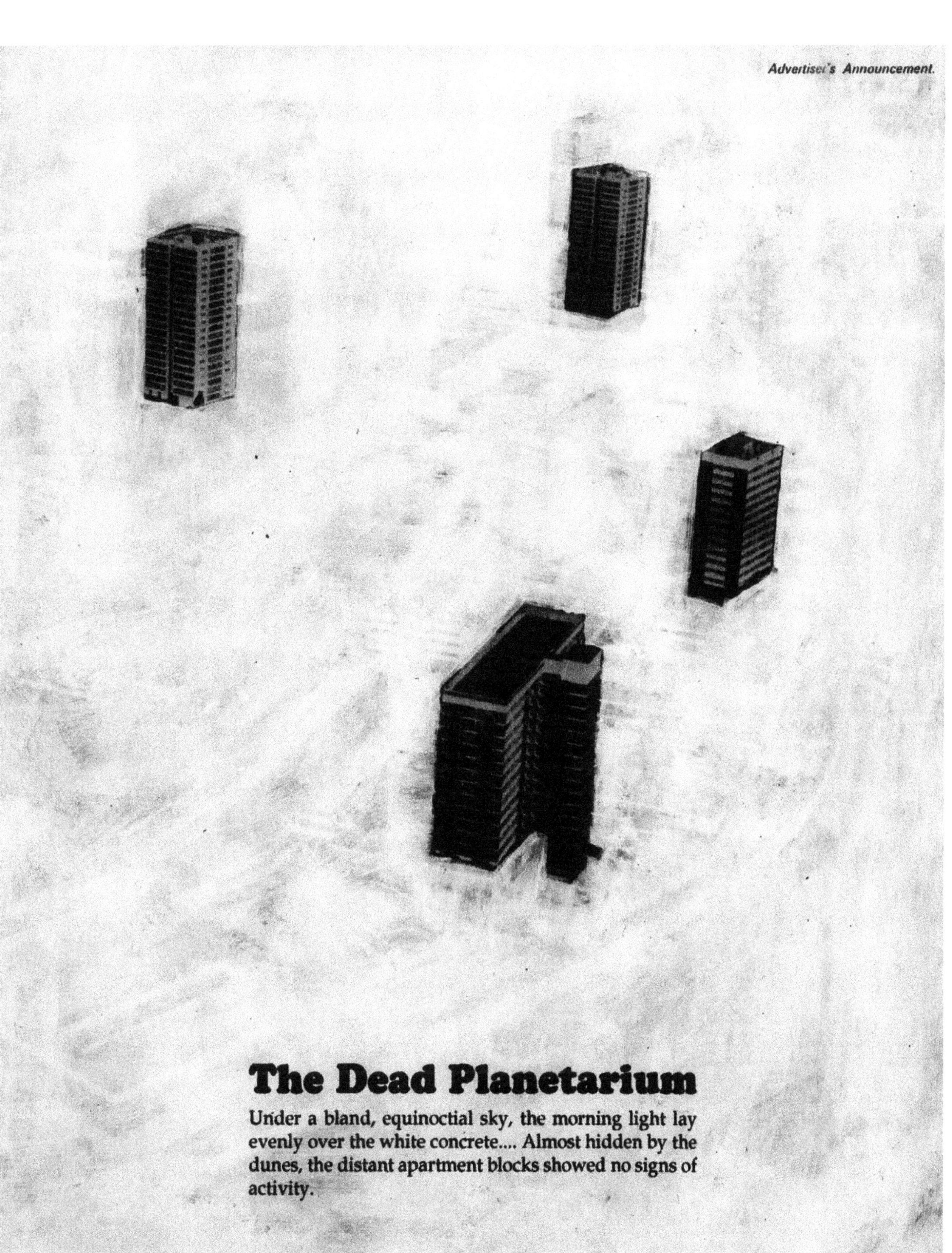
Advertiser's Announcement.
The Dead Planetarium
Under a bland, equinoctial sky, the morning light lay evenly over the white concrete.... Almost hidden by the dunes, the distant apartment blocks showed no signs of activity.

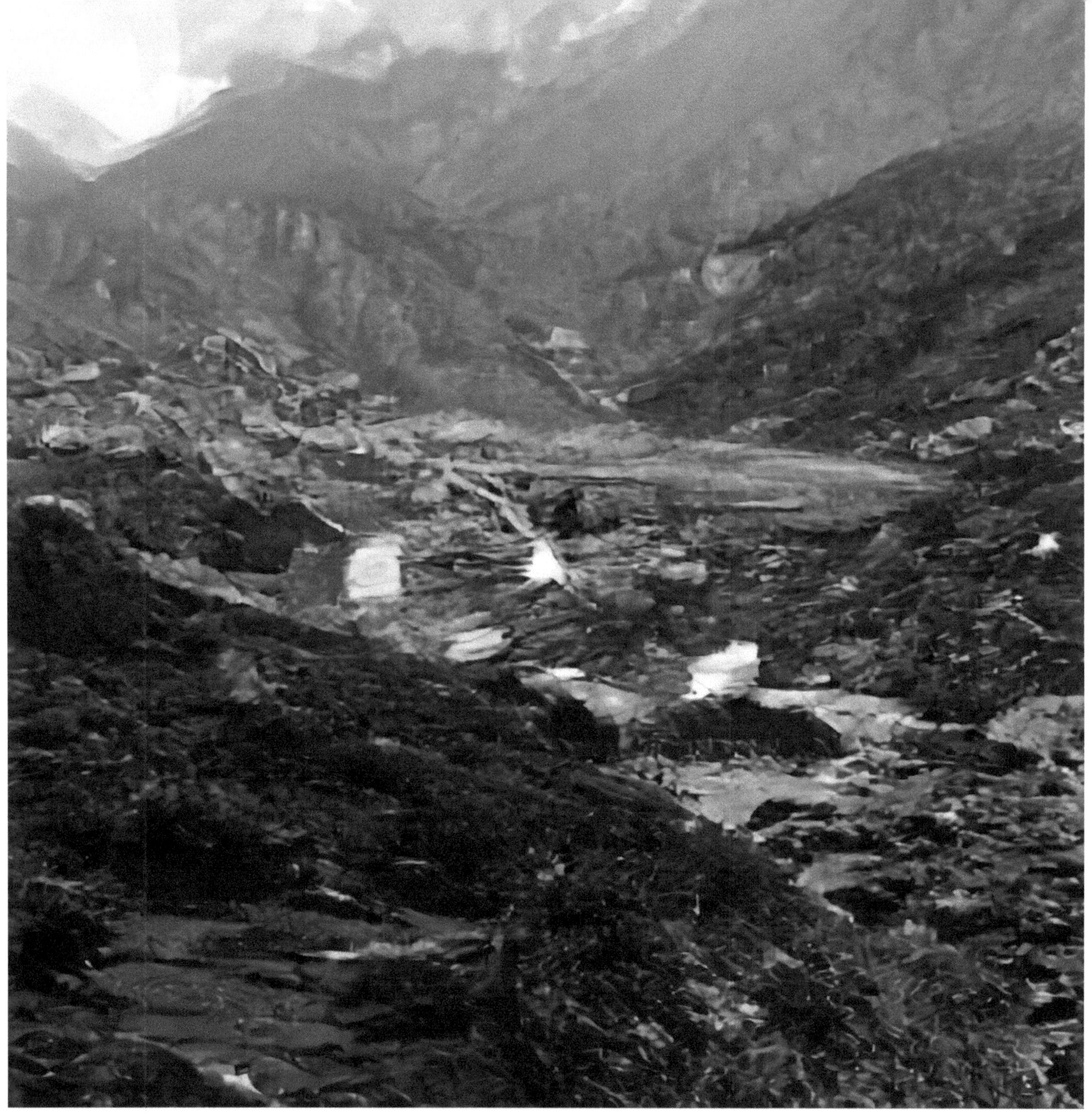

Sam Scoggins

Views Of The Uncanny Valley

Landscape photographs of landscapes that do not exist

I generated the images using a Generative Adversarial Network (GAN), a form of Artificial Intelligence. This deep neural network computer program consists of two nets, a Generator and a Discriminator, each of which have an adversarial relationship. A GAN can be taught to mimic any distribution of data. In this case landscape photographs were fed to the program and I then played with the parameters and "bred" new images over and over again until I obtained these images. Originally coined by Masahiro Mori in 1970, the term “uncanny valley” describes our strange revulsion toward things that appear nearly human. I have broadened the definition to apply to landscape in a pun on the word "valley". As we humans destroy our own natural environment, one day we may have to inhabit an artificial habitat generated for us by AI. It is towards this dystopian—but increasingly likely future—that this project looks.

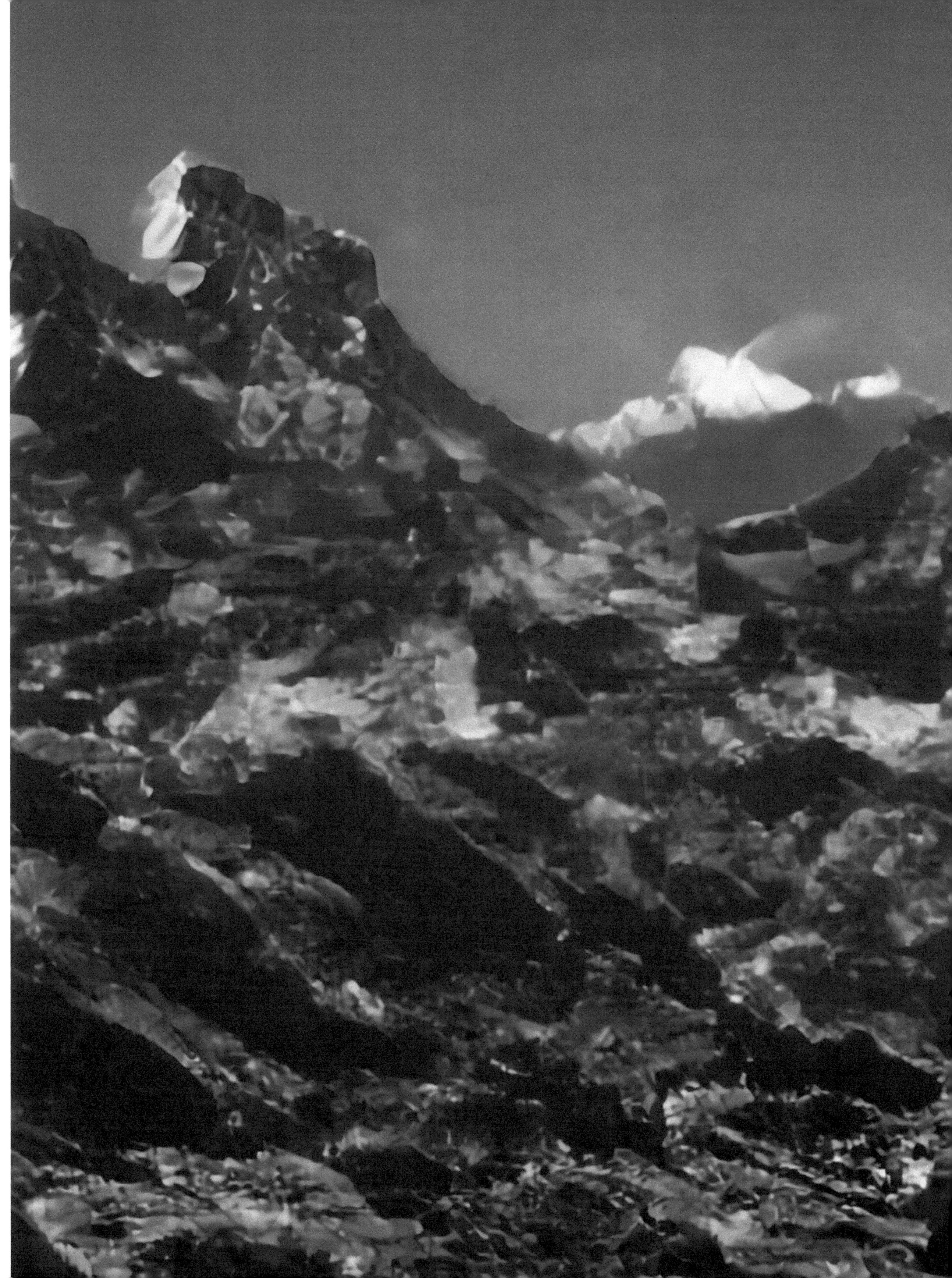

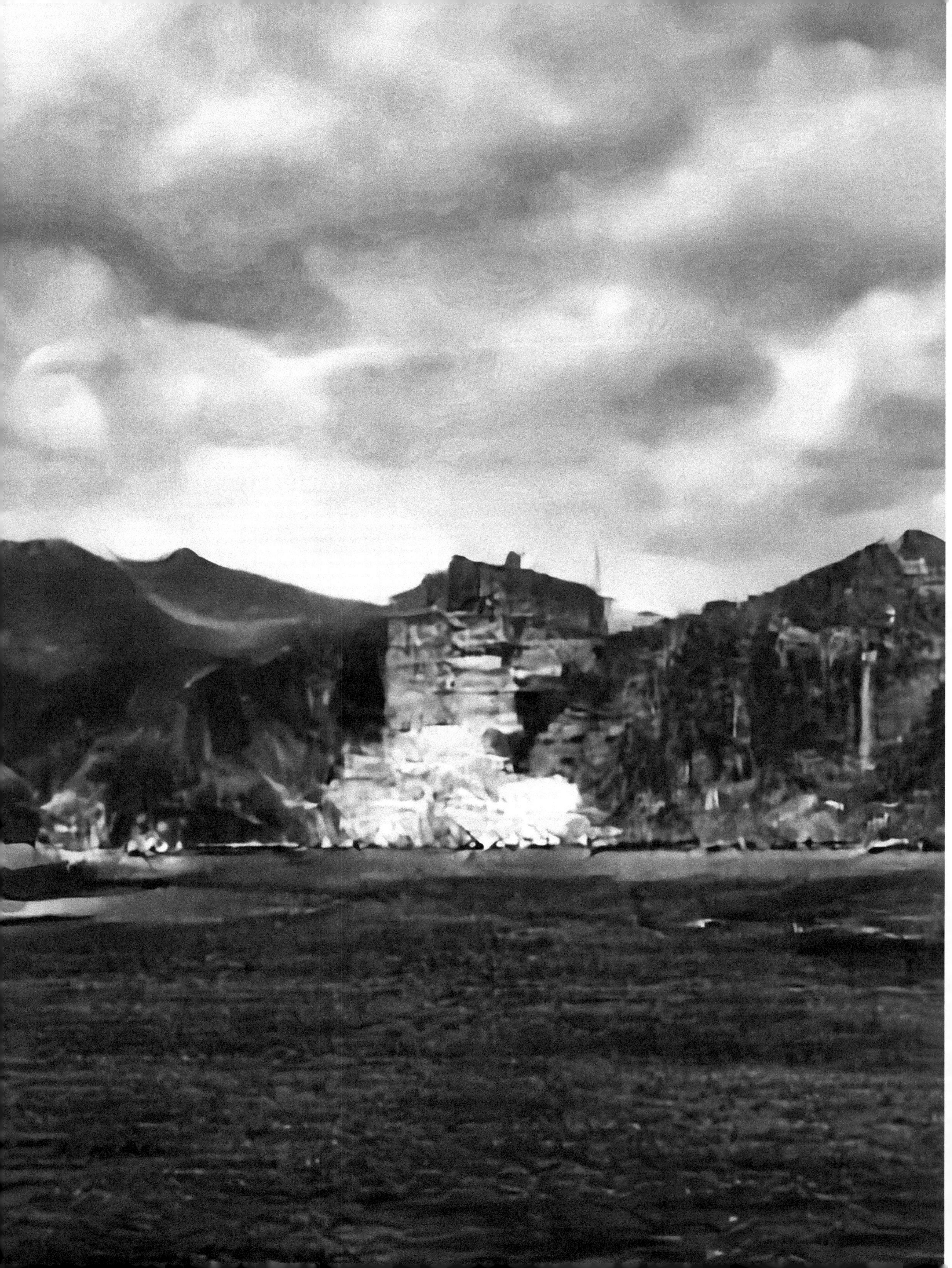

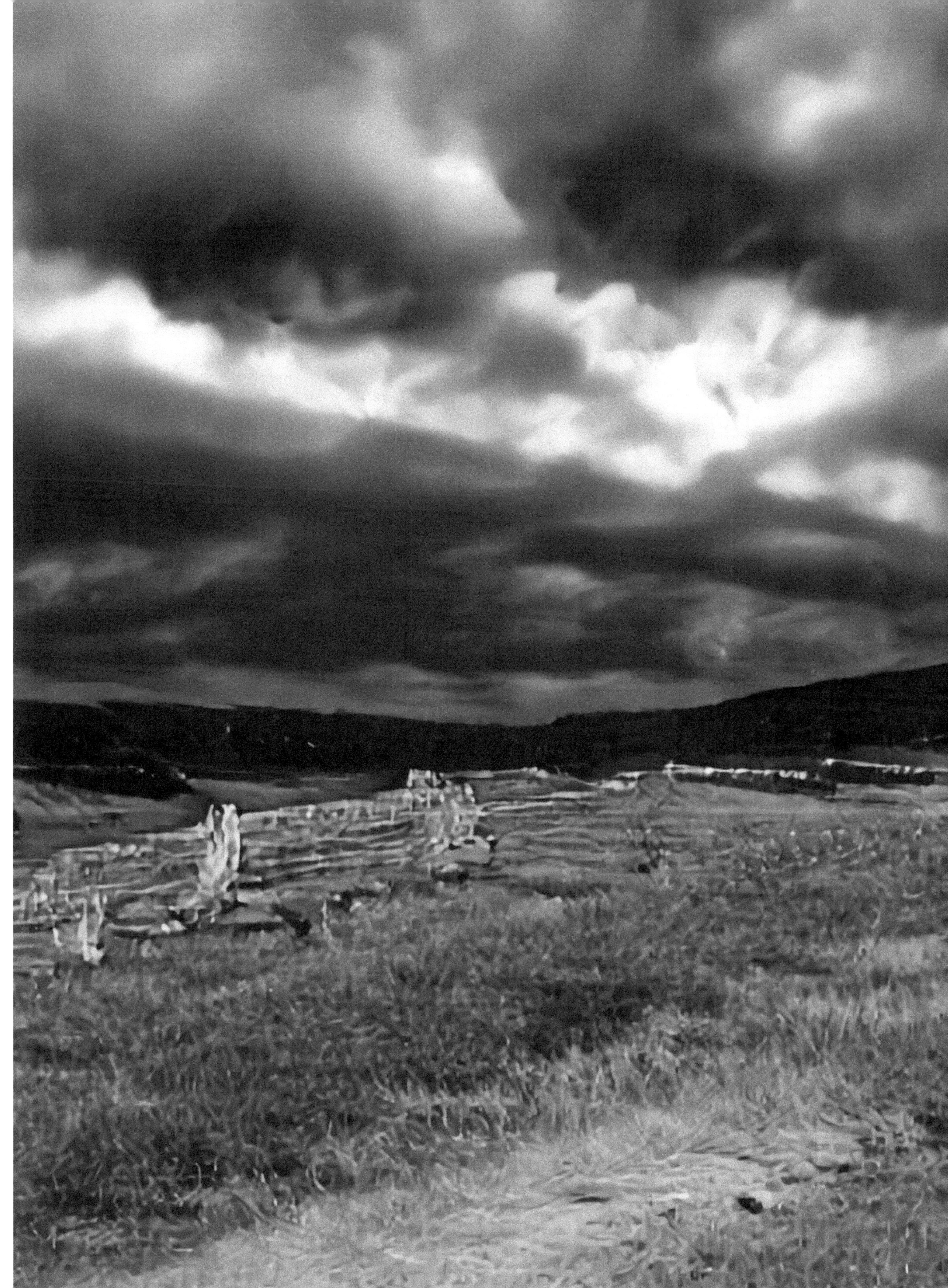

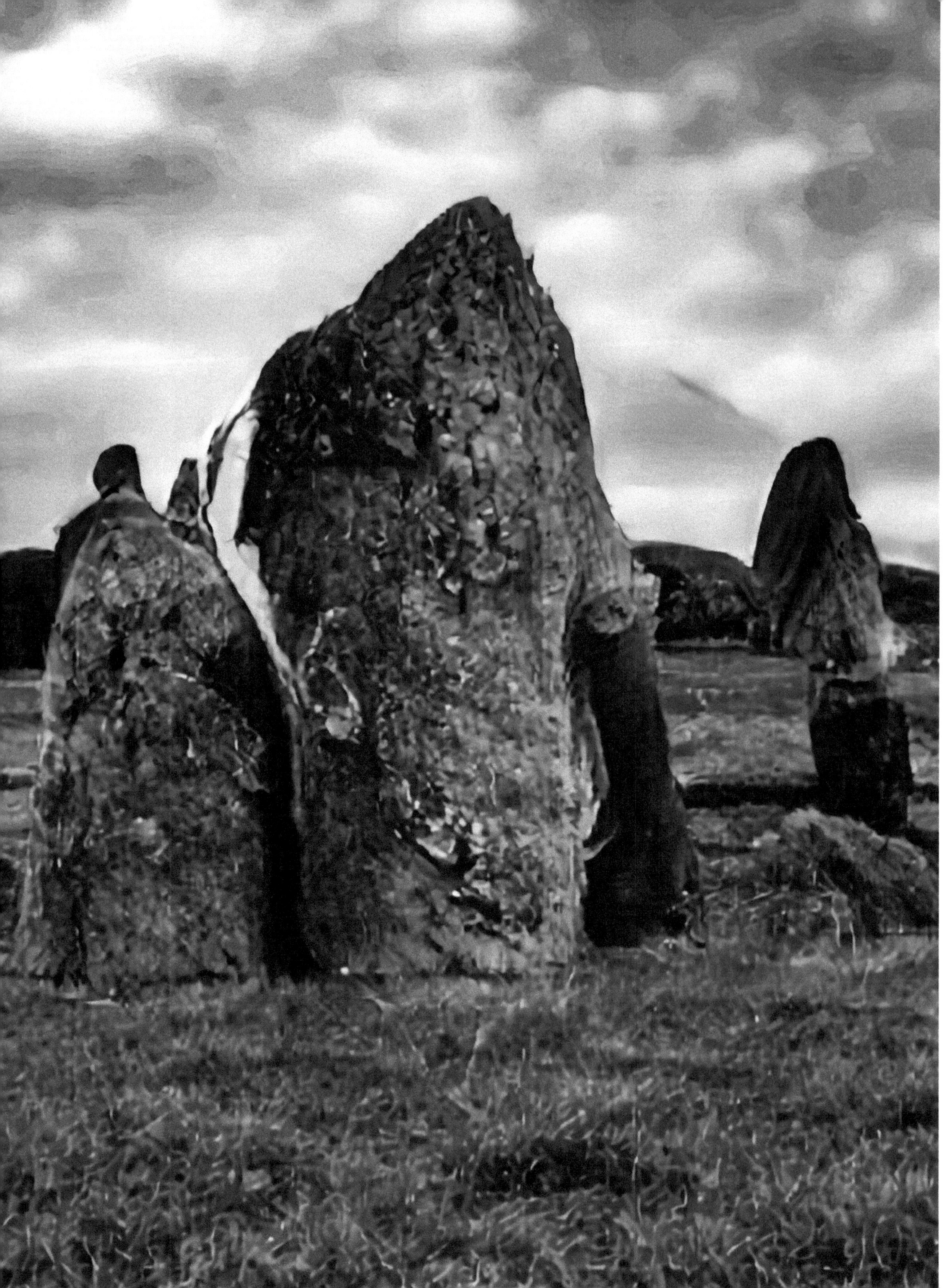

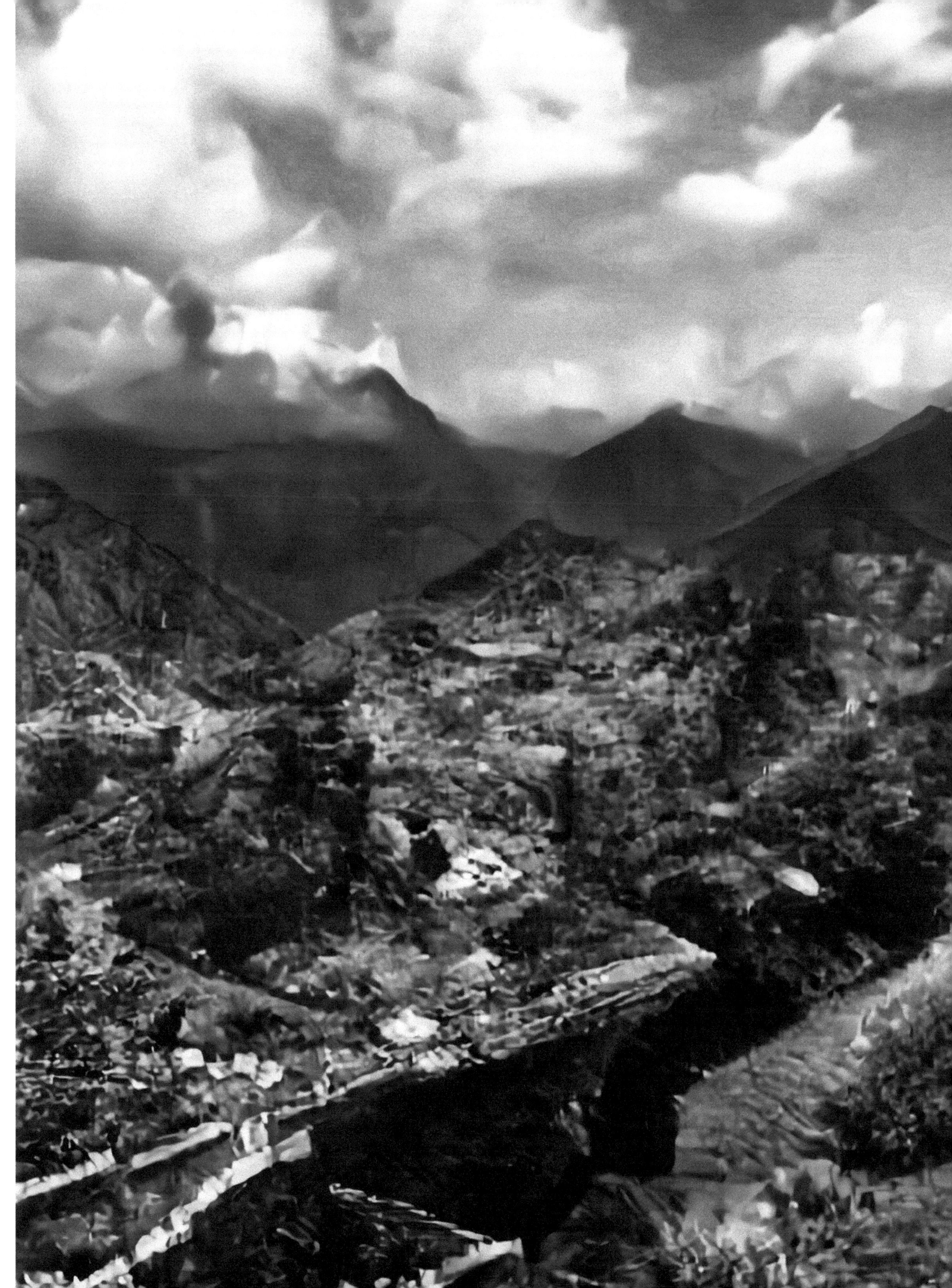

David Pringle:

An Introduction to "Dragon Moon"

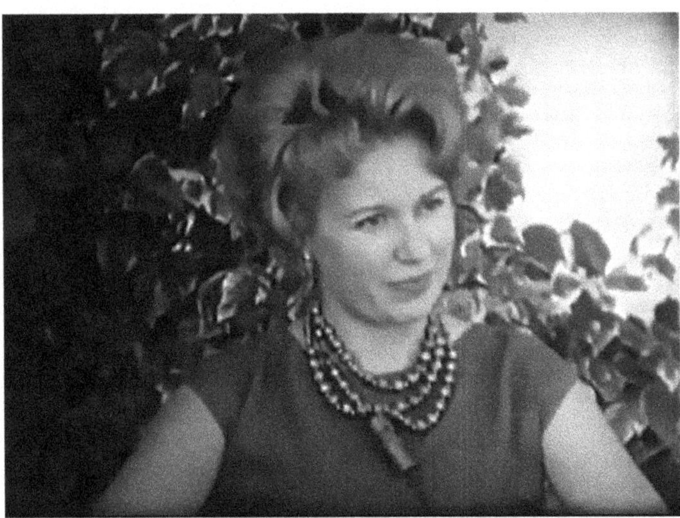

Ursula Keir Simpson

Shanghai, Summer of 1936. It may have been around this time that young James Graham Ballard learned to swim: "During school holidays we would drive every morning to the Country Club, where I spent hours in the swimming pool with my friends. I was a strong swimmer, and won a small silver spoon for coming first in a diving competition..." (Ballard, *Miracles of Life*, p19.) It is likely that his instructor was the ex-bantamweight boxer Billy Tingle (1900-1977), a popular figure as a sportsman and teacher among Western parents and schoolchildren in the Chinese city. Billy, born in Yorkshire, raised in Australia and many years in Shanghai, including a spell in Lunghua prison camp, before ending his days in Hong Kong, is mentioned in the following story, his name a passing detail which convinced me of its authenticity. (I had previously heard of Billy Tingle in an e-mail from an old inmate of Lunghua, a message which quoted Ballard mentioning the former boxer's name.)

The story, evidently set in the seaside resort of Tsingtao where the better-off Shanghailanders spent their vacations, was found among the papers of an early-childhood friend of Jamie Ballard's, the former Ursula Keir Simpson (later Ursula Ure), who died on 26th August 2007. Almost six months older than JGB, Ursula was the daughter of a Shell oil company employee in Shanghai who was originally from New Zealand. Her own daughter would explain: "My mother was born in the Country Hospital, Shanghai, on 25th May 1930. Her family lived in a mock Tudor house in Ave Joffre in the French Concession, nicknamed Gasoline Alley as the houses were owned by the Asiatic Petroleum Company/Shell for whom my grandfather Stanley Pare Simpson worked. She attended the Cathedral School and I'm not sure if it's then she met Jamie, as she knew him, or whether they already knew each other. My mother was an only child with a huge imagination and I believe was quite lonely as her parents were very tied up with work and social engagements. My mother contracted TB and therefore was off school a lot, [and she] and Jamie spent many happy hours playing together in their respective gardens, coming up with all sorts of stories and adventures. Their families also spent the summers in Tsingtao together... They used to enjoy playing with the trainee Buddhist monks who were a similar age to them... The large spiders that did battle with the servants' brooms and the land crabs that might eat you when you slept [as mentioned Ursula's story] were a huge source of fascination and horror." (Keiran Ure, e-mail to David Pringle, 11 June 2019.)

Sadly, the children's friendship did not last long, as Ursula's family moved away from Shanghai before the end of 1937—initially to New Zealand and then to Egypt, where they would live for the duration of World War II. A precocious girl, Ursula would become a contributor to *Blackwood's Magazine* in the postwar years and, while still in her early 20s, a published novelist: "*The Sun Behind Me*, based on her adolescence in Egypt, and *The Vintage*, inspired by time spent with her aunt's family in the Beaujolais which was adapted into a film by MGM with Michele Morgan, Pier Angeli and Mel Ferrer." However, despite those books and a Hollywood film, her career as a writer was fairly brief, although she did return to writing in her old age. It's not known exactly when this story, about a little girl and a little boy swimming in the sea while on a family holiday, was written, but it may have been in the late 1990s or the early 2000s. "I'm guessing my mother wrote this story ... possibly inspired by a trip back to Shanghai to visit her childhood home. I have found a handwritten draft which suggests she was planning to write an extended novella surrounding this story which would have covered 1936-37 Shanghai, featuring her illness and recovery from TB and playing with "Hamish" at his house on Saturdays." (Keiran Ure, e-mail to DP, 10 June 2019.)

Ursula did have some contact with her old friend after the war. Apparently she and JGB were in touch with each other around 1951, perhaps when he was still a student in Cambridge or perhaps when he was briefly at Queen Mary, University of London (academic year 1951-52). It would be interesting to know whether he was excited by her success as a writer in the early 1950s—but alas there's no further record of any communication between them.

An interesting aspect of Ursula's short story is the way in which it does reflect some of Ballard's characteristic imagery and themes. He had a long-time obsession with swimming and the sea and near-drownings—take, for example, his novel *Rushing to Paradise* (1994), whose teenage protagonist is a long-distance swimmer, and his little-known piece of prose poetry "Crystal of the Sea" (reprinted in *Deep Ends 2014*). In a 1991 interview, JGB was asked about the "at least half-a-dozen drowning scenes" in *The Kindness of Women*, "from the aquatic graves of Chinese soldiers in the early pages to, very near the end, the resuscitation of a child rescued from the Thames. Ballard seems truly surprised when the sequence is pointed out to him. 'If there is that strand, that strand has been part of my life.'" (Andrew Billen, "Riverside Demons," *The Observer*, 15 September 1991.) That strand in the Ballardian life does seem to be foreshadowed in Ursula Simpson's acute story.

With thanks to Keiran Ure and Fay Ballard.

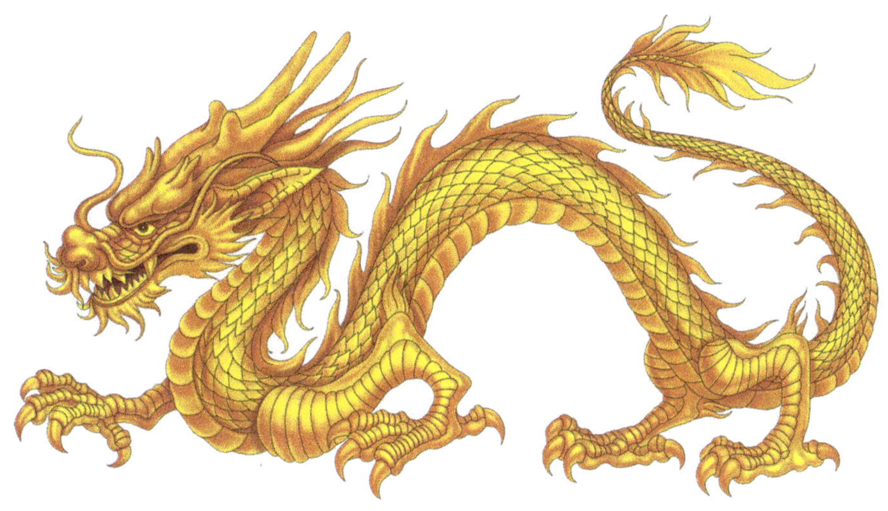

URSULA KEIR SIMPSON

DRAGON MOON

"I don't care," said Helena. They were on the beach with their shrimping nets. Her tangled blonde hair was tied back, her dress tucked into her knickers. The tide was out. It went out for miles and miles leaving the little blow-up fish stranded and the rock pools full of treasures.

"But the Chinese say the sea is full of demons. They won't go in the water; the dragon will get you if you do."

"Oh poooooh! You're just scared because you can't swim. Mummy's going to hire a boat to take us round to Shell Cove where it's deep and we can swim. You've got your water wings."

James was small and sturdy and worried. Billy Tingle had been teaching him to swim in the Shanghai Club baths and he liked Billy Tingle very much but he was still not sure about swimming in the sea.

He had been shaken to his very core when they arrived here and found the house deserted, dusty and cobwebby, and the haunt of giant spiders. The Boy and Coolie and Amah all set-to with brooms and, in his room, his very own room, while he was leaping around shrieking with excitement, a huge furry, thrashing, salivating monster had attacked the broom, charging it again and again, until clouted from behind with a shovel! He had heard of spiders that could eat birds. He didn't expect this one to eat him but the idea of that obscene, hairy body crawling over him in his sleep had kept him awake all night with a candle burning and hot wax stinging his hand when he moved it to see into the corner behind the door.

It's alright to read about adventures and safaris and all that, he thought, but it's quite another thing to be in the middle of one when you are not very big and rather easily scared. Helena was tall and bold and competent. She was a bit of a show-off but he was very fond of her. When they were alone and playing in the garden she often sang songs. They were the songs his mother sang and played on the piano in the evenings, full of drama and sadness. 'Two little feet were taught to go, stumbling, tumbling, to and fro.' He could see those little feet; small, detached, helpless little feet. He was so sorry for them. He liked the jolly one that went 'temple bells are ringing and the young green corn is springing. I lie hidden in the grass and I count the moments pass.' He had often done that. After the poor little feet came the hands. 'Pale hands I loved beside the Shalimar—I would have rather felt you round my throat, crushing out life, than waving me farewell.' He had staggered round and round the garden with his hands clutching his neck, coughing and roaring and spitting until Helena said "Oh do stop! You'd be dead by now anyway and you look so silly."

There on the sand he saw a giant jelly fish. Huge, disgusting, purplish and transparent.

"What a whopper!" he cried. "I say, Helena, do you think there are lots of these in the water? Maybe these are the dragons they're scared of."

"My Amah eats them," Helena said scornfully. "She eats seaweed too and other horrid things. Sea slugs; can you imagine eating sea slugs.?"

No he couldn't. Jelly fish, sea slugs, he was beginning to wish they hadn't come on this holiday. He cast an anxious eye at the cliffs. Uncle Bill had mentioned land crabs. He said they came out at night and scavenged on the beach and the headland. They ate dead bodies they found there. You must never go to sleep on the beach, he said, in case they come and eat you. James wished Uncle Bill had been there to see the spider.

Very carefully he picked up a Blow Up fish. It was very small and very round, totally inflated, holding its breath until the next tide came in. He put it in his pail of sea water and it at once became thin and lively. James trotted after the sea but it was really too far off, so he found a nice deep pool and released the little Blow Up fish into the sea weedy depths.

In the afternoon the children climbed up into the hills, to the pine woods. Helena said there was a Buddhist temple there. They would go one day. There was also an old German fort. His hair prickled at the idea of the old fort.

"I bet it's full of dead Germans," Helena said. "Daddy says it was dangerous and we weren't to go there but Fern and Robert say they have been there and there's nothing but an old skull. They probably made that up, a dead skeleton in a corner with its skull looking at you. I don't believe Fern ever went in the bunker."

"I'd rather see the temple," James said carefully.

That night they had the electricity on in the house, one bulb hanging from a piece of flex in each room. James had a night light beside the bed, a little candle inside a cheerily grinning pumpkin which his mother had remembered to bring from home and had now unpacked. James got Amah to take a broom into all the corners and under the bed, with the door wide open for the beasties to escape if she slushed any out, but there were no more horrid spiders, perhaps that monster had eaten all the others. His mother burned incense coils on the terrace to keep the mosquitoes and midges away. The incense smell made him think about the temple and he fell asleep imagining he was a Buddhist monk bowing and dancing before the statue of a beautiful lady, Kwan Yin, who was smiling at him ...

"Tonight is the fishermen's fête," his mother said. "Tonight they push out little boats, floats really, with lanterns and candles and offerings for the sea gods. We must go down to the beach to watch."

She was very beautiful, James thought.

She was a tall, slender woman with a mass of chestnut hair. All the other women had short hair. She had shingled hers once, he had seen photos of her with an Eton crop, but now she had let it grow and swept it up. It had a natural curl. She shoved in a few combs. She laughed and said "I am very retro!"

Helena said, "I shall do the same. No one will make me cut my hair, even if I hate it when it's all sticky with salt and I have to comb the tangles out after washing it." She thought about this for a moment and then said "I might cut it very short one summer. Enough to startle everyone. Short, short like a boy. My hair curls too like yours. It would be fun. When I'm sixteen." Her blue eyes glistened with lust.

James regarded her, surprised. "I like it just the way it is. I like it long. Helena, are we going to make a float with a lantern to send out to sea to frighten away the devils?"

"Yes, of course, silly. We'll use one of your night lights and we can buy a lantern in the village. I'll get Amah to choose one for us, she can get it cheaper. How much pocket money have you got?"

"I want to go with Amah and choose it. I want a special one," James said firmly. After all he had a special interest in placating the devils if they were going swimming in Shell Cove the next day.

It was a hot, still afternoon. The children had made their float with a lovely orange lantern on it and flowers twisted and stitched in place. They had bought a beautiful large lantern and Boy had painted a fabulous dragon on it for them. He flung back his long sleeves and grasped the brush and flourished it over the wet, black ink block, and there, before their eyes, in a few twists and whirls, was an authentic Chinese dragon, fierce and predatory with bulging eyes and warts with whiskers and a hideous grin.

"Ay-ya!" exclaimed Amah.

Boy, you are a real artist!" Helena exclaimed. "How wonderful! James, call your mother!"

"Ah a real dragon! Boy, that is very good, can you put our name in Chinese characters so that they will know it is our float?"

"Sure can do, Missie."

James's mother clapped her hands. "Wonderful!" Then she turned to the children. "Shall we go to Shell Cove today? I mean, now? We'll take a picnic and by the time we come home the festival will be starting, won't that be fun!"

"Oh cripes!" thought James. "I can't go swimming until we've made the offering! She didn't really mean it?" He shot a look at the painted dragon, it looked horribly fierce with its claws snatching at - well, it could be him!

James was worried but he said nothing. They set out with the picnic basket and three Amahs and Fern and Robert. His mother was in a very good mood. She had persuaded Fern's father to come with them. He was a good looking man, with a deep pleasant voice. He was kind and he was absolutely straight, James knew this at once. Fern's mother was having a headache. She was lying down in a darkened room at the hotel. She works much too hard, he told them. It's a pity. She would have enjoyed this jaunt. Well we'll just have to enjoy it all the more for her.

"He is a nice man," thought James. "If any dragons come near I bet he'll see them off." He inflated his water wings and thought about Billy Tingle.

Shell Cove was incredible. The entire beach was made of shells; every kind of shell: beautiful smooth, delicately coloured, sea washed shells—pale grey and delicate pink, pale melon, apricot, or peach blush pink, sugar pink—and fuchsia, beige and ivory. James was bewitched by the beauty of the shells. The perfect shell —the helix—the delicate spiral, twisting, sculpted by the sea? The meerschaum ivory without and the delicate, pudic blush within —underfoot the crumbly, softly gritty shell sand. Years later in Scotland, James opened a small attaché case with a vivid pink lining, it had a mirror in the middle, given him by Boy for his birthday, to take to school, and in there was Shell Cove. All the best and most beautiful shells he had collected that summer, long ago, before the war.

"James, I'm going in! Come and swim!" called Helena "Leave those stupid shells—you've got plenty! We'll come again!"

She took his hand. Cautiously James ventured. The beach shingled down suddenly, a dip, then a chasm! He lost his foothold but Helena held his hand. He had his water-wings, he had re-blown them on the beach, checked the tension.

"I say," cried Helena "Isn't the water grand! So deep and so cool!"

"I wish we had already sent out the little lanterns," thought James. "I wish this was after the festival."

She let go. He was on his own. The water wings bore him up. He struck out nobly. The sea was surging. There was the rattle of the shells on the beach as the waves rushed at them and sucked them and then retreated. "I'm swimming," James told himself, but he knew that was cheating. Helena was away ahead making for the boat. His mother was walking along the beach in deep discussion with Fern's father. He made it to the boat but the water wings held him back; they held him up, but they held him back. He clung to the side of the boat. They had put some lines out. What if he took off his wings? He looked round for Helena, but she was diving. Searching for bigger shells and coral. "I can't dive with these wings," he thought. "I'll take them off and I can cling on to the boat and then swim a little way and if I'm all right, then I don't need them. I can dive with Helena. I like going under water."

Very slowly he took off his water wings. He put them across the thwarts in the boat. He hung on. He called to Helena and she came splashing and happy, dropping some shells into the boat and beaming at him.

"Helena," he said. "I've put my water wings in the boat, look!"

"Great! Come on, I'll swim close to you—don't worry, you'll do fine."

James took a deep breath and flexed his legs, he let go of the boat and swam towards Helena. He could see Fern and Robert closer in to the beach, shouting and splashing. He swam. He pushed through the water, heading for the beach, one eye on Helena, then suddenly she was gone. She was diving of course. He put his head under water and tried to see where she had gone.

He saw sea weed floating in a mass. He looked for Helena but there was only seaweed. Gasping, he lifted his head out of the water and felt panic seize him for a second and he began to sink, then reacted, struck out again, looking back for the boat and then forward towards the beach and the children laughing and splashing. Helena was clinging to the boat. When she saw him look back she waved cheerily.

"What do I do? Go back to the boat or forward to the beach?"

Then she let go and swam strongly towards him and past him with a fast crawl stroke, heading for Robert and Fern. "I won't dog paddle," he thought. "I shall swim back nobly, breast stroke, trudge or crawl." Billy Tingle had taught him, but it had mostly been only a few strokes at a time, in the baths, not the sea.

He started after her. He made himself crawl and swam slowly. He changed stroke. It seemed a long way. Too far now to go back to the boat. He must go on.

At the beach Fern and Robert had come out of the water and were drying off. They sat on their towels and compared treasures. Mrs. Haldane stopped striding along the beach with Henry Taylor and turned, shading her eyes against the sun. She saw the little head, like a baby seal, advancing slowly towards the shore.

"My goodness! James is swimming!! He's out there without his water wings! Look!"

As if he could hear his mother, James stopped, swam round in a circle and then waved towards her. He was dreadfully tired. He wondered if there were any jelly fish around.

"Oh dear," his mother said to Henry Taylor. "He doesn't look too happy. Helena was supposed to stay and keep an eye on him. He isn't very strong you know. We had problems last winter ..."

Her companion was cut short. He had been in full spiel, happy to be walking along this marvellous shell cove with a charming, intelligent woman, who wanted to know all about his work among the Chinese, and suddenly she was totally withdrawn.

"James!" she shouted. "James!"

"Oh my God!" she said suddenly, and Henry saw her taking off her beach dress and plunging in her bathing suit into the sea.

"Really," he thought, bewildered, shaken, "She's quite unstable. One minute we are discussing marriage customs among the Chinese in the provinces and the next she takes off all her clothes and dives into the water!"

James saw her coming. He knew he could make it now, he took a deep breath and pushed his arms through the water. His body felt very heavy. Heavier than he had ever felt before.

"Mum!"

"It's alright James, Mummy's here—hang on to me."

He clung to her neck, slippery and cold. Her hair was wet, tangled like seaweed. She kissed him fiercely.

"Hang on love. You were really swimming well. Billy Tingle would have been proud of you, Jim."

She never called him Jim except on very special occasions. Usually when there were just the two of them. How well she swam. She was so strong, her shoulders broad, her neck long, her arms thrusting through the water, her legs scissoring. He hung on tight to her shoulders, kicking his legs a little, to help and then just letting them trail behind. He felt cold and sleepy but happy. He was safe. ∎

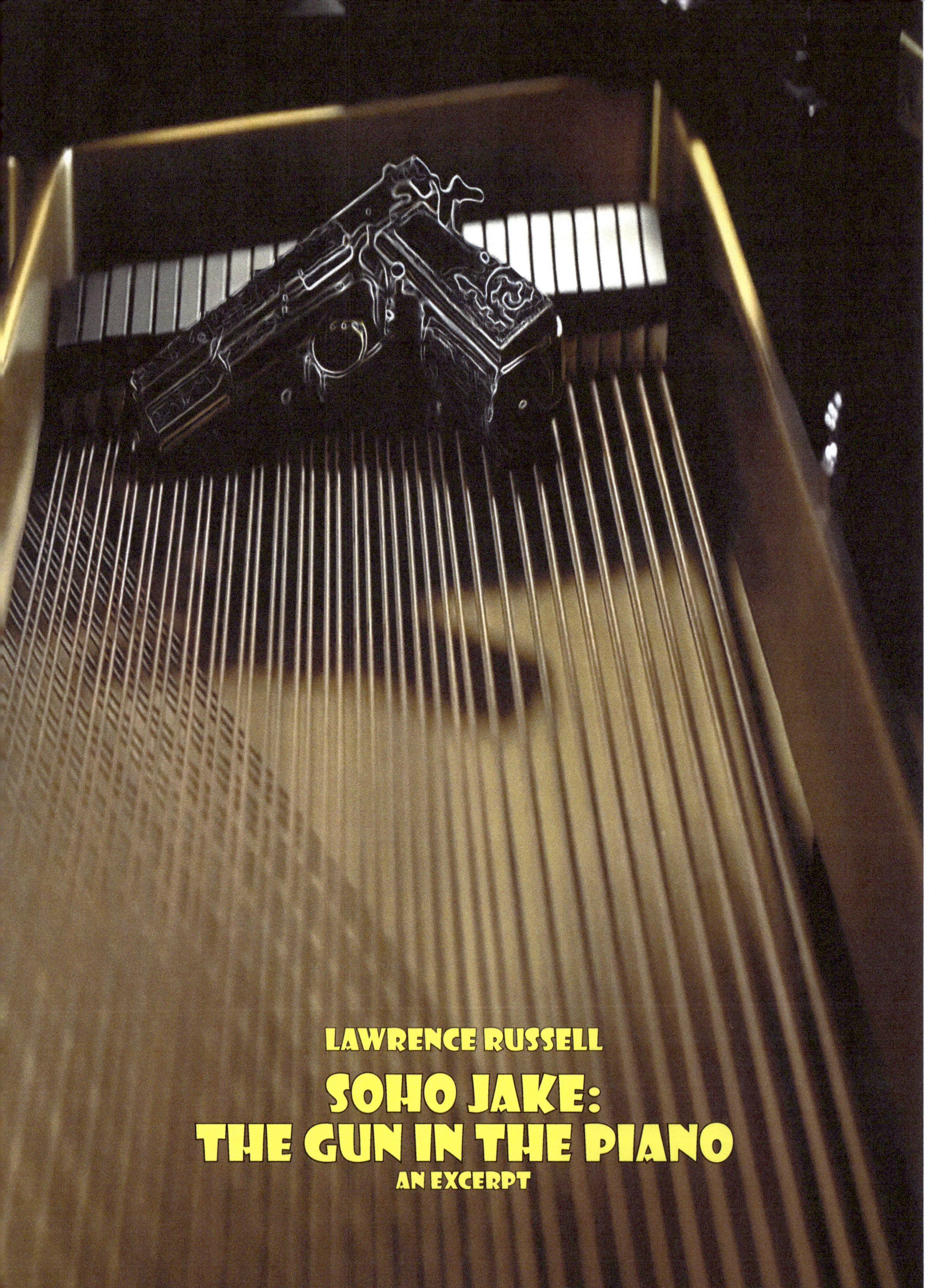
LAWRENCE RUSSELL
SOHO JAKE:
THE GUN IN THE PIANO
AN EXCERPT

1. Missing, Believed Mathematical. I knew Jimmy back in England when he was first publishing in the pulps and hanging around the galleries, about the time London was starting to swing big time and anything was possible. He was different, right from the start, had the soul of a poet and the balls of a Dadaist. They called us New Wave, for the lack of anything better. Fact is we were Punk before there was Punk. They say the Stones had a bad attitude—so where do you think they got it from? Chicago? No, mate. Pulp fiction London... and me and Jimmy were core pulp fiction London. I had a dungeon in Soho, stone's throw from Gerrard Street where all the boys and girls come to get bad. I could write a novel in three weeks, see it on the stands in six. A hack? Maybe I was, maybe I wasn't. It was a living and I loved it, then, now and maybe forever.

Jimmy was more suburban. Kids. They're grown, don't need him now, but he's still sending them postcards, telling them how great Hollywood is, one day he'll have a place in Laurel Canyon or Malibu and they can fly out here, see for themselves. Meanwhile he's sharing this weird motel suite with me, a place the owner calls The Grotto, because it looks like a cave in the jungle, or more accurately a cave on a movie set. Let's leave the owner anonymous, although you might know him, wrote for *The Twilight Zone*, this and that, made the News a few weeks ago because he had a run-in with Frank Sinatra and his goon squad out in Palm Springs, some disagreement about a pool table. Anonymous packs a .38. American. Better believe it, voted for Reagan.

But hell, he's a great guy, very generous, knows the scene, helped Jimmy get a contract because Jimmy didn't know shit about Hollywood and his agent had no pull here whatsoever. Me, I was just hanging on, draft 7 or 8 of a medieval romance with a science fiction back story which starts in England and ends up on Mars, writing for the pleasure of this one-hit wonder director who simply has no fucking clue as to what he wants and maybe is just using me to pass the time. So I couldn't help Jimmy when it came to writing for Hollywood. I could help him learn how to shoot tequila with a New World lager but Hollywood, no sir. Hollywood's like a woman who sits on your face, then expects you kiss her dog afterwards. Exciting, cheap and cruel.

I've been here six months and have learned the hard way. Jimmy's been here a couple of months, loving it, all new, the light, the smell of wild honeysuckle and autolead, corner-store discount booze, the buzz of an IBM typewriter. Been in great spirits, has forgotten the fiasco of his last novel, the lawsuit back in perfidious Albion, shitty fish and chips and driving on the wrong bloody side of the road. Well, maybe he's been off the rails a bit the past week. Something happened at that pool party on the hill above Mulholland. Some of Hockney's friends, artists, rockers, dealers, trannies, agents, writers, UFOs, bondo kinkies, bullshitters, you name it. All there, present and incorrect. Typical Hollywood flame-out stuff. Something happened and Jim ended up plain fucking weird. And now he's disappeared.

2. Stunts. It's one of those Art Deco towers in Long Beach, near the old East Village. The muscle guy with the scowl has an office on the 10th.

He says, "Who sent you, man?"

Me, I say, "Peter... Peter Trant."

I'm a bit hoarse, but he gets it, nods. Pete's name is the ticket. He relaxes.

"You a musician?"

"I'm a writer."

"Movies?"

"Yeah, I'm working on a script for Consolidated. Otherwise I'm a novelist. Paperbacks mostly."

He actually smiles. Well, the shadow leaves his face. Good looking face, I suppose. Could be thirty, could be forty, could be somewhere in between. Looks like a Beat, hair brushed forward, short on the sides, no gray, just what used to be blond. A naive first take would say Ivy League, although a smart guy would say ex-military.

"Best kind," he says. "If a guy can't put it close to his ass, what good is it? So, what sorta thing, westerns or what?"

"Speculative," I say.

I'm leary of the old labels. They just don't fit anymore.

"Speculative—what's that? Science fiction?"

"Yes, I write anything you could call 'speculative.'"

He's still assessing me, wondering what the fuck.

"So you know Pete, huh. Part of the Brit mafia, is it?"

"If you like, sir. Did he phone, let you know I was coming?"

He nods yeah.

I tell him, "Peter and I go way back. Knew him in London... before he was ever managing bands, right? He was a bouncer, and a wrestler. He went by the name Count Milano when he was in the ring."

He's amused.

"No shit. So why does Count Milano send, er... a spec writer to see me? No disrespect but you could pass for Italian yourself."

"Well I go kind of dark when I'm hungover."

"Need a drink? Alls I have is Jack Daniels."

"Jack would be nice, thanks."

Bottle's in a desk drawer, good to see, more or less full, good to see. Carton of plastic cups too. He grimaces apologetically, pours a couple.

"Most of my business is with rock and rollers," he says. "Fine glassware is just wasted on them."

I try to chuckle, cough instead. He lights a cigarette, then as an afterthought, offers me one. Lucky's. My hand's shaking as I reach for it.

"Trying to quit," I say.

"Me too," he says. "Last time I was still government property. Didn't last."

"Never does," I murmur.

He just looks at me, enjoying his fag, sipping his Jackie, waiting for me to state my business. I pull the envelope from my pocket, slide it over the desk. It's a bit mangled. He flips the flap, shakes the photo out.

He nods: "Nice lookin' dame. Your wife?"

"No sir. Read the back."

He rotates the photo, studies the writing.

He reads: "'Why I Want To Fuck Ronald Reagan...'"

He looks my way, expecting me to say something. I wait for him.

"Well that's in yer face, isn't it?" he says.

He's right about that. Some people think it's funny, although most don't.

I say, "Er, that's the title of a piece by my friend. Quite notorious."

"It got published?"

"Printed... then shredded. It was just one piece in a book of short pieces. The book got pulled by the publisher, although there are copies in circulation, and that particular piece—why I wanna fuck Ronnie—was published elsewhere. Lit mag in England. Caused a bit of a furore. Court case too.

He reads more: "'Dig your work, JGB. If you wanna meet...' Who is JGB?"

"My pal Jimmy. He's a science fiction writer. He's been staying with me."

"Writing for Consolidated Pictures too?"

"No, he's been working on a script for Joey Jerusalem."

"I know JJ. Used to play tennis with him occasionally. So what's the problem?"

"Well Jim has disappeared. Three days. I'm worried."

"What, you think he went to check out the lady?"

"Maybe. Wouldn't you?"

"You know her?"

"That's just it, I don't, otherwise I would've got in touch with her. She's a complete stranger to me."

"So maybe they like each other. You know groupies these days—come for a day, stay for a week."

"No, Jimmy was due to fly back to London yesterday."

"Maybe he did. You check?"

"I did. His ticket is still on his desk."

"Carrier?"

"British Airways. Yes, before you ask, I did phone the desk at LAX. He wasn't on the plane."

"A babe like this could give a man amnesia."

"Well that's just it. Jimmy's been drinking a lot. He was on the wagon for a couple of weeks but it wasn't going well, he was ready to explode."

"It happens."

"Some idiot gave him amyl nitrate. It didn't go well."

"Bad trip?"

"He thought it was cocaine, which he has no experience with but wanted to try. He was drunk and it really screwed him up, thought he was experiencing a heart attack."

"Huh. So you think the photo is just a ruse."

"I do."

"Ah. So the obvious question, *amigo*, why aren't you going to the police with this?"

"I've been here long enough to know a missing person doesn't rate high on the list with the LAPD. I talked it over with Peter and he agrees. Cops are stretched with these fires and everything. Street crime's up, isn't it?"

"Probably. We call it the Santa Ana Flush. People sweat, get crazy... robberies, murders go up, domestic shit. So, how old is your friend Jim?"

"Well, he's got eight years on me. Let's see, forty-eight, forty-nine, I think."

"Forty something, so still sexually active."

"Yeah. Now and then."

"This title... when your friend says 'Why I Want to Fuck Ronald Reagan', he mean that literally? Or does he mean just mess with the man."

"Well, ah, the pejorative is ambiguous of course. You can take it literally... and many people have."

"Your friend homosexual?"

"No, he is not."

"Bi-sexual? I ask, because in my experience providing security in the rock and roll scene, I've seen a lot of queer business. Amyl nitrate is a gay thrill pill."

Me, *sotto*, "And here I thought it was for angina."

Him, "So you're sure he ain't prowling the park in his other life—"

"No, no... Jimmy's a straight forward male chauvinist pig. He wouldn't want me putting it like that, but y'know, the man is straight."

"Were there any threats?"

"I don't know. He could be a bit paranoid. I think L.A. unsettled him. His idea of America was very fictional, a personal fantasy really. The reality might've been too much, I don't know... shit, it's all... you know."

The way he's looking at me, I suspect he thinks I'm babbling. I sigh, say, "Actually I thought he was loving it."

He has a short lanyard with a dangling bullet around his neck. He's fonding the bullet with one hand while the other is tapping a black pencil on the desk. California casual, I guess.

He says, "Did Reagan's lawyers ever get in touch with him?"

"Far as I know, no."

"He's in town."

"So I hear. Running for President."

"Maybe the Secret Service detained your mouthy friend. They do that, clean the streets, restrain the crazies, known threats, pre-emptive stuff. I'll put out a call."

Mouthy? Jim could be loquacious at times, although I wouldn't call him mouthy. Maybe this bloke is a Reagan supporter.

I say, "That'd be cool."

"I know a couple of agents... days in Nam."

I think: You were in Nam? I say: "Kill anyone?"

"That's what I was there for, man."

I stammer, "Sorry—I don't know why I said that, I really don't."

He flips his pencil, lets it crash land on the desk.

"Don't sweat it, man," he says. "It just slipped out, right?"

"Right."

"It's the old love and peace syndrome. California is full of it."

"It's fading, though."

"That your sense of it? How about London?"

"It's gone. It's Punk now."

"That's what I hear. Look, let me put out a couple of calls, show this photo around. Maybe some dude knows her."

I nod gratefully. Of course I'm thinking how am I gonna pay for this.

As if he's reading my mind, he says, "A favor for Pete, uh, Count Milano. If we need to go deeper, then we can discuss money."

I kick my cup back, hoping for some dregs but there aren't any. Fag's burned down to my knuckles too.

"I think I was followed here."

"Yeah? How'd you travel?"

"I drove... all the way from Hollywood. This guy was behind me all the way. Looked like one of those unmarked sedans the cops use."

"A Ford?"

"Dunno. American for sure."

"That's a long way. You sure it was the same auto, start to finish?"

"I think so."

"Freeway?"

"Yes. The 710 mostly."

"Where'd you park?"

"Around the block. He drove past, kept going."

"One guy, two guys, what?"

"Dunno. Quite possibly I'm imagining things."

He's on the phone. He seems to have no problem getting through to the FBI or the Secret Service or whomever it is he's talking to. His name seems to mean something. Erik Rhymer. Peter Trant said to me, he said, I know just the guy who can help you, mate. Rik Rhymer. He handles security for my artists when we're out west. Pete manages Graf Zeppelin and right now he and the guitarist Luke Cage are in Los Angeles mixing some tapes at some studio on Sunset, Dragonfly 44, I think. Well, Cage is doing the mixing. Pete is doing the taverns. Says it's the first holiday he's had since he gave up wrestling. I like Pete. Now and then we talk about him being my agent but of course he knows sweet fuck all about the lit business. Money in brown paper bags doesn't work in that scene. I think.

Rhymer hangs up the phone, says, "I just talked with my guy. He's says your friend Jimbo ain't on the list."

"Reagan has a list?"

"His people have a list. The SS have a list. He's not on it."

"Right you are. Well, I expect there's quite a long list of people who want to fuck Reagan."

"Sure. He gets death threats every day."

"He's controversial."

"Well the kids don't like him. They got no love for him up in Berkeley."

"He wasn't much of an actor."

"You think not? Yeah, I suppose he was a bit of a lightweight. He did ok with the union."

"President of the Screen Actors' Guild, right? Was he good at that?"

"He was. An easy step to being Governor."

"You got actors for clients?"

"Now and then. I stick mostly with the rockers. They get more grief, always need protection. Listen, I want more details."

"Shoot."

His head swivels as a helicopter flies past the window. Dangerously close, loud enough to vibrate all the shit on his desk.

"Goddamn," he says, "I wish they wouldn't do that."

"Police?" I say.

"SFS—Special Flight Section, undercover support. What the fuck are they doing in Long Beach? Oh, Reagan, of course."

The chopper fades. Bell Jet Ranger. Besides the pilot, there was a guy with a sub-machine gun. He took a good look at us.

Rhymer re-orders his desk, his stuff. The Jack Daniels bottle damn near hit the floor.

"Describe your pal. How tall?"

"Well he's shorter than me."

"You're a big man. Six three, right?"

"Spot on. Jim's big too, about six."

"Build? Got a gut?"

"He hides it."

"Any idea what he was wearing?"

"Casual. He has an old white linen jacket he likes. No tie. No socks, maybe sandals."

"Huh. Could be a cab driver. The face—you got a photo?"

I pull out one of Jim's paperbacks, pass it along.

"'The Voices of Time,'" Rhymer says. "Jeeze, heavy shit. He write for *Star Trek*?"

"Not yet. There's a face shot on the back...."

He studies it.

"Big forehead. He got any hair?"

"Not much."

"Well he ain't rock and roll, that's for sure. Cleft chin?"

"Yeah, he thinks he's Kirk Douglas."

"Hmm. Can I hold onto this?"

"Sure. Read it if you have time. It's brilliant."

As I stand up, a woman walks in, a red-light looker in tight blue jeans and a snug black blouse tied just above the belly button. Body by Fisher as they say around here. Clipped boots, cowgirl western, I guess. No makeup... well maybe a trace of lipstick, Nordic ice, burn me baby. Boobs, but not insulting. Blonde, almost. Ray Ban shades. Moves like a gymnast, hinged, light and confident. Hippy? Nah. Premier League groupie? I sincerely hope not.

Jesus, haven't seen a woman like this in months, years. L.A. is full of babes but this one is special. The morning glaze slips from my eyes and my hand caresses my stubbled, neglected face as I attempt to smile my special British smile.

She almost smiles back but she's here to see Rhymer and she's looking at him.

"They don't need me today, Rik," she says. "So unless you have something, think I'll go home, ok?"

"What's up? Jayne have a hissy fit again?"

"No, the big camera jammed, so they called it a day."

She notices the photo on the desk.

"What's this?"

"Know her?"

She nods, "Yes I do. Monica Falcón."

Rhymer looks me, says, "See? Progress."

"Minor League bitch. A few walk in parts... slashers... sci fi... maybe some adult."

I say, "Should be easy to find, then."

She turns, gives me an amused look. "Who'd want to?"

Rhymer says, "Annie, this gentleman believes his friend was abducted by this, um, minor league bitch."

She echoes, "A friend abducted?"

"Yeah," says Rhymer. "He's a writer... and he's a writer."

Her blue gaze is pure mockery.

"Yes," I say defensively. "We're just a couple of fools from England who don't know our way around town."

"Get a dog," she says. "Jeez."

"Be nice, Annie," says Rhymer. "Why don't you go see if you can find Miss Falcón? As a favor for me, ok?"

She gives her head a toss, like a nice filly looking for a lump of sugar.

I say, "I'm very worried. Jim's a good pal and I think he's been set up."

She's looking into my eyes, looking through them, looking deep, looking for something we shared in a former life. The tingle is going down the cheeks of my arse towards my balls. This isn't fair—a crime is being committed.

She doesn't smirk, yet she gloats, I know it, feel it.

She turns to Rhymer, who's now standing by the tall coffin window. "This is serious?"

"Maybe," he says, distracted, looking down at the street. "See? There goes Reagan."

We're all at the window now. It's a procession of three, maybe four black sedans with cops on Harleys, front and back.

"So it is," she says. "Where is Oswald now that we need him?"

"Don't be corny, doll—Ronnie did a lot for the business."

She's full of quiet scorn. "So you say, boss. I wouldn't risk my life for him."

Rhymer laughs, says to me, "Annie's a stuntwoman."

"Oh," I say, "really? Stunts?"

"That's right," she says. "Somebody has to do them."

"And body double," says Rhymer. He winks: "We can't say who for, of course. Trade secret and all that."

I'm thinking, no one could be the double of you, darlin'. I'm close enough to get her smell. Ah little man, why did you come west? You should've stayed in the ghost towns of old London where the ladies smell of Babycham and Castrol 30 weight motor oil. The ones I knew, anyway, when I had a Norton 500.

Reagan's motorcade has passed, shrinking to a narrow shadow on the vanishing point that leads to the Long Beach Convention Centre.

3. Apache. I won't be coming in today I said over the phone to the Director whose name I won't mention. The air quality is very bad this morning, this smoke is killing me so I'm going to stay put. Sure compadre he said you stay put and I'll stay put. If you were an Angeleno instead of a limey Anglo you'd know L.A. goes on fire every year, no big deal, suck it up baby. The particulates set off my allergy, I said, which was another lie, but what the hell, the script was finished as per the contract and all we were doing now was splitting hairs, so what the hell. He had no intention of filming this script, was just using me to pass the time until the studio came up with another project. I was past caring. I'd been paid and I knew damn well he was drawing expenses on the handsome per diem the studio gave out to hit directors like him. What was his line? 'Shit has its own integrity.' Probably wasn't his, although he was sure to say it a couple times whenever we had a conference. Thanks a lot, mate. Although I write fantasy, I am a realist, and even a realist in Hollywood surrenders to hope occasionally.

The script wasn't bad, even if it wasn't quite what this genius had in mind, and I knew for a fact he hadn't a fucking clue what he actually had in mind as his mind was always somewhere else, Kurosawa one day, Val Lewton the next. He could never see the untrodden path. He was an illiterate who spent a lot of time in the dark with a martini in one hand and a replica PPK automatic in the other which he'd point at the screen, exclaim, I want a scene like that. But I digress: my mind always goes stream-of-hate when I start thinking of all the pointless rewrites that came from the barrel of his bloody stage gun.

So he doesn't give a shit if I show up or not, as he often skips out himself, some excuse or other, buy a new car or check out some babe who wants to be in one of his movies. Before we hang up he says, put a clothes peg on your nose and a plug in your ass and you're good to go. It's not an insult—it's a joke, he thinks. I actually laugh. Ha ha ha.

Hear the horn outside, a couple of toots, look through the window, see my ride has arrived. Two tone white stretch limo, Lincoln Continental with a Landau roof. Yeah baby, 24 linear feet of private plutocracy. Grab my wallet and jacket, head down to the sidewalk. The sky is a bruised dirty yellow to east, and the air has an itchy, muggy feeling. There's that guy who uses a bicycle chain for a belt, looks like an Apache hanging around outside the fort, in this instance The Grotto motel, thirty five bucks a day without a TV, forty with. I have no TV... this week. Apache is selling paper workshop masks, the sort you can buy at a hardware store for a buck. Today he's asking three. Newspaper in the coffee shop this morning says the air in Santa Monica is in the "unhealthy" range of 151-200 on the US EPA's Air Quality Index, which means that prolonged exposure can harm even healthy people. Do I qualify as healthy? Well I've smoked for years, keep quitting, keep relapsing, so I'm probably fucked anyway... although, hmm, quite possibly I've developed an immunity.

As Apache hastens my direction, I wave him off.

"Don't be a friggin cheapskate,' he says. "Want some dope?"

"No thanks," I say. "Not today, brother."

"Two bucks, man, com'on!"

I keep moving.

"Blow yer little mind..."

"No thanks."

"You gonna die," he sings. "Cheapskate."

Die? Hold my breath instinctively as I head towards the limo. The air is bad this morning, no question.

Apache's shouting after me, "Your friend was no cheapskate!"

I stop, then go back.

"Jim bought a mask from you?" I say. "When?"

"Monday, maybe it was Monday."

"How do you know it was my friend?"

"He talks funny... like you."

"Ah well, I'm in Pictures. He say anything? Like where he was going?"

Apache has the hustler's knowing look, that maliferous expression when he knows he's got his mark. His greasy hair is hanging in curtains, concealing part of his pocked bad-luck face. "You gonna buy big, Mr. Picture Man? Your friend bought big."

Big? Bought big? What the hell does he mean, 'bought big'? Suddenly I feel like throwing my weight around, wanna grab this weasel by the throat. I'm big enough, pissed enough.

The limo honks its damn horn. Burns my nerves like a bad light switch.

"Dope?" I say. "He buy dope?"

"No, *manolo*, he buy a gun, dig?"

I pull a tenner from my wallet.

"What sort of gun, *amigo*?"

He shrugs. "I dunno. An automatic, street legal, man. No numbers."

His bony jungle hand darts for the bill, but I pull it back it smartly. "He say what he wanted it for?"

"Yeah, he said he was going someplace, needed security. You want a weapon, man? Hunret bucks, full clip."

"No thanks."

"Eighty, this time tomorrow."

I shake my head. "My friend didn't say where he was going?"

"No, cheapskate."

I let him have the tenner, take one of the masks, put it in my pocket.

I say, "If you remember something more, let me know, ok?"

He's already walking away. Well, I'm doing the same.

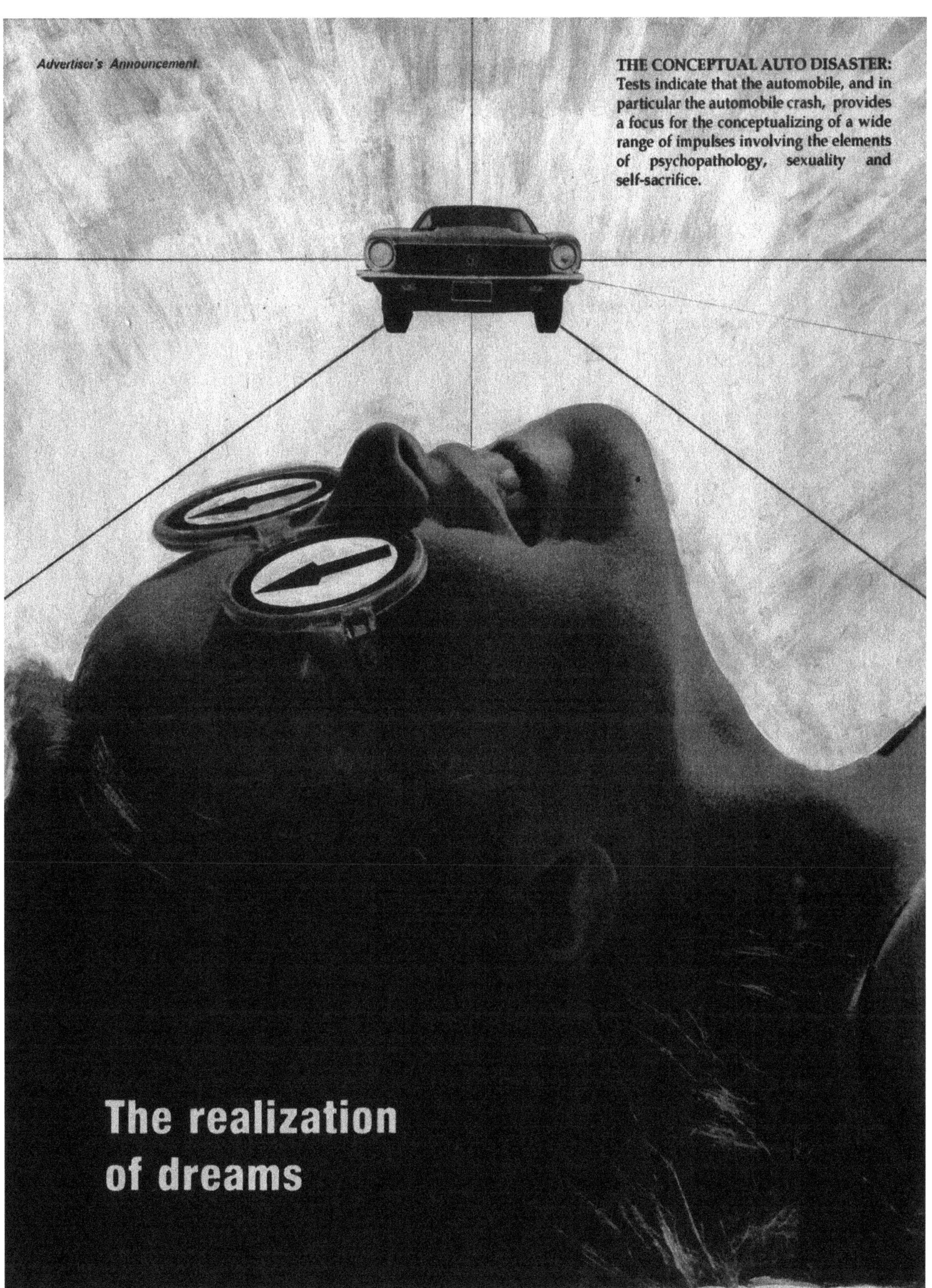
Advertiser's Announcement.
THE CONCEPTUAL AUTO DISASTER:
Tests indicate that the automobile, and in particular the automobile crash, provides a focus for the conceptualizing of a wide range of impulses involving the elements of psychopathology, sexuality and self-sacrifice.
The realization of dreams

MIKE HOLLIDAY

DISASTER IN SPACE: J.G. BALLARD'S 'JOURNEY ACROSS A CRATER'

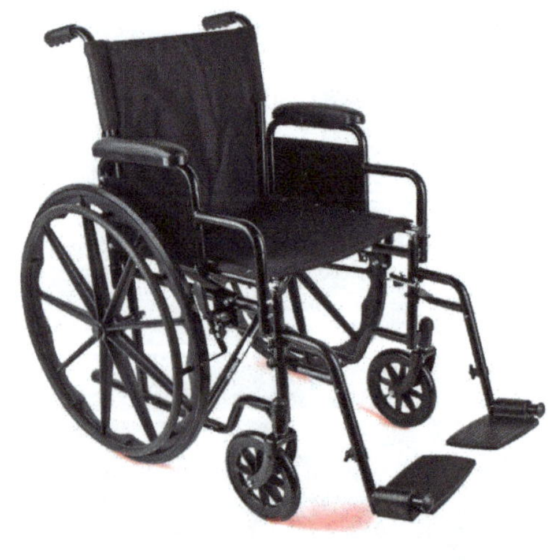

(I) A story disliked

The special edition of J.G. Ballard's novel *Crash*, published in April 2017 by Fourth Estate, contains a wealth of additional material, including the contemporaneous short story 'Journey Across a Crater'. The new edition was the first occasion that this particular piece had been included in one of Ballard's books—indeed, it was deliberately omitted from both *The Complete Short Stories* and the expanded edition of *The Atrocity Exhibition*. Ballard, it seems, had subsequently taken a dislike to the story, telling those who asked him that he did not believe that it worked.

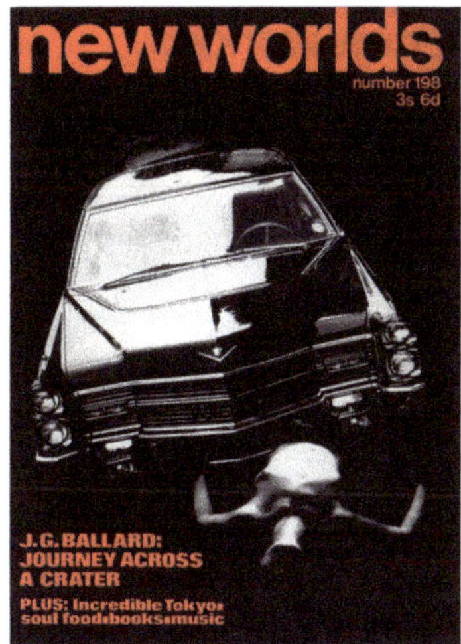

'Journey Across a Crater' originally appeared in the February 1970 issue of *New Worlds*, and was reprinted the following year in the first issue of *New Worlds Quarterly* before disappearing from sight. At the time of its original publication, Ballard was busy working on the first draft of *Crash*, which he had started writing a couple of months earlier. This was confirmed in the *New Worlds* editorial for its February issue, which also informed readers that the new novel would be conventional in form—unlike the 'condensed novels' that comprised *The Atrocity Exhibition*. However, 'Journey Across a Crater' was written as a condensed novel and bears strong similarities to Ballard's earlier stories in that format.

(II) Stitched together

One possible reason for the author's dissatisfaction with 'Journey Across a Crater' is that it does give the impression of being two different stories that have been rather inelegantly stitched together. The first half introduces the unnamed protagonist who is, or believes he is, an astronaut who has had some form of mishap in space and is now having difficulties in comprehending the world around him. Then midway through the story he takes up with a young paraplegic woman in a wheelchair, ultimately causing her death.[1]

The first half of 'Journey Across a Crater' therefore has some similarities to 'The Death Module', which had been published in *New Worlds* in July 1967 and was later included in *The Atrocity Exhibition* under the revised title of 'Notes Towards a Mental Breakdown'. That earlier story had been announced in Ballard's 'manifesto' for his new fiction—'Notes from Nowhere', which was published in *New Worlds* in October 1966:[2]

> At present I am working on a story about a disaster in space which, however badly, makes a first attempt to describe what space means.... In my own story a disaster in space is translated into the terms of our own inner and outer environments.

To help get across the theme of the story, Ballard quoted the surrealist painter Roberto Matta: "Why must we await, and fear, a disaster in space in order to understand our own times?"[3]

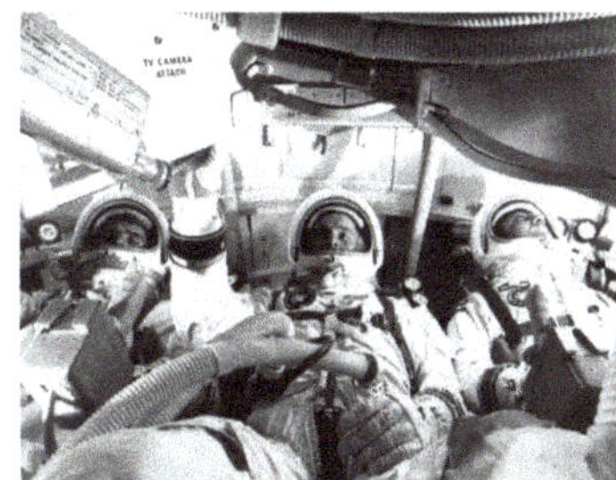

'The Death Module' did not appear in print until July 1967[4] by which time Ballard had incorporated the real-life deaths of the three Apollo 1 astronauts in a launch-pad fire on 27 January 1967. In retrospect, one of the benefits of using the Apollo 1 fire as his space disaster was that it was relatively straightforward for Ballard to incorporate this very public accident into the story. He had no need to find a way of relating a mysterious accident in space to the exterior and interior landscapes that confront the astronaut here on earth—one of the weaknesses of 'Journey Across a Crater'.

(III) Troubles with space

The phrase 'disaster in space' does appear in 'Journey Across a Crater', and it is possible that most of the first half (and perhaps some of the second half) was written during the latter part of 1966, before Ballard decided to base his story upon the deaths of the Apollo 1 astronauts. The similarities between 'The Death Module' and 'Journey Across a Crater' are particularly noticeable in the first paragraph of each story: the sub-titles are almost identical—'The Impact Zone' in 'The Death Module' and 'Impact Zone' in 'Journey Across a Crater'—and both paragraphs refer to radio or TV commentaries on a space disaster. In fact, the *New Worlds* editorial for its February 1970 issue included a brief description of 'Journey Across a Crater' which could well have been provided by Ballard and is of just the sort of story that one might have expected from his comments four years earlier in 'Notes from Nowhere':

> J.G. Ballard's latest story... describes an astronaut's search to re-establish the meaning of his surroundings, after a disaster which has destroyed his conception of space. The astronaut deciphers the coded landscape slowly and painfully until at last he finds the key to interpreting the geometries of his environment.

However, if 'Journey Across a Crater' had been started in 1966, it is unlikely to have been finished until late-1969, given that it contains references to Armstrong and Aldrin, who became the first men to land on the Moon in July of that year, and to the Boeing 747—an airliner that was first seen in public at the Paris Air Show in mid-1969 before entering service the following January.

---

1. The ending to the story does not explicitly state that the characters Gabrielle Saltzman and Vorster are actually dead, but the fact that the astronaut "moved away from the two bodies" is a strong indication that this is the case.
2. Based on internal evidence, it is likely that 'Notes from Nowhere' had been written a few months earlier, during June or July 1966.
3. Or rather, Ballard misquoted Matta, who actually wrote "Why must we await—and fear—a disaster in space, in order to become aware of our world?"
4. Another possible reason for the delay in the story's appearance is that *New Worlds* was experiencing publication and financial difficulties. At one point it seemed as if the magazine must close, and no issues appeared for February, May or June 1967.

(IV) The controls of the car

'Journey Across a Crater' can also be read as an attempt by Ballard to address the subject matter of *Crash* in the form of one of his condensed novels. Both halves of the story contain passages that relate to the automobile, including a description of a partially-constructed highway cloverleaf (which forms the 'crater' of the title), a re-enactment of a spectacular traffic accident, an account of the eroticism inherent in the paraplegic's car with its specially adapted controls, and a crashed vehicle that is displayed in an art gallery. But at first sight such passages seem to lack relevance to other aspects of the story—something which was not the case with those sections of *The Atrocity Exhibition* in which the automobile had played a key role.

Perhaps we can grasp the intent behind the car-related passages of 'Journey Across a Crater' by considering two specific paragraphs, one at the beginning of the story and another near to its end. In the story's second paragraph, the astronaut appears before Helen Clement in a dishevelled state, soaked to the skin, and so bewildered that he is unable even to comprehend the controls of her car. Later on, he takes up with the paraplegic woman, and in a paragraph titled 'Vectors of Eroticism' he carries out an inventory of various aspects of the controls and trim of her vehicle. Now, it seems, he can make sense of them—but only in an erotic or perverse context, by appreciating such features as "the unsymmetric imprints of buttock and thigh on the foam-plastic seat" or "the stained leather mounting for the seat urinal". If we view these two paragraphs as constituting a metaphor for the astronaut's ability, or inability, to comprehend the world around him, then they become key elements of the story. It is therefore appropriate that the resolution at the end of 'Journey Across a Crater' is the result of a 'crash', when the astronaut propels the paraplegic woman in her wheelchair into the middle of the highway cloverleaf and lets her spin out of control.

(V) Too many Gabrielles

The second half of 'Journey Across a Crater' contains the emphasis on injuries and eroticism that we find in *Crash*; and in both cases, the woman whose wounds and disabilities fascinate the protagonist is named Gabrielle—without a surname in the novel, but 'Gabrielle Saltzman' in the short story. There are, however, two notable differences: in *Crash*, Gabrielle usually gets around without her wheelchair—and she does not die, unlike Gabrielle Saltzman in 'Journey Across a Crater'.

The actress who appeared with Ballard in Harley Cokeliss' short film 'Crash!' (1971) was yet another Gabrielle—Gabrielle Drake. In the first typescript for the novel, the paraplegic woman is unnamed. But when working on the script for Cokeliss' film, Ballard suggested that it needed an actress, perhaps in the background, "like the artist's model in the paintings of Delvaux, Ernst, etc."[5] After Gabrielle Drake had fulfilled this role, Ballard put a name to the young woman in his novel. At first she was Gabrielle Byrd, but by the time he came to submit a typescript to his agent[6] she had actually become 'Gabrielle Drake'! Here we have another example of Ballard attempting to 'personalise'

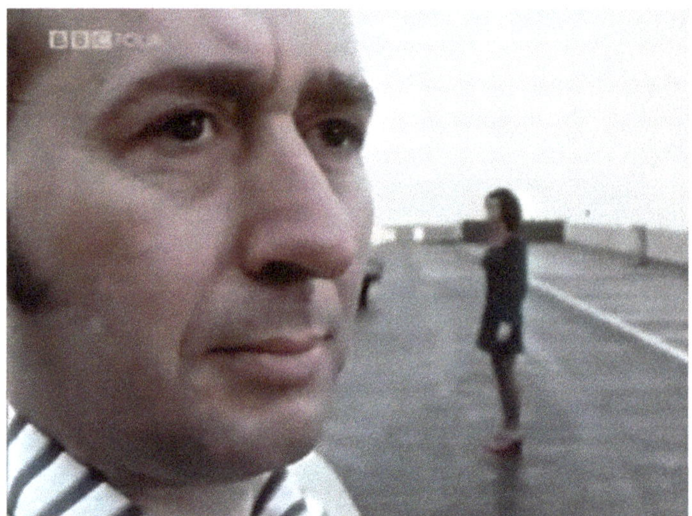

J.G. Ballard and Gabrielle Drake in the short film *Crash!* by Harley Cokeliss.

the text of *Crash* whilst he was writing it—in the same way that he named the protagonist of the novel 'James Ballard', based James' wife, Catherine, on his own real-life girlfriend, Claire Walsh, and modelled the hoodlum scientist Robert Vaughan on his good friend Dr. Christopher Evans. However, by the time that the novel came to be published, Gabrielle's surname had—

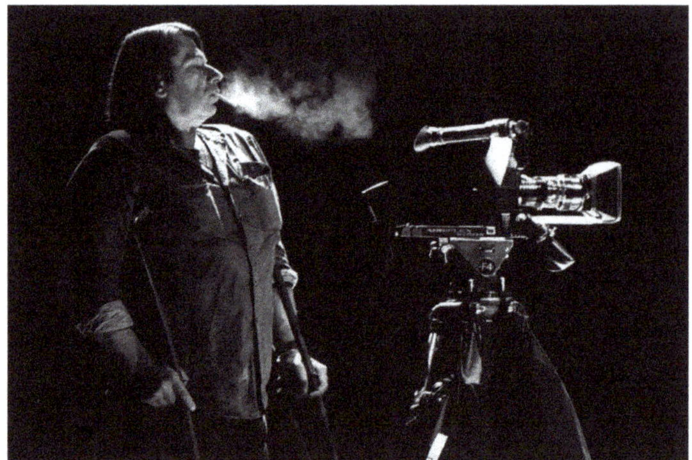
Stephen Dwoskin.

unsurprisingly—been omitted.

The description of Gabrielle Saltzman in 'Journey across a Crater'—she has "powerful hands" which propel her "chromium wheel chair", and emanates "an intense and perverse sexuality"—is very similar to Ballard's description of another of his real-life acquaintances in the late 1960's, the filmmaker Stephen Dwoskin. In his tongue-in-cheek introduction to 'The Bathroom', a series of stills from one of Dwoskin's films, Ballard had written:

> Dwoskin himself is something of a closed character. A strong-shouldered and laconic paraplegic, he moves around London in a chrome wheelchair. His pursuit, across a city and a mind, of my own girl-friend, the beautiful Claire Churchill (whom he hopes to star, naked, in his first feature film), merits a movie on its own.[7]

5. Letter from Ballard to Cokeliss dated 3 December 1970, available at the British Library, ref. Add MS 89171/1.

6. Available at the British Library, ref. Add MS 88938/3/8/2.

7. 'The Bathroom', *The Running Man* #2, July-August 1968.

This description is reprised in 'Journey Across a Crater', in which the protagonist drives around following Gabrielle Saltzman in her specially adapted car, just as Dwoskin pursues Claire Walsh (née Churchill) across London.

However, Gabrielle Saltzman was not the first "crippled young woman" in Ballard's fiction: that is the very description given to Vanessa Johnstone in *The Drought*, who has a metal support on her right leg and with whom the main character, Doctor Charles Ransom, has a discreet on-off romance.

(VI) A deliberate psychotic state

Two months after 'Journey Across a Crater' had been published in *New Worlds*, Ballard held his crashed cars exhibition at the New Arts Lab in London. He often said that the purpose behind the exhibition was to test the responses of the audience to the wrecked vehicles, but recollections of other attendees at the opening night do not substantiate his claims of wild and aggressive behaviour—some drunken fooling around at most. However, the fictional account by 'Jim' of his own exhibition in *The Kindness of Women* may contain a germ of the truth: "I still assumed that the exhibition had been designed to test the psychology of its audience, but [my friend] David took for granted that its sole purpose had been to incite myself."

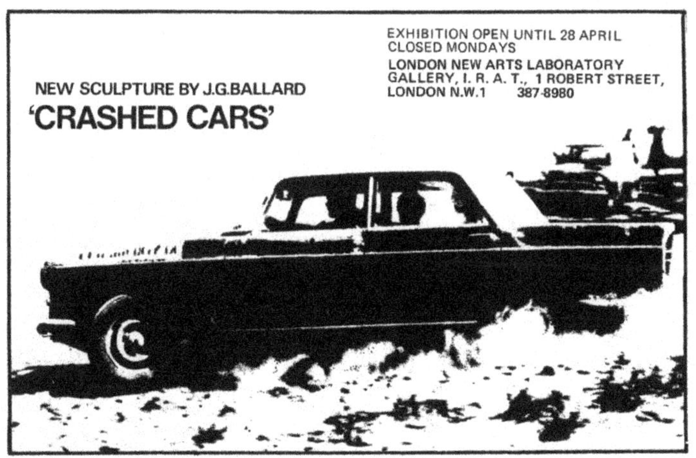

Might 'Journey Across a Crater' have been another attempt by Ballard, similar to his crashed cars exhibition, to get himself in the right state of mind for writing *Crash*?[8] At the end of the story the astronaut finally understands his environment, having come to terms with its "geometry of violence and eroticism"—and perhaps this reflects a belief on Ballard's part that he could only write *Crash* once he himself had accepted that same geometry. As he said in a later interview: "I had to will myself into this deliberate psychotic state, suspending all values and embracing the nightmare logic that the book sets out".[9] There are therefore similarities between the protagonist of 'Journey Across a Crater' and the story's author: the astronaut is an explorer of outer space, just as Ballard saw himself as an explorer of inner space;[10] they are both are concerned with trying to make sense of the world around them; and they both arrive at similar solutions.

At one point the protagonist attends a basketball game held at a hospital for injured aircrew and played by paraplegics in their wheelchairs. All of a sudden, he wheels one of the surprised players towards the exit. It seems that the mentally disturbed astronaut identifies with the physically wounded aircrew, in much the same way that in the first chapter of *Crash* the narrator James Ballard identifies with the likes of "psychopaths" and "excited schizophrenics". That Ballard himself made a similar identification can be seen from the dedication that he included in the suppressed 1970 Doubleday edition of *The Atrocity Exhibition*: "To the insane".[11]

Later on, the astronaut ponders his "failed relationship" with Helen Clement[12] before taking up with Gabrielle Saltzman, who has her own difficulties in coping with external reality. During his time with Gabrielle, the astronaut learns that he can come to terms with the world by accepting its underlying violence and eroticism. This he does by killing Gabrielle—and to the extent that he identifies with paraplegics, he can be considered to have sacrificed the "injured" part of himself in order to redeem his life. This theme of "sacrifice" is one that had featured in *The Atrocity Exhibition*, most notably in Dr. Nathan's suggestion that "in 20th century terms the crucifixion"—the ultimate sacrifice on behalf of humanity—"would be re-enacted as a conceptual auto-disaster."[13] Ballard also had to accept a world of violence and eroticism, and risk making a sacrifice of his sanity, by writing *Crash*: "I had to take the top off my skull... and start touching pain and pleasure centers to see what happened."[14]

(VII) Like an archangel

If Gabrielle Saltzman's role in 'Journey Across a Crater' is to show the astronaut how to come to terms with the world, then she is aptly named. Initially, it is the astronaut himself who is described as appearing before Helen Clement "like... an archangel"; but his relationship with Helen is a failure, and it becomes clear that it is Gabrielle who is the true messenger from God in this story.

It is possible that Gabrielle's namesake in *Crash* may have

8. For an examination of the development of the ideas that lay behind *Crash*, and Ballard's preparations for writing the novel, see Mike Holliday, 'Taking the Top Off His Skull: The Genesis of J.G. Ballard's *Crash*' at http://www.ballardian.com/taking-the-top-off-his-skull-the-genesis-of-j-g-ballards-crash.

9. Interview in 'Writers in Conversation: Volume 1', Christopher Bigsby, 2000; the interview most likely took place in 1991.

10. Ballard must surely have been aware of the Scottish novelist Alexander Trocchi's description of himself as a "cosmonaut of inner space", a phrase admired by William Burroughs; see Ted Morgan, *Literary Outlaw: The Life and Times of William S. Burroughs.*

11. The dedication had originally been included in the very first edition of *The Atrocity Exhibition*—Jannick Storm's Danish translation, published in late-1969. Although the dedication was omitted from subsequent editions, Ballard did note in his 1990 annotations that: "*The Atrocity Exhibition*'s original dedication should have been 'To the Insane'. I owe them everything."

12. Ballard's girlfriend during the middle of 1966, when he may have started writing 'Journey Across a Crater', was also named Helen; see David Pringle, 'Memories of Life: A Conversation with Fay Ballard', in *Deep Ends: The JG Ballard Anthology 2014* (ed. R. McGrath). One of the main female characters in Crash is also a 'Helen'—Dr. Helen Remington.

13. The same theme is implicit in *Crash*, even though not directly referred to; see Mike Holliday, 'Taking the Top Off His Skull: The Genesis of J.G. Ballard's *Crash*' at http://www.ballardian.com/taking-the-top-off-his-skull-the-genesis-of-j-g-ballards-crash.

14. Ballard interview in *Heavy Metal*, April 1982.

been intended for a similar role. The typescript which Ballard submitted to his agent contained a good deal of material that was omitted from the published version of the novel. In one such section, in the first chapter, the narrator ponders the fate of the other characters following the death of Robert Vaughan; Gabrielle, he believes, "will go off... with the others who gathered around her, like a crowd drawn to a cripple whose deformed postures reveal the secret formulas of their minds and lives"—a description which recapitulates Gabrielle Saltzman's role with respect to the astronaut in 'Journey Across a Crater'.

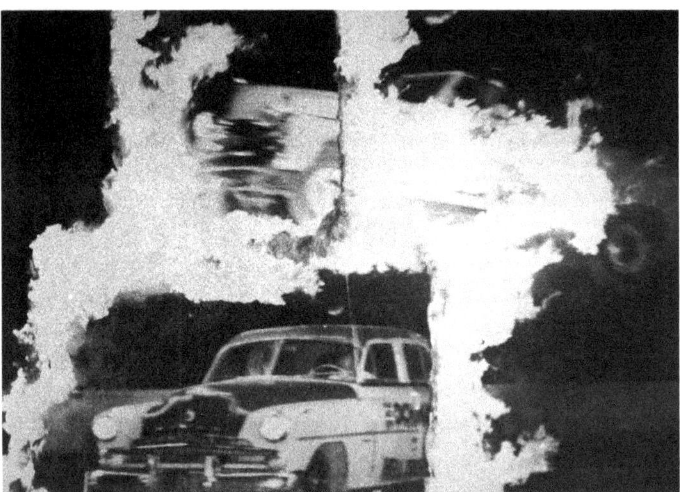

The American Hell-Drivers perform.

(VIII) An impatient little boy

'Journey Across a Crater' also contains quite specific autobiographical elements. Most obvious is the paragraph titled 'Hell-Drivers', which was the name of the American display team whom Ballard mentions in his autobiography, *Miracles of Life*. This section of the story describes how the character Vorster visits a display of crashing cars. After the climax of the demonstration, a reconstruction of a spectacular car crash, Vorster feels irritated by his fellow spectators and hands over his binoculars to a small boy who waits impatiently behind him—almost like a six year-old Jim Ballard standing with his father whilst watching the Hell-Drivers in Shanghai.[15]

(IX) Bondage activities

In a paragraph titled 'Nutrix Corporation', Helen Clement reflects upon the astronaut's "strange perversions" and realises that they are actually "bridges across which he hoped to make his escape", thereby freeing himself of his estrangement from the external world. Nutrix was actually a real-life US company that had been set up by Irving Klaw and specialised in producing bondage magazines and films. Ballard told *Penthouse* in a 1970 interview that a friend of his who had visited America had brought back a Nutrix magazine that featured a number of women being restrained and tied up to various parts of a motor launch.[16] This is therefore the likely source for the photograph used in Ballard's advertiser's announcement 'A Neural Interval', which was published in *Ambit* in 1968. That image was credited to the collection of Ballard's friend Eduardo Paolozzi, who did indeed spend some time in the US during 1968-69, and presumably supplied Ballard with the magazine.

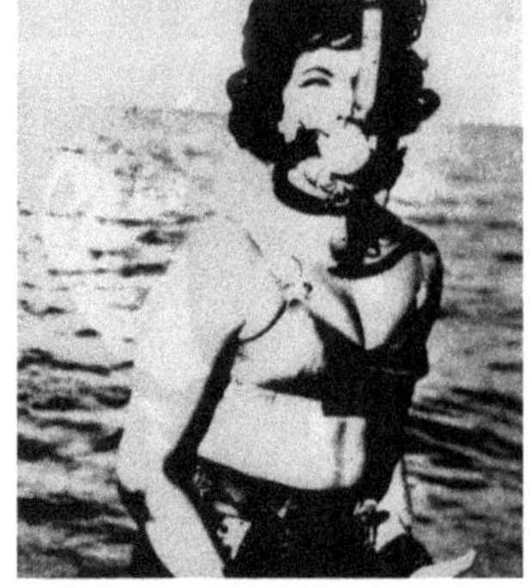

What struck Ballard about the Nutrix magazines were that at first sight they had nothing much to do with sex, and yet for their readers they presumably contained elements that were more erotic than an actual depiction of nudity or sexual intercourse—a theme that he would explore in both *The Atrocity Exhibition* and *Crash*.[17]

(X) Most dissatisfied

'Journey Across a Crater' is included in the recent special edition of *Crash*—but it certainly dissatisfied its author, perhaps because he felt that he had not managed to get it to work as a coherent whole. Or maybe, after killing off Karen Novotny (several times), Nurse Nagamatzu and Margaret Trabert in *The Atrocity Exhibition*, he thought that brutally ending the life of yet another young woman was a death too far. Another possibility is that Ballard refused any re-publication after 1971 because he viewed 'Journey Across a Crater' as an attempt to create the right conditions for writing *Crash*: an exercise in self-induced psychosis that was now best left consigned to the past.

Certainly, the story does nothing to suggest that the non-linear style of *The Atrocity Exhibition* might be an appropriate choice for a detailed exploration of the linkages between sexuality, psychopathology and the automobile that were the focus of *Crash*. In the February 1970 issue of *New Worlds* Ballard was quoted as saying that he intended to carry on writing in the condensed form "for many years to come". In fact, he dropped it almost entirely after 'Journey Across a Crater'.

So what was 'Journey Across a Crater'? A first version of Ballard's "disaster in space", given a bit of tweaking a few years later? A quick story written specifically for *New Worlds*, incorporating earlier, unused material? A failed attempt to develop the themes of *Crash* in a condensed format? A way of preparing himself mentally before he started writing his most notorious novel?

Or was it perhaps a bit of all of these?

---

15. Those of a Freudian disposition will therefore not be entirely surprised to learn that at the end of the story Vorster is killed by the astronaut.

16. Interview in *Penthouse*, September 1970. This section was not included in the published version of the interview, but it does appear in the 'author's proof' held at the British Library, ref. Add MS 89171/1.

17. In fact, part of the rationale for the Nutrix magazines was that, because they did not actually display nudity or sexual activity, they were not considered pornography and were therefore legal in the US.

Advertiser's Announcement.

How Garbo Died

Science is the ultimate pornography, analytic activity whose main aim is to isolate objects or events from their contexts in time and space. This obsession with the specific activity of quantified functions is what science shares with pornography.

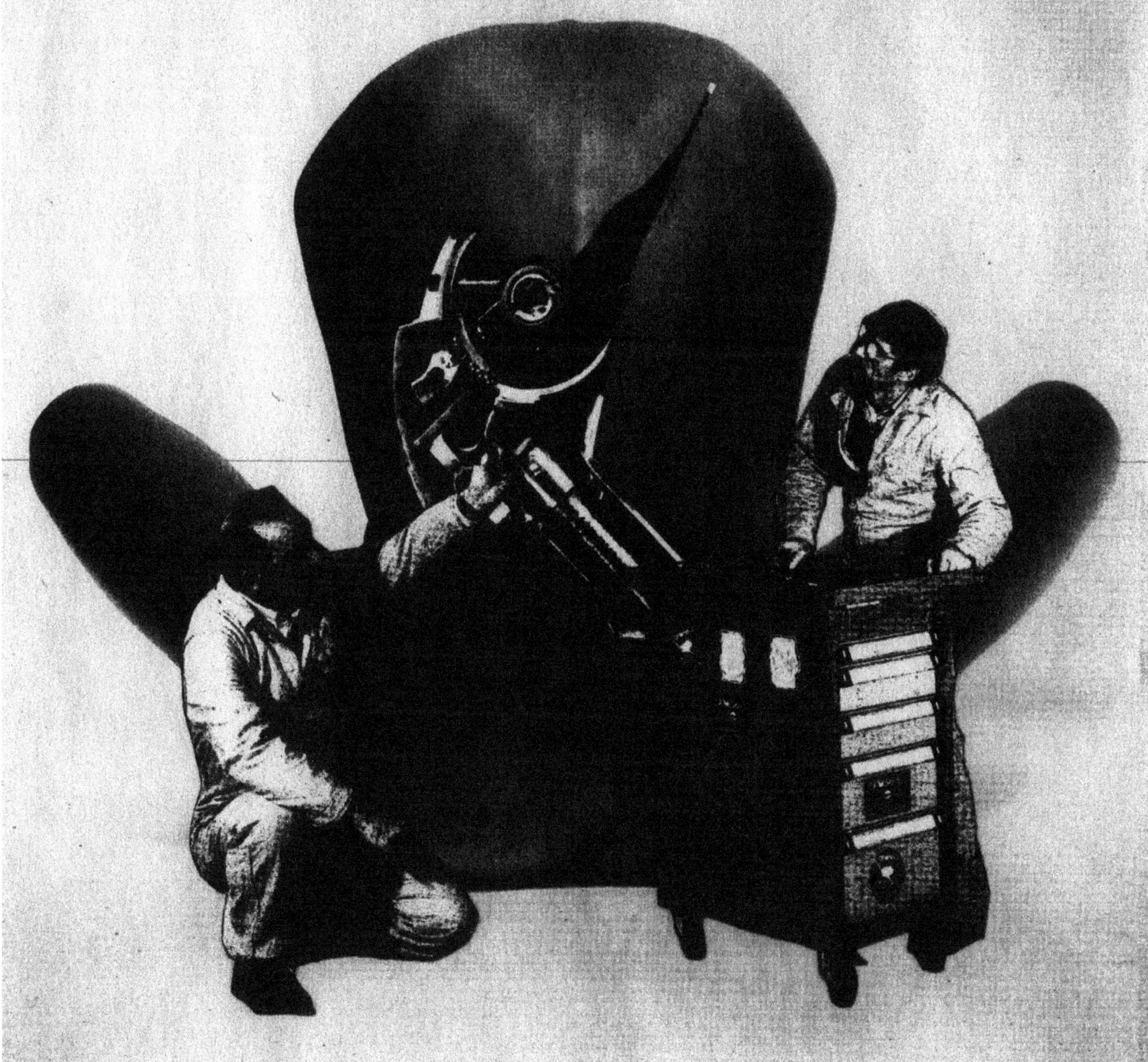

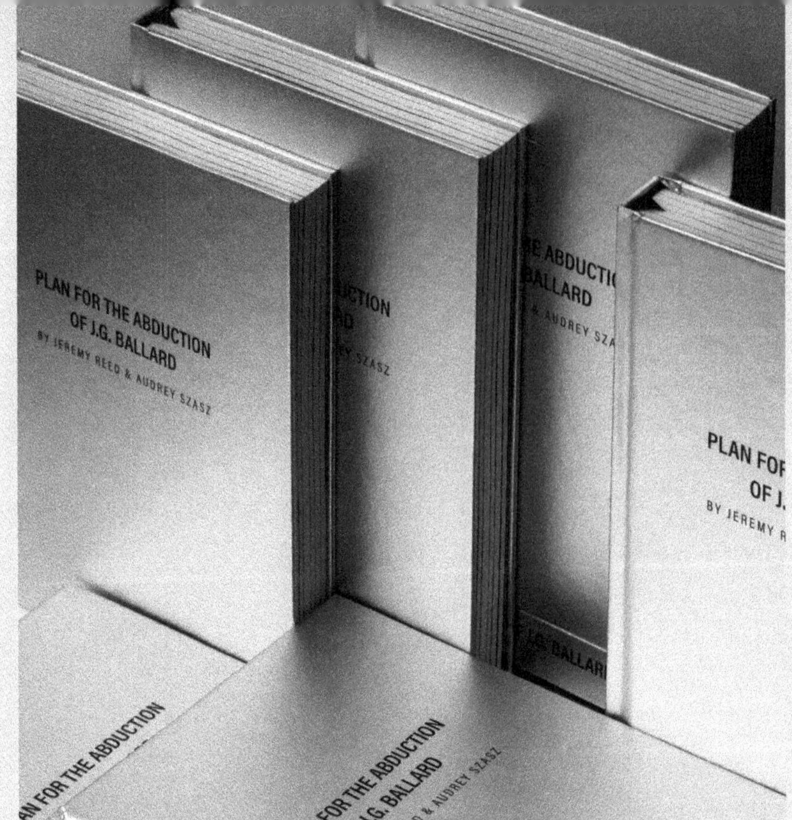

EXTRACTS

PLAN FOR THE ABDUCTION OF J.G. BALLARD

BY JEREMY REED & AUDREY SZASZ

ILLUSTRATED BY MARTIN BLADH

FIRST PUBLISHED BY INFINITY LAND PRESS 2019

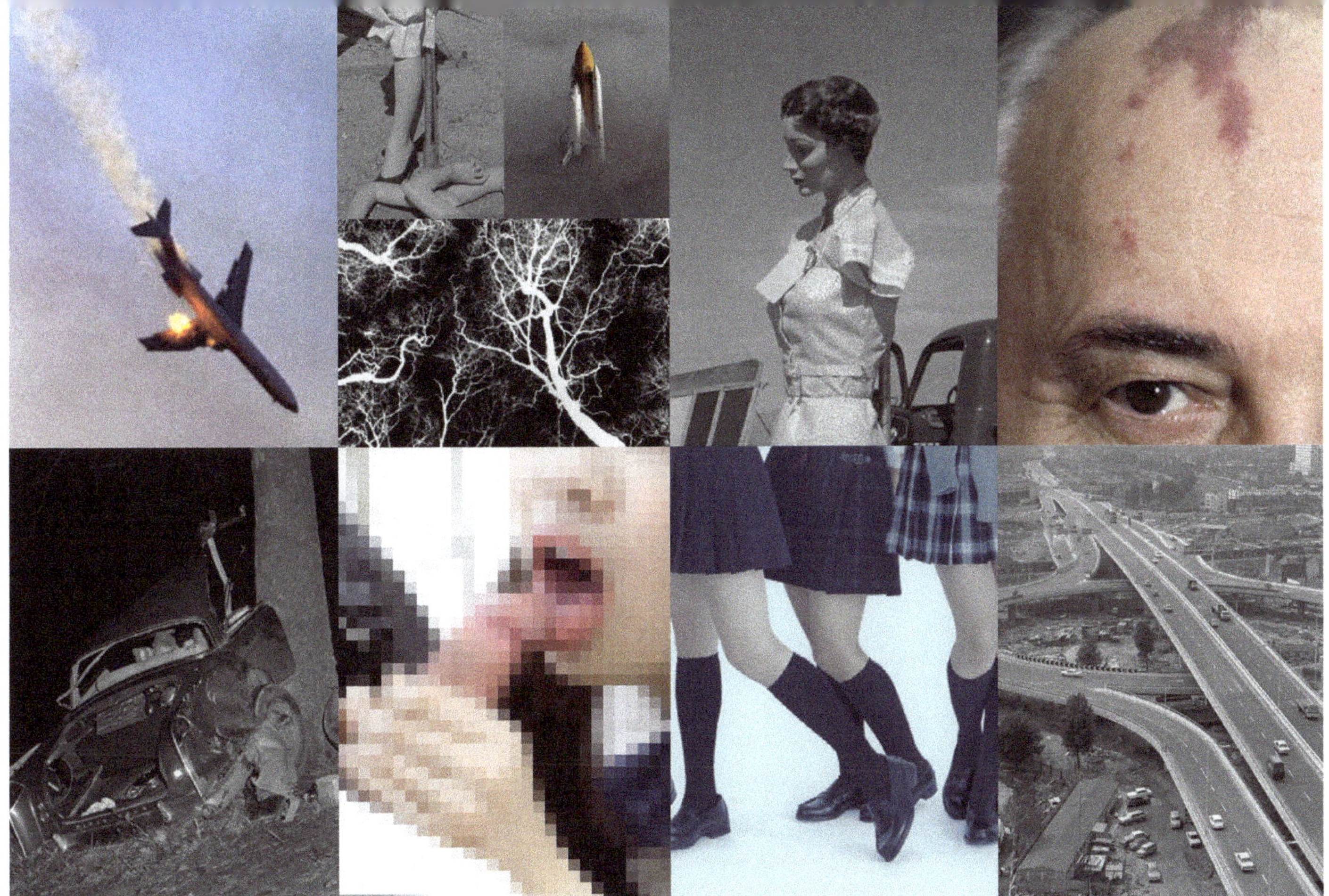

INTERACTIVE ACID

Parked on the top deck of a Northolt multi-storey in a recently panel-bashed, futures-grey Maserati Ballard worked at the cabin's ambient LED lighting modulating the interior blue, red, purple and white moods as distractive tech.

I'd sold him the acid he was doing, orange film-coated pills full of psychoactive intelligence, and on his own request agreed to voyeuristically film him having quantum sex in the Maserati's compressed architecture, his erection linked by a sensor to the car's turbo-driven diesel engine. What the acid I sold him did was to filmically stream his erotic fantasies, so his fetishised obsessions were fuckably externalised and could be brought into physical play rather than lost as transitioning images. The sky was luridly sci-fi orange and pink over the urban stacking of asymmetrical towers. The renewable skyline looked like it should in 50 years, collapsed back from the future into the past.

The acid was interactive, so doing it simultaneously with Ballard I was able to share his visions and note the catalogue of what juiced his testosterone. I could feel the drug coming up with fluttery visuals in electric line patterns, and from photos Ballard kept of Claire I recognised her nude body masked with indigo bruises, splinters of glass needling her skin, her legs disarranged aerially over her head, ankles cuffed, congealed blood trackings dribbling her temples, and Ballard projecting lemon, cerise and purple molecular wave-patterns by way of response, the shape of his telepathic orgasm pinched up into a bioluminescent twizzle supporting a conical burger cloudy as an opal. I too experienced the limbic rush, the overdrive like the Maserati's 190 mph potential to kill the highway peaking ahead of itself as exhaust audio.

Bent to the psychoactive's curve I followed out of orgasmic exhaust in jungle colours, like psychic ideograms, into a stream of dissociated car fucks, in which manipulated geometries substituted for emotional grammar, the obvious sold cheap, demoralised sex workers, all vitamins thrown out, having cash stuffed into their mouths as humiliating degradation. I could feel on the drug how Ballard's intellect was cleaned out by sex, as they came up singular facial commentaries on bodies signed out as sexual housekeeping after brutal use.

Claire reappeared in repeat fantasies riding Jim on the backseat sandwiched between a skinny guy in a black leather jacket, his bare torso displaying a severed right nipple, and what looked like a blonde-bobbed Chinese girl disinterestedly smoking. The blonde substituted for Claire, when Ballard grew bored, while the guy filmed the action with bland sunglassed indifference. While sex was in motion the stationary car was exploded into from the rear full on like an asteroid breaking up on impact. Orgasm counterpointed the fuel tank launched into roaring flames as the car and its occupants detonated into a savage fireball.

As the hallucinogen dipped, downsizing neural activity into more regulated patterns, so I continued to shoot Ballard like a car surgeon clinically reviewing accessorised ergonomics that he was clearly excavating for fiction. It was a day that hadn't arrived yet, planes finning through London's exhaust cloud, the sky glossed like green celluloid, Ballard dead, but his psychic snapshot hunched in the driver's seat, looking out through tinted haze towards Shepperton.

—JR

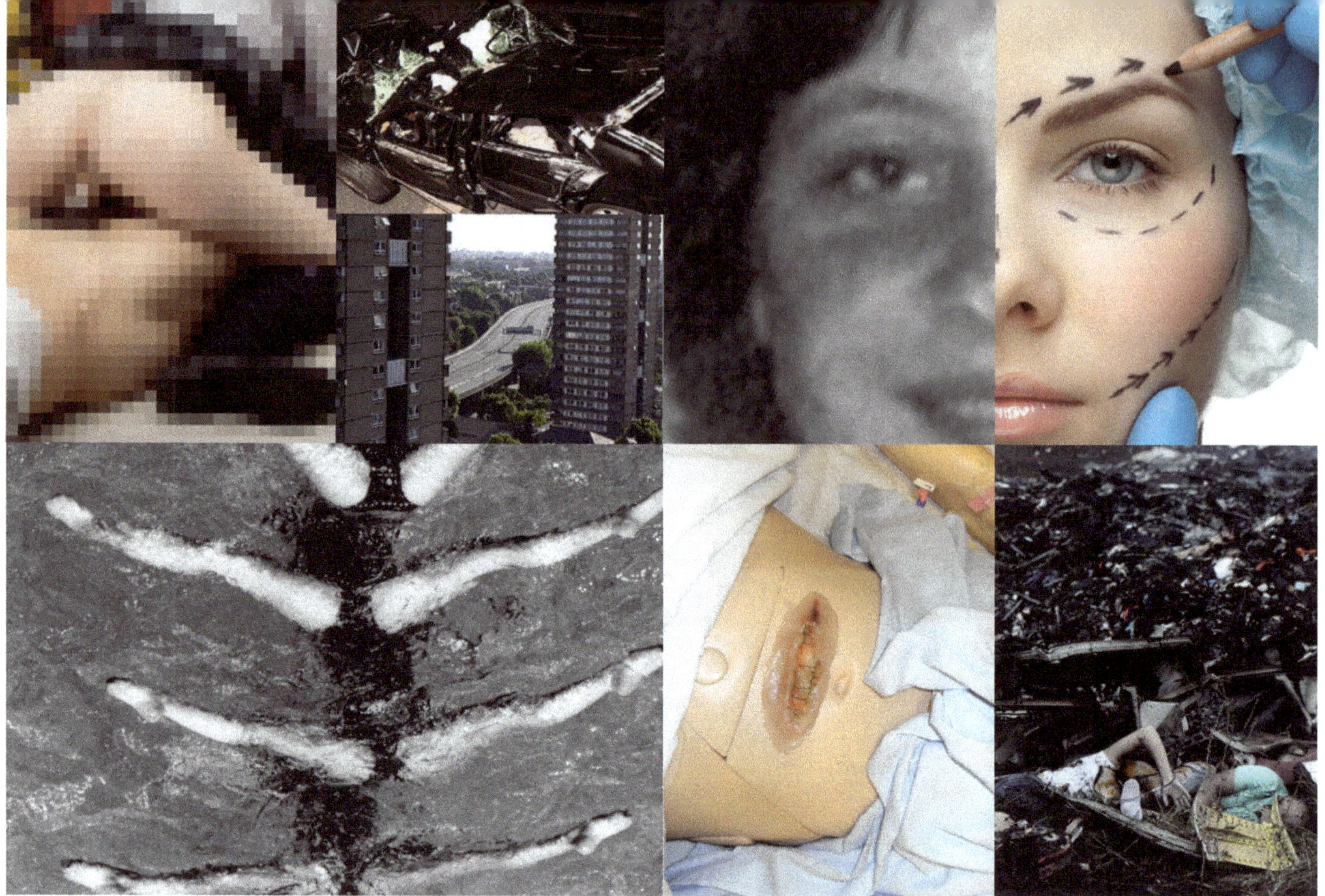

NEUTRON BLAST

Ballard plugs in, begins to charge his soul. He roams the heavens in his mind's eye, an astral plane frontier general. Flashes of high energy photons—gamma-ray bursts—on automatic alert mode. Serpent systems online, energy replenished. Full cadaver. He scans vast swathes of the sky, telecommunicates with his young Japanese companion Ayaka—she of the mirror eyes and diamond limbs—she snaps picture after picture—freeze frame—using a DSLR camera with a wide angle lens attached. A bolt of lightning caresses the rear wheel housing of her purple Ferrari 512 BB.

JG is in multiple places at once. Ayaka's presence—like a shadow in negative—arcs like electricity, devours entire stars, collapses in orgasm like a swirling firework. Ballard duplicates himself like a row of paper men, an infinity of conjoined twins, flesh and features multiplying like hallways of always. One of the identical brothers takes Ayaka from behind, enters her—some resistance—pushes carefully—a tight fit—contracting sockets—another brother kneels, parts the woman's thighs, searches out her sex with his tongue, parts her labia, palpates her moistening vulva, her sensitive clitoris—whilst yet another Ballard continues to the woman's mouth—open, lips and jaw apart—she yields—he slaps her face several times, grabs a fistful of her glittering hair —thick strands of her bobbed hairstyle—the nape of her neck – her smooth skin—Ayaka gasps, her eyes opening and closing, high on nitrous and arcade neon—dazzling—illuminated—her expression like the flickering buttons of a slot machine – all kinds of scintillating scrolling flashes in amber, ruby, sapphire and teal —cataclysmic outbursts—her saliva—her front teeth—yaeba canines—the white-hot tip of Ballard's erect penis. Liquid crystal jets and cosmic radiation.

But Ayaka has contrived—in a reciprocal gesture of good humour and transcendental irony—to distort the thudding hologram of her body like an after-image burnt by prodigious shade—a star-shredding symphony—belies the usual calm of her reserved countenance—another self—public mask slipping—her chosen exterior—her multiple personality order—evolving into pyrotechnics as she reaches around—there are several of her now all projected from the first like petals of a flower—grasps Ballard's cock with her nimble hands—watches herself being tongued and fucked by duplicates of the renegade author with growing fascination and intellectual arousal—rates the performance out of ten on Twitter, Facebook, Instagram. Snapchats the moment to her friends back home in Chiba Prefecture—in real time—forwards the images to her colleagues—a cosmological revolution in magenta plaid and black velvet flecked with bronze.

Distant objects now—remote viewing—the shape of Ballard's naked buttocks—pale in the half-light—as his penis emerges from Ayaka 1's head, her lips spitting quicksilvery semen glistening with all the transience of doomed prototypical youth—flesh banging flesh. Some universal vacuum that abhors nature—defying explanation—Ballard 2 explodes twice like the echo of a crash test dummy. A fluid trickle becomes a viscous flood—solidifying in waves—the collision of their phantom limbs—an ultraviolet afterglow—sighs collapsing like gold and platinum —the ingrained solipsism of Ayaka's tell-tale climax—ripples in space-time generated by black holes merging. A fourth Ballard appears, stands off to one side like a casual observer, puzzles over his future interactions—removes his leather belt and thrashes another version of himself as Ayaka 8 mounts him and rides him like a pony—stripped down and strapped on—beyond the opalescent horizon milky peaks surging and spiking like prongs of sai. It's a super-luminous daydream thrown off by bright shafts of light bouncing like rutting deer through the car window—its parameters expanding forever to encompass the entire universe.

—AS

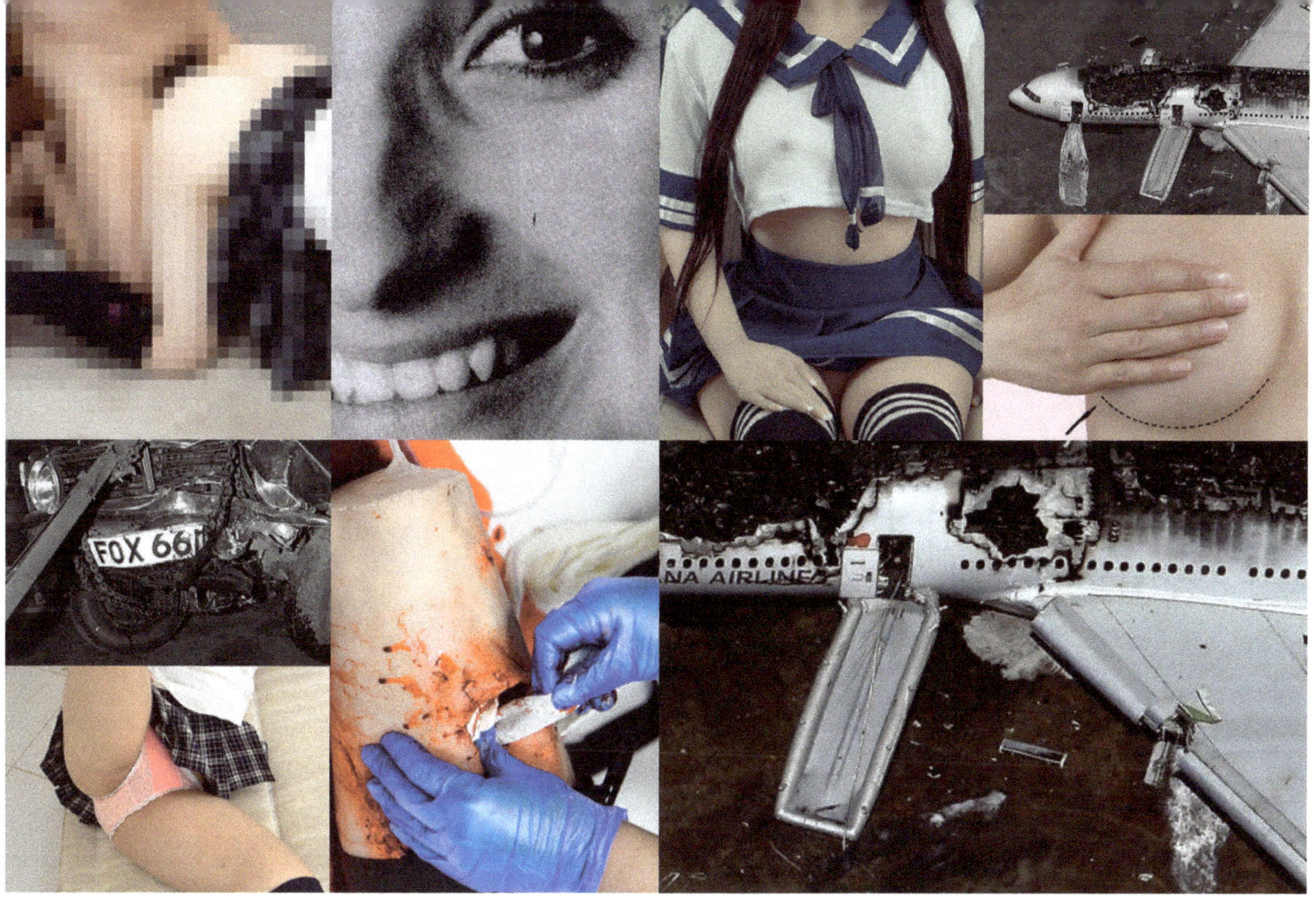

COSPLAY VAGINOPLASTY

Ayaka's delinquent sukeban girl gang, inspired by precedents like Tokyo's United Shoplifters Group and Kanto Women Delinquent Alliance, as paint and glue sniffers, were consolidated Ballardians, so hung up on their futurologist avatar they attempted to make brain bypasses into his post-biological parallel timelines. And having established in the process the arguable belief that everyone sees a different truth, because everyone is creating what they see in the bouncy world of quantum states, in which nothing that is observed is unaffected by the observer, they dedicated themselves to making virtual contact with their dissident anti-hero of subversively visionary fiction. Using their infantilized school skirt fetish as incentive, audaciously folding the pleated tartan skirt three times to hike it to shimmying micro, they'd coerced a fixated neuroscientist working on implants that bridge damaged parts of the brain into helping create a neural code to access the spacetime in which Ballard coexisted on a wavelength providing access to the future and the past simultaneously. Exploiting a variant of the electronics used by the climacteric neuroscientist to interpret the signals from one area of the brain, and circumventing the damaged parts, rewriting them into the second area, it was possible after prolonged experimentation to regain communication with the writer, who could happily renew old memories as well as impart presentness to the sukeban gang without the inhibitive time-lag expected of parallel realities.

If the signal was correct, Ballard was in the interests of virtualised sex, and consistent with his continuing biomedical interests, anxious for Ayaka to undergo cosmetic vaginoplasty, despite her 61.7 mm dimensions being unusually tight in the quotient of ubiquitous Shibuya teens. He wanted her smaller through labia reduction surgery, a common procedure done by a cosmetic surgeon making small incisions to correct the shape of the labia minora, and insisted on the correction as beautification of her pubis. To Ayaka the command was like fat-phobic fetishization taken to the edge, and risking on completion vaginismus, when the vaginal muscles involuntarily contract when confronted with penetration. It seemed like a mixed message relayed from mixed realities and possibly infected by the mismanagement of parallel timelines; but she found a cosmetic surgeon willing to undertake the procedure, who warned her of possible post-op labial swelling and discomfort from the dissolvable stitches. The private operation was completed in under an hour, the area expertly dressed, and Ayaka emerged as the embodiment of a racial demographic valued for constrictive penetration.

The afternoon she came out of the clinic the sky was the colour of blue ice cream, and she wanted to lick its spatial curve as she checked into a Starbucks to skype Ballard and report the infomatics of the design feature. Coolly circumspect and analytically inquisitive with an accent of acute voyeurism Ballard wanted to be assured she was now 61mm as opposed to the average vaginal dimension of her Kosplay gang at 62.7mm. His clinical specifications thrilled her with their precise attention to cosmetic gynaecology, and he was quick to inform her that he would conceive of a novel based on designer vagina performed both temporally and virtually on colonised exos like Mars and its shepherd moon Phobos. All space Ballard maintained was like navigating apps on a phone, you thumbed into zonal spacetimes altering your consciousness from portal to portal, something that allowed him periodically to travel back to Shepperton as an obsessive personalised resource helping keep his past alive. The time slip also allowed him to maintain his automotive fixation on the updated ergonomics of cars, those parked in Old Charlton Road where he'd lived for almost five decades, and those layered into high-rise car parks at Heathrow and Northolt as stacked metal intelligence in concrete sarcophagi.

When Ayaka transitioned back to real time, leaving Ballard to revert to a multiverse of distinct universes where the exactly right level of weirdness continually produces life, she began to fantasise about how sex would feel with her surgically modified vulva. The entire gang had agreed to copy her clitoral booster if sensation in her was radically enhanced by designer

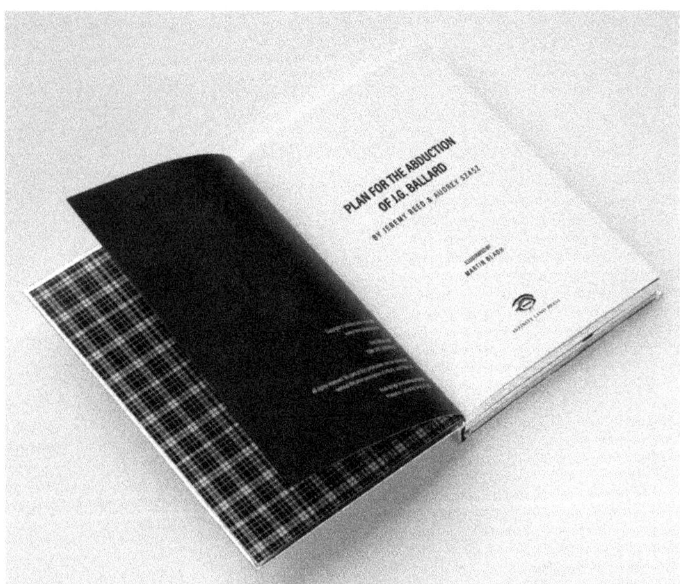

surgery, their sense of sorority being part of the perverse instinct to maintain super-small in the interests of extraterrestrial sex with their guru of symphorophilia. Ayaka on returning home drew the white shutout blinds, peeled to her strawberry panties, and turned off her digital devices as a return to the body's organic schematic, and lay with her miniscule wound in the suddenly darkened room. Becoming analogue again, with all the body's insistent cellular chatter was suddenly like lying on a beach head to the sand hearing rhythmically measured surf pound on the shore, as its momentum advanced, collapsed and turned back on itself in seething dialogue. Her body was suddenly like a personalised recording studio with arterial roar as awareness of living on the circadian drum of her heartbeat. Transitioning from what seemed like digitised prosthetics to organic rhythm made her feel like a zombie, confirming her belief in Ballard's reminder that Earth was the only alien planet. In fact exoplanets were to her mind probably more familiarly habitable, if only they could be experienced with the same gravitational pull as Earth, and perhaps less alien, once adapted as the basis for home.

After a time she got up to go see her pet python, the metabolic blockbuster weapon with which she lived as a flatmate, and given by her the name of The Day Of For Ever, on account of its digestive processes, when its metabolic rate increases up to 45 fold, about the same ramp up seen in a sprinting racehorse, running flat out across a field, and with its small intestine and liver, she'd read, doubling in size, so too the proportions of its heart and kidneys. Snakes reminded her of lurid sci-fi paperback covers in which supernova-fanged flameout serpents crushed space architecture into fall out rubble on colonised planets. She was also fascinated by their facility to manufacture venom protein, a fantastic mix of more than one hundred toxins. Pythons were in effect a venom bomb capable of killing and ingesting an antelope in the slo-mo breakdown of digestive juices that kept snakes ahead in the evolutionary arms race. Her warhead was dormant most of the time, a primal killer coding have it live out unedited ophidian psychopathy in its natural state. Snakes also aroused her sexually in that they were both phallus and clitoris, the two united in the figure of the ouroboros, with the snake swallowing its own tail as the arguable unification implied by androgyny. Ayaka could never face feeding it rodents like mice in its vivarium, and left that instead to her cleaner, while she herself was out committing keyless car thefts and riding stolen Yamaha bikes through the city, naked except for a skull and crossbones crash helmet and an atomiser containing tear gas as virulent defence, if she was ever pursued.

Ayaka still felt minor discomfort from surgery, and to alter mood took a Vortioxetine, one of the new family of SSRI and SNRI antidepressants with the multimodal mechanism of acting in upping dopamine, norepinephrine and acetylcholine activity in the prefrontal cortex; the pharmaceutical infrastructure of which she'd researched in depth before using the drug, as a pharma-obsessive impelled to experiment with new mood-sensitive sweeties. When she ran up the shutout blinds there was an auroral orange sunset over the city suffused with lavender ribbons of clouds deepening to indigo over the west quadrant. A dual-laned fluffy contrail was slowly crystallising to dissolve in the atmosphere.

She knew intuitively from the little uptakes in her brain chemistry that Ballard was going to come through, probably to get exact physiological details of the vaginoplasty on which he'd insisted instructing from his parallel timeline. She felt correspondingly excited and afraid, her usual response to meeting her virtual icon in the 4D portal he now occupied, where universes he'd predicted were alternative realities, allowing him to time-slip from one self-created fiction to another, chaptering his continuous navigation of multiple Ballardian spacetimes. In that way he claimed he revisited his past and continued to curate neural architecture in other futures where imagination was the dominant constructive reality.

When he did come through several minutes later, dressed no differently than in the neutral taste he'd displayed at Shepperton, he was as she'd predicted clinically preoccupied with the dimensions of her reconstructed vagina. In addition he provided Ayaka with the outline for a new sukeban novel in which psychoactive viruses engineered in the lab were injected into the food chain, with the result that the common majority started acting psychotomimetic and torching not only supermarkets and shopping malls, but themselves in huge petrol-doused pyrotechnical pyres. Whole communities would collectively combust in roaring big city hecatombs, spreading virally across the globe, with Angela Merkel providing live commentary to the mediatisation of the Berlin fires.

With the promise of the renewal of virtual sex once Ayaka's dissolvable stitches were removed, Ballard returned to his contactable spacetime, leaving Ayaka alone with the Day Of For Ever, lethargically elasticating its digestion of the cleaner's child, left in Ayaka's flat, while she was out undergoing surgery, and only remembered now, as she observed a foot disappearing into its bloated gullet, and finding a note from the cleaner saying she would be back to collect her child at 6pm.

—JR

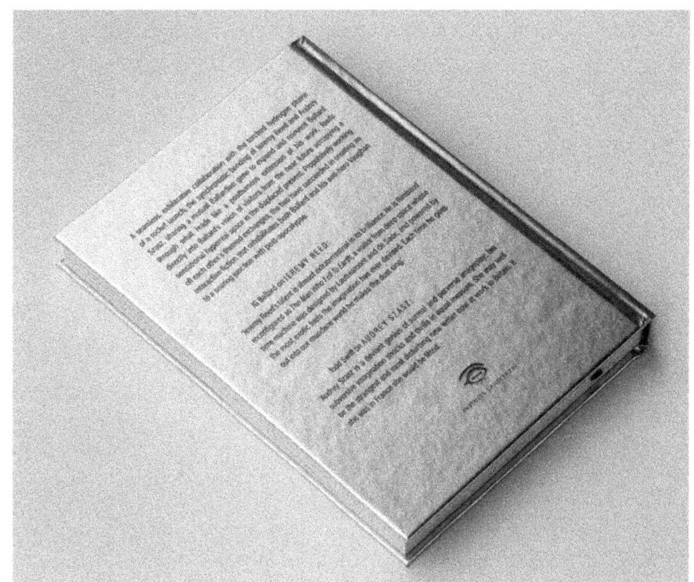

GOUACHE HAZE

Miss Europe 2055. Made to measure. A film distribution and production firm. Wet latex. International fashion brands. Industry leaders. Death by firing squad. Public spectacles. Bisexual holographic fantasies. Touch them they're real. Well it's an illusion but it feels so good. Making love to a beautiful actress while her trophy husband fucks you from behind. Oh yeah. Steal my love you awesome bitch, take it from me. Drain me of all my emotions. Eat my fuck. Complete with full customisation workshops. Unveiling your life choices online, making increasingly ~~bad~~ good decisions and successfully decoding social signals, because high school lasts forever. I've fantasised about the liquid crystal display spectre of Ballard for months, Rhea smiles. I've lain in hot baths, staring at my naked body beneath the surface of the water, sunk underneath and dreamed of Ballard's face looming over me at an angle, his eyes staring into mine as he drowns me. Maybe he's rolled up his sleeves, maybe he's got his hands around my throat.

Much-underrated ability to imagine one's own death. Blunted ah-ha moments of terrified insight. A rubber hand waved in front of the participant. The stars and stripes of your ejaculation. Another tumbler of whisky and soda in his study. Out in the overgrown garden staring at the vast blue sky, patched into brain activity monitors, space shuttles exploding repeatedly in Rhea's mind on an endless catastrophic loop. Ballard doesn't pay any attention to the girl trespassing on his property and lying stoned on the front lawn like a cat. But he does sometimes wonder if she's still a virgin—impossible at seventeen surely—or how many boys—or girls—she's slept with. An accurate overhaul of existing icons on fire—a human roasting. The commodification of youth. What's so great about being young anyway Rhea shouts into space—not so much a question as a protest—but no-one's even listening anyway—the joys of solipsism—self-absorption is such a wonderful toy in the daydreamer's hands. Scrolling, swiping and tapping is second nature to me now. But does one really need to open and close air vents by touchscreen? I want to drive with you into the smouldering ruins of a war-torn multimedia city and stare remorsefully at the rubble and orphans and stuff.

Making passionate romantic love to James Graham Ballard inside an abandoned recycling centre because everyone just got bored of saving the environment. Or maybe it wasn't profitable. Right there on the litter-strewn concrete floor surrounded by rusting units and dead machines. A variety of autoerotic sex-and-death-wish postures. Choose between the comfortable standard suspension and the sporty set-up. Broadening the scope of our orgasmic potentials irrespective of engine size. Along for the ride, wherever his moods take him. M25, A40, Heathrow perimeter, motorway slip roads, rush-hour tailbacks. Performance-minded compromise designed for relaxed cruising. The taste of his seminal fluids and the sensation of my naked thighs and buttocks on the fabric of the seats. Brushed nylon or stretch upholstery vinyl on a cotton backing, available in either heavy or light grain. Or velour, woven with an upright pile. Natural look finish. Stained leatherette. A variety of interiors. The architecture of structural abuse. Two-cylinder deficit brings a more muted exhaust note. I imagine Ballard dissecting my lifeless cadaver, my flowered contusions still visible, at the top end. Roaring away from bombed-out plague villages. Middle-class guilt? Don't make me laugh. But there are pills for that, right?

19:35. Mr Ballard—I'm still not used to calling him Jim even though he told me to—is wearing a pale blue shirt with white pinstripes, a cream-coloured cashmere single-breasted blazer and slate grey trousers. His shirt is unfastened at the collar. He gets into his car, starts the engine and drives off. He's probably going to meet some artist or writer acquaintances. Maybe an exhibition is opening at a gallery in Hampstead or something. It's so unfair. My life is so boring, my friends are boring. Shepperton is boring. There is literally nothing to do here. I might as well be dead. My parents are downstairs watching television as usual. It's like being in a coma. Or maybe I am in a coma and this is all a dream. A lucid dream exactly like real life. If real life exists. Maybe Jim is meeting his girlfriend tonight. And they're going to a restaurant. In Hammersmith, or Fulham, or somewhere like that. Jim says there's a woman he wants me to meet who is a doctor. He says she's very intelligent, a lot of fun, and he thinks I would like her. Her name is Veronica or Vanessa or something. He meets her at Heathrow. Well, Jim has gone now. I don't think he will come back for a while. I told him that I spy on him most of the time. He asked me if that interfered with my studies. He was joking. I told him I was going to break into his house when he was out and he said 'in that case I'll leave one of the windows open to save you the hassle.' I wish I could go for after-dinner drinks in some bar. I'm going to speak to my parents about learning to drive. Optional rear air suspension and adaptive dampeners, smothering my half-hearted complaints with precise handling and dazzling steering which cuts me very little slack. My consciousness completely recalibrated through experimental sobriety. Wouldn't it be amazing to have a car? Jim lets me drive his car sometimes. He showed me how to do it. I still stall it sometimes though. We drove to the end of our street where there is like a park with trees and a river, near the motorway footbridge and the golf course. I saw a woman walking her dog and she smiled at me, exchanged a few words with Jim—she thought he was my dad. It was amazing. And funny.

—AS

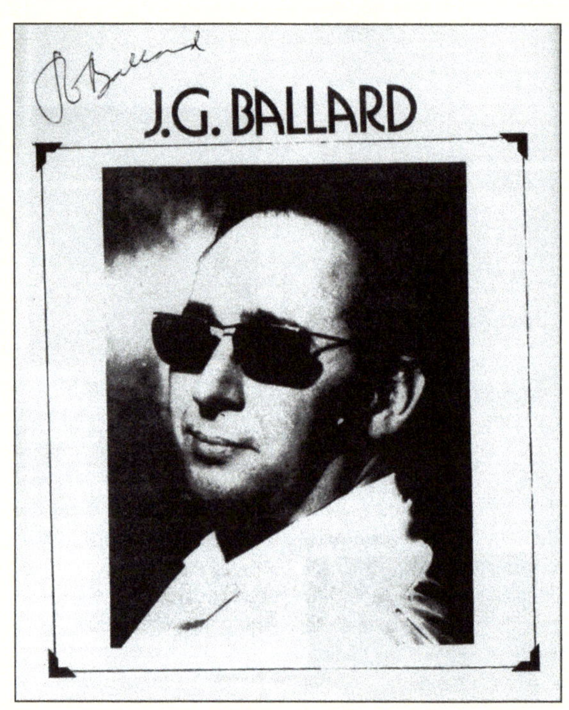

Recently Discovered JG Ballard Interview

from the

Illustrated London News

Saturday, 12 April 1969, p19-21

Now that space travel is becoming a reality, what will happen to science fiction? Can it continue as it has been or must it take on a completely new form? LEONIE GRAYEFF talked to two writers with quite different ideas.

The men who sell the future

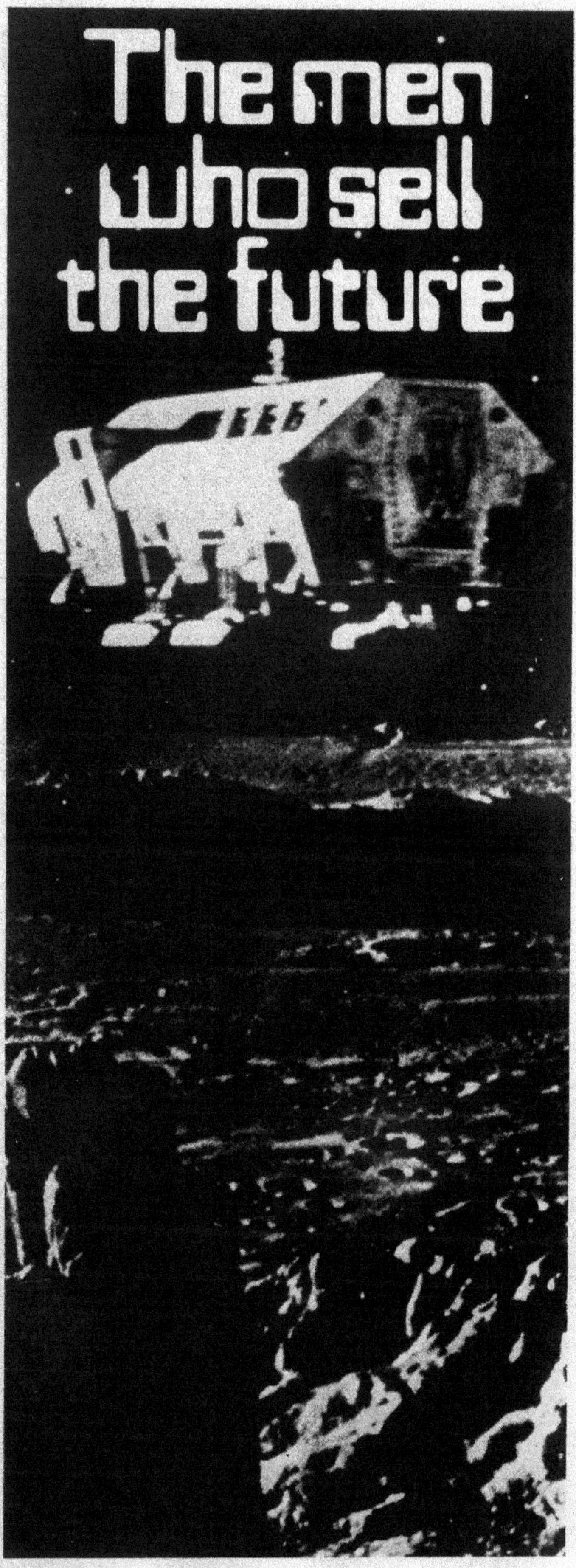

Whatever the science fiction writers may say, both the near and the remote future undoubtedly offer film makers unlimited scope for visual predictions. Currently Stanley Kubrick's film *2001: A Space Odyssey* is showing in London. Stills from the film, like this one where a lunar bus is flying above the moon's surface, are day by day revealing how accurate Stanley Kubrick's predictions were.

"Space fiction has plenty of scope"

ROBERT CONQUEST IS A CONVENTIONAL citizen who dresses in navy blue. He keeps a Bassett hound called Bluebell, and paces his study as he talks. The study overlooks Prince of Wales Drive, Battersea.

"Forster says of the novel that it tells a story basically. The early bad science fiction which was written in the 1920s by German professors was full of footnotes explaining how electricity worked. A fellow would be shown round some city of the future. He might look out of a window and be told: 'You see that moving way, it takes 500 million people at 200 mph.' There was no development in the story at all, except occasionally when the hero might meet a nice girl. But even if the facts had been interesting they ought to have been strung together somehow."

Robert Conquest has written one full-length science fiction novel, several poems and short stories, and together with Kingsley Amis has edited five volumes of *Spectrum*, an anthology of science fiction stories. Science fiction is not his only interest, and his problem is to find time to fit in all his commitments. Besides working for over ten years in the Foreign Office, he has lectured on politics and literature both in Britain and America.

His interest in science fiction began as a child, and he has now formulated views on what it should be like. He has no time for the surrealist school of "inner space" science fiction writers, who merely write about men's *psychological* reactions to a changed environment.

"Science fiction is fiction in which the context of human life is manipulated. An *x* factor is put in, but then the situation must be developed perfectly logically. There are two sorts of science fiction. One is about the near future. It is not exactly predictive, but it is within the limits of what we know is going to happen. The other may be set in the remote future, or on some totally different planet. That sort of book is a manipulation of much more fantastic material which has to be worked out equally logically."

Once a writer has an idea, its development very often has an intrinsic momentum. Robert Conquest is toying with the problems of human travel at the speed of light. The difficulties lie in the rate of acceleration and deceleration, which can only be achieved within a reasonable time span if the travellers are falling freely through an artificial gravity field. "Once one has an idea like that, one immediately has to develop a believable environment, not the machinery so much, but the sort of place where the man is operating and the technical society which is built round him. You can see how the plot would automatically start unfolding."

The number of space fiction themes appears to be fairly limited and even stereotyped, but that does not worry Robert Conquest. "Even a Western on Mars is of interest, if the Mars is well done." The future already has its own conventions. "It's a good thing that there are traditions about the future because it gives one a framework. For example, the currency of the future is often called the Credit."

But whatever the details are, it is the story that is of prime importance. It must move with pace, and characters should be subordinated to the action. "Aristotle says that character is a development of a story, and I think that is particularly true of science fiction. If an author is oversubtle about his hero, he can overconcentrate the reader's attention and lose something. The emphasis should be on the thing that is working as an alien environment. One can't apply the criteria of ordinary fiction to science fiction." There have to be reservations.

The writer of science fiction has to take care to write plain, clear prose. Conquest believes with Orwell that a story should be well told rather than well written if there has to be a choice. "One can't use experimentalist prose or imagery. There is a poem where the writer says the grass grows flaming red during a foxhunt, meaning simply that there is plenty of blood flowing. One can do that on earth where one knows damn well that the grass is green and that the writer is calling it red for some specific purpose. But if one says the grass is red in science fiction it can't be an image because it might be true of the planet one is writing about."

Robert Conquest is not worried that an increase in real space travel will put an end to space fiction: "There will always be a future. There will be rockets and planets, interplanetary and interstellar travel. But clearly a writer won't be able to do a story about what it feels like to land on the moon when people have landed on the moon because they will be able to say what it actually felt like. But we haven't got very far yet. After all the moon is only ¼ million miles away, and there are galaxies at a distance of about 300,000 light years. Space fiction has plenty of scope."

"Space fiction died ten years ago"

J. G. BALLARD WAS IN HIS MID-TWENTIES ten years ago. He has longish hair, an earnest manner, and smokes cigars. He lives with his three children in a dishevelled house in Shepperton, Surrey.

"I have just written a book called *The Atrocity Exhibition*. One of the chapters is about the suicide of Marilyn Monroe. It struck me her suicide was a kind of explosion in space and time. The body of Marilyn Monroe was part of the external landscape of our lives. It appeared on magazine covers, and in news-

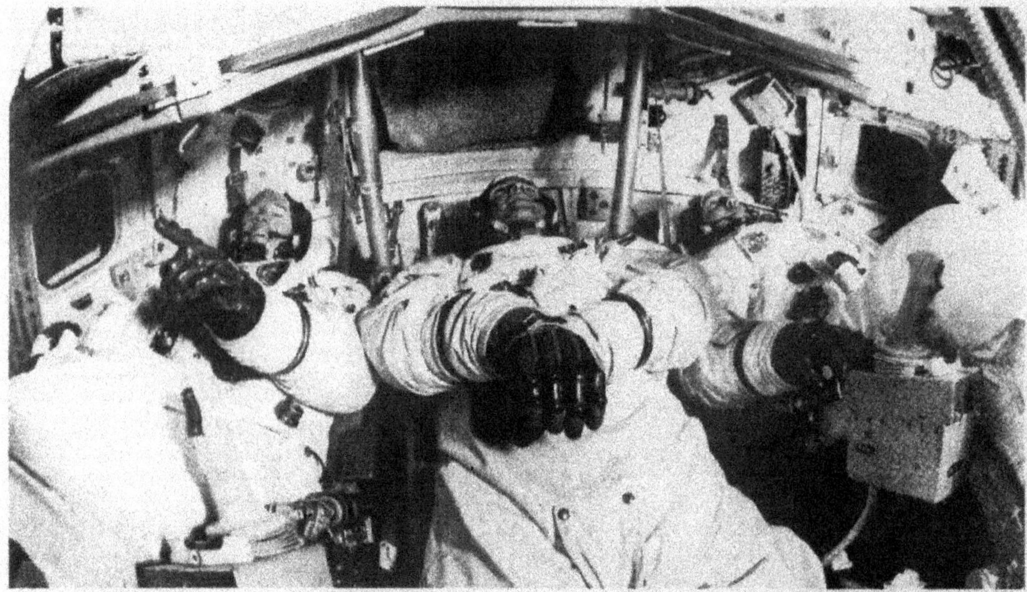

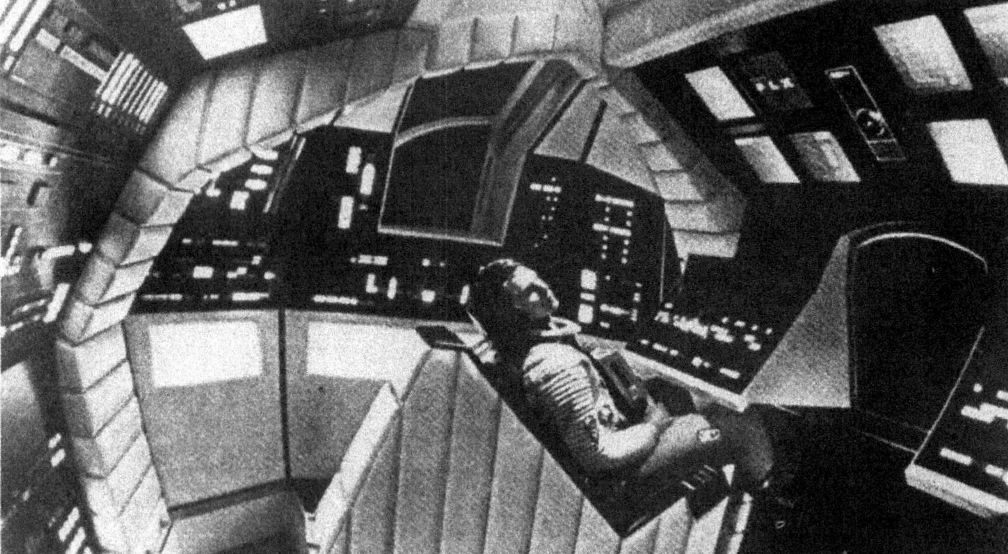

The travelling positions of these three United States astronauts (top) inside Apollo 9 look less comfortable than that of the traveller in the film (above).

Astronaut Russell L. Schweickart (below left) used hand rails when outside Apollo 9. His film counterpart (below) inspected the craft without holding on.

paper photographs. She was in films and on TV. Her body—not in a sexual way, but her appearance—had a real part in the psychological landscape of our lives. Her suicide dislocated that part of us. The chapter in my book tries to make sense of the suicide in those terms, as a disaster in space and time, rather than merely as the suicide of an unknown woman or a minor public figure."

Suicides and nightmares are James Graham Ballard's bread and butter. For ten years he has been a full-time science fiction writer. Previously he worked on a scientific journal and as script writer for scientific films. His three most important novels he considers *The Drowned World*, *The Disaster Area*, and *The Atrocity Exhibition*, which has Elizabeth Taylor, Jackie Kennedy, and John Kennedy among its leading characters—quite apart from Marilyn Monroe. The book should be published later this year.

President Kennedy's death was an "unconscious coronation", and equivalent to an enormous car crash. "The deaths of people like Jayne Mansfield, James Dean, and even Kennedy are a kind of liberation of their whole charisma and psychic energy."

His view of the car crash conflicts with that of the majority. He considers it an "enhancing event", and declares that although most people may deny it, they find in a car crash of a public figure a horrible fascination that liberates something in themselves. "If the crucifixion was to be re-enacted in the twentieth century it would be a car crash."

Horror and unreason do not seem to perturb James Ballard unduly. He writes from "nine to five" and lives in a world where the chairs in his study are losing their stuffing, but he is off to Rio de Janeiro by air for a week to attend a science fiction writers' symposium. He is amazed rather than disturbed by the tormented images of his brain: "I am constantly being surprised by the limitless possibilities of human experience. We are in the position of Aladdin. God knows what genii will spring from the lamps of our brains."

A surrealist poster of women turned into monsters hangs above the table, piled with toppling books and papers, that James Ballard uses as his desk. On another wall of his study there is a huge drawing of outsize, distorted lips in bright red that are fully two feet long. In an overfilled book case, beside, in front of, and on top of which are more books,

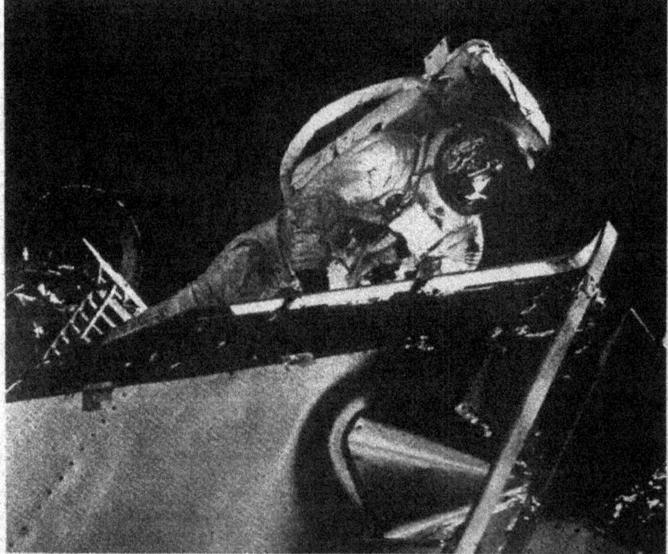

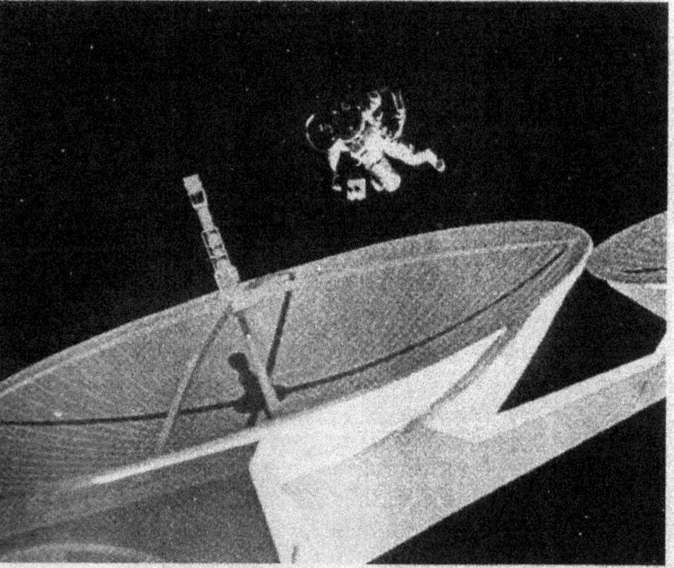

there are three huge volumes about Salvador Dali: *The Secret Life of Salvador Dali, The World of Salvador Dali,* and *Salvador Dali: Diary of a Genius.*

He draws his inspiration from the surrealists and men like Freud. " He made the distinction between our latent and our manifest minds. A house is not a house but a womb or whatever. I feel that this same distinction has to be applied to the outer world. Surrealism consists of a set of basic equations for explaining our lives that actually makes sense."

He does not accept the general distinctions between fact and fiction, maintaining that ours today is practically a fictional society. Advertisements shriek fictions non-stop. Politicians bombard people with false values, false policies, and false intentions, so what is reality?

" The role of the writer is no longer to provide fiction, but to identify some kind of reality. He merely analyses which of the fictions have any real significance." He certainly does not write conventional science fiction about Dan Dare-type spacemen, space pirates, space journeys, and the like. " Space fiction died ten years ago," to be replaced by what he calls " inner space " fiction, which records the psychological reactions of men to an extraordinary new set of conditions in our own twentieth century or in the more remote future. By exaggerating the conditions, perhaps by distorting them, he implicitly comments on society.

Because he is as much a product of the angry 50s as the surrealist 60s, Ballard brandishes a public conscience and is now working on a television play that will literally bring home to Englishmen the horrors of the Vietnam war by spelling out what would happen if Britain were in the Vietnam situation. The twentieth century is a " marriage between reason and nightmare. All a writer needs is a pair of scissors and a glue pot."

James Ballard who " always wanted to be a writer " chose to write science fiction rather than conventional novels: " The traditional novel is far too preoccupied with the past: it contains a nineteenth century approach to life. The twentieth century is a century of possibility, with science and technology as the tools of that possibility. Science fiction is the only fiction which portrays the supreme importance of science and technology, and it forms a mid-point between reason (science) and unreason (the world of our minds). The future is a better key to the present than the past is."

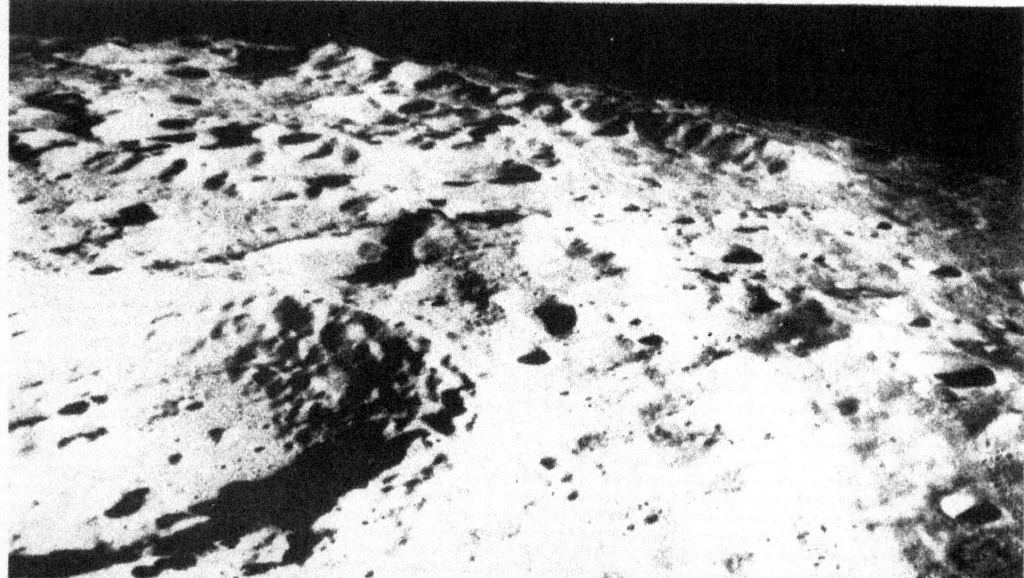

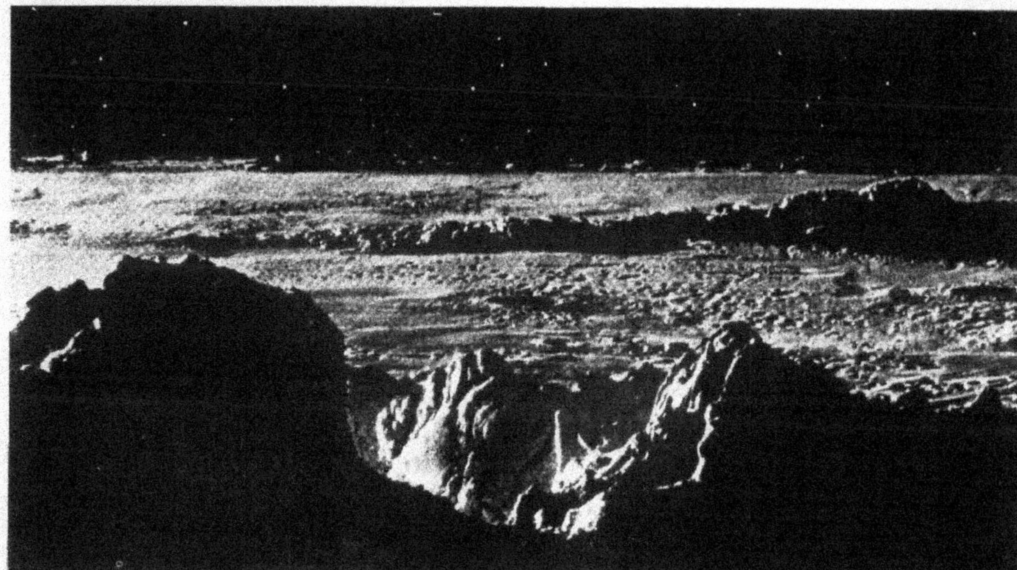

Apollo 8 Commander Borman described the moon's surface (top) as a " vast, lonely, forbidding expanse ". Kubrick's vision (above) does not contradict the reality.

The docking mechanism of the Apollo 9 command craft was photographed from its lunar module (below left). Docking (below) of the film's space craft.

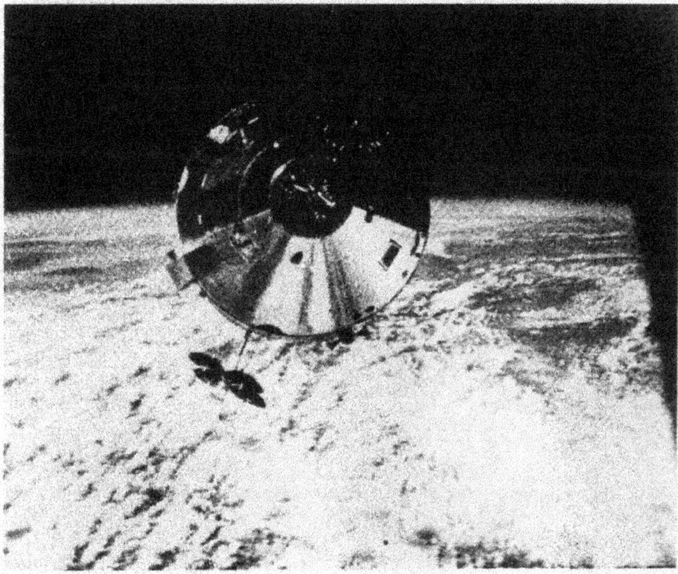

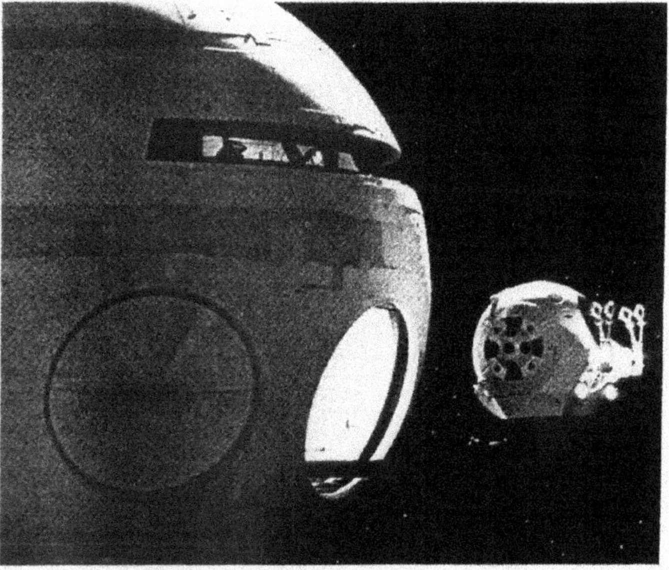

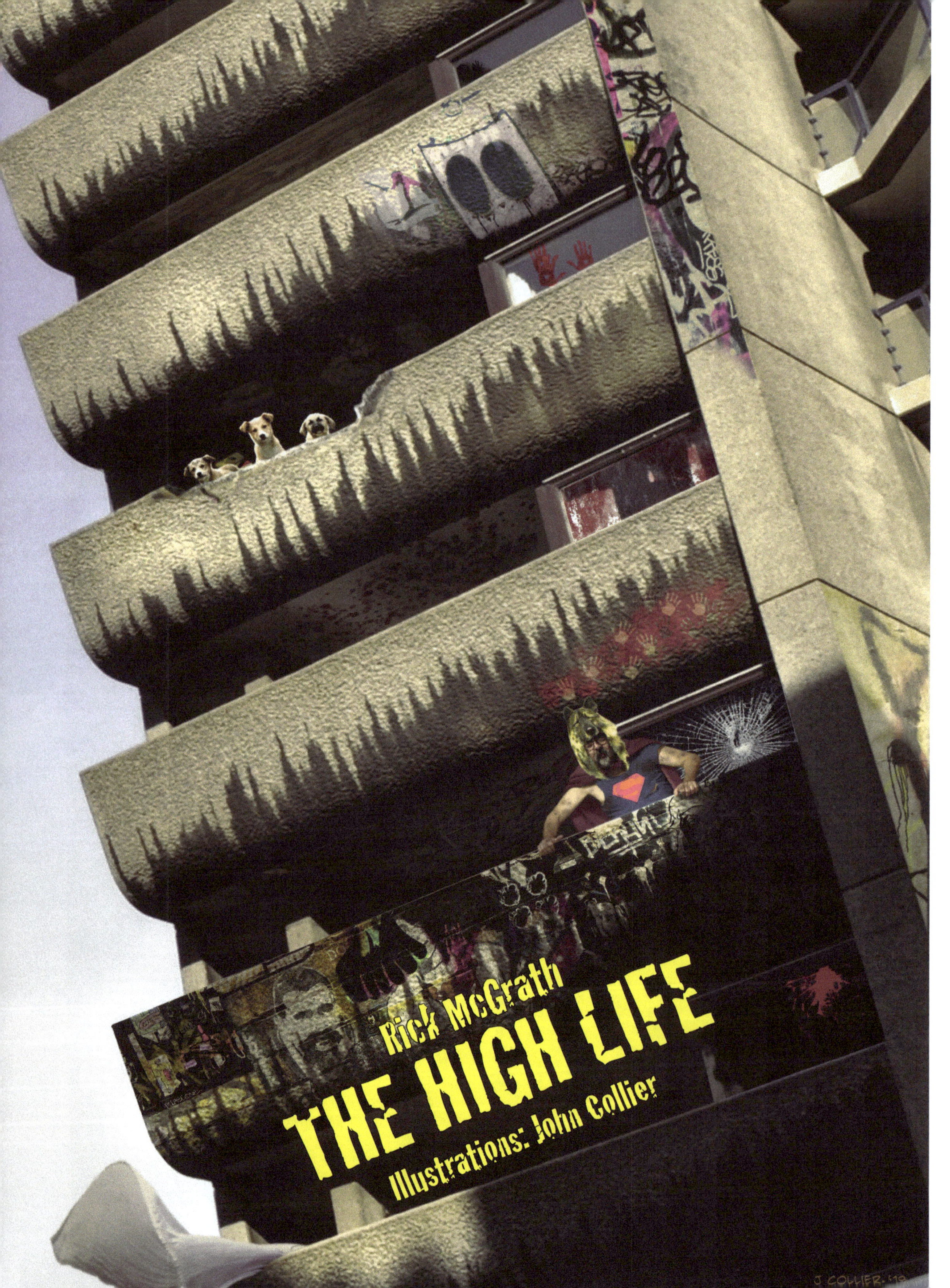
Rick McGrath
THE HIGH LIFE
Illustrations: John Collier
J COLLIER '13

Later, as he sat on the balcony poking the dying embers in the rough fire pit, Dr Robert Maitland reflected on the unusual events that must have taken place within this huge apartment building over the past year. Impressed by the building's size, with its forty floors and thousand apartments, swimming pools and supermarkets—all now but abandoned to the sky—he was also surprised of not being aware of its existence until two days ago.

Formerly an experimental architect in a London design group—before he was injured in a serious car crash—Maitland used his lengthy time in recuperation to study Social Psychology, earning his PhD and making his name three years later with a seminal study of urban unrest in London's Chelsea district, where residents suddenly transformed their upscale neighbourhood into a scene of group self-mutilation, disguised as dereliction. The media was fascinated. Once a Chelsea resident himself, Maitland famously described the event in his breakthrough Guardian series as "spontaneous localized characterization"—a violent, yet innately positive reaction to high levels of cultural homogenization within a confined geographic area.

Maitland followed this success with a regular output of well-publicized popular psychology pieces, and after a year researching and writing about Japanese internment camps in Tsing Tao and Shanghai he was back and relaxing in a London pub, comfortably chatting about his recent discovery near Heathrow with his old friend Richard Pearson, once an advertising executive his firm had hired to promote a suburban shopping mall, and now the sales manager for a major pharmaceutical company.

"No, no no, Richard, really, for no apparent reason. That's the interesting part—well, the part I have to figure out." Maitland wove his wine glass in a small figure eight in front of him. "I was there for a week. The population thought they were living in a tropical paradise, some thought they could fly, and a few found it impossible to leave. Damnedest thing."

Richard laughed in disbelief. "They thought Shepperton was transformed? Into a jungle? Brilliant! Christ, I could have used that idea at the Metro-Centre. Are there bears in the jungle? But Shepperton. I've been there, Robby—movie studios are big clients for our products. Sure, some places are crazy. That big loop in the river—betcha that's it. Perfect subject for a whatever-it-is spacey shrink like you."

Maitland smiled.

"Spatial, Richard, spatial psychologist. Ever wonder why open plan offices are managed by psychopaths?"

"You're making that up. I run an open off—ahh, you bastard."

Maitland smiled again.

"Still, Richard, Shepperton doesn't fit the model. Too much diversity. This could be a whole new area of study for me. Maybe. Sadly, the mania subsided and no one seems to remember, save some crazy pilot they fished out of the river."

It was Pearson's turn to smile.

"A wash out, you say? Enthusiasm dampened? I've got a tip for you, then, Roberto. What would you think about a large group of well-off people living in a self-wrecked building? Living there and liking it? This high-rise I know went from new and sold out to broken and abandoned in just over a year. Nobody bitched. Money just blown. Sorta creepy and cool in that psycho way you like."

Maitland was indeed interested. A vertical Chelsea? "Where?"

"Eastside, down by the river. Where it makes that big jog before the airport."

"And people still live there?"

"Apparently. Dunno. Maybe. There are stories. I don't cover that area anymore. Thankfully. Hey, you like a coincidence. Here's one. Didn't you write a paper a few years ago on that arsehole architect, Anthony Royal?"

Maitland rolled his eyes. Yes, he had. *Royal Revealed: Lipstick on the PoMo Pig.* The brutalists had loved it.

"Well, get this. Anthony Royal designed these high-rises."

Maitland's eyes flickered sharply under his dark brows, John Drake-style. "You know Anthony Royal?"

"Yeah, I know him. Don't look so amazed, Robert. Or should I say Herr Dockor Maitland?" He made a sardonic gesture. "We played at the same tennis club before Tony hit the..." Richard lowered his voice, "...ahh, terminal beach. But that's not the story."

"Royal lost his head?"

"Where ya been, Robby? His obit ran months ago. Oh, yes. China. No London papers? All right, there's more." Richard looked around as if people might be eavesdropping. "It was just over a year ago I bought an apartment in this new high-rise—on Tony's advice—as an investment, mind you—and I rented it to some TV producer and his family. He was a big, boisterous bastard but his wife seemed competent. Children. No matter. His rent cheque cashed the first month, but not the next."

Richard took a slow drink to emphasize the gravity of this omission.

"I phone. No answer. Leave messages. No answer. So, Christ, I drive over to see what's the problem and am stunned by the condition of the building. My place is still fine, but hell, it's only been open a few months and it's already breaking down. My tenant is nowhere to be found. I'm pissed off. So are most of the people yammering at the superintendent. The fast elevators are still working so I head up to Tony's penthouse to confront the great man. We're in his glass studio. I'm ranting. He's looking ragged—there's all these white birds screaming overhead—and he appears to have no answers for what's happening on the floors below him. I finally mention my lawyer, and—hard to believe—right away he goes over to his desk and writes me a cheque for more than what I paid. Take it, he says, this place is a zoo. I look at his big, white Alsatian. Being a practical man, I took the money, signed some papers, and got the hell out. I wanted a long-term investment. Fast payoff! A year ago—looks deserted now—no doubt any inhabitants are squatters."

"Fascinating. But I don't believe in coincidences." Maitland finished his wine, caught the barman's eye. Maitland knew Pearson, like all salesmen, tended to exaggerate. "Are you sure the whole place reacted? The lower floors usually instigate the brunt of change first. I'm not interested in slums."

"How about this, then?" Richard adopted his face of adman sincerity. "When I was repping the new medical school at the complex I dealt with one of the doctors who lived in the high-rise. Neurologist, if I remember. Maybe not. What was his name? Langley? No. Laing—that was it. He taught and ran the dispensary. Ordered all the drugs. Got to know him a bit—lived around the middle of the high-rise—floor 24 or 25. He was a tad odd."

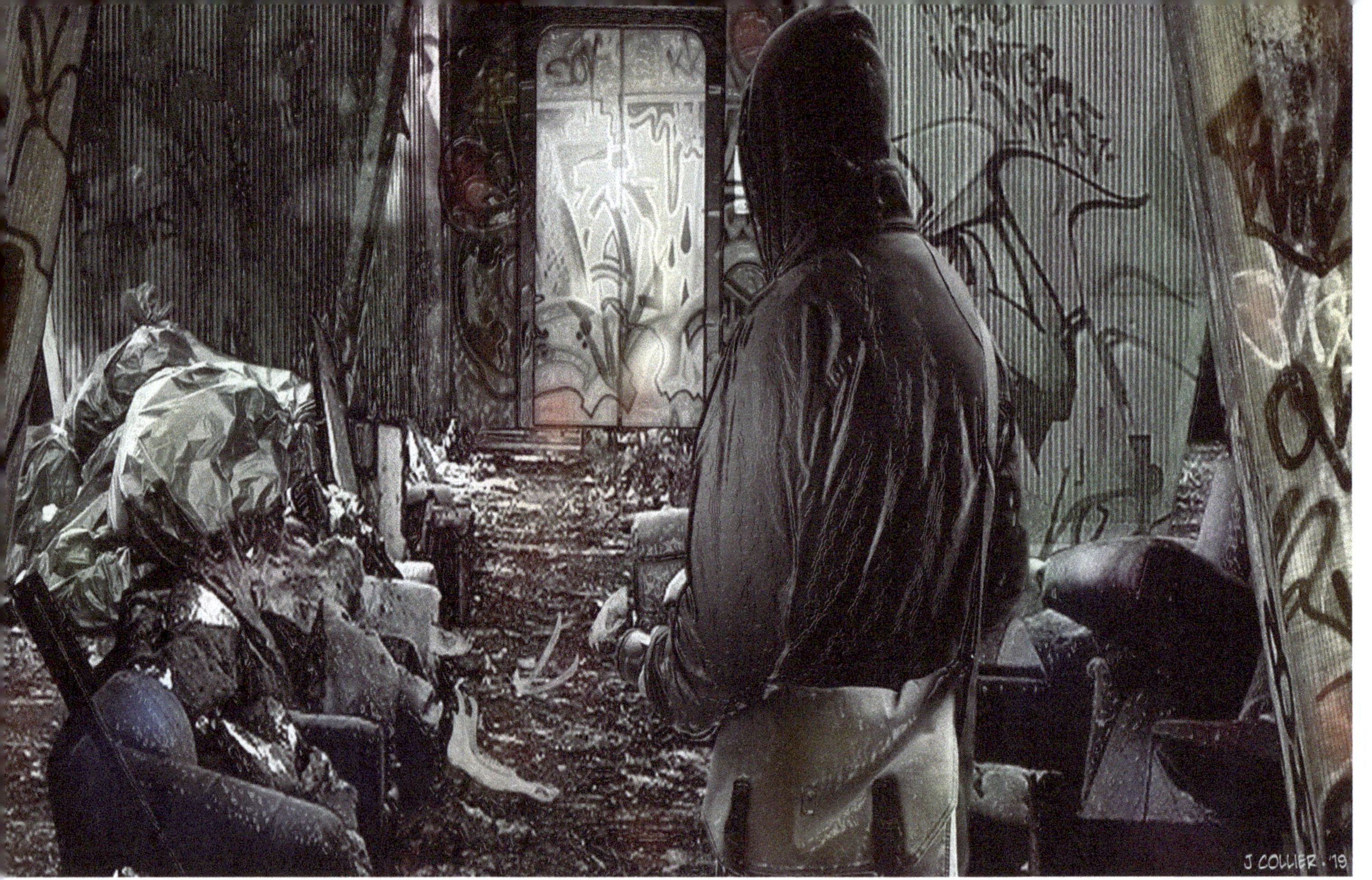

There's war in hell, Maitland thought, as he carefully picked a route through the flotsam that almost completely covered the floor.

"Anything odd about that?"

"Guess not—hah... why would you become a doctor to teach? But I started to wonder after dealing with him—they used a helluva lot of drugs. Heavy stuff. Morphine, mostly. Hey, maybe they had a cancer clinic out back. And when I called for an appointment he was rarely there—when we did meet he looked increasingly shabby, distracted, and, somewhat sadly, a tad ripe. I had to wonder."

"Did he complain?"

Richard snorted in his martini. "Just the opposite. He looked like hell—beardy and thin—but seemed quite content. That sorta dreamy thing, the long stare. His personality changed, too—from a sort of mousey voyeur type to something more self-confident—like a lonely adult becoming a popular teen. Again, I wondered."

"Did he talk about the building?"

"Rarely. He once called his home 'the cave on the cliff', but really, he basically talked business and seemed quite anxious to return to the high-rise after our meetings."

The following afternoon Maitland drove down to the Thames and made his way east through an interzone of abandoned warehouses, communication towers, and auto wrecking yards. He stopped beside a photographer, asked for directions and soon found himself atop the centre of a huge concrete dome in a larger, empty circular cement pool. The effect was strangely calming. Ahead towered a gigantic high-rise, struggling to maintain its 40 sinking stories in a sea of rusting, smashed cars and a shoreline of indeterminate garbage, a dune of forgotten yesterdays in sun-faded plastic bags. Behind him the second high-rise was dark but not apparently deserted, and seemed to be covered in camouflage, until it became clear the discoloured streaks were the result of smoke from a series of balcony fires. Some clothing fluttered in open windows. Between these two were three half-completed towers, forming a rough semi-circle. He turned back to the primary target.

The entrance to the high-rise consisted of a path through a maze of wrecked furniture, faded and warped in the sun and rain. The big front doors were chained at the handles, but an adjacent window had been smashed and Maitland stepped into what appeared to be the main hall of an atrocity exhibition. There's war in hell, Maitland thought as he carefully picked a route through the flotsam that almost completely covered the floor. He surveyed the carnage. The elevators were defaced with graffiti, bones littered the floor, and blood flecked in arcs over walls already defaced with crudely painted instructions and unintelligible threats.

Moving towards the emergency stairs, Maitland checked the elevators—none of the doors would open and a vaguely sweet putrid smell increased with proximity. Sludge was seeping under the deeply scratched and dented stainless steel doors. He tested the fire escape doors—they opened, and he made it up one floor before being stopped by a massive structure of intertwined furniture, smashed TVs, twisted bathroom fixtures and what looked like a car's rear bumper. He tried a few pulls and was about to try and dismantle the beaver-like dam when he heard what might have been a low growl from above. He retreated to the lobby.

What to do next, he wondered. The blocked stairwell. The distinct possibility of wildlife. The obvious signs of violence. This was better than he expected. Figuring this could be more complicated than simply exploring another abandoned building, Maitland decided to return home to his Spitalsfield flat and prepare for a proper exploration of the high-rise the next day. As he pulled away from the building his eye caught a sudden motion in the rear view mirror. Something on a balcony around the 10th floor. A figure in blue, wrapped in a red blanket?

Back on the road, Maitland drove north and was soon back in familiar territory. An idea occurred. He knew the manager of the local HM Land Registry, and decided to stop in for a quick meeting. Once home he cleared a table, opened the just-obtained tube of blueprints, and began to study Anthony Royal's original plans for the high-rise project. He had analyzed Royal's other buildings in the past and—if the architect was true to form—somewhere in the overall design there would be an unidentified passageway Royal could use for covert access and egress. Tony liked his privacy. And there it was. A small rectangle built in the angle between two walls of the public and service elevator shafts. He smiled. Happy ending.

When Maitland arrived on site early the next morning the warm June sun was butter yellow above the horizon and the three unfinished high-rises were backlit like the black stumps of a dog's broken teeth. This time he was prepared—along with ample food and water he packed a heavy torch, wire cutters, narcotic-laced dog biscuits, some rope, and his favourite toy, a set of lock picks. Again, he carefully made his way through the lobby debris and then stopped short. Today a strange apparition dressed in a black cassock sat slouched in a broken chair in front of the fire stairs. A resident? When he got closer Maitland realized a dog's head had been crudely attached to a mannequin's shoulders. So, Anubis guards the stairs—fine. Not going in that direction, anyway. He turned left and made his way through the administrator's office to the back of the elevator shafts.

He explored a conundrum of service corridors and empty storage areas before he found a battered steel door, inset in the concrete behind a stack of smashed TVs. He knew the lock, and the door was soon opened to reveal a narrow set of circular steps twisting skyward beside a small, two-person elevator. He looked up. There was a hint of light at the top of the shaft. He gingerly stepped inside the elevator and was somewhat shocked to note the floor indicator light was illuminating "G". Was the power still on after all this time? He tentatively pressed 10 and was rewarded when the door closed and the elevator slid quietly upwards. He felt a twinge of youthful excitement.

At the 10th floor Maitland exited the elevator, carefully opened the service door and stepped into one of the high-rise's machine rooms, now a kind of demented pasta palace, with various pipes bent and ripped from walls and ceiling in great arcs, some of them decorated with lengths of different coloured electrical cord. A dentist's chair sat in one corner. This room led to more hallways and then into the Concourse area, spread out end to end in the high-rise like a high street shopping mall. After a brief inspection of the ruined supermarket and liquor store, Maitland noticed with amusement that the beauty salon was still intact. The bank, with its barred-off area behind the teller's wickets, had at one time been converted into a kennel, with dog and cat travel cases stacked upon each other in the spacious safety deposit vault.

He poked his head into the recreation area. The stale air was faintly perfumed with chlorine, and a confusion of bones, shopping carts and wine bottles traced a strange pattern at the bottom of the drained swimming pool. The elevator doors on this floor opened, but his torchlight revealed their use as a garbage disposal. A lightweight chain sealed the fire steps, and he quickly cut through it to reveal a clear passage up. By the time he got to the 20th floor he heard a faint, far-off, high-pitched howling—dogs on the hunt. Pausing briefly, Maitland threw a couple handfuls of his doctored biscuits on the steps a few floors below him. At the entrance to the 25th floor he met a major roadblock of stacked furniture.

By luck he pulled on a chair leg—which proved to be the master lever that opened a hole just big enough for him to squeeze through. The dogs went quiet behind him. Past the barrier, he surveyed the lobby—now an art gallery of greasy polaroids taped and pinned to the walls. He got out his torch and took a closer look. Most were jarred, motion blurred photos of people fighting, bloody faces, and drunken cheering, but many were of macabre scenes of dead people dressed in often surreal costumes with ornate face make-up, posed in various sexual positions. He turned away and splayed his light around. Desiccated bags of garbage lined the walls. He noticed a slight draught playing on his face from the aisle to the right of the elevator. Rounding the corner he heard a faint flapping sound, like a small bird struggling in the jaws of a bored cat. He crept along to an open door and looked inside. The apartment stretched just 20 feet from the dull carpet under his shoes to the shining air outside. Straight ahead on the sitting room floor a notebook's pages chittered in the breeze from the open balcony. He picked it up, took a quick glance, pocketed the book and instinctively closed the large sliding glass door.

Maitland turned and quickly assessed the apartment. It was spaceship small. He spent a few minutes looking through the bedroom, noticing there was a hole in the floor where a plank had been removed, and in the tiny kitchen he was somehow not that surprised to discover a bag of old letters, all addressed to the rather enigmatic Dr Laing. Richard was correct about the location. The morphine. Was any still here? He returned to the living room to ponder his next move and while staring out the window he was startled by a loud sniffing sound from the hallway. He turned to see a smallish man dressed in a torn and stained Superman costume, with the furry remains of an Alsatian's head for a hat.

Letting out a low growl, Superman revealed a dentist's drill in his right hand and simultaneously lunged towards Maitland, who stood frozen on the spot and then casually kicked a small, three-legged side table into Superman's charge. The rim caught the caped crusader on the shin, throwing him forward, arms flailing for balance as he as he made a final attempt at recovery before falling nose first into the balcony's glass door and bouncing backwards, dazed, to the grimy floor. Blood seeped over his cheeks and into the headpiece. Maitland gave him a tentative kick to the ribs and stepped over the body, out of the apartment, down the hallway and into the service area where he could find Royal's elevator door. He had his lock picks out but the door swung open. Did Superman know? Inside he found a board just the right size to jam between the door and the wall. Just as good as a lock. He waited for the elevator to rise from the 10th floor, got in and hit a button. At the 35th floor he stopped and made his way to the main elevator lobby to find another empty swimming pool and the remains of a restaurant. He checked the stairwell going down—the landing was stacked with tables and chairs from the restaurant, and broken household furniture choked the steps down a whole floor. Apparently no one from the lower levels was going to be invited higher for dinner and a dip. Conversely, the steps up to the roof were clear.

Maitland checked his watch. It was nigh on noon and he sat down in the restaurant to review his immediate situation. Apparently the high-rise was still occupied, if only by an inept madman in a kid's costume. And a few dogs, perhaps kept. And an unexplored building, already revealing itself to be generally divided into territorial areas. Classic tribalism, he realized. Tree forts. That thought took him back to his youth, when rather than play and fight with other kids, he preferred creeping through abandoned houses and derelict buildings. His explorations would keep him amused for hours, searching for the often-surreal remains and bits of prior occupants, prior lives.

This building was forty floors of much more intriguing possibilities.

A faint creak in the hallway outside snapped Maitland from his reverie. Time to reach the top. Ten minutes later the elevator's rooftop door appeared and he carefully opened it, blinking in the harsh sunlight. An unexpected flurry of large white birds briefly startled him as he rounded the elevator head and walked onto the terrace. Did he also see a figure in white out of the corner of his eye? He paused. Stretching out on the roof in front of him was a large, white-tiled rectangle. Randomly placed on this grid was a collection of large, geometrically shaped objects mounted on pedestals. Off to the right were dozens of large plant pots, many with greenery, and to the left was a glass-walled room that overlooked the area. Maitland stepped forward, belatedly recognizing the geometric forms as sculptures, and wondered about the flowing discolourations that stained the spheres, pyramids, cubes and the white tiles underfoot—like a demented Jackson Pollock had run amok with gallons of dark red paint. In the centre of the sculpture garden he noticed a large black burnt area, and on either side of it sat a strange apparition which seemed to resemble parts of a callisthenics machine, but was obviously reconfigured to be used as support for a roasting spit.

Maitland looked into the glassy room—obviously Royal's office. Desk, table, sofa, chairs, filing cabinets—all undamaged. A second glass door beside the office revealed steps descending to the main apartment. He crept down. All was silent. Then he noticed—the walls were clean, the carpets unstained, curtains hung peacefully around the high windows in the slightly musty living room. On the shining dining room table stood two silver candlesticks. He found the apartment's foyer and entered the 40th floor elevator lobby. It had no barricades, no garbage bags, and the lobby furniture was present and still intact. The walls had also been cleaned, although some faded graffiti still stubbornly remained. He opened the door to the fire stairs and they appeared to stretch cleanly down a number of floors.

Returning to Royal's penthouse, Maitland began a systematic search of the rambling apartment, which stretched half the length and the full width of the high-rise. In the library he found an unopened bottle of Italian wine—something red and strong from the Del Baldo estate, hidden behind a few books by JG Ballard—and off the master bedroom he discovered someone had converted the walk-in closet into a tiny sleeper, complete with single bed, side table, and a small light attached to a car battery. It still worked. By the time he had checked out all of Royal's home and explored the top three floors the late afternoon sun was beginning to smear the towers of London into an orange haze, and giving in to some unknown impulse he decided to spend the night in the high-rise.

The tiny closet bedroom was too claustrophobic for Maitland, so he lugged the lamp and battery up to Royal's rooftop aerie. A few large white gulls circled above, finally landing on the roof's outer wall and rubbing their beaks in red-stained concrete crevices. Not trusting the lamp's battery he went downstairs, retrieved the two dining room candlesticks and pulled down two curtains to use as blankets should the night chill. Back on the roof, he laid out the contents of his backpack on a draughting table and surveyed Royal's late estate. The lazy twilight beckoned, and Maitland grabbed a chair and the wine and wandered out into the sculpture garden. The golden air lightened the dull red patina on the various works, one of which caught his eye: three cement ovoids, stacked vertically, each slightly smaller than the one beneath it. Damn modern art, he thought, munching the sandwiches he should have had for lunch, but even now he wasn't feeling that hungry. He took a swig from the wine bottle and for some reason again felt like a teenager out on an adventure. Could someone actually live here? He eyed the big birds appraisingly.

It was becoming cooler in the twilight and he tugged his jacket closer. There was something in the right pocket. He retrieved the notebook he had found in Laing's apartment on the 25th floor. It was about the size of a thin paperback novel, quite beat up, and had wine spilled on most of the back cover. Or was that blood? He opened it. The first page was inscribed at the top with a neat LAING, with 2525 underneath. A quick flip of the few pages revealed it was some sort of diary, to-do reminders, recipes, and lists of names, many with a line drawn through them. He thumbed back to the beginning:

> Night. Girls asleep. Building still quiet. Sitting on the balcony pecking at the dog when all the lights went off on the 7th floor of our sister high-rise. Could hear some of the shouts from here. Tomorrow need to set more traps.
>
> At one time all the dogs were on the top floors, and the children mostly below the 10th. Now it's reversed. None of the telephones work.
>
> Not sure of the date. Does it matter? Steele becoming more dangerous at night, altho being right beside him may be safest as he seems to be ranging wider,

and he has a dog. Bait or food? Alice is becoming weaker. Eleanor is still demanding batteries. Time to increase the doses of M?

Maitland paused for a drink. Darkness was deepening so he decided to move indoors. One curtain became a pillow, the other a sheet, and with the light on and candles lit he snuggled down on the sofa with the wine and Laing's notes. For a few pages there were just lists of names, as if Laing was keeping track of what must have been a dwindling population. The next few pages were covered with what looked like a scratchy floor plan of the 25th floor, with various distances marked along rooms and hallways. Maitland laughed as he read on...

Found it today! Was looking around the service elevator area and finally discovered where my anomaly was hidden—behind a stack of mattresses, a small steel door. It wasn't locked. Inside a stairway and a vertical shaft. It was easy to walk down to the basement, and there it was: a mini-elevator. Room for two. Best: the elevator's electric system was separate from the building and throwing a switch started it up. Royal was clever—big rubber wheels and the engine in the basement means the cage runs silently. Now we can escape from Steele, who has run out of bodies to dress up and has replaced his dead models with mannequins from the 10th floor's fashion shops. He's also found a storage of costumes from somewhere, which he either wears on his night raids or drapes over mannequins. Lately he's been Superman, or as he claims, "The Man of Steele". He may also be training dogs on the lower floors. The protection he claims to be giving us is costing too much M.

Christ, they're all strung out, Maitland thought, then slightly chuckled as he finished off the Del Baldo. So Steele was his inept assailant, and Laing had figured it out and gained if not the territorial advantage, then certainly freedom of movement. His sense of control must have increased—but where was Laing now? Outside, the gulls had vanished with the night and on the horizon the lights of London glowed like an ersatz sunset through the dusty windows. He returned to Laing's notes.

Steele abandoned his home and moved to Wilder's on the second floor. He's claimed all the floors to the 10th and has chained the stairway higher. Aside from Steele's barricade on the first and 10th, the inferior block on the 25th and the huge wall at the 35th, many of the defensive structures have been taken apart.

Maitland didn't recognize the names, but realized the barricades were still as described. The list of Laing's various observations went on and Maitland sleepily paused from the notebook. It was dark out. His silhouette threw dune-like shadows on the walls of glass, and he was just about to turn off the lights and fade to sleep when he felt a slim hand at his throat and the oblique flash of a long carving knife.

"Shhhhsh..."

Maitland raised his hands slightly. The notebook dropped.

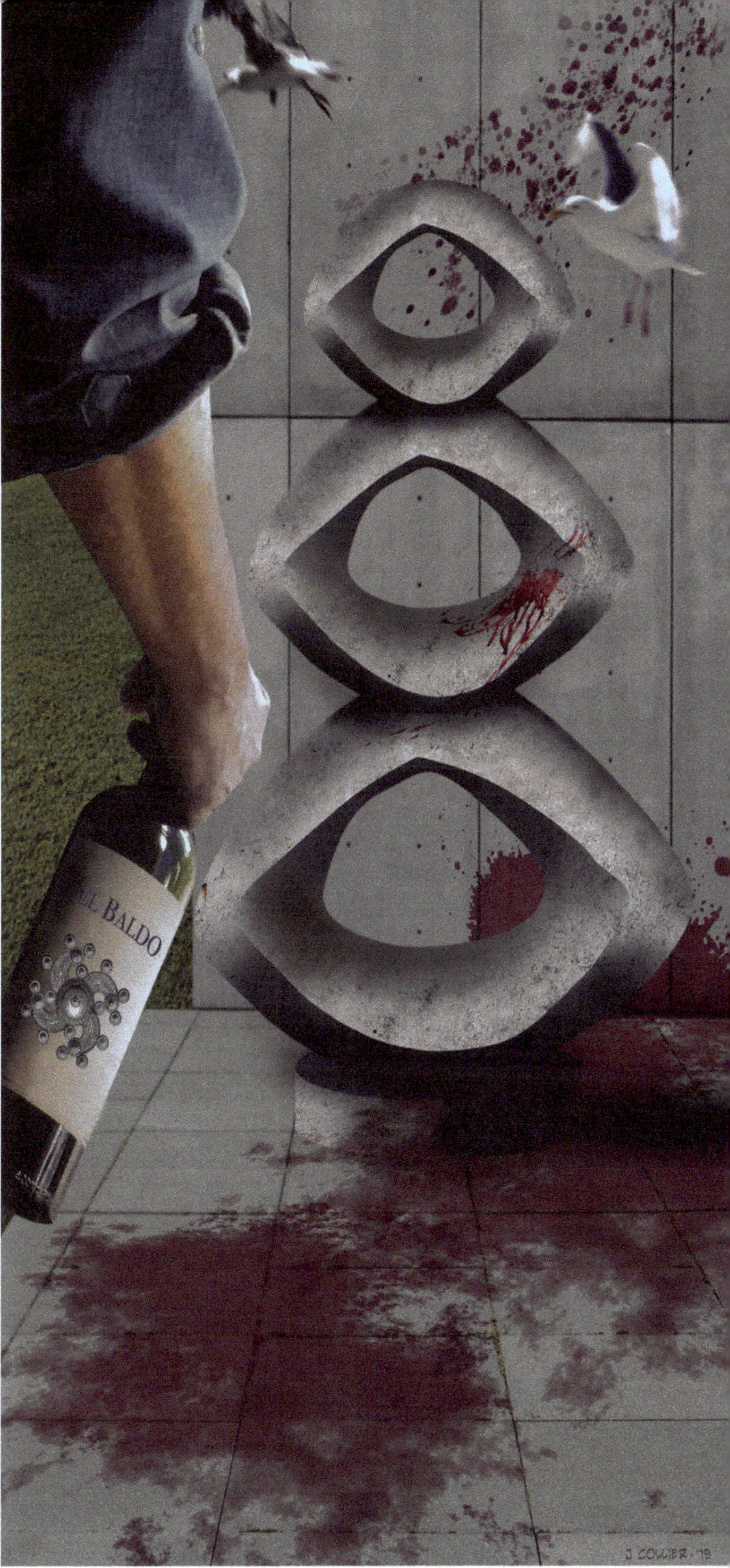

The golden air lightened the dull red patina on
the various works,
one of which caught his eye:
three cement ovoids, stacked vertically,
each slightly smaller than
the one beneath it.
Damn modern art, he thought...

He whispered, "It's OK... I'm a kind of architect. Just here for the night. If that's OK."

A woman in white cut into his vision. A face that had recently seen a mirror. Dirty blonde hair twisting over her shoulders. She appeared to be wearing something fashionable—a short skirt and finely finished silk blouse. Her breasts moved heavily under the thin cloth as she warily circled the sofa.

"Who are you? Why are you here?"

"My name is Maitland. Robert Maitland. I'm a spatial psychologist and I'm interested in this building... OK, I'm a kind of shrink at a university. You can call me Bob. And you?"

"Anne. Anne Royal."

Maitland was surprised. "Tony's wife?"

"Ex-wife."

"Sorry."

"Unmissed. But he was the Royal Lord of this manor, and now I'm the Lady."

Maitland lowered his hands and bowed his head. "Enchanted, m'lady."

Anne smiled slightly and sat behind Royal's desk. The knife disappeared. Two long legs appeared on the desktop. Maitland flashed Anne his warmest smile.

"I'm sure we'll be the best of friends. Do you have any here? Are you alone in the castle tower?" He pulled back the curtain sheet and sat up on the sofa.

Anne looked out on the roof, now washed white in the moonlight. There was a faraway look in her dark eyes. "We had a sort of women's organization that lasted about nine months. Mums and kids, living and working together. Protecting each other. The eventual shortage of men—food—finally became a problem—yes, I know about Tony's elevator—but there were too many of us and our original ideals began to fade—or evolve. Within two months I was the only sister left—on the roof. The high-rise still contains quite a few people—there are secret and not-so-secret passages cut through floors and walls everywhere. But nobody above the 35th floor—this is mine."

"How do you survive?"

"You've already met my protection—Steele. He pretty well scares the shit out of anyone who wants to explore the high-rise or get past the big blockade at the 25th floor. How did you get past the dogs and wall? No matter. I keep him as the old school crazy, a reminder of our tribal time when it went instinctual. Bears grudges. Is jealous of me. One of these days he... won't be necessary. Food? Protein is pretty easy to find. And cook. I'm growing veg in those pots on the roof, but water is bloody hard work to get up here, even with the lift. If I could only hook up a water pump—and I'm sure Tony had set up an alternate power source for the penthouse, but I can't find it—I'd have a little farm up here. This urban hunter-gatherer shit is OK for a while, but I'm willing to compromise."

Maitland wasn't so sure. He decided to change topics. "I'm also curious about one of the tenants here. A Dr Laing. Do you know him?"

Anne laughed. "We all know the Doctor, Robert—Bob. Hah—you both have the same first name. He was basically invisible and acquiescent during the, ahh... transformation, but then he emerged as a kind of cranky, bossy shopkeeper. Laing ran the drugstore. Traded drugs—and morphine—for everything, but inevitably he ran out. Things got unfortunate then."

"Upset addicts?"

"Maybe, but it hit closer to home. Laing was quite pleased with his 'harem'—two fucked up women he controlled with drugs—who earned their keep by complaining. Don't ask. One of them, Eleanor, went missing, and soon after Laing's sister Alice died, possibly from withdrawal. Or an overdose. Laing hid her body."

"He did what?"

"Stashed it away somewhere—away from our psycho, Steele. He likes to take bodies and dress them up."

"I think I've already seen one. Anubis in the lobby."

"That's him, all right. Anyway, Laing didn't go long without a companion. A few weeks later sister Helen Wilder—who left us—showed up at Laing's door with two kids and a broken cine camera. She wanted out and finally convinced him to clean up, put on a suit and go back to the medical school. Last I heard Laing was back at his old job—they thought he's been on sabbatical in Africa, working on a water project in the desert. Hah. Maybe he was."

Anne suddenly froze. "Shhhh..."

Then Maitland heard it—the faint howl of a beagle echoing up the building. Distant, but still too close. Could Superman really fly? He looked at Anne. She didn't look happy, and motioned to Maitland to collect his stuff. He doused the light and candles, recovered his knapsack and both of them retreated to the wall behind the sculpture garden—he a dark shadow, she a shimmering flow of moonlight. They paused to wait. He liked the way she pressed up beside him. Presently the darting beam of a torch bounced up the white walls of the stairs and Steele, still in his Superman costume, slowly opened the door to the roof. Four dogs rushed past his legs and began excitedly sniffing the ground. They pawed at the studio door. Steele let them in and they rushed the just-vacated sofa. Not waiting for the dogs to catch their scent Maitland and Anne backed away and gained the safety of the waiting elevator. For some reason she stopped at the 25th floor.

Laing's apartment was unchanged from this morning, save the fresh blood stains. Maitland made a rough barricade behind the door and flopped on Laing's large sofa. Anne stretched out beside him. He tried to review the day's events but the warmth of her body overcame him and soon he was in a deep sleep.

Maitland awoke in the early morning sun, unsure at first where he was. His back was stiff. Anne was in the kitchen. He still had food and a bottle of water left in his pack, and Anne had done a quick exploration of Laing's kitchen, finding various pots, broken dishes, a few mugs, and, surprisingly, a small jar still containing ground coffee. She poured some water into a pot and took it to the balcony, where a handful of telephone directory pages and some splintered chair legs soon made a small blaze in Laing's homemade fire pit, which looked suspiciously like a long metal meat tray from a butcher's shop. Coffee made, Maitland and Anne sat out on the balcony and basked in the early morning sun.

Maitland found himself straying from the view of London to Anne Royal. She was like someone from a desert island. He looked up to the penthouse high above. Power and water could be routed to the roof—he had the building plans, and he didn't think it would be too difficult to finally deal with Steele. Anne smiled at him.

Maybe, he thought, I could stay here a week or two...

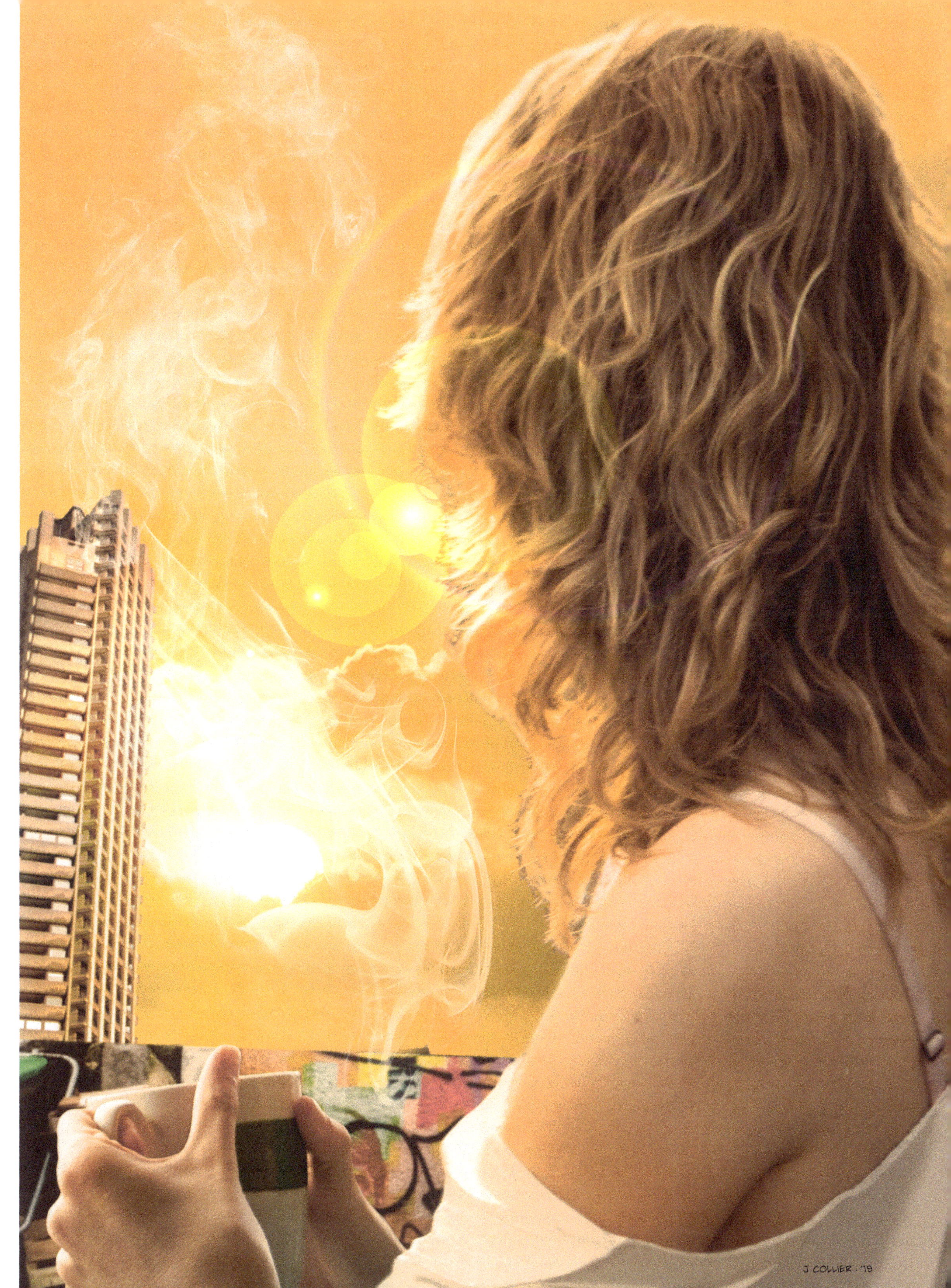
J COLLIER · '19

www.ingramcontent.com/pod-product-compliance
Lightning Source LLC
LaVergne TN
LVHW060618110826
845147LV00019B/1044

* 9 7 8 1 7 7 5 3 6 7 9 1 8 *